The Cambridge Companion to Ancient Athens

Named for a goddess, epicenter of the first democracy, birthplace of tragic and comic theater, locus of the major philosophical schools, artistically in the vanguard for centuries, ancient Athens looms large in contemporary study of the ancient world. This *Companion* is a comprehensive introduction to the city, its topography and monuments, inhabitants and cultural institutions, religious rituals and politics. Chapters link the religious, cultural, and political institutions of Athens to the physical locales in which they took place. Discussion of the urban plan, with its streets, gates, walls, and public and private buildings, provides readers with a thorough understanding of how the city operated and what people saw, heard, smelled, and tasted as they flowed through it. Drawing on the latest scholarship, as well as excavation discoveries at the Agora, sanctuaries, and cemeteries, this *Companion* explores how the city was planned, how it functioned, and how it was transformed from a democratic *polis* into a Roman city.

JENIFER NEILS is the Director of the American School of Classical Studies at Athens. She has authored and edited several books on ancient Athens, including *The Parthenon Frieze* (Cambridge, 2001), *The Parthenon from Antiquity to the Present* (Cambridge, 2005), and *Goddess and Polis: The Panathenaic Festival of Ancient Athens* (1993).

DYLAN K. ROGERS is Lecturer in Roman Art and Archaeology at the University of Virginia, and previously served as the Assistant Director of the American School of Classical Studies at Athens. He is the author of *Water Culture in Roman Society* (2018) and a co-editor of *What's New in Roman Greece?* (2018)

Online resources for this title can be found at: www.cambridge.org/ NeilsRogers

CAMBRIDGE COMPANIONS TO THE ANCIENT WORLD

Other Titles in the Series

The Cambridge Companion to Ancient Athens

Edited by

JENIFER NEILS
American School of Classical Studies at Athens

DYLAN K. ROGERS
University of Virginia

CAMBRIDGE
UNIVERSITY PRESS

University Printing House, Cambridge CB2 8BS, United Kingdom

One Liberty Plaza, 20th Floor, New York, NY 10006, USA

477 Williamstown Road, Port Melbourne, VIC 3207, Australia

314–321, 3rd Floor, Plot 3, Splendor Forum, Jasola District Centre, New Delhi – 110025, India

79 Anson Road, #06-04/06, Singapore 079906

Cambridge University Press is part of the University of Cambridge.

It furthers the University's mission by disseminating knowledge in the pursuit of
education, learning, and research at the highest international levels of excellence.

www.cambridge.org
Information on this title: www.cambridge.org/9781108484558
DOI: 10.1017/9781108614054

First published 2021

Printed in the United Kingdom by TJ Books Limited, Padstow Cornwall

A catalogue record for this publication is available from the British Library.

Library of Congress Cataloging-in-Publication Data
Names: Neils, Jenifer, 1950– editor. | Rogers, Dylan Kelby, editor.
Title: The Cambridge companion to ancient Athens / edited by Jenifer Neils, Dylan Rogers.
Description: Cambridge ; New York, NY : Cambridge University Press, 2021. | Series: Cambridge companions
    to the ancient world | Includes bibliographical references and index.
Identifiers: LCCN 2020037668 (print) | LCCN 2020037669 (ebook) | ISBN 9781108484558 (hardback) |
    ISBN 9781108723305 (paperback) | ISBN 9781108614054 (epub)
Subjects: LCSH: Athens (Greece)–Civilization. | Athens (Greece)–Antiquities.
Classification: LCC DF275 .C27 2021 (print) | LCC DF275 (ebook) | DDC 938/.5–dc23
LC record available at https://lccn.loc.gov/2020037668
LC ebook record available at https://lccn.loc.gov/2020037669

ISBN 978-1-108-48455-8 Hardback
ISBN 978-1-108-72330-5 Paperback

Additional resources for this publication at www.cambridge.org/NeilsRogers.

Contents

vi   *Contents*

Online resources for this title can be found at: www.cambridge.org/
NeilsRogers

Contributors

Geoffrey Bakewell, Professor of Greek and Roman Studies, Rhodes College

Robert A. Bridges, Jr., Secretary Emeritus, American School of Classical Studies at Athens

John McK. Camp II, Director, Agora Excavations (American School of Classical Studies at Athens), and Stavros Niarchos Foundation Professor of Classics, Randolph-Macon College

Leda Costaki, American School of Classical Studies at Athens, and Dipylon Society

Sylvian Fachard, Professeur d'archéologie classique, Université de Lausanne, and American School of Classical Studies at Athens

Valentina Di Napoli, Assistant Professor, University of Patras, and Swiss School of Archaeology in Greece

Katherine B. Harrington, Postdoctoral Teaching Fellow, Florida State University

Edward. M Harris, Emeritus Professor of Ancient History, Durham University, and Honorary Professorial Fellow, University of Edinburgh

Danielle L. Kellogg, Associate Professor of Classics, Brooklyn College, and the Graduate Center, City University of New York

James Kierstead, Senior Lecturer in Classics, Victoria University of Wellington

John H. Kroll, Professor Emeritus, University of Texas at Austin, and Research Associate, Herberden Coin Room, Ashmolean Museum

Mark L. Lawall, Professor of Classics, University of Manitoba

David M. Lewis, Lecturer in Greek History and Culture, University of Edinburgh

Maria A. Liston, Associate Professor of Anthropology, University of Waterloo, Ontario

Elizabeth A. Meyer, T. Cary Johnson, Jr. Professor of History, University of Virginia

Margaret M. Miles, Professor Emerita of Art History and Classics, University of California, Irvine

Jenifer Neils, Director, American School of Classical Studies at Athens

Kirk Ormand, Nathan A. Greenberg Professor of Classics, Oberlin College

Olga Palagia, Professor Emerita of Classical Archaeology, National and Kapodistrian University of Athens

John K. Papadopoulos, Professor of Archaeology and Classics, University of California, Los Angeles

Cynthia B. Patterson, Professor of History, Emory University

Robert K. Pitt, College Year in Athens

David M. Pritchard, Associate Professor of Greek History, University of Queensland

Dylan K. Rogers, Lecturer in Roman Art and Archaeology, University of Virginia

Susan I. Rotroff, Jarvis Thurston and Mona Van Duyn Professor Emerita, Washington University in Saint Louis

H.A. Shapiro, Dietrich von Bothmer Research Scholar, Greek and Roman Department, Metropolitan Museum of Art, and Professor Emeritus of Classics, Johns Hopkins University

Tim Shea, Assistant Professor of Classics, University of North Carolina at Chapel Hill

Tyler Jo Smith, Professor of Classical Art and Archaeology, University of Virginia

Ann Steiner, Shirley Watkins Steinman Professor of Classics, Franklin & Marshall College

George Steinhauer, Ephorate of Piraeus

Jutta Stroszeck, Director, Kerameikos Excavations, German Archaeological Institute, Athens

Anna Maria Theocharaki, independent scholar, and Dipylon Society

Panos Valavanis, Professor Emeritus of Classical Archaeology, National and Kapodistrian University of Athens

Abbreviations

Agora	*The Athenian Agora.* 1953–present. Princeton.
AJA	*American Journal of Archaeology.* 1885–present. Boston.
ArchDelt	Αρχαιολογικόν Δελτίον/*Archaiologikon Deltion.* 1885–1892, 1915–1933/35, 1960–present. Athens.
BAPD	Beazley Archive Pottery Database (www.beazley.ox.ac.uk/ pottery)
CQ	*Classical Quarterly.* 1907–present. Cambridge.
Delos	*Exploration archéologique de Délos.* 1914–present. Paris.
FGrH	Jacoby, F., ed. *Die Fragmente der griechischen Historiker.* 1923–1958. Berlin.
FHG	Müller, C. *Fragmenta Historicorum Graecorum.* 1841–1870. Paris.
IG	*Inscriptiones Graecae.* 1895–present. Berlin.
JHS	*Journal of Hellenic Studies.* 1880–present. Cambridge.
JSAH	*Journal of the Society of Architectural Historians.* 1941–present. Oakland.
Kerameikos	*Kerameikos: Ergebnisse der Ausgrabungen.* 1939–present. Berlin.
PAE	Πρακτικά της εν Αθήναις Αρχαιολογικής Εταιρείας/*Praktika tis en Athenais Archaiologikis Etaireias.* 1837–1849, 1858–present. Athens.
PCG	Kassel, R., and C. Austin, eds. *Poetae Comici Graeci.* 1983–2001. Berlin.
SEG	*Supplementum Epigraphicum Graecum.* 1923–present. Leiden.
ZPE	*Zeitschrift für Papyrologie und Epigraphik.* 1967–present. Bonn.

Athens: An Introduction

JENIFER NEILS

> O glorious Athens! violet-crowned, worthy of song, bulwark of
> Greece, city of the gods.
>
> Pindar, fr. 76

Inhabited from the Stone Age to the present, Athens is one of the oldest continuously inhabited cities in the world. We know it best from the Classical period (500–300 BC), because in addition to its impressive archaeological remains, such as the Parthenon, a vast variety of informative inscriptions and texts, from philosophical dialogues to comic jokes, attests to its importance. The names of its most famous citizens – Aischylos, Aristophanes, Perikles, Plato, Sokrates, Solon, Themistokles, Thucydides – are not unfamiliar to the educated public. Long after Pindar (fr. 76), Athens remained well known in European history as the "bulwark of Greece," having routed the Persian menace not only once at Marathon, but also a second time at Salamis. Many of the institutions invented by the Athenians – democracy and theater being the obvious ones, but also practices such as jury pay, impeachment, and a 'tomb for the unknown soldier' – are still with us today.

Like all cities, Athens was and is in a constant state of evolution. With its succession of native Greek and foreign overlords, its alternating periods of population explosion and severe contraction, its modern infrastructure projects resulting in the exposure of ancient urban structures, and its periodic inflows of foreigners and exoduses of locals, both seeking new horizons, it has been ever changing over time. And yet in many ways much remains the same – and this continuity is striking. With its steep cliffs and mighty walls, the Akropolis remained a citadel for thousands of years, from which Athenians defended their city beginning in the Late Bronze Age until the successful conclusion of the Greek War of Independence in 1830. The fourth-century BC marble stadium used for the ancient games at Athens is now the end point for the running of the modern 'authentic' Marathon every year. Today one reads XAIPE ("greetings") on festive cards and on doormats, the same expression carved on marble gravestones and painted on ceramic drinking cups in antiquity. The Greek language

1

continues to be read and spoken, not only in churches, as was the fate of Latin, but also in everyday life.

While scholars, both in this book and in general, privilege the Athens of the Classical period, the city went through many iterations before becoming the capital of Greece in 1834. Ruled by so-called tyrants in the sixth century BC, it was the first Greek city to establish a democracy, in 508 BC. After being conquered by Alexander the Great's father, Philip II, in 338 BC, the city lost much of its independence but gained stature as a university town, a locus of culture and learning. That reputation in turn inspired admiring Romans, especially the emperors Augustus (27 BC–AD 14) and Hadrian (AD 117–138), to embellish the city with temples, arches, a forum, concert hall, library, and aqueducts. While the city shrank considerably in the subsequent Byzantine and medieval periods, churches were added to the cityscape, which retained many of its antiquities either in situ or embedded as spolia into new structures. Even during the four centuries of Ottoman domination (1458–1833), many of the ancient structures retained their integrity, while a building as revered as the Parthenon was converted into a mosque.

Athens was fortunate in having many chroniclers in antiquity, from the historian Herodotos to its own native son Thucydides. Less well known but also important are the so-called Atthidographers, whose works survive only in fragments; from the late fifth century to the middle of the third, they wrote about local history in texts called *Atthides*.[1] In the Classical period the city was chock-full of inscriptions on stone, many of which survive, mostly in fragments that epigraphers have painstakingly pieced together. More than 7,000 have been found in the excavations of the Athenian Agora alone. These constitute a mine of information about civic life, law, property, treaties, religion, and finances of all kinds. The many references in this volume to the publication abbreviated as *IG* (*Inscriptiones Graecae*) clearly demonstrate the indispensability of inscriptions to the study of all aspects of Athenian life.[2]

While we know a great deal about the city, an essential question is why Athens, and not another *polis*, became the epicenter of Greek civilization. There were certainly many diverse factors that converged at the right time in the right locale. One of the most telling myths of the ancient Athenians is their staunch belief in their autochthony – the notion that they were

[1] See Harding 2008.
[2] A useful online source for Attic inscriptions is that compiled by S. Lambert beginning in 2012: www.atticinscriptions.com.

literally born from Attic soil, and were not invaders. This belief was consistent with a particularly patriotic attachment to their land, such that they would actually desert the land in order to save it, as they did before the famous sea battle of Salamis.[3] The early Athenians were not great colonizers on the scale of other Greek city-states. They were well protected by the surrounding mountains and had substantial natural resources (water, fertile soil, silver mines) to make them relatively prosperous at home. They emphasized education for their male youth so as to become informed citizens; Plato's Academy could be called the first institution of higher learning. Citizens also had civic lessons in the Theater of Dionysos, where tragedies and comedies were not simply entertainment but political commentary of a high order. Religion, including a belief in the special patronage of the goddess Athena as expressed in the city's name, sanctuaries, and coinage, was also a unifying factor, since it permeated all aspects of life from birth to death.[4] These and many other topics constitute the contents of this *Companion*, whose purpose is to elucidate the cultural and social institutions of one of the most remarkable cities of the ancient world, and the marks they left both in texts and on the ground.

The opening chapter (Shapiro) demonstrates what we can glean about the life of an ordinary Athenian citizen in the late sixth century BC from extant inscriptions, imagery on vases, and Herodotos. Part I (Chapters 2–10) surveys the physical nature of Athens, beginning with its emergence in the eighth century BC, and then presents its surrounding countryside, urban plan, sacred spaces, civic center, natural resources, and structures for both the living and the dead. Part II (Chapters 11–14) deals with the inhabitants, both human and animal, of ancient Athens. The institution of slavery, common to all ancient societies, is not treated in a single chapter but is referred to throughout the book, given the challenges of documenting the life of slaves archaeologically, even though they were a fact of life in ancient Athens. The business and commercial activities that took place, from the port of Piraeus to the marble quarries of Mt. Penteli and the silver mines of Laurion, comprise Part III (Chapters 15–20). Classical Athens is known for its legendary contributions to culture, namely theater, competitive sport, religion, the *symposion*, and philosophy; these topics are covered in Part IV (Chapters 21–26). Finally, the political institutions that also made Athens famous in antiquity – civic associations, the rule of law, and the military training that led to the victories at Marathon and

---

[3] For more on this topic see Meier 1998.
[4] See Meyer 2017.

Salamis – are described in Part V (Chapters 27–29). A coda (Chapters 30–33) introduces more recent visitors who made an indelible impact on the cityscape: Roman conquerors, travelers from Western Europe who first documented the antiquities of the city, the nineteenth-century architects who transformed it, and the archaeologists who have laid bare the buried past. In every chapter an effort has been made to link the texts to the antiquities still visible in the city, so that the visitor, armchair or on-the-spot, can relate these customs and institutions to the physical remains.

Nearly two hundred years of archaeological exploration continue to add to our portrait of ancient Athens. Surprises still pop up, like a Late Bronze Age gold ring with a bull-leaping scene suggestive of the hero Theseus' adventure in Crete. The excavations for the Athens Metro, the new airport, and the Akropolis Museum, and most recently the cultural center at Phaleron, have uncovered buildings, artifacts, and burials which will continue to occupy scholars for decades to come.[5] Such finds suggest that there is still much to learn about this city, its history and monuments. A city truly "worthy of song" and worthy of this new volume.

Note to the Reader

This edited volume is the second in a series of Cambridge Companions to ancient cities.[6] Many of the authors generously met together in Athens with the editors to share ideas and improve the content of the volume. Ancient Greek orthography has been followed as much as possible to spell proper names as the Greeks would have, except in instances (e.g. Thucydides) when such spellings might be unrecognizable to the general reader. Suggested readings and a select bibliography follow each chapter. The various maps of Attika, the city, the Agora, and the Akropolis should be consulted throughout for locating features mentioned in the text. Owing to the constraints on printing illustrations here, readers will find additional figures in the text (indicated as Web Fig. or Web Map) on a companion website, with further digital resources for studying and understanding ancient Athens: www.cambridge.org/NeilsRogers.

---

[5] Publications of these finds can be found in Parlama and Stampolidis 2000, Kaza-Papageorgiou 2016, and Eleftheratou 2019.

[6] The first is *The Cambridge Companion to Ancient Rome*, edited by Paul Erdkamp (2013). In various ways, notably its organization, it served as a model for this *Companion*.

The editors thank Beatrice Rehl for initiating this project and for providing much sage advice along the way. The Blegen Library of the American School of Classical Studies at Athens served as our editorial base camp, and we dedicate the book to two important denizens of the School, Pandora and Atticus.

Further Reading

Histories of Athens dealing with specific periods are: Anderson 2003 for the Early Classical period and the emergence of democracy; Meier 1998, Munn 2000, and Samons 2007 for the Classical period; and Habicht 1997 for the Hellenistic and Roman periods. An overview of the major monuments in their historical context can be found in Camp 2001 and Goette 2001. Topographical studies include Travlos 1971 and Greco 2010–2015 (with more to come). A thorough study of the Akropolis monuments is Hurwit 1999. For religion in ancient Athens see Parker 1996. The institution of slavery is thoroughly explored by Wrenhaven 2012 and Lewis 2018.

Bibliography

Anderson, G. 2003. *The Athenian Experiment: Building an Imagined Political Community in Ancient Attica, 508–490 BC.* Ann Arbor.

Camp, J.M. 2001. *The Archaeology of Athens.* New Haven.

Eleftheratou, S. 2019. *Μουσείο Ακρόπολης: η ανασκαφή.* Athens.

Goette, H.R. 2001. *Athens, Attica and the Megarid: An Archaeological Guide.* London.

Greco, E., ed. 2010–2015. *Topografia di Atene. Sviluppo urbano e monumenti dalle origini al III secolo d.C.* 5 vols. Athens.

Habicht, C. 1997. *Athens from Alexander to Antony.* Cambridge, MA.

Harding, P. 2008. *The Story of Athens: The Fragments of the Local Chronicles of Attika.* Oxford.

Hurwit, J.M. 1999. *The Athenian Acropolis: History, Mythology, and Archaeology from the Neolithic Era to the Present.* Cambridge.

Kaza-Papageorgiou, K. 2016. *The Ancient City Road and the Metro beneath Vouliagmenis Avenue.* Athens.

Lewis, D.M. 2018. *Greek Slave Systems in Their Eastern Mediterranean Context, c. 800–146 BC.* Oxford.

Meier, C. 1998. *Athens. A Portrait of the City in Its Golden Age.* New York.

Meyer, M. 2017. *Athena, Göttin von Athen: Kult und Mythos auf der Akropolis bis in klassische Zeit.* Vienna.

Munn, M. 2000. *The School of History: Athens in the Age of Socrates.* Berkeley.

Parker, R. 1996. *Athenian Religion: A History.* Oxford.

Parlama, L., and N.C. Stampolidis, eds. 2000. *Athens: The City beneath the City: Antiquities from the Metropolitan Railway Excavations*. Athens.

Samons, L.J. 2007. *The Cambridge Companion to the Age of Pericles*. New York.

Travlos, J. 1971. *Pictorial Dictionary of Ancient Athens*. New York.

Wrenhaven, K.L. 2012. *Reconstructing the Slave: The Image of the Slave in Ancient Greece*. London.

1 | #Leagros: An Athenian Life

H.A. SHAPIRO

On a summer afternoon in the year 520 BC, a teenage boy wandered into a potter's workshop in the center of Athens. Leagros had grown up in the neighborhood, which went by the name Kerameis, a reference to the potters who made it the center of their thriving industry. A dozen years later, when the statesman Kleisthenes reorganized all of Attika into a democracy, Kerameis, located just to the northwest of the Agora, would become one of the 139 official demes or townships which made up the confederated city-state of Athens. In the standard practice of the democracy, Leagros would be officially known as "Leagros son of Glaukon from Kerameis" (*Leagros Glaukonos ek Kerameion*).

The boy was already well known to the potters and painters in the workshop from many earlier visits, but this time they were struck by how he had grown into an exceptionally handsome youth of fifteen. He especially caught the attention of the youngest painter in the shop, Euphronios, who was at the beginning of his career and perhaps not much older than Leagros. After perfecting his skills decorating a few red-figure drinking cups, Euphronios had started work on his most ambitious project to date, a large calyx-krater for mixing wine and water at the *symposion*, the elite all-male drinking party (Fig. 1.1).[1] His choice of subject was equally ambitious: a scene of young athletes in the *palaistra* that would stretch across both sides of the broad vase. The two panels would comprise five young athletes, a trainer (the only clothed figure), and four small slave boys helping out in various ways. One could imagine Euphronios sitting in a corner of the *palaistra* making sketches of the male figure in a whole range of poses, sketches he would later transfer into the new medium known as red-figure. There are also touches of cheeky humor: one athlete on the far left is caught in the act of tying up his foreskin with a strip of leather (a practice known as infibulation, perhaps intended to protect the penis like a jockstrap), as one of the slave boys observes him with fascination, while the trainer points directly at another athlete's genitalia, perhaps advising him that he needs to do the same.

---

[1] Berlin, Antikensammlung F 2180; BAPD no. 200063.

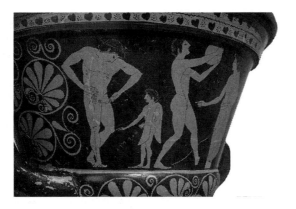

Fig. 1.1 Detail of Leagros inscription, Attic red-figure calyx-krater attributed to Euphronios, ca. 520 BC, Berlin, Staatliche Museen, Antikensammlung F 2180. © ArchaiOptix, Wikimedia Commons/CC-BY-SA 3.0 DE

This is not just some idealized or anonymous gathering in the *palaistra*, for Euphronios has written names beside six of the figures that identify real Athenians of the period: the athletes Polydamas, Hegesias, Antiphon, and Lykos; the trainer Hipparchos; and a slave boy, Tranion. Above the youth infibulating himself, the painter has written *Leagros kalos* (Leagros is handsome). (This phenomenon is known as a "tag-kalos," and it could be considered the ancient equivalent of the hash tag.) This figure has no inscription naming him, as the other athletes do, so perhaps the inscription *Leagros kalos* does double duty, both naming and praising him. Over the next ten years or so, Euphronios would continue to praise Leagros on at least a dozen more vases, almost half of all the surviving works signed by or attributed to the painter. It appears that a friend and rival of Euphronios named Smikros noticed his fascination with Leagros and poked fun at it on a different vase by depicting the two as an amorous couple, the somewhat older Euphronios wooing a young Leagros.

This fictional vignette of Leagros wandering into the shop of Euphronios is partly inspired by a scene in the novel *The Praise Singer* (1978), by Mary Renault, the British writer who drew a huge following for her updated retellings of Greek myths.[2] A scene in *The Praise Singer*, which is a retelling of the life of the poet Simonides (ca. 557–467 BC), takes place in a potter's shop a few years earlier than our encounter of Leagros and Euphronios,

[2] Her books include *The King Must Die* and *The Bull from the Sea*, both about the hero Theseus, and *The Persian Boy* and *Fire from Heaven*, both about Alexander the Great, all of them set in a milieu that often recalls Oxford in the 1920s and, not incidentally, with a keen eye for the homoerotic ambience that is palpable in Euphronios' *palaistra* scene and the *kalos* inscriptions.

ca. 525 BC. It is narrated by Simonides recalling a *symposion* he attended hosted by Hipparchos, brother of the Athenian tyrant Hippias. The potter's shop belongs to Exekias, the greatest master of the earlier black-figure technique:

> "I was in Exekias' shop [says Hipparchos]. He painted me that wine-cooler, which I don't think will displease me however fashions change. That day, however, I was there to order a small dedication to Eros." The handsome youth (a new one) who shared the couch returned his glance with charm, but no vulgar simpering, and touched his wine-cup, doubtless inscribed with "The Beautiful" [i.e. *kalos* in Greek] and his name. "I had attended to that, and was idling about the shop when I heard the master roaring at a pupil who'd been working, it seemed, industriously in his corner. People say my curiosity will be the death of me someday." He turned on us his winning smile. "So I went over, in time to hear the culprit told that if he thought he had all day to spend in foolery, he had better make room for someone else who'd value his place. By now I was craning over Exekias' shoulder. The young man was holding an oil-jar, on which he'd drawn a Greek and a Phrygian dueling. As you'll have guessed, he amused himself by painting the background black, and reserving the figures. It was the very best Ilissos clay, that bakes a soft glowing red. Seeing Exekias just about to dash it to the ground, or maybe at his pupil's head, I caught back his arm crying, "Fire it! Fire it, my friend, and let me see." (Renault, *The Praise Singer* 107)

Thus was the red-figure technique invented, with assistance from the tyrant, who then shows off to his guests a set of red-figure *kylikes* (drinking cups), and in so doing, starts a trend. The inventor is identified in the novel as Psiax, who was indeed among the earliest painters we know by name who worked in red-figure.[3] And he was most likely not a young apprentice, but an experienced artisan who came of age working in the black-figure technique, perhaps even alongside Exekias, as Renault suggests. A few years later, Euphronios and a small circle of painters referred to as the Pioneers would bring red-figure to a peak of grandeur and technical perfection that was rarely if ever matched in the long history of the technique.

Renault imagines that the youths named as *kalos* on the vases were in attendance at the *symposia* of the rich and powerful and even shared a couch with their older admirers. If so, Leagros would have been an unusually popular *symposion* guest, and everything we know about him

---

[3] Though an Athenian artist known to scholars today as the Andokides Painter (after two vases by his hand signed by Andokides as potter) probably made the discovery a few years before Psiax.

from the vases does suggest as much. Given the paucity of attestations in the literary sources, the vase inscriptions naming Leagros, with or without *kalos*, take on an outsized importance in our attempts to establish the contours of his life. Even that most fundamental fact of an individual's biography – the year of his birth – is largely an inference from the assumption that he should have been entering adolescence at the time he is first named as *kalos* on early works of Euphronios, ca. 520, yielding a birth year of ca. 535.[4]

If, however, we follow the traditional chronology, Leagros came of age in a period – the 520s and early teens – that was remembered as a kind of Golden Age in Athens (or Age of Kronos, as Aristotle put it in the *Constitution of the Athenians* 16.7). The tyrant Peisistratos had died in 528, ensuring a smooth transition in power to his two sons, Hippias and Hipparchos. The word *tyrannos* in Greek does not have most of the negative connotations of the modern word and basically refers to the means by which a man seized power in a *polis* – by force of arms – and not to the nature of his rule. In the case of Peisistratos, after two short-lived attempts to take power in Athens, starting in ca. 561, on the third try, in 546, he succeeded in consolidating his power and held it until his death almost twenty years later. It was a period marked by largely peaceful relations with other Greek states and prosperity at home, thanks in part to the thriving pottery industry and massive exports to Etruscan and other buyers.

While Hippias held the reins of power in the same benevolent spirit as his father, his younger brother served as a kind of Minister of Culture (Plato, *Hipparchos* 228b–229d). Among his many initiatives, he reorganized the musical competitions at the Panathenaic Festival, so that the professional bards, known as rhapsodes, would perform the Homeric poems in the correct sequence. In the same spirit of edifying the populace, he commissioned large numbers of herms, marble shafts topped with the bearded head of the god Hermes (Web Fig. 1.1), to stand as milestones throughout the Attic landscape and adorned them with gentle exhortations of his own composition ("Don't deceive a friend"). He once displayed his passionate commitment to poetry by staging a daring rescue. In 522,

---

[4] It should be noted, however, that in recent years a growing minority of scholars have argued for lowering the date for the introduction of red-figure by about ten years, on the basis of pottery chronology derived from material found in the Athenian Agora. Such a shift would not actually affect anything we know about Leagros' later life and would even make his death in battle at a rather advanced age somewhat less implausible (see below).

Polykrates, tyrant of Samos, was suddenly overthrown, and the members of his glittering court were in jeopardy. Among these was the famous poet Anakreon, so Hipparchos dispatched a ship to bring him safely to Athens, where he lived out the rest of his long life (until ca. 486) and seems to have had a major impact on the cultural life of the city – so much so that almost fifty years after his death, an honorific portrait statue was set up on the Akropolis.

When Anakreon arrived in Athens, he was already famous throughout Greece as the poet par excellence of love and life's other pleasures. His extravagant style of dress, brought from his Ionian homeland of Teos, was noted by the vase-painters and imitated by fashionable Athenians. The primary venue for the performance of his poems was not at public festivals or contests, but in the private setting of the *symposion*. Whether he regularly attended elegant *symposia* hosted by Hipparchos, such as the one described by Mary Renault, is not recorded anywhere in our sources, but it is certainly not beyond the realm of possibility.

A few years after his remarkable scene of athletes exercising in the *palaistra*, Euphronios produced an equally intimate glimpse of such an elegant *symposion*, on a krater of impressive proportions.[5] Here the subject matter and the shape are in perfect accord, since just such a vase would be used to serve the wine at a *symposion*. Four symposiasts recline on two luxurious couches (*klinai*), and the painter identifies the participants as real Athenians of the period: Ekphantides, Thoudemos, Melas, and a youth identified as Smikros, presumably the painter who would later return the compliment (if it was so intended) by pairing Euphronios with Leagros. Ekphantides, captivated by the music, throws back his head and a few words spill out of his mouth, a hymn to Apollo that has been associated with Anakreon. Even if the poet is not present at the *symposion*, his poetry is. Finally, on the reverse, between a lampstand and a lyre hanging on the imaginary wall, are the words *Leagros kalos*. It may not be accidental that these words are placed just beside the figure of a handsome nude slave boy who rushes to fetch more wine for the assembled guests.

The *kalos* inscriptions naming Leagros are of special interest, in several respects, not only because there are so few references to him in other sources, but because they comprise an utterly unique group within the large corpus of *kalos* inscriptions, which extends for over a century (ca. 550–425 BC). First, the number of inscriptions naming Leagros is of an

---

[5] Munich, Antikensammlung 8935; BAPD no. 275007.

order of magnitude greater than for anyone else – currently over sixty, compared to about thirty for the next most popular, Chairestratos. (Leagros' son Glaukos is a close third.) And they are not limited to a particular painter or workshop, as is the case with many other *kalos* names (e.g. the inscriptions *Chairestratos kalos* are virtually all on vases by the painter Douris). Though Euphronios' devotion to Leagros is unmatched by other painters, the name does appear on vases attributed to at least five others, including several black-figure vases that are contemporary with the work of Euphronios.

Secondly, the vases naming Leagros seem to stretch over a longer span of time than those for any other *kalos*, a roughly twenty-year period that, in the conventional dating of red-figure, would be ca. 520–500 BC. By definition, no one could remain a beauty into his thirties. Perhaps we should entertain a more neutral definition of the expression, something like "Leagros is a fine fellow." Or there may be a more banal explanation, that once the great Euphronios had elevated Leagros to the status of "number one fair-haired boy," other painters saw a commercial advantage in appropriating his name.

A third unusual aspect of the *Leagros kalos* inscriptions is especially difficult to interpret, namely that, in addition to the sixty in the standard formula, there are about fifteen that omit the word *kalos*. And instead of a handsome young athlete or some other figure who could plausibly be Leagros, we find a whole range of improbable subjects: satyrs (with or without maenads), *hetairai* (high-class prostitutes), and a bearded reveler vomiting, among others. In a sense, these are the reverse of the tag-*kalos* inscriptions. There is also the unique inscription in a scene of two half-naked *hetairai* playing the party game of *kottabos*, in which the drinker would fling the dregs of wine at the bottom of her *kylix* at a target. The player might dedicate the toss to a particular individual, say, to the object of one's affection. Here the *hetaira* cries out, "This one's for you, Leagros!"[6] The implication that Leagros was as popular with Athenian women of a certain class as with his male admirers adds a new dimension to his gradually emerging personality.

Beazley coined the term "tag-*kalos*" for those cases where a proper *kalos* inscription stands close to a youth who could plausibly be understood as the individual named in the inscription, like the young athlete infibulating himself on the early krater by Euphronios (Fig. 1.1). This is an important

---

[6] St. Petersburg, Hermitage 644; BAPD no. 200078.

distinction, since *kalos* inscriptions also appear in all manner of scenes (e.g. mythological ones) with which the inscription has no possible association. The sixty-plus Leagros *kalos* inscriptions appear in every kind of scene, mythological and non-mythological, but it is intriguing that several hint at the same bad-boy image that we shall find in the 'portraits' of Leagros: a boy punished for masturbating, a youth participating in a wild orgy, and other forms of sexual intercourse.

It is tempting to lay out the vases that name Leagros without *kalos*, along with some of those with *kalos*, in chronological order to try to create a portrait as he ages from adolescence to early middle age. Toward the end of the sequence, for example, is a solitary drinker looking rather paunchy and dissolute, labeled Leagros. Could it be that by this time Leagros had become a byword for a high-living aristocrat who lost his good looks to an over-indulgence in wine, women, and other pleasures?

Once Leagros' name disappears from the vases ca. 500 BC, we lose track of him for some years. There is no record of his having served in the Athenian army during either of the two Persian invasions, in 490, when a small Athenian force famously beat back a much larger Persian army at Marathon, or in 480/79, when the Greeks, led by Athenian commanders, won a series of victories both at sea (Salamis, Mykale) and on land (Plataia). Yet, since the latter campaigns required the mobilization of all able-bodied Athenians, and judging from what we know of his later life and death, it is hard to imagine that Leagros did not serve in some capacity.

Leagros was also politically active. Indeed, he was a candidate for official ostracism, indicating he was like virtually all Athenian men of his class. This is vividly illustrated by a cache of eighty-six *ostraka* (inscribed sherds) bearing his name. Part of a much larger group of about 6,000 discovered in the excavations of the Kerameikos in the 1960s, the eighty-six sherds represent a relatively large number and suggest that Leagros was well known in Athens (and had many enemies).[7] Most *ostraka* consist of nothing more than a name scratched on a potsherd, sometimes with the individual's patronymic or demotic, but several of those naming Leagros son of Glaukon add an extra word or two that make them rather suggestive. One voter wrote, "because he was a traitor," but in what sense? Had he perhaps been an associate of the great Themistokles, who, after leading the Greeks to victory at Salamis, fell out of favor, was himself ostracized in 472, and sought refuge at the Persian court? It seems likely that Leagros was a

---

[7] See Brenne 2018.

candidate for ostracism just a year later, in 471. Another sherd calls him *baskanos*, which may mean that he was a gossip, or brought bad luck, or even that he practiced the dark arts of magic. Of all the *ostraka*, only one gives Leagros' deme, but it does so not in the usual formula (*ek Kerameion*), but as *Kerameus*. Since this is also the word for potter, some consideration should be given to the idea that Leagros not only *lived* among the potters, but may even have been the proprietor of a potters' shop. This could be a lucrative business in the days of Athens' great commercial success in the marketing of pottery abroad.

Aside from the *kalos* inscriptions on vases and the *ostraka*, Leagros enters into the archaeological record in a most spectacular fashion. The American excavations of the Athenian Agora uncovered the foundations of a monument that is often mentioned in our literary sources: the Altar of the Twelve Gods (see Map 6.2). This is also perhaps the only monument from Archaic Athens that can be dated to the exact year, 522/1 BC. The date is arrived at by combining the report in Thucydides (6.54.6) that the altar was set up by Peisistratos, grandson of the elder tyrant and son of Hippias, during the year he was Eponymous Archon (chief magistrate) of Athens, with an inscribed "Archon list" of the late fifth century, indicating that Peisistratos the Younger held the office in that year. The excavation also revealed a rectangular block, set right against the foundation of the altar, with the inscription "Leagros son of Glaukon set this up to the Twelve Gods" (Web Fig. 1.2). The inclusion of the patronymic makes it certain that the dedicator is our man.

The Altar of the Twelve Gods was another project of the tyrant family that was intended to benefit the Athenian populace in several ways. Standing in the open, in the northwest sector of the market square, it marked a kind of ground zero from which distances within Attika were measured. The herms erected by Hipparchos (the uncle of the altar's dedicator) would have stood halfway between the altar and the outlying demes. In later times, we are told, the Altar of the Twelve Gods functioned as a place of refuge for those fleeing persecution (Herodotos 6.108; Lycurgus, *Against Leokrates* 93). Altars in general were thought to protect those in distress – it was forbidden to harm a suppliant who was sitting on or otherwise clinging to an altar – but the Altar of the Twelve Gods had tremendous religious significance apart from this.

Athens was not the only city in the Greek world with a Dodekatheon (Shrine of the Twelve Gods). While we tend to assume that the Twelve are equivalent to the Olympians, because that is the number recorded in later times, it is far from certain that Peisistratos the Younger had in mind the same Twelve as, for example, the Olympians on the east frieze of the Parthenon, carved almost a century later.

The original form of the Altar of the Twelve Gods is also not certain – possibly an open-air shrine surrounded by an enclosure wall – but it was surely damaged in the Persian sack of Athens in 480 and restored or remodeled after that. It is therefore hard to know whether Leagros set up his dedication before or after the Persians arrived, or whether its current location against the foundation of the altar is the original one. But judging from the letter forms and other criteria, it will have been set up within a few years either side of 480. Even more intriguing is the question of the dedication itself, i.e. what stood atop the inscribed base? Preserved dowel holes suggest a standing figure with the right foot slightly advanced. Typically, a statue dedicated to a divinity represents that divinity, so a dedication to the Twelve Gods on a small base presents a problem. Could the dedication have been a statue of Leagros himself? A well-known red-figure cup depicts a mature man contemplating a statue of a young athlete on a two-stepped base (Fig. 1.2).[8] The words *Leagros kalos* form a semi-circle at the top of the picture field. Raubitschek made the intriguing suggestion that the scene shows Leagros as a middle-aged man (he would have been in his mid-50s when he made the dedication) admiring the image of his younger self. Aside from the chronological issue – the cup is dated ca. 500, well before the date of Leagros' dedication – it is hard to think of a dedication by an individual in the form of a statue of himself.

The last occurrence of Leagros' name in our sources is in Herodotos' account of the years following the Greek victories of 480/79, when the Athenians, often under the leadership of Kimon, tried to wipe out the last vestiges of a pro-Persian presence in the Aegean and consolidate their growing hegemony. One notable failure in this process was the attempt to establish an Athenian colony at Ennea Hodoi (Amphipolis), on the Thracian coast opposite the northern Aegean island of Thasos, in the face of stiff opposition from the native population. Leagros was elected one of the ten generals (*strategoi*) for the year 465 and, with his colleague Sophanes, was sent to Thrace. The enterprise was abandoned after an Athenian defeat at Drabeskos, in which Sophanes was killed (Herodotos 9.75; Pausanias 1.29.5; Schol. Aischines 2.31). Though the fate of Leagros is not recorded, it is likely he fell in the battle too, for this is the last we hear of him. A casualty list inscribed on stone, a portion of which was found in the

---

[8] Baltimore, Johns Hopkins Archaeological Museum Inv. B5; BAPD no. 201626.

Fig. 1.2 Tondo with Leagros inscription, Attic red-figure cup attributed to the Kiss Painter, ca. 500 BC, Baltimore, Johns Hopkins Archaeological Museum B5.
Courtesy of the Johns Hopkins Archaeological Museum. Photograph: J.T. VanRensselaer

Agora, gives the names of some of the men who fell with Leagros and Sophanes at Drabeskos. If it seems improbable that a man aged seventy (assuming a birth year of 535) was serving as *strategos*, we may recall Tellos, the Athenian whom Solon described to King Kroisos of Lydia as the happiest man ever: "He lived to see children born to each [of his sons] . . . and he had a glorious death [in battle]" (Herodotos 1.30).

Leagros never attained the level of fame and distinction of his contemporaries Themistokles or Aristides the Just. Plutarch would not have thought to write his biography. In all of the literature of the fifth century, there is only a single mention of him, in Herodotos, who records that Leagros served as *strategos* but neglects to tell us his fate. And yet he is better known to us than the vast majority of his fellow Athenians. Most of the youths named as *kalos* on the vases are otherwise unattested. Similarly, the majority of the names that turn up on the *ostraka* are unknown. With his dedication to the Twelve Gods, Leagros was immortalized in the heart of the city of Athens in a way that can be said of very few others.

Leagros lived through a period of remarkable upheaval in his native city. After an idyllic childhood in the Golden Age of the Peisistratid tyranny (and fleeting fame for his youthful good looks), as a young man he experienced the violent fall of the tyrants and the rocky birth of a democracy. In middle age he saw his country invaded twice by Persian armies and his city reduced to rubble in 480. If he was a favorite of the vase-painters in his youth, he had enough enemies in old age to be targeted by many of them for ostracism. Finally, at an age when most men enjoy a quiet retirement, he led an Athenian army into a disastrous battle far from home in the North Aegean. Though there is much more about this larger-than-life personality that we would like to know, it can fairly be said that only in Athens could such a wide range of archaeological, epigraphical, and literary evidence be woven together to bring a man like Leagros back to life.

Further Reading

The most convenient, succinct summary of the evidence for the family of Leagros is Davies 1971. The vases inscribed *Leagros kalos* are catalogued in an Appendix to Beazley 1963, and their significance is discussed by Robinson and Fluck 1937, Boardman 1992, and Shapiro 2004. Leagros' role in the traditional chronology of red-figure vase-painting is challenged by Francis and Vickers 1981 and, more convincingly, by Rotroff 2009. The Altar of the Twelve Gods and the Leagros Base have a long publication history, best summarized, with new observations, by Gadbery 1992.

Bibliography

Beazley, J.D. 1963. *Attic Red-Figure Vase-Painters*. 2nd edn. Oxford.

Boardman, J. 1992. "Kaloi and Other Names on Euphronios' Vases." In *Euphronios: Atti del Seminario Internazionale di Studi, Arezzo 27–28 Maggio 1990*, eds. M. Cygielman et al., Florence, 45–50.

Brenne, S. 2018. *Die Ostraka vom Kerameikos. Kerameikos* 20. Berlin.

Davies, J.K. 1971. *Athenian Propertied Families*. Oxford.

Francis, E.D., and M. Vickers 1981. "Leagros Kalos." *Proceedings of the Cambridge Philological Society* 207: 97–136.

Gadbery, L.M. 1992. "The Sanctuary of the Twelve Gods in the Athenian Agora: A Revised View." *Hesperia* 91: 447–489.

Raubitschek, A.E. 1939. "Leagros." *Hesperia* 8: 155–164.

Robinson, D.M., and E.J. Fluck 1937. *A Study of the Greek Love Names*. Baltimore.

Rotroff, S.I. 2009. "Early Red-Figure in Context." In *Athenian Potters and Painters, Vol. II*, eds. J.H. Oakley and O. Palagia, Oxford, 150–160.

Shapiro, H.A. 2004. "Leagros the Satyr." In *Greek Vases: Images, Contexts, Controversies*, ed. C. Marconi, Leiden, 1–11.

Additional resources to accompany this chapter can be found at: www.cambridge .org/NeilsRogers

PART I

The Urban Fabric

2 | *Asty* and *Chora*: City and Countryside

SYLVIAN FACHARD

Not all Athenians lived in Athens. Like every *polis* of the Greek world, the Athenian state (*polis*) was composed of an *asty* (the city of Athens) and a *chora* (the territory known as Attika). Ancient Greek cities maintained strong links with their countryside. In the Classical period, roughly half of the population lived outside Athens, in small towns, villages, seaports, hamlets, country estates, and farmsteads. On the one hand, people who lived outside the city center would regularly walk to the city to shop, visit family and friends, take part in the political assemblies, attend festivals, or sell their products in the Agora. On the other hand, many Athenians living in the city were originally from a village in rural Attika and kept a hereditary link with the place of origin of their ancestors. Many city dwellers owned and exploited land on their family estate, which they regularly visited and from which they obtained revenue. The festivals taking place in the important shrines of the *chora* would attract large crowds from the city and from other places in Attika. A male citizen fulfilling his military service as an ephebe would have spent one year guarding the borders of Attika and policing the countryside, which provided him with a mental map of the Attic *chora*. The constant movement of people and goods promoted the city as the central demographic, political, and economic hub, but the *polis* would never have been able to sustain such a population without its territory. Athens and Attika form an organic whole, and one cannot study Athens without its *chora*.

The territory was defined by political borders (*horia*), which marked the spatial limits of the state's political, economic, and legal authority. Athens was exceptional in that it had an unusually large territory (2,400 km^2), which ranked among the four largest of the Greek world. The Classical *chora* included the entire Attic peninsula, limited to the north by the Parnes mountain range, and surrounded by the waters of the Saronic and Euboean gulfs, which connected Attika with the wider Aegean (Map 2.1). The country had many constraints: it was dominated by limestone mountains with no deciduous trees and hills covered by maquis shrubland; it received little precipitation and had no perennial rivers forming large deltas or broad alluvial valleys. Compared to Thessaly or Macedonia, Attika was

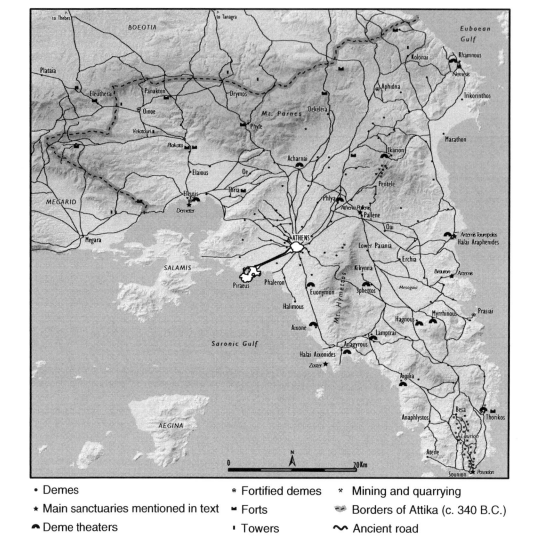

- Demes
- ★ Main sanctuaries mentioned in text
- ▲ Deme theaters

- ◉ Fortified demes
- ◄ Forts
- ı Towers

- ✳ Mining and quarrying
- ～ Borders of Attika (c. 340 B.C.)
- ∿ Ancient road

Map 2.1 Map of Attika.
Source: S. Fachard

less productive from an agricultural point of view. Still, it was far from being poor, as 40 percent of the land could be exploited for agriculture (mostly olive, vine, and barley), enough to sustain roughly 100,000–120,000 people. Moreover, the dry hills and thin soils of Attika hid mineral treasures: pristine Pentelic marble, the material signature of its most renowned architectural achievements; fine clay for producing the local ceramic repertoire, which was in high demand over the entire Mediterranean; and, above all, the Laurion silver mines, whose exploitation in the fifth century contributed significantly to the city's military and economic dominance in the Aegean.

So despite the natural constraints, Athens was able to control an important territory and to sustain an unusually large population, which progressively gave the city an edge in Central Greece and the Aegean in the Classical period. With a population of 200,000–300,000 individuals, of whom 30,000–40,000 were male citizens, Athens was the most populous *polis* of Classical Greece. This was a prodigious source of power at a time when most *poleis* could only field a few hundreds or thousands of hoplites on a battlefield.[1] But how did it get there? How did Athens manage to incorporate such a large *chora* in the midst of fierce regional competition? How was this territory settled, organized, and defended?

Settling Attika

The political unification of such a large *chora* is a complex, multifaceted, and gradual process, and it still remains unclear how Athens progressively acquired and politically unified this territory. For ancient authors, the unification (*synoikismos*) of Attika was achieved by the mythical figure of Theseus.[2] However, if there is any truth in this tradition, such a unification would have not survived the demise of Mycenean Attika, so the formation of Attika as a political territory must have taken place in the Early Iron Age. Athens appears to have been the only substantial settlement in the Attic peninsula to show resilience between the Bronze Age and the Early Iron Age (see Papadopoulos, Chapter 3 in this volume), but by the Late Protogeometric period (925–900 BC), secondary sites were being founded in various areas of Attika by groups seemingly sharing a common material culture. In the Geometric period, the funerary evidence suggests that Athens enjoyed steady demographic growth, and by the end of the eighth century larger communities were occupying and exploiting the most fertile areas of the Attic peninsula (Eleusis, Aphidna, Thorikos, Vari, Brauron, the Mesogaia). At this stage, it remains unclear how these communities interacted with Athens. Were they part of the same polity or were they independent? By 700 BC, was Athens already recognized as a central authority ruling over a defined territory? Those questions cannot be answered. However, a date ca. 620 BC provides a secure *terminus ante quem* for the legal notion of

---

[1] Bresson 2016, 60–61.
[2] See Thucydides 2.15.2–3; Plutarch, *Theseus.*

Athens controlling a political territory. Drako's law on homicide, which required those convicted of involuntary homicide to leave "Attika" until they were pardoned by the relatives of the victim, indicates that Athens controlled a territory which corresponded to the extent of its legal authority.

In the following decades, Attika seems to have experienced population growth, which created social inequalities and problems in land tenure. At the beginning of the sixth century, issues related to land holdings, ownership, and agriculture were addressed by the lawgiver Solon, who allegedly banned the export of Attic products except olive oil. This perhaps suggests that the land could no longer support the population of Athens, which had to rely on foreign imports – a situation that the *polis* would endure for many centuries. In the second half of the sixth century, a period dominated by the tyrannical regime of Peisistratos and his sons, major investments were made in the *chora*. Roads were improved, the shrine at Eleusis was surrounded by walls and received a new Telesterion, and festivals acquired a new dimension (Great Dionysia, Eleusinian Mysteries, Panathenaia). These policies boosted an increased sense of "national (state) unity," now symbolized by Athens' first civic silver coinage bearing the famous owl motif. (See Kroll, Chapter 18 in this volume.) By the end of the sixth century, over 100 communities of various sizes and importance were scattered throughout the Attic peninsula, forming the demographic backbone of Athens and bonded by a more inclusive sense of citizenship. Following the fall of tyranny, the political and civic reforms adopted under the leadership of Kleisthenes (508/7) would finally cement this cultural, political, and military unity, provide Athens with an impressive civic and political organization for centuries to come, and reinforce a strong spatial and territorial unity between *asty* and *chora*.

The Civic and Political Organization of Attika in the Classical Period

Often considered to be the father of Athenian democracy, Kleisthenes implemented (with his team) an impressive package of reforms: an increase in the number of the Attic tribes (*phylai*, from four to ten, now named after Attic heroes); the institutionalization of 139 demes (*demoi*, understood as local communities living on their own land); the creation of thirty *trittyes* made of demes belonging to the three regions of Attika (the coast, the inland, and the city) – three *trittyes* forming a tribe, one from each region. (See also Kierstead, Chapter 27 in this volume.) Each Athenian adult male was registered as a citizen in his deme under his demotic (the latter being hereditary), which granted him the right to attend the Assembly (*ekklesia*). The distribution of the entire male population within demes, *trittyes*, and tribes from all over Attika restrained the influence of old regional power groups and intermingled the Attic population within a new political system, highly participatory for the standards of the time, isonomic in nature, and, as many would claim, "democratic" for the first time. Each deme sent a number of representatives (*bouleutai*, chosen by lot) to the Council (*boule*) according to the size of its population at the time of the reforms. Kleisthenes fixed the number of *bouleutai* at 500, fifty from each tribe serving in rotation as *prytaneis* of the Council during the calendar year. Therefore, every citizen from the remotest part of Attika had his say in the Assembly and had a fair chance of being appointed to the Council or elected to office. This innovative and highly participatory system created political and social ties within an unusually expansive territory.

Thus, the base of this complex pyramid was formed by the demes. The latter embodied communities as well as blocks of territory which were settled, exploited, and delimited, in some cases, by boundaries. Therefore, one must imagine the entire Attic peninsula as a mosaic of 139 deme territories of various demographic and territorial sizes. Some demes had a large population living in an urban settlement that would have been equivalent to many small freestanding independent *poleis* in other regions of the Greek world. Others were composed of a small village or a group of hamlets and farmsteads. But each deme had a communal meeting point, elected a *demarchos* (the word for "mayor" in Modern Greek) in charge of municipal affairs, maintained a roster of its citizens, followed its own calendar, took care of local business, and worshiped its local heroes and gods. Many demes had their own agora, comparable in function to the Athenian Agora, but much smaller in terms of size and volume of trade. Deme agoras are recorded at Eleusis, Dekeleia, Rhamnous, Erchia, Besa, Sounion, and Halai Aixonides, but it is reasonable to believe that many more demes had their own marketplace (Myrrhinous, Steiria, and Thorikos, among others). The latter could be a source of revenue for the deme, and the existence of local agoras clearly testifies to the vitality of the Attic rural economy. Some demes also had their own theater (nineteen are attested by various sources). The earliest, which is found in the silver mining town of Thorikos, has a rectilinear orchestra and dates to the end of the sixth century. At Ikarion, on the shady slopes of Mt. Penteli, the small theater held dramatic performances, and the deme was traditionally identified with Dionysos' first landing in Attika. Other theaters are found at

Eleusis, Piraeus, Acharnai, Euonymon, Sphettos, and Myrrhinous. The deme theaters of Attika were multipurpose spaces: they were used not only for dramatic performances (Rural Dionysia), but also for civic and political meetings, and perhaps even as local courts, thus serving diverse functions within the deme, *trittyes*, and tribes to which they were variously interrelated.

In many ways, the deme was a microcosm of the *polis*. Thanks to the institutional structure of the deme, communities retained their local identity and some form of autonomy, while fully participating in the civic and democratic process of the *polis*.

Living in the *Chora*

The most populous deme was Acharnai (twenty-two *bouleutai*), situated some 12 km northwest of Athens (Map 2.1). In his play *The Acharnians*, Aristophanes portrays its male inhabitants as "sturdy old men, tough as hardwood, stubborn Marathon fighters, men of maple" (178–185). They were deeply attached to their place of origin and suffered from evacuating their fields and homes when the Spartans ravaged Attika during the Peloponnesian War. Many of them were woodcutters and charcoal-makers, exploiting the pine-covered slopes of Mt. Parnes and transporting their products to the city, while others were peasants and artisans. The topography of the deme remains unclear, as multiple finds appear scattered over a large area, suggesting that this populous deme had several hubs of settlements, one of them centered around a theater which would have accommodated the needs of the deme assembly and served as the deme's political center.

Another large deme, but with a more pronounced urban and nucleated character, was Eleusis, situated 21 km west of Athens, where the Sacred Way ended. The settlement was dominated by the Sanctuary of Demeter, but an important population (eleven *bouleutai*) lived around the shrine. The site had been fortified in the sixth century, and part of its population lived within the walls, in a condensed network of streets and houses. Given its position at the western gate of Attika, on the coastal road to Megara and the Isthmus, Eleusis was of great strategic importance for the Athenians, who constantly upgraded its fortifications. In the fourth century, it became the military headquarters for the defense of the territory and the seat of a garrison for ephebes and mercenaries.

Situated at the southernmost promontory of Attika, Sounion is mostly known for its dramatically sited fifth-century marble Doric temple dedicated to Poseidon. Yet the shrine and another dedicated to Athena, which occupy the summit plateau of a steep hill surrounded by the sea, was part of a larger settlement with houses and streets laid out on an orthogonal grid. The deme center was fortified during the Peloponnesian War and served as a naval base for triremes patrolling the strategic sea routes off Cape Sounion. The deme was also a commercial hub and a gateway to the Laurion silver mines, and no less than three agoras are attested within the deme territory.

Rhamnous, situated in northeast Attika and the coast facing the island of Euboea, is arguably the best-preserved Attic deme center. The site occupies a small promontory overlooking two small anchorages. It was fortified and used as a naval base by the Athenians during the Peloponnesian War to patrol the waters of the Euboean Gulf. Within the walls are the notable remains of a very densely occupied habitat, with houses, shops, a banker's stand, a small shrine to Aphrodite, a military mess, and a network of paved streets fitted with drains. A central agora with a portico and a small theater was used for the deme assembly and for the display of inscriptions related to the daily life of the community. The latter comprised many soldiers and mercenaries, as Rhamnous was used by the Athenians as a garrison and military headquarters for the defense of the coast. Inscriptions honor generals and garrison commanders for providing security to the community, for defending their crops, or even for freeing individuals abducted by pirates. The road leading out of the main gate and ascending the surrounding slopes was lined with impressive grave monuments comparable to those found in the Kerameikos in Athens. The road connected the settlement with the Sanctuary of Nemesis, whose temple was burnt by the Persians and rebuilt in the course of the fifth century.

But not all Attic demes were characterized by a dense urban fabric nor fortified (in fact, only nine out of 139 had fortifications). Many were villages of various sizes, groups of hamlets, loose conglomerations of buildings, houses, gardens, and shrines, or even farmsteads and country estates scattered around the territory of the deme. Myrrhinous, for example, occupied the eastern end of the Mesogaia plain along the important road leading to the harbor of Prasiai (now Porto Raphti). Recent excavations have uncovered many remains scattered over a large area, including a deme agora, a Sanctuary of Zeus Phratrios which served as a meeting place for the *demotai*, shrines to Aphrodite and Artemis Kolainis, farmsteads, various buildings, and a dense network of roads, some of them lined with funerary enclosures. With six councilors, Myrrhinous was a medium-sized deme, whose inhabitants appear to have lived scattered around a loose conglomeration of public buildings, dwellings, and shrines that served as the political center of the deme.

Similarly, Halai Aixonides, in the modern suburb of Voula, had a settlement spread out over a large area, with different loci of settlement and commercial activities. In one sector, excavations have revealed an entire neighborhood with an irregular plan comprising several streets separating houses, workshops, small shrines, a clubhouse (*lesche*), and empty plots identified as gardens. The largest house included a round tower and a bathroom with a waterproof floor. At some distance to the south was the deme agora, featuring a large open space with a rock-cut cistern, surrounded by workshops, shops, a small tavern, and a shrine.

However many demes were more modest and much smaller in size. The smallest demes sending one or two *bouleutai* to the Council must be pictured as groups of hamlets or even scattered individual houses and farmsteads. In this respect, the small deme of Atene, west of Sounion, did not have a nucleated center but was constituted instead by a dispersed pattern of habitation, dominated by wealthy farmsteads exploiting agricultural estates.

These various snapshots offer some idea of how life and settlement were organized within demes in the Classical period, but demes were living organisms which evolved throughout the Hellenistic and Roman periods. This means that deme populations fluctuated and settlement patterns within demes changed accordingly. Because of emigration within Attika (from one deme to another, from the city to the countryside and vice versa), fluid movement of people and goods, changing settlement patterns, and varied models of rural exploitation, it is impossible to know precisely how many people lived permanently in the Attic *chora*. However, a range of 100,000 to 150,000 appears plausible for the Classical period. This peak in occupation is followed by a gradual population decrease through the Late Hellenistic and Roman periods in the *chora*, but the causes of this occupational and demographic drop remain only partially understood.

The Sacred Landscape

The demes formed the basis of Attic religious practices, as each deme had its own calendar of sacrifices for gods and local heroes, its own priest(s), and its own sanctuaries. This prodigious diversity was nevertheless cemented by strong religious and social ties across Attika, through leagues of neighboring demes, phratries, the *trittyes*, and the tribes, as well as the overseeing of the *polis* in religious affairs and its direct involvement with the largest festivals and shrines of "Panathenian" status. Regarding the latter, few territories of the Greek world counted as many shrines of monumental character and religious importance. Indeed, while most *poleis* had one important rural "extra-urban" sanctuary (as they are often called), such as the Heraion for Argos or the Artemision for Ephesos, Attika had three sanctuaries of "Panathenian" status (Eleusis, Sounion, and Brauron), that is with strong connections to the Athenian state in terms of cult practices (festivals), administration, and finance, as well as popularity within the broader Attic population. Other shrines enjoyed a more confined influence, such as the Sanctuaries of Nemesis in Rhamnous, Apollo at Cape Zoster, Athena at Pallene, and Artemis Tauropolos at Halai. Some of these shrines, despite their more regional character, nevertheless appear to have been linked with the religious authorities of the *polis* at varying degrees. The cult of Athena Pallenis, for example, was directly administered by a league of nearby demes (Pallene, Gargettos, Acharnai, and Paiania), but the archons of the cult were chosen by the King Archon in Athens. The Sanctuary at Cape Zoster, with its *naiskos* dedicated to Apollo, Artemis, and Leto, was apparently of a more local influence, but his priest enjoyed *proedria* in the Theater of Dionysos and honors by the Council and the People. Small leagues or associations of demes (Tetrakomia of Phaleron, Marathonian Tetrapolis), performed their own rites, followed their own sacrificial calendars, and appointed their cult officials and servants, even sending, in the case of the Tetrapolis, sacred ambassadors to Delphi and Delos. Compared to other *poleis*, the large number of Attic sanctuaries for which we have archaeological, architectural, epigraphical, and literary evidence is unique.

Road Network and Transportation

Such a complex social, political, religious, and territorial organization would not have been possible without an efficient network of communication allowing people, animals, and goods to move swiftly throughout Attika. In the last two decades, archaeological discoveries have changed our picture of the Attic road network to the point where it now appears to be among the densest and best documented of the ancient Greek world. While archaeological evidence records stretches of roads dating back to the Bronze Age, the first communication network was gradually set up in the Geometric and Archaic periods. In the sixth century, the importance of the road network for the unity of Attika appeared obvious to the Peisistratids. They established the Altar of the Twelve Gods in the

Athenian Agora as the zero point from which all distances to villages should be measured and placed herms on the roads at mid-distance between the demes and the city (Plato, *Hipparchos* 228d; see Map 6.2). The network became fully developed in the Classical period, connecting every single deme with the *asty* (Map 2.1). The largest roads were carriage-able (*amaxitos odos*), reaching widths of 3–6 m, and could accommodate carts. Many excavated stretches of roads display a succession of hard layers of composite materials delimited by side walls. Particular care was taken along the Sacred Way to Eleusis, which was marked by *horoi* (boundary stones) and fitted with bridges. In the fourth century, a man named Xenocles built a stone bridge near Eleusis at his own expense, for conveying safely the sacred objects of the procession and facilitating the gathering of pilgrims during the Mysteries, accommodating at the same time the local inhabitants and the farmers (*IG* II^2 1191). This network of highways was supplemented by an even denser number of non-carriageable paths used by pack animals (donkeys and mules), which were more common than carts. Many of these paths were engineered, requiring retaining walls, regular surfaces, zigzags on steep slopes, and even rock carving.

In the fourth century, a board of five *hodopoioi* was in charge of road maintenance and employed a workforce of public slaves to build and maintain the road network (*Constitution of the Athenians* 54.1). The road network was subsequently maintained and even selectively improved in the Hellenistic and Roman periods. The success of Athens' political and territor-ial organization relied heavily on the mobility of its citizens who participated in the administration of the state and the wider political debate. Good roads allowed people to travel in and out of the city quickly, safely, and more comfortably. Efficient roads also boosted commerce and facilitated economic exchanges between the demes and the *asty*. Several routes built in the mountainous borderlands opened up isolated areas, improved access to remote natural resources (wood, charcoal, resin, pitch), and facilitated the movement of troops guarding and defending the borders of Attika. Thus, there were strong political, social, religious, and military incentives for building an efficient road network. Overall, this dense communication network indicates a strong level of political authority and state cohesion.

Defending and Policing the *Chora*

Such a vast territory, with its population, resources, infrastructure, and overall wealth, could not remain unprotected. Athens obviously had a standing army, and the city was protected by city walls that were constantly upgraded. But how could the polis defend its large *chora*, offer protection to the rural population, and secure its agricultural resources? Relations with Boeotia and Megara, Athens' neighbors, were often tense and periodically marked by conflicts. The high level of infrastructure built in the *chora* attracted foreign raiders (*Hellenica Oxyrhynchia* 12.5), and natural resources and cattle situated in the borderlands were often subject to encroachments and raiding.

In the second half of the fifth century, Athens fortified several deme centers (Eleusis, Oinoe, Aphidna, Rhamnous, Sounion) and strategic locations (Panakton, Thorikos), which received a garrison (*phroura*). The latter was composed of soldiers and *peripoloi*, who were in charge of patrolling the borders of Attika under the command of a peripolarch. By the end of the fourth century, the defense of Attika had been perfected. Older defenses had been updated or enlarged, and a new fort built at Phyle. Towers at Velatouri and Plakoto monitored the Oinoe road, connecting Eleusis with Oinoe and Thebes. Smaller rubble forts placed in isolated positions offered bases for patrols in the borderlands. Institutionally speaking, the defense of the territory (*phylake tes choras*) was part of the political agenda and regularly addressed at meetings of the Assembly. Athens also reformed its military organization. Young recruits called ephebes were required to undergo military training over two years, spending one of them patrolling and guarding the borders of the *chora* in the garrison forts. The defense of the territory was under the responsibility of a "general of the territory" (*strategos tes choras*) based most of the time in Eleusis, while the defense of the coastline was assumed by another general based in Rhamnous (*strategos tes paralias*). Both were under the command of the hoplite general. The main tasks of the garrisons were to police the countryside, patrol the borders, monitor people entering the *chora*, protect agricultural resources and infrastructure, and defend the rural population of Attika.

Conclusions

Athens progressively succeeded in acquiring a large *chora* and setting up a territorial organization that constitutes one of the most impressive examples of early state complexity. By the Classical period, an important rural population lived scattered over 100 rural demes, farming the land and exploiting its natural resources. The impression of a "full countryside" is corroborated by two different intensive field surveys conducted at Atene and Oinoe, showing that a peak in occupation was attained in the Late Classical and Early Hellenistic periods. Archaeological research throughout Attika reveals intense signs of activity and agricultural exploitation well beyond the deme centers, suggesting a bustling and active landscape.

Yet, there are still major gaps in our knowledge. Compared to the city and its prestigious monuments, Athens' countryside has often been ignored or treated superficially. There is no overall archaeological map of Attika for studying its occupational history, and few systematic excavations have been conducted outside rural sanctuaries. But the dramatic rise of rescue excavations by the Greek Ministry of Culture as a result of the large-scale construction works undertaken in Attika in the last two decades has brought an extraordinary wealth of new information regarding Attic archaeology. Hopefully, this élan will lead to more systematic excavation and survey. The more we know the Attic countryside, the better we will understand the *polis* of Athens.

Further Reading

For a well-illustrated overview of the archaeology of Attika, see Travlos 1988. On the political and territorial organization of Attika (demes, *trittyes*, tribes), the classic work remains that of Traill 1975 and 1986 and Whitehead 1986. On specific aspects of deme organization, settlement, and land-holding, as well as public and sacred land ownership, see Osborne 1985 and Papazarkadas 2011. Comprehensive studies of individual demes are Lohmann 1993 (Atene), Petrakos 1999 (Rhamnous), Goette 2000 (Sounion), and Kellogg 2013 (Acharnai). On the deme theaters, see Paga 2010. On the religious landscape of Attika, see Parker 1987 and 1996, Paga 2016, and Shear 2016. On the rural landscape, see Lohmann 1992, 1993, and 1995, Jones 2004, and Oliver 2006 and 2007. For survey work, see Lohmann 1993 and Knodell et al. 2017. On Attic roads, see Lohmann 2002, Korres 2009, and Fachard and Pirisino 2015. Many aspects of the Attic economy are treated by Bresson 2016; for a general overview, see Fachard and Bresson forthcoming. On rural fortifications and the defense of Attika's borderlands, see Ober 1985, Oliver 2007, Munn 2010, and Fachard 2017.

Bibliography

Bresson, A. 2016. *The Making of the Ancient Greek Economy: Institutions, Markets, and Growth in the City-States.* Princeton.

Fachard, S. 2017. "The Resources of the Borderlands: Control, Inequality, and Exchange on the Attic-Boeotian Borders." In *Économie et inégalité: ressources, échanges et pouvoir dans l'Antiquité classique,* Vandœuvres, 19–73.

Fachard, S., and A. Bresson. Forthcoming. "Athens and the Aegean." In *The Cambridge Companion to the Ancient Greek Economy*, ed. S. von Reden, Cambridge.

Fachard, S., and D. Pirisino. 2015. "Routes out of Attika." In *Autopsy in Athens. Recent Archaeological Research on Athens and Attika*, ed. M. Miles, Oxford, 139–153.

Goette, H.R. 2000. *Ο αξιόλογος δήμος Σούνιον: landeskundliche Studien in Südost-Attika*. Rahden.

Jones, N.F. 2004. *Rural Athens under the Democracy*. Philadelphia.

Kellogg, D.L. 2013. *Marathon Fighters and Men of Maple: Ancient Acharnai*. Oxford.

Knodell, A.R., S. Fachard, and K. Papangeli. 2017. "The Mazi Archaeological Project 2016: Survey and Settlement Investigations in Northwest Attika (Greece)." *Antike Kunst* 60: 146–163.

Korres, M., ed. 2009. *Αττικῆς οδοί: Αρχαίοι δρόμοι της Αττικῆς*. Athens.

Lohmann, H. 1992. "Agriculture and Country Life in Classical Attika." In *Agriculture in Ancient Greece*, ed. B. Wells, Stockholm, 29–57.

1993. *Atene: Forschungen zu Siedlungs- und Wirtschaftsstruktur des klassischen Attika*. Cologne.

1995. "Die Chora Athens im 4. Jahrhundert v. Chr.: Festungwesen, Bergbau und Siedlungen." In *Die athenische Demokratie im 4. Jahrhundert v. Chr. Vollendung oder Verfall einfer Verfassungsform? Akten eines Symposiums 3.–7. August 1992, Bellagio*, ed. W. Eder, Stuttgart, 515–553.

2002. "Ancient Roads in Attika and the Megaris." In *Ancient Roads in Greece, Proceedings of a Symposion Organized by the Cultural Association Aigeas (Athens) and the German Archaeological Institute (Athens) with the Support of the German School at Athens, November 23, 1998, Athens*, ed. H.R. Goette, Hamburg, 73–91.

Munn, M. 2010. "Panakton and Drymos: A Disputed Frontier." In *Attika: Archäologie einer "zentralen" Kulturlandschaft: Akten der internationalen Tagung vom 18.–20. Mai 2007 in Marburg*, eds. H. Lohmann and T. Mattern, Wiesbaden, 189–200.

Ober, J. 1985. *Fortress Attika: Defense of the Athenian Land Frontier, 404–322* BC. Leiden.

Oliver, G.J. 2006. "Hellenistic Economies: Regional Views from the Athenian Polis." In *Approches de l'économie hellénistique*, eds. R. Descat, Saint-Bertrand-de-Comminges, 215–256.

2007. *War, Food, and Politics in Early Hellenistic Athens*. Oxford.

Osborne, R. 1985. *Demos: the Discovery of Classical Attika*. Cambridge.

Paga, J. 2010. "Deme Theaters in Attika and the Trittys System." *Hesperia* 79: 351–384.

2016. "Attic Sanctuaries." In *A Companion to Greek Architecture*, ed. M.M. Miles, 178–193, Chichester.

Papazarkadas, N. 2011. *Sacred and Public Land in Ancient Athens*. Oxford.

Parker, R. 1987. "Festivals of the Attic Demes." In *Gifts to the Gods. Proceedings of the Uppsala Symposium 1985*, eds. T. Linders and G. Nordquist, Uppsala, 137–147.

1996. *Athenian Religion: A History*. Oxford.

Petrakos, V.C. 1999. *Ο δήμος του Ραμνούντος: Σύνοψη των ανασκαφών και των ερευνών 1813–1998*. Athens.

Shear, T.L. 2016. *Trophies of Victory: Public Building in Periklean Athens*. Princeton.

Traill, J.S. 1975. *The Political Organization of Attika. A Study of the Demes, Trittyes, and Phylai, and Their Representation in the Athenian Council*. Princeton.

1986. *Demos and Trittys: Epigraphical and Topographical Studies in the Organization of Attika*. Toronto.

Travlos, J. 1988. *Bildlexikon zur Topographie des antiken Attika*. Tübingen.

Whitehead, D. 1986. *The Demes of Attika, 508/7–ca. 250 BC: A Political and Social Study*. Princeton.

3 | The Emergence of the *Polis*

JOHN K. PAPADOPOULOS

> Before this [i.e. the *synoikismos* of Attika under Theseus] what is now
> the Akropolis was the city, together with the region at the foot of
> Akropolis toward the south.
>
> Thucydides 2.15.3

> And, finally, the Akropolis, because the Athenians had there in early
> times a place of habitation, is still to this day called by them polis or city.
>
> Thucydides 2.15.6

Around 1200 BC, the great Bronze Age palatial centers of Greece were
destroyed. Shortly thereafter the major Mycenean settlements – Mycenae,
Tiryns, Pylos, Orchomenos, and Gla – were all but abandoned, and these
once-great centers never developed into leading city-states (*poleis*) of the
Greek world. Among the Mycenean citadels, only Athens and Thebes
developed into leading *poleis*. We do not know much about Thebes during
the post-palatial Bronze Age and the early stages of the ensuing Iron Age
(1200–700 BC), but over 200 years of illicit and systematic exploration of
Athens have brought the archaeology of the city into much clearer focus.

The Landscape of the Living and the Dead

What marks out Athens in the Early Iron Age, in contrast to many other
sites, is not only clear continuity from the Bronze Age, but a steady rise of
population throughout the Early Iron Age into the Archaic period. By the
Late Archaic period, Athens becomes a leading city-state and in the early
fifth century BC, the largest *polis* that the Greek world would see before the
rise of mega-cities in the Late Classical and Hellenistic eras.

   The topography of Mycenean Athens was centered on the same rock where
the Neolithic, Early, and Middle Bronze Age villages were located. Although
Athens has yet to yield firm evidence of the trappings of a Mycenean palatial
center (no Linear B tablets, no frescoes, no tholos tombs),[1] the continual use

---

[1] Save but a gold ring with a bull-leaping scene, and the tholos tomb at Menidhi.

and reuse of the Akropolis through the Classical, Hellenistic, Roman, Byzantine, and Ottoman periods all but eradicated the scant vestiges of earlier periods. What survives best are traces of the Mycenean Cyclopean wall around the Akropolis, together with the so-called Pelargikon, a lower fortification wall on the west, northwest, and southwest slopes of the hill (Web Map 3.1). More notably, the Cyclopean wall was multiphased and substantial, architecturally similar to the primary entrance at Tiryns with its large bastion jutting out to the west. Although it is clear that throughout the prehistoric period other areas around the rock were settled, particularly to the south, the Akropolis remained the nucleus, the focus of the Bronze Age settlement, first and foremost a citadel. This strategic aspect of the Akropolis was a feature throughout the more than six-thousand-year history of Athens, and one that continued into the Early Iron Age.

Continuity from the Bronze Age into the Early Iron Age is also clear in the many tombs, especially those in the cemeteries closest to the Akropolis. But rather than beginning with the burials of the Athenian elite nearest the Akropolis, one must start with the most well-explored cemetery, the Kerameikos, in order to establish an enduring feature of the landscape of Athenian death. The area of the Kerameikos excavated by the German Archaeological Institute becomes a full-fledged burial ground at the transition from the Bronze Age into the Early Iron Age, with the tombs of the Pompeion Cemetery, north of the Eridanos River (Web Map 3.2). Some 148 Submycenean tombs have been uncovered in this cemetery alone, mostly inhumations in simple pit or cist graves. In the ensuing Protogeometric period (ca. 1050–900), a new burial ground was established on the south bank of the Eridanos, farther to the west. During the Geometric period (ca. 900–700), tombs were laid out in the same area as the Protogeometric cemetery, with extensions to the north and east; during these periods both inhumations and cremations were practiced, cremations primarily for adults. In the Archaic period (ca. 700–480), graves, together with their associated "offering ditches" (*Opferrinne*) and "offering places" (*Opfergrube* or *Opferplatz*), extended from the Tritopatreion to Peiraios Street in the areas south and north of the Eridanos and continuing northeast to Eleftherias Square and beyond.

Although it is believed that the group(s) that buried their dead in the Kerameikos beginning in the Submycenean period must have lived somewhere to the north of the Akropolis, there is, to date, no evidence of any such habitation in the vicinity of these tombs. The Kerameikos was, first and foremost, a burial ground. What is clear is that, by the Geometric period, Athens had developed a system of roads linking the principal settlement – the area on and around the Akropolis – with the Attic countryside. This is gleaned from the many tombs of the period, including those of the Kerameikos, concentrated near the known gates of the later Themistoklean Wall, where Early Iron Age tombs, as well as cemeteries of later periods were also placed. The Kerameikos was only one of these many cemeteries.

As was the case in the Kerameikos, the Early Iron Age tombs in the area of the later Agora belong to one of several cemeteries. There are at least four well-defined burial grounds, most of which begin in the Late Bronze Age and continue well into the Early Iron Age (Map 3.1). The first is on the north slope of the Areopagos, closest to the Akropolis, which included some of the richest and most prominent tombs of the Bronze Age and the Early Geometric period: the Tomb of the Rich Athenian Lady (Tomb 15), the "warrior" grave (Tomb 13), and the "booties" grave (Tomb 11). Diachronically, this cemetery extends in time from Late Helladic (hereafter LH) IIIA, with an unbroken sequence of tombs from LH IIIC into the Late Geometric and Subgeometric periods. The nearby cemetery on the Kolonos

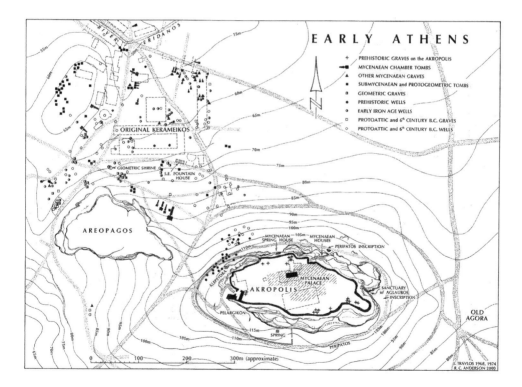

Map 3.1 Plan of early Athens showing the Akropolis, the original Kerameikos (later Classical Agora), and the Late Bronze and Early Iron Age cemeteries.
Courtesy of the American School of Classical Studies at Athens: Agora Excavations

Agoraios above the later Agora preserves two Mycenean chamber tombs dug into the eastern flank of the hill, and there followed numerous tombs dating from Submycenean down to Late Geometric/Subgeometric times. It is likely that much of the Kolonos Agoraios was originally covered by considerably more Late Bronze and Early Iron Age tombs, but later building activity, including the Classical temple known as the Hephaisteion, coupled with the fact that the modern surface here was only a few centimeters above the preserved level of the tombs, accounted for the destruction of many of the earlier burials.

To what extent the cemetery along the south bank of the Eridanos in the Classical Agora represents one cemetery or several different burial grounds is impossible to determine, and given the sheer quantity of later building activity in this area – including the Hellenistic Stoa of Attalos, Roman Odeion of Agrippa, and the transplanted Temple of Ares – we may never know. The tombs uncovered in this area range in date from LH IIB, through LH IIIA/B and LH IIIC, into Submycenean and various phases of the Protogeometric period. The last of the four Agora cemeteries, that to the north of the Eridanos, is still under excavation by the American School of Classical Studies. As of the summer of 2019, ten burials have been unearthed in what must be a cemetery along the banks of the river, all immediately north of the building identified as the Stoa Poikile. The tombs begin in LH IIB/IIIA, and this may be a cemetery dating primarily to the Bronze Age, although there is one tomb, in the upper fill of a well, that is Early Geometric.

The Agora cemeteries share the same burial customs of, and echo the pattern seen in, the Kerameikos, where there are several clearly distinct cemeteries, each separated by major topographical features such as the hills of the Areopagos and Kolonos Agoraios, or the Eridanos, the same river that separates at least two, if not three, of the Agora cemeteries. The Agora and the Kerameikos cemeteries are not the only large cemeteries in Athens. One of the largest Early Iron Age cemeteries found in the modern city is located on the grounds of the Presidential Guard barracks, where seventy-six tombs of the Submycenean and Protogeometric periods were excavated. What is significant is that the pattern seen in the Agora, Kerameikos, and Presidential Guard cemeteries is not one confined to Athens. It is found in most large Early Iron Age sites that have been extensively excavated, such as Lefkandi, Knossos, Iolkos, Ialysos, Old Smyrna, at Zagora on Andros, and the hamlet of Vitsa Zagoriou in Epirus.[2]

---

[2] See Papadopoulos and Smithson 2017, 17–18.

Among the various cemeteries in Athens that have been explored, it is those in the area of the Agora that display the most continuity and resilience over time. These cemeteries begin at an early stage of the Mycenean period (LH II) and continue right through into the Early Iron Age and Archaic periods. Consequently, Early Iron Age Athens was not a series of disparate hamlets each with its own burial plots, but, like other contemporary settlements, a clearly circumscribed proto-urban nucleus, centered on the Akropolis.

The pattern seen in the distribution of tombs and cemeteries outlined above is one that suggests that the early Athenians organized their cemeteries by kin groups, that their burials were formalized, and that the society of the period was already highly stratified. We may never know the precise makeup of these kin groups, but it is no accident that the earliest and most lavishly furnished of the Late Bronze and Early Iron Age cemeteries were those closest to the Akropolis.

Whether understood as a village or as a town, the proto-urban nucleus was the Athenian Akropolis. The overlap of Early Iron Age burials with Mycenean tombs, both in the area of the Classical Agora and to the south of the Akropolis, is remarkable. Taking the evidence of the settlement and cemeteries together allows us not only to posit continuity, but to open the door to an interpretation that seeks the origin of the Greek city – at least in the case of Athens – in an older, more prehistoric past. Such an interpretation would suggest that the collapse of Mycenean palatial society played a major role in the formative political experiments that were to follow, thereby contributing more directly to the formation of the *polis*.

The pattern of continuity seen in the tombs and in the central importance of the Akropolis through time is not only an archaeological phenomenon, but is echoed in our literary sources. Thucydides does not mince his words. In the passages of Book 2 cited at the beginning of this chapter, he clearly states that what is now the Akropolis was the city, together with that region at the foot of the hill, toward the south. He also notes that because the Athenians had established there in early times a place of habitation, the Akropolis is still called by them, to this day (the fifth century BC), *polis* or city.

There is also the more enigmatic passage in Herodotos (7.140) that describes Athens, at the time of the Persian Wars, as "circular" or "wheel-shaped." Indeed, the manner in which the Late Bronze and Early Iron cemeteries of Athens surround the Akropolis defines a circular or wheel-shaped settlement. Taken together, the evidence of Thucydides and Herodotos is compelling, as it refers to the topography of the pre-Persian

War town in which Thucydides was brought up, and which Herodotos knew. By combining the literary evidence with the archaeological, we encounter an Athens that exhibits clear continuity, and a growing population through time, following the troubled times at the end of the Bronze Age. Consequently, Athens is one of those few places that emerges, relatively unscathed, as a major player following the collapse of the Mycenean palatial world.

At the lower end of the time scale, there remains the issue of when, precisely, the Athenian Akropolis became a sacred space devoted to the goddess Athena. Although some scholars have argued that the Akropolis was first set aside as the principal sanctuary of Athena in the second quarter of the sixth century BC, others assume that the citadel became a sanctuary by about 750; the evidence at hand, however, is not conclusive. Moreover, given the nature of the published Early Iron Age material from the Akropolis, it is not impossible that the Akropolis was, for a time in the Early Iron Age, both a sanctuary and a settlement. As we shall see, what changes the topography of Athens radically does not date to the Bronze or Early Iron Age, but to the period immediately after the defeat of the Persians at Salamis in 480.

The Emergence of the Athenian *Polis*

As to what occurred in Athens at any specific time in the Late Bronze and Early Iron Ages, we have little to go on, both on the Akropolis and its surrounds, given the palimpsest of later occupation. But a useful proxy, in broad brushstrokes, is the distribution of sites from LH IIIB (i.e. the last phase of palatial Mycenean) into the Geometric period, determined on the basis of survey.[3] Settlements in Greece drop from 306 in LH IIIB to 132 in LH IIIC (post-palatial) to 95 in Protogeometric, rising to 166 in Geometric times; cemeteries tell a similar, but not quite the same, story: 450 (LH IIIB), 205 (LH IIIC), 245 (Protogeometric), and 332 (Geometric) (the greatest disparity being the number of Protogeometric settlements as opposed to cemeteries). In a more nuanced, and regionally sensitive, overview we find clear continuity from palatial to post-palatial Bronze Age into the Early Iron Age in those areas that witness the greatest growth: Attika, with Athens; Boeotia, with Thebes.[4]

---

[3] See Murray 2017, 141, table 3.12.

[4] Provided by Knodell forthcoming, based on data from central Greece and comparing the number of sites in the eighth century with those in the earlier stages of the Iron Age. While

One way to explain this growth of settlement is to look for key developments in the Early Iron Age, and how Athens, in particular, contributed to each of these and how it fared through time. Enumerated elsewhere are four significant developments in the history of Greece during the Early Iron Age,[5] and Athens played a defining role in all four. The first emerges precisely in the phase of experimentation at the transition from Bronze to Iron Age and follows a pattern already established in the Bronze Age. The contrast between palatial and non-palatial Greece in the Bronze Age mirrors the contrast, in the Early Iron Age, between the Greek *polis*, on the one hand, and the *polis*-less tribal states based on kinship, on the other, or *polis* vs. *ethnos*.[6] Although this contrast becomes most marked in the Archaic period and later, its origins are firmly rooted in the Late Bronze Age, with important developments during the collapse of Mycenean palatial society well into the Early Iron Age. The resilience of Athens as a Mycenean state to survive the collapse and to continue to grow through the ensuing phases is a phenomenon shared by few other sites. While Mycenae, Tiryns, Gla, Orchomenos, and Mycenean Iolkos at Dimini fizzle into insignificance, Athens (and Thebes) develop into full-fledged city-states.

The second important development is Greeks leaving Greece. The movement of peoples, together with their material culture, was an enduring and continuous process throughout the Mediterranean, and one that had important ramifications for Mediterranean history. Greek overseas mobility and settlement must be seen together with similar movements by other Mediterranean peoples, especially the Phoenicians, as this movement acts as a catalyst for various developments throughout the entire region. In comparison to other Greek city-states, Athens was not a primary colonizer – its only colony in South Italy, Thurii, is late, dating to the fifth century BC, and Sigeion in the Troad, according to tradition, was won by the Athenians from its original Mytilenaean colonists – but Athens loomed large in the foundation myths, however real or imagined, of Ionia and the Ionian migration. It was these foundation myths that not only sustained

certain areas in the study region experience marginal growth, like Euboea and Phokis, and others, such as east Lokris and Phthiotis, experience a decline in the number of sites, and Thessaly sees a significant drop (from thirty-two to nineteen), Attika and Boeotia experience a veritable explosion of settlements (twenty-one to fifty-two sites in Attika, twenty-three to fifty-one in Boeotia). While there are many reasons that could account for these patterns, it is striking that the two regions were Attika and Boeotia.

[5] Papadopoulos 2014.
[6] Papadopoulos 2016.

the *polis* but permitted the construction and negotiation of its very under-pinnings: cultural and civic identity.

Ironically, the upside of Athens not being a primary colonizing force is that its population grew and prospered in its own territory. Here the contrast between Athens and Euboean Chalkis could not be greater: Chalkis, together with other erstwhile *poleis*, established numerous col-onies, and won control of the Lelantine Plain from Eretria after the Lelantine War, but was compelled to cede part of its territory to Athenian cleruchs (settlers) in 506 BC, and after its defeat by the Athenians in 446, Chalkis became a tribute-paying ally. Indeed, Athens was to take cleruchies, a special sort of colony in which the settlers kept their original citizenship and did not form completely independent com-munities, to dizzying heights from the end of the sixth century BC through the period of the Delian League in the mid-fifth century.

The third issue relates to the second: it is the quest for metals, the very commodities that define our periodization (Bronze and Iron Ages), and their procurement. The crucial development, however, extends beyond technological innovation, especially the reasons for the adoption and use of iron, the vicissitudes of supply, and the mechanics of regional networks for the procurement of metals. Rather, more significant in the long run is the structuring of commodities of value that ultimately leads to an eco-nomic system of exchange that is not limited to elites. Iron and bronze play a significant role, but perhaps more important is the often overlooked metal of the Early Iron Age, silver. Here the importance and control of the Laurion mines by Athens cannot be underestimated. If there is ever just one compelling reason for the unification of Attika under Athens, it is the control of these mines. The culmination of this development is the inven-tion of coinage, an innovation that was to have global consequences. Although coinage first occurs in the context of Lydia and east Greece during the course of the later seventh century BC, and takes off among the Greek city-states in the sixth century BC, the search for structured commodities of value goes back to the Early Iron Age.

The fourth great Early Iron Age innovation represents no less of a revolution: literacy. It is not just the adoption of the Phoenician alphabet or of a technology of writing that is important, but rather the introduction of alphabetic writing to the unique cultural context of Early Iron Age Greece. Various places in the Aegean contributed to this story, not least Euboea, Methone, and Phrygia, but the Dipylon *oinochoe* (Web Fig. 3.1) found in the Athenian Kerameikos, is still among the very earliest (Late Geometric Ib: 750–735 BC) and longest inscriptions in alphabetic Greek.

It proclaims, "He who, of all the dancers, now performs most elegantly." As noted elsewhere the adoption and adaptation by the Greeks of the Phoenician alphabet to develop their own meant that writing, for the first time in world history, was not limited to a scribal class serving a ruling or religious elite.[7] Writing became a tool that could be exploited by anyone. Eventually, any male citizen could scratch on a potsherd the name of whomever he wished to ostracize from Athens.

The Bigger Picture

In our conventional chronology, the Early Iron Age extends to about 700 BC. But if we look beyond a periodization defined by pottery styles – that is, when a Geometric style is ostensibly replaced by a more figurative one – there is no watershed that we can point to at or around 700. If there is social or cultural change, it happened earlier, around 770/750 BC, when some scholars see a renaissance of sorts in the material culture of the Greek world, with Athens leading the way, though to what extent this was a radical change is moot. In a similar vein, the collapse of the palatial Mycenean way of life occurred at the end of LH IIIB, when most of the citadels were destroyed. Yet, on the basis of pottery styles, Mycenean-type ceramics continue up to that time when Mycenean, or Submycenean, painted pottery is replaced by Protogeometric. But what were the social forces at play at play around 1050 BC that led to this new stylistic development? What was the watershed? Notwithstanding the increasing use of iron for weaponry, even though bronze remained unchallenged as the votive commodity of real value, whatever happened ca. 1050 was more of a whimper than a bang in comparison to what occurred at the end of LH IIIB. It was the collapse of the Mycenean palatial economy around 1200/1190 BC that ushered in a new type of entrepreneur, one not restrained by Mycenean "big men." The archetypal wanderer-entrepreneur is Odysseus, the master of guile and deception: "I am become a name; for always roaming with a hungry heart" (Alfred Tennyson, *Ulysses* 11–12). There is thus a watershed at the very end of LH IIIB, one that played out across various parts of Greece, though not all of Greece; the *ethne* of northern and western Greece, or those of the northern Peloponnese, and many of the islands, especially in the east and north Aegean, were never part of this

---

[7] Papadopoulos 2014.

watershed. Athens, however, was right in the thick of it, one of those few palatial economies that remained resilient after the putative collapse.

The next watershed in Greek history involves a uniquely Athenian story, dating to September of 480 BC after the Athenian victory at Salamis. The most fundamental change in Athenian topography comes in the aftermath of the Persian sack. Having twice defeated the might of the Persian army

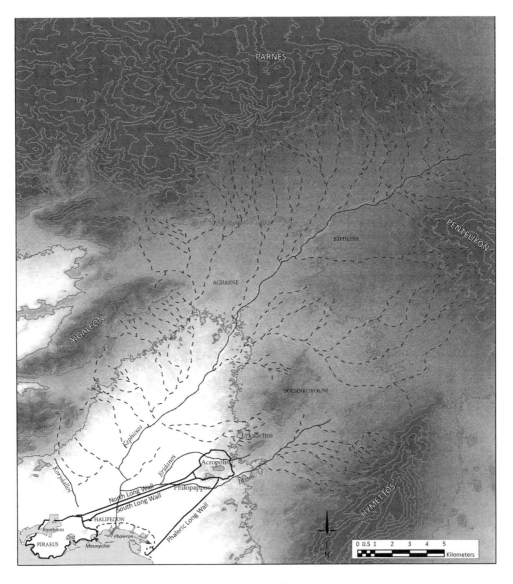

Map 3.2 Map of the Athens basin, including major fortifications.
Source: M. Chykerda

and navy, a combined force much larger than their own, the Athenians, almost single-handedly and in their own territory – at Marathon in 490 and the Straits of Salamis in 480 BC – defeated the Persians. The Athenian *polis* emerged as a major player on the world stage, ready to take on the Spartans, and all of Greece, on their own terms, ready to dispel the Persians from Europe, ready to embark on empire, and ready to provide their city with an architectural presence that would ensure its later archaeological and cultural visibility. In the period immediately following Salamis, the social, political, and architectural reforms of Kimon and Perikles irrevocably transformed the landscape of central Athens. This included the building program on the Akropolis, and a new Agora, which replaced the Archaic agora on the east side of Athens. But this was only part of the story. With the construction of the Themistoklean Wall around Athens, by moving the new harbor to Piraeus from Phaleron, and by connecting Athens to the Piraeus, via the Long Walls (Map 3.2), the Athenians not only doubled the footprint of their *polis*, they created the largest *polis* that the Greek world would see. In this way, the Athenian *polis* emerged during a period defined by two watersheds: the collapse of the Mycenean palatial economy and the Persian Wars.

At its very center stood the Athenian Akropolis. Physically and spiritually, it ceased to be just a citadel and just a sanctuary; it became the focus of a new Athenian identity, one that was never lost from human view or memory. It became a metonymic monument and the enduring symbol of the nascent Greek state after the War of Independence in 1834.

Further Reading

For a good overview of Early Iron Age Athens (Submycenean to Archaic), consult Dimitriadou 2019. For the Mycenean Akropolis, see Iakovidis 2006 (with more recent bibliography in Papadopoulos and Smithson 2017). For the topography of Early Iron Age Athens, see Papadopoulos 2003 (with references to critical earlier work); for the cemeteries of the period in the Kerameikos and Agora, see Morris 1987, Knigge 1988, Papadopoulos and Smithson 2017 (with discussion of resilience theory), and Papadopoulos forthcoming. For the collapse of the Mycenean economy and what follows, Murray 2017 is the most recent; for central Greek settlement and demographics, Knodell forthcoming is invaluable. For periodization in the Early Iron Age, Kotsonas 2016 is important; critical developments of the period are fully discussed in Papadopoulos 2014. Among earlier studies, the overviews by Snodgrass 1971 (cf. also his collected papers, Snodgrass 2006) and Coldstream 1977 remain important.

Bibliography

Coldstream, J.N. 1977. *Geometric Greece*. London.

Dimitriadou, E.M. 2019. *Early Athens: Settlements and Cemeteries in the Submycenaean, Geometric, and Archaic Periods*. Los Angeles.

Knigge, U. 1988. *The Athenian Kerameikos: History, Monuments, Excavations*. Athens.

Knodell, A.R. Forthcoming. *Societies in Transition in Early Greece*. Berkeley.

Kotsonas, A. 2016. "The Politics of Periodization and the Archaeology of Early Greece." *AJA* 120: 239–270.

Iakovidis, S.E. 2006. *The Mycenaean Acropolis of Athens*. Athens.

Morris, I. 1987. *Burial and Ancient Society: The Rise of the Greek City-State*. Cambridge.

Murray, S.C. 2017. *The Collapse of the Mycenaean Economy: Imports, Trade, and Institutions 1300–700* BCE. Cambridge.

Papadopoulos, J.K. 2003. *Ceramicus Redivivus: The Early Iron Age Potters' Field in the Area of the Classical Athenian Agora*. Princeton.

2014. "Greece in the Early Iron Age: Mobility, Commodities, Polities, and Literacy." In *The Cambridge Prehistory of the Bronze and Iron Age Mediterranean*, eds. A.B. Knapp and P. van Dommelen, Cambridge, 178–195.

2016. "Komai, Colonies, and Cities in Epirus and Southern Albania: The Failure of the Polis and the Rise of Urbanism on the Fringes of the Greek World." In *Of Odysseys and Oddities: Scales and Modes of Interaction between Prehistoric Aegean Societies and Their Neighbours*, ed. B.P.C. Molloy, Oxford, 435–460.

Forthcoming. "Athens, 1200–600 BCE." In *The Cambridge Companion to the Greek Early Iron Age*, ed. C. Antonaccio and J. Carter, Cambridge.

Papadopoulos, J.K., and E.L. Smithson. 2017. *The Early Iron Age: The Cemeteries. Agora* 36. Princeton.

Snodgrass, A.M. 1971. *The Dark Age of Greece: An Archaeological Survey of the Eleventh to the Eighth Centuries* BC. Edinburgh.

2006. *Archaeology and the Emergence of Greece*. Ithaca.

Travlos, J. 1971. *Pictorial Dictionary of Ancient Athens*. New York.

Additional resources to accompany this chapter can be found at: www.cambridge .org/NeilsRogers

4 | City Streets, Walls, and Gates

LEDA COSTAKI AND ANNA MARIA THEOCHARAKI

A common perception of the ancient Greek city is of a clean, unlittered environment with thoroughfares meeting at right angles, based on the Hippodamian plan, contained within its boundary walls, and entered via monumental gateways. Ancient Athens could not be more different from this ideal image. Its streets were not grand avenues following a logical grid plan, some of its fortifications were long corridors stretching to the sea, and it had at least one double gate. What these urban elements may have lacked in physical appearance they more than made up for in historic aura. These were the streets walked upon by mythical founders and legendary heroes, ancestral figures and historical leaders, their footsteps reenacting religious processions and athletic events upon age-old sacred ways. They led to significant public spaces, which served as settings for civic orations and philosophical dialogues. Streets were both an integral part of the city plan and a lively stage where primarily male Athenians spent a considerable portion of their everyday lives.

The Streets

The geomorphology, especially the hills and the natural boundary of the Ilissos River, as well as the water sources, dictated the lines of the original paths, which subsequently became the main streets of the urban network. In the direction of the countryside and the sea, the location of the Attic demes, the harbors, and the major extra-urban sanctuaries were the connecting points of the road system. Eventually, the development of the street network within the city was related to issues of land property, city administration, and urbanism. The most decisive element in the formation of the street plan was the construction of the city wall in 479/8 BC, which permanently defined urban space, consolidated internal spatial organization, and separated burial grounds from the rest of the city. It is striking that the urban area enclosed by the Themistoklean Wall was rather small, ca. 2 km^2; one could easily walk from one edge of the city to the other in half an hour.

The street plan is the backbone of the city plan; it structures urban space, whether to define the boundaries of private property or to provide access to places and to facilitate circulation (Map 4.1). Some old paths and streets acquired symbolic meaning that was reinforced and perpetuated by rituals and processions, while streets leading to public buildings and sanctuaries attained a more monumental character with ramps and stairways. Streets constantly interact with roadside structures, defining their limits and challenging their survival. Numerous examples of encroachment onto street space exist, which explain why the state was interested in protecting road space.

Although the overall street layout was rather meandering with narrow, winding streets, it was not hard to orient oneself, since certain features, namely the hills (Akropolis, Lykabettos, Western Hills), were visible from all around. The Akropolis, as it rises above the rest of the city, naturally dictated a set of ring roads around the slopes starting with the Peripatos, or walkway encircling the citadel. This pattern was "mirrored" in the periphery of the city, where a set of three ring roads ran around the constituent parts of the fortifications: along the inner side of the city wall, between the city wall and the *proteichisma*, and outside the moat. These outer ring roads allowed circulation around the city, fundamental for moving troops quickly from one point to another, but also for everyday traffic to bypass the city center, not unlike today's motor beltways. Basic arteries led from the gates to the center, offering a direct view to the Akropolis and a natural unobstructed flow of direction toward the center. Other streets crossed the city, joining gate to gate, especially on the north–south and east–west axes. In general, streets associated with gates display some degree of regularity, which may be the result of extensive public works of the second half of the fourth century BC. Some regularity in the street plan can also be observed in flatter areas, such as the southern part of the city, where the streets appear to have been laid out in a more systematic way.[1] In these areas, streets meet at right angles and form regular crossroads and orthogonal housing plots, while in the rest of the city, junctions of streets present a great variety in form, affecting the plan of houses which are thus set in wedge-shaped plots (see Harrington, Chapter 9 in this volume).

Continuous habitation and use account for the diachronic character of the street layout, especially in the residential districts. Before the Hellenistic and Roman periods, even widespread destructions such as the Persian sack of the city in 480/79 BC did not seriously affect the street network.

---

[1] See Korres 2009, 81–82.

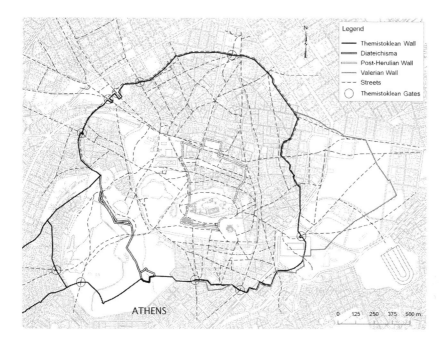

Map 4.1 Map of Athens, with reconstructed walls, streets, and gates based on excavated remains.
© Dipylon Society/Stamatina Lampraki

However, large-scale building projects, such as the laying out of the Roman Agora or the construction of the Library of Hadrian, brought more radical changes to the street pattern, since they cleared large surface areas in the civic center, thus eradicating earlier structures and streets.

The stratigraphy of the streets attests to leveling and cleaning operations, dumping of materials, and covering over of preexisting structures, and is the most vivid witness of the constant flow of people, cultures, and historic events. One of the oldest streets of Athens was the route later known as the Panathenaic Way. It is perhaps the only excavated street with identifiable Neolithic surfaces of use, and one of the few with surfaces of Middle Helladic and Late Helladic date. The South Road and the North Road of the Agora, two streets with a long history along natural paths, also preserve prehistoric road surfaces, while the Mycenean chamber tombs in the southern part of the city (along modern Demetrakopoulou and Veikou Streets) provide indirect evidence for the existence of old streets. From the Geometric period, and especially from the Archaic period on, examples of excavated street surfaces increase throughout the city. Streets have been excavated within designated archaeological sites and in more than 300 modern rescue excavations in the city.

In terms of technical characteristics, the defining elements of an Athenian street are the retaining walls and the road surfaces (Web Fig. 4.1).[2] Most streets were of packed dirt, while very few examples of paved streets have been excavated. The composition of the road surfaces may include sand, gravel, pebbles, sherds, and debris used for filling that contained all sorts of refuse material, from bones and shells to *ostraka* and figurine fragments, but also anything that one might unintentionally lose on the street, most frequently coins. In some cases, reused architectural members and pieces of sculpture have been revealed within street surfaces. The most striking example of Archaic sculpture used in the construction of a street came to light along the Sacred Way in the Kerameikos, in the area outside the Sacred Gate. The 2002 excavations revealed a marble kouros, a fragment of a marble sphinx, two marble lions, a fragment of a marble column with an Ionic capital, and a fragment of a poros Doric capital, all in secondary use set in the course of the Sacred Way and scarred with wheel ruts. The relevant road surface is associated with the construction of the first phase of the Sacred Gate (479/8 BC). One cannot help but compare this practice in road building with the similar and contemporary practice of using spolia in the construction of the Themistoklean city wall (see below).

The retaining walls of the street consisted of two parallel walls that contained the road surfaces and defined the edges of the street. They may have belonged to roadside buildings or may have been freestanding walls of various masonry styles and building materials. Retaining walls, like fortifications, were continuously repaired, and this may account for differences in masonry noticeable in the same wall. Also, their height rose as road surfaces rose, and this can be indicative of their dating and life span. The average width of an Athenian street was 3.50–4.50 m, though there are two notable exceptions: the Panathenaic Way, which in the Hellenistic period reached a width of 29 m, and the Dromos (Kerameikos Road) from the Dipylon to the Academy which was, at least outside the city gate, 40 m wide. Both of these avenues were used for religious and athletic events, such as the racing of chariots, which justified their unusual width. Another notable Athenian street, the Street of the Tripods, was also wider than average (ca. 6 m). It has been estimated that a width of 2 m was sufficient for the passage of pack animals, but there are even narrower streets (alleys) ca. 1–1.20 m wide. Roads leading to and from city gates seem to have received a more formal delineation in the second half of the fourth century, with extensive repair works and an increase in their width.

---

[2] For the technical characteristics of Athenian streets, see Costaki 2006, 39–92.

There is evidence that the urban street network was used by wheeled traffic, since wheel ruts have been preserved on the hard-packed dirt surfaces, as well as on the bedrock when it served as a road surface, as one can still see on the road through the deme of Koile, between the hills of the Muses and the Nymphs.[3] Impressive wheel ruts are also visible on the paved surface of the Panathenaic Way of the Roman period. It is certain that wheeled traffic from the harbor at Piraeus and the Attic countryside would enter the city from the various gates, especially the Piraeus Gate and the Dipylon, carrying goods and heading toward the Agora. Heavy wheeled traffic would have been directed from the quarries at Penteli, Hymettos, and Piraeus to the center of the city for the various building projects over the centuries.

The variety of types of drains and water pipes that were installed along the streets attests to the existence of a developed water management system, the origins of which date to the Archaic period (see Stroszeck, Chapter 8 in this volume). In the Makriyannis plot south of the Akropolis, where excavations preceding the construction of the new Akropolis Museum and the Metro station brought to light an extensive residential district, the streets were furnished with a central drain with side drains cutting through the retaining walls and emptying into it.[4] Water manage-ment and street construction are interconnected public works, also associ-ated with the fortifications, since the moat around the city wall was used for the disposal of wastewater. Large stone-built drains ran perpendicular to the ring road, cut through the *proteichisma* and emptied into the moat. Some narrow streets, occasionally paved and following the natural down-ward slope, served as drainage alleys (Web Map 4.1).[5]

As attested in Aristotle's *Constitution of the Athenians* (50.1–2, 51.1, 54.1; *Politics* 1321b 20–27), the state was responsible for the maintenance of the streets. Literary sources refer to *hodopoioi*, *agoranomoi*, and *astynomoi*, officials charged with maintaining and supervising the streets. Among their duties were the regular leveling and clearing of the streets, especially in preparation for religious festivals and processions, as well as ensuring that roadside buildings did not encroach onto street space, including overhanging balconies and drains. In the archaeological record there is evidence of the continuous resurfacing of the streets; some streets

---

[3] Costaki 2009, 103–104.
[4] Parlama and Stampolidis 2000, 32–37; *ArchDelt* 55 (2000) B', 49–56; *ArchDelt* 56–59 (2001–2004) B', 147–151.
[5] Like the one excavated on 19–25 Parthenonos Street; see *ArchDelt* 29 (1973–1974) B', 44–47.

have as many as several dozen successive road surfaces. A clear and serviceable street network was of paramount importance for the survival of the urban plan. At the same time, citizens were expected to repair the retaining walls bordering their properties and not to neglect keeping the streets unobstructed. Boundary markers (*horoi*) of streets further highlight the city's interest in protecting street space. About twenty *horoi* of roads have come to light in Athens and Piraeus, but the majority of them were not found in situ. Other inscribed boundary markers set up on the sides of streets reveal the frequent conflict between private and public space. However, these boundary stones did not remain visible for long, since they were usually buried in the rising street layers or were damaged by passing traffic.[6]

Few streets are known by name; most of the preserved names derive either from the name of the destination (e.g. *Acharniki hodos* is the road heading to the northern deme of Acharnai, *Phaleriki hodos* is the road to Phaleron) or from the cultic use of the street (e.g. Panathenaic Way, the street used by the procession during the Panathenaic Festival, or *Hiera Hodos*, the Sacred Way to Eleusis). The Street of the Tripods was an exceptional street in the heart of the city leading from the Prytaneion to the Sanctuary of Dionysos on the south slope of the Akropolis (Pausanias 1.20.1). It took its name from the choregic tripods that the winners of the dithyrambic contests of the Dionysia (*choregoi*) set up on monuments along the street. These roadside structures combined architecture, sculpture, and inscriptions, creating a unique setting where Athenians liked to stroll (Athenaios, *Deipnosophistai* 12.60 [542–543]) and comment as they read the inscriptions carved on them.

The combination of images, writing, and symbolism was only paralleled by the Street of the Tombs in the Kerameikos and the Dromos of the Demosion Sema (state burial ground). There, the funerary monuments of individuals and their families or the tribal monuments of those who had fallen in battle also offered a complex setting of imagery and commemoration for passersby. One could not only admire the ideal Athenian citizen as portrayed on the tombstones, but could also read the names of the deceased on the gravestones. (See also Shea, Chapter 10 in this volume.) This interaction of inscribed roadside monuments with pedestrians is very distinctive of Athenian streets and fundamental in the shaping of Athenian identity. On a symbolic level, the streets of Athens

---

[6] Costaki 2006, 95–97.

highlighted the connections made by a society between past and present. Athenians exploited writing, sculpture, and architecture in intricate ways creating powerful *lieux de mémoire* along major routes of the city.

In the Hellenistic and Roman periods, some streets in the center of the city received monumental articulation by the addition of arches, marble paving, or colonnades along their sides.[7] One of the most impressive colonnaded streets led from the Dipylon Gate to the Agora and perhaps also along the north side of the Agora toward the Library of Hadrian. Another such monumental colonnaded street on the east–west axis has been reconstructed east of the Roman Agora at the top of a monumental stairway south of the Tower of the Winds.[8] So far, no such examples of monumentally articulated streets have been excavated on the north–south axis. The reason may be that the large Dipylon Gate was considered the primary entrance to the city. The streets in and around the Agora, being the most frequented, attracted the most roadside monuments ranging from statues to shrines, arches, trophies, and inscribed dedications, a fact described by Pausanias and verified by excavations.

Streets were conceptualized as a stage for civic or religious activities. Processional routes involved large crowds of people, animals, and a certain degree of theatricality accentuated by elements now lost, such as music or torchlight. Athenian city streets may have been humble in construction, resembling for the most part the dirt roads of pre-industrial societies, but around the civic and religious center, they, along with fortifications and gates, had the ability to promote, through public display, collective ideals and collective memory, historical consciousness, and civic identity.

The Walls

It has been said that people, not walls, make a city. But in the case of ancient Athens, walls, streets, and gates were an integral part of the city since its earliest days and continued to shape the urban experience during various stages of growth, destruction, recovery, and decline. Walls are generally based on the local topography, following the lines of higher elevations, but the ranges surrounding Athens (Aigaleos, Parnes, Pentelikon, Hymettos) are far from the Akropolis, which always formed

---

[7] One could consider the Greek stoa bordering the streets as a predecessor of the colonnaded street of the Roman era.

[8] Korres 2009, 85–86.

the focal point of urban life. Rising high above the surrounding plain, it was defended with massive fortifications since the Late Bronze Age, and was in continuous use, with perennial repairs, up until the Greek War of Independence (1821–1830). The later city wall around Classical Athens defined the boundaries of the *asty*, while the primary channels of communication determined the placement of gates.

Aristotle (*Politics* 1330b18) states that a democracy prefers a fortified plain (as opposed to monarchies and oligarchies, which prefer citadels), and the longest walls of Classical Athens were built in low-lying areas. As will be seen in the following account, the city walls of Athens consisted of the enceintes surrounding the inhabited areas of Athens and its main harbor 6–7 km away, three long walls extending to the ports of Phaleron and the Piraeus, and a cross-wall known as the *diateichisma* over the low hills west of the Akropolis. The connection between the inland *asty* and its harbor through the Long Walls remained intact throughout the Peloponnesian War, and so the Athenians were assured of the city's sea power. In addition, the fortified urban complex secured the population from the countryside during Spartan invasions or at times of emergency.

Although there may have been an earlier city wall, the earliest surviving circuit wall of Athens is that known as the Themistoklean Wall. Built rapidly after the devastation caused by the Persian invasion of Athens in 480/79 BC, it enclosed an area extending outside the earlier city borders, as Thucydides (1.93.2) states, "in every direction" (Map 4.1).[9] It was built in great haste, perhaps within a year, and everyone in the city of Athens helped in this task. Sections of the enceinte have come to light within the archaeological sites of the Kerameikos, the hills of the Muses, the Pnyx and the Nymphs, the Olympieion, and in at least 180 rescue excavations in modern Athens.[10]

Estimated to have been ca. 6,400 m in length, the Themistoklean Wall had a double-faced stone socle with inner fill and mudbrick superstructure, and was founded directly on bedrock, often disturbing tombs of the Geometric period. The stone socle ranged in width between 2.50 and 3.25 m and did not exceed 1.20 m above ground level. The wall's original height must have reached about 6–10 m. Besides mudbrick, building materials consisting of spolia, such as architectural members of poros limestone or marble, funerary *stelai*, bases of statues, and fragments of

---

[9] There are no securely attested physical remains of a pre-Themistoklean circuit wall, and so the debate over its existence is still open.

[10] Katsianis et al. 2018, 179–181.

sculptures roughly hacked for reuse, all of Archaic date. The testimony of Thucydides (1.93.2) that "there are many *stelai* from grave monuments and worked stones built in" has been well attested by the archaeological evidence.

Archaeological research can confirm that safeguarding the defensive capability of the walls was a constant concern of the state. The Athenians first repaired their walls in the period of the Peloponnesian War, probably following the great earthquake of 426 BC (Thucydides 3.87.4), using polygonal limestone blocks, lightly tooled. The next building phase is traditionally linked to the period of Konon, ca. 395–391 BC. Newly quarried hard limestone blocks were used, some distinctively large and dressed in broached or furrowed work with drafted joints.[11] Following the victory of Philip over the Greeks in the Battle of Chaironeia in 338 BC, a systematic effort was undertaken under the leadership of Lycurgus and Demosthenes (*On the Crown* 248; *Against Ktesiphon* 3.14, 17, 23, 27, 28, 31) to modernize the fortifications against the powerful siege techniques of the Macedonians. The text of an inscription (*IG* II^3 429.1–46) concerns repairs of the walls at Eetioneia, the rest of Piraeus, and the Long Walls (see below), and we can reasonably assume that these projects would have also included work on sections of the Athenian circuit wall. It was then that the use of catapults was introduced to Athenian *ephebes* (*Constitution of the Athenians* 42.3).

Another building inscription from the end of the fourth century BC (*IG* II^2 463) preserves a decree ordering specific repairs to be carried out on the walls of the *asty*, the Long Walls, and the walls of Piraeus. This major renovation project was led by Demochares in the years 307–304, when the city was under the control of Demetrios Poliorketes. This early Hellenistic circuit wall was augmented by new towers, and the interior faces of the wall were outfitted with stone stairways or ramps that gave access to wall-walks protected by battlements. Two principal outworks surrounded the main wall: the *proteichisma* and a defensive moat. The *proteichisma* was a wall of lesser thickness built in isodomic masonry of conglomerate stones set alternately in courses of headers or stretchers. The moat was up to 11 m deep and 12.5 m wide, at its maximum dimensions (Fig. 4.1).[12]

---

[11] However, if the Athenian enceinte remained intact after the victory of the Spartans in the Peloponnesian War in 404 BC, as Conwell has proposed, and only large sections of the Long Walls and the circuit wall of Piraeus were destroyed, this elaborate masonry could possibly belong to later fortification works undertaken in the years following the battle of Chaironeia in 338. See Conwell 2008, 105.

[12] For the structural characteristics of the Hellenistic wall in Athens, see Theocharaki 2011, 138–146.

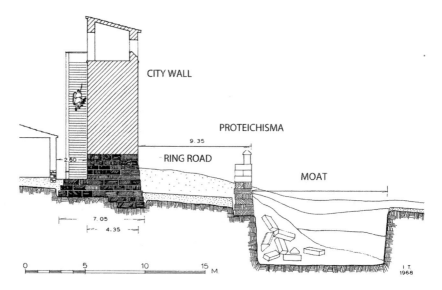

Fig. 4.1 Cross-section of the Athenian fortifications.
Source: Travlos 1971, fig. 228, adapted; courtesy of the Archaeological Society at Athens

Among the several remains of the Hellenistic fortifications in modern
Athens, a stretch of solid stone masonry 2.50 m high is preserved at 6
Dragatsaniou Street (Web Fig. 4.2).[13] It is about 5 m thick, which makes it
one of the widest stretches of the Athenian fortifications: the internal face
of the wall was widened to 6.85 m for the construction either of steps
leading to towers and battlements or of a ramp for lifting ballistic
machines. Instances of all-stone walls found in other parts of the city have
been documented with a height ranging between 6 and 9 courses. The
original height of the Hellenistic Dipylon reached about 10 m.[14]

Following the defeat of the Piraeus and the fort at Mounychia in 295/4
BC, Demetrios Poliorketes attempted a second siege of Athens and forced
the impregnable city to surrender through starvation. Immediately afterwards, he installed a garrison at the peak of the Hill of the Muses where he
built a fort (Plutarch, *Demetrios* 34.5; Pausanias 1.25.8), which was successfully besieged by the Athenians a few years later (287). Once the
Athenians gained their independence (287–263/2), they had no reason to
keep the fortified area between the *asty* and the occupied harbor (295–229).
They built the *diateichisma*, a ca. 850-meter-long cross-wall, running from

---

[13] The preserved sections of the city wall are presented in Theocharaki 2020, 281–315.
[14] Gruben and Müller 2018, 68.

the Macedonian fort up to the Hill of the Nymphs (Map 4.1).[15] It had a double-faced socle and a mudbrick superstructure. The faces of the socle were built in isodomic masonry of conglomerate blocks, and cross-walls divided the interior into compartments filled with earth and rubble. This so-called compartment wall reduced the size of the enceinte marking the Athenians' decision to abandon the Long Walls,[16] and it redefined the city's southwest boundary until the end of antiquity. Houses were deserted or destroyed to make way for its construction, and the pattern of land use as well as the landscape changed radically: by early Hellenistic times, the preexisting residential area had become a burial ground. An all-stone extension of this wall, known as the White Poros Wall, was added in the second century BC on the Pnyx Hill, slightly farther west of the *diateichisma*, reinforced by a series of buttresses along its inner face.

Military operations in Athens in the following decades proved that the fortifications provided sufficiently robust defense. In 262, at the end of the Chremonidean War, the city surrendered only after a long siege, and a new Macedonian garrison was installed on the Hill of the Muses (*FGrH* 244 F44). After many years of peace, Athens withstood another attack, this time in 200 BC by King Philip V of Macedon, who was not able to breach the Dipylon Gate (Livy 31.24.9). Sections of the Themistoklean city wall suffered extensive damage during the invasion of the Roman general Sulla, after he broke through the city wall between the Sacred and the Piraeus gates in 87/6 BC (Plutarch, *Sulla* 14.1–2).

Another extensive fortification was put up during the reign of the emperor Valerian (AD 253–260) or his son Gallienus (AD 260–268), designated as the Valerian Wall (Map 4.1). A double-faced wall made of spolia, this huge public work has been associated with an unprecedented issue of Athenian coins connected to Gallienus' visit to Athens in AD 264. The new fortification extended to the east outside the earlier Themistoklean course to include a flourishing part of the city, which had developed under Hadrian in the early second century AD. The Valerian Wall, however, did not protect the Athenians against the Germanic tribe known as the Herulians, who devastated the city in AD 267. In the first decades after the Herulian invasion, a much smaller circuit was constructed

---

[15] Thompson and Scranton (1943, 337) originally associated the building of the Compartment Wall with the building inscription *IG* II² 463 dated to 307/6 BC, where a *diateichisma* is mentioned (lines 52–54). During the course of later investigations, ceramic finds re-dated the remains of the wall to a period after this inscription, specifically between 300 and ca. 280 BC (Thompson 1982, 146, n. 44; Conwell 2008, 177–182).

[16] Conwell 2008, 191, 204.

on a new line. The so-called Post-Herulian Wall extended to the north of the Akropolis and also enclosed parts of the southern slope (Map 4.1).[17] The city gradually spread outside this wall, and by the early Byzantine period the old Valerian Wall had acquired a renewed defensive role. A new type of nearly square towers in mortared rubble then appeared, with sides about 5 to 6 m long, not structurally connected to the wall. The established date of these towers is Justinianic (sixth century AD; Procopius, *On Buildings* 4.2.23–24), yet, one cannot rule out the possibility that some had been constructed shortly before the Visigoth King Alaric's invasion of the city in AD 395.

The Long Walls

Reliance on Athenian naval strength was a fundamental principle in the city's defensive planning as early as the fifth century, and so Themistokles was determined during his term as archon (493/2 BC) to build the walls of the city's harbor at Piraeus. His strategy against the Persian threat, should defense of the *asty* prove impossible, was for the Athenians to take refuge behind the Piraeus' circuit wall, from where they would have quick access to their impregnable fleet (Thucydides 1.74.4, 1.93.7). Few circuits are likely to have rivaled in size and thickness the walls that Themistokles had planned for the Piraeus; they were built entirely of stones that were clamped together on the outside with iron clamps and lead. From the mid-fifth century onwards, Piraeus had become the Athenians' principal economic and military harbor, and communication with Athens had to be safeguarded. (See Steinhauer, Chapter 16 in this volume.) Pursuing Themistokles' strategic planning, Kimon and Perikles focused on the creation of a distinct fortified zone, formed by the twin Athens–Piraeus Long Walls together with the sections of the two circuit walls at either end. The movements of troops were facilitated, and the uninterrupted importation of food was ensured.

The first two Long Walls, namely the North and the Phaleric (462/1 and 458/7 BC) crossed the broad coastal plain that separated the *asty* from its harbors at Piraeus and Phaleron (Map 4.2). The later Middle, or South, Long Wall (around 443/2 BC) ran almost parallel to the North at a distance of 183 m. All three Long Walls functioned until the Dekeleian War

---

[17] Frantz 1988, 125–141.

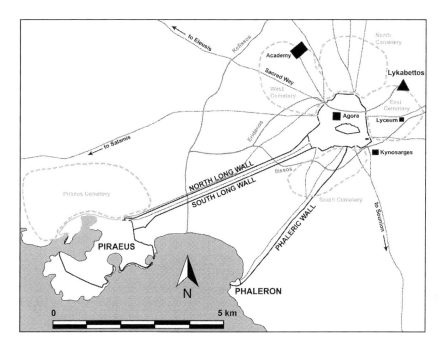

Map 4.2 Map of the Long Walls from Athens to Piraeus and Phaleron, with extra-urban streets, cemeteries, and rivers.
Source: D. Weiss adapted in part from Travlos 1971, fig. 213, courtesy of the Archaeological Society at Athens

(413–404 BC), when the Phaleric line became permanently obsolete.[18] Large sections of these huge constructions with stone socle and mudbrick superstructure were dismantled in 404 after the Peloponnesian War. Ten years later, Konon rebuilt the twin structures (ca. 395–391 BC) with hammer-dressed blocks in trapezoidal masonry; another rebuilding in solid-block isodomic masonry was implemented by Lycurgus in 337, and, some thirty years later, repairs were carried out by Demochares (307–304 BC). The Long Walls were abandoned in early Hellenistic times after the building of the new fortifications across the Pnyx range.

The Gates

At least ten gates built during the original construction phase of the Themistoklean Wall were placed on the axis of preexisting roads

---

[18] Conwell 2008, 100.

(Map 4.1).[19] The Sacred Way from Eleusis and the Kerameikos Road led to the Sacred Gate and the Dipylon Gate, respectively. Two additional roads of pre-Themistoklean date, the one to the west of the Olympieion propylon and the other on modern Erechtheiou Street, corresponded to another two gates built in the original phase of the Themistoklean Wall, as documented by excavated physical remains of the gates themselves. Other examples include the arteries that coincide with modern Leokoriou, Georgiou, Herakleidon, and Phalerou Streets and would have led to gates in the city wall. Another two gates might have been placed on the line of roads that followed natural passes oriented toward the city wall: the road through the deme of Koile followed the gulley between the hills of the Muses and the Nymphs in the direction of Piraeus, and the pass southwest of the Hill of the Muses heading to Phaleron.

The ten generally accepted ancient names for the gates of the Athenian city wall are: *Hiera* (Sacred Gate), *Dipylon* (*Thriasiai* or *Kerameikai*), *Hippades*, *Acharnikai*, *Diocharous*, *Diomeis*, *Itoniai*, *Melitides*, *Demiai*, and *Peiraikai*. At the end of the nineteenth century, we gained two additional names for gates from epigraphical evidence: one is referred to as *halade* (*IG* I³ 84.35–36); the other gate led to the Baths of Isthmonikos (*IG* I³ 84.36–37). The identification of these names with the gates of the Themistoklean circuit in its original or later phases remains largely unresolved. Comprehensive reviews of the corresponding names and gates were proposed by Judeich (1931) and Travlos (1971), who suggested fifteen gates. In the present state of research, ten gates in the city wall can be dated to the initial period of construction with a certain degree of confidence. Another fifteen gates or posterns can be identified on the evidence of roadways connecting the urban center with areas outside it that date to later periods, although some of those might have been constructed in the original phase of the Themistoklean city wall.

The Themistoklean Gate consisted of an enclosed forecourt that was open toward the countryside and closed toward the city. It was designed on a clear strategic plan that did not alter over time, namely to trap the enemy in the court area. The defenders fought from the battlements, which went around the walls of the gate, and from two square outer towers. In the case of the Dipylon Gate, the towers were four, and the outer western one projected further forward than the respective eastern tower. This particular

---

[19] The positions of the gates in the Themistoklean course are discussed in Theocharaki 2020, 233–280.

design exploited the fact that the attackers had their unprotected sides exposed to the tower, an element of warfare that was used in the earliest days of Athens' fortifications, that of the Bronze Age 'Cyclopean' wall on the Akropolis.

Conclusion

The fortifications and the streets of Athens remained throughout the history of the city the most permanent and unchanged features of the urban form. Once built, the Themistoklean Wall remained in use with continuous repairs and modifications for over eleven centuries, proof of its successful layout and effective design. Both walls and streets structure space and define the urban area and direct circulation, having an impact on everyday life in the city. They are associated with the survival of the city, physical and economic, and the security of the inhabitants. For this, it was a major concern of the state to keep them in good shape and to oversee their administration. Two elements so vital for the history and topography of ancient Athens may remain invisible in the modern urban landscape, buried beneath modern buildings, parking lots, and Metro stations; however, they are well documented in the archaeological record of hundreds of excavations.

Further Reading

A web-mapping platform with all published archaeological remains revealed in rescue excavations in Athens from the nineteenth century onwards will be launched in 2020 by the Dipylon Society for the Study of Ancient Topography (https://dipylon.org). Costaki 2006 and 2009 offers a comprehensive study of Athenian streets, discussing technical matters and urban planning issues. Information on stretches of the city walls and the streets excavated in rescue excavations can be found in the reports of the Archaeological Service published annually in the *Archaiologikon Deltion* (in Greek).

For fortifications in Athens, Theocharaki 2020 provides the definitive study of the city walls throughout the centuries, assembling literary sources and archaeological evidence. The study of the fortifications in the Kerameikos has been recently enriched by the final publications of the Dipylon and Sacred Gates (Gruben and Müller 2018 and Kuhn 2017, respectively). Conwell's 2008 monograph throws new light on the Long Walls, arguing that they were effective whenever the Athenians were confident in the safety of their fleet. Judeich 1931 and Travlos 1960 and 1971 provide the best overview of the location and names of the city gates and a general discussion of the city streets.

Bibliography

Conwell, D.H. 2008. *Connecting a City to the Sea: The History of the Athenian Long Walls*. Leiden.

Costaki, L. 2006. "The *Intra Muros* Road System of Ancient Athens." PhD dissertation, University of Toronto.

2009. "Οδικό δίκτυο των Αθηνών." In *Αττικής Οδοί: Αρχαίοι δρόμοι της Αττικής*, ed. M. Korres, Athens, 96–111.

Frantz, A. 1988. *Late Antiquity:* AD *267–700. Agora 24*. Princeton.

Gruben, G., and K. Müller. 2018. *Das Dipylon. Kerameikos 22*. Wiesbaden.

Judeich, W. 1931. *Topographie von Athen*. 2nd edn. Munich.

Katsianis, M., S. Lampraki, A.M. Theocharaki, M. Pigaki, L. Costaki, and E. Papaefthimiou. 2018. "Reconnecting a Fragmented Monument through Digital Mapping: The City Walls of Athens." *Studies in Digital Heritage* 2.2: 177–195.

Korres, M. 2009. "Οδικό δίκτυο γύρω από την Ακρόπολη." In *Αττικής Οδοί: Αρχαίοι δρόμοι της Αττικής*, ed. M. Korres, Athens, 74–95.

Kuhn, G. 2017. *Das Heilige Tor. Kerameikos 19*. Wiesbaden.

Parlama, L., and N.C. Stampolidis, eds. 2000. *Athens: The City beneath the City: Antiquities from the Metropolitan Railway Excavations*. Athens.

Theocharaki, A.M. 2011. "The Ancient Circuit Wall of Athens: Its Changing Course and the Phases of Construction." *Hesperia* 80: 71–156.

2020. *The Ancient Circuit Walls of Athens*. Berlin.

Thompson, H.A. 1982. "The Pnyx in Models." In *Studies in Attic Epigraphy: History and Topography Presented to Eugene Vanderpool*, Princeton, 133–147.

Thompson, H.A., and R.L. Scranton. 1943. "Stoas and City Walls on the Pnyx." *Hesperia* 12: 269–383.

Travlos, J. 1960. *Πολεοδομική εξέλιξις των Αθηνών*. Athens.

1971. *Pictorial Dictionary of Ancient Athens*. New York.

Additional resources to accompany this chapter can be found at: www.cambridge.org/NeilsRogers

5 | The Akropolis

PANOS VALAVANIS

The Akropolis, a rocky outcrop with an elevation of 156 m above sea level, remains today as the most visible and prominent feature of the city. In area about twice the size of a soccer field (approximately 250 × 110 m), it has, since prehistoric times, been the nucleus of life in Athens. Originally, its sole functions were habitation and defense, but in the historic period it became a monumental sanctuary with three temples to the city's tutelary goddess Athena. The Classical buildings of the Akropolis were unusual in being entirely of marble, in their combination of Doric and Ionic elements, and in three instances the plan of a double cella facing both east and west (Map 5.1).

The Early Akropolis

The first solid evidence of a sanctuary (bronze and clay figurines and tripods) has been dated to the early eighth century, a period when all of Attika appears to have been formed into a city-state, leading to the establishment of a major religious center on the Akropolis. Fragments of marble and clay tiles, along with two poros (i.e. limestone) column bases, could be the remains of an early temple, possibly dating to the early seventh century. This early temple would have stood on the north part of the rock, most likely in the location of the Mycenean palace, and enshrined the olivewood *xoanon*, an aniconic cult image which was believed to have fallen from the sky. A seventh-century Gorgon made of a bronze sheet has been associated with this temple, either as an acroterion or pedimental ornament.[1] More recently, remains have also been identified of large terracottas, attached or freestanding, including a half-life-size statue of Athena.[2]

---

[1] Or with an early representation of Athena Parthenos, although a recent proposal associates it with a tripod attachment, see Doronzio 2018, 46–47.
[2] Moustaka 2018.

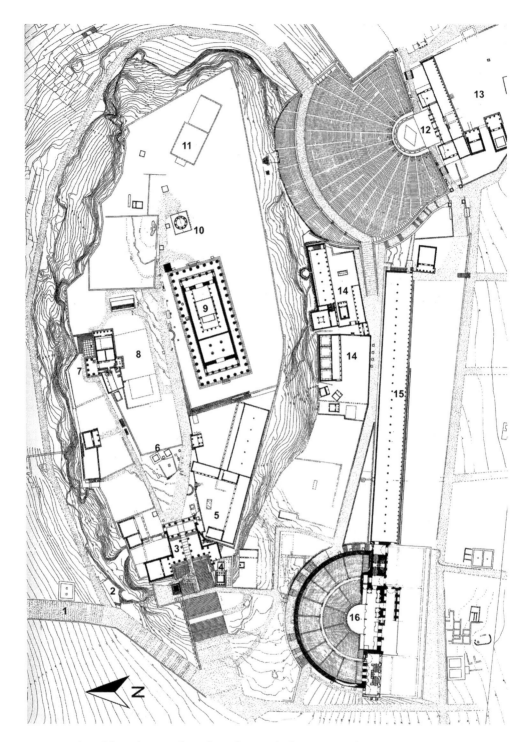

Map 5.1 Plan of the Athenian Akropolis and its south slope. 1. Panathenaic Way.
2. Klepsydra. 3. Propylaia. 4. Temple of Athena Nike. 5. Sanctuary of Artemis Brauronia. 6. Statue of
Athena Promachos. 7. Erechtheion. 8. Foundations of the Old Temple of Athena Polias (also known as
the Old Athena Temple). 9. Parthenon. 10. Monopteros of Roma and Augustus. 11. Sanctuary of
Pandion. 12. Theater of Dionysos. 13. Sanctuary of Dionysos. 14. Sanctuary of Asklepios. 15. Stoa of
Eumenes II. 16. Odeion of Herodes Atticus.
Courtesy of M. Korres, adapted by D. Weiss

The Akropolis was monumentalized for the first time in the early sixth century, but its appearance has been the subject of much debate. The most plausible view is that there were two temples by this time, reflecting two complementary aspects of the goddess. The best-known remains of these temples are poros architectural sculptures found broken in pits to the south and southeast of the Parthenon, known as the Tyrants' and Persian fills. Their themes are lions tearing bulls apart, serpents, and the labors of Herakles. Usually dated to the second quarter of the sixth century, they are associated with the reorganization of the Great Panathenaic Festival in 566/5. The most impressive remains are attributed to the so-called Hekatompedon (100-footer) or, more correctly, the Archaic Parthenon, a Doric temple of 6 × 14 columns. Other parts of smaller poros sculptures and architectural members have been dated to the mid-sixth century and are usually attributed to small Doric structures of uncertain location and function, possibly temples for smaller deities or heroes.[3]

The early sixth century also saw the first monumental temple building and the provision of improved access to the Akropolis with a great ramp 90 m long and 11–12 m wide. It not only facilitated the Panathenaic procession but also allowed for easier transport of the massive architectural members for the new buildings. This construction was followed by the founding of the cult of Athena Nike atop the Mycenean bastion, in the form of a statue on a poros base and an inscribed altar. What is known from inscriptions as the *archaios neos* ("old temple" [of Athena Polias]), of which the foundations to the south of the Erechtheion are preserved along with parts of the marble pedimental composition with a Gigantomachy and Athena as protagonist, was a Doric peripteral temple with 6 × 12 (or 13) columns. Opinions differ as to its dating and founders. It was most probably begun by the sons of the tyrant Peisistratos around 520 and completed by the early years of the democracy under Kleisthenes, since its sculptures, connected to Antenor or Endoios, appear to be later than the corresponding sculptures of the Temple of Apollo at Delphi, which have been reliably dated to 510 BC.

---

[3] More recent research (Klein 2015) has revealed the existence of fourteen clay roofs and seven marble simas, which date to between the early sixth and early fifth centuries. Owing to the fact that there was not sufficient room for all these buildings on the Akropolis, it is rightly argued that many of them would have been in the lower city, where they were deliberately broken into small pieces so they could be more easily transported. After the Persian destruction and the erection of the south wall of the rock, they were used as fill in order to raise the ground, a process which required approximately 40–45,000 m^3 of earth.

Other characteristic remains from the Archaic Akropolis include the large number of expensive votive offerings from the city's aristocratic families, manifestations of their piety and fierce social competition. The majority are statues of *korai* (around 200), *kouroi*, and horsemen, along with many *perirrhanteria*, or water basins. Though fewer in number, there were also votives from traders and craftsmen, since in one of her aspects, as Athena Ergane, the goddess was the protectress of manual workers.

The Older Parthenon, construction of which began shortly after the Battle of Marathon (490) as a thank-offering to the goddess for the great victory, was to be the first all-marble temple in mainland Greece, thanks to the discovery of the quarries on Mt. Penteli just a few years earlier. It was built on a massive limestone platform (78 m long and 11 m deep), probably a work of the Kleisthenic period, ca. 500 BC, on which the Classical Parthenon would stand some years later.[4] Construction of the Doric temple (6 × 15 columns) had progressed to the setting of the second or third column drums when it was destroyed by the Persians, along with the Old Temple of Athena Polias and a half-finished propylon. The spolia were buried in deposits or built into the north wall of the Akropolis, either for practical reasons or to be visible from the Agora below as a stark reminder of the depredations of the barbarians, forming one of the earliest landscapes of memory.

The Classical Akropolis

Following the wars with the Persians and despite its total devastation, Athens took the historical center stage with enormous confidence and unprecedented vigor, which largely stemmed from its key contribution to the Greek victories. Generated also by the wealth amassed from the Persian spoils, this new dynamism was manifested in many ways, among them a new fortification wall of the Akropolis, which not only reinforced the stronghold but also expanded the usable surface of the sanctuary by 25 percent.[5] The north wall was a work of Themistokles and Perikles, while the south wall was built by Kimon.[6]

In the aftermath of the Persian destruction, the necessary continuation of the worship and housing of the cult statue was served either by a *naiskos*

---

[4] Korres 2018, 125.

[5] According to recent measurements, the area of the Akropolis was initially 22,660 m^2 (17,830 m^2 of free space) and after the expansion was 28,240 m^2 (21,110 m^2 free space). See Valavanis et al. in Neils and Palagia forthcoming.

[6] On the buildings of Kimon, see Di Cesare 2015.

in the location of the later Erechtheion (Pre-Erechtheion, ca. 470), or by the restoration of the *opisthodomos* of the Old Athena Temple, which according to ancient sources also sheltered the treasury of the city and the Delian League. This old relic was burned down in 406, when worship was transferred to the then-completed Erechtheion, and the treasury was moved into the west room of the Parthenon. Meanwhile, the ravaged Akropolis continued to be the main religious sanctuary of the city, as evidenced by the momentous works of the period of the so-called Severe style (480–450). Around 460, on the initiative of Kimon or, according to a more recent view, a little later, a colossal (most likely 9 m high) bronze statue of Athena Promachos was erected as a thank-offering to the goddess for the victories of the Athenians over the Persians.[7] This was the first public work commissioned by the city from the sculptor Pheidias and perhaps the first work of the Periklean program.

The most innovative manifestation of this dynamism was the gradual implementation, starting in 450, of an extensive building program on the Akropolis (Fig. 5.1). The program, possibly designed by Perikles himself in collaboration with his political and artistic associates, envisaged the construction of three temples in honor of the three aspects of the goddess Athena (Polias, Parthenos, Nike) and a monumental propylon. With interruptions, the building program lasted the entire second half of the fifth century. There has been much discussion about what is Periklean in this program and what is not. It appears most likely that there was an original master plan, which was implemented in stages by the Athenian state. But according to a more recent view, the Erechtheion was not part of the original plan, and the Parthenon was the natural successor of the Old Athena Temple, with the *xoanon* initially being placed beside the new chryselephantine statue of Athena Parthenos.[8] However, due to the many misfortunes that befell the Athenians after the start of the Peloponnesian War (Thucydides 1.23.1–3), such as the plague and the earthquake in 426, which also caused significant damage to the Parthenon, the Athenians believed that these phenomena reflected the wrath of the gods, especially of Poseidon, who was held responsible for earthquakes. So, in order to appease their anger, they decided to build a new temple for his worship, the Erechtheion, to which the *xoanon* of Athena Polias was transferred, thereby depriving the Parthenon of its cult dimension.

---

[7] Palagia 2013.
[8] Shear 2016, 370–375.

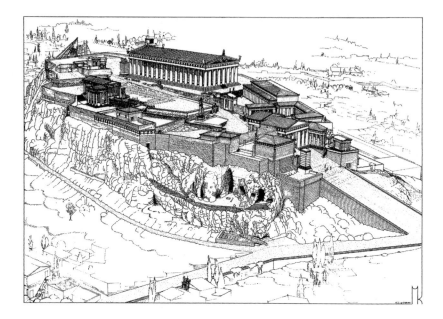

Fig. 5.1 Reconstruction of the Athenian Akropolis from the northwest in the Hellenistic period.
Courtesy of M. Korres

The Periklean architectural program had multiple objectives. First, it was to reflect the piety of the Athenians and serve as a thank-offering to Athena and the other deities who had contributed greatly to their military victories. Second, it would restore the appearance of the city's religious center, and third, it would place art – monumental architecture and sculpture – at the service of Athens' political propaganda, making known throughout the ancient world the city's claim to Panhellenic hegemony. The first works, the Parthenon (447–432) and the Propylaia (437–432), were constructed in a relatively short space of time and possibly inaugurated by Perikles himself. The Erechtheion (possibly 421–415 or earlier in the 430s in a program parallel to the Propylaia, and certainly 410–406) and the Temple of Athena Nike (432 or 426–424) were erected in stages during lulls in the Peloponnesian War, in difficult economic circumstances.

The Parthenon

The Parthenon is the most characteristic monument of Classical culture, since it is inextricably linked to the era and the circumstances in which it was erected; an era marked by the birth of the democratic state, the enthusiasm and vision of an entire people after victorious wars, the emergence of great leaders, the accumulation of ample capital, and the availability of inspired artists and outstanding craftsmen.

Iktinos and Kallikrates were appointed as co-architects of the edifice, while the general supervision of the project was assigned to Perikles' friend, the sculptor Pheidias, who was also commissioned to create the colossal chryselephantine statue of Athena, which was to be set up in the new temple. Construction was funded with the 'sacred monies' of Athena and unexpended balances from other works, while the statue was paid for from the public treasury. The financial administration of the project was entrusted to a board of six *epistatai*, or overseers, citizens with considerable expertise in handling huge sums of money, which rotated annually but had a permanent secretary, a certain Antikles. On the basis of building inscriptions, we know that work began in 447 with the cutting of the first marble at the quarry on Mt. Penteli, that the temple took ten years to complete, and that by 433/2 the roof was in place.

The Parthenon is a Doric peripteral temple with a peristyle of 8 × 17 columns (composed of eleven drums and weighing 75–80 tons each) and a hexastyle amphiprostyle cella. It is one of the largest Classical temples, 69.50 m by 30.88 m, i.e. having an area of more than 0.2 ha. It had a height of just over 20 m, almost the same as that of the Temple of Zeus at Olympia, which had been finished by 457 and with which the Parthenon appears to have 'competed' in many respects. It was built of 16,500 marble members of different sizes, from enormous architraves 4.30 m long and weighing 5–10 tons to marble rooftiles approximately 9,000 in number, with a total weight of 350 tons.

Following a tradition on the Akropolis, the cella was divided into two separate chambers of unequal size. In the eastern room, which was the largest, an unprecedented architectural backdrop was created in the form of a pi-shaped, two-tiered Doric colonnade, which enclosed the statue of Athena Parthenos. This room had an extraordinary width for its time of almost 20 m, corresponding to the five center interaxials of the seven on the façade. This innovation may have been an initiative of Pheidias, who wanted his gold-and-ivory statue of Athena to be displayed in a spacious chamber. The same motive is also indicated by the fact that the ceiling of the cella was raised to the maximum possible limit below the roof and was 1.35 m higher than the roof of the outer colonnade. The sunlight passing through the marble tiles enhanced the illumination of the coffers and the statue, which was additionally illuminated by the two windows on either side of the cella door. Another impressive feature is the staircase which was built into the east cella wall and led to an attic between the ceiling and the roof. The ceiling of the western chamber was supported by four Ionic or, possibly, the first Corinthian columns, at a height of 12.50 m. This square room served as the treasury of the city (acting like a modern central bank), and as a storeroom for many other offerings and spoils of war (e.g. the throne set up by Xerxes on Mt. Aigaleo).

The northern *pteron* of the Parthenon incorporated an earlier single-chamber *naiskos* with its circular altar, of which the attribution to Athena Ergane and its date (mid-sixth century?) remain in question. The *naiskos* predates the Classical temple, and when the latter was expanded to the north, the older shrine had to be preserved.[9]

In the architecture of the Parthenon, three features stand out in particular. The first is the mixture in the Doric order of many Ionic and Cycladic traits, the most apparent of which are the octastyle façades, the Ionic frieze, and the columns of the western chamber. In addition, though less conspicuous, the slender proportions of the columns, Ionic and Lesbian moldings, astragals and other ornamental motifs on the geisons and the simas, are all elements of an architectural idiom known as the Attic-Doric order.

The second striking architectural feature of the Parthenon is its harmonious and balanced proportions. This is immediately apparent to the visitor who, on exiting the Propylaia, beholds the temple for the first time at an angle of 45 degrees and perceives the balanced relationship among its three dimensions (Web Fig. 5.1). Of course, this effect would not have been as apparent in ancient times as it is today, owing to the presence of surrounding walls and the propylon of the Sanctuary of Artemis Brauronia. Moreover, a ratio of 9:4, considered a relationship of inner harmony, is found in many separate architectural members of the temple, although not to the extent initially believed.

The third feature is its refinements (i.e. the very subtle and imperceptible deviations from strict regularity), seen mainly in the curvature of horizontal surfaces and the inclination of vertical members. In fact, no line of the monument is straight and no surface flat. The curves begin in the stylobate of the temple, its four sides gradually becoming 'domed,' and are carried

---

[9] This conscious tendency to preserve older places or forms of worship is widely observed also in other Classical buildings on the Akropolis, either with their incorporation into the later works or the adaptation of their design on the basis of architectural tradition.

upwards to all the horizontal members of the entablature (architrave, frieze and cornice) on all four sides, indeed not only to the *peristasis* (colonnade) but also the walls of the cella. Similar deviations are evident also in the columns, which taper upward and lean slightly inward, while the corner columns lean inward twice. It has been ascertained that the inclination applied to each one of the eleven drums of the columns would have required 3,500 more hours of work for a multidrum column compared to a monolithic one. The absolutely perfect joining of the drums was achieved by the use of surface plates (i.e. circular or rectangular marble slabs weighing about 500 kg), which were painted and placed on the worked surfaces in order to reveal any areas that might require further processing.

All of these features, scarcely discernible at first glance, cannot possibly have been for the purpose of making visual corrections or compensating for optical illusions, as supposed since ancient times. Some believe that they form part of a 'secret' web that permeates the entire construction and serves aesthetic ends, utilized to give life and movement to the monument, endowing it with inner harmony and hidden dynamism. Recent studies, however, conclude that the purpose was twofold, both practical and aesthetic: "The refinements were applied in order to gracefully resolve certain technical problems of the building, to achieve geometric concordance between the forms of its structural elements, as well as the smooth transition from one element to the other, so as to constitute an organic whole."[10] In addition, it has been found that the design and execution of the fluting took into account the angle of incidence of sunlight on the column surface, not only to accentuate the 'muscular' quality of the columns but also to give even a distant observer a sense of their three dimensions in different lighting, depending on the time of day. All these devices served to highlight the plasticity and sculptural merit of the Parthenon far more than in any other architectural creation. In general, the design of the temple and its execution constituted a mathematical, intellectual, and technical achievement of the highest quality.

The Sculptures of the Parthenon

The sculptural ornamentation of ancient Greek temples served three distinct purposes: (a) religious-cultic, since it usually narrated events from the life of the deity being worshiped, with the aim of deepening piety;

[10] Zambas 2010.

(b) decorative, since it adorned architectural surfaces and thereby enhanced the aesthetic value of the building; and (c) politico-ideological, because the mythological themes were generally symbolic and echoed significant historical events of the city, thereby inculcating patriotism and the dissemination of political ideology.

The planning and overall responsibility for the sculptural decoration of the Parthenon lay with Pheidias, who proved to be peerless at incorporating themes and those ideas that the city wished to promote. In its execution, modern research discerns two designers and nine sculptors, among them two of his renowned pupils, Agorakritos and Alkamenes. Pheidias himself may have worked only until 438, because afterwards he went to Olympia to create the chryselephantine statue of Zeus.[11] The master sculptor certainly took advantage of all the possibilities afforded by the monument, since for the first time sculptures adorned both pediments, the ninety-two metopes, the entire inner frieze (160 m long), and the six acroteria. This excess was deemed necessary in order to showcase as many themes (that is, as many messages) as possible.

The forty-eight to fifty statues on the two pediments, carved between 437 and 432, appropriately represented mythological scenes associated with the goddess. The east pediment, above the entrance, depicted the miraculous birth of Athena, but the precise poses of the central figures are unknown.[12] Among the many hypothetical reconstructions proposed, it seems likely either that Zeus and Athena were depicted on either side of the vertical axis of the pediment, or that there was a central triad of three standing figures (similar to the group in the east pediment of Olympia), with Zeus in the middle, Hera to his left and Athena to his right, in accordance with the *Homeric Hymn to Athena* (1.7–1.16). Extending to the edges were the other Olympian deities, standing, seated, or reclining, depending on their placement in the pediment.

The west pediment showed, for the first time in ancient art, the struggle between Athena and Poseidon over their claims to Athens, which probably ended with the intervention of Zeus in the form of a thunderbolt. The choice of Athena is obvious, while that of Poseidon as her adversary is difficult to interpret. At any rate, an intention to highlight the enmity

---

[11] It is also not unlikely that some of the sculptors who executed the west pediment of the Temple of Zeus at Olympia also worked on the later Parthenon.

[12] Due to their removal in Christian times to make way for an apse, when the Parthenon was converted into a church. See Palagia 1998. See also Williams 2013 on the east pediment in general.

between them is not likely when the god of the sea was the patron deity of Athenian naval power, and the two gods were jointly worshiped in the Erechtheion, which was also the site of the 'sacred tokens' of their contest. The theme may be connected with the role of the Athenian fleet and of the *thetai*, the poorer citizens of Athens, who manned the ships and helped consolidate democracy and Athenian supremacy. The ultimate purpose seems to be the reconciliation of Athena and Poseidon, who joined forces to protect Athens during the Persians Wars. To the left and right of the central composition, after the chariots of the two gods, are the families of mythical Attic heroes and early kings, who were also the referees of the divine contest. Various interpretations have been put forward regarding the identity of these figures, with most proposing members of the two legendary families of Athens, that of King Kekrops on one side and Erechtheus on the other.

The old mythological episodes depicted on the pediments were now given new, symbolic content, so as to become integrated into the politico-ideological messaging of the temple's decoration. What is emphasized, first of all, is the presence and decisive role of Athena in the history of the city. From the dynamic creative moment of her birth on the east pediment, to her clash with Poseidon on the west pediment, all that takes place on the divine level is aimed at the glorification of Athens. The Athenians seek to show that the Panhellenic Athena was essentially *their* goddess or their goddess alone. Striking is the juxtaposition of the Athenian Akropolis on the west to Mt. Olympos on the east. The east pediment and the east frieze depict all the Olympian gods, in surely the most magnificent family portrait in ancient art. The Athenians garner the attention of all the gods because they are at the epicenter of the Hellenic world. They seek to show that the gods are born, care deeply about, and even clash over this, their beloved city. On the west pediment, the divine quarrel is emphatically accompanied by the presence of the city's early kings and progenitors who, by choosing the victor of the divine contest, demonstrate their power and emphasize the central importance of Athenian autochthony.

Each side of the temple's ninety-two metopes (fourteen on the ends, and thirty-two on the flanks) depicted a different mythical battle. The east side, above the entrance, featured the Gigantomachy; the west side, the Amazonomachy; the north side, scenes from the Fall of Troy; and the south side, the Centauromachy. All the metopes on the east and west sides, as well as twelve on the north side, are almost entirely destroyed, since their figures were deliberately chiseled away. This defacement is usually attributed to Christians, who attempted to obliterate the 'graven images' when the Parthenon was converted into a church.[13]

The mythical clashes on the metopes have been interpreted as an allegory of the Greco-Persian wars. That is to say, there exists a parallelism between the historical and the mythical battles, and therefore also a correlation between their historical weight and their importance, a notion that was already apparent in the wall paintings of the Sanctuary of Theseus (Theseion) and the Stoa Poikile in the Agora. In particular, the Gigantomachy symbolizes the consolidation of universal order, while the Centauromachy alludes to the punishment of barbarian impiety. Similarly, the Amazonomachy on the west side was seen as a mythical parallel to the Battle of Marathon and symbolized the defense of the city against foreign invaders. The adversaries in the metopes are, on the one hand, the barbarians, the foreigners, the invaders, the challengers (giants, Amazons, centaurs, Trojans), and on the other, the gods, the Greeks, the Athenians, the civilized. Generally speaking, in the metopes, as in many other figurative representations on the Akropolis, the element of *agon* (struggle) is paramount, thus presenting life as a perpetual interplay of opposing forces, or victory and defeat as merely temporary and easily reversed.

The Parthenon frieze, consisting of 114 blocks, depicts, according to the traditional view, a real event, the procession of the Panathenaia, the city's most important festival, held every four years in honor of the goddess Athena. Three temporal and spatial stages of this procession are depicted on the frieze, not as an actual but a notional portrayal. For this purpose, a total of 360 human figures are mustered (not counting the deities), along with more than 180 horses. The west side presents the preparatory stages and marshaling of the procession, probably outside the city. The two long sides, the north and the south, feature the parallel unfolding of the procession with horsemen and chariots, in an almost mirror-image arrangement, taking place inside the city (see Fig. 29.1). Just before the center is the most popular contest of the Panathenaia, the *apobates* race, an important component of Athenian identity and therefore deserving of such prominence (see Web Fig. 24.2). The preponderance of horsemen has also been linked to the new cavalry units created by Perikles at the time.

The east side of the temple depicts the symbolic convergence of the two files on the Akropolis itself, with the most important element of the entire festival, the *peplos* of Athena (see Fig. 24.2). According to one view, the

---

[13] The only relatively undamaged metope (North 32) seems to have survived owing to the resemblance of its two female figures to those of the Annunciation of Mary.

religious leader of the city, the *archon basileus*, with the aid of a child, has just folded the old *peplos*, marking the end of the procession and the commencement of rituals for the acceptance of the newly woven *peplos*. At the same time, the transfer of two stools by two girls (*arrhephoroi*) means the preparation for the rite of Theoxenia for the Olympian gods who, rendered on a larger scale and divided into two groups, seem to have turned their backs to the procession, a rendition perhaps indicating that they are seated in a semicircle and are invisible to mortals.[14]

Masterpieces of art usually invite numerous different interpretations. This applies especially to the frieze, one of the most heavily laden – with multiple symbols and meanings – works in the history of art. One of the most insightful interpretations, based on the number and arrangement of the horsemen on the two long sides, suggests that the monument simultaneously expresses the past and the present of Athens, the origin but also the continuation of democratic governance. The fact that all the scenes are represented in dynamic motion implies that the celebration is repeated every four years and will continue forever. Meanwhile, recent research has added a further dimension. Because the frieze shows an idealized rather than actual representation of the Panathenaic procession, it is proposed that, apart from the east side, it represents not only this procession, but a selective conflation of religious events from all of the city's festivals, hence an expression of Athenian devotion to all their gods, referring to the words of Perikles in his Funeral Oration (Thucydides 2.35.1–2, 2.46.2), which was delivered a few years later (430).[15] In general, the presentation of the Panathenaic procession on the Parthenon frieze is the most conspicuous show of civic grandeur, manifested before the community itself and before all of Greece.

The apexes of the two pediments were crowned with floral acroteria in a combination of acanthus fronds and palm leaves which, creating curves in the form of an anthemion, extended the temple façades skyward by more than four meters. The four corner acroteria fulfilled the same role, although instead of anthemia, as believed in the past, they are now thought to have been large marble Nikai, or Victories, in flight.[16] Their characteristic movement forwards and outwards not only created dynamic plastic extensions of the sculptural decoration but also alluded symbolically to the victorious character of the monument and the city.

---

[14] Neils 2001 and 2005, 114.
[15] Shear 2016, 401–404.
[16] Korres 2018, 133.

The chryselephantine statue of Athena Parthenos, the work of Pheidias, was an imposing creation, whose colossal size (12.75 m tall), splendor, and elaborate decoration defined the essential nature of the goddess and accentuated her importance for Athens. Apart from the cutting in the temple floor in which the supporting wooden mast was placed, nothing remains of the statue itself. However, its form is well known from detailed descriptions of ancient writers (e.g. Pausanias 1.24.5–7) as well as from around 200 minor replicas and depictions in all media. In front of the statue, a rectangular pool of water served both to prevent the drying of the ivory and also to reflect light upon the statue. The original work was assembled on a plastered wooden armature, to which pieces of carved ivory were attached for the face and arms, while the drapery was fashioned from gold plates weighing 1,150 kg. The divine figure and its various accessories (statue of Nike in her right hand, helmet, shield, sandals, base) were also exceptional for their lavish sculptural ornamentation featuring more or less the same themes as the sculptural decoration of the temple exterior. This fact lends considerable weight to the view that Pheidias, the creator of the statue, was also the artist who conceived and designed the decoration of the entire edifice.

The wealth of images on the outside of the Parthenon then alluded to the wealth of precious metal that was inside – the chryselephantine statue of Athena and the treasures of the Goddess – thus becoming a visible proclamation of the wealth and power of the Athenian state, which by the middle of the fifth century had in fact become the wealthiest polity in the Greek world.[17]

The Propylaia

The Propylaia (437–432 BC, Web Fig. 5.2), designed by the architect Mnesikles, has many features in common with the Parthenon, such that the same construction team may have worked on both buildings. The outstanding achievement of its creator is illustrated by the fact that he managed, in an extremely difficult site on the rock, not only to solve the many architectural problems but also to impart temple-like splendor to a secular gate building. The originality of the design lies in the fact that a monumental structure was constructed from five architectural units in a pi

---

[17] Marconi 2009, 168.

shape, turning the Parthenon's inner pi-shaped colonnade inside out. The doubling of the width of the access ramp to 21 m provided those entering with an impressive sightline, while those departing would have been able to see, far off on the horizon, Salamis and the narrow straits where the great naval battle was won, as well as the harbor of Piraeus, as landmarks of Athenian sea power.[18]

The central building consisted of two sections of unequal height because of the sloping ground, which had hexastyle Doric temple façades that echo those of the Parthenon porches. In the cross-wall dividing the two sections there were five symmetrical gates of descending height, which gave the building its plural form (*Propylaia*). The central gate was the widest and had a sloping surface to accommodate the procession of sacrificial animals. The threshold of the smallest (north) gate shows greater wear, an indication that it was used more by pedestrians, whereas the others would normally have remained closed. In the west portion, the passageway is flanked by three Ionic columns on each side, possibly imitating the Ionic columns of the western chamber of the Parthenon. To the left of those entering was a small wing with a three-columned portico and off-center doorway; it housed paintings of mythological content (hence its name, Pinakotheke, i.e. picture gallery) and seventeen couches. It clearly functioned as a place of leisure (*lesche*) for official visitors and/or the holding of *symposia* after celebrations on the Akropolis. Particularly impressive is the ceiling of the Propylaia with its massive beams, huge architraves, and polychrome marble coffers, the recent restoration of which led to the first modern reconstruction of a ceiling on the Akropolis buildings (Fig. 5.2).

The original design of Mnesikles envisaged two more large halls to the northeast and southeast of the main building, but the plan was never completed, for reasons that are debated. The existence also of many unfinished surfaces throughout the building evidence the interruption of the Propylaia's construction, either due to the outbreak of the Peloponnesian War, which would have put a strain on the city's finances, or, according to a recent view, because the *ekklesia* – swayed by political opponents of Perikles – refused to approve the budget for the last year.[19]

[18] Martin-Mcauliffe and Papadopoulos 2012, 342–347.
[19] Shear 2016, 311–327.

Fig. 5.2 Restored Ionic capital and coffers of the Propylaia.
Courtesy of T. Tanoulas

The Temple of Athena Nike

Athena Nike's shrine (Web Fig. 5.3) was situated near the entrance to protect
the Akropolis as did the earlier Mycenean bastion. Kallikrates had been
commissioned to build the temple of the goddess of victory, from as early
as the mid-fifth century, but, because priority was given to the Parthenon
and the Propylaia, work did not start for about twenty to twenty-five years.
However, during the first phase of the Peloponnesian War, and following the
Athenian victories of 426/5, its construction was accelerated on the initiative
of Kleon for purposes of political propaganda. First, and along with the
Propylaia, the Mycenean rampart was sheathed with walls of poros limestone, both to embellish the approach to the Akropolis and to increase the
upper surface of the bastion. On top, an amphiprostyle tetrastyle Ionic
naiskos was erected with a shallow, single-room cella. Instead of a gate wall,
the temple had three openings, a central doorway and two flanking windows,
closed by metal grilles. The monolithic Ionic columns, each 4 m high,
resemble those of the Propylaia, although only half their size.

The sculptural decoration, by the workshop of Agorakritos, had many
themes in common with the Parthenon and served the ideological objectives of Athenian policy. The east pediment depicted a Gigantomachy, the
west pediment an Amazonomachy, the east frieze an assembly of the gods.
But here for the first time, historical themes appear on the other three
friezes: a battle between Greeks and Persians, as well as one between

Greeks, placing them among the earliest historical reliefs of Greek sculpture. The sculptural decoration was augmented by massive acroteria, a possible total of ten gilded winged Nikai, who held wreaths or spoils of war, further emphasizing the victorious character and the triumphal mood of the sculptural decoration of the temple.

This triumphal mood was completed by a sculpted parapet, 34 m in length, which served as a guardrail for three sides of the bastion. It depicted about fifty winged Nikai erecting victory trophies consisting of Greek or Persian weapons and preparing sacrifices of bulls. During the same period, the north, west, and south walls of the bastion were covered with Spartan shields, as in the stoas of the Agora. These shields were spoils from the capture of 120 Spartan warriors on the island of Sphakteria in 425, an unprecedented event that was fully exploited by Athenian political propaganda. All these visual elements, alluding to victories and supremacy, constituted a striking first impression for visitors ascending the Akropolis, even before they entered the sacred precinct.

The Erechtheion

The Erechtheion (Web Fig. 5.4) was the most important temple on the Akropolis, because it housed the *xoanon* of the goddess, which every four years was recloaked with a new *peplos* following the Panathenaic Festival. It is a peculiar and complex structure, for, although a temple, it lacks symmetry and regularity. It consists of three different architectural units that stand on four levels with a height difference of more than 3 m and has four façades with different roofs and colonnades. Despite the spatial and architectural difficulties, the architect (most probably Mnesikles, because of many construction features in common with the Propylaia) succeeded not only in giving cohesion to the building, but also turning it into one of the most graceful works of ancient Greek architecture.

The singularity of the Erechtheion is due to many factors, which also constituted challenging conditions for its creator. First, it was built on the north edge of the rock, next to the wall, clearly in order to leave an open space in the center of the Akropolis for watching the sacrifice of the Panathenaia. Second, the temple had to accommodate the worship of Olympian deities associated with the 'sacred tokens' (i.e. the indications of their divine presence on the Akropolis), such as the olive tree of Athena, and the marks left by the trident and the saltwater spring of Poseidon, or by the thunderbolt of Zeus. Third, the building also had to incorporate the tombs of early kings and heroes from the city's mythological past, since their presence underpinned Athenian autochthony.

These ancient relics had to be integrated into a single, majestic edifice in order to take on an emblematic quality, as necessitated by ideological and artistic considerations at the time. By bringing together all these outdoor remains under a common roof, the Erechtheion became the repository for the traditions of Athenian existence. The cella was divided laterally into two parts. The east chamber was dedicated to Athena Polias and enshrined the *xoanon* of the goddess. It had an Ionic hexastyle portico and two windows on either side of the doorway, one of which was recently restored in the Akropolis Museum. In front of the *xoanon* stood an ever-burning golden lamp made by Kallimachos, the smoke from which exited through the trunk of a bronze palm tree. The west chamber, which was probably laid out on different levels, accommodated the other cults. The two projecting porches on the north and south sides of the building housed and simultaneously highlighted some of the 'sacred tokens.' The north porch, so impressive in its architectural and decorative richness, covered evidence relating to King Erechtheus, while the Porch of the Maidens above the tomb of King Kekrops evinced the devotion of the Athenians to their great ancestors. Lastly, on the west façade, which had four engaged Ionic half-columns set in antis, windows were created during repair work at the time of Augustus, overlooking the open-air sanctuary of the heroine Pandrosos, which included an Ionic stoa, the altar of Zeus Herkeios, and the sacred olive tree of Athena. In the north and south walls of the temple, there were three narrow light openings, which were in alignment with similar ones in the north citadel wall, clearly for the purpose of sending some message to the city in the framework of nighttime cult rituals.

The Maidens (Caryatids) have been dated to 420–415, and their presence above the tomb of Kekrops has been interpreted in various ways. The more plausible interpretations suggest that they represent the *choephoroi*, who, holding libation vessels, pay tribute to the mythical king, expressing the Athenians' reverence for their forefathers, in the same manner as the corresponding Athenian maidens on the east frieze of the Parthenon, who were in the service of Athena Polias.

The Erechtheion frieze, with a length of 60 m, reliably dated to 409–406, ran along the upper walls and porches of the temple, giving it a sense of unity. For artistic or economic reasons, it consisted of individually carved white marble figures, which were affixed onto a dark background of Eleusinian stone slabs, a method also seen in the sculptural decoration of cult statue bases of the Pheidian circle. Although fragments of more than

100 figures (mainly female) have survived, it has not been possible to identify the subject, of which there may have been more than one. It has been suggested that it depicted scenes from myths relating to Erechtheus or to Ion, progenitor of the Ionians, as portrayed in the contemporary homonymous tragedies of Euripides. These themes have been associated with an Athenian reversion to time-honored myths, in the aftermath of the crushing defeat in the Sicilian Expedition (415–413) and the collapse of their hegemony.

Ideology and Politics in the Monuments of the Akropolis

While preserving the more ancient architectural remains (e.g. the Mycenean wall, Archaic propylon, retaining walls of the Old Temple, etc.) as elements of a landscape of memory, it appears that the entire tradition of the Sacred Rock and of the earlier temples was incorporated in both the architecture and the sculpture of the new buildings on the Akropolis, in a deliberate management of the past. Only now, the old forms, traditions, and values were given a new visual aspect on an artistic and ideological level, which augmented their symbolic potency, so that, as public iconography, they could dynamically transmit the new messages of power which the city wished to communicate to its people, its allies, and its enemies. The old mythical exploits of the Athenians deliberately reference recent successes. The mythological past, as a landscape of memory, served the democratic but also the hegemonic present of Athens in perpetuity.

This uniform conceptualization and structured web that connected themes, groups, and figures is evident in the Parthenon, the Erechtheion, and the Temple of Athena Nike. These political messages served (a) to demonstrate that Athens was the city beloved by the gods, (b) to substantiate Athenian autochthony, and (c) to extol the role of the Athenians in the struggles against and victories over mythical and historical enemies, with the aim of justifying their Panhellenic hegemony. These two values, struggle (*agon*) and victory (*nike*), which denote the virtues of the Athenians, are two motifs which unify the many figures and diverse subject matter on all the monuments. Generally speaking, the sculptural decoration constituted the fullest expression of all the accomplishments of the Athenian past and present: military, political, religious, and cultural. In short, the great works on the Akropolis, as in the words of Perikles' Funeral Oration, exalt the triumphant power. Whether all these

messages discerned in the monuments by modern scholars would have
been apprehended by most visitors to the Akropolis in ancient times is
doubtful. But the splendor and grandeur of the works would certainly
have instilled in them civic pride and self-confidence, prerequisites for
any major collective endeavor.

These magnificent conceptions of Perikles and his circle, and their
implementation by the Athenian democracy, not only attained their object-
ive of establishing Athens as the capital of the Greek world, but also
achieved something that even their creators themselves could not have
imagined: they surpassed time itself to become unparalleled works of
crowning moments of intellectual and artistic expression in the history
of civilization.

Postscript

After the Classical period, the Akropolis saw a number of changes,
additions, and destructions. After the Herulian attack on Athens (AD
267), a fire damaged the Parthenon, and afterwards the interior colonnade was repaired using material from a long Hellenistic two-story stoa,
a repair attributed to either Julian (AD 361–363) or to Herculius, the
Praetorian Prefect of Illyricum (about AD 402–410). And the turbulent
history of the Akropolis after the ancient period witnessed its original
role as a fortress, with its inclusion in the late Roman wall, which was
built after the Herulian sack of the city. This was followed by the
conversion of the Parthenon and the Erechtheion into Christian
churches (sixth century AD) and the use from time to time of the
Propylaia as the seat of religious and political leaders, especially from
AD 1204 onwards, when Athens was occupied by Franks. In AD 1460,
during the visit of Mehmet the Conqueror, the Parthenon was converted
into a mosque.

All these changes and reuses caused considerable damage to the
Akropolis buildings, but nothing compared to the great catastrophe that
befell the Parthenon on September 26, 1687, during the siege of the
Venetians under the command of Francesco Morosini. A cannon shell
caused a huge explosion that blew out the central portion of the building,
leaving it in ruins. Subsequently, the appearance of the monuments on the
Akropolis deteriorated due to the removal of materials for the construction
of houses and the small mosque inside the Parthenon (around 1700), the

looting of the sculptures by Lord Elgin (1801–1803), and sieges during the Greek War of Independence. This long and destructive phase ended with the surrender of the Akropolis to the Greeks on April 30, 1833, which also led to the commencement of efforts to convert it from a fortress into a monument.

Further Reading

The bibliography on the Akropolis of Athens is vast and thus very difficult to study fully. That said, the books by Hurwit 1999 and 2004 and Holtzmann 2003 continue to be essential and irreplaceable. For this reason, the selected bibliography presented here is mostly from 2004 onwards; for a general bibliography on the Athenian Akropolis, see Sassu 2012. The most important recent books taking general approaches and making many new contributions are those by Neils 2005, Barringer and Hurwit 2005, Shear 2016, Meyer 2017, and Rous 2019, along with the article of Valavanis in Neils and Palagia forthcoming. Greco 2010 provides a summary of research data and a good bibliography on all the monuments, while the latest collections on the Hellenistic and Roman periods is Krumeich and Witschel 2010. The investigations and papers by scholars of the restoration of the Akropolis monuments continue to provide new material (e.g. Lambrinou 2019 and Manidaki 2019), as well as the honorary volumes for Manolis Korres (Zambas et al. 2016) and Charalambos Bouras (Korres et al. 2018), along with Palagia and Sioumpara 2019 and Neils and Palagia forthcoming.

Bibliography

Barringer, J.M., and J. Hurwit, eds. 2005. *Periklean Athens and Its Legacy. Problems and Perspectives*. Austin.

Di Cesare, R. 2015. *La città di Cecrope. Ricerche sulla politica edilizie cimoniana ad Atene*. Athens.

Doronzio, A. 2018. *Athen im 7. Jahrhundert v. Chr. Räume und Funde der frühe Polis*. Berlin.

Greco, E., ed. 2010. *Topografia di Atene. Sviluppo urbano e monumenti dalle origini al III secolo d.C. Tomo I: Acropoli – Areopago – Tra Acropoli e Pnice*. Athens.

Holtzmann, B. 2003. *L'Acropole d'Athénes: Monuments, cultes et histoire du sanctuaire d'Athéna Polias*. Paris.

Hurwit, J.M. 1999. *The Athenian Acropolis: History, Mythology, and Archaeology from the Neolithic Era to the Present*. Cambridge.

2004. *The Acropolis in the Age of Pericles*. Cambridge.

Klein, N. 2015. "The Architecture of the Athenian Acropolis before Pericles: The Life and Death of the Small Limestone Buildings." In *Cities Called Athens*.

Studies Honoring John McK. Camp II, eds. K.F. Daly and L.A. Riccardi, Lewisburg, 137–163.

Korres, M. 2018. "Ἡ αρχιτεκτονική του Παρθενώνος. Εισιτήριος λόγος του ακαδημαϊκού κ. Μανόλη Κορρέ." *Πρακτικά της Ακαδημίας Αθηνών* 93: 122–137.

Korres, M., S. Mamaloukos, K. Zambas, and F. Mallouchou-Tufano, eds. 2018. *Ἥρως Κτίστης: Μνήμη Χαραλάμπου Μπούρα*. Athens.

Krumeich, R., and C. Witschel, eds. 2010. *Die Akropolis von Athen im Hellenismus und in der römischen Kaiserzeit*. Wiesbaden.

Lambrinou, L. 2019. "The Parthenon's North Colonnade: Comments on Its Construction." In *New Directions and Paradigms for the Study of Greek Architecture: Interdisciplinary Dialogues in the Field*, eds. P. Sapirstein and D. Scahill, Leiden, 21–38.

Manidaki, V. 2019. "New Evidence for the Construction Phases of the Parthenon Peristyle: Anomalies at the Southwest Corner." In *New Directions and Paradigms for the Study of Greek Architecture: Interdisciplinary Dialogues in the Field*, eds. P. Sapirstein and D. Scahill, Leiden, 39–55.

Marconi, C. 2009. "The Parthenon Frieze: Degrees of Visibility." *Res: Anthropology and Aesthetics* 55/56: 156–173.

Martin-Mcauliffe, S.L., and J.K. Papadopoulos. 2012. "Framing Victory: Salamis, the Athenian Acropolis, and the Agora." *JSAH* 71: 332–361.

Meyer, M. 2017. *Athena, Göttin von Athen: Kult und Mythos auf der Akropolis bis in klassische Zeit*. Vienna.

Moustaka, A. 2018. "Θραύσματα πήλινων γλυπτών των αρχαϊκών χρόνων από την αθηναϊκή Ακρόπολη." In *Terracotta Sculpture and Roofs: New Discoveries & New Perspectives*, ed. A. Moustaka, Athens, 109–126.

Neils, J. 2001. *The Parthenon Frieze*. Cambridge.

    ed. 2005. *The Parthenon from Antiquity to the Present*. Cambridge.

Neils, J., and O. Palagia, eds. Forthcoming. *From Kallias to Kritias. Classical Culture: Athens in the Second Half of the 5th c. BC*. Cambridge.

Palagia, O. 1998. *The Pediments of the Parthenon*. Leiden.

    2013. "Not from the Spoils of Marathon: Pheidias' Bronze Athena on the Acropolis." In *Marathon: The Day After*, eds. K. Bourazelis and E. Koulakiotis, Athens, 117–137.

Palagia, O., and E. Sioumpara, eds. 2019. *From Hippias to Kallias: Greek Art in Athens and beyond, 527–449 BC*. Athens.

Rous, S.A. 2019. *Reset in Stone: Memory and Reuse in Ancient Athens*. Madison.

Sassu, R. 2012. "Bibliografia Acropoli di Atene." *Thiasos* 1: 11–23.

Shear, T.L. 2016. *Trophies of Victory: Public Buildings in Periklean Athens*. Princeton.

Williams, D. 2013. *The East Pediment of the Parthenon: From Perikles to Nero*. London.

Zambas, C. 2010. "The Beauty of the Monuments and the First Years of the Restoration of the Acropolis." In *Dialogues on the Acropolis*, ed. C. Koutsadelis, Athens, 388–409.

Zambas, C. et al., eds. 2016. *ΑΡΧΙΤΕΚΤΩΝ. Honorary Volume for Prof. Manolis Korres*. Athens.

Additional resources to accompany this chapter can be found at: www.cambridge .org/NeilsRogers

6 | The Agora: Public Life and Administration

JOHN MCK. CAMP II

> You will find everything sold together in the same place at Athens:
> figs, witnesses to summons, bunches of grapes, turnips, pears, apples,
> givers of evidence, roses, medlars, porridge, honeycombs, chickpeas,
> lawsuits, first-milk, puddings, myrtle, allotment machines, irises,
> lambs, water-clocks, laws, indictments.
>
> Athenaios, *Deipnosophistai* 14.640b–c

In one sense, public life in ancient Athens was intensely participatory.
From early times, the Athenians were expected to take part in running
the state. The lawgiver Solon (640–558 BC) made it mandatory, whenever
there was a contentious issue to be resolved, that everyone had to take one
side or the other (Plutarch, *Solon* 20; *Constitution of the Athenians* 8.5) and
the concept that the citizens of Athens were to 'rule and be ruled' in turn
was a pillar of the later democracy. On the other hand, public life was
also highly exclusive; left out, for the most part, were women, slaves, and
metics (resident foreigners from other countries and other Greek cities). In
a population of hundreds of thousands, only tens of thousands (male
citizens) had the right to vote and any significant role in the daily administration of the city.

Our information concerning the public administration of Athens is
unusually detailed, thanks primarily to the recovery in 1890 of part of the
text of Aristotle's *Constitution of the Athenians*. In addition to outlining the
history of eleven successive constitutions (Chapters 1–41), and providing a
detailed account of the mechanics of empaneling huge Athenian juries for
the lawcourts (Chapters 63–69), Aristotle gives a detailed description of
Athenian officials and their functions in the second half of the fourth
century BC (Chapters 42–62). From this we learn that the city required
some 350 officials, the huge majority chosen by lot, most to serve for a
single year. The only exceptional positions, where the task required special
experience and therefore election, were treasurers, generals, some lesser
military officers, and water commissioners. The only other elected officials –
where character seems to have been a factor – were those in charge of
young men at the *gymnasia*. In addition to these individual officials and

boards of administrators, e.g. *poletai* (state auctioneers), *astynomoi* (guardians of the city), *agoranomoi* (market officials), *epimeletai* (overseers of various activities), secretaries, etc., there were 500 counselors serving in the council known as the *boule* for a year, and hundreds of jurors empaneled whenever the lawcourts sat to hear cases.

Considerable additional light is shed on the public administration of Athens by the unparalleled epigraphical record for the city: literally thousands of primary documents inscribed on stone, illuminating and supplementing what we learn from Aristotle, the orators, and other literary sources. A properly functioning democracy requires extensive public archives so that those about to come into office will be able to fulfill their duties. *Traditiones* record the annual expenditures and handing over of money or equipment (such as official weights and measures) to incoming officials, while honorary decrees praise outgoing officials for their good service to the state. A monarchy or oligarchy may not be so committed to informing its citizens as to how – or how well – the city is being run, and by whom.

The Agora

The physical center of much of this public activity was the Agora, a large open meeting place where many or most Athenians gathered every day. Early on it was multifunctional, and most public activities and spectacles were held here: markets, elections, dramatic performances, athletic events, military drills, and religious processions. It was logical, therefore, to site the principal public buildings needed to run the city around the sides of this square, where so many citizens congregated on a daily basis. Over time, facilities were provided for the three main branches of the government: executive, legislative, and judicial. The Agora was considered the physical center of the city, as indicated by the altar dedicated within the square to the Twelve Gods in 522/21 BC. Thereafter, this altar was regarded as the central milestone of the city, from which all distances from Athens were measured (*IG* II^2 2640 and Herodotos 2.7.1–2; see Web Fig. 1.2).

The traveler Pausanias (active in the second century AD) and several other sources suggest that there was an earlier agora, recognizable and marked by the Prytaneion – the traditional center and communal hearth of any Greek city. This earlier agora is unexplored, lying under the modern district of Plaka, perhaps some 500 m to the east of the Agora under discussion here, which lay northwest of the Acropolis, on ground sloping down from the north slopes of the Areopagos Hill to the Eridanos River. The square itself was defined by a series of marble boundary stones (*horoi*) set wherever a street came into the open space; two of them, inscribed "I am the boundary of the Agora," have been found in situ along the west side of the square. This Agora, in use throughout the Late Archaic, Classical, and Hellenistic periods (ca. 520 until ca. 10 BC), has been under excavation by the American School of Classical Studies at Athens since 1931 (Map 6.1).

The development of this civic center for the Athenians was somewhat haphazard, with buildings and monuments added gradually over time from the late sixth (Map 6.2) through the fourth centuries BC. Even in antiquity, the city was thought to have been poorly laid out: "The city itself is totally dry and not well-watered, and badly laid out on account of its antiquity. Many of the houses are shabby, only a few useful. Seen by a stranger, it

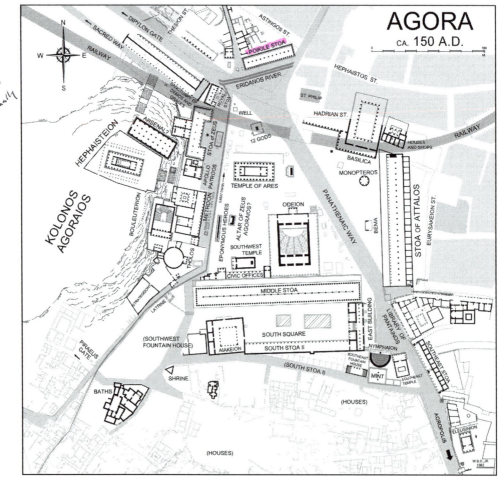

Map 6.1 Plan of the Athenian Agora, ca. AD 150.
Courtesy of the American School of Classical Studies at Athens: Agora Excavations

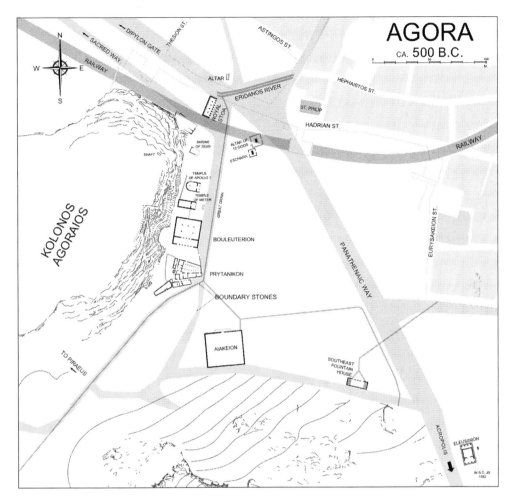

Map 6.2 Plan of the Athenian Agora, ca. 500 BC.
Courtesy of the American School of Classical Studies at Athens: Agora Excavations

would at first be doubtful that this was the famed city of the Athenians"
(Pseudo-Dikaiarchos, *FGrH* 59). Only later, well down in the Hellenistic
period, do we see some attempt to create an organized public space, defined
primarily by long colonnades (stoas), such as those found in the contemporary agoras of the east Greek world, as at Ephesos, Miletos, Priene,
Pergamon, and Magnesia.

From the time of the creation of the Kleisthenic reforms which are usually
defined as a starting point for the Athenian democracy in 507 BC, most
government activities – executive, legislative, judicial, and administrative –
were accommodated in and around this square and its adjacent buildings.

Executive

The senior magistrate of the democracy, known as the Eponymous Archon, held office, according to Aristotle, at the Prytaneion in the earlier, traditional agora to the east. Next was the *archon basileus* (King Archon), responsible for most legal matters and the laws, who served also as second in command of the state and as a high priest of the city. He held office in the Royal Stoa, built of limestone at the northwest corner of the square in the late sixth century BC (see Web Fig. 28.1). It was a small Doric colonnade, with eight columns across the front and four down the middle. Within its shelter, the King Archon adjudicated indictments for impiety, including those charging Sokrates with various offenses in 400–399 BC (Plato, *Theaetetus* 210d and *Euthyphro* 2a). On the steps of the building was the *lithos*, the oath-stone of the Athenians, where the King administered the annual oath of office to all Athenians about to assume a magistracy. By the end of the fifth century, the entire constitution of Athens had been written up on many marble *stelai* that were set up in and in front of the Royal Stoa, the whole law code inscribed and publicly displayed for any citizen to consult.

The third-ranking archon, the polemarch (war archon), held office in the *polemarcheion* or *Epilykeion*, a building which has not yet been identified, though it probably stood near the Agora. The six lesser archons, known as *thesmothetes*, were also housed in a building named after them (*thesmotheteion*), which has not been recognized.

As noted, many of these high officials were allotted rather than elected. Perhaps as a counterbalance, the Athenians created an annual electoral opportunity to vote an official out of, rather than into, office. The procedure was known as ostracism. Once a year, the Athenians would meet in the Agora and answer a simple question: is anyone a threat to the democracy? If a simple majority voted yes, then they dispersed; several weeks later they reassembled in the square, this time bringing with them an *ostrakon* (Fig. 6.1), on which they had scratched the name of the individual they thought was a problem. The man with the most votes lost, and he was exiled for ten years, which was thought to interrupt or end any poor political behavior. The procedure was used for much of the fifth century (480s to 417 BC), and almost all prominent Athenian statesmen (e.g. Themistokles, Kimon, Xanthippos, Aristides) – except Perikles – spent time exiled from Athens and its political arena.

Fig. 6.1 *Ostraka* cast against Aristides, Themistokles, Kimon, and Perikles, Athenian Agora, fifth century BC, Agora P 9973, P 9950, P 18555, P 16755.
Courtesy of the American School of Classical Studies at Athens: Agora Excavations

Legislative

For making laws, the Athenians resorted to two legislative bodies: the *ekklesia*, an assembly of citizens (all of whom were male), which met approximately every ten days at the Pnyx, a large meeting place on the ridge southwest of the Agora, and the *boule*, a council of 500 citizens, appointed by lot to serve for a year, who met on most days in the Agora. Their meeting place was the Bouleuterion, built along the west side of the square, soon after the institution of the democracy and its new council, in 507 BC. The meetings were run by the *prytaneis*, a revolving executive committee made up of fifty members from each of the ten tribes, each tribal contingent serving in rotation for a period of thirty-six or thirty-five days. During their elongated month in office, the *prytaneis* were fed at public expense in an adjacent building, the Tholos. In addition, one-third of the *prytaneis* were expected to sleep in the building overnight. That way, if urgent news arrived at a difficult hour, the messenger did not have to go down unlit, unmarked streets, searching for the allotted archon of that year; he could go directly to the Tholos, where he would find seventeen citizens, serving as *prytaneis*, available to address any issue. So, in a sense, the Bouleuterion and Tholos together served as the functioning heart of the democracy, where responsible officials were on duty twenty-four hours a day. The Tholos was built in around 470 BC, after the Persian destruction

Fig. 6.2 Model of the Tholos, showing the possible restoration of the roof with diamond-shaped tiles.
Courtesy of the American School of Classical Studies at Athens: Agora Excavations

of Athens (Fig. 6.2). Its unusual round shape perhaps suggests that all fifty diners sat on a bench running around the circumference of the interior, a democratic arrangement where there was no hierarchy in seating nor any head of the table. Originally the meals served in the Tholos were not lavish, presumably consisting of bread, cheese, olives, and garlic, though meat or fish were probably added to the menu toward the end of the fifth century. Examples of the state tableware have been found, marked with a delta/epsilon ligature standing for *demosion* (public property) to ensure that the diners did not walk off with the crockery after their meal (see Fig. 25.1). (See Steiner, Chapter 25 in this volume.)

Later in the fifth century, the *boule* moved into a newly constructed meeting-hall, built just to the west of the old Late Archaic Bouleuterion, which continued to house the archives of the city, though its name was changed to the Metroon, a sanctuary of the mother of the gods.

Judiciary

The Athenians were a litigious people, and their democracy was founded on the independence and effectiveness of the popular courts, the *dikasteria*. (See Harris, Chapter 28 in this volume, especially for a discussion on the terminology of the *dikastai*.) Since the time of Solon, early in the sixth century BC, access to the courts by all levels of society was regarded as essential. The minimum Athenian jury was 200, and courts of 500 and more were not unheard of. Aristotle's *Constitution of the Athenians* (63–69) describes in detail the empaneling of an Athenian jury, and the excavations have brought to light much of the paraphernalia associated with the process: *kleroteria* (allotment machines; see Fig. 28.1) used to choose the jury at the start of a case, *pinakia*, the thin strips of bronze carrying a potential juror's name and tribe, ballots used by the jurors to record their votes, water clocks (*klepsydrai*) to time the speeches (see Web Fig. 28.2), and containers listing the documents stored inside them which were to be presented to the jurors.

There were many lawcourts in Athens, but only a few can be recognized today. A small cluster existed at the northeast corner of the Agora square, their remains covered by the later Stoa of Attalos. The identification is based on the discovery of a casual 'ballot box' cobbled together from two drain tiles set upright, in which were found seven of the inscribed round bronze ballots used by the jurors when voting on a case (see Fig. 28.2).

Just south of the Agora is the steep, low rocky hill known as the Areopagos, site of one of the earliest governing bodies and lawcourts of the city, also called the Areopagos. This council was made up of retired archons, and like the House of Lords in England, gradually lost its power, eroded away over decades by the slow rise of democracy. The court, however, remained useful as one of the four homicide courts of the city. Other courts in Athens, though known by name (e.g. Heliaia, Parabyston, Trigonon, Phoinikion, and Batrachion), are less easy to identify, in part because our usually reliable guide, Pausanias, describes them all at once, rather than in his usual topographical order.

Other Administrative Buildings

Other aspects of public life and administration were housed in and around the Agora; sometimes there are actual physical remains, and sometimes they are known primarily from the written sources. An example of the former is South Stoa I, built in the second half of the fifth century BC along the south side of the square. A Doric colonnade some 80 m long gave access to sixteen rooms, set side by side along the length of the building. Several of the rooms were equipped as dining rooms, and both the size and location suggest a public building. Dining at state expense is known for the nine archons, high priests, ambassadors, crowned athletic victors, and the *prytaneis* (executive committee) of the *boule*, while some other officials were paid for their maintenance while in office. The rooms of South Stoa I could have served both as offices and as dining areas for many of the small boards and commissions charged with the daily running of the city. A Hellenistic inscription found in one of the rooms adds its weight to this interpretation. It is a record in 222/1 BC, recording the handing over of a set of the official weights and measures from the board of *metronomoi* (commissioners of weights and measures) to the incoming board of the following year. The number of officials listed by name, five *metronomoi* and two secretaries, matches exactly the number of dining couches which could be accommodated in one of the rooms. Another indication that official commercial activity was carried out is the large number of bronze coins, just under 200, that were found in the building. Generally, coins are found in streets, drains, private houses, and shops; they are much rarer in public buildings, and the unusually large number found here suggests that the stoa was used to house activities and officials concerned with the economics of the city. Another set of official weights and measures was said to be kept in the Tholos as well, and a set of official weights of bronze, labeled as public (*demosion*), with inscriptions and symbols (knuckle-bone, shield, tortoise) indicating their weight, have been recovered, along with lead equivalents used by merchants in the market.

To the east of South Stoa I was a building plausibly identified as one of the mints of Athens, built around 400 BC. Signs of burning, water basins, the bottoms of furnaces, and other debris all suggest that considerable industrial activity took place in the building, while dozens of unstruck bronze coin blanks or flans were found as well. Lacking was the slightest trace of silver, suggesting that the famous Athenian owl coins, admired throughout the Mediterranean and beyond for the purity of their silver, were minted elsewhere.

Other official buildings housing Athenian administrators are listed as being in or near the Agora, though they have not yet been associated with specific remains. These include the Poleterion (offices of the state auctioneers), the Strategeion (office of the generals), and the Thesmotheteion (office of the six lesser archons). As noted, the archives were housed in the Metroon, which earlier had served as the Bouleuterion. Other officials are attested, though with no specific indication that they were housed in the Agora, such as the *sitophylakes* or *sitonai* (grain commissioners), water commissioners, *agoranomoi* (market inspectors), and the like.

Military Headquarters

Military administration and activities were also accommodated in the Agora. A cluster of dedications, inscribed honors, and reliefs found at the northwest corner of the square suggests the proximity of the Hipparcheion, the office of the cavalry commanders, the hipparchs and phylarchs.

Also recovered in the vicinity was a well containing several series of lead strips carrying inscriptions used in the annual assessment of the knights (*hippeis*), those who claimed to have a horse worthy of fighting in the cavalry. The owner's name and a description of the horse's brand and color, along with a monetary value, are listed on each of these lead tablets, following inspection by the officers. Money was provided to the owner to help maintain the horse, and the value indicates a form of insurance should the horse be lost in battle. A fragment from the comic poet Mnesimachos indicates that the roadway and open spaces of the Agora were used for training the cavalry: "Go forth, Manes, to the Agora, to the herms, the place frequented by the phylarchs, and to their handsome pupils, whom Pheidon trains in mounting and dismounting" (Athenaios 9.402). In a remarkable correlation of archaeology and text, the lead archives were accompanied by several clay tokens, stamped with the name of this same Pheidon, the hipparch assigned to supervise the Athenian island possession of Lemnos. Also attested for the Agora were the offices of the ten generals, one from each tribe, who met in a building known as the Strategeion. Its location is still unknown.

Other Public Structures

Given the large number of citizens participating in public life, crowd control must have been an issue, and enclosures made of ropes or wooden fences were used on various occasions. Parts of the Agora would be fenced or roped off when an ostracism was taking place, as were the large juries in the lawcourts. An example of such an enclosure, a *perischoinisma*, has been found just east of the Altar of the Twelve Gods. It consisted of a series of square stone blocks embedded in the road fill of the Panathenaic Way, with cuttings in their tops to anchor wooden posts to which the ropes would be affixed. The area enclosed measures ca. 12 by 14 m. The installation seems to be the one mentioned by Plutarch (*Moralia* 847a), next to the Altar of the Twelve Gods. Its location, straddling the road, suggests it was used to control crowds going in or out of the main square.

Basic amenities had to be provided for the hundreds of visitors, both those with and without business, places where the curious, the idle, and the social could spend their free time. Water and shelter were the two main requirements. Fountain-houses at the southwest (fourth century BC) and southeast (sixth century BC) corners of the square provided abundant clean, fresh water, piped in over long distances. Shade was available in numerous stoas which ringed all sides of the square throughout its history. Some stoas were places of official business and may not have been available to everyone at all times. Others were designed to house those with nowhere else to be. The Stoa Poikile (Painted Stoa) was the principal example of this latter type, perhaps the most public building in the city (see Fig. 21.2). Erected in ca. 470 BC, it was decorated soon thereafter with handsome paintings done on wooden panels, which gave the building its name. In a sense, the building may be regarded as among the earliest known examples of a public art museum, facing onto the public square with its open, colonnaded façade.

The traveler Pausanias, who visited Athens in ca. AD 150, describes four paintings, all showing Athenian military exploits, both mythical and historical, in the Stoa Poikile. The panels were not removed until the fourth century AD. The stoa served various other functions as well: as a place of entertainment by sword-swallowers (Apuleius, *Metamorphoses* 1.4), for arbitrations (Demosthenes 45 [*Stephanos* 1], 17), as a lawcourt (*IG* II^2 1641 and 1670), and for proclamations concerning the Eleusinian Mysteries (Schol. Aristophanes, *Frogs* 369 ff). It was the haunt of philosophers, and in particular Zeno, whose regular use of the building led to both him and his followers becoming known as the Stoics.

In short, the Agora of Athens, like that of all Greek cities, was the center of commerce, spectacle, and social interchange, and the open space and adjacent buildings provided the venues for a host of daily activities. It was distinctly Greek, as not all ancient societies had need of such a center. Herodotos (1.153) quotes King Cyrus of Persia as saying:

> "I never yet feared men who have a place set apart in the middle of their city where they lie and deceive each other. If I keep my health, these men will have their own problems to worry about, not those of the Ionians." This threat he uttered against all Greeks, because they have agoras and buy and sell there; for the Persians use no agoras, nor do they have any.

This concept of a large, central public square was passed on from Greece through the *fora* of Imperial Roman cities to most European capitals. In Athens, the Agora served also as the center of most government activity, where democracy was invented and practiced by its citizens over the course of two centuries.

Further Reading

The excavations of the Athenian Agora have been well published. Over sixty volumes and 450 articles have appeared thus far, and more are in preparation.

The majority of articles are published in *Hesperia*, the journal of the American School of Classical Studies at Athens. The website of the Athenian Agora Excavations (www.agathe.gr) provides online access to numerous resources, including archival excavation materials, plans, and full publication lists of the excavations. On the early years of these excavations see Dumont 2020. For more on the ancient sources related to the Agora, see Pausanias (Book 1, especially chapters 3–18), Aristotle's *Constitution of the Athenians* (*Athenaion Politeia*), and Wycherley 1957. For general resources on the Agora, consult Thompson and Wycherley 1972, Camp 1992, Mauzy 2006, Camp and Mauzy 2009, Camp 2010, and Gawlinski 2014. On the lawcourts, see Boegehold 1995 and Townsend 1995, along with Lang 1990 on ostracism. For more on the numerous inscriptions of the Agora, see Bradeen 1973, Meritt and Traill 1974, Lalonde, Langdon, and Walbank 1991, Woodhead 1997, and Geagan 2011.

Bibliography

Boegehold, A. 1995. *The Lawcourts at Athens: Sites, Buildings, Equipment, Procedure, and Testimonia. Agora* 28. Princeton.

Bradeen, D. 1973. *Inscriptions: The Funerary Monuments. Agora* 17. Princeton.

Camp, J.M. 1992. *The Athenian Agora: Excavations in the Heart of Classical Athens*. London.

 2010. *The Athenian Agora: Site Guide*. 5th edn. Princeton.

Camp, J.M., and C. Mauzy, eds. 2009. *The Athenian Agora: New Perspectives on an Ancient Site*. Mainz.

Dumont, S. 2020. *Vrysaki: A Neighborhood Lost in Search of the Athenian Agora*. Princeton.

Gawlinski, L. 2014. *The Athenian Agora: Museum Guide*. 5th edn. Princeton.

Geagan, D. 2011. *Inscriptions: The Dedications. Agora* 18. Princeton.

Lalonde, G., M.K. Langdon, and M.B. Walbank. 1991. *Inscriptions: Horoi, Poletai Records, Leases of Public Lands. Agora* 19. Princeton.

Lang, M. 1990. *Ostraka. Agora* 25. Princeton.

Mauzy, C. 2006. *Agora Excavations 1931–2006: A Pictorial History*. Athens.

Meritt, B.D., and J.S. Traill. 1974. *Inscriptions: The Athenian Councilors. Agora* 15. Princeton.

Thompson, H.A., and R.E. Wycherley. 1972. *The Agora of Athens: The History, Shape, and Uses of an Ancient City Center. Agora* 14. Princeton.

Townsend, R. 1995. *The East Side of the Agora: The Remains beneath the Stoa of Attalos. Agora* 27. Princeton.

Woodhead, A.G. 1997. *Inscriptions: The Decrees. Agora* 16. Princeton.

Wycherley, R.E. 1957. *Literary and Epigraphical Testimonia. Agora* 3. Princeton.

7 | Athenian Inscriptions

ELIZABETH A. MEYER

For much of its history, Athens was a city of words on stone: from the Late Archaic period (sixth century BC) to Late Antiquity, Athenian stone-cutters, and those of Athens' territory, Attika, carved or scratched more than 20,000 inscriptions, far more than any other Greek *polis* (city-state). As a consequence, starting in the fifth century BC, there was much more for an Athenian to see and read than others could elsewhere. The range of inscription-type was wide, too, although the distribution of inscriptions across the city was rather less so: one would see many more inscriptions in Athens' cemeteries and on the Athenian Akropolis than elsewhere. Such a proliferation of inscriptions has prompted some basic historical questions: Why so many? Why some types of inscription more than others, why in some locations more than others? Do the sheer numbers imply a higher literacy rate in Athens than elsewhere, a higher degree of religiosity, or some fundamental connection to the Athenian democracy? And, perhaps more imponderable, what was the experience of walking through the inscribed city?

Funerary Inscriptions

By far the most common type of Athenian inscription – as true, also, elsewhere – was the epitaph. Archaic Athens produced actual grave monuments, inscribed *stelai* (standing rectangular stones, usually) with reliefs or full-size funerary sculpture of young men and women (*kouroi* and *korai*), at times on inscribed bases; after a pause in the making of private memorials between 480 and 430 BC, grave *stelai* with relief sculpture returned, as did simpler forms of commemoration, tall *stelai* with only a name. After 317–307 BC, when sumptuary laws of the Athenian tyrant Demetrios of Phaleron cracked down on opulent – large and, or, sculptured – grave monuments, both types were supplanted by memorials in the form of undecorated little columns or *columellae*. (See Shea, Chapter 10 in this volume.) On the other hand, Athens was unusual in producing, from some time in the 480s through the end of the fifth century (and thus overlapping with the gap in private stone epitaphs), city-sponsored lists of war dead called by scholars 'casualty lists' (*IG* I³ 1194–1281). These lists could be quite long, especially during the latter years of the Great Peloponnesian War with Sparta (431–404 BC), and seem to have been erected in prominent locations along the major road leading into the city from the northwest, through a section of the Kerameikos cemetery identified as the Demosion Sema, or 'public memorial.'

If walking through an Attic cemetery was much like walking through a more modern one, complete with family enclosures and the occasional tumulus or tall *stele* calling for the viewer's attention, then walking past the casualty lists might have evoked the same pity, solemn tenderness, and sense of loss that standing before a World War I memorial in a small town in Britain does, and likely inspired the same desire to touch that the thousands of names inscribed on the Vietnam Memorial in Washington, DC do. Quiet moments depicted on a type of funerary vase known as a *lekythos* show men and women looking sadly at grave monuments (one even, it seems, a casualty list),[1] reaching out to them, tying ribbons around them, and leaving offerings. The great Athenian leader Perikles wanted the Athenians to see in their war dead the greatness of Athens and the uniqueness of her genius, but all responses were not necessarily so political and so specific. One does not need to have known the dead to be moved by their memorialization: the dead speak to everyone.

Religious Dedications

Dedications to gods and heroes are the second most common type of inscription, and here again, Athens follows a pattern found in many other Greek city-states. Like epitaphs, dedications are some of the earliest inscriptions found in Athens. Dedications were gifts to the gods, and expected as a form of thank-offering and acknowledgment that the divinity had smiled upon, and thus assisted, a human endeavor – or as an offering in the hope of the same, or as a simple expression of religious feeling. Dedications were usually valuable objects, or at least valuable to the donor (they did not necessarily have to be expensive); they could be a prize won in a competition or custom-made to be a gift, and were themselves often inscribed. As a consequence, not everything that was dedicated has

---

[1] Amsterdam, Allard Pierson Museum 2455; BAPD no. 4215.

survived, since more costly items could be looted, stolen, and – if metal – melted down. But many of the bases on which the more costly offerings, such as bronze tripods or statues, were placed do survive, certainly enough to make clear that these expressions of honor and reverence to the gods were very common and very important. Almost all of these were found on the Athenian Akropolis, where the city's goddess Athena was worshiped in three forms (Athena Polias 'of the City,' Athena Parthenos 'the virgin,' and Athena Nike 'victory') and had a statue in a fourth (Athena Promachos 'foremost in battle'); but other divinities, such as Artemis Brauronia and the divinized Athenian king Erechtheus, also had their dedicated areas on the Akropolis. The entire Akropolis came to be seen as a sacred space ("all of the Akropolis is sacred," said Demosthenes [19.272]) and a dedication itself (Pausanias 5.21.1); it attracted a multitude of individual offerings, hundreds and hundreds over the centuries, many of which were stored in the Temple of Athena Parthenos itself. All such gifts belonged to the divinity as well, and so could (if, for example, broken) be repurposed within the sanctuary but not, without special permission or inviting a charge of sacrilege, sold outside it.

Athenian treasurers, elected yearly, were responsible for the oversight of the gifts dedicated in the sanctuary, and in a formal ceremony inventoried these gifts and passed them on to the next year's treasurers, an act that produced an inscribed list (called a *paradosis*, a handing-over); officials also supervised the inventorying and melting-down of broken dedications, resulting in inscriptions called *kathaireseis* or cleanings. Both types (as well as a third type, a one-time inventory of treasures called an *exetasmos*) were also placed on the Akropolis. To walk on to the Akropolis was thus to enter the divine realm where different rules applied. This was true of all sanctuaries, the word for whose space – a *temenos* – literally meant "cut-off" space. The Akropolis was an area deliberately separated from regular existence: behavior in it was governed by sacred regulations, it was home to temples and altars, and it bristled with permanent dedications that honored the gods and conveyed the piety of the donor, also named. The closest modern parallel to entering this sacred space is probably entering an old English or European church, the type with soaring architecture that imposes a different sensory experience on the viewer, and with votive plaques and family chapels and more temporary offerings, such as candles, that mark previous acts of piety, some lasting, some not.

The gods could be honored with far more than purpose-crafted dedications and lists that reflected the devoted and honest handling of those gifts. As also elsewhere, gods in Athenian sanctuaries were honored with inscriptions that we might be tempted to call secular: acts of the city-state itself, such as laws, decrees, treaties, and even regulations for foreign states from the time when Athens ruled an empire. Athens would, over the centuries, produce hundreds of these inscriptions. Such abundance makes Athens unique; and most of these inscriptions were erected on the Akropolis as well. It was once thought that sanctuaries like that of the Akropolis merely served as a practical archive for *poleis*, a convenient place to display or simply store stone versions of these important state documents, but the frequently encountered heading "Gods," as well as the reliefs of gods and heroes that often adorn these so-called document *stelai,*[2] suggest what their placement on the Akropolis underlines: these inscribed documents were also conceived, at some level, as a gift to the divinity, an achievement of the Athenians bestowed upon her in honor of her assistance and reflecting on her glory. This placement reminds us that we draw a line between sacred and secular that the ancients did not, and that the modern experience of visiting a church marks only the beginning, but not the end, of what walking on the Akropolis would have been like. Athens' glory was Athena's glory, and the Akropolis encompassed, conveyed, and displayed it all.

Civic Inscriptions

Athenian legislation took two forms, both inscribed. One type was Athenian laws, called *thesmoi* or *nomoi*. (See Harris, Chapter 28 in this volume.) In their earliest form, under Drako in the late seventh century BC, they were said to have been inscribed on wood, specifically wooden 'axles' (*axones*); a somewhat later set of laws, those of Solon in the early sixth century, began life (as, probably, did Drako's), I have argued, as pillars of a very ancient temple on the Akropolis.[3] One of Drako's laws was reinscribed from its *axon* onto a stone *stele* at the end of the fifth century BC (*OR* 183), along with a sacred calendar (and some other fragmentary laws survive as well), all as part of a seven- or eight-year effort to revise and reinscribe Athens' existing laws. 403/2 BC, the year this effort finished, also marked the moment when the passage of *nomoi* – legislation of more general, and sometimes of specifically religious, application – became more

---

[2] For the reliefs of documentary *stelai*, see Lawton 1995.
[3] For my argument that Athenian *thesmoi* were initially published on wooden columns, see Meyer 2016.

complicated, and the second type of Athenian legislation, *psephismata* ('things pebbled,' i.e. things voted on), known and already numerically preponderant from the middle of the fifth century, became the absolutely common way in which the Athenian Assembly handled its legislative business. Only ten inscribed *nomoi* survive, at least so far, while from the mid-fifth century 270 or so inscribed decrees before 403/2 survive, and around 600 from 403/2 to 322/1 BC.[4]

Although decrees could cover a variety of topics, such as a cleruchy (citizen settlement) on the island of Salamis (the earliest decree known, from the late sixth century BC: *IG* I[3] 1), the creation of a new priestess (to Athena Nike 'Victory,' *OR* 137), or the imposition of regulations on the subject-allies at the height of the Athenian Empire in the fifth century (*OR* 131, Chalcis), the majority of surviving Athenian decrees are honorific, granting privileges to foreigners in thanks for some valuable action taken by them that benefited the Athenians, such as supplying cheap grain in a time of scarcity. This habit of honoring foreigners became particularly visible in the closing decade of the Peloponnesian War, when it functioned as a useful instrument of Athenian diplomacy,[5] and never ceased thereafter. Athenians start to honor fellow Athenians only much later, starting around the 340s BC, although a statue to the victorious general Chabrias was erected in the Athenian Agora after 376 BC.[6]

Inscribed laws and decrees, along with treaties, found their home on the Akropolis, or, at least, for the most part. At the very end of the fifth century, several of the *nomoi* produced by the seven- or eight-year effort at revision were brought down from the Akropolis, reinscribed, and erected in the Stoa of the King Archon, one of Athens' nine annually chosen chief magistrates: this was a major change. Previous inscriptions in the Agora had been limited to its speaking boundary stones ("I am the boundary stone of the Agora"),[7] to the couplet inscribed under the statues of the two Tyrannicides, Harmodios and Aristogeiton (*IG* I[3] 502; Web Fig. 20.1), valorized by the Athenians for their killing of Hipparchos (who was, according to the historian Thucydides, not the tyrant himself but his brother), to an inscribed archon list (*IG* I[3] 1031); and to a copy of the decree reassessing the allies' tribute in 425 BC, set up in the Council-House with another copy on the Akropolis (*OR* 153). (The great inscribed tribute

---

[4] Lambert forthcoming, 3.
[5] Liddel 2010.
[6] *Agora* 18, C146.
[7] *Agora* 19, H25–27.

list itself, standing more than 2 m high and covered with lists of the one-sixtieth taken from the allies' tribute and offered to Athena, was placed on the Akropolis, another glorious achievement attributed to the goddess; *OR* 119.)

The Agora never surpassed the Akropolis as a place to display inscriptions, but came to play a significant and specialized role. The so-called Charter of the Second Athenian Naval League (*RO* 22) was placed next to the statue of Zeus Eleutherios ('of freedom') in front of his Stoa in the Agora, reflecting not so much the 'public' or 'democratic' nature of the Agora as the importance of the 'freedom' – autonomy – which the Charter granted to the new allies, with Zeus's epithet and statue reinforcing this crucial aspect of the agreement. The *poletai*, official sellers of confiscated property and leasers of state-owned lands and mines, had a building in the Agora, and fragments of leases and lists of confiscated property have also been found there.[8] In the third century BC, ephebes – Athenian males between the ages of 18 and 20 who trained for war and served the city – were sometimes listed and honored with inscriptions erected in the Agora. But as Stephen Lambert has emphasized, the Agora as such did not become a default location for the erection of inscriptions; instead, the inscribed fourth-century laws that have been found there, such as the law on the grain tax and the law on testing the silver coinage (*RO* 26 and 25), were placed in the Agora because their placement was determined by their specific contextual application (what Lambert calls the driver): these laws were erected in the Agora because that is where the business they regulated took place, and in this way participants were directly reminded of the ways in which business was to be performed. For a similar reason, a law forbidding the Areopagos Council to meet if there was a tyrannical coup (*RO* 79) was erected at the entrance to the Areopagos, and several decrees that honored foreigners active in the grain trade were erected in Athens' port of Piraeus.[9]

Epigraphic Style

All of these types of inscriptions – epitaphs, dedications, legislation (in its various forms), and other state-related inscribed documents – were intentional monuments: commissioned, paid for, and placed where their

---

[8] *Agora* 19, P1–56, L1–16.
[9] Lambert 2018, 42 (two laws in the Agora), 33–34 (Areopagos), 35–39 (Piraeus).

grieving relatives, respectful donors, deferential *polis*, or grateful honorands wished them to be placed. As befitted such more-than-utilitarian monuments, they were constructed with great care and beauty. Sculpture and reliefs (of high artistic quality, as the current presence of inscriptions with such adornments in museums stresses) were often present, and the lettering has its own attractive aspects. Most of the laws and other documents from 480 to ca. 300 BC were laid out in what is called the *stoichedon* (*stoichos* means "row") format, a type of checkerboard arrangement in which one letter is carved in each box, symmetrical both horizontally and vertically.[10] This style created a visual uniformity, especially on the Akropolis, and imparted a visual knowledge of what kind of document an inscription in this format was likely to be; it tied together these smaller *stelai* and appealed to the eye.

This sense of graceful and even spacing carries over into inscriptions that were not dense blocks of text inscribed in *stoichedon* format, contributing to a kind of recognizable Athenian scheme of lettering that finds its way into non-stone media, such as vase-painting, as well. The shapes of the letters themselves changed over time – in particular, the letter *sigma* went from having three bars to four, and the letter *rho* lost its 'tail' – and the Attic alphabet (which had no eta or omega, and also wrote some other letters differently) was replaced by the Ionic (which did), officially in 403/2 BC but in practice unofficially, if sporadically, some time before that. But the carvers always did their work with meticulous attention and with remarkably few mistakes. There was enough work for enough of them, by the end of the fifth century, that various hands – that is, of individual carvers – can even be identified.[11]

There were yet other types of inscription – some still on stone, others on materials such as lead and potsherds – that the Athenians also produced. 'Legislation' – rules, sacred regulations, honorific decrees – as well as dedications could also be inscribed by smaller units within the Athenian *polis*, such as the Attic demes (self-governing villages, *RO* 159) or phratries (literally 'brotherhoods,' *RO* 5), just as local sanctuaries attracted, understandably, their own dedicatory inscriptions and sacred regulations. These were usually set up in the demes, not the central city of Athens. Graffiti is also a form of inscribing, and Athenians scratched obscenities on pieces of pottery and on buildings ("fucker" on an orthostate reused in the

---

[10] For the *stoichedon* style, Austin 1938/1973 is still the standard.

[11] For letter-cutters, see the body of work by Tracy, of which the most recent, on the carvers of the fifth century, is Tracy 2016.

foundation of the Painted Stoa comes to mind) with no less enthusiasm and lack of imagination (if with less access to paint) than their modern counterparts.[12] Around 2,000 very early examples of this sort of 'inscribing' have been found in the hills south of Athens, crudely scratched into rocks by, apparently, herders of sheep and goats: some are practice-alphabets, some drawings (those of ships have been published), some one-line statements.[13] Athenians also cursed their enemies by writing on lead so-called curse-tablets, which they buried in graves (so as to reach their underworld enforcers in an expeditious fashion). The most famous fifth century examples of this more ephemeral type of inscribing are provided by names scratched on potsherds, *ostraka*, as part of the Athenian process of ostracism, whereby the 'winning' politician would be required to leave Athens and Attika for ten years, but would keep his property (see Fig. 6.1). Great caches of these inscribed potsherds have been found in the Kerameikos excavations, and more than 1,400 also in the Agora – the total from both locations now stands at more than 10,500, with more no doubt to come – probably swept together and buried after the ostracism had taken place. These gave the names of many famous fifth-century Athenian politicians (Perikles, Kimon, Themistokles), as well as some men entirely unknown to history. Very striking is one set, against Themistokles, apparently written in the same hands, suggesting a conspiracy to facilitate his expulsion from the city by preparing *ostraka* ahead of time, and presumably written not just for efficiency but for those who themselves could not write.[14]

Literacy

The profusion not only of stone inscriptions but also of these more ephemeral types of writing have encouraged scholars to see Athens as a city of extraordinarily high literacy. The broad evidence of writing is better here than anywhere else in Greece, and seems – with graffiti, *ostraka*, and curse-tablets – to reach further down in society than can be seen anywhere else in the ancient world except, perhaps, Pompeii. Nonetheless, it is not entirely clear that the Athenian citizenry was largely literate. As the

---

[12] See *Agora* 21.
[13] For numbers and drawings (in this case of ships), see Van de Moortel and Langdon 2017, and for alphabets, Langdon 2005; the entire assemblage of these rock inscriptions is to be published by Langdon.
[14] The Kerameikos *ostraka* are published by Brenne 2018, those of the Agora (including the Themistokles *ostraka*) in *Agora* 25 and Sickinger 2017.

example of the Themistokles *ostraka* suggests, even the most humble writing, in a *polis*-procedure that seems to take it for granted that citizens could write, could be performed by one citizen for another; and curse-tablets, seemingly the most private of written acts, could be written for a client by a *goes* (a magician). Only with graffiti can we be relatively sure that there was no intermediary. Stone inscriptions, or even the wooden 'notice-boards' nailed to the Monument of the Eponymous Heroes in the Agora, could be read by one person to a group of others (see Web Fig. 27.1). So not only is an estimate of the level of literacy beyond reconstruction; we cannot even be sure that many Athenians could read, much less write.

Democracy required participation – turning up, listening, speaking, fulfilling magistracies and other positions distributed by lot, clearly in some cases with the help of scribes and secretaries – but not necessarily personal literacy. Even what has been called the hortatory principle – "we honor this person and his achievements so you, the reader of this inscription, will feel compelled to benefit the city as well," a clause in an inscription to inspire a necessarily literate population to benefaction – is found in honorific inscriptions starting only in the 340s BC, and, again, could actually work through another's reading as well as one's own. There were always work-arounds.

What about the deeper level of what citizens 'needed to know'? The immense volume of Athenian epigraphy has suggested that stone inscriptions were erected because they conveyed, and were intended to convey, information to citizens, functioning as an important indicator of the transparency of governance to the governed. This is an attractive proposition, especially when one thinks of financial documents, such as the great tribute list, the treasurers' yearly *paradoseis* of temple treasures, the inscriptions on the Akropolis that recorded the expenditures, in columnar formats, of money spent (much of it sacred) on temples and buildings, and (in *stoichedon*) Athena's loans to the city of Athens (with interest). But such transparency did not extend even to financial matters that we would think most crucial in democratic governance, such as how the tribute collected was actually spent, or what happened to the goddess's income (from rented lands, for example), rather than how carefully the goddess's gifts were treated. The driver (if one may use Lambert's term, again) of Athenian inscribing was not fundamentally the Athenian democracy, but Athenian piety, which erected epitaphs to the dead and dedicated gifts and attestations of a wide range of Athenian achievements to the gods. That is why the Akropolis remained the magnetic center for so many types of inscription, not only those one would expect (dedications), but also those whose presence there seems odd to us (laws, inscriptions, treaties, regulations, financial documents), and especially after 450 BC. For not only did the Periklean building project begin then, but also the impressive and acknowledged power of Athens over the cities and islands of the Aegean in her Empire. Within the Athenians' strong impulse to expressions of piety and reverence, imperial domination provided a new category of achievement, and a more powerful, less ambivalent one than the democracy itself.

Conclusion

Still, Athens was a city of words. Even if stone inscriptions were highly symbolic rather than directly functional, they would have made a substantial impression on both Athenians and visitors. Other sanctuaries, such as Delphi and Olympia, impressed with their glittering monuments but in the fifth and fourth centuries had much less visible writing: Athens was the first to populate her great city-sanctuary with so many standing inscriptions, the first to assert that inscriptions were themselves worthy gifts. Themselves works of art, often large, ornamental, carefully carved, and in lettering styles that helped to establish uniformity in the sanctuary across its large space, freestanding inscriptions conveyed a quintessentially Athenian view that words alone could convey Athenian piety and power. Walking on the Athenian Akropolis would, therefore, be much like walking into Napoleon's mausoleum in Paris, where his sarcophagus rests on a mosaic in the shape of a sun inside a victory-wreath, with the names of his eight major battles inscribed in a circle; the sarcophagus was surrounded by twelve victory statues; ten relief-plaques depicted his great achievements; and access was granted by a bronze door made from the cannon taken at Austerlitz. Words, objects, and images all told one story, that of Napoleon's stupendous greatness. Or, perhaps even better, it would be like walking into a museum exhibit devoted to a theme or a period of history, with both well-lighted precious objects and much well-written and significant wall-text: both objects and text tell the story, one with as much care and eloquence as the other, but neither capable of conveying the entirety of the achievement by itself. Yet the further advantage of inscribing, in Athens, is that one could touch the object, run your fingers over the inscription, and sense as well as see the wonder, the reverence, the greatness.

Further Reading

The study of Athenian, and Attic, epigraphy is old. The great collection of (most) Greek inscriptions is *Inscriptiones Graecae*, where volume I^3 covers Attic inscriptions down to the year 403/2 BC, and *IG* II/III^2 the years thereafter. This latter set is being republished: *IG* II/III^3 1.2, 1.4, and 1.5 (laws and decrees 352/–322/1, 300/ 299–230/29, and 229/8–168/7 BC), *IG* II/III^3 4.1 (public and choregic dedications), and *IG* II/III^3 5 (Late Antiquity). *IG* publishes in Greek with commentary in Latin, and with no translations in the printed versions; I have therefore chosen as specific examples here mostly inscriptions that can be found in Rhodes and Osborne 2003 (*RO*) and Osborne and Rhodes 2017 (*OR*), which constitute rich collections, with English translations and commentaries, of specific inscriptions, many of them Athenian. For ease of accessibility, excellent translations and brief commentaries, and a rapidly growing body of inscriptions (added to quarterly), see Lambert's www.atticinscriptionsonline.com. The other major source of Athenian inscriptions is the Agora series, of which *Agora* 18 (*Inscriptions: The Dedicatory Monuments* [2011]), *Agora* 19 (*Inscriptions: Horoi, Poletai Records, Leases of Public Lands* [1991]), *Agora* 21 (*Graffiti and Dipinti* [1976]), and Agora 25 (*Ostraka* [1990]) are cited here. This essay is also much indebted to Lambert forthcoming, an excellent overview of Athenian epigraphy with greater attention to some other sub-genres of Athenian inscriptions (mortgage-*horoi*, cavalry tickets, etc.) and to some technical details (history of epigraphy, dating, letter forms, onomastics and prosopography, the science of epigraphy) than there was room for here.

For Athenian epitaphs, there is no good overview, but for an argument addressing the great increase of Athenian epitaphs in the fourth century, see Meyer 1993. For inscribed Akropolis dedications from the Archaic period, Keesling 2003; for Akropolis 'inventories' (*paradoseis, kathareseis, exetasmoi*), Harris 1995. For inscriptions as honors to the gods, Meyer 2013, which also investigates earlier theories of democratic functionality, as well as significant placement on both Akropolis and in the Agora; for the latter, see also Shear 2011, and (especially) Lambert 2018, who lays out the bigger (more long-term) picture and cites the (few) factors that 'drive' the erection of inscriptions away from the Akropolis. For format as conveyer of knowledge, Meyer 2017. For honorific inscriptions as a significant element of Athenian foreign policy, Liddel 2010. On the relationship of literacy and democracy, Missiou 2011 is optimistic; of Athenian Empire to Akropolis inscribing, Moroo 2016.

Bibliography

Austin, R.P. 1938/1973. *The Stoichedon Style in Greek Inscriptions*. Oxford.

Brenne, S. 2018. *Die Ostraka vom Kerameikos. Kerameikos* 20. Berlin.

Harris, D.R. 1995. *The Treasures of the Parthenon and the Erechtheion*. Oxford.

Keesling, C. 2003. *The Votive Statues of the Athenian Acropolis*. Cambridge.

Lambert, S.D. 2018. "The Locations of Inscribed Athenian Laws and Decrees in the Age of Demosthenes." In *Inscribed Laws and Decrees in the Age of Demosthenes. Historical Essays*, ed. S.D. Lambert, Leiden, 19–46.

Forthcoming. "Attic Epigraphy." In *The Oxford Handbook of Greek Epigraphy*, ed. N. Papazarkadas, Oxford.

Langdon, M.K. 2005. "A New Greek Abcedarium." *Kadmos* 44: 175–182.

Lawton, C.L. 1995. *Attic Document Reliefs. Art and Politics in Ancient Athens.* Oxford.

Liddel, P. 2010. "Epigraphy, Legislation, and Power within the Athenian Empire." *Bulletin of the Institute of Classical Studies* 53: 99–128.

Meyer, E.A. 1993. "Epitaphs and Citizenship in Classical Athens." *JHS* 113: 99–121.

2013. "Inscriptions as Honors and the Athenian Epigraphic Habit." *Historia* 62: 453–505.

2016. "Posts, *Kurbeis*, Metopes. The Origins of the Athenian 'Documentary' Stele." *Hesperia* 85: 323–383.

2017. "Inscribing in Columns in Fifth-Century Athens." In *Writing Matters. Presenting and Perceiving Monumental Inscriptions in Antiquity and the Middle Ages. Proceedings of the Symposium, 10–12 October 2013*, eds. I. Berti, K. Bolle, F. Opdenhoff, and F. Stroth, Berlin, 205–261.

Missiou, A. 2011. *Literacy and Democracy in Fifth Century Athens.* Cambridge.

Moroo, A. 2016. "The Origin and Development of the Acropolis as a Place for Erecting Public Decrees: The Periclean Building Project and its Effect on the Athenian Epigraphic Habit." In *The Parthenon Frieze. The Ritual Communication Between the Goddess and the Polis*, ed. T. Osada, Vienna, 31–48.

Osborne, R., and P.J. Rhodes. 2017. *Greek Historical Inscriptions 479–404* BC. Oxford.

Rhodes, P.J., and R. Osborne. 2003. *Greek Historical Inscriptions 404–323* BC. Oxford.

Shear, J.L. 2011. *Polis and Revolution. Responding to Oligarchy in Classical Athens.* Cambridge.

Sickinger, J.P. 2017. "New Ostraka from the Athenian Agora." *Hesperia* 86: 443–508.

Tracy, S.V. 2016. *Athenian Lettering of the Fifth Century* BC: *The Rise of the Professional Letter-Cutter.* Berlin.

Van de Moortel, A., and M.K. Langdon. 2017. "Archaic Ship Graffiti from Southern Attica, Greece. Typology and Preliminary Contextual Analysis." *International Journal of Nautical Archaeology* 46: 382–405.

8 | Water and Water Management

JUTTA STROSZECK

> [A city] must possess, if possible, a plentiful natural supply of pools
> and springs, but failing this, a mode has been invented of supplying
> water by means of constructing an abundance of large reservoirs for
> rain-water so that a supply may never fail the citizens when they are
> debarred from their territory by war ... The health of the
> inhabitants ... depends upon ... using wholesome water-supplies ...
>
> Aristotle, *Politics* 7.10.2–3 (1330b)

Sufficient water of good quality is indispensable for human existence and a
prerequisite for the development and flourishing of any city. Thus, water
installations are among the first kinds of evidence for a human presence in
an area. The earliest traces of a settlement at Athens are to be found on the
northwestern slope of the Akropolis during the Late Neolithic period
(3500–3200 BC). Obviously, the first inhabitants of the area had observed
that the water table was close to the surface around the Empedo spring
(later to become the Klepsydra). By digging wells in the local bedrock,
water could be stored for some time. Subsequently, these earliest devices
led to a better understanding of methods for storing water in cisterns.
With the growing population and over time, the need for more water
ultimately generated new technical solutions, in particular, new water
conduits bringing water from the springs on the slopes around the
Athenian plain toward the city. The quantity and quality of water were
subject to change during the seasons and influenced by various factors,
such as precipitation and climate. In the following survey of the water
supply and water management in ancient Athens, the evidence from
excavation is supplemented by a number of texts by ancient authors
and inscriptions.

Athens has a typical Mediterranean subtropical climate, with hot and
dry summers and mild winters. Short but heavy rainfalls occur mainly in
autumn and winter. The groundwater table is influenced by precipitation,
rising during the winter and dropping in the summer. In general, the city
was not well provided with water resources, and Athens repeatedly suffered
from droughts. The two main periods of drought were during the late

eighth to seventh and during the fourth centuries BC.[1] Sanctuaries for Zeus Ombrios (Zeus who commands rain), situated on Mt. Hymettos and Mt. Parnes, demonstrate that the need for water induced Athenians to pray there for rain during the seventh century BC.[2] The philosopher Dikaiarchos (*FHG* 2 fr. 59), who lived in Athens during the late fourth to early third century BC, called the city "completely dry, not well provided with water."

Springs and Rivers

Several springs emerge on the slopes of the hills around the Athenian plain and of the Akropolis. This can be explained by the geological formation of karstic calcareous limestone (or marble) on top of a harder and impermeable formation, an aquifuge layer of marly 'Athenian' schist. The latter forces the intruding surface water to form springs that emerge on the lower slopes of the mountains slightly above the schist layer.[3] The strongest spring on the Akropolis is the perennial Empedo on the northwestern slope. A second spring on the north slope was architecturally enclosed during the Late Mycenean period. On the south slope, there is a spring in the healing Sanctuary of Asklepios, and a fourth one, once sacred to the nymphs, lies further to the west. On top of the rock, there was Poseidon's well (Pausanias 1.26.5) or the sea (*thalassa*) in the Erechtheion, a sacred spring that was said to be filled by sea water (Herodotos 8.55; Aristophanes, *Wealth* 656–657).

The rivers of ancient Athens originate from such springs. The three main rivers in the Athenian plain are the Kephissos, the Ilissos, and the Eridanos (see Map 4.2).[4] These rivers play an important role for the groundwater table within the Attic plain and in particular within the boundaries of the ancient city. The Eridanos emerges from a main spring on the west slope of Mt. Lykabettos. The Ilissos' and the Kykloboros' sources are springs on Mt. Hymettos, while the Kephissos' springs are situated on Mts. Penteli and Parnes to the northeast of the Athenian plain. More springs are situated in the Athenian plain itself, and their water usually is absorbed by the courses of the rivers. The most important and prolific of all springs in the area of the city, the Kallirhoe ('the fair-flowing' that later received the more technical name Enneakrounos, 'the nine-water-spouted')

---

[1] See Camp 1982.
[2] Pausanias (1.24.3) reports seeing a statue of Ge on the Akropolis, asking Zeus for rain.
[3] Tanoulas 2017, 175, 183, fig. 1.
[4] There are also major creeks (dry valleys), for instance the Kykloboros, the Skiron brook, and the *Rema tis Pikrodafnis*, of which the ancient name is not known.

emerges in the Ilissos bed to the southeast of the Akropolis. Because of the abundant water it produced, it became proverbial, as Kratinos, a writer of old comedy in the fifth century BC, stated: "the flood of his words, springs splashing twelve spouts to his mouth, an Ilissos in his throat" (*PCG* 4 fr. 198).

The Kephissos springs are situated in the ancient deme of Trimeneia, an area east of modern Kephisia. In its course, the river passes the northern part of the Attic plain close to the Kolonos Hippios and the Academy and discharges into the bay of Phaleron. The water of this river was used for the irrigation of the olive plantations in the Attic plain, among them, the sacred grove of Athena in the Academy (Sophokles, *Oedipus at Kolonos* 685–686). Near Phaleron, close to the river mouth, was a sanctuary for the river god Kephissos, founded by Xenokrateia at the end of the fifth century BC (*IG* II^2 4548).

Most important for the development of the city of Athens, the source of the Ilissos River is situated on the northwestern slopes of Mt. Hymettos, near the Kaisariani monastery. The river ran through the southern part of the Attic plain and discharged directly into the sea near Phaleron (Strabo 9.1.24), or joined the Kephissos at some point. Near the Kallirhoe spring, there was a bridge in front of the stadium built in the fourth century BC by Lycurgus, and several sanctuaries dotted its banks.[5] The Kallirhoe spring emerges a little to the west of this bridge. Still farther to the west, there was the public washing area of the Athenian launderers and tanners that used the river's waters (*IG* I^3 1257). A dedication of the Athenian washers of about 350–340 BC is preserved on a relief found at the Ilissos, now in Berlin, bearing the inscription, "the washers set this up after praying to the Nymphs and for all other gods" (*IG* II^2 2934). The cult of the Ilissos as a god is attested by numerous inscriptions (*IG* I^3 369e l. 89; *IG* I^3 383 l. 206).

The Eridanos is the shortest of the Athenian rivers. Its springs emerge to the west and the south of Mt. Lykabettos, from where the river ran through the walled area of the ancient city toward the west of the Attic plain, where it united with the Kephissos. During the fifth century BC, the river was channeled, and it passed through the city wall within the Sacred Gate.[6]

Rivers form the landscape and influence to a large extent the urban planning of a settlement. Ancient *gymnasia* like Plato's Academy, Aristotle's Lyceum, and the Kynosarges *gymnasion* were established close to the course of rivers, as were a number of bath-houses (see Map 4.2). By

---

[5] Greco 2011, 480–483.
[6] Not far to the west of the Sacred Gate, there was a creek called Skiron (Pausanias 1.36.4).

nature, rivers often function as boundaries. In Greece, roads tended to follow the course of rivers. Special attention was paid to the location where rivers could be crossed by fords and bridges.[7] As a rule, these developed into landmarks where important sanctuaries and tombs were erected.

All rivers, at some point, flooded neighboring areas, posing a significant threat to the crops and the inhabitants inside and outside the city walls. The Athenians tried to cope with this challenge in various ways. To avoid danger of flooding, dry valleys were filled up, and artificial river beds were built within the city, channeling the course of the rivers or parts of them in order to manage the sudden abundance of water in inhabited areas during heavy rainfalls. Overflow channels were built that led the water away from the rivers. Structures of this kind have been found along the Eridanos in the Kerameikos and in the area of the Academy.[8]

According to ancient thought and religion, water, in particular fresh drinking water of springs and rivers, was protected by the divine. While Poseidon ruled over the saline seas and Zeus over precipitation, a large number of other deities were responsible for the protection of sweet drinking water. The nymphs ensured the quantity and the purity of springs and wells. Major springs had individual female names, such as the Kallirhoe and the Empedo in Athens. The rivers, on the other hand, were perceived as male gods and represented as reclining male figures; an Athenian river, for example, was represented thus in the north corner of the Parthenon's west pediment.

Wells and Cisterns

Given the scarcity of springs, the most important access to drinking water in Athens was provided by wells. More than twenty wells northwest of the Akropolis provide us with the first evidence for human inhabitation during the Late Neolithic period (3500–3200 BC). From then on, and more so since the sixth century BC, many hundreds of wells were dug all over the ancient city and outside its walls, particularly in the area to the south of the Ilissos. There were public wells, private wells, and wells that belonged to sanctuaries. At the beginning of the sixth century BC, regulation was necessary. Plutarch quotes a law of the great statesman Solon around 600 BC:

---

[7] Bougia 1996.

[8] Strabo (16.1.9) describes a similar system of overflow for the Euphrates and the Nile Rivers.

> Since the country was not supplied with water by ever-flowing rivers, or lakes, or copious springs, but most of the inhabitants used wells which had been dug, he made a law that where there was a public well within a *hippikon*, a distance of four furlongs [ca. 710 m], that should be used, but where the distance was greater than this, people must try to get water of their own; if, however, after digging to a depth of ten fathoms [ca. 18 m] on their own land they could not get water, then they might take it from a neighbor's well, filling a five gallon jar [a *hydria* of six *choes*, ca. 20 liters] twice a day; for he thought it his duty to aid the needy, not to provision the idle. (*Solon* 23)

Being a common everyday feature, only few individual wells in Athens are mentioned in ancient texts. An exception was the drawing well in the garden of the Sanctuary of Zeus near the Olympieion. Pliny the Elder (*Natural History* 31.3) refers to the temperature of its water: it was said to have an extraordinary cool temperature in periods of drought and warmer temperatures on foggy days.

An inscription dating to the second half of the fifth century BC gives insight into the economy of well water.[9] Following an economic dispute about the use of the waters of the Halykos well in the Attic deme of Lamptrai, the Delphic oracle settled the matter, providing regulations that were inscribed on a stone that was put up by the well:

(1) The right to drinking water should be paid with 1 obol (the cost of about 3 liters of wine) per year, to be given to the sanctuaries of the nymphs. Those who do not pay the obol had no right to drink.
(2) Drinking without paying the nymphs was fined with 5 drachmas (the equivalent of 30 obols worth five days' wages for a skilled worker).
(3) Leading away water [for irrigation?] cost 1 obol per amphora.
(4) In case someone leads away water without paying for each amphora, the fine is 50 drachmas to the sanctuaries of the nymphs.[10]

This rare case highlights the water economy in rural Classical Athens and the importance of well water for drinking and even for irrigation.

In addition to digging wells and using tapped spring water, the Athenians made use of the possibility to harvest and store rainwater both in public and private buildings. The earliest cisterns in Athens, apart from the basin built in the Mycenean *krene* on the north slope of the Akropolis,

[9] Athens, Epigraphical Museum 13181. *Stele* of white marble. Height 89 cm. See *SEG* 23.76.
[10] Bousquet 1967, 94.

were built during the late sixth century BC. A flask-shaped underground cistern on the south side of Kolonos Agoraios was filled in at the latest between 585 and 575 BC, and constitutes proof for the fact that this type of cistern, which later became abundantly popular in Athens, was in fact gradually developed in the course of the sixth and fifth centuries.[11] Another cistern, dating to the end of the sixth or to the early fifth century, was situated within the Sanctuary of Athena on the Akropolis, just to the east of the Archaic Propylon.[12] The trapezoidal construction consisted of two chambers and received its water from a surface channel hewn into the bedrock that collected rainwater. It was destroyed during the Persian sack of Athens in 480 BC. In the fifth century, cisterns slowly became more popular in Athens. For instance, the Dipylon bath was equipped with an elaborate underground cistern system that was destroyed at the end of the century. In the second half of the fourth century BC especially, cisterns were dug in most, if not all Athenian houses, very likely by highly specialized work teams. They combined an almost standard architecture dug 3–7 m into the ground with the application of hydraulic mortar and a hydrophobic polishing that covered the entire inner surface of the cisterns.[13] Connections between two or more such chambers in the form of underground tunnels were a common feature; the storage volume capacity could thus be increased (Fig. 8.1). These cisterns, together with the many wells, constituted a distinct underground profile for Athens that was created and controlled by water engineers, but the installations also needed regular maintenance. There may be many reasons why these cisterns abruptly ceased to be built after the Sullan siege of 86 BC. Most probably, this mirrored changes in society that were closely related to the effects of the Roman conquest.

Water Pipes

During the last quarter of the sixth century BC, Peisistratos' sons undertook a major project for the Athenian water supply. They installed a pipeline system that led water from the area of the Ilissos springs on the slopes of the Hymettos southeast of the city into the city and beyond, toward the

---

[11] Klingborg 2017, 57, 180 no. 94.

[12] Klingborg 2017, 57, 200 no. 157; Tanoulas 2017, 184, fig. 2 ('Pre-Mnesiklean').

[13] A more or less flask shape of the cistern chamber with a circular floor, walls narrowing towards the neck and a small mouth (diameters vary between 48 and 90 cm).

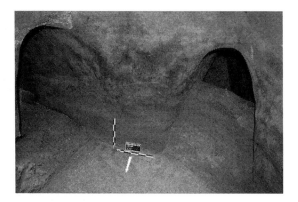

Fig. 8.1 Interior view of cistern system (Z 1-23-24), Kerameikos.
Source: J. Stroszeck

area of the Academy and the western hills of Athens. At the starting point, a collection basin should be assumed, although it has not been found. The main conduit initially followed the course of the Ilissos bed, while the branch channels were placed mainly below the ancient road system of Athens. Between the head waters and the area southeast of the Akropolis, the water conduit had the form of a deep tunnel with rectangular opening shafts that were dug from the surface at regular distances. In other words, the Archaic water engineers used a technique for which today the Arabic word *qanat* is commonly used. As far as we know, this kind of water technology was first invented in the Near East in the early first millennium BC, and owing to their effectiveness, *qanat* channels are still in use today.

Interlocking clay pipes carried water throughout the city. Thousands of such pipes were produced for this purpose by Athenian potters whose business benefited vastly from this undertaking, and they also profited by the water flow reaching their workshops that were situated mainly between the Dipylon Gate and the area of the Academy. From that period on, clay water pipes, drawing vessels, and other water devices made of clay were also used as containers for the burials of neonates and very young children, indicating the ready availability of the prefabricated parts. Some of the Peisistratid clay pipes from the northern branch pipeline were inscribed with the letters XA or the name Charon.[14] This is probably the name of the water architect who proudly had parts of his work signed. In the late sixth century BC, when the first water conduit in Athens was brought into service, many black-figure water vessels (*hydriai*) were decorated with the

---

[14] Tölle-Kastenbein 1994, 50, nos. 4 and 5, figs. 68, 69.

Fig. 8.2 Kallirhoe fountain-house, Attic black-figure *hydria* fragment, ca. 520 BC,
Athens, National Archaeological Museum Akr. 732.
Courtesy of G. Kavvadias

depiction of women fetching water from beautiful fountain-houses
adorned with sculpted water spouts (Fig. 8.2), obviously a celebration of
the augmented quality of life offered by the innovation.

The Athenian water conduit system was repaired and enhanced several
times. In each renovation, the pipes used were slightly different in dimensions (between 52 and 71 cm) and decoration. Sections of these pipelines
have been found during excavations in the city, the best-preserved sections
being in the Olympieion, the Agora, and the Kerameikos areas.

Fountains and Fountain-Houses

In an attempt to store and provide access to water for the purpose of
survival during siege and for public or cultic use, Athenians built fountain-
houses (*krenai*) on the spots where springs emerged. The earliest structure
of this kind in Athens is a rock-hewn spring chamber on the northeastern
slope of the Akropolis, built during the Late Mycenean period (around
1250–1100 BC). It combines the older feature of a rock-cut well with an
attempt to collect and store the water of the well in a basin. It was accessible
by a steep, rock-cut staircase leading down from the surface on the
Akropolis about 25 m, toward a drawing basin that was constructed on
top of a well. The well had a top diameter of 2 m but widened toward the
bottom to a width of 4 m. The water in the basin was collected by

infiltration from the aquifer above the schist layer. After about one generation of use, the structure was filled in and abandoned.[15]

The Empedo spring farther to the west on the Akropolis north slope was found and architectonically enlarged at the same time as the aforementioned well-house. But in contrast, because of its uninterrupted perennial water inflow, this *krene* was repeatedly refurbished. After its enlargement during the fifth century BC with an L-shaped paved court in front of a water basin with a balustrade, it was called the Klepsydra (hidden water, or 'water clock'). Even after the destruction of the entrance to the well house in the first century AD by a massive rock, the *krene* continued to be used, and it was refurbished again in the third and sixth centuries AD. On the south side of the Akropolis, the spring to the west of the later Sanctuary of Asklepios was refurbished during the sixth century BC. For this purpose, a part of the rock was cut off. Like the Mycenean *krene* cut into the north slope, this one collected water in a drawing basin erected above a well cut into the bedrock. In the last quarter of the fifth century BC, the space of this spring was marked by a boundary stone (*horos krenes*; IG I^2 874). It may have had a porch with three columns and a balustrade in front of the drawing basin.[16]

During the reign of Peisistratos' sons in the late sixth century BC, the Kallirhoe spring in the Ilissos valley was beautifully rebuilt as a magnificent fountain-house. It probably had nine waterspouts continuously providing freshwater as well as a colonnaded porch. Two Athenian black-figure *hydriai* show this fountain-house, accompanied by the inscription "Kallirhoe" (Fig. 8.2) and "ΚΑΛΙΡΕ."[17] Thucydides (2.15.3–4) relates that after the Peisistratids had built the fountain-house, this spring was called Enneakrounos. By the time of Pausanias (ca. AD 150), this was the only spring in Athens: "There are wells all over the city, but only this one spring" (Paus. 1.14.1).[18]

The dating of the water conduit systems and their refurbishments is in part possible by the dates provided by the excavations of the splendid public fountain-houses or *krenai* that adorned the endpoints or in-between

---

[15] Travlos 1988, 72–75, fig. 96.

[16] Travlos 1988, 61, no. 114, 138–141.

[17] Athens, National Archaeological Museum, Akr. 1.732; BAPD no. 306479. London, British Museum B 331; BAPD no. 302273. See Travlos 1988, 204 ff., figs. 267, 268; Tölle-Kastenbein 1994, 91, no. 4.

[18] Pausanias uses the name Enneakrounos for the Southeast Fountain in the Agora, that was provided with water from a pipeline. See also Paga 2015.

outlets of the pipelines. Like the fountain-houses made for springs, the *krenai* made for the pipelines were roofed structures with a marble colonnade and paved entrance porches. They were supplied by the water conduits and equipped with one or more collecting basins. Water spouts were either on the back wall or on the front balustrade of the basins. The spouts were decorated with sculptures of various forms, mostly animal heads (Web Fig. 8.1). A common feature is also the open space in front of the entrance, so people could use these structures simply for drinking as well as collecting or drawing water. A large number of Athenian black-figure vase-paintings appear in the period of the first installation of the pipeline under the rule of Peisistratos' sons (527–510 BC), celebrating this improvement. On these representations, jars, mostly *hydriai*, are placed or held in front of the water spouts (Fig. 8.2).[19]

The public benefit provided for the citizens of Athens by the pipeline was highly visible through the erection of these fountain-houses. This is further emphasized by the locations where they were erected. Two of them, the Dipylon Krene and the Panops Krene (built in the first half of the fourth century BC), mentioned by Plato (*Lysis* 203a), lay close by the city wall and next to a gate. This position makes it probable that these were integrated into the defensive strategy of the Athenians, as their water could be used to extinguish the flames if the wooden gates were set on fire. Another two fountain-houses flanked the western and eastern ends of the south side of the public space of the Agora (Southeast- and Southwest Fountain-Houses, built in the late sixth and first half of the fourth centuries, respectively, see Map 6.1), while the Dionysia Krene represented on an Athenian red-figured *kalpis* (water jar) was probably connected to the southern branch of the pipeline.[20] It was situated prominently in the area of the Theater of Dionysos and was probably originally built in the sixth century. Smaller and later fountains were situated on the Areopagos, on the foot of the Hill of the Muses (the so-called Pan Krene), and within the Hellenistic Stoa of Attalos and the South Stoa II in the Agora. Legislation prohibited the contamination of fountain water, and severe penalties for pollution and violation were set up.[21]

---

[19] Compare with Aristophanes (*Lysistrata* 237 ff.), who mentions *krenai* and *hydriai*.
[20] Rome, Villa Torlonia 73; BAPD no. 200171. See Tölle-Kastenbein 1994, fig. 167.
[21] Compare with an inscription preserved from Minoa on Delos (*Delos* 5.133).

Baths

As a direct consequence of the sustainable water supply provided by the pipelines, bath-houses of both public and private character were erected in Athens. The earliest had to be situated outside the city walls like that outside the Dipylon Gate, which was connected to a branch conduit diverting water from the northern pipeline.[22] Another bath-house has been found at the Piraeus gate. Private baths just outside city gates are also known by inscriptions: one owned by Isthmonikos was located south of the Akropolis (*IG* I³ 84 = *IG* I² 94 Z. 30 f., dated 418/417 BC) and another one owned by Diochares was to the east of the city (*IG* II² 2495, dated 338–326 BC). Only from the Hellenistic period onwards were bath-houses allowed inside the city. For instance, the bath-house at the northwest foot of the Areopagos was first built during the second century BC.[23] In sum, the living standards of the Athenians were vastly improved in many respects by these pipelines.

Wastewater Management

Wastewater management is always connected to and supplements the establishment of the freshwater supply. The earliest datable wastewater management of the city of Athens can be found in the Agora during the early fifth century BC, when a monumental drain was installed. It is square in section (1 × 1 m), the side walls were made from polygonal conglomerate blocks, the floor consisted of limestone, and the cover slabs of yellow limestone. The channel collected drainage water from the southwestern entrance area and led it north along the western side of the Agora. Near the northwestern entrance, it joined a massive channel built for the Eridanos, which carried the water farther westwards through the Sacred Gate.[24] Over the centuries, this main drainage system was supplemented and enlarged by many other wastewater channels, usually oval in section and built from two U-shaped clay parts positioned on top of each other. As a rule, these channels were laid below the streets, either on the side or under the middle of the road, and manholes were built at regular intervals for their maintenance. Like a certain type of well, these were constructed from clay cylinders

[22] Lucore and Trümper 2013, 281; Stroszeck 2014, 98, no. 17.
[23] Camp 1990, 187, no. 73, fig. 127; Lucore and Trümper 2013, 284.
[24] Camp 1990, 59–61, no. 11, fig. 27.

equipped with foot holes. This type of wastewater channel that first occurs during the fourth century BC. When necessary, these channel systems were repaired, but sometimes a whole new system was installed on a lower or higher level below ground. The latest datable system of this kind was established during the late fifth or sixth century AD. Private wastewater management is first traceable in fifth-century Athenian residences. Rectangular, walled basins that are sometimes situated in the courtyards or near the entrances were very probably drainage pits (*koprones*).[25] In later periods, private houses were connected to public waste water channels.

The Roman Period

During the Sullan siege of Athens in 86 BC, the city's water installations, water conduits, well-houses, and bath-houses were severely damaged and in part never recuperated. According to Vitruvius writing in the first century BC (8.3.60), water from the pipelines in Athens was so bad, it was only suitable for bathing or other uses, while drinking water had to be drawn from wells. Gradually, water was managed according to Roman methods. Together with other buildings, a fountain-house was established near the old ones on the south side of the Agora in the first century BC. In the first century AD, a public latrine was erected near the Roman Agora, and between the first and the third centuries AD, more than twenty-four bath-houses were erected everywhere in the city. (See also Rogers, Chapter 30 in this volume.) In response to the growing demand for fresh water, a new water conduit system was begun during the reign of the emperor Hadrian (AD 117–138) and finished around AD 140. It carried water from the Kephalari spring on Mts. Parnes and Penteli toward the city in a very impressive underground aqueduct that arrived at a central distribution cistern. In front of this reservoir, a beautiful colonnaded marble Nymphaeum was erected on the slope of Mt. Lykabettos. A large Nymphaeum in the ancient Agora, near the ancient Southeastern Fountain-House, was also connected to this pipeline. It consisted of a richly decorated semicircle with marble paneling and was adorned with statues of members of the imperial family.

---

[25] Travlos 1988, 342.

Conclusions

The importance of water management and related structures in ancient Athens can hardly be overstated. It was a major concern of Athenian political leaders in the Archaic and Classical periods. The democratic *polis* kept track of its water management through an honorable office called the 'supervisor of the waters.' Before 480 BC, Themistokles himself, the great Athenian statesman and general at the Battle of Salamis, was entrusted with this function for some time (Plutarch, *Themistokles* 31). He also was inscribed into the deme Phrearrhioi (a place name meaning 'well specialists'). From the penalty payments assessed from transgressors of the water laws, Themistokles dedicated in an Athenian sanctuary a bronze statue of a young maiden carrying water (*hydrophoros*), a beautiful work of art, that – like the famous statue of the Tyrannicides in the Agora – was looted by the Persians in 480. Throughout the centuries, the city of Athens managed water in such a way as to ensure the health of its inhabitants, to sustain agriculture and industry, and to provide an essential resource in case of siege. Their shrewd handling of water and its distribution probably contributed to the success of the *polis* over the many years of its existence in ways that are not immediately evident but nonetheless essential.

Further Reading

For more on springs, rivers, and nymphs of Athens, see Ammermann 1996, Brewster 1997, Larson 2001, and Kypraiou 2004. On the water supply of Athens, consult Camp 1977 and Chiotis 2011. For more on wells and cisterns throughout the city, see Klingborg 2017 and Stroszeck 2017. Glaser 1983 and Longfellow 2011 (9–13) offer good overviews of Greek fountains and fountain-houses, along with Paga 2015 on the Southeast Fountain-House of the Agora. For more on Greek bathing, see Lucore and Trümper 2013. On fountains of Roman Athens, see Longfellow 2011 and Leigh 2018, with bibliography therein. See Christaki et al. 2017 for a discussion of Athenian water supply until the nineteenth century AD.

Bibliography

Ammermann, A.J. 1996. "The Eridanos Valley and the Athenian Agora." *AJA* 100: 699–715.

Bougia, P. 1996. "Ancient Bridges in Greece and Coastal Asia Minor." PhD dissertation, University of Pennsylvania.

Bousquet, J. 1967. "Deux inscriptions attiques." *Bulletin de Correspondance Hellénique* 91: 90–95.

Brewster, H. 1997. *The River Gods of Greece: Mythos and Mountain Waters in the Hellenistic World.* London.

Camp, J.M. 1977. "The Water Supply of Ancient Athens from 3000 to 86 BC." PhD dissertation, Princeton University.

   1982. "Drought and Famine in the 4th Century BC." In *Studies in Athenian Architecture and Topography*, Princeton, 9–17.

   1990. *The Athenian Agora.* Princeton

Chiotis, E. 2011. "Water Supply and Drainage Works in the Agora of Ancient Athens." In *The Agora in the Mediterranean from Homeric to Roman Times*, ed. by A. Giannikouri, Athens, 165–180.

Christaki, M., et al. 2017. "Water Supply Associated with the Development of the City of Athens from the Hellenistic Period until the End of the 19th Century." *Water History* 9.4: 389–410.

Glaser, F. 1983. *Antike Brunnenbauten (KPHNAI) in Griechenland.* Vienna.

Greco, E., ed. 2011. *Topografia di Atene. Sviluppo urbano e monumenti dalle origini al III secolo d.C. Tomo* II: *Colline sud-occidentali – Valle dell'Ilisso.* Athens.

Klingborg, P. 2017. "Greek Cisterns: Water and Risk in Ancient Greece, 600–650 BC." PhD dissertation, University of Uppsala.

Kypraiou, E. 2004. *Eridanos: The River of Ancient Athens.* Athens.

Larson, J. 2001. *Greek Nymphs. Myth, Cult, Lore.* Oxford.

Leigh, S. 2018. "The Monumental Fountain in the Athenian Agora: Reconstruction and Interpretation." In *Great Waterworks in Roman Greece: Aqueducts and Monumental Fountain Structures*, ed. by G.A. Aristodemou and T.P. Tassios, Oxford, 218–234.

Longfellow, B. 2011. *Roman Imperialism and Civic Patronage: Form, Meaning, and Ideology in Monumental Fountain Complexes.* Cambridge.

Lucore, S.K., and M. Trümper, eds. 2013. *Greek Baths and Bathing Culture: New Discoveries and Approaches.* Leuven.

Paga, J. 2015. "The Southeast Fountain House in the Athenian Agora: A Reappraisal of its Date and Historical Context." *Hesperia* 84.2: 355–387.

Stroszeck, J. 2014. *Der Kerameikos in Athen. Geschichte, Bauten, und Denkmäler im archäologischen Park.* Bad Langensalza.

   2017. "Wells in Athens: The Contribution of the Kerameikos Wells." In *Cura Aquarum in Greece*, ed. by K. Wellbrock, Siegburg, 43–88.

Tanoulas, T. 2017. "Waterworks at the Northwest End of the Athenian Acropolis from Prehistory to Date." In *Cura Aquarum in Greece*, ed. by K. Wellbrock, Siegburg, 175–191.

Tölle-Kastenbein, R. 1994. *Das archaische Wasserleitungsnetz für Athen und seine späteren Bauphasen.* Mainz.

Travlos, J. 1988. *Bildlexikon zur Topographie des antiken Attika.* Tübingen.

Additional resources to accompany this chapter can be found at: www.cambridge.org/NeilsRogers

9 | Housing and the Household

KATHERINE B. HARRINGTON

One of the great paradoxes of Athenian archaeology is that although the residents of ancient Athens spent more time in their houses than in any other buildings, these structures have received far less scholarly attention than more durable and monumental public and religious buildings.[1] The archaeology of Athenian houses has the potential, however, to inform us about several fundamental aspects of ancient life. The mostly commonly used ancient Greek word for house, *oikos*, refers to the physical structure of the house, as well as to the family which inhabited it and all their movable and immovable property, including household slaves. This concept is akin to accepted anthropological definitions of the household as a cooperative social and economic unit, but the *oikos* is composed not just of people, but also material goods.[2]

The inherent physicality of the *oikos* thus means that it is well suited to archaeological investigation. Though the literary record also describes other types of residential buildings, such as *synoikiai*, or tenement houses, occupied by more than one household, such structures have been difficult to identify archaeologically. This chapter focuses on the surviving evidence for Athenian houses and trends in scholarship relating to domestic life in fifth- to third-century BC Attika, including both the urban core of the city (*asty*) and the countryside (*chora*).[3]

Architecture and Construction

Athenian houses were constructed in a manner similar to houses elsewhere in mainland Greece. House walls were typically built of mudbrick elevated on a low stone socle to prevent erosion from below. Some Athenian

---

[1] I would like to acknowledge my great debt to the work of Barbara Tsakirgis (1954–2019), whose work on the houses excavated by the Agora Excavations will continue to be fundamental to the study of Athenian houses.

[2] Hence, it is the root of the English word economy.

[3] Because of the limited nature of the surviving evidence for Archaic houses, this period will be covered in less detail.

households had their own wells, typically located in the courtyard, while others used public wells. Decoration of walls was relatively limited, though painted plaster sometimes adorned *andrones* (men's dining rooms) and courtyards. Most interior floors were of packed dirt, but courtyards were often paved with flagstones or chips, and *andron* floors sometimes featured pebble mosaics or other paving. The roof frame was constructed from wooden beams, which carried heavy terracotta pan and cover tiles embedded in clay. Roofing a house was a serious and expensive business, and a standard to ensure the proper size of commercially available tiles was even set up in the Agora in the first century BC.

In ancient texts, Athenian houses were notoriously humble, with the houses of the wealthy indistinguishable from the houses of the broader population (e.g. Demosthenes, *Olynthiac* 3.25). While this literary trope of moderation may be an exaggeration, archaeological evidence suggests that Classical and Early Hellenistic Athenian houses were not typically elaborate, nor were those of other contemporary *poleis*. Greek domestic structures, although they increased steadily in size from the Early Iron Age to the Classical period, generally remained relatively modest until the Late Classical and Early Hellenistic periods, when house sizes increased dramatically, especially for the very wealthy.[4]

While references to house architects and other construction specialists exist in the literary record, other references suggest that the occupants may have played some role in planning and potentially even in constructing domestic structures (Xenophon, *Symposion* 4.4, *Cyropaedia* 8.2.5, *Oikonomikos*; Pausanias 4.27.7). Previously built houses were also bought, sold, leased, and used as security on loans, as recorded epigraphically.[5] Rooftiles, doors, and door and window frames were considered part of the property of the *oikos* and thus could be removed and transported to a new house.

Survival and Recovery

A properly roofed and plastered mudbrick structure can have an exceptionally long use-life, though mudbrick will melt once left uncovered. This was the fate of many rural and suburban houses, which slowly decayed after abandonment and were sometimes later further damaged by farming

[4] Morris 2007, 104–125.
[5] Fine 1951; Pritchett 1956, 261–276.

or modern construction. Within the urban core of Athens, where space has always been at a premium, many Classical and Hellenistic houses were deliberately destroyed in antiquity to make way for a variety of building projects – including the construction of newer houses. Given the long history of occupation in the city, many ancient houses lie beneath a warren of wall socles, drains, streets, and other features from later periods, which is most easily visible in Athens today in the exposed excavations below the Akropolis Museum.[6] The cycles of building and rebuilding from antiquity to the present day have greatly limited our ability to understand earlier domestic architecture.

Research priorities have also influenced the degree to which we are able to use domestic assemblages to understand daily life in Athens. Much archaeological work in Athens and Attika has focused on the monumental buildings of public and religious life. Excavated domestic structures thus typically lie on the edges of public centers (e.g. within the purview of the excavations of the Agora and the Kerameikos or the partially excavated residential quarter at Sounion). Other houses were only partially recovered during rescue excavations, such as the preparations for the Akropoli Metro station or the residential quarter excavated in Ano Voula (ancient Halai Aixonides). Some residential areas of Attika were part of specifically targeted research excavations, including Rhamnous, the industrial quarter of Thorikos, the Vari House, and the Dema House.

Complete domestic assemblages are rare in household archaeology for other reasons as well. Houses were generally kept relatively clean, with waste discarded outside the house, and except in rare cases of natural disaster (e.g. the Bronze Age settlement of Akrotiri on Santorini, preserved by volcanic eruption) or warfare (e.g. the unusually rich assemblages of Olynthos, destroyed by Philip II in 348 BC), people typically took their material goods with them when they moved, or abandoned household items were later scavenged by others. What remains in the archaeological record is often limited to wall foundations, roof collapse, floors, and objects too large to move easily or too small to be noticed in clean up.

Though well-preserved and fully published domestic assemblages are rare in Attika, several examples can provide insight into the range of objects used in private buildings. Lynch studied the domestic pottery of a Late Archaic house which had been dumped in a well (Agora Well J 2:4) as a part of rebuilding efforts after the Persian War.[7] Another possible

[6] Eleftheratou 2019.
[7] Lynch 2011.

residence, Bau Z, next to the Sacred Gate and just inside the city walls, has been completely excavated and the large number of finds published by room.[8] While this building served at least some residential function in all three of the first phases, the large size of the building and the high number of drinking and serving vessels and loom weights have inspired varied interpretations. In its earlier phases, it could have been a *synoikia* (Web Map 9.1), and some scholars argue that in the third phase it also served as a brothel, a tavern, an inn, and/or a weaving workshop. (See Ormand, Chapter 26 in this volume.)

Understanding the material world of domestic life in ancient Athens is thus challenging. Beyond excavated domestic assemblages, several other categories of evidence can shed light on domestic objects. One set of Athenian epigraphic documents records household inventories, namely the Attic Stelai erected after the seizure and sale of the property of men found guilty of profaning the Eleusinian Mysteries and mutilating the herms in 415/14 BC.[9] Though the inventory lists are fragmentary, they do provide a record of some household goods and their prices, such as chairs, couches, beds, doors, rugs, and curtains. Attic vase-paintings can also provide some information on domestic furnishings and household objects, and are a particularly useful source of information for organic objects such as wooden furniture and textiles which do not generally survive in the archaeological record. Still, domestic architecture is rarely depicted in ancient art, and we must be wary of assuming that household scenes represent snapshots of actual daily life and not generalized or idealized visual idioms.[10]

House Form

Given these challenges, much work on Athenian houses has relied primarily on architectural form. While there is great variety in the forms of Attic housing, some commonalities in spatial arrangement can be discerned. Rooms were typically organized around a central courtyard, and the house often had only one entrance from the street, a form Nevett has termed

---

[8] Knigge 2005.
[9] See Pritchett 1956.
[10] For an assessment of the literary, iconographic, and material sources for Greek domestic furniture and furnishings, see Andrianou 2009.

the "single-entrance, courtyard house."[11] Except for the most isolated rural houses, dwellings generally shared party walls with their neighbors, creating a dense urban cityscape, even in the rural deme centers.

The courtyard house is well adapted to the climate of Greece, allowing circulation of air during the hot summers and penetration of light into as many rooms as possible. In his influential cross-cultural study of house forms, however, Rapoport noted that culture, rather than environment, is typically the primary determinant of house form, and indeed, societies situated in similar climates have created a variety of dwelling types.[12] Thus, Athenian house forms should also tell us something about social organization and cultural priorities.

One early study that sought to demonstrate how Greek houses reflected larger social and political developments was Hoepfner and Schwandner's *Haus und Stadt im klassischen Griechenland* (1986). Noting that at many cities with orthogonal grid plans houses tended to conform to a set size and shape (*Typenhäuser*), the authors argued that the conformity of the houses reflected the value of *isonomia*, equality before the law. This notion has come under criticism in subsequent years, as it is difficult to demonstrate that particularly strong notions of democracy or equality existed within cities with *Typenhäuser*, such as Olynthos and Priene, and democratic Athens certainly had a wide variety of house sizes and forms. In fact, the size, shape, and internal arrangement of rooms within Athenian houses could vary greatly within a single city block, as can been seen in the six houses excavated at the edge of the Athenian Agora (Web Map 9.2). Some of this variety resulted because Athenian city blocks respected traditional paths through the city and no street grid plan was established. Though the urban core of Athens was not orthogonally planned, Hippodamos of Miletos famously provided the rectilinear grid plan for the port of Piraeus, but it cannot be convincingly demonstrated that the more regular plan of the port somehow better reflects notions of equality than the winding streets of the *asty*.[13] (See also Steinhauer, Chapter 16 in this volume.)

Gender and Spatial Negotiations

While the spatial organization of Athenian houses does not directly reflect the system of government, other aspects of social life certainly were

[11] Nevett 1999, 103.
[12] Rapoport 1969.
[13] For a critique of Hoepfner and Schwandner, see Shipley 2005, 369–371.

encoded into domestic architecture in subtle ways. Classical Athenian texts speak of strongly gendered domestic roles, and indeed, the house has been interpreted as a primarily female space, with much of male life assumed to take place outside on the political stage and in the farm fields. The house itself is often described using terms for the men's quarters (*andronkonitis*) and the women's quarters (*gynaikonitis*). Yet the context and authorship of these ancient texts – typically court speeches or philosophical texts written by wealthy men – suggest that the authors are presenting an idealized, normative view of gender relations which may not reflect reality for every family. Social status and identity also impacted expected behaviors and use of domestic space beyond a simple division of male and female.[14]

Identifying men's and women's quarters on the ground has been notoriously difficult, not only in Athens but also across Greece. Certainly, many activities of daily life were gendered, but these activities may not have taken place in 'men's quarters' or 'women's quarters.' Women were typically tasked with textile production and childcare, as well as food preparation. Many of these tasks would have taken place in the heavily trafficked courtyard of the house. In wealthier households, much of this labor would have been done by female slaves, but citizen and metic women also engaged in domestic work. These activities have left material traces in the archaeological record in the form of loom weights, spindle whorls, baby feeders, children's toys, cooking pots, and braziers. Yet, the spatial patterning of these objects in excavated houses indicates that female labor was not confined to only one part of the house. For example, built hearths were rare and cooking equipment was generally movable, suggesting that permanent kitchens were not typically part of Athenian houses. One room which can be considered gendered is the *andron*, the dining room where the primarily male *symposion* took place. Though guests at the *symposion* were male, entertainers such as flute-girls, dancers, or sex workers were female. An *andron*, typically identified by its square shape, offset doorway, raised berth for couches, and, sometimes, a paved floor, was not present in every house, but several have been identified in Attika.

The organization of single-entrance, courtyard houses does not prioritize strict separation of men and women within the household, but rather the privacy of the household unit by minimizing contact between the women of the household and unrelated males. Rather than being secluded in one part of the building, women likely had access to the entire house

---

[14] Goldberg 1999, 146.

unless male guests were visiting. Then, the women could retire to the less accessible rooms, while the guests were entertained in the *andron*. Nevett has noted that the courtyard, *andron*, and anteroom to the *andron* were often the only rooms with painted wall plaster and paved floors. These decorative features served to impress guests, but also to provide them with visual clues as to which parts of the house were socially acceptable for them to visit.[15]

Visual privacy from the outside world was evidently a priority in the spatial organization of Athenian houses. Though the lack of standing house walls in Athens limits our understanding of exterior windows, information from text and stone-built houses in northwestern Greece (e.g. Orraon) suggests that these were generally small and placed relatively high on the walls. The interior courtyard provided access to outdoor space shielded from the prying eyes of the neighbors, while the single-entrance controlled access, both physical and visual, and protected household property. Given that houses in the *asty* and many deme centers shared party walls, privacy was not complete, however. Household activities could be observed via glimpses through the door and visits to neighbors, as well as through sound and smell.[16]

The arrangement of space in an Athenian courtyard house is quite different from the linearly organized rooms in Early Iron Age houses, which lacked the transitional space of an internal courtyard and were sometimes surrounded by an exterior yard for work and recreation instead (e.g. Skala Oropou). This shift from linear to central plans may reflect a reorganization of women's roles and a greater priority on control of women's movements concurrent with the development of the *polis*. This change suggests an increased concern over women's interactions with males not belonging to the household, which in turn was due to the importance of legitimate children within citizen families.[17]

Ultimately, the use of domestic space in Athens was flexible and varied depending on the time of day and social identities of those present. Most items of furniture were movable, and few rooms seem to have had a permanently fixed function. Various activities of household life might take place in different rooms depending on the season, time of day, presence of visitors, and stage of the household lifecycle.

---

[15] Nevett 1999, 70.
[16] Harrington 2015.
[17] Nevett 1999, 167.

Domestic Industry

The spatial flexibility of Athenian houses is also demonstrated by the high number of houses which combined workshop space with residential space. While the ideal citizen-farmer of Xenophon (*Oikonomikos* 4) spent much of his time outside of the house working the fields, many men ran businesses from their houses, including banking, tavern keeping, and various forms of manufacturing. Many industries could also involve wives and other members of the household. In fact, economic activity in Classical Athens was often organized at the household level and some workshops were situated within or immediately adjacent to houses. Some literary texts describe workshops employing many slaves (Lysias 12.19; Demosthenes 27.9), but most manufacturing was likely carried out on a much smaller scale. Certain heavy industries, such as ceramic production, were typically situated in non-residential workshops outside of the city walls (see Rotroff, Chapter 19 in this volume), but a wide variety of industrial activities did take place in the heart of the city in residential areas. Outside of the *asty*, industry and domestic life could similarly be combined, such as the presence of industrial installations in domestic areas of the mining district of Laurion or the residential ceramic workshops complexes of the demes of Euonymon and Aixone.

This combination of domestic and workshop space was especially common in the so-called Industrial District below the Areopagos. This neighborhood produced abundant evidence for marbleworking, metalworking, coroplasty, and other industries. Some of the excavated buildings were small, non-residential workshops, but others combined living and working space. The best example of this is House C'–D' (Map 9.1), a structure that was originally two separate houses, which were combined in the fourth century BC by knocking down a small section of wall. While the House C side had a typical domestic assemblage, the hearth in House D was used for metal working, and marble working chips were also found in the courtyard.[18] The spatial organization of this house prioritized a separation between 'living' and 'working' space, but this was not always true in Athenian domestic workshops. The House of Simon the Shoemaker at the edge of the Agora had sandal-making supplies scattered throughout its ground floor, for example.

---

[18] Young 1951, 202–228; Tsakirgis 2005, 76–77.

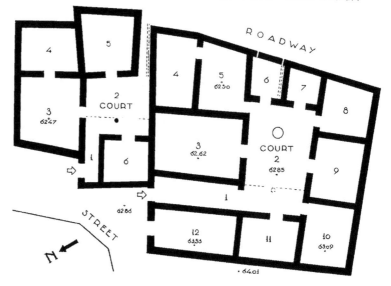

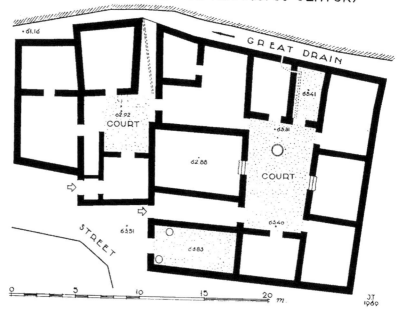

Map 9.1 Houses C and D before and after the removal of a wall to create one large structure, Street of the Marble Workers, Athenian Agora.

Courtesy of the American School of Classical Studies at Athens: Agora Excavations

Religion and Ritual Practice

While religious practice at public festivals, temples, and shrines is better known, literary texts also attest to the importance of domestic religion. In particular, the house was associated with Hestia and the hearth. Literary evidence portrays the house as the domain of various other gods too, including Zeus Ktesios (Zeus of the storeroom), Zeus Herkeios (Zeus of the courtyard), Apollo Patroos (patrilineal Apollo), Apollo Agyieus (Apollo who protects entrances), and Hermes (another protector of entrances). The domestic manifestation of these Olympian gods could differ greatly from their more familiar, public aspects. For example, Zeus Ktesios was worshiped in the guise of a pot, while Hermes protected the house in the form of an ithyphallic herm set near the doorway (e.g. see Web Fig. 1.1).

Despite an abundance of literary evidence, domestic cult has rarely been attested archaeologically in Athens. Though domestic altars have been recovered at other sites, no examples have yet been found in Athens; similarly, permanent built hearths are rarely found archaeologically in Athenian houses. Other evidence of private religion has been unearthed, however. Bau Z contained a small *naiskos* for Kybele, as well as several saucer pyre deposits. As recently discussed in detail by Rotroff, some domestic workshops in Athens participated in ritual practices involving the deposition of miniature vessels, particularly pyre saucers, beneath the floor of the structure, often in association with traces of burning. These 'saucer pyres' were found most commonly in residential and non-residential workshops associated with various industries. The rituals may have been apotropaic, designed to ward off evil from the workspace given the economic consequences of failure during craft production. The presence of similar ritual activity in workshops devoted to a variety of industries suggests some social connection among the inhabitants. These practices possibly represent the beliefs of metics, who were particularly common in manufacturing industries because they could not own property.[19]

The limited archaeological evidence for domestic religion in Athens is not surprising, given the ephemeral or non-tangible nature of many of the associated ritual actions, such as pouring libations, marking ritual boundaries with salt or oil, burning incense, or making offerings of grain. The sights, sounds, and smells of ancient ritual are challenging to investigate

---

[19] Rotroff 2013, 88.

archaeologically, but the literary and iconographic records of these actions suggest that we should not underestimate their importance.[20]

Ritual activities related to life stages such as birth, marriage, and death also fell under the purview of the household and often took place within the house. Upon the birth of a baby, an object announcing the gender was hung on the door (wool for a girl and an olive branch for a boy), while during the marriage ritual, the bride and her dowry were transferred physically and symbolically between houses. The *prothesis*, or viewing portion, of a Greek funeral also took place within the house, and the funeral procession led from the house to the cemetery beyond the city wall. This marked a final severing of the physical association between the individual and the *oikos*, though the members of the household, especially women, maintained ritual support for the deceased family member after the death by visits to the cemetery.

Public religious festivals, too, had components which took place within the home. For example, the Adonia saw women climb to their rooftops to plant gardens of lettuce and fennel in broken pieces of pottery and enact mourning rituals for Adonis. During the Anthesteria, the new vintage of wine was opened in the storerooms, the house was decorated, and all members of the household – including slaves and children – consumed wine. In these ways, ritual actions in the domestic sphere reflected, subverted, and reinforced wider social practices.

Houses in the Attic *Chora*

While much archaeology has focused on the urban core of Athens, settlement areas of several rural deme centers have also been surveyed or excavated, as have isolated examples of farmsteads. Given that as much as two-thirds of the population of the polis of Athens may have resided in the *chora* during the Classical period, houses in these areas round out our picture of domestic life in the *polis* of Athens.

Many rural demes had densely settled centers which functioned as small villages within the larger *polis* (Web Fig. 9.1). Houses in deme centers often had many similarities with houses in the *asty*, though there were some differences in spatial organization and use. In general, *andrones* were less common, which suggests that the *symposion* may have been less important

---

[20] Morgan 2007, 121–124.

in the *chora*. Differences in social interaction and cultural priorities can also be seen in the decreased emphasis on privacy and control of access in some rural deme houses; several houses at Halai Aixonides and Thorikos had two entrances, for example. At Thorikos, rooms were typically larger than those of townhouses and were often arranged sequentially, rather than radiating from the courtyard. Thorikos was unusual in many respects, given the mining focus of the site and the comparatively higher number of slaves who must have lived and worked there.

Beyond the urban blocks of the rural deme centers, evidence of occupation also exists in the countryside in the form of sites typically described as farmsteads, which in one recent definition broadly consist of a class of "rural sites which could support either year-round or temporary occupation by a free or slave labor force engaged in agricultural activity for either subsistence or economic gain."[21] Early scholarship focused on the literary record, which suggested that farmers lived in nucleated settlements and commuted out to their fields each day. Yet with the advent of pedestrian survey in the later twentieth century, field walkers have documented the remains of structures, agricultural installations, and ceramic scatters across the landscape, suggestive of more intensive occupation.

The few farmsteads which have been excavated contained ceramic assemblages similar to urban houses. In Attika, the most well-known examples are the Dema House and the Vari House (Map 9.2). In spatial organization, these buildings are similar to urban *pastas* houses, with a single entrance and rooms arranged off a courtyard. However, these structures do not share party walls with other buildings, and the courtyards are unusually large. Finds were rare but included domestic objects like spindle whorls and loom weights, and in the case of the Vari House, beehives. The Atene Survey in southern Attika also documented several well-preserved farmsteads, some of which had large courtyards, exterior yards, and threshing floors. Several of the farmsteads in Atene even have identifiable *andro27nes*. Most rural dwellings in Attika were much smaller and less elaborate, however.

One notable feature of some farmsteads is the presence of a tower. Towers were also present in some houses in rural deme centers, such as Thorikos and Rhamnous, though they do not appear in the *asty*. Noting that many of the farmstead towers could be locked from the outside, Morris and Papadopoulos have argued that they were used to secure

[21] McHugh 2017, 1.

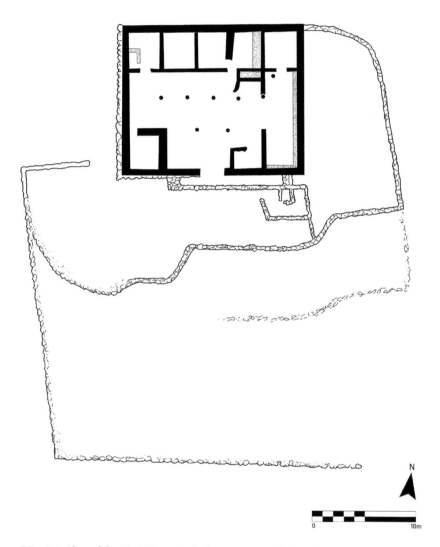

Map 9.2 Plan of the Vari House, including exterior walled yard and terraces.
Source: Jones et al. 1973, fig. 4, adapted by M. Durusu-Tanrıöver

agricultural slaves during the night and to surveil their work during the day.[22] Other scholars have argued for a more varied role. Towers, expensive to build and conspicuous in the landscape, might have fulfilled diverse functions, including surveillance, protection, ostentatious display, storage, agricultural processing, and various domestic purposes, depending on the needs of the particular farmstead.

[22] Morris and Papadopoulos 2005.

Though most scholars now agree that the Attic countryside was more populated than the textual record suggests, there is still debate over how farmsteads were used and if they were occupied year-round or only seasonally during sowing and harvesting. Agricultural labor included wealthy landowners, subsistence farmers and their families, farm bailiffs, dependent laborers, and slaves, though the experience of life in the countryside was very different for each of these groups of people. Who occupied these structures and for what portion of the year remain open questions; use may have varied by building and time period. Our understanding of rural domestic life will expand with greater coverage of Attika by intensive archaeological survey.

Conclusions

Houses were the most ubiquitous buildings in ancient Athens. Yet until recent decades, the archaeology of daily life was considered merely the neutral backdrop to larger social, political, and religious developments. Recent research, however, has demonstrated how houses and household life both influenced and were influenced by larger societal trends, providing a microcosm of ancient Athenian life. The diverse domestic structures of the *asty* and the *chora* speak to a range of ancient lifestyles for citizens, slaves, and metics. The spatial organization of houses can inform us about gender relations and notions of privacy, while examining the domestic economy sheds light on smaller-scale economic units, which, in aggregate, had a considerable impact on the larger economy of the city. Similarly, examining domestic ritual can round out our picture of ancient religion and shed light on individual (or household) belief systems. The *oikos* has often been considered the building block of the *polis*, and household archaeology helps us understand these connections.

Further Reading

The most comprehensive account of Greek houses generally is Nevett 1999. On rescue excavations in Attika, see Parlama and Stampolidis 2000, Kaza-Papageorgiou 2016, and Eleftheratou 2019. For town planning, see Hoepfner and Schwandner 1986 and Shipley 2005. On gender in Greek houses, see Jameson 1990, Nevett 1994 and 1999, and Goldberg 1999. Tsakirgis 2005 is a good introduction to household industry near the Agora. For domestic religion, see Morgan 2007, and for saucer pyres specifically, see Rotroff 2013. On depictions of domestic life on

Athenian vases, see Oakley 2020, 7–46. In the *chora*, see Nevett 2005 on 'suburban' houses and McHugh 2017 on farmsteads.

Bibliography

Andrianou, D. 2009. *The Furniture and Furnishings of Ancient Greek Houses and Tombs.* Cambridge.

Eleftheratou, S. 2019. *Μουσείο Ακρόπολης: η ανασκαφή.* Athens.

Fine, J.V.A. 1951. *Horoi: Studies in Mortgage, Real Security, and Land Tenure in Ancient Athens.* Princeton.

Goldberg, M.Y. 1999. "Spatial and Behavioral Negotiations in Classical Athenian City Houses." In *The Archaeology of Household Activities*, ed. P.M. Allison, London, 142–161.

Harrington, K.B. 2015. "Privacy and Production: Sensory Aspects of Household Industry in Classical and Hellenistic Greece." *Archaeological Review from Cambridge* 30: 63–69.

Hoepfner, W., and E.-L. Schwandner. 1986. *Haus und Stadt im klassischen Griechenland.* Munich.

Jameson, M.H. 1990. "Domestic Space in the Greek City-State." In *Domestic Architecture and the Use of Space: An Interdisciplinary Cross-Cultural Study*, ed. S. Kent, Cambridge, 92–113.

Jones, J.E., et al. 1973. "An Attic Country House below the Cave of Pan at Vari." *Annual of the British School at Athens* 68: 355–452.

Kaza-Papageorgiou, K. 2016. *The Ancient City Road and the Metro beneath Vouliagmenis Avenue.* Athens.

Knigge, U. 2005. *Der Bau Z. Kerameikos* 17. Munich.

Lynch, K.M. 2011. *The Symposium in Context: Pottery from a Late Archaic House near the Athenian Agora.* Princeton.

McHugh, M. 2017. *The Ancient Greek Farmstead.* Oxford.

Morgan, J.E. 2007. "Space and the Notion of Final Frontier: Searching for Ritual Boundaries in the Classical Athenian Home." *Kernos* 20: 113–129.

Morris, I. 2007. "Archaeology, Standards of Living, and Greek Economic History." In *The Ancient Economy: Evidence and Models*, eds. J.G. Manning and I. Morris, Stanford, 91–126.

Morris, S.P., and J.K. Papadopoulos. 2005. "Greek Towers and Slaves: An Archaeology of Exploitation." *AJA* 109: 155–225.

Nevett, L.C. 1994. "Separation or Seclusion? Towards an Archaeological Approach to Investigating Women in the Greek Household in the Fifth to Third Centuries BC." In *Architecture and Order: Approaches to Social Space*, eds. M. Parker Pearson and C. Richards, London, 89–112.

1999. *House and Society in the Ancient Greek World.* Cambridge.

2005. "Between Urban and Rural: House-Form and Social Relations in Attic Villages and Deme Centers." In *Ancient Greek Houses and Households:*

  Chronological, Regional, and Social Diversity, eds. B.A. Ault and L.C. Nevett, Philadelphia, 83–98.

Oakley, J.H. 2020. *A Guide to Scenes of Daily Life on Athenian Vases*. Madison.

Parlama, L., and N.C. Stampolidis, eds. 2000. *Athens: The City beneath the City: Antiquities from the Metropolitan Railway Excavations*. Athens.

Pritchett, W.K. 1956. "The Attic Stelai: Part ɪɪ." *Hesperia* 25: 178–328.

Rapoport, A. 1969. *House Form and Culture*. Englewood Cliffs.

Rotroff, S.I. 2013. *Industrial Religion: The Saucer Pyres of the Athenian Agora*. Princeton.

Shipley, G. 2005. "Little Boxes on the Hillside: Greek Town Planning, Hippodamos, and Polis Ideology." In *The Imaginary Polis: Symposium, January 7–10, 2004*, ed. M.H. Hanson, Copenhagen, 335–403.

Tsakirgis, B. 2005. "Living and Working around the Athenian Agora: A Preliminary Case Study of Three Houses." In *Ancient Greek Houses and Households: Chronological, Regional, and Social Diversity*, eds. B.A. Ault and L.C. Nevett, Philadelphia, 67–82.

Young, R.S. 1951. "An Industrial District of Ancient Athens." *Hesperia* 20: 135–288.

Additional resources to accompany this chapter can be found at: www.cambridge.org/NeilsRogers

10 | The Archaic and Classical Cemeteries

TIM SHEA

Stop and mourn beside the marker of the deceased, Kroisos,
whom violent Ares once struck down on the front lines.

IG I³ 1240

Travelers to Athens in the middle of the fourth century BC would have encountered funerary monuments crowding the roadside with increasing frequency as they approached the ancient city walls. Large burial enclosures, known as *periboloi*, supported by retaining walls with impressive masonry and adorned with sculpture, were the most costly and conspicuous form of burial marker in Classical Athens (see Fig. 12.2). Behind these monumental *periboloi*, burials were added, either marked individually or unmarked. Cemeteries tended to proliferate in flat, undeveloped areas of the city stretching back from the roads and were also home to sanctuaries and industrial activities, such as ceramic and bronze-casting workshops. The Kerameikos, named for the ceramic workshops in its vicinity, is the classic example, with its large burial enclosures lining the roads branching out of the Sacred Gate. Cemeteries do not appear to have been reserved, planned spaces, but developed gradually in non-residential areas. Athens had several urban cemeteries around its city walls, and each had its own character.

Funerary Commemoration in Archaic and Classical Athens

The basic burial unit for citizens was the family plot. There do not appear to have been definitive rules for who was included or excluded; sometimes siblings and their children were included, other times spouses and parents. At no point in the Archaic and Classical periods was every family member in a given *oikos* (family unit) commemorated with an individual funerary monument, nor were they necessarily commemorated on an inscribed tombstone.[1] Funerary commemoration was selective and was used to

---

[1] As Closterman 2007, 646 notes, "no *peribolos* tomb traces all descent lines or commemorates siblings in every generation."

create an impression of the larger family's membership and household identity, rather than to give every individual member his or her due.

In the Archaic period, permanent funerary monuments were used sparingly. The tumulus, a large earthen mound built over one or more burials, was perhaps the most conspicuous element in the landscape. The largest tumuli in the Kerameikos, Grave Mound G and the South Hill, were massive earthworks.[2] Tumuli such as these were sometimes marked with sculpted monuments, which took the forms of marble *kouroi, korai,* and *stelai* with reliefs or painted decoration (Web Fig. 10.1; see Fig. 20.1 for an example of a votive *kouros*). Sometimes freestanding sculpture was used to adorn the tomb; extant examples include lions, who stood as guardians, marble discuses for pentathletes, and freestanding columns. Freestanding funerary sculpture rarely, if ever, stood directly over the burials themselves or on top of the tumulus; instead, these monuments were set up along the major roadways, which structured Athenian burial grounds more than any topographical feature. Inscriptions on the bases of monuments beckoned passersby to stop and read – and mourn – for the deceased, so placement along roads with foot and cart traffic was highly desirable.

By the end of the sixth century BC, burials were already clustering along major roads on the edges of the city that would be enclosed by the Themistoklean Wall in 479.[3] During the cleanup of the debris from the Persian sack of Athens in 480 and the subsequent rebuilding program, the roadside monuments that had stood in front of burials were repurposed as building materials in the city walls and road beds (Thucydides 1.90.3–4). This depopulation of monuments in the funerary landscape seems to have contributed to conservativism in funerary commemoration for the better part of the fifth century. This trend had started already by 500 BC, perhaps with changing attitudes toward forms of commemoration that came with the Kleisthenic reforms and the establishment of the democracy. Many have attributed the cessation of conspicuous forms of funerary commemoration to an anti-sumptuary law referenced by Cicero (*De legibus* 2.64). Whatever the reason, fewer than fifty tombstones dating to the *Pentakontaiteia* (480–430 BC) have survived; most were simple inscribed

---

[2] Grave Mound G measured 40 m in diameter and 5 m in height in antiquity, while the South Hill measured 34 m in diameter and 4 m in height. See Stroszeck 2017, 173–176.

[3] The clustering of burials at the limits of the Themistoklean Wall by the late sixth century was first demonstrated by Morris 1987. For a recent overview of the excavated remains of Archaic cemeteries, see Dimitriadou 2019.

Fig. 10.1 *Stele* of Alexileos of Lampsakos, 440–410 BC, Athens, National Archaeological Museum 2591.
Source: T. Shea

stelai, while some preserve remnants of sculpted and painted decoration (Fig. 10.1).[4]

At the end of the fifth century BC, sculpted and painted memorials reappear in greater numbers throughout Athenian cemeteries. Athenian citizens and foreign residents would mark burials differently depending on the context of their death and the family's means. *Periboloi* could be delineated with walls constructed of impressive masonry, as much as 3–4 m in height. The most basic form of burial marker in a *peribolos* setting is the humble *horos.* These roughly carved stones typically had the portion that was visible above ground smoothed with a tooth chisel and inscribed with the word *horos* (boundary) in large letters.[5] Sometimes the stone was labeled as the *horos* of a plot or burial, and in some cases the name of the

---

[4] Stears 2000.

[5] For a recent overview of funerary *horoi,* see Stroszeck 2013.

deceased whose burial was marked appears in the genitive. While these *horoi* may seem like the least costly form of tombstone, they delineated a piece of land to be used for burial that could be passed from generation to generation, and the cost of such plots could be quite substantial. In Aischines' oration *Against Timarchos* (1.99, 346/5 BC), the prodigality of Timarchos is demonstrated by the fact that he sold property in the deme Alopeke – about 11 or 12 stades from the city walls – that his mother had asked him not to sell, and if he were to do so, to at least let her be buried there before he did. Timarchos sold the plot of land for 2,000 drachmas. When compared to the daily wage of a specialized worker on the Akropolis at the end of the fifth century BC of 1–2 drachmas per day, it becomes clear that this amount was out of reach of a large portion of the population of Athens. The simple boundary stone, then, stands for much more than the cost of the stone itself; a plot in a prime location would have been a conspicuous expenditure, even if humbly marked.

After a family had secured a plot for burial, they might have chosen to adorn it with a permanent tombstone. Plots containing tombstones with sculpted reliefs were invariably close to roads, while burials marked with tombstones with painted scenes have been found set back several meters from the road. Because sculpted monuments were likely more costly than painted counterparts, they appear more often in roadside plots. Tombstones from the Kerameikos excavations dating to the last third of the fifth century BC have a rather narrow range of forms: shallow *naiskoi* with standing or seated figures in relief (see Fig. 12.1), vase group *stelai* (*stelai* that depict in low relief one or more vases, usually *loutrophoroi*, *lekythoi*, or *alabastra*), and *stelai* with relief or anthemia with painted scenes. Foreign residents were also setting up tombstones, some with a sculpted molding or painted decoration, others made from repurposed stones, like that of Nautes of Torone made from a marble rooftile fragment.[6]

The *naiskoi* of the late fifth century tend to depict one or two figures, therefore representing only one or two generations of the family. Men and women are shown performing a narrow range of gendered roles. Women are usually seated in interior scenes, reaching out to or embracing children or grandchildren, beside a domestic slave holding open a *pyxis*, or holding a mirror (see Fig. 12.1). Young, beardless men are often holding a strigil, a marker of participation in the *gymnasion*, as in the *stele* of Eupheros from

[6] Athens, National Archaeological Museum 2588. *IG* I³ 1377; Stears 2000, 30–31, Fig. 2.2.

the Kerameikos (Fig. 10.2).[7] Above the pedimental anthemion of his *stele* are vestiges of papyrus scrolls in added paint. Together, these iconographical clues signal that the young Eupheros was still in the midst of his education in the *gymnasion*. Perhaps he was a lover of books, so much so that his family made sure to include them on his tombstone. The attributes of adult men include a beard, a himation, and a walking stick. On marble vases, especially *lekythoi*, the iconography is drawn more from the iconographic tradition of their ceramic white-ground counterparts, which often depict family members visiting the grave and men in military garb.

In the fourth century BC, the number of funerary monuments increased, peaking in the period between 360 and 330. The scale of monuments also increased over the century, with life-size figures in high relief appearing across Attika by the 320s. The range of iconography in the fourth century is quite expansive, when one considers both sculpted and painted scenes.[8] In general, there are some broad categories of tombstones that appear in the archaeological record: marble vases, guardians of the plot (such as sirens or Molossian hounds), inscribed *stelai* with a crowning molding and/or anthemia and rosettes (*Namenstelen*), *stelai* with carved reliefs in a recessed square or rectangular window (*Bildfeldstelen*), and *naiskoi* (see Web Fig. 20.4). Undecorated inscribed slabs were another common type of tombstone.

The iconographic repertoire also expanded by the mid-fourth century BC. Unlike earlier examples from the late fifth and early fourth centuries BC, *naiskoi* often depict three generations of the family. For instance, the *naiskos* of Hierokles from the coastal deme of Rhamnous housed four life-size portraits in high relief of Hierokles (I), his sons Lykeas and Iophon, and Demostrate, Iophon's daughter-in-law. This *naiskos* was one of possibly nine different monuments that adorned a massive enclosure, which also included two marble *lekythoi*, two *Namenstelen*, and two other *naiskoi* likely flanking either side of the central large *naiskos*. Four generations of the family were referenced in the inscriptions on the various monuments in the *peribolos*. Also in the fourth century, military iconography returned to the private family plot. The *naiskos* of Aristonautes, found in excavations on Peiraios Street near the Kerameikos, shows the deceased life-size, striding forward, wearing a cuirass and Phrygian-style helmet (Web Fig. 10.2).[9] Children's tombstones become much more popular in

---

[7] Athens, Kerameikos Museum P1169. Bergemann 1997, *naiskos* no. 9.
[8] For painted decoration preserved on tombstones, see Posamentir 2006.
[9] Athens, National Archaeological Museum 738. Clairmont 1993, Vol. 1, 460; Bergemann 1997, *naiskos* no. 603.

Fig. 10.2 Detail of the *stele* of Eupheros, 430–420 BC, Athens, Kerameikos Museum P 1169.
© Hans R. Goette

the fourth century as well (see Fig. 14.2). Typically, children were often shown with their pets; boys tended to be shown with their dogs, while girls are depicted with doves or hares.

Because of the conspicuous consumption of colossal funerary monuments, such as the so-called Kallithea Monument (ca. 320 BC) erected by metics from Istria on the Black Sea (modern-day Romania), a second anti-luxury decree was passed in 317/16 BC.[10] Cicero relates that Demetrios of Phaleron, when he was the regent of Athens, restricted the form and size of tombstones: only small columns (*columellae*) no taller than three cubits, tables (*mensae*) resembling altars, and small basins (*labella*) were permitted. These simple nondescript columnar monuments became the most popular new form of funerary commemoration and remained so until the Roman period, when grave *stelai* returned to Athens.

Inscriptions

Archaic funerary inscriptions appear on both the bases of monuments and the monuments themselves. (See also Meyer, Chapter 7 in this volume.)

[10] *SEG* 24.258.

Sometimes, poetic epigrams beckoned the viewer to reperform and rededicate the monument on behalf of the deceased and to mourn for them, such as that of Kroisos quoted at the beginning of the chapter.[11] Usually the name of the deceased appears by itself, often in the genitive, identifying the marker or memorial (*sema* or *mnema*) as belonging to the deceased. In some cases, the name of the dedicant and their relationship to the deceased was provided as well; usually the dedicant was a parent, child, sibling, or spouse. The deceased's father's name or patronym was sometimes provided to identify him or her more precisely. The use of the patronymic form was more common in the urban cemeteries than it was in the Attic countryside. Artists' signatures also appeared on Archaic funerary monuments, but they were never used on Classical ones.

There is some continuity in the use of inscriptions from the Archaic to the Classical period. Poetic epigrams return in the last quarter of the fifth century. The basic inscriptional formula for citizen men was the name (*nomos*) + the name of the father in the genitive case (patronymic) + the name of the deme in which he is registered as a citizen (demotic). For citizen women, the formula is the same, except that it was her father's or husband's demotic that was inscribed. Children's name usually occur without a patronymic and always without a demotic, since the child would have died before registry as a citizen or marriage to a citizen could have taken place. For foreign residents, the foreign *polis* or *ethnos* to which he or she belonged (*ethnikon*) was often present in place of the demotic (e.g. Fig. 10.1). These inscriptional formulae were in use by the end of the fifth century and were standard practice by the fourth century BC. However, since in the fifth century many tombstones lack demotics, they have been variously interpreted as citizens or foreign residents. Because burial plots were privately owned, most cases in which tombstones bore only the name, with or without a patronymic, likely represent citizen burials.

Cemetery Organization

The outbreak of the Peloponnesian War had a lasting impact on the funerary landscape of Athens. Families residing in rural demes across Attika who had long resisted moving to the city center were now flocking there in large numbers because of the threat of Spartan invasions

[11] Day 2010.

(Thucydides 2.13.7). The safest place in all of Attika was within the city walls of Athens – the fortifications built under Themistokles, the Long Walls connecting the city to the harbor of Piraeus, and the fortifications around Piraeus itself (see Costaki and Theocharaki, Chapter 4 in this volume). This influx of people put a strain on the market for permanent plots in the urban cemeteries. During the first decade of the war, funerary *horoi* and *periboloi* first appeared. For families who had lived for generations in rural demes, it was necessary to purchase plots of land for burial. Some families may have left behind burial plots in their home deme, some of which had their own large cemeteries, such as that of Merenda, the ancient deme of Myrrhinous. It is no wonder then that some of the earliest instances of the use of a demotic were used by citizens from demes outside of the urban center.[12]

A funerary *horos* found north of the National Gardens nicely encapsulates the need of families moving to the city center to procure new burial plots.[13] The inscription, usually dated to the last quarter of the fifth century BC, reads: "Boundary stone of the burial plot of Glyke from Marathon, who was living in the city. She was the sister of Eschation son of Kallias" (*IG* I³ 1136). This *horos* marks the plot of a citizen woman who moved from Marathon to the city (*asty*), where she was living at the time of her death. She had probably died unmarried and orphaned, leaving her brother Eschation as her *kyrios*, responsible for her burial. To keep others from encroaching on Glyke's plot, Eschation had the corners marked with boundary stones. Rarely were *horoi* this explicit, but the handling of Glyke's burial was likely a common practice during the Peloponnesian War and into the fourth century BC as the urban population of Athens grew.

It is unclear from literary testimonia who determined the land designated for burial. Presumably, by the late fifth century BC most permanent burial plots were bought and sold like any other piece of property.[14] The ownership of property was restricted to citizens and select foreign residents and metics who had been expressly given the right to own property (*enktesis*). Some unrestricted or open-access cemeteries no doubt existed

---

[12] One of the earliest tombstones from Athens that preserves a demotic marked the burial of Phaidron, son of Lysistratos from Acharnai (*IG* I³ 1303, 450–425 BC). His tombstone was found near the Dipylon Gate.

[13] Athens, Epigraphical Museum 10184.

[14] Zelnick-Abramovitz (2015, 63) argues that ownership of graves and burial plots was private and, in the case of religious or political associations, collective from the fourth century BC onward.

where anyone could bury their dead. Burial grounds with open access would have been necessary on a practical level to deal with ritual pollution associated with death (*miasma*). The administration of cemeteries is hinted at in some ancient literary sources. By the fourth century, the demarch was responsible for disposing of unclaimed bodies either by tracking down relatives or in the case of slaves, notifying their master (Demosthenes 43.57–58). If the body went unburied, the demarch was responsible for contracting out the burial of the body with as little cost to the deme as possible. In fourth-century Athens, the *astynomoi* were responsible for the burials of unclaimed corpses on the streets and used public slaves to carry them out (*Constitution of the Athenians* 50.2). How these two bodies of officials – one at the deme level and one at the *polis* level – handled ambiguous cases is unclear, but it does appear that the disposal of bodies to mitigate religious pollution was a primary concern.

Most of the *periboloi* belonged to citizen families, like that of Eschation and Glyke of Marathon, and the land was likely privately owned. Because foreign residents and slaves were unable to own property, the mechanisms by which these groups were incorporated into cemeteries is relatively obscure. One of the most notable examples of a *peribolos* started by foreign residents is that of the Messenians in the Kerameikos.[15] The plot went into use around 350 BC and enclosed an area of approximately 145 m^2. The earliest burial marker belongs to Parthenios, son of Philoxenos of Messene. Since some fifty simple burials were added to the precinct over the course of the second half of the fourth century, it cannot represent merely a family group. Knigge was the first to suggest that the plot was purchased by Parthenios, who as a *proxenos* may have had the right to own property in Athens;[16] he then allowed other Messenians access for burial. Knigge's proposal is supported by the fact that, in all the cemeteries where foreign residents' tombstones have been found, they tend to bury in groups.[17]

The basic building blocks of the cemeteries of ancient Athens, then, were the *periboloi* that lined the major roads leading to and from the city center and the Piraeus. These seem to have been privately or collectively owned pieces of land. The general layout of Classical cemeteries was straightforward. The most expensive plots, with the most elaborate masonry and the largest-scale sculptural programs, abutted the roads and were concentrated

---

[15] Stroszeck 2017, 193–195, no. 32.

[16] Knigge 1991, 117–121, no. 21.

[17] This phenomenon occurs in the East, West, and Piraeus cemeteries in the fifth and fourth centuries BC (Shea 2018).

near the gates of the city. Behind these *periboloi* in undeveloped areas, burials were added individually or in small groups and were sometimes individually marked. It could be that these open cemeteries were in a legal gray area – unused plots of land whose value decreased as the number of burials increased to the point that no one dared lay claim to them.

The Topography of Cemeteries in Classical Athens

The cemeteries of ancient Athens developed around the road and fortification network of the city. Proximity to roads served a twofold purpose: allowing monuments to be seen by passersby and enabling family members to visit the graves with easy access. Reference is made to these cemeteries based on their cardinal direction in relation to the city, except in the case of the cemetery north of Piraeus, referred to here as the Piraeus cemetery (Maps 4.2 and 10.1).

Only two large sections of the major urban cemeteries are now easily accessible. The first is the Kerameikos, which preserves a portion of the western cemetery outside the Sacred and Dipylon Gates. Its Street of the Tombs is the single best location to experience the scope of the sculptural programs and the scale of fourth-century funerary *periboloi*. The continuation of this cemetery was excavated during the Athens Metro project, when 1,191 graves were found (Map 10.1, no. 1).[18] In addition to clusters of individual burials, the excavations uncovered two mass burials, which have been interpreted as victims of the plague that ravaged the city in the early years of the Peloponnesian War.[19] The Classical cemetery extended down the Sacred Way (the modern Iera Odos) at least as far as the Botanical Gardens, where tombstones were found in large numbers.

The Kerameikos highlights the lack of strict zoning when it came to Athenian cemeteries (Map 10.1, no. 2). Just outside the Dipylon Gate is the best-preserved Greek bath-complex in Athens. First built in the fifth century, the bath and its large cistern system was in use until the third century BC.[20] In addition, several pottery kilns from the sixth and fifth centuries BC have been found in the area of the Kerameikos and its wider

---

[18] Parlama and Stampolidis 2000, 264–389.

[19] Owing to the scale of the excavation and the importance of the material uncovered, the planned location of the Kerameikos Station was moved to its current location in Gazi.

[20] Lucore and Trümper 2013, 281. See also Stroszeck, Chapter 8 in this volume.

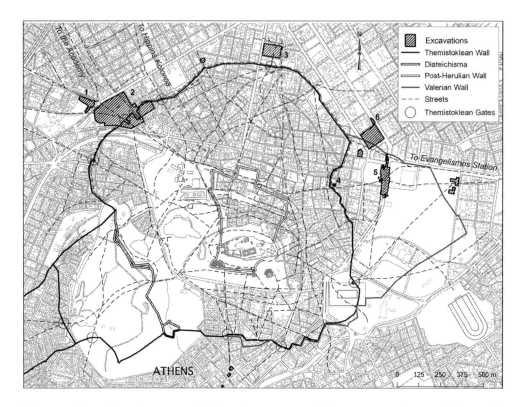

Map 10.1 Map of the urban center of Athens showing some of the excavations that revealed parts of ancient cemeteries. 1. Kerameikos Station Excavation. 2. Kerameikos Archaeological Park. 3. Kotzia Square Excavations. 4. Diochares Bath-House. 5. Syntagma Station Excavation. 6. Amerikis Shaft Excavation.
© Dipylon Society/Stamatina Lampraki, adapted by T. Shea

environs.[21] Sanctuaries were also embedded within the stretch of cemetery; a sacred enclosure along the Street of the Tombs contained the Sanctuaries of Artemis Soteiria and Apollo Paian, as well as one of Pan, the Nymphs, and the Anatolian lunar deity Men.[22] The nature of these cults is obscure, but the Apollo cult appears to have been a hydromancy cult, with an oracular ritual tied to one of the wells cut into the bedrock. Tiles lining the well preserve the inscription: "Come to me, Paian (Apollo), bearing the true oracle."[23] While the sanctuary was elaborated in the first or second century AD, an earlier iteration may have been in place by the Classical or Hellenistic period.

[21] Monaco 2000, 70–80, pl. 37–38.
[22] Stroszeck 2017, 120–123, no. 24.
[23] Stroszeck 2017, 122.

The portion of the western cemetery preserved within the Kerameikos demonstrates the polyvalent aspect of the ancient cemeteries of Athens.[24] Activities that were polluting or disruptive to residential communities, such as pottery kilns, were pushed outside the city walls. Bath-houses, where one would want to bathe before heading into town for business, were also located just outside the city gates. Trümper has proposed that public bathing had a dubious reputation in the Classical period, which may have been a contributing factor to the placement of bath-houses outside the walls.[25] A sanctuary like that of Apollo that relied on oracular pronouncements derived from a well cut into the earth may have also benefited from a setting embedded within a heterotopia, such as a cemetery. The cult of Pan and the Nymphs, more common in rural areas, was fittingly placed near the walls where city meets countryside. As Bakewell demonstrates in Chapter 21 of this volume, *gymnasia* were also founded outside of the city, and the roads leading out to the Lyceum and Academy were lined with burials.

The second location where a large portion of an ancient cemetery can be visited today is in Kotzia Square, where part of the northern cemetery is preserved. Portions of the moat (*proteichisma*) and ring road near the northern gate of the Themistoklean Wall, identified as the Acharnian Gate (see Map 10.1, no. 3), can be seen under the National Bank of Greece on the southern side of the square. As in the Kerameikos, burials lined this important road leading north toward the deme of Acharnai. Approximately 680 burials were excavated in the square, along with portions of the roads, and third- and fourth-century AD ceramic workshops.[26] The burials have been dated by excavators from the ninth century BC to the third century AD, but the majority date to the Classical period. The cemetery of Kotzia Square was part of a larger cemetery that stretched at least as far as Omonia Square, where tombstones were found during building construction projects at the end of the nineteenth century. Additionally, a group of five tombstones was found during the construction of the sewage system for Athinas Street, connecting Kotzia Square with Omonia Square.

While one can still visit portions of the western and northern cemeteries, the eastern cemetery has only been exposed in informal excavations during construction or rescue excavations, mainly to the north of Syntagma

[24] Patterson 2006 gives an excellent description of Athenian cemeteries as multiuse spaces.
[25] Trümper 2013, 39.
[26] Pitt 2011–2012, 29; *ArchDelt* 43 (1988) B', 22–29.

Square, and extending out as far east as the Evangelismos Metro station (see Map 10.1, nos. 4–6).[27] Much like the western cemetery preserved in the Kerameikos, remnants of a bath-house, often referred to as the Diochares Bath-House, have been excavated close to the course of the Themistoklean Wall. In the Syntagma station excavations, remnants of seven bronze-casting pits were found in the vicinity of a bronze sculpture workshop. Hundreds of Classical burials have been uncovered in rescue excavations, including those during the construction of the Metro system in the Amerikis Shaft. The eastern cemetery serves as a useful parallel for the cemetery in the Kerameikos: bath-houses, industrial activities, and burials all structured by the roads leaving the city gates.

Along the road network reaching from the city to Piraeus, burial clusters and tombstones have been excavated along the roads leaving from the southern and southwestern gates of the city wall. The cemeteries continued along the Long Walls that connected the city with the port of Piraeus. Over fifty Classical tombstones – mostly *stelai*, marble vessels, and *naiskoi* – have been found in excavations in the neighborhoods of Petralona, Kallithea, and Moschato. North of Piraeus itself lay one of the largest cemeteries of Classical Athens, portions of which were excavated in the nineteenth century (see Map 4.2). Piraeus' northern cemetery was never published, formally or otherwise, so the distribution of burials is largely obscure. Most of what we know about this cemetery comes from the tombstones reportedly found there. Clairmont (1993) lists 245 tombstones in his topographical index as coming from Piraeus, many of which are housed in the Archaeological Museum of Piraeus. Piraeus boasted a diverse immigrant community, which is reflected in the corpus of tombstones that survives from the area. Men and women from large coastal port cities from Anatolia to the Black Sea to North Africa to the Western Mediterranean are represented among the tombstones from Piraeus. (See also Steinhauer, Chapter 16 in this volume.)

Finally, the area along the Dromos or Academy Road that ran from the Dipylon Gate to the Academy seems to have been the preferred location for the placement of the mass burials of cremated remains of soldiers who died in battle and the casualty lists that commemorated them (see Map 4.2).[28] Thucydides described the burial of those who died in the first year of the Peloponnesian War as being placed in the Demosion Sema, located in the

---

[27] For an overview of the evidence for the East Cemetery, see Dillon and Shea 2017.

[28] For an overview of the remains of the mass burials of the war dead and the use of the Academy Road as the preferred location of publicly funded burials, see Arrington 2010 and 2015.

most beautiful suburb of the city, where they always buried the war dead, except those who died at Marathon (Thucydides 2.34.5). Patterson has argued that the term *demosion sema* (literally, publicly funded burial) does not refer to a specific location in the Athenian landscape, and that we should not imagine a large, reserved 'national cemetery' existing in ancient Athens.[29] Instead, Arrington has demonstrated that the evidence for mass burials and the casualty lists that stood in front them clustered along the road to the Academy, creating a "neighborhood of graves" interspersed with private burials and other activities.[30] Land for burial was likely appropriated or purchased piecemeal as mass burials and single burials were added over time. Just to the northeast of the Academy Road, the road leading out of the so-called Leokoriou Gate toward the Kolonos Hippios has been shown by Arrington to have been associated with the burial of elite families, and iconography associated with horses and horsemanship on monuments found in the area hint that the deceased may have been members of the cavalry.[31]

The cemeteries of Athens enveloped the city and stretched outwards in all directions as they followed the road network of the city. Cemeteries were rarely used only for burial. The incremental nature of their development allowed for pockets of industrial activity, the occasional bath-house, and small-scale sanctuaries to be embedded within them. Family plots seem to have been an important structural element, which reflected ideal notions of the family unit, while the reality of those personalities and relationships often remain obscure.

Further Reading

The study of Athenian cemeteries continues to be a vibrant field of study. For a recent overview of Athenian cemeteries in the Early Iron Age and Archaic periods, see Dimitriadou 2019. For the Classical cemeteries, see Morris 1992, Parlama and Stampolidis 2000, Marchiandi 2011, and Stroszeck 2017. For the study of cemetery management and the procurement of burial plots see Zelnick-Abramovitz 2015. For comprehensive collections of Classical tombstones, Clairmont 1993 and Bergemann 1997 and 2001 are good places to begin, but Conze's multi-volume study (1893–1911) is still useful today. For tombstones that have been found more recently in rescue excavations, see Bardani and Papadopoulos 2006. For painted

---

[29] Patterson 2006, 53–56.
[30] Arrington 2015, 75.
[31] Arrington 2010, 529–532.

tombstones, see Posamentir 2006. For an overview of the public cemetery and the monuments associated with it, see Arrington 2010 and 2015.

Bibliography

Arrington, N. 2010. "Topographic Semantics: The Location of the Athenian Public Cemetery and Its Significance for the Nascent Democracy." *Hesperia* 79: 499–539.

2015. *Ashes, Images, and Memories: The Presence of the War Dead in Fifth-Century Athens*. Oxford.

Bardani, V., and G. Papadopoulos. 2006. Συμπλήρωμα των επιτύμβιων μνημείων της Αττικής. Athens.

Bergemann, J. 1997. *Demos und Thanatos*. Munich.

2001. *Datenbank der attischen Grabreliefs des 5. und 4. Jahrhunderts v. Chr.: Projekt Dyabola*. Munich.

Clairmont, C. 1993. *Classical Attic Tombstones*. Vols. 1–7. Kilchberg.

Closterman, W.E. 2007. "Family Ideology and Family History: The Function of Funerary Markers in Classical Attic Peribolos Tombs." *AJA* 111: 633–652.

Conze, A. 1893–1911. *Die attischen Grabreliefs*. Berlin.

Day, J. 2010. *Archaic Greek Epigram and Dedication: Representation and Reperformance*. Cambridge.

Dillon, S., and T. Shea. 2017. "Sculpture and Context: Towards an Archaeology of Greek Statuary." In *Greek Art in Context: Archaeological and Art Historical Perspectives*, ed. D. Rodríguez Pérez, Abingdon, 19–29.

Dimitriadou, E.M. 2019. *Early Athens: Settlements and Cemeteries in the Submycenaean, Geometric, and Archaic Periods*. Los Angeles.

Knigge, U. 1991. *The Athenian Kerameikos: History, Monuments, Excavations*. Athens.

Lucore, S.K., and M. Trümper, eds. 2013. *Greek Baths and Bathing Culture: New Discoveries and Approaches*. Leuven.

Marchiandi, D. 2011. *I periboli funerari nell'Attica classica. Lo specchio di una "borghesia."* Athens.

Monaco, M.C. 2000. *Ergasteria: impianti artigianali ceramica ad Atene ed in Attica dal protogeometrico alle soglie dell'ellenismo*. Rome.

Morris, I. 1987. *Burial and Ancient Society: The Rise of the Greek City-State*. Cambridge.

1992. *Death-Ritual and Social Structure in Classical Antiquity*. Cambridge.

Parlama, L., and N.C. Stampolidis, eds. 2000. *Athens: The City Beneath the City. Antiquities from the Metropolitan Railway Excavations*. Athens.

Patterson, C. 2006. "'Citizen Cemeteries' in Classical Athens?" *CQ* 56: 48–56.

Pitt, R. 2011–2012. "Archaeological Exhibits from Recent Excavations in Athens." *Archaeological Reports* 58: 28–9.

Posamentir, R. 2006. *Bemalte attische Grabstelen klassischer Zeit*. Munich.

Shea, T. 2018. "Mapping Immigrant Communities through Their Tombstones in Archaic and Classical Athens." PhD Dissertation, Duke University.

Stears, K. 2000. "The Times They Are A'Changing: Developments in Fifth-Century Funerary Sculpture." In *The Epigraphy of Death: Studies in the History and Society of Greece and Rome*, ed. G.J. Oliver, Liverpool, 25–58.

Stroszeck, J. 2013. "Sema, Mnema, Mnemeion und Theke: zu inschriftlich begrenzten Gräbern im Kerameikos." In *Griechische Grabbezirke klassischer Zeit: Normen und Regionalismen*, ed. K. Sporn. Munich, 7–27.

2017. *Ο Κεραμεικός των Αθηνών. Ιστορία και Μνημεία εντός του αρχαιολογικού χώρου*. Bad Langensalza.

Trümper, M. 2013. "Urban Context of Greek Public Baths." In *Greek Baths and Bathing Culture: New Discoveries and Approaches*, ed. S.K. Lucore and M. Trümper, Leuven, 37–62.

Zelnick-Abramovitz, R. 2015. "Whose Grave Is This? The Status of Grave Plots in Ancient Greece." *Dike* 18: 51–98.

Additional resources to accompany this chapter can be found at: www.cambridge.org/NeilsRogers

PART II

Inhabitants

11 | Population and Social Structure

DANIELLE L. KELLOGG

In a speech of Demosthenes (*Against Euboulides*), the speaker Euxitheos attempts to convince an Athenian jury that he has been unfairly disenfranchised by Euboulides and his cronies in a recent purge of the citizenship lists. To bolster his claims to citizen status, Euxitheos discusses numerous aspects of Athenian society. These include economic strata (and the prejudices arising from poverty), family history and marriage relations, service in the Athenian armed forces, burial practices, and a number of social and political groups with which he was affiliated. Taken as a whole, Euxitheos' defense paints a picture of a web of overlapping, competing, and cooperative interests and groups that together comprised Athenian society – and also a system which was prone to manipulation in the hands of unscrupulous men, a situation made more possible by the large size of the Athenian citizen population.

The Population of Athens

Determining the population of a given *polis* in antiquity is always a proposition fraught with challenges. Even after decades of debate, no consensus has been reached as to the adult male citizen population of Athens in any period, much less the total population of Athens and Attika, which would have included children, women, slaves, and metics as well. Part of the difficulty lies in the methods employed by ancient historians and demographers to calculate population. Scholars have used various data such as the bouleutic quotas of demes, army figures, estimates of the carrying capacity of Attika and the amount of grain imported to Athens, or even a combination of methods. Another problem lies in our source materials, which are scattered, can contradict one another, and under-represent or ignore whole groups such as minor children, women, or slaves.

Such difficulties are magnified by the changes in the population of Athens over time. It is generally accepted that the population of Athens was at its highest in the years just before the Peloponnesian War (431–404 BC), and that the war and other demographic changes resulted in a

159

reduction of the population that was never made up. Thus, the population of Athens was lower in the fourth century than it had been in the fifth, and lower still in the Hellenistic period – but besides agreeing on this very general picture of demographic decline, scholars have reached widely divergent figures as to the actual population.

Most attempts to reckon with the population of Athens deal in some way with the question of the bouleutic quotas, the number of representatives that each of the 139 Attic demes sent to serve on the Council of 500 (boule) each year. Scholars apply known demographic models to the quotas to come up with a minimum number of adult male citizens meeting the criteria which the polis must have had available to be able to provide that requisite number of representatives each year.[1] They then extrapolate from this data to suggest an estimated population for an individual deme or for Athens as a whole, often supported by evidence gleaned from ancient texts, archaeological finds, or epigraphic materials. Much of the disagreement among scholars lies either in different interpretations of the source materials or in the nature of this extrapolation and resulting population estimates.

In the last twenty years, the estimates about the population of ancient Athens have largely been divided into two camps along ideological lines. On one side, scholars have argued for relatively low population figures, putting the population of adult male citizens somewhere between 30,000–40,000 in the fifth century and around 20,000–30,000 in the fourth, with the total population of Athens and Attika being somewhere around 250,000 in the fifth century and 120,000–150,000 in the fourth.[2] Leading the other side of the debate has been Hansen, who since 1985 has repeatedly argued that the population numbers for Attika have been systematically underestimated. He has postulated that, in order for the Athenian political system to be able to function after the high number of casualties associated both with the Peloponnesian War effort and with the plague, there must have been at least 60,000 adult male citizens in Athens in the years before 431 BC. A number this high would mean that the total citizen

[1] The usual demographic model employed is that of Coale and Demeny 1966, Model West mortality level 4, growth rate 0.5 percent. As Osborne 1985, 43–44 notes, according to this model, for every new bouleutes of 30 years of age, there would have needed to be some sixty-five males in the total population. This calculation assumes a lifetime limit of one term of service in the boule. If citizens could serve twice in their lifetime (for which the evidence is limited), a minimum male population of 32.5 males for every one bouleutes is required. See Akrigg 2019, 9–37 on the limitations of the Coale–Demeny model as applied to ancient Athens.
[2] See, for example, Osborne 1985, 42–46.

population of Attika – including free Athenian women and children of both sexes, but excluding metics and slaves – would have been in the neighborhood of 200,000 individuals.[3] In the fourth century, Hansen has argued for a total population figure (including non-citizens) of 300,000.[4] Most recently, Akrigg has thoroughly reexamined the arguments, demographic models, and evidence for the population of Athens, and has reached conclusions similar to Hansen's – a male citizen population of 60,000 or so *at minimum* in the 430s, and around 30,000 during the fourth century.[5]

By default, opting for numbers much closer to the minimums presupposes a very high rate of political participation – nearly 100 percent – among eligible male citizens.[6] Scholars who support the higher estimates have argued that a participation rate that high in the centralized *polis* bureaucracy is so unlikely as to be unworthy of consideration, and the evidence suggests that the population of Athens must have been much higher than the minimum figures, so that many more citizens were available for political service than were in fact absolutely required. Recently, the higher numbers have been meeting with wider acceptance, and scholarship on other, related questions, such as those involving the food supply of Athens, have provided oblique support for this position.[7] It seems that the total population of Athens – men, women, and children, including both free people and slaves, citizens and resident foreigners – must have been over 300,000 and perhaps even approaching 400,000 in the fifth century, and somewhere between 200,000 and 300,000 in the fourth. An inescapable conclusion is that the population of Athens was an order of magnitude larger than any other ancient Greek *polis*.

Social Structure

Athenian society was marked by a complex web of groups and identities to which people belonged, which alternately marked out and emphasized

[3] This assumes a sex ratio of males to females that is roughly one-to-one.
[4] The bibliography is vast. See, for example, Hansen 1985 and 2011 *passim*.
[5] Akrigg 2019, *passim*; see especially 38–88 for arguments about the size of the citizen population.
[6] Especially if *bouleutai* were permitted only one term of service in their lifetime. There is limited evidence for second terms of service for some *bouleutai*, especially in later periods, but the extent of this phenomenon is poorly understood.
[7] For example, Moreno 2007, 10 and 31; Akrigg 2019, 171–243 on the implications of population size and demographic change.

various aspects of life in ancient Athens. These groups could be social, religious, military, economic, or political; could be defined by gender, descent, profession, or social or economic class; and could overlap, complement, cooperate, or compete with one another. However, Athenian life did not recognize hard-and-fast boundaries between these different spheres, and sometimes groups whose primary sphere of influence or function was, say, religious, could also have political or economic functions.[8] One prime example of this fluidity is the *genos* of the Salaminioi, whose members were spread across numerous Attic demes. The Salaminioi administered or were involved in several cults, owned other properties (including saltpans and an agora) that funded their activities, and formed a religious-political group which eventually split into two branches after a dispute.[9] Context is important in recognizing the primary aspect of these social groups and identifications in various spheres of Athenian social reality, as the same phenomenon might appear to be religious when viewed from one angle and political from another. Although often presented as a dichotomy between opposing statuses, it is becoming increasingly clear that these categories must rather be thought of as a continuum.[10]

This apparent complexity of Athenian social reality is further complicated by the limits of the source materials for modern scholars. Because the various statuses and organizations available to the inhabitants of Attika were a well-established cornerstone of ancient Greek life, they were generally not explicated in great detail, and our knowledge of them often comes from times when such statuses underwent change due to political or other circumstances or when social norms and statuses were perceived to have been somehow violated.[11] Moreover, studies of Athenian society inevitably reflect modern historiographical and political concerns: earlier studies of Athenian citizenship often focused on questions that can be deemed constitutionalist (What were the legal criteria for citizenship? What was the role of citizenship in legal and political institutions? What perquisites and obligations defined citizenship?). More recent studies have turned more toward considerations of gender, economic status, and other factors that may have affected the expression of such rights, obligations, and privileges in Athenian life.

---

[8] This is particularly true of associations that pre-dated the Kleisthenic democracy and whose role changed over time. See, for example, Lambert 1993, 25–57 and Ismard 2018 on phratries.

[9] See especially Lambert 1997 and Taylor 1997 on the evidence for the Salaminioi.

[10] See Kamen 2013, *passim*.

[11] For example, much of our knowledge about the Salaminioi comes from the mediation of the dispute between the two branches of the *genos*.

At the core of Athenian civic identity were the legal divisions: free/ unfree, citizen/non-citizen. Even these, however, were subject to dispute. Perikles' Citizenship Law of 451/50 required legitimate descent from both an Athenian citizen father and citizen mother for the acquisition Athenian citizenship. However, the status of 'citizen' is often bound up in the exercise of political and legal privilege in the Athenian *polis*, spheres from which women were unilaterally excluded. What, then, defines a female 'citizen'? Obviously, citizenship encompassed far more than the ability to participate in the political and legal spheres. Similarly, in a famous passage from the writer known as the Old Oligarch, he claims that it is impossible to tell a citizen from a slave or metic at Athens:

> Now among the slaves and metics at Athens there is the greatest uncon-
> trolled wantonness; you cannot hit them there, and a slave will not stand
> aside for you. I shall point out why this is their native practice: if it were
> customary for a slave (or metic or freedman) to be struck by one who is
> free, you would often hit an Athenian citizen by mistake on the assump-
> tion that he was a slave. For the people there are no better dressed than
> the slaves and metics, nor are they any more handsome. (*Constitution of
> the Athenians* 10)

Although the Old Oligarch's claims must be taken with a grain of salt, it is clear that anxiety existed in Athens about who 'belonged,' and that a constant negotiation of statuses was taking place. At various points in Athenian history, revisions of the citizenship rolls took place to 'weed out' individuals who may have undeservedly accessed citizen status and the perks that came with it. Demosthenes' *Against Euboulides*, mentioned above, concerns the claims of one Euxitheos, who is attempting to regain his citizen rights after being deprived of them in one such revision. Conversely, the same speech makes clear that, in times of crisis, the rule requiring citizen descent on both sides could be relaxed in order to help swell depleted citizenship rolls (Demosthenes 57.30); there were at least two periods of such exemption in the years between 430 and 403 BC.

The complexity and fluidity of Athenian social practice defies attempts to distill the question of the social structure of the *polis* into an easily digestible snack. Rather, an examination of some *polis* sub-groups that were important in constructing social, political, and religious identities may help to explicate Athenian social structure. The discussion that follows focuses primarily on those associations which defined the social practices of Athenian citizens, as it was the citizenry which had the most direct influence on the range of statuses and hierarchies that operated within the Athenian *polis*.

Phratries, *Gene*, and Other Associations

A prime example of an organization that straddled the lines between the civic and religious spheres is the groups known as phratries. (See also Kierstead, Chapter 27 in this volume.) Phratries were *polis* sub-groups whose membership was hereditary and which were often associated with specific localities; their characteristic function was as a community of support beyond the family unit. Many (but not all) phratry names ended with the patronymic suffix *-idai*, indicating a belief that the phratry members were in some sense descended from the eponym, although such relationships were, and remain, largely obscure. The phratries in Athens pre-dated the introduction of democracy at the end of the sixth century BC, and recently Ismard has argued persuasively that the phratries and other associations of Archaic Attika were prime movers in the elaboration of civic identity before the inception of the Kleisthenic democracy.[12] Although their legal status as determiners of citizenship waned after the reforms of Kleisthenes, their influence in this respect continued, and the phratries played a significant role in the mediation of status during the Classical era. In particular, the phratries mediated questions relating to legitimacy of descent, upon which questions of citizenship and inheritance rights were predicated.[13]

The male children of phratry members underwent a dual process of phratry introduction as part of religious initiation rituals. In infancy, they would have been introduced to the phratry at the ceremony of the Meion, and then inducted during their adolescence at the Koureion. The Meion involved a sacrifice, shared with the members of the father's phratry, which seems usually to have taken place during the infant's first year of life; presumably the *phrateres* could reject the infant if they suspected it was illegitimate.[14] The Koureion involved the sacrifice of a lamb in the phratry when a boy had reached the age of fifteen or sixteen; the name seems to indicate that the adolescent boy ceremonially cut his hair at the time of the sacrifice, marking his transition to adulthood. Again, phratry members who wished to challenge the boy's claim to legitimate birth (and thereby to phratry membership and, ultimately, citizenship) could do so.[15] There is

---

[12] Ismard 2018. See also Humphreys 2018, 25–61 for a slightly different interpretation of the role of phratries in citizenship and inheritance in the pre-Kleisthenic period, although she also emphasizes their importance to citizenship.

[13] See Humphreys 2018, 580–617 on the functions of phratries after the inception of democracy.

[14] Cf. Humphreys 2018, 298–299.

[15] Humphreys 2018, 302–304.

some evidence to suggest that female children were sometimes introduced to their fathers' phratries, and new wives were introduced to their husband's phratries at the Gamelia; these ceremonies would have taken on greater significance after the adoption of Perikles' Citizenship Law of 451/50, requiring citizen descent in the female line as well as the male. In addition, there might be a separate process of scrutiny (*diadikasia*) for male members of a phratry, in which the phratry could vote on a candidate's eligibility. These ceremonies admitting members to the phratries normally took place at the annual festival of the Apatouria, during which the cults of Zeus Phratrios and Athena Phratria received religious observance.

A fragment of Philochoros (*FGrH* 328 F 35) preserves a law, conventionally dated to the fifth century BC,[16] which requires *phrateres* to accept individuals who belonged to other particular *polis* sub-groups: "But the *phrateres* were obliged to accept both the *orgeones* and the *homogalaktes*, whom we call *gennetai*." A *genos*, the members of which were known as *gennetai*, was a group of families who identified themselves through the use of a collective plural name. The names of Athenian *gene* (pl.) were largely patronymic in form, implying collective descent from a fictive or real ancestor, but could also be geographical or occupational in origin. Although debate exists as to the roles of the *gene*, many of them seem to have 'possessed' ancestral priesthoods or other cultic responsibilities, and Humphreys argues that "the crystallization of small lineages into named, corporate gene seems to be associated essentially with hereditary rights to office."[17] In similar fashion, the *orgeones* were members of a cultic society that observed rites for particular heroes or gods. A group of *orgeones* maintained a sacred precinct for the god or hero to whom they were devoted, and the evidence suggests that they had officers, funds, and periodic meetings at which they held religious observances such as sacrifices and feasts, but also tended to other, more mundane, matters such as the enrollment of new members or the passage of decrees related to their activities. It has been hypothesized that the law preserved by Philochoros relating to these groups has its origins in the role that such groups played in the determination of Athenian citizenship status during the sixth century,

---

[16] See Lambert 1993, 46–48. Ismard 2018, 155 dates the law to the "Kleisthenic period." Humphreys 2018, 26 argues that it is early sixth century.

[17] Humphreys 2018, 633. The debate over the roles of Attic *gene* stems partially from the fact that, by the late fourth century (the period from which we have the most evidence), the word *genos* had acquired a technical meaning, denoting a corporate group which held certain rights to priestly offices; this terminology did not necessarily pertain in earlier periods, even though named descent groups certainly played a role in Athenian socio-religious contexts.

before the Kleisthenic reforms standardized acceptance by the demes as the gateway to legal citizenship.[18]

The orators demonstrate that membership in a *genos* or a group of *orgeones* could be used as evidence that the individual in question possessed the requisite qualifications of descent (Demosthenes 57.23–25; Isaios 2.14–17, 7.13–17). Membership in a phratry was also used in this way in cases where the citizenship or right of inheritance of an individual was called into question. Because of the role of the phratries as gatekeepers on questions relating to legitimacy, descent, and membership in the religious and social communities that the phratries represented, they also came to be of great significance in determining who was eligible for citizenship; phratry membership could be used as de facto proof of an individual's right to the franchise. Thus, despite the religious and social nature of phratry membership, existing as it did outside and before the Kleisthenic democratic system, it nonetheless had great importance in the civic and political realms as well.

A similar elision of the boundaries between spheres of influence in Athenian society and practice can be found in the organizations known as the *hetaireiai*. The *hetaireiai* in Athens were associations that combined social functions with the advancement of political careers and agendas. The members of a *hetaireia*, typically young, upper-class males, would strive to further the political and legal ambitions of their members by providing mutual assistance in the lawcourts and in marshaling votes at elections. *Hetaireiai* played significant roles in some of the most pivotal events of late fifth-century Athens: Plutarch informs us that Alkibiades and Nikias persuaded their supporters to vote against Hyperbolos instead of one another in the last ostracism apparently performed in Athens (Plutarch, *Nikias* 11, *Alkibiades* 13, *Aristides* 7). Similarly, the Mutilation of the Herms in 415 was linked to a *hetaireia* that involved the orator Andokides (Andokides, *On the Mysteries* 37–69), while the underground political machinations that preceded the two brief periods of oligarchy in Athens at the end of the fifth century were conducted in part among the *hetaireiai* (Thucydides 8.48.3–4, 65.2, 92.4; Xenophon, *Hellenika* 2.3.46; Lysias 12.43–45). The potentially political ramifications of these social organizations were recognized by the Athenian state when, in the revision of the law code in the early fourth century, provisions were inserted to protect the

[18] Ismard 2018, 155–159.

polis from the actions of *hetaireiai* which were intended to subvert the democracy.

Economic and social status also played a role in determinations of the social structure in Athens, and was linked with the political structure of the *polis* as well. Although de iure every adult male citizen in full possession of his citizen rights in Athens could participate equally in the operations of the democratic government,[19] de facto the ability of many Athenians to participate rested at least in part on their economic status. A significant number of Athenian citizens on the poorer end of the spectrum would have experienced barriers to political participation. Taylor notes that "being a representative on the *boule,* for example, presumably required near per-manent residence in the city for a year if the office was to be seriously performed (although see Demosthenes 22.35–37 or the *Constitution of the Athenians* 30.6 for hints that this was not always the case)."[20] Citizens from rural Attika, who could not afford the time away from their means of living, would necessarily have had fewer opportunities to participate in the centralized apparatuses of the Athenian democracy, although they could have engaged in local political activities upon occasion. One thing which seems to be lacking in Classical Athens is the notion of a hereditary 'aristocracy' of the sort experienced in Europe of the Medieval and Post-Medieval periods. Although kinship relationships and the support of other powerful individuals did contribute to political or social success in Athens, these factors did not remain stable over time. Hereditary membership in a *genos,* for example, might entitle one to control over or participation in certain religious cults, but this did not necessarily correlate with material wealth or political influence. Moreover, this picture is complicated by the social aspects of status and demographic change over time. Inherited wealth (in the form of land) and status did not guarantee social or political success; the performative aspects of Athenian society, where much depended upon oratorical or military prowess, allowed for a certain degree of social mobility into or out of the upper ranks of Athenian social and political strata which were not protected by hereditary considerations.[21]

---

[19] That is, not having experienced *atimia*, a form of disenfranchisement that deprived him of the ability to carry out the functions of a citizen; this penalty could be imposed temporarily or in perpetuity in response to various crimes or for failing to pay a debt to the *polis.*

[20] Taylor 2007, 86.

[21] Duplouy 2015, 61. Kennedy 2014, 19 notes that the passage of two laws after 403 BC to undo the exceptions that had been made during the Peloponnesian War to Perikles' Citizenship Law indicates that "citizenship and inheritance did not necessarily go hand in hand."

Women

Gender also played an obvious role in the rights, obligations, and privileges accorded to individuals in ancient Athens, whether they were citizens or metics, enslaved, or free. There has been much debate over the status of women in Athenian society, particularly as it pertains to legal rights and obligations. It is clear, despite Loraux's famous claim to the contrary, that Athenian women were considered citizens; however, they experienced serious limitations in the political and legal sphere which so often dominates consideration of ancient citizenship.[22] Athenian women could not participate in the political sphere, they were excluded from the courts, they could not serve in the military, and there were limitations on the size of economic transactions that they could participate in without male supervision, although it seems that this last prohibition was not always enforced. The ideology of female seclusion, so prominent in our ancient sources (Lysias 3.6; Thucydides 2.45.2), should be seen as more of a social ideal than a practical rule; in practice, only the wealthy could have followed it to any extent, and women of lower socio-economic strata would have regularly engaged in activities outside the home, although doing so could open them up to attacks on their status, as seen in Demosthenes' *Against Euboulides*. The religious sphere was one in which women freely operated; there were numerous responsibilities and rituals in which women were not only prominent but indispensable, such as the twenty-nine Athenian women and girls participating in the Panathenaic procession on the east frieze of the Parthenon.

Metics

The position of metics and slaves in the social structure of Athens is both at once simpler to define and also more difficult to elucidate in all the shades and gradations of status that could pertain. In its broadest sense, the term *metoikoi* referred to two relatively distinct bodies of individuals: freeborn foreigners who were official residents of Attika, and former chattel slaves who were no longer obligated to their prior owners. While both groups had some of the same rights and obligations under Athenian law, it is clear that freeborn foreigners were considered a more privileged group than freed

---

[22] Loraux 1993, 8; Blok 2017, *passim.*

slaves.[23] The official legal status of the metic seems to date back to the 460s BC, and required foreigners who had been resident in Athens for longer than a specified time to pay a specific tax known as the *metoikion*, which was set at 12 drachmas per year for men and 6 drachmas for women. In the fourth century, metics were also required to register themselves and their families with the polemarch, who heard legal disputes involving metics and who was responsible for keeping the official records of metics in Attika.[24]

Like citizens, metics were obligated to obey the laws of the city and to serve in the military if called, but unlike citizens they possessed no political rights. They were required to have a citizen *prostates*, or patron, to assist them in their dealings with the legal system of Athens, but cases involving metics were subject to different procedures and held in different courts than those solely involving citizens. Marriage between citizens and metics was permitted during the fifth century, even though Perikles' Citizenship Law would necessarily discourage the practice, but in the fourth century such marriages were outlawed entirely.[25] Demosthenes (57.48) tells us that metics could not hold religious office in Athens, nor could they participate in any cults whose operations fell under the domain of associations only open to citizens, such as those cults operated by the *gene* of Athens. However, the evidence indicates that metics were allowed limited religious participation in some observances; *IG I*[3] 244C.4–10 indicates some ceremonies in the deme of Skambonidai in which metics could participate, while both male and female metics had defined roles in the procession of the Panathenaia. Metics also could not own land in Attika, although they had the right to freely dispose of any movable goods and property which they possessed.

Metics who were thought to have provided some tangible benefits for the Athenian *polis* could be rewarded with various privileges. Prominent among these were the rights of *enktesis* and *isoteleia*. *Enktesis* allowed the recipient to own landed property in Attika, while *isoteleia* conferred the right of equal taxation with citizens – specifically, exemption from the *metoikion* and any other taxes to which metics were subject.

---

[23] Kamen 2013, 44–46; that freed slaves were distinguished from freeborn foreigners is also implied by the passage from the Old Oligarch above, since he lists slaves, metics, and freedmen individually.

[24] Kamen 2013, 43–61; Kennedy 2014, 12. Kamen further notes that wealthy metics might also be liable for the *eisphora*, a property tax extracted from wealthy citizens and non citizens alike, and were subject to liturgical obligations (2013, 53).

[25] Kamen 2013, 49–50; Kennedy 2014, 12–20.

Slaves

Chattel slaves were at the bottom of the Athenian social structure, although there was a spectrum of privilege even among the unfree. Although Greeks who found themselves on the losing side of a war could be enslaved by other Greeks, in practice the evidence indicates that most of the slaves in Athens were of foreign origin. Very early in Greek history, slavery began to play an important role in economic development, so it should not be surprising that the number of slaves in Athens was quite high, comprising probably between 15–35 percent of the total population of Attika.[26] (See also Lewis, Chapter 15 in this volume.) Slaves in Athens were not only stripped of nearly all legal or political rights, but were also deprived of *time* (honor), thus rendering them devoid of any social status as well.[27] This is notable in the extensive rights of physical abuse that owners possessed over their slaves; some sources suggest this even extended to killing slaves (Antiphon 6.4), but even if this is not true it is clear that physical and sexual violence toward the enslaved was considered ideologically unproblematic (Lysias 1.12, 18–22). Slaves were considered fully alienable property under Athenian law, and slave ownership could be passed to one's heirs; and generally the law was skewed in favor of the rights of Athenian slave owners.

Conclusions

While Athenian social structure had many similarities with institutions and associations in other Greek *poleis*, there were also many ways in which Athens could be considered atypical. First, the unusually large size of the Athenian *polis* would necessarily have impacted how Athenian society functioned. Second, the democratic ethos and political system of Classical Athens influenced the roles and operations of the religious, social, and descent groups that comprised Athenian society. The integration of these different spheres combined to create a sociopolitical system that was, at once, recognizably Greek, and yet at the same time wholly Athenian.

---

[26] Kamen 2013, 9.

[27] On the legal status of slaves in Athens, see Lewis 2015, 6–8. Kamen 2013, 8–31 discusses the different status aspects of slavery in Athens.

Further Reading

The available literature on the population and social structure of Athens is vast and continues to multiply; for that reason, what follows is necessarily selective. For questions of population, a good place to begin is Akrigg 2019, as he references much of the earlier literature on both sides of the population debate. Much of the work on Athenian society has been focused on various groups and statuses. For the phratries, the standard work is still Lambert 1993, but see also Humphreys 2018. For a general examination of status categories in Athens, see Kamen 2013. On questions of gender and citizenship, see Blok 2017. For wealth and poverty, see Taylor 2017, and Kierstead and Klapaukh 2018. On associations in Athens and their connections with citizenship, see Jones 1999, Ismard 2010 and 2018, and Humphreys 2018. On questions of kinship relations, see Humphreys 2018. On metics, the standard work is still Whitehead 1977; for metic women, Kennedy 2014. For slavery, see Vlassopoulos 2009, Lewis and Canevaro 2014, and Lewis 2018.

Bibliography

Akrigg, B. 2019. *Population and Economy in Classical Athens*. Cambridge.

Blok, J. 2017. *Citizenship in Classical Athens*. Cambridge.

Coale, A.J., and P. Demeny. 1966. *Regional Model Life Tables and Stable Populations*. Princeton.

Duplouy, A. 2015. "Genealogical and Dynastic Behaviour in Archaic and Classical Greece: Two Gentilician Strategies." In *Aristocracy in Antiquity: Redefining Greek and Roman Elites*, eds. N. Fisher and H. van Wees, Swansea, 59–84.

Hansen, M.H. 1985. *Demography and Democracy: The Number of Athenian Citizens in the Fourth Century* BC. Herning.

    2011. "How to Convert an Army Figure into a Population Figure." *Greek, Roman, and Byzantine Studies* 51: 239–253.

Humphreys, S.C. 2018. *Kinship in Classical Athens*. Oxford.

Ismard, P. 2010. *La cité des réseaux: Athènes et ses associations, VIe–Ier siècle av. J.-C.* Paris.

    2018. "Associations and Citizenship in Attika from Solon to Kleisthenes." In *Defining Citizenship in Archaic Greece*, eds. A. Duplouy and R. Brock, Oxford, 145–159.

Jones, N.F. 1999. *The Associations of Classical Athens: The Response to Democracy*. Oxford.

Kamen, D. 2013. *Status in Classical Athens*. Princeton.

Kennedy, R.F. 2014. *Immigrant Women in Athens: Gender, Ethnicity, and Citizenship in the Classical City*. New York.

Kierstead, J.C., and R. Klapaukh. 2018. "The Distribution of Wealthy Athenians in the Attic Demes." In *Ancient Greek History and Contemporary Social*

Science, eds. M. Canevaro, A. Erskine, B. Gray, and J. Ober, Edinburgh, 376–401.

Lambert, S.D. 1993. *The Phratries of Attika*. 2nd edn. Ann Arbor.

1997. "The Attic Genos Salaminioi and the Island of Salamis." *ZPE* 119: 85–106.

Lewis, D.M. 2015. "Slavery and Manumission." In *The Oxford Handbook of Ancient Greek Law*, eds. E. Harris and M. Canevaro, Oxford.

2018. *Greek Slave Systems in their Eastern Mediterranean Context, c. 800–146 BC*. Oxford.

Lewis, D.M and Canevaro, M. 2014. "Khoris Oikountes and the Obligations of Freedmen in late Classical and early Hellenistic Athens." *Incidenza dell'antico* 12: 91–121.

Loraux, N. 1993. *The Children of Athena: Athenian Ideas about Citizenship and the Division between the Sexes*. Princeton.

Moreno, A. 2007. *Feeding the Democracy: The Athenian Grain Trade in the Fifth and Fourth Centuries BC*. Oxford.

Osborne, R. 1985. *Demos: The Discovery of Classical Attika*. Cambridge.

Taylor, C. 2007. "A New Political World." In *Debating the Athenian Cultural Revolution: Art, Literature, Philosophy, and Politics 430–380 BC*, ed. R. Osborne, Cambridge, 72–90.

2017. *Poverty, Wealth, and Well-Being: Experiencing Penia in Democratic Athens*. Oxford.

Taylor, M. 1997. *Salamis and the Salaminioi: The History of an Unofficial Athenian Demos*. Leiden.

Vlassopoulos, K. 2009. "Slavery, Freedom, and Citizenship in Classical Athens: Beyond a Legalistic Approach." In *Slavery, Citizenship, and the State in Classical Antiquity*, eds. K. Vlassopoulos and D. Geary. *European Review of History* 16:3: 347–364.

Whitehead, D. 1977. *The Ideology of the Athenian Metic*. Cambridge.

12 | The Athenian Family

CYNTHIA B. PATTERSON

The family was the basis of the Athenian *polis*, both structurally and conceptually. Athenians entered into and participated in the life of the city as members of Athenian families. For example, candidates for the office of archon were asked, "Who is your father, and of what deme? Who is your father's father? Who is your mother? Who is your mother's father, and of what deme?" and also whether they had family tombs, paid their taxes, and treated their parents well (*Constitution of the Athenians* 55). In addition to this structural connection (i.e. the family as a 'building block'), the *polis* imagined itself as a kind of family. This strong metaphor underlies the Athenian myth of autochthony, in which all Athenians were siblings born from their common 'mother earth.' It also expresses the legal privilege of membership in the *polis* (or 'citizenship') as "having a share," the same term that is used of the inheritance of family property. The prominence of family language and ideology in Athenian public discourse makes the project of locating the historical Athenian family challenging, but also particularly rewarding, given the variety and richness of the surviving sources. Perspectives provided by three different sources – marriage and inheritance law, tragic drama, and funerary monuments – can together work to 'triangulate' the Athenian family and give us a picture that has depth and complexity even if 'reality' is still elusive. And, as will be seen, although family membership was the basis of citizenship in Athens, the families of ancient Athens were not exclusively Athenian.

First, however, a brief word about terminology. In this chapter, the term family refers to the functioning household (*oikos*) and also its supportive kin structure, which, following the Athenian definition of "closeness of birth" (*anchisteia tou genou*), extended to children of cousins of the head of a household. Thus, I draw on two distinct but complementary senses of family: the first (*oikos* or *oikia*) denoting the house itself, as well as those who live together inside and manage the house and everything connected with it (i.e. the household); and the second (*genos*) denoting the bilateral lines of connection that created a kinship web unique to each Athenian household. This kinship web should be distinguished, however, from the *fictive* kin groups, called *gene* (plural of *genos*) and phratries (brotherhoods), who as managers or officiants of religious cult or traditions could play key roles in Athenian society. (See Kellogg, Chapter 11 in this volume.) Such use of the language of kinship, confusing to the modern eye, is further evidence of the conceptual centrality of the family in Athenian political society.

Family Law

Family law was a key part of Athenian law from its earliest formation. The laws of the semi-mythical lawgiver Drako, whose fierceness was legendary (thus our 'draconian'), are lost except for sections of the law on homicide that were reinscribed in the late fifth century. Of particular relevance here is that law's articulation of the role of the family members "to the degree of sons of cousins" (i.e. coinciding with the relationship later called *anchisteia tou genou*) in both the prosecution and the pardon of acts of homicide (*IG* 1³ 104.15, 22), providing the earliest evidence for what we might call the legal definition of the Athenian family in the sense of kin.

The Athenian family comes more fully into view, however, with the emergence – traditionally a generation later – of Drako's historical successor Solon, a statesman and poet who took the helm of the Athenian *polis* at a time of economic and social strife in which "the many were enslaved to the few" (*Constitution of the Athenians* 5.1). To this dire situation, Solon responded with a code of laws through which, most importantly, he established the freedom of the Athenian land and her "children." In his own words:

> I took up the markers fixed in many places – previously she [the land] was enslaved, but now is free. Many I brought back to Athens ... Those at home, suffering the outrages of slavery and trembling at the whim of their master, I freed. This I achieved by the might of law, combining force, and justice. (*Constitution of the Athenians* 12.4)

Solon's law code restored the households of Attika; his laws acted to secure the integrity of families and the ability of households to maintain and transmit their property within Attika. Although Solon's law code itself does not survive today, it was known in antiquity, as were his verses. The Aristotelian author of the *Constitutions of the Athenians* draws on both, with a predictable interest in political principles of the public institutions of assembly and lawcourts. Plutarch, on the other hand, writing in the early second century AD but having at hand sources now lost, offers in his *Life of*

Solon a wider range of details about Solon's social, religious, and family law that complement the Aristotelian view and establish the enduring importance of Solon's legislation for the stability and integrity of Athenian families. A third source for Solonian family law is the fourth-century speeches from the Athenian courts, particularly in cases involving inheritance and property. It should be noted that the Athenians had the habit of attributing all of their laws to Solon; thus, in speaking of Solonian family law we speak of what is properly called a Solonian legacy.

Solon's legislation established the protection of the person and freedom of the *oikos* as interlocking privileges of Athenian citizenship – of "having a share in the polis of Athens." The connection between public and private welfare is clear in one of Solon's more vivid poetic images:

> The public Ruin invades the house of each citizen, and the courtyard doors no longer have strength to keep it away, but it overleaps the lofty wall, and though a man runs in and tries to hide in chamber or closet, it ferrets him out. (Fr. 4)

Debt and enslavement were not the only threats to the integrity of the *oikos* addressed by Solon. Another was the danger of a man dying childless and heirless, leaving the property to be carved up by others. The prevention of an 'empty *oikos*' is the focus of a number of laws associated with Solon.

According to Plutarch (*Solon* 21.2), Solon gave every male citizen the right to make a will, *if* he had no legitimate children. The rule prior to Solon, says Plutarch, was that in such a circumstance the property would be split up among the kin (*genos*), but Solon now "made every man's estate truly his own." If, however, such a man made no will, Athenian law (perhaps Solonian) created or adapted a sequence of inheritance that moved bilaterally, with preference for the male in each degree, to the limit of children of cousins. But what if a man had only a daughter (or daughters) who was unmarried on his death? A number of fourth-century Athenian orations, written for the litigation of inheritance disputes, suggest that in this situation the law required that the heiress, termed an *epikleros* or one who "is upon the property," should be married to her closest male relative, following the same web of bilateral kin identified by *anchisteia tou genou.*[1]

---

[1] The rule is generally taken to be Solonian. Aristotle for his part suggested that Solon might have intentionally made the rules vague so as to give more authority to the lawcourts that interpreted them; later, Plato undertook to clarify them.

The interest of the *polis* in the marriage of the heiress drew Plato's attention as he outlined the inheritance law of his new city of the *Laws*. The "second best" city of the *Laws* will have a fixed number of households (5,040, to be precise). If it happened that a man died with only an unmarried daughter or daughters, Plato rules that the interest and security of the estate must be privileged and the daughter(s) married to those closest in kinship (proceeding bilaterally, as in the Athenian *anchisteia tou genou*) who do not already possess one of the *polis'* fixed number of estates. But then he adds a comment "from the lawgiver" to the deceased father, asking for his forgiveness "if he [the lawgiver] arranges [the marriage] with an eye on only two considerations: close kinship [*anchisteia*] and the security of the estate." Further considerations that ordinarily a father would have taken into account, namely "to select from among the entire citizen body someone whose character and habits qualify him to be his own son and his daughter's husband" – these considerations "will have to be passed over" (*Laws* 11.924c–d). Although these words do not by any stretch of the imagination suggest a recognition that the daughter herself might have preferences, the concerns of Plato's imaginary father about his daughter's marriage can nonetheless remind us that the legal 'persona' of the family may present a partial and so misleading view of the motivations, not to mention emotions, of family members.

Plutarch's account of Solon's legislation on the heiress and her marriage offers further details. The husband of an heiress (*epikleros*), we are told, should have intercourse with her at least three times a month; and, if he proves impotent, she should be allowed to marry his nearest kinsman (*Solon* 20.3). Plutarch, who apparently found this legislation intriguing, also notes Solon's directive that the bride and groom should be shut in the bridal chamber and eat a quince together – and concludes not unreasonably that Solon's goal was that the *oikos* not be left without legitimate children and heirs.

Marriage is thus assumed as a key institution in Solon's family law, but is not itself defined. Legislation focuses on the questions of how and to whom the heiress should be married, not the marriage process itself.[2] Another Solonian rule emphasizing the centrality of marriage for the integrity of the family is his apparent exclusion of the illegitimate child (specifically the *nothos/e*) from inheriting from his (or her) father. In *Birds* (lines 1661–1666), Aristophanes 'quotes' for comic effect a Solonian law to

---

[2] This remains true of later Athenian law; see Patterson 1998.

demonstrate to Herakles that as a child of a god and a mortal he is a *nothos* and will not inherit. (Poor Herakles, more brawny than brainy, is taken by surprise by this legalistic gambit.) Solon also, according to Plutarch (*Solon* 22.4), freed the *nothos* from the obligations of supporting his parents, so not only separating the bastard child from his parents, but also discouraging the male parent from taking on extramarital relationships.

Although there is no evidence that Solon legislated on citizenship per se, Plutarch attributes to him (and finds puzzling) a law stating that citizenship *cannot* be given *except* to those who come as exiles to Athens, *with a household* and to practice a craft (Plutarch, *Solon* 24.4). Although there does not seem to be any known example of an immigrant family entering the citizen body in this way, the rule is notable in its language. The evidence for the openness of Athenian society needs more attention, given the usual emphasis on its exclusivity. The family of families that was the Athenian *polis* was on occasion, like the individual family, willing to 'adopt' new members.

In the mid-fifth century, the Athenians voted, on the proposal of Perikles, that anyone who "was not born from two citizens (*astoi*) should not have a share in the polis" (*Constitution of the Athenians* 26.4). The motivation and consequences of this law, generally known as Perikles' Citizenship Law, continue to be debated. First, the negative phrasing is important and should remind us that the law provides not a definition of "having a share" in the *polis*, but simply a necessary condition for being a shareholder, namely two Athenian parents. Did the Athenian parents have to be married? In my view, this is a question that misses the point of the law which, using the language of inheritance ("having a share"), requires that heirs of the "family" (that is the Athenian *polis*) must have two Athenian parents. We can equate "have a share in the *polis*" with "be a citizen," but doing so risks missing the power of the metaphor that underlies the law as proposed by Perikles. Emphasizing the family language of the law also suggests strongly that just as legitimacy was required for family inheritance so it is required for *polis* inheritance or citizenship. Making this metaphor a part of *polis* law is, in my view, the most significant feature of Perikles' law. The fact that Plutarch (*Perikles* 37.2) referred to the law as "about *nothoi* (bastards)" is a further indication of the strength of the *polis* as family metaphor: the child of "mixed parentage" is now in the position of the *nothos/e* (i.e. he/she is excluded from both inheritance and privileges of "family" membership). If we want to call Perikles' law a citizenship law, then we need to recognize that citizenship, like family participation, is gendered but still inclusive of both male and female members – an important corollary of the Athenian metaphor of the *polis* as a "family of families."

The metaphor may also help us understand the way in which the Athenian family writ large could accept new members. Just as adoption was a regular inheritance strategy among Athenian families without heirs or without sons (in which case an adopted son could marry a daughter and so prevent the crisis of an unmarried heiress), so the city could create a new citizen/sibling when the need or opportunity arose. Both the adopted child and the 'adopted' citizen were *poietoi* – created rather than born into their place in family or state. Athenian inheritance cases are replete with the complicating claims of adopted heirs, who, it should be noted, are generally adopted as adults. Athenian adoption is not a system with the primary goal of caring for the parentless child or fulfilling the childless couple's desire for a child. It is, rather, a support for the inheritance structure of the *oikos* and so the *polis*.

Athenians then employed the idea and language of adoption when they brought non-Athenians as 'siblings' into the *polis*, both as groups (e.g. the Plataians in 427 or the Samians in 405, both rewarded for their loyalty to Athens) or individuals (e.g. the banker and ex-slave Pasion, rewarded for his generosity to the city). The story of Pasion and his family is often taken as an 'exception that proves the rule' of Athenian exclusivity. But perhaps we need to look more carefully at the evidence. When Pasion's son, Apollodoros, prosecuted the ex-slave and ex-prostitute Neaira on the charge of illegitimately acting as citizen, he says emphatically to the jury that Neaira was "neither born an *aste* nor made a *politis*" ([Demosthenes], *Against Neaira* 107). It may be that the *making* of *politai* (and *politides*) was a more common occurrence than generally thought, even if not one that we hear much about.

One specific area of family responsibility was the burial and commemoration of the dead, in which the participation of female members of the family was particularly important. Plutarch attributes to Solon a law forbidding the laceration of flesh at funerals, which would seem to be aimed at women (*Solon* 21.4). But more significant evidence comes from a law quoted by Demosthenes (*Against Makartatos* 62) and attributed to Solon:

> The deceased shall be laid out in the house in any way one chooses, and they shall carry out the deceased on the day after that on which they lay him out, before the sunrise. And the men shall walk in front when they carry him out and the women behind. And no woman less than sixty years of age shall be permitted to enter the chamber of the deceased, or to

follow the deceased when he is carried to the tomb *except those who are within the degree of children of cousins* [my emphasis].

The language of the law needs to be read carefully for what it says and does not say. The law does not exclude women from involvement in the burial of members of their family; rather, using the same network of close kin that we have seen earlier, it affirms the right to participate for all women within this network of kin relations, and seems to allow non-related women over the age of sixty to participate as well. Perhaps the latter are imagined to be experienced mourners whose presence adds solemnity to the ritual—and whose age makes their public appearance less of a concern. Indeed, the burial responsibilities of female members of the family drew women into the public realm, despite real or imagined concerns about the dangers of public exposure.[3] An Athenian painted black-figure *pinax* (plaque) from the sixth century BC shows the *prothesis* (setting out) of a dead family member, with each member of the attending family duly labeled and noted, such as the mother (*meter*) holding the head of her deceased son (Web Fig. 12.1).[4]

The Athenian *polis* also took on responsibility for burial of its citizens, most prominently those who died in battle. Sometime in the early fifth century the Athenians took the step of bringing their war dead home to Athens – instead of burying them on the battlefield – in order to celebrate their common public burial. The public ritual is best known through the description provided by Thucydides in Book 2 of his narrative of the "great war" of Athens with the Peloponnesians and has sometimes been viewed, in the context of family/city relations, as having the effect of stripping the family (and particularly women) of their traditional responsibility for the mourning and burial of dead kin. But a more careful reading of the evidence suggests a less adversarial relationship of *polis* and family. By instituting the public funeral, the Athenians guaranteed that the dead would be honored and buried at Athens, in the presence of their kin; during the three-day celebration, the public funeral provided a significant role to family members in the mourning of the dead.[5] In addition, families were free to set up their own memorials, even if the ashes of the dead family member were interred in the public tomb, or the so-called Demosion Sema

---

[3] Cf. Perikles' advice to widows that their "greatest glory" was not to be talked about by men in either praise or blame (Thucydides 2.45).

[4] Paris, Louvre MNB 905; BAPD no. 463.

[5] Thucydides 2.34 specifically mentions the presence of female kin, cf. also his advice to widows noted earlier (above n. 3) at 2.45.

(Thucydides 2.34). The spheres of family and state were fundamentally intertwined in Athens; the dangers of antagonism between them were thus especially acute and are often explored at the Theater of Dionysos – nowhere more starkly than in Sophokles' dramas focusing on the family of Oedipus.

Drama

Sophokles turned and returned to the story of the family of Oedipus throughout his long career spanning the second half of the fifth century BC. Three of his surviving plays present different moments in this disaster-filled family history: first in *Antigone*, produced in 441 BC; then again in *Oedipus Tyrannos*, probably produced ca. 429 BC, and finally in *Oedipus at Kolonos*, produced posthumously and bringing Oedipus to his final rest at Kolonos, the poet's home deme. What can a story of a mythical family, whose acts of incest, patricide, fratricide, and suicide so clearly violated all the norms of family behavior, tell us about real Athenian families? It is not an easy question, and some might be tempted to bracket the evidence of Athenian tragedy as 'not historically relevant' and move on to more transparent and direct sorts of evidence. But this would be to miss the power of the voices of members of the families of drama as they try to make sense of the horrific events myth has set for them. The words of Oedipus, Antigone, and their family surely touched deeply held values of the Athenian audience. The violations of family norms and the consequences that are portrayed in the drama illuminate in dark relief the principles of family structure and responsibility put forth in Athenian law. In this regard, Aristotle's somewhat obscure comment in the *Poetics* that in tragic plots "things probable though impossible should be preferred to the possible but implausible" (1460a26–27) may offer some guidance, if we put together his comments to suggest that the mythic plot of Sophokles' Theban plays may be 'impossible.' The response and emotions, however, of the characters surely make the story plausible.

If we can allow Plato's *Laws* to illuminate relevant Athenian law (written and unwritten), we can see with particular clarity the cultural enormity of Oedipus' crimes – incest and parricide. In Book 8 of the *Laws*, Plato's "Athenian" expresses a wish that the citizens of his new city-state would have the same attitude toward the sorts of sexual behavior he finds objectionable – essentially same-sex and adulterous relations – as they have toward acts of incest, which require no written law because for "most people" these acts "are absolutely unholy, an abomination in the sight of the gods" (838b).[6] Similarly, Plato considered the "deliberate and wholly wicked" murder of close relatives "most detestable in the sight of heaven" (872d), and people must believe that Justice herself stands on guard against such acts. Nonetheless, the Athenian does offer a specific statute punishing those who kill deliberately, and with premeditation, their parents, siblings, or children. Such a one should be executed and his body be thrown out "where the three roads meet outside of the city" (873b).[7] However, it should be noted that when considering homicide committed either "in anger without premeditation" or "in anger with premeditation," the law, as proposed by Plato's Athenian, requires not execution but that the killer be purified and go into exile for three years, and never again share in religious festivals or common meals with remaining members of his (or her) family.[8]

In the logic of myth, however, parricide is simple and not qualified by issues of intent or emotional condition; similarly, the incest between mother and child cannot be mitigated by considerations of 'who knew what when.' After discovering, through his own determined investigation, that he is himself the murderer he sought and the husband of his own mother, Oedipus can only judge himself cursed: "cursed in my birth, cursed in marriage, cursed in the lives I cut down with these hands!" (1184–1185). And later, after discovering his mother/wife's suicide, and blinding himself with her golden dress pins, he speaks even more strongly if that is possible, saying that he is "a great murderous ruin" (1331–1332) and "loathed by the gods" (1345–1346). He is a pariah who should be expelled, killed, "cast into the sea" (1411–1412).

Yet, when the self-blinded Oedipus engages with his young daughters (Antigone and Ismene), whom their uncle Kreon brings out to see him because he knows "the joy they gave [their father]" (1476), Sophokles allows Oedipus to speak as a father. He first insists that he did not knowingly become both their father and brother, and then laments the hurt and suffering that they would experience; he asks, "Where are the public gatherings you can join?" (1489), and then "Who will marry you?"

[6] In the *Republic,* when considering the possibility that his system of child-rearing might make it possible for a biological brother and sister to unknowingly commit incest, Plato in an earlier point in his life allows that this might be allowed, "if the Pythia approves" (461e). His views apparently had hardened in old age, but still held to the point that some kinds of behavior were most properly the domain not of human, written law but of religious piety.
[7] Plato here moves to the masculine singular.
[8] Plato here amplifies a distinction made in Drako's homicide, between "willing" and "unwilling" acts of homicide, which he applies even to acts committed against close kin.

to which he answers "Not a man on earth. Your doom is clear: you'll wither away to nothing, single, without a child" (1502). These are paternal emotions that the audience would have had no trouble recognizing. Even more remarkable are Oedipus' comments on his own exposure as an infant. First, when he is interrogating the shepherd, Oedipus expresses surprise that Jocasta would have ordered her own child to be killed: "Her own child, how could she?" (1175). Later, when speaking to Kreon before his daughters are brought to him, Oedipus asks to be sent to die on Kithaeron, the very place, he says, where his own mother and father would have had him die (1452–1453). I suggest that, in these comments, Sophokles' Oedipus speaks outside of the mythic domain and directly to the act of infant exposure and infanticide as it occurred in his own fifth-century world, drawing attention to the potential emotional cost of such an act, whatever might be its motivation.[9]

The end of *Oedipus Tyrannos* leaves Oedipus' fate uncertain. His attempt to hold on to his daughters is dismissed with Kreon's "your power ends here" (1523). *Antigone*, written roughly a decade before, but in narrative sequence the last of the three plays, takes up the story just after the double homicide of Oedipus' sons (and brothers), Eteokles and Polyneikes, and the assumption of rule by Kreon, who is at once their maternal uncle and half-brother, and Oedipus' maternal uncle and brother-in-law. Oedipus himself is dead, and Antigone and Ismene have reached the marriageable age, from the perspective of the Athenian audience – probably their mid-teens. They are also, from the Athenian tradition, heiresses as the sole surviving members of the family of Laius. Ironically, as the nearest surviving male relative (specifically their maternal uncle), Kreon is responsible for their marriages. The metaphor of family and *polis* is thus collapsed onto a single figure of authority who rules as *strategos* (general) and subordinates all interests to the security of the *polis*. For Kreon, there is only one loyalty. Thus Polyneikes, who died attacking his native city with Argive allies, must be left unburied, while Eteokles, who fought on behalf of Thebes, is given a hero's burial. Antigone, however, refuses to accept Kreon's single-minded focus on the *polis*. As the play unfolds, Antigone's actions reveal her determination to uphold the values of the family in the face of Kreon's attempt, in her words, to treat as enemies "those whom we love most" (10). Her sister disagrees, but Ismene's reluctance makes Antigone's shouldering full responsibility as

---

[9] On infanticide see Liston, Rotroff, and Snyder 2018, 119–125.

the surviving heir of her family all the more striking. Against the starkness of the mythic tale in which they are caught, Sophokles' characters give voice to the emotions that bound Athenian families together and allow us a view of their experience that expands that provided by law or legal cases.

Grave Monuments

A third perspective for triangulating the Athenian family is provided by surviving grave monuments commemorating the dead. (See Shea, Chapter 10 in this volume.) In one sense, these monuments, set up by and for real family members who lived and died in Athens, offer our most direct evidence for the biographies of Athenian families. Yet, the monuments also follow conventions of style and form, both in sculpted reliefs and inscribed names or tributes, which can make them appear generic. Nonetheless, the choices a family made in setting up a particular monument in a particular place can often provide insight into Athenian family ideology and – at moments – experience.

The evidence for family tombs in Athens in the Archaic period (before ca. 500 BC) is limited. The most prominent form was a tumulus, which covered individual burials and could be marked with sculpted or painted reliefs. In addition, however, individual funerary *stelai*, often of sons or daughters who had died young, stood along the roadways entering the city and presented to the viewer the grief of the family (particularly the parent) left behind. In the Late Archaic-Early Classical era, there was a marked reduction in stone funerary monuments in Athens. Whatever the explanation for the change, the white-ground *lekythos* emerged as a primary vehicle for commemoration, with exquisitely painted scenes of family members, often with attending slaves, visiting the tombs of their deceased kin. Do the images of these quite substantial tombs represent what the family would like to imagine but cannot provide? Both the character and the location of the actual burial remain obscure, but there is a new emphasis on relationships of the household which anticipates the styles of later Classical monuments.

In the later fifth century, Athenians began again to set up funerary *stelai* notable for family scenes featuring the engagement of family members, often marked with a handshake that connects the living to the dead (although often it is difficult to be certain which is which). By the fourth century, scenes with multiple household members are common, including in many cases figures who can be identified as household slaves. When an

Fig. 12.1 Grave *stele* of Ampharete with her grandson, ca. 430–420 BC, Athens,
Kerameikos Museum P 695.
© Hans R. Goette

inscription survives on the stone, the relief can speak more clearly, as in the
grave *stele* of Ampharete and her grandson (Fig. 12.1).[10] That the child is
Ampharete's grandson would not be known without the *stele*'s inscription:
"I hold the son of my daughter, whom I used to hold on my knees when we
both saw the light of the sun: now, dead, I hold him, dead too." Here the
combination of a text with a monument provides emotional depth to the
scene and makes it particularly effective in relaying the experience and the
love of a maternal grandmother.

It is important to note that Athenian family tombs could be located on
private suburban or rural property as well as set up to face the public road.
However, given that family land might at some later date be sold, there
were consequences, for such family tombs might end up on another
family's land. An example of this situation appears in a speech by

---

[10] Athens, Kerameikos Museum P 695. See Clairmont 1993, no. 23.

Demosthenes (*Against Kallikles* 55), although we only hear one side of the dispute and it is possible that public land may be involved. Did descendants retain some right of access to tombs, either on private or public land? Also worth noting is the problem of identifying the process by which a family and, as we will see, even non-Athenians, could acquire or claim land for a family member's tomb outside their own deme holding.[11]

Finally, the most prominent and public of Athenian family tombs are the *peribolos* tomb enclosures, which in the late fifth and fourth centuries came to line the roadways of Athens. Some 250 such enclosures with their road-facing monuments have been found throughout Attika, along the roads entering unwalled deme communities as well as outside the gates of the Athenian city center. Considerable progress has been made on the publication and interpretation of these impressive tombs, with the result that they are now a primary source for understanding the self-presentation of the Classical Athenian family. The burials and memorials of the *peribolos* tombs create portraits of Athenian families that emphasize, on the one hand, continuity (although only rarely does a tomb continue more than three generations) and, on the other, flexibility in the creation of family identity and connections. In the well-known *peribolos* of Dexileos in the Kerameikos, for example, the initial monument was a cenotaph for the young Dexileos, a member of the Athenian cavalry who died in battle in 394 BC and was buried in a public tomb. Later, his family added more monuments and created the tomb enclosure now facing the road and including grave markers for his brother Lysias, his sister Melitta, with her husband Nausistratos, and then for Lysias' son Lysanios and his grandson Kalliphanes (Fig. 12.2). Such selective inclusion is also evidenced in other *periboloi*.

Nearby, the *peribolos* of Dexileos was another remarkable tomb enclosure known as the Tomb of the Messenians. It included eight grave markers of various sorts commemorating the Messenian Philoxenos, his two sons, Dion and Parthenios, two female relatives (one named Philoumene and one unnamed), and three females who are apparently slaves, Anna, Dorkas, and Sophrone. Here we can consider the possibility that slaves were buried in the tomb enclosures of their owners, a practice that should not be surprising given their role in the household and also a reported Athenian law that required a master to carry out the burial of his (or her) slaves (Demosthenes, *Against Makartatos* 57). In addition, the tomb enclosure of the Messenians contained around fifty-five unmarked burials dating from

---

[11] For examples and discussion of both issues see Zelnick-Abramovitz 2015.

Fig. 12.2 View of *peribolos* tomb of Dexileos, Kerameikos, fourth century BC. Note the direction of the two *stelai* facing toward the road, while the earlier cenotaph of Dexileos is set obliquely to take advantage of its corner position.
© Hans R. Goette

the mid-fourth through the first quarter of the third century BC. The prominent position of the Messenian tomb and the diverse character of those commemorated and buried in its confines present a useful challenge to common assumptions about the exclusivity of Athenian society and Athenian families. These themes can be followed out in other monuments; and when put together with texts both legal and literary, they help deepen our perception of the way in which the 'family of families' that was ancient Athens could yet recognize in death those who belonged to a more extended community that included foreigners and slaves – not in relationships of equality by any means, but with nonetheless a measure of humanity.

Thus, to draw together the three sections of this chapter, the Athenian family can be approached from the perspectives and genres of prescriptive law, dramatic theater, or funerary commemoration. None is without its own viewing angle, and none provides us with a simple true picture, but together they can take us some way toward an appreciation of the interests, challenges, and experience of families in ancient Athens.

Further Reading

The Greek (and especially Athenian) family continues to be the focus of a wide range of discussion. For the perspectives developed in this chapter, see especially Patterson 1998, Closterman 2006, and Cohen 2011. Humphreys 1980 remains an important and fundamental article for the topic.

Bibliography

Clairmont, C. 1993. *Classical Attic Tombstones.* Vols. 1–7. Kilchberg.

Closterman, W. 2006. "Family Members and Citizens: Athenian Identity and the Peribolos Tomb Setting." In *Antigone's Answer: Essays on Death and Burial, Family, and State in Ancient Athens*, ed. C. Patterson, Lubbock, 49–78.

Cohen, A. 2011. "Picturing Greek Families." In *A Companion to Families in the Greek and Roman Worlds*, ed. B. Rawson, Malden, MA, 465–487.

Humphreys. S.C. 1980. "Family Tombs and Tomb-Cult in Classical Athens." *JHS* 100: 96–126.

Liston, M.A., S.I. Rotroff, and L.M. Snyder. 2018. *The Agora Bone Well.* Princeton.

Patterson, C. 1998. *The Family in Greek History.* Cambridge, MA.

   ed. 2006. *Antigone's Answer: Essays on Death and Burial, Family, and State in Ancient Athens.* Lubbock.

Zelnick-Abramovitz, R. 2015. "Whose Grave Is This? The Status of Grave Plots in Ancient Greece." *Dike* 18: 51–98.

Additional resources to accompany this chapter can be found at: www.cambridge .org/NeilsRogers

13 | Death and Disease

MARIA A. LISTON

Athens offered a healthy environment in antiquity, with good water supplies, adequate food resources, and a generally mild climate. Yet, unchecked by effective prevention or treatment, bacteria, viruses, and parasites eventually affected most Athenians, either temporarily or permanently, over the course of their lifetimes. Urban crowding, constant air pollution from fires used for heating, cooking, and light, and garbage disposal practices that were convenient but not sanitary ensured that the ancient people of Athens suffered from an array of diseases and died of causes that are easily preventable today. Accidental injury and muscle strain would have been common when humans provided most of the power for household subsistence, manufacturing, and transportation. Large animals could be used for the most arduous tasks, but they brought an even higher risk of injuries to the humans around them.

Human burials have been found in excavations across Athens, and it is these skeletons that provide us with direct insight into the medical conditions of ancient Athenians. The excavations in the Athenian Agora and the Kerameikos have supplied the greatest number of skeletons, but newer excavations for the Athens Metro, the Akropolis Museum, and the Stavros Niarchos Foundation Cultural Center in Phaleron all contribute to our understanding of the lives, diseases, and deaths of ancient Athenians.

However, not every skeleton can provide personal information on diseases and causes of death. Soft tissue trauma can kill by damage to the internal organs or excessive bleeding, but will leave no mark on the bones. Most diseases that afflict humans are relatively short in duration; people either recover or die, with no record left on their bones. In particular, many acute viral and bacterial diseases, such as staph and strep infections, common colds, influenza, dysentery, and cholera, rarely leave evidence. The diseases common to children, such as measles, mumps, chicken pox, diphtheria, and polio, also either kill the child quickly, or they survive with little or no skeletal evidence of the affliction. Catastrophic epidemics, such as the great Plague of Athens in the fifth century BC or the waves of disease that mark the Justinianic Plague of the sixth century AD may leave evidence in the form of mass graves, but offer no direct clues on the skeletons.

Analyses of pathogen DNA are beginning to identify some of these diseases, but preservation of DNA is poor in the climate of Athens, and such studies are expensive and prone to contamination. Cemeteries are full of skeletons that appear to have no obvious signs of stress, but there are also many diseases and stresses that do leave marks on bone, and traumas often affect the skeleton in recognizable ways.

Disease and Death in Childhood

The most dangerous time for any child is birth. Throughout the history of ancient Athens, nearly half of infants would die, many of them in their first week. This high infant mortality rate was not unique to Athens, but was typical of all societies prior to the nineteenth century, and did not significantly decrease until the development of antibiotics and sanitary childbirth practices. Excavations in various parts of Athens have yielded vivid evidence of this sad reality for Athenians. In the Archaic cemetery at Phaleron, the first port of Athens, 30 percent of the burials were pots containing infant remains.[1] In the Kerameikos and Kotzia Square cemeteries, hundreds of infants and young children were found buried in ceramic containers.[2]

At times, both the infant and its mother would be lost, and wealth was no protection from the hazards of pregnancy and childbirth. Located at the edge of what was later the Athenian Agora, an Early Geometric grave, known as the Tomb of the Rich Athenian Lady, is one of the wealthiest graves ever excavated in Athens. It contained many ceramic vessels as well as jewelry made from gold, bronze, and glass – a very rare item at that early date. Close examination of the cremated remains showed that this was the burial of a woman, 30–35 years old when she died. But mingled with her bones were the tiny remains of a fetus, probably about 34–36 weeks into the pregnancy (Web Fig. 13.1). It is not clear if the woman died while giving birth, or was pregnant and died of other causes, but it is a reminder that even the richest Athenians were not safe from the dangers of pregnancy and birth.[3]

Even more graphic evidence comes from a well in the Agora excavated on the slopes of the Kolonos Agoraios, near the Temple of Hephaistos.

---

[1] See Prevedorou and Buikstra 2019.
[2] See Lagia 2007.
[3] Liston and Papadopoulos 2004.

Here, in 1937–1938, archaeologists discovered the remains of at least 457 infants, together with over 150 dog and puppy skeletons, deposited in the mid-second century BC. It took over seventy years for the science of juvenile osteology and pathology to develop to the point that these remains could be effectively studied.[4] It is now clear that many, if not most of the infants died of natural causes. Many had developed bacterial infections, possibly meningitis, probably caused by cutting or dressing the umbilical cord with unsanitary materials. Others had skeletal birth defects, including nine cleft palates (Web Fig. 13.2) and an infant with a deformed left arm. Analysis of their ages at death indicated that nearly all had died before they were eight days old, the age at which the first formal acknowledgment of a newborn Athenian took place, in a ceremony called the Amphidromia. Since most of these infants died before this age, it appears that they were disposed of in the well, possibly by the midwives who would have attended the birth, carried away the placentas, and cared for the mother in the postpartum period. When the infant died before the Amphidromia, it is likely that the same midwives were given the task of disposing of the bodies. A convenient, but hidden abandoned well on the hill outside of the Agora seems to have been used for this sad task.[5]

In some cases, a skeleton preserves indications of stress during childhood that persist into adult life. For example, stresses in a child's life can interrupt the formation of the teeth, leaving horizontal grooves called Linear Enamel Hypoplasias (LEH). In many children from the Athenian Agora excavations, there are multiple grooves in the teeth, indicating repeated stress throughout the growing years. The permanent adult teeth, which begin to develop at around the time of birth, are most affected. This record of stress during growth survives as long as the tooth does, preserving a record of childhood developmental stress. Lack of proper nutrition is another typical example of childhood stress. Although the winters in Athens are mild, there were probably some food shortages among the poorer populations. In addition, at the end of the long hot summers, before the fall grains and fruits matured, food may have been in short supply. We also know from medical writers such as Hippokrates and Galen that diseases with fevers and rashes were common among children. It is generally impossible to identify these specifically, but many were probably the same childhood diseases that were common causes of misery and death until the advent of modern vaccines.

[4] Liston, Rotroff, and Snyder 2018.
[5] This is not an isolated case, as a similar phenomenon was excavated at the site of Messene.

In addition to the teeth, growth interruptions in childhood also affect the bones. In the long bones of the legs and arms, stress from disease and malnutrition results in dense lines that can be seen on radiographs, where the growth of the bone paused during the stress. That period of growth may not be made up, resulting in the child being small for its age, or short stature in adults. In an extreme case, a child found in the Agora excavations who died in the Protogeometric period had a dental age of 11–12, while bone lengths indicate the size of a six-year-old child.[6] Because there was no evidence of any genetic or systemic growth disruption, it appears that this child suffered repeatedly from stresses before death.

Dietary Disease and Anemias

Nutritional diseases were a constant threat in antiquity, when simply getting sufficient calories was a challenge for many poor people and the role of balanced nutrition was little understood. Medical practice was largely based on humeral theory, which attempted to balance the supposed hot/cold and wet/dry qualities of foods, with little perception of their nutritional values. Our analyses of the quality of the diet are complicated by the fact that the graves of high-status individuals, who would have had access to better nutrition, are much more likely to be preserved and excavated than those of poorer people. One of the great contributions of the ongoing analysis of over 1,900 ordinary graves from the eighth-to-fourth-century BC cemetery at the port of Phaleron is that it will give much better insight into the lives of the non-elite in ancient Athens (see Map 4.2).

Nutritional deficiencies do leave signs on bones. At times, the poorer Athenians probably subsisted on little more than grains, either boiled or made into bread. (See Steiner, Chapter 25 in this volume.) As a result, vitamin C deficiencies were probably common. Scurvy affects the connective tissues of the body, including blood vessels. Bruising and bleeding in the tissues surrounding the bones and teeth are common, and this in turn results in the production of porous new bone formations on the affected surfaces, evident especially in young children.

Various forms of anemia also plagued the Athenians, although not to the extent seen in other parts of Greece. Anemias can be identified in bone through the expansion of blood-cell-producing diploe, found in particular on the upper back of the skull and inside the eye orbits. An anemic child

---

[6] Papadopoulos et al., 2018.

will develop very porous bone surfaces, which can persist, with some remodeling, into adulthood. However, it is impossible to determine the cause of the anemia. Blood loss from internal parasites or therapeutic bleeding, genetic anemias, and iron-deficient diets can all result in similar bone lesions, and it is difficult to distinguish the underlying causes.

Zoonoses

Most ancient Athenians lived in close contact with animals. (See Smith, Chapter 14 in this volume.) Without refrigeration to prevent meat from spoiling, animals had to be slaughtered close to the consumers who would eat them, and large numbers of animals were required for both private and public sacrifices to the gods. Even goats and sheep kept for milk and cheese production would live much closer to people than the farm animals of the modern world. As a result, there was a much greater chance of catching zoonoses, diseases whose natural reservoir is in another species. One of the most common of these zoonoses was brucellosis. It is described in the Hippocratic writings as undulant fever, that is, a fever that rises and falls on a twenty-four-hour cycle. This differed from malaria, described accurately as tertian (three-day) and quartian (four-day) fever. Brucellosis is caused by bacteria that infect various animal species, but the most common variants that humans may catch are carried by sheep and goats, or cattle. There is evidence of both of these variants in Athens. In fact, from the same second-century BC well that contained the 457 infants, there are also the skeletons of an adult male and a child. The adult had evidence in his vertebrae that probably indicates *Brucella melitensis*, the species most often carried by goats and sheep. The child had extensive evidence of destructive lesions in his spine that strongly resemble the damage caused by *Brucella abortus*, the species carried by cattle (Fig. 13.1).

Cancer

Cancer was once believed to be a disease of modern peoples, linked to both extended life spans and higher rates of environmental pollutants. But more recent research has shown clearly that cancer was very much present in ancient Greece.[7] The Athenian Agora burials have a rich record of bone

---

[7] See Siek 2019.

Fig. 13.1 Vertebrae of a child aged 8–10, Agora Bone Well, second century BC. Arrows indicate lesions associated with brucellosis.
Source: M.A. Liston

tumors. Benign lesions are fairly common, occurring in many individuals. Most would have had little or no impact on life, but one individual developed a large benign tumor that expanded into his right eye socket and nasal cavity, crowding and compressing other tissues of the face.[8] Malignancies also are present, both in primary bone cancers and metastatic disease that originated in other organs and spread to bone, thus preserving a record of the affliction. A woman who died violently in the Herulian sack of Athens in AD 267 (see below) was suffering from metastatic cancer that had spread to her skull at the time of her death. Multiple lesions where the cranial bone had been eaten away, in one case penetrating all the way through the braincase, indicate that she suffered from extensive metastasis (Fig. 13.2). Her age, in her late thirties, suggests breast cancer as a likely origin, but many cancers of organs can metastasize to the bone. A middle-aged man from the Athenian Agora also exhibited extensive metastatic lesions across his left hip and femur that appear to be osteosarcoma, possibly originating from prostate cancer.[9]

Trauma and Warfare

War casualties were frequent throughout most of Athens' history, and yet direct evidence for combat injury and death in battle is relatively rare. Mycenean Bronze Age graves offer the best evidence for the impact of war

[8] Smith 2010.
[9] Bourbou 2003.

(a)   (b)

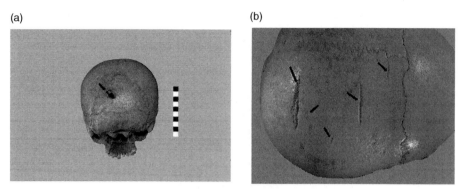

Fig. 13.2a–b Adult woman killed in the Herulian sack of Athens of AD 267, Athenian Agora: (a) posterior skull, the arrow indicates bone cancer lesion; (b) top of the skull, the arrows indicate perimortem blade cuts.
Source: M.A. Liston

on both the elite and non-elite, civilians and soldiers. On the one hand, a survey of seven Athenian 'warrior graves' containing high-status bronze weapons found that the associated skeletons show no evidence of skeletal injury from warfare, and only two had significant skeletal trauma, in both cases injuries that could easily have resulted from falls or accidents. On the other hand, two Mycenean graves of individuals who were *not* buried with weapons showed clear evidence of weapon injuries, blade wounds, and skull fractures.[10] It has recently been suggested that these wounds were the result of high-velocity impacts from sling bullets. In general, Bronze Age skeletons that lack any high-status grave goods more often show evidence of war-related trauma, including fractures and wounds from weapons, while those whose families could afford to bury them with expensive bronze weapons rarely show injuries. Contrary to the view presented in battle scenes in the *Iliad*, in actual Bronze Age warfare, high status may often have protected most combatants from risk of injury.

In the historic periods in Athens, there is also very little evidence of casualties in warfare. The Athenians buried their war dead at public expense in the Demosion Sema, which was located somewhere outside the city walls on the road to Plato's Academy. (See also Shea, Chapter 10 in this volume.) A number of inscriptions and *polyandria* (burials of multiple individuals) have been found in that area, but there is no definitive identification. Moreover, few of the human remains found in the various military graves have ever been studied or published. As a result, our

[10] Smith 2009.

evidence for the impact of warfare comes not from the warriors, but from some of the victims killed in attacks on the city. These are not from the famous sacks of Athens by the Persians in 480 BC and by the Roman general Sulla in 86 BC. Only from later invasions, by the Herulians in AD 267 and a later attack by Slavs in the sixth century AD, do we have conclusive skeletal evidence of civilian residents killed in warfare.

Four wells in the Agora excavations have produced remains of individuals killed in the Herulian attack. Given that these war dead were buried so casually, in the midst of debris from the cleanup after the attack, it is unlikely that they are from citizen families. The four women and two children all have facial fractures that suggest they were subdued by blows to the face. One woman was hit repeatedly on the top of the head with a dull blade that failed to break her skull but would have caused terrible bleeding (Fig. 13.2), another woman's throat was cut, and the third woman has no clear cause of death, but was struck in the back with a long blade at least twice. Both children's skulls were crushed. The violence of the event is vividly preserved in the skeletal remains. The one adult male skeleton from the attack died even more violently. A blow to his face broke his nose, knocked out two front teeth, and fractured the bones behind his right eye. New blade cuts, with no evidence of healing, are found on his right upper arm, left shoulder, and lower left arm, this time cutting almost through the radius (Web Fig. 13.3). Another major blade wound fell on his left shin. None of these wounds would have killed him immediately, although blood loss and shock would have ended his life quickly.

The warfare that Athens experienced almost continuously during its history also contributed to the disease load endured by citizens. In particular, the Peloponnesian War contributed to the devastating Plague of Athens. Fleeing from the Spartan armies ravaging the countryside, the population of Attika was crowded into the city and between the Long Walls extending to the harbor at Piraeus. The resulting overcrowding and poor sanitation contributed to the spread of the most devastating plague recorded in the city's history. The Plague also impacted the arts, in particular tragedy, and probably influenced the construction of the Sanctuary of Asklepios, the god of healing, on the south slope of the Acropolis in 419/18.[11]

There was little direct evidence outside of literary sources for the Plague of Athens until construction of the subway station near the Kerameikos

---

[11] Mitchell-Boyask 2008.

cemetery revealed a mass grave of 150 bodies dating to the period of the Peloponnesian War (431–404 BC). The circumstances of the burial suggest they were interred over a very short period of time, around 420–430 BC, and may have been victims of the famous Plague of Athens, an epidemic described in detail by the Athenian historian Thucydides (2.47–48, 3.87), who caught the disease and survived it.

Analysis of DNA from the teeth of three individuals in the mass grave has identified typhoid fever as a possible cause of the Plague.[12] But Thucydides' description makes it clear that this was a 'virgin soil' epidemic, devastating a population that had no immunity to it. That does not fit well with typhoid, which was probably endemic, circulating at low levels constantly and occasionally flaring up under the right conditions. So, while the people of Athens were no doubt suffering from typhoid fever during the war years, some other disease was also killing them in great numbers.[13] Smallpox is a good candidate and would fit the description given by Thucydides fairly well, but definitive identification of the cause of the Plague still eludes us.

Lifespan and Age at Death

Despite disease and violence, some individuals managed to survive into old age. Like most ancient populations, Athenians rarely lived beyond their sixties, and most died much younger. But rarely is not the same as never, and there are occasional examples of individuals who survived into extreme old age, probably into their eighties. However, the scattered cemeteries in Athens from across several millennia make it impossible to develop accurately representative mortality profiles for any time period.

For Athenians who survived to old age, health problems continued and were not unlike those of today. Arthritis is common in the spines and major joints of most older individuals (i.e. those who survived beyond about forty years of age). Women, in particular, suffered from osteoporosis as they aged. A woman found in the Athenian Agora who died in her fifties suffered the collapse of vertebral bodies, resulting in compression of her rib cage, and a fracture of her right wrist, probably from a fall. A man in his forties, also from the Agora, suffered from hemochromatosis, a genetic disease that causes excessive buildup of iron. His symptoms included

[12] Papagrigorakis et al. 2006.
[13] Littman 2009.

osteoporosis and advanced arthritis in his spine, knees, and hands. Because of his underlying disease, it is likely that heart disease or liver cancer was his ultimate cause of death; but like so many others, we will never know definitely how he met his end.

Archaeology and the study of skeletons from excavations have made great contributions to our knowledge and understanding of the lives of the ancient Athenians.[14] Archaeological sciences have given us the ability to analyze the diets and migration patterns of the population, identify their diseases and injuries, and understand the real impact of wars that were once known only through historical sources. Using the constantly evolving techniques that blend science and archaeology, we can answer questions that have long confounded us, and reach a more holistic, nuanced understanding of Athens' past.

Further Reading

A recent exhibition at the Museum of Cycladic Art on ancient health practices and cults has summary essays on various aspects of health and disease (Stampolidis and Tassoulas 2014). Two collections of papers on ancient health provide a wide range of perspectives on the topic (Hope and Marshall 2000; King 2005). The Phaleron Archaeological Project being conducted at the Malcolm Weiner Laboratory for Archaeological Science of the American School of Classical Studies at Athens has, as of this writing, begun to move from cleaning and preparation to publication of 1,200 skeletons. This enormous cemetery of the early port of Athens will provide an unparalleled view of the lives of ordinary Athenians, slaves, and convicted criminals. Updates are available on the project website: http://phaleron.digital-ascsa.org/.

Bibliography

Bourbou, C. 2003. "A Survey of Neoplastic Disease in Ancient and Medieval Greek Populations." *Eulimine* 4: 181–188.

Hope, V.M., and E. Marshall, eds. 2000. *Death and Disease in the Ancient City.* London.

King, H., ed. 2005. *Health in Antiquity.* London.

Lagia, A. 2007. "Notions of Childhood in the Classical Polis: Evidence from the Bioarchaeological Record." In *Constructions of Childhood in Ancient Greece and Italy*, eds. A. Cohen and J.B. Rutter, Princeton, 293–306.

---

[14] See Liston 2012 for understanding women's lives in ancient Greece through skeletal remains.

Liston, M.A. 2012. "Reading the Bones: Interpreting the Skeletal Evidence for Women's Lives in Ancient Greece." In *A Companion to Women in the Ancient Mediterranean*, eds. S.A. James and S. Dillon, Malden, MA, 125–140.

Liston, M.A., and J.K. Papadopoulos 2004. "The Rich Athenian Lady Was Pregnant: The Anthropology of a Geometric Tomb Reconsidered." *Hesperia* 73.1: 7–38.

Liston, M.A., S.I. Rotroff, and L.M. Snyder. 2018. *The Agora Bone Well*. Princeton.

Littman, R.J. 2009. "The Plague of Athens: Epidemiology and Paleopathology." *Mount Sinai Journal of Medicine* 76: 456–467.

Mitchell-Boyask, R. 2008. *Plague and the Athenian Imagination: Drama, History, and the Cult of Asclepius*. Cambridge.

Papagrigorakis, M.J., C. Yapijakis, P.N. Synodinos, and E. Baziotopoulou-Valavani. 2006. "DNA Examination of Ancient Dental Pulp Incriminates Typhoid Fever as a Probable Cause of the Plague of Athens." *International Journal of Infectious Diseases* 10: 206–214.

Papadopoulos, J.K., and E.L. Smithson, eds., with M.A. Liston, D. Ruscillo, S. Strack, and E. Dimitriadou. 2018. *The Early Iron Age: The Cemeteries*. *Agora* 36. Princeton.

Prevedorou, E.-A., and J.E. Buikstra. 2019. "Bioarchaeological Practice and the Curation of Human Skeletal Remains in a Greek Context: The Phaleron Cemetery." *Advances in Archaeological Practice* 7: 60–67.

Siek, T. 2019. "Reconsidering Palaeoepidemiological Investigations in Palaeo-Oncology." PhD dissertation, University College London.

Smith, S.K. 2009. "Skeletal Evidence for Militarism in Mycenaean Athens." In *New Directions in the Skeletal Biology of Greece*, eds. L.A. Schepartz, S.C. Fox, and C. Bourbou, Princeton, 99–110.

2010. "Differential Diagnosis and Discussion of a Large Nasal Neoplasm from a Late Bronze Age Athenian Male." *International Journal of Osteoarchaeology* 20: 731–736.

Stampolidis, N.C., and Y. Tassoulas. 2014. *Hygeia: Health, Illness, Treatment from Homer to Galen*. Athens.

Additional resources to accompany this chapter can be found at: www.cambridge .org/NeilsRogers

14 | Animals in Athenian Life

TYLER JO SMITH

> So we can clearly infer that plants exist for the sake of animals as they
> develop, and animals for the good of humankind.
>
> Aristotle, *Politics* 1256b15 (trans. Mynott 2018, 65)

The city of ancient Athens was literally teeming with animals. From tiny
insects and pests to large beasts of burden, and the known terrestrial,
aquatic, and avian species between these extremes, animals had many uses,
meanings, and roles within the human sphere and as part of the urban
environment. The evidence relating animals to Athens is abundant.
Ancient authors, such as the comic playwright Aristophanes and the
philosopher Aristotle, writing for different audiences and at different times,
provide insights about the classification, behaviors, and characteristics of
various animals – domestic and tame, wild and feral. Ancient inscriptions
record prices, quantities, and legal aspects of certain animals in both
religious and secular circumstances. The visual arts, especially the many
figure-decorated vases produced in Athens (though often found elsewhere),
along with large-scale public sculptures and small-scale figurines, offer a
great deal of information about the variety of animals known in Athens
throughout antiquity. At the same time, it is clear that painters, sculptors,
and other artists, were not always creating their representations based on
personal experience or observation of the animal kingdom. Some relatively
rare animals, such as the lion, are common in art but their iconography is
heavily derived from the arts of other cultures; while the camel, an exotic
non-Greek beast, known for its tasty milk and meat to Aristotle (*History of
Animals* 6.26, 578a15–17), was given assorted forms by vase-painters (Web
Fig. 14.1) most of whom may never have cast their eyes on one. The
archaeological record, particularly the excavated materials from the
Akropolis, the Agora, and the Kerameikos, also add significantly to the
story of animals in Athens, and include both material man-made objects
and faunal remains, the bones of once living, breathing creatures. It should
be emphasized, however, that these diverse sources of evidence, when
combined, by no means present a cohesive or consistent picture of animals
in the ancient city. Indeed, one person's pet was another person's pest.

That being said, the texts, images, and objects surviving from antiquity, especially those created in Athens, belonging to the city, or both, enable us to question the complex world of human–animal relations. A less obvious, but no less important area of interaction involves the use of animals as secondary products: sheep for milk and wool, goats for their skins (cf. Euripides, *Cyclops* 76–81), bone, horn, or shell employed for making tools, musical instruments, and works of art. Indications of these practices also survive in written and material form, and invite us to question the extent to which humans exploited animals for personal and communal benefit. By focusing on selective evidence, mainly from Archaic and Classical times (sixth to fourth centuries BC), we shall consider animals in daily life, mythology and religion, and performance and competition. Such broad categories are not able to capture every aspect of this immense subject, and many pertinent issues must remain beyond our present scope (e.g. ethical treatment, animals as food, breeding, veterinary medicine). Rather, these themes have been selected based on the amounts and types of information available, the ways they enlighten us about the place of animals in human life, and the various conditions in which they brought humans and animals together in the city.

Daily Life

Athenians experienced animals in many parts of their everyday life, at work, at rest, and at play. People coexisted with live animals in domestic settings and public spaces, as livestock in the marketplace, as transport in the crowded streets, even in the lawcourts (cf. Aristophanes, *Peace* 996–1016; Plutarch, *Moralia, On the Genius of Sokrates* 10; Antiphon, fr. 57–59), but also through material culture and the visual arts animals of many kinds were manifest. As early as the tenth century BC, a Geometric *pyxis* (circular box) with a multiple horse-handle lid was deposited in an Athenian grave alongside clay models of horses, fowl, and a donkey weighed down with jars.[1] Such an assemblage not only testifies to the potential importance of these animals for the living and the dead, but also enables us to make useful observations about how the individual creatures played different roles and upheld symbolic meanings: the stately, upright horses bespeak the elite status of the grave's occupant, the donkey (or mule) is forever used as labor, and the fowl (perhaps ducks) may be

---

[1] Kurtz and Boardman 1971, 38–40, fig. 3.

admired either as pets or for their inherent versatility given their ability to fly, swim, and walk.

Sculpted animals displayed on the Akropolis, both as architectural decoration and as offerings, or in the Kerameikos as grave-markers, place them at an arguably high level of importance in the Athenian imagination and in the cityscape. Consider how the large and impressive limestone lioness killing a bull, from a temple pediment on the Akropolis dated around 570–560 BC, might have been perceived by its contemporary ancient audience.[2] Were these creatures viewed as symbolic illustrations of power/aggression or victory/defeat, as a commentary on ritual practices or local myths, or as the inescapable forces of nature? A rather different example from the Akropolis takes the form of a crouching marble hunting hound of the late sixth century, perhaps one of a pair dedicated to Artemis Brauronia, who had a sanctuary there.[3] Would the striking, realistic posture of the sculpted animal have marked it as a creature to love and nurture or, rather, something to fear and avoid? After all, Agorakritos, the sausage-seller in Aristophanes' *Knights*, a satirical play that won first prize at the Lenaia festival of 424 BC, alludes to a biting guard dog, perhaps the Molossian breed (cf. *Lysistrata* 1213–1215; cf. *Thesmophoriazousai*, 414.7; see Web Fig. 20.3). By comparison, a grave monument in the Kerameikos was topped with a massive, charging bull, sending a clear message of power and prestige.[4]

More mundane examples of the everyday animal world abound in Athenian vase-painting, though the exact setting is truly anyone's guess: a parade of cattle encircles an eclectic grouping of wild and fantastical beasts on an Attic plate of ca. 650 BC found in the Kerameikos;[5] dolphins and fish swim convincingly about the interior of a mid-sixth century black-figure cup discovered at faraway Gordion.[6] Early fifth-century artists working in red-figure select a pastoral scene, or one of animals in the wild, as decoration on molded vessels in the shapes of animal parts: a lobster claw and a horse hoof.[7] The addition of a human participant to some scenes adds little to these non-narrative moments. Such is the case when a boy with a fishing pole balances on the edge of a rock while making his

---

[2] Athens, Akropolis Museum 3. Boardman 1978, 154, figs. 190–192.
[3] Athens, Akropolis Museum 143. Boardman 1978, fig. 271.
[4] For Dionysios of Kollytos, mid-fourth century, see Kurtz and Boardman 1971, 136, 238.
[5] Athens, Kerameikos Museum 74. Boardman 1998, fig. 201.
[6] Berlin, Antikensammlung 4604; BAPD no. 300736.
[7] Bérard 1989, figs. 6–8.

catch, on the inside of a late-sixth century red-figure cup.[8] Unsurprisingly, a pair of oxen, the animals deemed best suited for the job (Aristotle, *Politics* 1.1 1252b12), pull a plow in order to assist human male workers in a rare agricultural scene shown on the exterior of a black-figure cup of ca. 575–560, perhaps representing a festival of Demeter, such as the Thesmophoria.[9] Another version of the subject from the mid-fifth century, a red-figure bell-krater has been associated specifically with the Bouzygia, the sacred plowing held annually at the foot of the Akropolis.[10]

Specific classes of large animals, among them bovines (cows, oxen, bulls) and equids (donkeys, mules, horses), were connected to certain tasks and related to well-defined everyday activities. Work-animals, such as oxen (castrated bulls), were by no means relegated to the countryside and, like horses, the economic aspects of owning them have been much discussed. It is important to note that when Solon restructured the Athenian class system around four divisions related to wealth and agricultural production, he named the two upper social tiers *zeugitai* and *hippeis*, terms derived from the words for oxen and horse, respectively. Furthermore, both of these animals were dedicated in sculpted form on the Akropolis, as was a bronze heifer of the Early Classical artist Myron, whose realism was the subject of many epigrams: "O bull, in vain do you nudge this heifer. For it is lifeless; Myron the cow-sculptor has deceived you" (*Greek Anthology* 9.734).

Apart from agricultural labor, oxen were used for transporting heavy loads within the city. One inscription helpfully records that Eudemos of Plataia was honored in Athens in 330/29 BC for donating generous funds and, importantly, 1,000 yoke of oxen to facilitate moving the building material for the Theater of Dionysos and the Panathenaic Stadium (*IG* II^2 351). Mules and donkeys, as noted above, were used to carry loads, such as the famous one who, after helping to build the Parthenon, could be seen eating freely from the city corn-sellers in his retirement (Plutarch, *Cato* 5.3); they also moved people, such as the pair toting the cart of a bride and groom on a well-known *lekythos* by the Amasis Painter.[11] The physical features, behavior, and noisy braying of these beasts, not to mention their associations with Dionysos, made them the subject of fables and proverbs

---

[8] Boston, Museum of Fine Arts 01.8024; BAPD no. 201573.
[9] London, British Museum 1906.12-15.1; BAPD no. 300834. The opposite side shows women dancing at an altar and a seated goddess.
[10] Cambridge, Harvard University 60.345; BAPD no. 214755.
[11] New York, Metropolitan Museum of Art 56.11.1; BAPD no. 350478.

(cf. Aristophanes, *Wasps* 191; Plato, *Phaedrus* 260c) as well as the focus of humorous images on many Athenian vases. A series of red-figure examples show satyrs, the half-man and half-equine followers of Dionysos, acting as stable hands dutifully feeding and tending to donkeys.

Horses enjoyed a particularly high status in Athenian society. They are also among the best-represented in texts and images and perhaps the most studied of all ancient animal groups. The overall importance of horses in the city is nowhere better in evidence than on the Parthenon frieze (see Fig. 29.1), designed by Pheidias in the 430s, where the impressive cavalcade of riders has been connected to the city's Panathenaic procession. As much-loved and valued possessions – some might even argue 'pets' – horses were given names by their owners, with "Xanthos" meaning "Blonde" (the name of Achilles' mount) among the most frequent equine appellation on Athenian vase inscriptions. Male-centered activities, such as warfare, hunting, and equestrian sports (discussed below), required horse investment and ownership. (See also Pritchard, Chapter 22 in this volume.) The Classical author and student of Sokrates, Xenophon, wrote extensively about horses and horsemanship (as did Simon, a slightly earlier Athenian author), covering everything from purchasing and training, to grooming, mounting, riding, and also showing, parading, and equipping for battle. His mid-fifth-century treatise *Hipparchikos* (*On the Cavalry Commander*) details an officer's duties, but also advises about the character and condition of his mounts: "You must see that they are docile, because disobedient animals assist the enemy more than their own side" (1.3). Discoveries of fourth-to-third-century inscribed lead and clay tablets in the Kerameikos and the Agora provide details of horse procurements, prices, and replacements. In vase-painting and sculpture, there is no shortage of horse-themed scenes, including those related to warfare and the hunt: equestrian hunting for big game surges in the mid-sixth century; horsemen, *ephebes*, and foreigners walk beside or ride their mounts on Late Archaic red-figure cups; Classical funerary monuments portray splendid riders (cf. Web Fig. 20.7). In both these cases, the combined human–horse motifs may well reflect the current political situation and the prominence of horses in the elite lifestyle. Recall that Plato in his *Laws* (7.823e–824a) recognizes the horse–hound–human trio as the noblest form of hunting, both physically and strategically.

Animals of more modest sizes played fundamental and varied roles in several areas of Athenian domestic life. The *symposion*, the drinking party attended by aristocratic males, for which so many Athenian vases were produced, was also an occasion for the giving of gifts between older and younger male couples. These 'love-gifts' took animal forms, both living and dead. Common choices seen on vases are the rooster or the hare – though Aristophanes mentions the horse, hunting dogs, geese, and quail (*Wealth*, 153ff; *Birds*, 707) – and these amorous offerings are common additions to scenes of male courtship and *komos* (revelry). Another species associated with the *symposion* setting is dogs of slender build, perhaps Laconian hounds (cf. Xenophon, *On Hunting* 4.1), who await scraps below the tables and dining-couches, or who stand at the feet of their owners or an otherwise engaged loving couple. Not surprisingly, the horse is alluded to at the *symposion*, both in literature (Xenophon's *Symposion* is set after the horse race of the Great Panathenaia) and in art, as on a black-figure *oinochoe* from Athens, where one is chosen as a decorative motif on the side of the wine-mixing *krater* set in the center of the scene.[12] The stately and statuesque beast is overtly juxtaposed with a surrounding group of worse-for-wear drunken revelers. Some molded vessels suitable for wine consumption took the shape of an animal's head (e.g. boar, lion, dog, donkey, stag).[13] One striking example is a half-ram and half-donkey mug, embellished around the rim with playful satyrs, themselves hybrid creatures (Fig. 14.1). The wineskin (*askos*), used to transport wine in large quantities, is shown as the plaything of rowdy youths and lusty satyrs on decorated drinking vessels, and it would in actuality have been made from goatskin.

The keeping of pets in the home was clearly a preoccupation of the ancient Greeks, and Athenian sources provide ample evidence, and even criticism of the practice (cf. Theophrastos, *Characters* 5.9, 21.6, 21.9). Alkibiades let loose a quail hidden under his cloak into the Assembly and also snipped the tail of his own beautiful dog, two animal episodes causing quite a kerfuffle (Plutarch, *Alkibiades* 9–10.1). Another celebrated dog story is that of Xanthippos, father of Perikles, who left his pet behind when escaping the Persian invasion of Athens in 480. The distressed canine swam to Salamis behind his master's trireme and, dying upon arrival, was given a heroic burial (Plutarch, *Themistokles* 10.9–10). Although no single word for 'pet' exists in ancient Greek, companion or personal animals, as they are sometimes called, included dogs, rabbits, and birds.

[12] Athens, National Archaeological Museum 1045, attributed to the Xenokles Painter; BAPD no. 302454.

[13] Most notable are those from the workshop of the potter Sotades (mid-fifth century) with painted figure scenes highlighting the animal kingdom or myths involving human–animal hybrids.

(a)

(b)

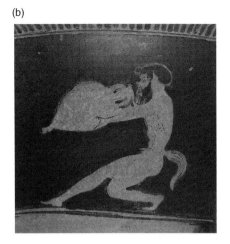

Fig. 14.1a–b *Rhyton* in the form of a dimidiated donkey and ram with satyrs, attributed to Sotades, ca. 450 BC, (a) ram head, (b) detail of satyr with amphora, Baltimore, Walters Art Gallery 48.2050. Courtesy of The Walters Art Museum, Baltimore

All are found in locally produced artistic depictions, and their status as pets may be designated by the human attention they receive, by the addition of material objects (i.e. collars, leashes, cages), or by their inscribed names. Dogs small and large are especially prominent. One series of late fifth-century Athenian red-figure *choes*, small jugs associated with the Anthesteria festival in honor of Dionysos, were given to very young boys to drink their first sips of wine. Many such vessels show children playing on the floor with small, fluffy Maltese-type dogs, no doubt their own family pets,[14] and a similar breed is seen on an Attic grave *stele* for Melisto dated ca. 340 BC (Fig. 14.2). Larger dogs, such as the hounds mentioned above in reference to hunting and the *symposion*, are also found in scenes of warriors departing home, though whether they can even be considered pets in the modern sense remains open to question. Xenophon, in his *Kynegetikos* (*On Hunting*), discusses hunting dogs in depth, including their breeding, rearing, and even their naming. A hunting variety joins his deceased master and other members of the household on the later fourth-century Ilissos *stele*;[15] while the evidence for dogs buried with or

[14] Cf. *Agora* 30, no. 735. The term "Melitean" is inscribed above the dog on an Athenian red-figure amphora (ca. 500); Calder 2011, 83.

[15] Athens, National Archaeological Museum 869. Kaltsas 2002, no. 382.

Fig. 14.2 Melisto, Attic marble grave *stele*, ca. 340 BC, Cambridge, Harvard Art Museums 1961.86.
© President and Fellows of Harvard College; courtesy of the Harvard Art Museums/Arthur M. Sackler Museum, Alpheus Hyatt Purchasing and Gifts for Special Uses Funds in Memory of Katherine Brewster Taylor, as a tribute to her many years at the Fogg Museum

deposited alongside humans suggests that they were thought to continue to serve as both guardians and companions of the deceased in the afterlife.[16] A similar variety of medium-build dog (i.e. long legs, sharp nose, curly tail), is added to scenes of human labor – preparing and transporting fish, selling olive oil – but it is impossible to judge if these well-behaved animals are simply passing by in hopes of a treat, or if they are the true companions to one of the human figures in the scenes. Other pets include hares, as already mentioned in connection with the hunt and male courtship, while birds (songbirds, geese) are common in female domestic settings on vases and in the hands of young girls on grave-markers. House cats are difficult to identify in the textual record, being sometimes confused with weasels, and they are rarely portrayed in art. Their status as pets, as opposed to pest-control, is somewhat ambiguous. A few vases show small cats in obvious indoor contexts (e.g. music lessons, chasing mice), and their playful yet cautious nature is well-articulated. The diminutive animal

[16] On animal burials: Calder 2011, 81–84. MacKinnon in Campbell 2014, 274.

seated below a bird cage on a late fifth-century Attic grave *stele* showing a man and a boy, is usually identified as a cat, and thus an accepted member of the household.[17] There is also evidence of exotic pet-keeping by the Athenians. Large, wild felines, probably cheetahs, seem to have been in vogue among elite youths, who collared and walked them on leashes.

Mythology and Religion

Animals were closely associated with the ancient Greek gods, goddesses, and heroes, both through mythological stories and in relation to religious cults. Sokrates appropriated the expression "by the dog" to avoid taking sacred names in vain. Artemis was goddess of the hunt and overseer of the animal world in her role as *potnia theron* (mistress of animals). In Athenian art, she is frequently represented in the company of dogs, deer, felines, or avian fauna. A sanctuary to Artemis Brauronia stood on the Akropolis, and was connected to the rural Attic sanctuary of Brauron, where aristocratic young girls from Athens "played the bear," a metaphor for possible initiation rituals occurring under the goddess's tutelage (Aristophanes, *Lysistrata* 644–645). Other deities had a single animal associated with them, such as the eagle for Zeus, the sow for Demeter, or the dog for Hekate; Athena's owl represented her symbolically on local coinage (see Figs. 18.1 and 18.2) and on fifth-century 'Owl *Skyphoi*.'[18] The epithets of a given god or goddess could highlight certain animal associations, such as Poseidon Hippios and Athena Hippia, both denoting their oversight of horses and horse-related activities.

Some myths involving the gods are rife with animal symbolism, such as one told in the *Homeric Hymn to Hermes*, where the young god steals the cattle of Apollo, but is then forgiven after creating the beautiful-sounding tortoise-shell lyre (*chelys*). Or, Artemis who exacted revenge on Aktaion after, according to later sources, he accidentally came upon her bathing and so was mauled by his own hunting dogs, a grisly event depicted by vase-painters. Another set of deities associated with the city, through myths and cult, are those taking human–animal hybrid forms: Kekrops, the mythical first king of Athens (not a god per se, but the founder of many cults), had the upper body of a man and the lower body of a serpent; the rustic god

---

[17] Athens, National Archaeological Museum 715. Kaltsas 2002, no. 287.

[18] *Agora* 30, nos. 1312–1322.

Pan, introduced to Athens after the Persian Wars and worshiped in a
grotto on the north slope of the Akropolis, had the hindquarters, legs,
and horns of a goat; Acheloos, a personified river-god, was often shown in
Athenian art as a man-headed bull with a long bushy beard.

One deity with especially strong ties to animals was Dionysos, god of
wine and drama. The goat was special to him and to his worship, and the
Greek word tragedy (*tragedos*) actually translates as "goat-song." His male
followers, the satyrs, were animal–human hybrids, being half-equine and
half-man (Fig. 14.1). In art, satyrs can be seen in sexual pursuit of unsus-
pecting animal victims (including goats), as well as playfully riding on the
backs of ithyphallic donkeys – a possible allusion to the story of the Return
of Hephaistos to Olympos, in which the god of the forge, transformed by
the intoxicating effects of wine, rode rather unceremoniously on a similar
randy mount. Maenads, the female devotees of Dionysos, played the part of
the chorus in Euripides' *Bacchae*, performed at the at City Dionysia in 405
BC, where they express a collective desire to dance like a fawn having
escaped from the hunt (lines 866–872), though only after Pentheus asserts
that they will be "hunted down, out of the mountains like the animals they
are" (lines 227–228). On numerous vase-paintings, such wild women drape
animal skins over their clothing, wear snakes like crowns, or carry the
reptiles in their hands. Euripides' description of maenads who went into
the hills and, possessed by the power of Dionysos, dismembered a live bull
with their bare hands (*sparagmos*) is comparable to the scene on an earlier
red-figure vase from the mid-fifth century in which the victim is a fawn.[19]
The *Homeric Hymn to Dionysos* recounts the god's ability to transform
himself into a wild animal (lion, bear), and his power to turn fearful pirates
into dolphins – the likely subject adorning the inside of a black-figure cup
signed by Exekias.[20]

Greek mythology, known through texts and imagery, had no shortage of
episodes involving heroes overcoming animal and monster menaces.
Themes of aggression and conflict, in which the ancient hero emerges
victorious over a beastly foe, belong to a tradition of othering non-Greek
human enemies (e.g. Trojans, Persians). Struggles with sea creatures, such
as Tritons, or the hunt for the ferocious Kalydonian boar, afforded the
opportunity for Athenian artists to highlight human strength over animal
adversaries. The Centauromachy, involving half-man and half-horse centaurs battling the Lapiths, was popular on vases, but also prominent in the

---

[19] Paris, Cabinet des Médailles, 357, attributed to the Achilles Painter; BAPD no. 213822.
[20] Munich, Antikensammlungen 2044; BAPD no. 310403.

city, appearing both on the south metopes of the Parthenon, and in a wall-painting by Mikon in the Sanctuary of Theseus (Pausanias 1.17.2–3). The heroes Herakles and Theseus were especially important to the city of Athens, emerging in the Archaic and Classical periods respectively, and both defeated terrifying, remote animal enemies. Herakles' first labor, the fight with the Nemean lion, a particular favorite of vase-painters, gave him his signature lion-skin armor and lion-head helmet; and most of his remaining labors involved animal rivals: Lernean hydra (nine-headed snake), Keryneian hind, Erymanthian boar, Stymphalian birds, Cretan bull, mares of Diomedes, and the retrieving of the canine Kerberos from the Underworld. Theseus killed the Krommyonian sow, captured and sacrificed the Marathonian bull, and most notably slayed the Cretan Minotaur, a half-bull, half-man monster. Thereby he spared the further martyring of Athenian youths and maidens. Importantly, the labors of Herakles and the deeds of Theseus were chosen to decorate the metopes on the Hephaisteion, a temple constructed above the Agora during the second half of the fifth century, and the Centauromachy was depicted on part of its Ionic frieze.

Animals were central to Athenian religious life, and to forging successful relationships between the individual, the community, and the divine. The blood sacrifice of domestic animals, such as sheep, goats, and bulls, is well attested in ancient inscriptions, referenced in literary texts, and, to an extent, depicted in art. Burnt faunal remains, such as those from the fifth-to-fourth-century Altar of Aphrodite Urania in the Agora, isolate individual species (sheep/goat, pig, fish) and their numbers (at least seventy-nine).[21] Mostly, these sacrifices occurred at specific times throughout the calendar year, during festivals held to honor specific deities, and were the main occasions for meat consumption. Some animals, such as young sheep and goats (predominant in Attika) were selected based on type and seasonal availability. Special occasions necessitated animal slaughter, such as the Athenian sacrifice of a she-goat for Artemis for every Persian killed at Marathon (Xenophon, *Anabasis* 3.2.12). Likewise, individual and family sacrifices must also have been practiced, as Sokrates reminds Krito in the end (cf. Plato, *Phaedo* 118a): "we owe a cock to Asklepios."

The visual arts again emerge as a significant category of evidence for the practice of animal sacrifice, but the often-idealized nature of such scenes suggests that we should exercise caution in linking them to real life. Several

---

[21] Jameson 2014, esp. 204.

Fig. 14.3 Bronze figurines (from left) of a lion, boar, dog, and raven, from the Akropolis, sixth to fifth century BC, Athens, Akropolis Museum X 6657, X 6699, X 6692, X 6669.
© Akropolis Museum, 2009. Photograph: Nikos Daniilidis

black-figure examples make Athena the destination of the procession leading heifers to an altar, and it is tempting to relate such scenes to the Panathenaia, while another series showing large bovines grouped around an altar has been connected to the Bouphonia, a summer festival in honor of Zeus Polieus.[22] The post-kill phase is preferred by most painters, who display the entrails of the animal being roasted over a flaming altar. The inclusion of a *bucranion* (bull's skull) in some scenes emphasizes the already consecrated sanctuary setting, as do the perched or flying birds in many scenes, who await a tasty morsel or a chance to build their nests (cf. Euripides, *Ion*). Votive dedications in animal form were perhaps inexpensive substitutes for real victims, such as bronze versions found on the Akropolis (Fig. 14.3) or the golden cicadas dedicated to Pan, a symbol of Athenian autochthony (Thucydides 1.6.3). Sculpted reliefs with animals were dedicated at various sanctuaries throughout the city. Some represent Zeus Meilichios as a bearded, coiled snake, while another features a full menagerie, including a snake near the deity, a horse's head in the window, and a pig and goose being brought in as victims.[23] Another serpent, this one larger than life, was coiled at the feet of Pheidias' ivory and gold cult statue of Athena Parthenos, and was said to represent Erechthonios, an autochthonous early king of Athens (Pausanias 1.24.5–7).

[22] E.g., Munich, Antikensammlungen 1824; BAPD no. 330554.
[23] Athens, National Archaeological Museum 3873. Kaltsas 2002, no. 487.

Performance and Competition

Animals were related in many ways to private performances and public spectacles in ancient Greece. Music and dance had overt animal associations, because animals (including insects) corresponded to these areas of human culture through sound and movement (cf. Aristotle, *On the Movement of Animals*). Dolphins played a part in stories connected with the invention of dithyramb and hymns to Dionysos, and their aquatic movements were likened to ecstatic and circular dancing. An Attic black-figure cup (ca. 570) shows a dolphin with human arms playing the *aulos* (double-pipes), a clever reminder that *aulos* was the ancient word for a dolphin's breathing hole and that these creatures were known as "*aulos-loving*" (Aristophanes, *Frogs* 1313–1319).[24] The analogy was taken to another level by vase-painters around 500 BC who decorated *symposion* vessels with armed men riding on dolphins, often to the tunes of the *aulos*, suggesting the performance of pyrrhic dancing at city festivals and foreshadowing dramatic choruses.[25] A contemporary red-figure *pelike* also joined poetic performance and animals by portraying men pointing at flying birds and exclaiming: "Look, a swallow ... it's already spring," in possible reference to the "Swallow Song" sung throughout Greece.[26] All types of staged dramas, performed competitively during festivals for Dionysos, took advantage of animal themes, allusions, and imagery. Tragic playwrights used animal metaphors to address many aspects of human feeling, character, and behavior. Birds, for example, were used to interpret signs, as in Sophokles' *Antigone*, but in other plays to express the desire to escape difficulty, or to emphasize human emotion, as when Hekuba is compared to a distraught mother bird in Euripides' *Trojan Women* (lines 826–832). Aristophanes included animal imagery, live animals, and choruses playing animals in his comedies (*Frogs*, *Birds*, *Wasps*, *Knights*). Human performers in animal costumes on Athenian vases indicate similar themes, such as the bird-costumed dancers on a vase (Web Fig. 14.2) dated just slightly before the introduction of comedy at the City Dionysia in 486. Satyr-plays featured the familiar Dionysian hybrids as a convincingly costumed chorus and were also sometimes illustrated in vase imagery.

---

[24] Rome, Villa Giulia 64608; BAPD no. 505.
[25] Lissarrague 1990, 115–120, further connects these examples to the *symposion*.
[26] Steiner 2013.

Finally, athletic and equestrian competitions, including those held during the Great Panathenaia, incorporated animals in various ways. The festival procession, which ran from the Kerameikos through the Agora to the Akropolis, provided the opportunity for impressive animal displays by the cavalry, the *apobatai* leaping from racing chariots, and packs of sacrificial victims. The city's hippodrome staged horse- and chariot-racing, while the Anthippasia, a mock cavalry battle (Xenophon, *On the Cavalry Commander* 3.11–12), commemorated in a relief carving of ca. 400 from the Agora,[27] combined military skill and equestrian expertise. The high regard for elite equestrian victors, is attested by a mid-fifth-century inscription (*IG* I³ 131) declaring that Athenian winners at Olympia, Delphi, and Nemea, were allowed to dine at state expense in the Prytaneion; one imagines Alkibiades in this light after he took first, second, and fourth in chariot-racing at the Olympics of 416 (Thucydides 6.16.1–4). In Athens, the monumental prize amphoras awarded to athletic and equestrian victors at the Panathenaia presented Athena holding a round shield, wearing her snaky aegis, and standing between roosters mounted on columns. Like warriors' shields shown on numerous Greek vases, which exhibit animals (e.g. bull, lion, scorpion, wasp, bird, dolphin), the patron goddess's shield was emblazoned with a real or imaginary being (e.g. snake, Pegasos), signs of both protection and strength. The roosters framing Athena on the amphoras from ca. 540 onwards have been connected to the "fighting spirit of Athens" and the military prowess of the goddess herself.[28] Cock-fighting is attested in art and in texts, becoming a state-sanctioned activity after Themistokles staged one to rally his troops before the battle of Salamis (Aelian, *On Animals* 2.28). A statue base from Athens (ca. 510 BC) offers a tamer version of the animal *agon*, in which an angry dog provokes an agitated cat, and both are being held on leashes by youths.[29] As a human–animal episode, one wonders whether it represents a planned or chance encounter in a private or public setting.

Conclusion

Animals played a part in many areas of ancient Athenian life. By looking at texts, images, and objects, it becomes clear that animal interactions, both

---

[27] Athens, Agora I 7167. *Agora* 14, no. 72.

[28] Popkin 2012, 216–221.

[29] Athens, National Archaeological Museum 3476. Boardman 1978, fig. 242.

with one another and with humans, could be either positive or negative and took place in an array of different settings and venues. The three thematic categories explored briefly here (daily life, mythology and religion, performance and competition) attest the complexity and nuance of animals as a subject, and affirm that our evidence for animals in the ancient city is inevitably screened through a human lens. More than simply existing "for the good of humankind" as Aristotle propounds, animals inhabited the urban landscape, the domestic sphere, the stage, and supernatural world. Their variety was as great as the areas of human life they served. Our ancient evidence illustrates, unambiguously, that Athens was very much a city of animals.

Further Reading

The growing field of Animals Studies has encouraged recent publications on many aspects of ancient Greek (and thus Athenian) animals; e.g., bovines by McInerney 2010, who reflects on their symbolic value and their many functions within ancient Greek culture; birds by Mynott 2018. The best general introduction is Campbell 2014, with chapters organized according to theme, and covering much that is mentioned here, as well the economy, magic, communication, husbandry, metamorphosis, zoology, etc. For classification, terminology, and species, see Calder 2011; Korhonen and Ruonakoski 2017; and the user-friendly collections of Kitchell 2013, and Lewis and Llewelyn-Jones 2018. Fauna are covered by MacKinnon (in Campbell 2014); Ekroth and Wallensten 2013; and see Liston et al. 2018, for dogs found deposited with infants in a second-century BC well in the Agora. For animal fossils and their connections to mythology, see Mayor (in Campbell 2014). Both Kalof 2011 and Campbell 2014 place Greek animals into a wider ancient context. Hybrid creatures in Athenian literature and art are well covered in Padgett 2003 and Aston 2011, while animal-shaped vessels from Athens and elsewhere are the topic of a recent exhibition and well-illustrated catalogue (Ebbinhaus 2018).

Bibliography

Aston, E. 2011. *Mixanthrôpoi: Animal–Human Hybrid Deities in Greek Religion*. Liège.

Bérard, C. et al. 1989. *A City of Images: Iconography and Society in Ancient Greece*. Princeton.

Boardman, J. 1978. *Greek Sculpture: The Archaic Period*. London.

  1998. *Early Greek Vase Painting*. London.

Calder, L. 2011. *Cruelty and Sentimentality: Greek Attitudes to Animals, 600–300 BC*. Oxford.

Campbell, G.L., ed. 2014. *The Oxford Handbook of Animals in Classical Thought and Life*. Oxford.

Ebbinhaus, S. 2018. *Animal-Shaped Vessels from the Ancient World: Feasting with Gods, Heroes, and Kings*. New Haven.

Ekroth, G., and J. Wallensten, eds. 2013. *Bones, Behaviour, and Belief: The Zooarchaeological Evidence as a Source for Ritual Practice in Ancient Greece and Beyond*. Stockholm.

Jameson, M.H. 2014. *Cults and Rites in Ancient Greece: Essays on Religion and Society*. Cambridge.

Kalof, L., ed. 2011. *A Cultural History of Animals in Antiquity*. Oxford.

Kaltsas, N. 2002. *Sculpture in the National Archaeological Museum, Athens*. Athens.

Kitchell, K.F. 2013. *Animals in the Ancient World from A to Z*. London.

Korhonen, T., and E. Ruonakoski. 2017. *Human and Animal in Ancient Greece: Empathy and Encounter in Classical Literature*. London.

Kurtz, D.C., and J. Boardman. 1971. *Greek Burial Customs*. London.

Lewis, S., and L. Llewelyn-Jones. 2018. *The Culture of Animals in Antiquity: A Sourcebook with Commentaries*. London.

Lissarrague, F. 1990. *The Aesthetics of the Greek Banquet: Images of Wine and Ritual*. Princeton.

Liston, M.A., S.I. Rotroff, and L.M. Snyder. 2018. *The Agora Bone Well*. Princeton.

McInerney, J. 2010. *The Cattle of the Sun: Cows and Culture in the World of the Ancient Greeks*. Princeton.

Mynott, J. 2018. *Birds in the Ancient World: Winged Words*. Oxford.

Padgett, M. ed. 2003. *The Centaur's Smile: The Human Animal in Early Greek Art*. New Haven.

Popkin, M. 2012. "Roosters, Columns, and Athena on Early Panathenaic Prize Amphoras: Symbols of a New Athenian Identity." *Hesperia* 81: 207–235.

Steiner, D. 2013. "Swallow This: A *Pelike* within Late Archaic Song and Visual Culture." *Helios* 40: 41–70.

Additional resources to accompany this chapter can be found at: www.cambridge .org/NeilsRogers

PART III

Business/Commerce

15 | Labor and Employment

DAVID M. LEWIS

> In small towns the same workman makes chairs and doors and plows
> and tables, and often this same artisan builds houses, and even so he is
> thankful if he can only find employment enough to support him. And
> it is, of course, impossible for a man of many trades to be proficient in
> all of them. In large cities, on the other hand, inasmuch as many
> people have demands to make upon each branch of industry, one
> trade alone, and very often even less than a whole trade, is enough to
> support a man: one man, for instance, makes shoes for men, and
> another for women; and there are places even where one man earns a
> living by only stitching shoes, another by cutting them out, another by
> sewing the uppers together, while there is another who performs none
> of these operations but only assembles the parts.
>
> Xenophon, *Cyropaedia* 8.2.5 (trans. Miller)

For almost all of Attika's population at any given point in time during the
Classical period, the typical day was spent at work. Contrary to primitivist
ideas that the vast majority of the population labored as poverty-stricken,
self-sufficient subsistence farmers, recent research has shown both how
agricultural life was intimately bound up with market exchange, and how
non-agricultural workers (including miners and quarriers, woodcutters,
charcoal-makers, artisans, fishermen, merchants, wholesalers, retailers,
and purveyors of a wide range of services) constituted a large and dynamic
component of the population. Indeed, probably only around half of
Attika's population was directly involved in farming.[1]

Farmers and Market Gardeners

Whether one lived in the city (broadly defined as the zone around Athens
and Piraeus, linked together by the Long Walls) or the countryside, the
basic unit of the economy was the *oikos* (household). This term covers both
the physical house as well as its human and animal members, its land, and

---

[1] See Bresson 2016, 142–145; Fachard and Bresson forthcoming.

movable property. The *oikos* was the basis of economic production, and its functioning involved several kinds of resource allocation. (See also Harrington, Chapter 9 in this volume.) The most basic was production for domestic consumption. A small farmer and his family growing cereals (most commonly barley; wheat was less well adapted to Attika's arid climate), vines, and olives, and keeping a few animals, might be able to consume much of this produce, convert animal products such as wool into clothing, and dispose of surpluses and acquire items which they lacked by barter with neighbors. But in Classical Attika, such a picture of isolation and self-sufficiency underplays the real importance of market exchange: Athens regularly imported an enormous amount of grain, easing the pressure to maximize cereal production; more farmland could therefore be given over to cash crops such as vines and olives.[2] Pseudo-Aristotle (*Economics* 1344b32–34, 1345a18–20) characterized the Athenians as practicing a form of *oikonomia* where the market played a crucial role, especially small households, which tended to sell their produce rather than store it. This tallies with the picture of farming presented in Aristophanes, where, for example, Khremes in the *Ekklesiazousai* (817–822) talks about selling his grapes in town for cash and using the money to buy flour.

Land in Attika was mostly in private hands, and the typical small farmer was an owner-occupier, not a tenant.[3] The farmer's work was shaped by residential patterns, inheritance patterns, and seasonality. In some demes, farmers lived in scattered farmsteads (see Map 9.2), while in others, nucleated settlements predominated.[4] Distance from the fields influenced the intensity of labor that could be applied to a given plot. Partible inheritance led to intergenerational fragmentation of landholdings, but land could be bought and sold, to some degree counteracting this tendency. In a small mixed farm, different crops and tasks occupied the farmer throughout the year, as Table 15.1 shows.

The smallest farms were worked by the owner and his family, but slavery was pervasive, and on many modestly sized farms a couple of slaves would aid the farmer in his work. Members of the elite typically owned larger holdings and would not personally engage in manual work, labor generally being provided by slaves overseen by bailiffs (*epitropoi*), themselves often of

---

[2] On the relationship between olive cultivation and the ancient Greek economy, see Foxhall 2007.

[3] We do have some limited evidence for private leasing, and much more for land leased by institutions such as demes and sanctuaries. See Pernin 2014.

[4] For scattered settlements, see Lohmann 1992; for nucleated ones, see Osborne 1985. See also Fachard, Chapter 2 in this volume.

Table 15.1 *Agricultural year of Attika.* Source: adapted from Foxhall 2007, 127

Modern Month	Attic Month	Agricultural jobs
Sept.–Oct.	Boedromion	Manuring & field cleaning; Vintage & pressing; Fig harvest; Watering
Oct.–Nov.	Pyanepsion	Ploughing & sowing cereals & legumes; Trenching; manuring; pruning other fruit trees; planting new trees; Olive picking & pressing (every other year); trenching; manuring, pruning olive trees
Nov.–Dec.	Maimakterion	(Ploughing & sowing cereals & legumes cont.); Lambing & kidding
Dec.–Jan.	Poseideon	Lambing & kidding
Jan.–Feb.	Gamelion	Fallow ploughing; Sheep & goat milking & processing
Feb.–Mar.	Anthesterion	Weeding cereals; Vine & tree digging & pruning
Mar.–Apr.	Elaphebolion	(Weeding cereals cont.); Grafting
Apr.–May	Mounichion	Earthing up trees; Watering young trees
May–June	Thargelion	Cereal & winter legume harvest *barley wheat*; Earthing up tree & vine trenches; Fig fertilising; Milk & milk processing
June–July	Skirophorion	Fallow ploughing; Watering young trees & vines
July–Aug.	Hekatombaion	(Fallow ploughing cont.); Threshing & crop processing for storage
Aug.–Sept.	Metageitnion	Fig harvest *fresh dried*

slave status. Elite landholdings were especially geared toward production for the market.[5]

Market gardens were to be found in the belt of land immediately surrounding Athens and Piraeus.[6] Vegetables were a key part of the diet and could be bought in the Agora (Aristophanes, *Knights* 676–682), although this market was strongly affected by the seasonal availability of different greens (Aristophanes fr. 581;[7] Theophrastos, *Characters* 14.9). The gardens that supplied this market were intensively cultivated and regularly irrigated from wells, or from streams using shadufs (*keloneia*) (Aristophanes fr. 697; [Aristotle], *Mechanics* 857a). According to Antisthenes of Rhodes (*ap.* Diogenes Laertius 7.5), when the philosopher Kleanthes arrived in Athens at the end of the fourth century with only 4 drachmas in hand, he worked for wages drawing water at night in a market garden to fund his philosophical studies.

The Non-Agricultural Population

Around 200 differentiated occupations were practiced in Classical Attika, most of them in the non-agricultural sector, although farming remained the single largest occupation. This degree of specialization reflected the high level of market demand exerted by a comparatively egalitarian distribution of wealth across the free population, and relatively high living standards.[8] Two kinds of specialization should be noted: horizontal and vertical. The most extensive type, horizontal specialization, refers to the number of individual specialists producing goods, selling goods, or offering services. There were specialist potters to produce pots, fishermen to catch fish, barbers to cut hair, and so forth. Vertical specialization refers to the number of specialized artisans collaborating in the production of a single item. Due to the relatively low level of technology, highly complex forms of production were rare and vertical specialization limited.[9]

The bulk of non-agricultural workers lived in the city, but workshops have been discovered in some country demes;[10] nor should we neglect

---

[5] On elite landholdings, see Osborne 1991; Lewis 2018, 173–176, 180–193; cf. Bresson 2016, 142–174.

[6] Carroll-Spillecke 1992.

[7] Here and hereafter, references to comic fragments follow the *PCG*.

[8] Taylor 2017, 69–114.

[9] On the two types of specialization, see Harris 2002.

[10] Sanidas 2013, 111–122.

forestry workers such as charcoal-makers (Aristophanes, *Acharnians* 212; Menander, *Epitrepontes* 407f), woodcutters (*IG* I^3 1361), and pine-torch cutters (*IG* II^2 1557.29). Many coastal dwellers were involved in fishing: some local products were proverbial, such as Phaleric sprats (Aristophanes, fr. 520; *Acharnians* 901; cf. *Birds* 76) or perch from Anagyrous (Plato Comicus fr. 175; Kallias Comicus I fr. 6). For most citizens and metics (resident foreigners), self-employment was the norm for several reasons. One was technological: the relatively simple craft technology prevented the development of highly elaborate forms of 'vertical specialization,' which in turn could have led to the development of large 'firms' with many specialized workers and managers. A second was cultural: Athenians tended to avoid long-term employment as the workers of fellow citizens unless compelled by extreme poverty (Xenophon, *Memorabilia* 2.8; Demosthenes 57.35). Third was the prevalence of slavery; acquiring a slave was a common aspiration. In Lysias 24.6, we hear of a petty artisan who complains that he had not yet managed to acquire enough money to buy a slave to help relieve him of his work. In Athens the employer–employee relationship was often synonymous with the master–slave relationship.

The Slave Population

Slaves were relatively cheap in Classical Athens, meaning that the acquisition of slave labor was a realistic aspiration for most citizens. The richest men might own fifty or more slaves, but a middling family would typically own a couple, such as the farmers we often encounter in the plays of Aristophanes, or the minor artisans listed in the building accounts of the Erechtheion, who often work alongside one or two of their own slaves (*IG* I^3 476). It was a sign of indigence not to own a single slave. Slaves were largely recruited from abroad, especially from Anatolia, Syria, Thrace, and the Black Sea. They made up a large component – perhaps over a third – of Attika's population, rather higher than was the case later in Rome.[11]

The effect that slavery had on the link between work and leisure is significant. As Lysias' client realized, the acquisition of a slave injected flexibility into his daily routine. This, of course, required exploiting the slave as much as possible: in one calculation, Xenophon proposed making slaves work for 360 days per year (*Ways and Means* 4.23), redolent of a

---

[11] On the role of slaves in Athens, see Lewis 2018, 39–48, 167–194.

proverb later quoted by Aristotle (*Politics* 1334a20): "no leisure for slaves." That said, the extent to which masters were successful in extracting a maximum of labor from their slaves ought not to be exaggerated, and slaves found various ways to shirk or negotiate the burden of unpaid work imposed by economically parasitic masters. Slaves were employed in a wide range of occupations from drudgery in the mines to relatively skilled and upwardly mobile occupations such as banking. Perhaps ca. 1,000 slaves in Athens were *demosioi*, publicly owned slaves, who performed a wide range of labor roles, from looking after public roads to testing coins, acting as a kind of police force, and working in the state archive.[12]

Miners and Quarriers

Attika's most valuable resource was silver, which was mined in the Laurion district. Miners extracted argentiferous lead, and then separated out the silver in several stages. The workforce at Laurion was mainly composed of slaves, perhaps around 11,000 in the 340s; the concentration of industry in silver mining affected the wider economy of southern Attika, where cash-crop-oriented production fed the slave workforce and charcoal-burning on an industrial scale fed the fuel-hungry smelting process. (See also Kroll, Chapter 18 in this volume.) Attika also contained numerous quarries, the most famous of which was at Mt. Penteli, northeast of Athens. It was marble from here that was used to construct the Classical buildings of the Akropolis, and workers and oxen dragged rough-hewn blocks along a specially constructed road (*lithagogia*) into Athens for finishing.[13] Throughout the Classical period, a vibrant industry in stone sculpture existed. (See Palagia, Chapter 20 in this volume.)

Artisans

A number of workshops have been excavated in Attika, most of them concerned with ceramics, metalworking, and stonemasonry.[14] Yet as

---

[12] Ismard 2017, 35–56.

[13] See Korres 2001.

[14] Sanidas 2013, 41–121; for an introduction to these three forms of production, see Hasaki 2012; on manufacturing more generally, see Acton 2014. See Rotroff, Chapter 19 in this volume on the ceramic industry.

Aischines (1.124) pointed out, *ergasteria* (workshops) were generally not tailor-built for specific forms of industry. A shop rented out to a doctor might be termed a 'surgery,' but if he moved out and a smith moved in, it would subsequently be termed a 'foundry,' or if a fuller moved in, a 'laundry,' or if a carpenter, a 'carpenter's shop,' and so forth. Of the wide range of petty industries known from literary and epigraphical sources, only a very few are archaeologically detectable. One archaeological resource of great value, however, is iconography; more precisely, a trend in Late Archaic and Early Classical vase-painting that occasionally took as its subject matter the work of artisans, providing a wealth of technical details, although one should not treat these images as straightforward snapshots of daily life.[15]

One highly skilled occupation was that of the perfume-maker, on whose craft Theophrastos' *On Odors* provides many insights.[16] Top-end perfumes required expensive imported ingredients; one slave in charge of such an operation managed to rack up a debt of five talents with his suppliers and moneylenders (Hyperides 3.6–9). Another skilled job lay in the production of books for sale: scriveners (Kratinos fr. 267) copied out the works of famous writers, which could be bought in the Agora (Eupolis fr. 327; Plato, *Apology* 26d–e).

Woodworking industries are known from textual and iconographic sources.[17] For example, Aristophanes (*Knights* 464) refers in passing to cartwrights, a key industry essential for the transport of goods and materials. A fourth-century inscription detailing what went into the production of a wagon (*IG* II^2 1673.11–44) reveals much about the business networks of these artisans, who had to subcontract with (and buy raw materials and component parts from) a variety of other specialists, such as rope-makers, ironmongers, and timber wholesalers, not to mention the muleteers needed to transport raw materials to the construction site.

Another important industry was the processing of animal hides into a very wide range of commodities, from footwear to boxing paraphernalia, saddles and harnesses, and even sex toys.[18] This involved various stages. Hides first had to be tanned; the most famous tannery was owned by the demagogue Kleon (Aristophanes, *Knights* 43–45). The industry was malodorous and polluting: one inscription bans the tanning of hides near the

---

[15] Vidale 2002.

[16] Reger 2005.

[17] Vidale 2002, 149–168.

[18] See Dercy 2015.

Ilissos River (*IG* I³ 257). Tanned hides were then sold to various craftsmen, such as bridle-makers (Xenophon, *Memorabilia* 4.2.1) or shoemakers. Sokrates' tendency to walk around barefoot was highly unusual, and the massive demand for footwear spawned an elaborately organized industry, where a degree of 'vertical specialization' developed.

Market Vendors

Much labor in Attika involved buying and selling. (See also Lawall, Chapter 17 in this volume.) The non-agricultural population by definition depended on the market for survival, for it did not produce its own food but had to make or sell goods or services in order to acquire the money to pay for the necessities of life. Coinage was introduced to Attika in the second half of the sixth century BC; by the fourth century, Attika was heavily monetized, with many small denominations of coin suitable for everyday transactions. One drachma – the amount that many of the workers on the Erechtheion were paid per diem – was worth 6 obols; each obol was in turn worth 8 *chalkoi* (coppers). (See Kroll, Chapter 18 in this volume.) It is worth pointing out, however, that the idea of a 'standard' daily wage is quite misleading. Loomis has published an invaluable collection of evidence for wages in Classical Attika: these are mainly culled from inscriptions where the state contracted with private artisans, transporters, etc. and paid them a fee.[19] The wage (*misthos*) paid by the state was calibrated to match what a worker could expect to earn per day *on average*; but for artisans making and selling goods, vendors hawking their wares, or the purveyors of various services, the amount they earned each day would have been highly variable.

Market exchange took place in various venues and contexts. The densest cluster of vendors was, of course, in the central Agora of Athens, which was subdivided into sections based on the commodity sold. Life as a market vendor was precarious: it is a sausage-seller that Aristophanes chose as his quintessential proletarian in the *Knights*; and Davies has recently reconstructed the position of fishmongers who, working on credit, had to tailor their sales strategies in order to sell as much of their stock as dearly as possible, so that they could repay the loan sharks (*obolostatai*) on which their trade depended yet have enough profit left over on which to live.[20] This sharp-eyed profit-seeking was decried as *chrematistike* by wealthy

---

[19] Loomis 1998.
[20] Davies 2016.

philosophers whose survival was not dependent on learning the art of what Xenophon called "buying cheap and selling dear" (*Memorabilia* 3.7.6). The once-popular view that profit-seeking was a marginal behavior can no longer be upheld; nor was the pursuit of profit hampered by primitive accounting techniques.[21]

The central Agora was not the only marketplace in Attika: several city demes had their own agoras, and there were others in country demes, not to mention a major marketplace in Piraeus. In addition, there were shops from which commodities could be sold (e.g. Alexis fr. 18), and some vendors were itinerant, selling their wares on the go (Diphilos fr. 87; Antiphanes fr. 69). Vendors thus sold their wares in diverse locations and in different ways.

Piraeus and Maritime Traders

The largest expense in Athens' public finances was its navy: 200 triremes fought at Salamis in 480, and the fleet grew even larger by the late fourth century. Each trireme had a complement of 200 men, 170 of them rowers. Although Athens almost never fielded its full force, the economic implications of maintaining such an enormous fleet for a pre-modern city-state should be clear. (On military expenditures, see Pritchard, Chapter 22 in this volume.) That includes not only the imported materials (wood, rope, sailcloth, bronze) that went into the ship itself, but the cost of paying its crew (about one talent per month at sea), and the various support industries and services that grew up in Piraeus: there were sail-stitchers (Aristophanes, *Thesmophoriazousai* 935), rope-makers (*IG* II^2 1673.18–19), rope-sellers (*IG* II^2 1570.24), smiths (*IG* II^2 1554A.10–11), barbers (Plutarch, *Nikias* 30), keepers of tenement houses (Thucydides 3.74.2) and brothels (Aristophanes, *Peace* 165), wine-shops (*IG* II^2 1554A.22-3), and bath-houses (Isaios 6.33), auctioneers (Demosthenes 44.4), and muleteers (*IG* II^2 1558B.48), to name just a few.

Piraeus also represented the conduit through which imports and exports flowed. Athens' most important import was, of course, grain. But the comic poet Hermippos (fr. 63) outlines a sample of some of the many other items that flowed into Athens during the late fifth century: silphium and hides from Cyrene, fish from the Hellespont, pork and cheese from Syracuse, sailcloth, rope, and papyrus from Egypt, incense from Syria, cypress from

---

[21] Faraguna 2008.

Crete, ivory from Libya, raisins and figs from Rhodes, slaves from Phrygia and Pagasai, nuts from Paphlagonia, palm fruit from Phoenicia, and textiles from Carthage. These imports were then bought by wholesalers and resold to consumers in the Agora by a wide variety of retailers;[22] but raw materials were also bought by artisans who worked them into more complex products. The importance of imports for Attika's artisans can better be grasped if we consider ventures such as the shield-manufactory of Kephalos, a metic from Syracuse dwelling in Piraeus and father of the orator Lysias (Lysias 12.19; Plato, *Republic* 327b). Most of the labor and raw materials for his shields came from overseas and had to be acquired from wholesalers: slaves (Kephalos owned some 120), willow (Theophrastos, *Enquiry into Plants* 5.7.7), leather and glue, and bronze, never mind the tools required to turn these materials into the finished product.

These imports were brought to Piraeus by maritime traders (*emporoi*) and shippers (*naukleroi*); and the port served as the hub for mariners of various sorts, including oarsmen hiring their labor to the state. Most sailing occurred in the clement months from April through November, with a lower intensity of activity in the winter. (See also Steinhauer, Chapter 16 in this volume.)

Services

For many residents of Attika, work meant selling their services. One of the most important service areas was in transport. Porters carried loads of all kinds; simple yoke-poles were typically used to carry bulky loads (Aristophanes fr. 886; Plato Comicus fr. 50). For larger loads, one could hire a muleteer (*IG* II² 10B.4; 1558.33–36, 47–48; Plato, *Lysis* 208b), a cart, or a wagon ([Xenophon], *Constitution of the Athenians* 1.17).[23] There was a hire market at Kolonos Agoraios next to the Temple of Hephaistos, where unskilled workers could be hired for odd jobs (Kratinos fr. 281; Pherekrates fr. 142). Cooks also hired themselves out to cater at special occasions (Menander, *Aspis* 216ff.).

Prostitution was big business in Athens, ranging from *pornai*, whose services could be bought for a few obols to rather more exclusive *hetairai*, affordable only for rich men (Xenarchos fr. 4; cf. Xenophon, *Memorabilia* 3.11.1–4). (See Ormand, Chapter 26 in this volume.) Other notable services

---

[22] Bresson 2016, 306–317.
[23] Raepsaet 2002.

included barbershops (Aristophanes, *Wealth* 377–378; *Ekklesiazousai* 302), bath-houses (*Constitution of the Athenians* 2.10; Theophrastos, *Characters* 4.15, 9.8), private schools (Demosthenes 19.249), doctors (Menander, *Aspis* 339–342), banks (Demosthenes 36.29–30), and fullers (Theophrastos, *Characters* 10.14, 18.6).

The Labor of Women

Whereas *schole*, leisure from manual labor, was a key marker of the male cultural and economic elite, the same cannot be said of their wives, mothers, and sisters, who played a crucial role in economic life. Both Aristophanes (*Lysistrata* 15–19) and Xenophon (*Oikonomikos* 7.33–42) underscore the key organizational role that women played in the co-ordination of the human and material resources of the *oikos*. Above all, one of the most important areas of the economy – textile production – was largely in the hands of women of all statuses and classes.[24] The production of (predominantly) wool and linen garments was an extremely time-consuming task. Apart from the production of the major garments (e.g. *himation*, *chiton*, and *peplos*), specialist artisans might produce textiles by other processes – ribbon-weavers, for instance (cf. Eupolis fr. 262); or hatters, such as Thettale, who on one occasion made felt hats for the public slaves at Eleusis (*IG* II[2] 1672.70–71). Another important textile product was fishing nets; we find two net-weavers, Kittos and Euphrosyne, as the target of a curse tablet from Early Hellenistic Athens, along with their work and workshops (Pollux, *Onomastikon* 7.179).

   Whereas elite writers stress the sequestered nature of their womenfolk, the same is not true of lower-class women, whose economic activities were manifold and often conducted outside the household, such as market vendors, midwives, wet-nurses, tavern-keepers, and makers of garlands; women also lent a hand at times with agricultural work.[25]

Attitudes to Work

The importance of slavery should not lead us to think that work was despised by most Athenians. For conservative philosophical elements of

[24] Spantidaki 2016.
[25] Brock 1994.

the leisured elite, manual work was contemptible, especially the so-called banausic (vulgar) trades (Xenophon, *Oikonomikos* 4.2–4; Aristotle, *Politics* 1277b33–1278a13). These were minority views that had little if any effect on economic life. The archaic attitudes of Hesiod and Solon – that one should work hard and strive to maximize output and grow wealthy, so long as one did not act unjustly – represent popular thinking on economic life, and that goes for the elite as much as for the broader *demos* (Hesiod, *Works and Days* 11f., 320 ff.; Solon fr. 13 [West]; cf. Xenophon, *Oikonomikos* 1.4, 2.5–6, 2.10, 11.8, 11.10). That philosophical views about the shamefulness of working in manual trades were not shared by most of the population is clear from the many artists' signatures on vases, statues, and other craft products, which make it clear that artisans took pride in their work, gaining wealth and status through displays of skill.[26] Hesiod's remark (*Works and Days* 25) on the rivalry between competing potters was just as true of Athens at the dawn of the Classical period, when we find the vase-painter Euthymides signing off one virtuoso piece with *hos oudepote Euphronios* ("As never Euphronios," a dig at a rival vase-painter's inferior skill). The same outlook is evident in Xenophon's discussion of Sokrates' meeting with the corselet-maker Pistias, who prided himself on making the best-fitting armor in town (*Memorabilia* 3.10.9–15).

Conclusion

Labor in Attika was a complex affair. A wide range of specialties existed, with their own special technical knowledge, most of which was passed on from master to apprentice without being recorded, and thus has passed out of history. Intimations of the remarkable degree of technical skill attained by Athenian artisans can be gained nowadays by visiting museums where durable remains such as sculpture and fine pottery can be viewed. Yet these few survivals represent the tip of a vast iceberg, a lost economy of staggering complexity whose workforce cannot be reduced to a few familiar examples – the farmer, potter, vase-painter, sculptor. For individual workers, much of the texture of life was determined by the nature of their occupation; daily practice in the movements of work made their hands more dexterous and their particular skill set more refined, whether they

---

[26] See Hurwit 2015.

made vases or lyres, hammered out hoplite helmets, or wove elaborate textiles. Yet none of these occupations was isolated: work provided a constant impetus for social interaction, through sourcing raw materials, repairing tools, subcontracting with other workers in the production of composite products, or selling goods and services.

Further Reading

Much has changed in the last two decades regarding general views of the ancient Greek economy; a splendid, detailed, and up-to-date *vade mecum* is Bresson 2016. On the range of occupations in Attika, see Harris 2002, with supplements in Lewis 2020. Taylor 2017 provides an overview of the working population of Athens' living standards; Lewis 2018, 167–193 discusses the slave population, whilst Brock 1994 discusses the labor of women. Spantidaki 2016 provides a wide-ranging study of textile production. Hasaki 2012 is a useful entry-point to the study of the crafts of potter, smith, and mason, while Sanidas 2013 provides a catalogue of excavated workshops. On masons, Hochscheid 2015 is fundamental. See Vidale 2002 for a detailed study (with many images) of the iconography of artisans, along with Oakley 2020, 47–70 for depictions of workshops on Athenian vases. Acton 2014 contains useful discussion of manufacture but should be used with caution (see the useful review of Rotroff in the *Bryn Mawr Classical Review* 2015.04.23).

Bibliography

Acton, P. 2014. *Poiesis: Manufacturing in Classical Athens*. Oxford.

Bresson, A. 2016. *The Making of the Ancient Greek Economy: Institutions, Markets, and Growth in the City-States*. Princeton.

Brock, R. 1994. "The Labour of Women in Classical Athens." CQ 44.2: 336–346.

Carroll-Spillecke, M. 1992. "The Gardens of Greece from Homeric to Roman Times." *Journal of Garden History* 12.2: 84–101.

Davies, J.K. 2016. "Aristonikos and the Fishmongers." In *Studies on Wealth in the Ancient World*, eds. F. Santangelo and E. Bissa, London, 21–32.

Dercy, B. 2015. *Le travail des peaux et du cuir dans le monde grec antique*. Naples.

Fachard, S., and A. Bresson. Forthcoming. "Athens and the Aegean." In *The Cambridge Companion to the Ancient Greek Economy*, ed. S. von Reden, Cambridge.

Faraguna, M. 2008. "Calcolo economico, archivi finanziari e credito nel mondo greco tra VI e IV sec. a.C." In *Pistoi Dia Tèn Technèn: Bankers, Loans, and Archives in the Ancient World*, eds. K. Verboven, K. Vandorpe, and V. Chankowski, Leuven, 33–57.

Foxhall, L. 2007. *Olive Cultivation in Ancient Greece: Seeking the Ancient Economy*. Oxford.

Harris, E.M. 2002. "Workshop, Marketplace, and Household: The Nature of Technical Specialization in Classical Athens and its Influence on Economy and Society." In *Money, Labour, and Land: Approaches to the Economies of Ancient Greece*, eds. P.A. Cartledge, E.E. Cohen, and L. Foxhall, London, 67–99.

Hasaki, E. 2012. "Workshops and Technology." In *A Companion to Greek Art*, eds. T.J. Smith and D. Plantzos, Malden, MA, 255–272.

Hochscheid, H. 2015. *Networks of Stone: Sculpture and Society in Archaic and Classical Athens*. Oxford.

Hurwit, J.M. 2015. *Artists and Signatures in Ancient Greece*. Cambridge.

Ismard, P. 2017. *Democracy's Slaves: A Political History of Greece*. Cambridge, MA.

Korres, M. 2001. *From Pentelicon to the Parthenon: The Ancient Quarries and the Story of a Half-Worked Column Capital of the First Marble Parthenon*. Athens.

Lewis, D.M. 2018. *Greek Slave Systems in their Eastern Mediterranean Context, c. 800–146 BC*. Oxford.

   2020. "Occupational Hazards: Gauging the Extent of Horizontal Specialization in the Classical Athenian Economy." In *Professionals and Skilled Labour in Ancient Greece and Rome*, eds. E. Stewart, E.M. Harris, and D.M. Lewis, Cambridge, 129–174.

Lohmann, H. 1992. "Agriculture and Country Life in Classical Attica." In *Agriculture in Ancient Greece*, ed. B. Wells, Stockholm, 29–57.

Loomis, W.T. 1998. *Wages, Welfare Costs, and Inflation in Classical Athens*. Ann Arbor.

Oakley, J.H. 2020. *A Guide to Scenes of Daily Life on Athenian Vases*. Madison.

Osborne, R. 1985. *Demos: The Discovery of Classical Attika*. Cambridge.

   1991. "Pride and Prejudice, Sense and Subsistence: Exchange and Society in the Greek City." In *City and Country in the Ancient World*, eds. J. Rich and A. Wallace-Hadrill, London, 119–146.

Pernin, I. 2014. *Les baux ruraux en Grèce ancienne: corpus épigraphique et étude*. Lyon.

Raepsaet, G. 2002. *Attelages et techniques de transport dans le monde gréco-romain*. Brussels.

Reger, G. 2005. "The Manufacture and Distribution of Perfume." In *Making, Moving, and Managing: The New World of Ancient Economies*, eds. Z. Archibald, J.K. Davies, and V. Gabrielsen, Oxford, 253–297.

Sanidas, G.M. 2013. *La production artisanale en Grèce. Une approche spatiale et topographique à partir des exemples de l'Attique et du Péloponnèse du VIIe au Ier siècle avant J.-C*. Paris.

Spantidaki, S. 2016. *Textile Production in Classical Athens*. Oxford.

Taylor, C. 2017. *Poverty, Wealth, and Wellbeing. Experiencing* Penia *in Democratic Athens*. Oxford.

Vidale, M. 2002. *L'idea di un lavoro lieve. Il lavoro artigianale nelle immagini della ceramica greca tra VI e IV secolo a.C*. Padua.

16 | Piraeus: Harbors, Navy, and Shipping

GEORGE STEINHAUER

> Themistokles was the first to have the audacity to suggest that the Athenians should attach themselves to the sea and in so doing laid the basis for their empire.

> He was of the opinion Piraeus was more useful than the upper city.
>
> Thucydides 1.93

The Making of Piraeus

Among the great Greek sea powers of Corinth, Samos, and Aegina, Athens was a latecomer. For a very long period, Athens was the civic center of a large agricultural state ruled by an aristocracy of landowners, with the majority of the population living in hamlets and villages, the antecedents of the Attic demes. Athens also did not take part in the overseas adventures of the great Greek colonization. The small harbors on the western and eastern coasts of Attika were restricted mainly to fishing and local trade.[1]

From the eighth to the fifth century BC, the main harbor of Athens was at Phaleron (see Map 4.2), a site easily accessible from Athens by a direct road, but as it was open to the south winds and had shallow waters, it was unsuitable for larger ships. The recent excavation of an extensive Archaic cemetery near the shore of Phaleron testifies to a large but poor population, possibly of seamen and fishermen. No trace of ancient constructions of any kind has been found; however, a sonar underwater scanning of the bay provides indications of a large pier with an east–west orientation, starting from the western cape of Phaleron near the point where the Phaleric Wall allegedly ended.[2]

---

[1] Exceptions were rare. One of these, Steiria in the bay of Port Rafti, was an important harbor in Late Roman times, and of course there were the ports of the Laurion region (Thorikos, Pountazeza, Limani Pasa), which, it has been suggested, imported wood for metallurgical furnaces, and exported lead or shipped it to Piraeus.

[2] Some Roman foundations noted in the vicinity, around the chapel of Agios Georgios prove the existence of a Roman port there, used by merchant ships, like St. Paul's.

The dynamic turn of Athens toward the Aegean had been anticipated by private overseas enterprises of the leading Athenian families by the mid-sixth century. However, the decisive step was only taken in 493/2 BC, when the leader, Themistokles, during his archonship, persuaded the people to fortify the isolated rocky peninsula of Piraeus, in whose strategic location and natural harbors he recognized the prerequisites for a future Athenian maritime empire. Yet the plan was not fully implemented until 483/2 BC, when, on the eve of and with the premonition of the second great Persian invasion, it was decided to use the year's surplus of 100 talents from the silver mines for the construction of 200 triremes (cf. Fig. 29.2). Two years later, these vessels saved Greece in the Battle of Salamis and helped Athens acquire the leadership of Delian League in the subsequent battles for the liberation of Ionia. The gradual trans-formation of the Athenian leadership of the League in 478 BC into an Athenian empire, culminating in the transfer in 454 BC of the League's treasury to Athens, went hand in hand with the development of the new port into both a naval stronghold and the commercial capital of the Athenian *mare nostrum*.

To prevent any future danger of Athens being cut off from its military and supply center of Piraeus, the statesman, Kimon, constructed two Long Walls to Piraeus and Phaleron (Map 4.2). A grandiose project, it was finally completed in the 460s by Perikles with the construction of a more easily manned, walled corridor which was a stade (184 m) wide. (See Costaki and Theocharaki, Chapter 4 in this volume.) This linked the two poles of the 'bipolar' city, practically transforming it into an island invulnerable to attack by land. Piraeus, the old rustic deme of approximately 500 citizens, was by then on its way to becoming a large and powerful urban center. It was planned anew by Hippodamos of Miletos, an eccentric philosopher of Perikles' circle, thus acquiring immortality as a model city and the only proven work of the 'father' of town planning.

The debacle of 404, at the end of the Peloponnesian War, was a severe blow to the port. Its fortifications and its shipsheds were destroyed, and as a consequence of the commercial recession, the city was deserted by foreigners. Piraeus became no more than "a big nutshell without a kern" (Philiskos, *PCG* 7 fr. 356). Its revival began in 394 with the rebuilding – with Persian funds – of the harbor, its fortifications, and the Long Walls. The dockyards, in contrast, were slower to expand, so that in 377/6, Athens had no more than 100 triremes. In 354 BC, after its definitive failure to recover supremacy in the Aegean, the state was practically bankrupt (Demosthenes 10.37).

The keystone of the recovery policy of Euboulos and Lycurgus in the third quarter of the fourth century BC consisted of restructuring public finances and encouraging private investment in trade, mining, and agriculture. Thanks to the economic importance of the local market, and the banking facilities and administrative expertise of the Emporion (the commercial section of the city), Piraeus became once again, as in the glorious days of the past, the most profitable trading center of the Aegean. The return of the metics (resident foreigners) was encouraged through tax exemptions, housing facilities, and a range of administrative measures, including favorable legal regulations and the right to build their own temples. The rising prosperity from trade and agriculture helped the Athenian economy compensate for the loss of the tribute with taxes (*eisphorai*) on private revenues, and made possible the Lycurgan policy of classical grandeur which was realized in the astonishing growth of the fleet to 379 triremes in 337/8 and to 370 triremes, 43 *tetrereis*, and 7 *pentereis* in 325/4, and the building of the shipsheds and the famous arsenal of Philon.

For most of the third century, the Piraeus was under Macedonian control and consequently separated from Athens. Its liberation in 229 BC was immediately followed by the rebuilding of the fortifications, but not of the Long Walls. Piraeus' importance as a military naval base for a virtual enemy explains the long siege by Sulla in 86 BC and his rage against the city.

The Remains of Ancient Piraeus

The wall and the gates of the Piraeus fortifications are the best-preserved and the most impressive monuments of the city (Map 16.1). The Themistoklean fortification was highly praised by Thucydides (1.93) for its size (5 m in width, and a height that at the northern section reached 18.5 m), as well as its careful compact stone construction. Only parts of the foundations have been preserved, those of the wall joining the Asty Gates, and of the northern wall east of the Eetioneia Gate on the fortified hill north-northwest of the port and some very small portions recovered along the coast behind the Kononian wall of 394 BC.

The two Asty Gates, built only 100 m apart, served for communication with Athens, respectively outside (the western gate) and inside (the so-called in-between gate) the Long Walls. Notwithstanding the similarity of their general features, the two mighty flanking towers and the internal courtyard are not contemporary. In the ruins of the towers of the older

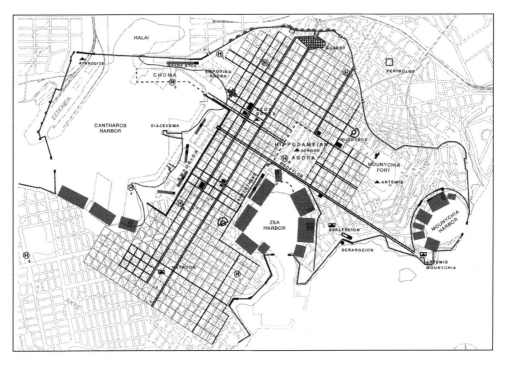

Map 16.1 Map of Piraeus.
Source: G. Steinhauer

outer (western) Astikos pylon, two phases of construction can be clearly
discerned, which correspond to the two major periods of the fortification of
the Piraeus: the oval towers of the initial Themistoklean phase which were
replaced during Konon's reconstruction by rectangular ones. It was only
after the building of the corridor of the Long Walls in the 460s BC that the
need for a second (the in-between-the Walls) gate, arose, so that its round
towers must be dated either before the completion or, more likely, after
their abandonment. There was an analogous strategic interest in building
the Eetioneia Gate on the homonymous hill overlooking the entrance to
Piraeus both from the sea and the land side. This is a simple type of gate
flanked by two towers, without an internal courtyard, which still preserves
its original intimidating aspect thanks to the 3–5 m height of the towers
and the defensive ditch with the piers of its removable bridge. The initial,
partly uncovered (Themistoklean) fortification was a continuation of the
northern fortification of Piraeus which crossed westwards the harbor. The
fort was built by the oligarchs of 411 BC, but it has now disappeared. Most
of the ruins now visible belong to the Kononian reconstruction, with the

Hellenistic additions of a bastion and the encasement of the orthogonal Kononian structures into the existing round towers. A well-preserved stretch of about two kilometers with 5 × 5 m towers every 50 m of the seaside wall still defiantly faces the Aegean. It is also datable to the same Kononian phase.

Especially in contrast to Athens, one of the wonders of Piraeus is the Hippodamian town plan (Map 16.1). The name Hippodamos is associated by Aristotle (*Politics* 2.8 p. 1267b 7; 1268a 15, 8.11 p. 1330b 24) with the idea of a clear separation and demarcation of the public, private, and sacred areas of a city. For most modern architects and archaeologists, the 'Hippodamian' urban plan is based on a rational, orthogonal network of roads and squares, and the uniform parceling out of the houses.

Some light can be shed on the Hippodamian partitioning of Piraeus by the boundary stones (*horoi*) found at different places in the city, demarcating the areas of the overall sections of the city and the main public areas of the dockyards, the Emporion, the civic Agora, etc. The general plan of the city has been recovered mainly through archaeological work of the last thirty years. It was based on the division of the central part of the peninsula into a grid of rectangular house blocks 40 × 46 m each, consisting of eight plots of land, measuring 20 × 11.50 m, thus equaling 230 m². These conditioned the form – not necessarily prescribed by the town planner – of a more or less uniform house type, alternating in same cases with tenement houses (*synoikiai*). Every two or four blocks eventually formed a district with overall dimensions of 80 × 92 m or 250 × 275 m.

On the ground, the model was made by setting up a system of roads. The ordinary roads that defined the house blocks and served the traffic between them had an average width of 5 m, and the main streets defining and connecting the residential districts 8.29 m. Two pairs of large streets (*plateiai hodoi*) with a breadth of 15 m forming a cross across the peninsula constituted the main thoroughfare that defined and linked the public sectors of the city. The north–south axis linked the trade center (Emporion) and the Makra Stoa with the Hippodamian market, the dockyards of Zea and Mounychia, the Mounychia fort, and the Sanctuaries of Artemis Mounychia and Asklepios, while the east–west axis lead to the Asty Gates. The crossroad of these axes was marked by the main Sanctuary of Zeus Soter (Map 16.1). The tiring uniformity of this ideal plan was varied by the graduated construction imposed by the ground, especially of the hill of Mounychia, where, owing to the slope, which exceeds 10 percent, the houses were built on successive natural or artificial embankments. The residential quarter was equipped with an equally well-planned drainage system with tunnel shaped ducts hewn into the rock on the axis of the traverse north–south roads. However, the city suffered severely from a shortage of water. Because springs and wells were extremely rare, the private houses depended for their water supply on a system of cisterns, of which a great number have been found. Thucydides (2.48.2) tells us about the panic created during the Peloponnesian War by the rumor "that the enemies had poisoned the wells, as there were no fountains yet."

A basic constituent of the Hippodamian plan of Piraeus is the main arterial road, which links the three harbors of Kantharos, Zea, and Mounychia with the Hippodamian Agora, and at the same time connects the main sacred areas of Zeus Soter, Asklepios, and Artemis Mounychia. Of the two basic public sectors of the Piraeus, the Emporion occupied the central section of the eastern and part of the northern sides of the port Kantharos, while the dockyards were spread out on the two small closed harbors of Zea and Mounychia at the western and eastern foot of the fortified hill of Mounychia and on the southern end next to the mouth of Kantharos. The internal layout of each harbor followed the shape of the coastline and consequently was independent of the regularity of the Hippodamian scheme, to which each was adapted by means of its proper enclosure wall.

The headquarters of the Athenian naval base (*neorion*) was very probably located at Zea, a mid-sized perfectly round basin with a narrow and sinuous entrance. It was situated in a perfect strategic position abutting on the Hippodamian Agora, the civic center and the mustering station of the army, midway on the street connecting the Mounychia port with the Great Harbor of Kantharos. Zea was the largest naval port, covering 55,000 m^2 and, as of 330/29 BC, it housed 196 triremes in its shipsheds. This was more than half of the Athenian fleet; the rest were in Kantharos (94) and Mounychia (82). Furthermore, Zea boasted such famous buildings as the arsenal for the ship tackle designed by Philon.

The shipsheds (*neosoikoi* or "houses of the ships") were intended for storage of the inactive triremes and shelter from rain, sun, and ship worms, thus keeping them ready for war. They were the prerequisite of naval power and a source of great pride for the Athenian democracy, and were in fact praised as being works equal to the Parthenon and the Propylaia (Demosthenes 22.76). The best documented shipsheds of the Zea harbor were long, parallel colonnades, grouped in pairs under a common roof (*neosoikoi homotegeis*) and formed complexes of ten or twenty shipsheds with a continuous back wall. On their longitudinal axis they had a stone and wood sloping ramp starting from the water's edge (1.52 m wide, with an inclination of ca. 5°). Passages (ca. 2.05 m wide) on each side of the ramp were provided for the hauling and maintenance crews. The length of the shipsheds is now estimated at approximately 54 m. The archaeological evidence for double *neosoikoi* of 89 m helps to fit the epigraphically attested number of 190–200 triremes into a shoreline measuring only 950 m, before the rise of the sea level.

On the northwest side of the harbor, dominating the monumental colonnaded seafront of the *neosoikoi* stood the famous Skeuotheke or Arsenal of Philon. It was constructed from 347–325 BC for the storage of the hanging gear for 134 warships and was highly praised up to Roman times. The building was already known and even reconstructed in detail, well before 1988, when its foundations were uncovered and identified, thanks to the precise and minutely detailed specifications of the architect in his *syngraphe*, or contract (*IG* II² 1609). It was a long narrow building measuring 130 by 18 m, and 10 m in height, divided by two rows of thirty-five square pillars into a central nave. Low walls with lattice gates corresponding to the thirty-four intercolumniations separated the central gangway, a *diodos toi demoi*, allowing the citizens to inspect the contents from two side aisles, which were divided into seventy-eight compartments each furnished with wooden shelves in the loft for ropes and cables, and a chest for the sails.

Opposite, at the north entrance of the Arsenal, a main gate with a court delimited by four boundary stones of the *demosion propylon* formed the monumental gate to the Hippodamian Agora, the city's main market (*he agora ton demoton*), with the old council house (*bouleuterion*), the Temple of Hera, and the market police. We know that the Agora was used occasionally as a place for marshaling the army, very likely also for the warship's crews too, before they embarked for the Choma (in the main harbor) where the final inspection by the *boule* would take place. The site of the office of the supervisors of the dockyard (*epimeletai ton neorion*), who kept the annual detailed list of ships, is unknown, although the existence of this office is reported in a very important series of inscriptions (*IG* II² 1604–1632), found at the southern end of the Emporion.

The Great Harbor (*Megas Limen*) or Kantharos (perhaps named after the two-handled drinking vessel), with an area of 530 km² was the largest (larger than the Vieux Port of Marseille) and one of the safest natural ports of the Mediterranean. It was well protected from the dangerous south winds by the Piraeus peninsula and from the western and northwestern winds by the hills of Aigaleos. The harbor's projecting fortified rocky hill of Eetioneia northwest and the adjoining marshes (*ho en halais pelos*;

Xenophon, *Hellenika* 2.4.34) offered good protection against attacks from land. The entrance to the port was guarded by two towers (by night connected with a chain; *IG* II² 1032) and marked by two lighthouses at the end of the opposite Eetioneia and Piraike peninsulas.

The Kantharos had a double function as a commercial and a military harbor. From a scholiast on Aristophanes' play *Peace* (line 145) and an Augustan inscription (*IG* II² 1935) pertaining to reparations of the port installations, we learn of its main features. These were: the shipsheds (*neoria*), partly discovered between the entrance to the port and the Emporion; the "five porticoes" (*stoai*) around the port of the Emporion and probably on the opposite (i.e. the northwest) side of the port, at the foot of the Eetioneia hill; the dockyards (*psyktrai*), for the construction and repair of the ships; and finally, crowning the hill, the Sanctuary of Aphrodite.

The Emporion, or the commercial harbor, occupied a well-defined zone of ca. 1.5 km² along the eastern side of the Kantharos, a site chosen because it was so well suited to the purpose. It was the sole flat area of the port, was well protected from the south winds with easy access to the nearby city gates, and it had a rich subterranean water table feeding a number of ancient and Late Antique fountains. The land side of the zone was demarcated by an enclosure wall accompanied by a series of stone boundary markers (*horoi*) inscribed "limit of the Emporion and street." Its purpose was both financial (to ensure the control of export, import taxes, and port fees) and urban, that is, to adapt the Emporion to the regular Hippodamian plan and to isolate the residential area from the port and its activities and people. Its limits on the seaside were designated by two *horoi* bearing the inscription "of the ferryboat anchorage," actually found in the sea at the two north and south ends of the mooring place.

The physiognomy of the Emporion was determined, according to our sources, by two features: the large pier, the *Diazeugma* in the middle, and the five porticoes mentioned above. The correct reading of the excavation report of one portico (the first from the south) found in the nineteenth century and the discovery of the traces of three more, as well as some traces of the ancient quay during construction works in the 1980s, show that these porticoes were not aligned along the absolutely straight Emporion waterfront as had been assumed by modern archaeologists, but instead followed the line of the ancient shoreline boxed by the modern wharfs but still recognizable in the Venetian map of Piraeus of 1689 and in Curtius' map of 1841 (Map 16.2).

The heart of port life literally beats in the middle of the Emporion. There, opposite the *Diazeugma*, where Theophrastos imagined his

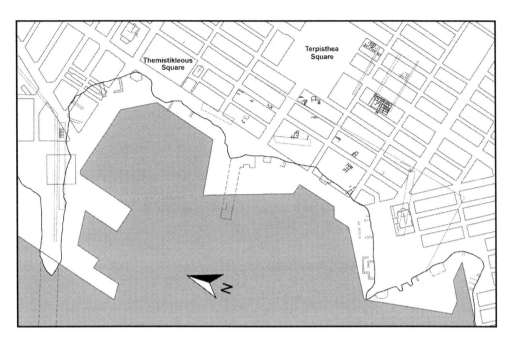

Map 16.2 Plan of the Emporion district, Piraeus.
Source: G. Steinhauer, adapted by D. Weiss

'arrogant' character standing and boasting of his profits from sea trade, stood the *Deigma* (the Sample), probably one of the five porticoes or perhaps an open-air enclosure where, immediately after the arrival of the ships, samples of the merchandise offered for sale were displayed. In front of that structure, around the statue of Poseidon and the tables of the money changers and lenders, most of the inscriptions regarding trade regulations or honoring foreign benefactors were erected. The rest of the porticoes probably served as office rooms of the Overseers (*epimeletai tou emporiou*) and the administrative personnel of the Emporion, while some were used as magazines and retail shops, workshops, and resting places.

The management of such an extensive and active site, with more than twelve ships unloading every day while others were moored outside, required specialized installations such as cranes and skilled operators, stevedores, and boatmen, to say nothing of services such as inns, taverns, and brothels related to the entertainment of sailors, for whom the port was the place in which, then as today, they had to spend most of their time.

The Emporion dealt exclusively with overseas commerce. A long list of goods from all over Greece and the Mediterranean arriving in Piraeus is provided by the comic poet Hermippos of the fifth century. The most important commodities imported were grain, the raw materials used in shipbuilding (such as wood, flax, and pitch), and slaves. (See also Lewis, Chapter 15 in this volume.) In fact, more than half the volume of the trade in the Piraeus port consisted of grain imports. Because the supply of the Athenian population was a matter of very serious concern for the Athenian state, the grain trade was very closely supervised by special agents (the *sitophylakes*) and a separate section of the Emporion was exclusively devoted to it. The core of this *sitikon emporion* was the so-called Long Portico (*Makra Stoa*), a small part of which, in fact five compartments, each consisting of a room 6 × 4 m and an adjoining corridor 6 × 2 m, has recently been excavated at the northern part of the port, next (at a distance of only five meters) to the fortification wall connecting Piraeus to the Eetioneia (Map 16.1). Usually identified with the Alphitopolis stoa of Aristophanes' *Acharnians* (Schol. Aristophanes, *Acharnians* 548), this portico was the place where the imported corn and barley (at least that which was not transported to Athens) was stored, and where the distribution of grain to the crews before the departure of the fleet and to the people in dire times took place (Demosthenes 52). Given the role of the *trittyes* in organizing the deme, both in the Council and in mobilization, we may assume that the same principle was applied to the distribution of grain. In this, case every shop in the stoa would have been designated for the storage and sale of the grain of a single *trittys*, and the building would have had thirty such compartments and a total length of 200 m, thus justifying the name of Makra ("Long") Stoa. The importance of this portico for the grain supply of the city and its advantageous position on the Choma pier at the point closest to Eetioneia explain the attempt of the oligarchs in 411 to attain control of the stoa by incorporating it into the adjacent wall (Thucydides 8.90).

It is very likely that the area west/southwest, immediately next to the Long Stoa, was the "seaman's market" (*agora ton nauton*), which was situated "on the Choma, in front of the Makra Stoa" (Demosthenes 52). Another name for this market was the "commercial market" (*emporike agora*), in which "there was the Long Stoa, where stands a market place for those living near the sea" (Pausanias 1.1.3) and where crews made their final purchases before the departure of the fleet. A lively picture, full of noise, activity, and the odors of the port during these preparations, is given by Aristophanes in the *Acharnians* (544–554):

> But you want to launch your three hundred ships straight into the sea, and there would be noise, the city full of soldiers, as the selection was been

made by the trireme captain and the wages were being distributed; with gilding over the statues of Pallas Athena, the Makra Stoa would be resounding from the people gathering there, they would be distributing grain, there would be sacks, leather thongs, they would buy jars, olives, garlic, onions in net bags, you would see garlands, sardines, flute-players, blistered hands, on the other side, you would see in the shipyard oars being scraped, nails being hammered, leather thongs being hitched to the oars, flutes singing, signalmen whistling, all happening together.

The People of Piraeus

In keeping with its idiosyncratic nature as a cosmopolitan trade center, the population of the Piraeus was predominantly of mixed origin and of a varying economic and social status, fluctuating sharply according to the season and in line with changing political and economic conditions. As demonstrated by the grave markers of the Piraeus cemeteries, only a small part of the approximately 30,000 free people living permanently in Piraeus were actually from Piraeus; the majority came from different demes of Attica. About 20 percent were metics, mostly from Greek, Cypriot, and Levantine cities, not to mention the considerable temporary population of (*paremidemountes*) foreign merchants and sailors. Athens, according to Isokrates in the mid-fourth century (8.21), "was full of *emporoi, xenoi,* and metics." (See also Shea, Chapter 10 in this volume.)

Socially, two categories were predominant, both of which were equally foreign to the conservative middle-class landowning characters found in the plays of Aristophanes.[3] There were the wealthy merchants and factory owners like the metic Kephalos, Lysias' father, bankers like the liberated slave Pasion, and the majority of the well-to-do metics. At the other end of the social scale was the large mass of the *thetes*, the poor people, manual laborers such as fishermen, workers, landless artisans, and poor deracinated villagers who had abandoned their fields to settle in the city responding to the call of the leaders of the popular party (*Constitution of the Athenians* 24.1). As a consequence of the growing dependence of the Athenian Empire on this mass of approximately 20,000 *thetes* and metics required to man the fleet, "power passed into the hands of sailors, boatswains, and pilots" (Plutarch, *Themistokles* 19.4). Because the maintenance of the fleet and the payment of the crews depended, in the fifth century, to a

---

[3] For example, Dikaiopolis in the *Archarnians*, Trygaios in the *Peace*, or Strepsiades in the *Clouds*.

large degree (about 40 percent) on the tribute of the allies, these same naval people, the people of Piraeus, became the most eager supporters of the democratic regime (*mallon demotikoi*; Aristotle, *Politics* 5.2, p.1303b, 10–12) and of its external policy, which was vehemently denounced alike by aristocrats (*Constitution of the Athenians* 1.2) and conservative-minded Athenians, such as Aristophanes in many of his plays.

The most severe verdict on this busy modern polis was pronounced by Sokrates in Plato's *Gorgias* (518e–519a), centered on industry and money making, and its ethnically and socially mixed democratic population:

> Thanks to Themistokles and Kimon and Perikles the authors of the city's woes – who they say made it great – prosperity and democracy depend more and more on the fleet; the Athens of former times is dominated by the poor. It has filled up with shipyards, walls and taxes and other such rubbish and has developed into a city which no longer knows moderation, justice and restraint.

No wonder that for Plato (*Laws* 11.919d) the ideal city should be a minimum distance of 80 stades from the sea, which is exactly twice the actual distance of the *asty* from Piraeus.

Further Reading

The classic reference (with the older bibliography and a good plan of Piraeus) is still the Piraeus section of Judeich's 1931 *Topographie von Athen*. Garland 1987 offers a useful study of the history and different aspects of the city. Von Eickstedt 1991 gives an exhaustive list of all Piraeus excavations up to 1988. For the Hippodamian planning, see Hoepfner and Schwandner 1994, with a map of the suggested Hippodamian plan and an appendix on the Skeuotheke by Steinhauer. For supplementary remarks on the town plan of Hippodamos, see Gill 2006, Steinhauer 2007, and Longo 2008. The Zea Shipsheds have now been exhaustively published by Lovén 2011 and Lovén and Sapountzis 2019; that can be paired with Pakkanen 2013 and Rankov 2013. The Long Walls are published by Conwell 2008. For the new excavations in the Emporion, see Steinhauer 2012. For the Eetioneia, see Steinhauer 2003. For the important Piraeus stone quarries, see Langdon 2000. On ancient ships and seamanship, the old book of Casson 1971 is still very helpful. On the organization of the Emporion, see Stanley 1976, and for the navy Jordan 1975, Gabrielsen 1994, and Hale 2009, along with Pritchard, Chapter 22 in this volume.

Bibliography

Casson, L. 1971. *Ships and Seamanship in the Ancient World*. Princeton.
Conwell, D.H. 2008. *Connecting a City to the Sea: The History of the Athenian Long Walls*. Leiden.

Gabrielsen, V. 1994. *Financing the Athenian Fleet: Public Taxation and Social Relations*. Baltimore.

Garland, R. 1987. *The Piraeus from the Fifth to the First Century* BC. Ithaca, NY.

Gill, D.W.J. 2006. "Hippodamus and Piraeus." *Historia* 55.1: 1–15.

Hale, J.R. 2009. *Lords of the Sea: The Epic Story of the Athenian Navy and the Birth of Democracy*. New York.

Hoepfner, W., and E.-L. Schwandner. 1994. *Haus und Stadt im klassischen Griechenland, Neubearbeitung*. 2nd edn. Munich.

Jordan, B. 1975. *The Athenian Navy in the Classical Period: A Study of Athenian Naval Administration and Military Organization in the Fifth and Fourth Centuries* BC. Berkeley.

Judeich, W. 1931. *Topographie von Athen*. Munich.

Langdon, M.K. 2000. "The Quarries of Piraeus." *ArchDelt* 55, A', 235–250.

Longo, F. 2008. "L'impianto urbano del Pireo tra dati reali e proiezioni immaginarie." In *Atene e la Magna Grecia dall'età arcaica all' Ellenismo*, eds. A. Stazio and S. Ceccoli, Taranto, 137–155.

Lovén, B. 2011. *The Ancient Harbours of the Piraeus: The Zea Shipsheds and Slipways*. Aarhus.

Lovén, B., and I. Sapountzis. 2019. *The Ancient Harbours of Piraeus: Volume* II. *Zea Harbour: The Group 1 and 2 Shipsheds and Slipways. Architecture, Topography, and Finds*. Aarhus.

Pakkanen, J. 2013. "The Economies of Shipshed Complexes: Zea, A Case Study." In *Shipsheds of the Ancient Mediterranean*, eds. D. Blackman and B. Rankov, Cambridge, 55–75.

Rankov, B. 2013. "Piraeus." In *Shipsheds of the Ancient Mediterranean*, eds. D. Blackman and B. Rankov, Cambridge, 420–488.

Stanley, P.V. 1976. "Ancient Greek Market Regulations and Controls." PhD dissertation, University of California, Berkeley.

Steinhauer, G. 2003. *Η οχύρωση και η πύλη της Ηετιώνειας*. Piraeus.

2007. "Ο Ιππόδαμος και η διαίρεσις του Πειραίως." In *Atene e l'Occidente: i grandi temi*, eds. E. Greco and M. Lombardo, Athens, 191–209.

2012. "Ancient Piraeus. The City of Themistocles and Hippodamus." In *Piraeus: Center of Shipping and Culture*, eds. G. Steinhauer, et al., Piraeus, 18–123.

Von Eickstedt, K.-V. 1991. *Beiträge zur Topographie des antiken Piräus*. Athens.

17 | The Archaeology of Markets and Trade

MARK L. LAWALL

For more than a century, archaeological excavation in the city of Athens has concentrated on a region explicitly marked off by boundary stones labeling it "The Agora of the Athenians." These excavations have recovered countless artifacts related to the commerce of the city, from small balance weights to massive stoas that house small shops. As with so many aspects of Athenian life, literary sources, ranging from comic playwrights and the Attic orators, to philosophers and later lexicographers and commentators, provide a richly detailed picture of the Athenian marketplace. Market officials – *agoranomoi* (market inspectors), *epimeletai* (overseers of various activities) of the Agora, *sitophylakes* (grain commissioners) and *metronomoi* (overseers of weights and measures) – oversaw the activity. Whether from temporary stalls or permanent buildings, sellers of similar commodities tended to cluster together in known, specific locations. Buyers knew just where to go on their shopping trip: to "the wine," "the garlic," "the edibles (*opson*)," and so on (Pollux 9.47–48).[1] The commodities mentioned run the gamut from pots and vegetables (Aristophanes, *Lysistrata* 557–558) to shoes (Lysias 24.20) and haircuts (Lysias 23.3). Some merchants probably lived up to the negative stereotypes often written about the denizens of the Agora, such as, "Or, being a barman or barmaid, cheats with the standard measure for the *chous* and the *kotylai*" (Aristophanes, *Thesmophoriazousai* 346–347). With such a wealth of relevant texts, the archaeological evidence runs the risk of being relegated to illustration. Archaeology, however, also offers an important perspective on changes to Athenian markets, marketing, and trade over time that are difficult to reconstruct from the texts alone.

Scholars have long debated how the Greek economy ought to be classified and understood in comparison to modern economies. (See Lewis, Chapter 15 in this volume.) This focus on classification encouraged a singular view of ancient markets well adapted to using textual evidence ranging in date across many centuries. And yet, events of Athenian history

---

[1] This passage dates to the second century AD, but in part referring to testimonia from Eupolis, a comic playwright of the late fifth century BC.

should raise an expectation of change. Solon's reforms in the areas of agriculture, trade, and craftwork suggest changes to local production and foreign trade. The introduction of coinage likewise should have had a profound impact on Athenian markets and society as a whole. (See Kroll, Chapter 18 in this volume.) Even the location of the Athenians' Agora moved from the east side of the Akropolis to the present site at the north sometime around 500 BC. (See Papadopoulos, Chapter 3 in this volume.) The influx of rural populations into the city during the Peloponnesian War is famously given an economic tinge by Aristophanes in his comedy *Acharnians*. Athenian efforts to maintain commercial standing in the turmoil of the fourth century are made clear in legal speeches (e.g. [Demosthenes] 35.51, quoting a law on return of grain ships to Athens), texts offering economic advice (e.g. Xenophon, *Ways and Means*), and inscribed laws from the Agora.[2] The Athenian economy was not a mono-lithic, static entity. More recent interest in documenting the mechanisms and performance of economies encourages scholars to pay greater attention to change. In this sense, the archaeology of Athenian markets, marketing, and trade has an important contribution to make to the broader field of ancient economic history.

The present chapter offers an overview of the evidence related to Athens' economic history from prehistory through the Late Hellenistic period. Coverage is, of necessity, uneven. Prehistoric Athens has far less to offer in terms of direct evidence for commerce – a scatter of imported pottery and rare luxury goods such as ivories and jewelry. The Early Iron Age and Archaic periods have much to offer in terms of artifacts related to trade and markets but still relatively little in terms of the physical locations. For the Classical and Hellenistic periods, by contrast, both the physical locations and the artifacts of commerce are on full display.

Pre-Classical Athens

Athens and Attika are obviously well positioned to participate in shipping routes crossing the Aegean either from Asia Minor or from Crete. Early Bronze Age sites on both the east and west coasts of Attika, such as Tsepi near Marathon and Agios Kosmas south of Athens, show clear links with the Cyclades. Very sparse finds within Athens include imported Cycladic

---

[2] For example, Agora I 7180, the law on silver coinage; Agora I 7557, the grain-tax law.

and Anatolian pottery as well as obsidian. In the Middle Bronze Age, the finds from well deposits on the north slope of the Akropolis, include substantial amounts of imported Cycladic and non-Attic pottery from the mainland of Greece. Mycenean fortifications and the famous spring on the Akropolis along with the extensive cemetery in the area of the Agora excavations all attest to Late Bronze Age prosperity and importance. Some indication of Athens' prominence in Aegean trade in the Late Bronze Age is offered by exports of Attic pottery to Kea and Melos after the eruption of Thera seemingly interrupted Minoan trade with these areas. A wide array of sources is attested in the exotic goods found in elite Late Bronze Age burials at Perati in southeastern Attika; recent research emphasizes the importance of social connections east to the Levant and Anatolia as attested by these imports. Such social connections likely greased the wheels of commerce that brought bulk goods from overseas as well. So far, however, archaeological research in Athens has revealed only scattered examples of imported shipping containers, for example, so-called Canaanite jars from the Levant.

The relative prosperity of Athens in the Early Iron Age is attested by the extensive series of graves, including some quite rich in grave goods, spanning the Late Helladic through Geometric periods. While there is ample evidence for pottery production in the city, evidence for the processes of marketing and trade remains scarce. Some vessels, including larger amphoras and *hydriai*, preserve markings applied by the potter. These can include both numerical notation and other symbols, even ahead of the adoption of the new alphabet in the eighth century. While the specific meanings of these notations are not known, they do point to a degree of organization on the part of the potters and, perhaps, their customers.[3]

Once the alphabet is adopted and graffiti appear on Attic pottery, we get a somewhat clearer indication of Athenian marketing practices. The very large Attic SOS transport amphoras (so called because of the distinctive decoration on their necks; Web Fig. 17.1) often carry graffiti indicating personal names, but numerical graffiti are rare on these jars. Apart from their size (nearly 70 cm high for early examples, 50 cm in diameter, with a capacity of roughly 76 liters), these jars are also noteworthy for their stability; they have a wide, heavy ring base. Such large, named or personalized Attic jars might well have moved within aristocratic circles of the

---

[3] Interestingly, however, most of the numerical notations from this period appear on non-Athenian pottery, outside Athens.

emerging sympotic class, as in earlier centuries, a further example of social connections facilitating commerce.

Such practices in terms of the mix of social and commercial exchange may have continued well into the seventh century. During this period, even though Athens did not engage widely in the extensive process of Greek settlement overseas, Athenian foreign networking is well attested by the influence of eastern Mediterranean artistic styles on Athenian practices, an influence that, some scholars argue, was more direct in the case of Athens than, for example, nearby Corinth. Moving into the sixth century, Attic transport amphoras shrank to more manageable proportions, and they lost the ability to stand unsupported. As such, these jars, like others across the Mediterranean, were increasingly suited for stacking in large numbers in the deep holds of merchant vessels or in storerooms. Athenian exports of fine decorated pottery expanded greatly in this period, seemingly at the expense of the Corinthian fine-ware industry.

Through the seventh and sixth centuries BC, remains of physical structures related to markets in Athens are lacking. The record of amphora imports to the city in the Archaic period also remains fairly sparse. Fragments of local Attic and Corinthian amphoras are fairly common, and there is a scattering of pieces from Chios, the region of Lesbos, and other sites along the eastern Aegean coast. Other accoutrements of trade are similarly rare: only three bronze weights dated to the Archaic period are published from the Agora excavations. Rather than seeing such poverty of the archaeological record as an indication of a lack of prosperity in Archaic Athens, a safer conclusion may be that we are not yet looking in the right place for Archaic Athenian markets.

Classical Athens

By the early years of the fifth century BC, the epicenter of marketing and trade in Athens had shifted from the old agora to the east of the Acropolis to the region of the modern excavations at the foot of the north slope. While buildings and other structures serving the political and cultic functions of the area were readily identified (see Camp, Chapter 6 in this volume), the physical infrastructure of the marketplace was more elusive. With the clustering of political and cultic structures along the west side of the Agora, the eastern half was thought more likely to have served as the area for ephemeral market stalls. The difficulty in identifying market structures may have been the result of a greater interest in filling out the roster of public buildings and the presupposition of what a 'Classical market building' should look like: a Hellenistic stoa!

Two buildings in the southwestern corner of the excavation area were initially identified as the State Prison and the Strategeion (see Map 6.1). Both preserve the remains of multiple rooms opening off a central corridor. Over various phases of use, starting in the first half of the fifth century, these buildings offer evidence for craft work and other commercial activity. The building thought to be the jail of Sokrates more likely housed a sculptor's workshop (hence the unfinished statuette of the philosopher) and perhaps an apothecary (hence the collection of medicine vials). The area of the so-called Strategeion, also a building with rows of rooms, has recently offered up discarded piles of transport amphoras, some with commercial graffiti. Running eastward from this western commercial area is South Stoa I with the Mint at its eastern end, both likely part of the late fifth-century commercial landscape of the area. The Stoa may have been intended for the offices of officials, overseeing markets and other jurisdictions, rather than for the shops themselves. This suggestion is based both on the use of off-center doors, more appropriate for dining than for shopping, and on the discovery of a late third-century inscription referring to the *metronomoi* found in the building. The Mint, of undeniable commercial importance, is the production site for Athenian bronze coinage, which helps to illustrate the tools of exchange in the retail setting of the Agora. (See Kroll, Chapter 18 in this volume.) Farther to the east, a complex of buildings in the southeast corner of the excavated area was the site of wine-selling, bone working, and terracotta production over the last decades of the fifth and beginning of the fourth century. Following the Panathenaic Way toward the northern corner of the Agora, one would pass the crowded, ramshackle, late fifth-century buildings attributed to the influx of rural population into Athens during the Peloponnesian War. Beyond these structures, however, there are further multi-room buildings whose fifth-century phases may have already seen use as shops or workshops. To this more permanent commercial infrastructure should be added the more temporary, or at least less robust, wicker and wood stalls attested in Classical literary sources.

This same geographical shift in the location of the Agora that seemingly encouraged the construction of these various shops around the open area also resulted in a striking change in the archaeological record related to activity in the area. While plenty of pottery is found discarded into out-of-use well shafts and other convenient dumping sites in the Iron Age and Archaic periods, the Late Archaic and Classical periods offer evidence for

Table 17.1 *Athenian amphora imports, 480–475 BC*

	Dates of deposits (BC)	Many	Some	Few
Persian sack cleanup	480	Chios, Northern Greece (NGR)	Attika, Corinthian A (Cor A), Southeastern Aegean (SEA)	Klazomenai, Lesbos, Adriatic-Ionian Sea (= 'Corinthian Type B'), Punic, Italy
Classical	480–450	Chios, NGR	Adriatic-Ionian Sea, SEA	Cor A, Lesbos
	440–380	Chios, Mende, NGR, SEA	Adriatic-Ionian Sea, Lesbos, Central Greece (CGR),	Cor A, Erythrai, Punic, Italy
	360–340	Chios, NGR, SEA	Adriatic-Ionian Sea	Lesbos, Mende
Hellenistic	325–240	NGR, SEA, possible Pontic	Chios, Cor A, Italy, CGR	Adriatic-Ionian Sea, Lesbos, Pontic
	230–170	Rhodes, Knidos (only at end of period)	Punic, CGR	Kos, SEA, Chios, NGR, Italy, Adriatic-Ionian Sea, Pontic, CGR
	170–175	Knidos	Kos, Italy, Erythrai, SEA, Rhodes	Chios, Pontic, Punic

The ranges of closing dates used here are defined by the points at which significant change is apparent between groups of roughly contemporary deposits. For example, deposits closed between 440 and 380 BC all show similar numbers and types of amphoras but show different numbers and types than are seen in deposits closed between 360 and 340 BC. Given that many of these deposits were excavated decades ago and retention of sherds has varied over that time, general categories are used here in place of specific counts: "Many" (roughly ten or more rim or base fragments), "Some" (five to nine rims or bases), and "Few" (fewer than five rims or bases).
Source: M.L. Lawall

discard from a retail shop specializing in pottery (especially *lekythoi*), from bone-working establishments, from marble workers studios, from a shoe-maker, and from merchants selling goods contained in transport amphoras.

While transport amphoras already offer significant evidence for markets and trade in pre-Classical Athens, the evidence from the Classical period is far more plentiful (Table 17.1). The well deposits attributed to cleanup following the Persian sack in 480 BC provide the first large assemblages of amphoras and show clearly the cosmopolitan nature of Athenian imports (Fig. 17.1). Chios and the broader region of northern Greece including the Chalkidiki, Thasos, and the Thracian mainland dominate the import record. Substantial numbers are also seen from a wide range of southern Ionian and Carian producers, including Miletos and offshore Samos. Other

Fig. 17.1 Amphoras found in a well deposit filled during the cleanup after the Persian Sack, 480 BC, in the Athenian Agora, from left: Corinthian Type A, Northern Aegean, Corinthian Type B, Klazomenian, Northern Aegean, Ionian, Attic. Agora P 12795, P 24892, P 24126, P 24872, P 24887, P 24870, P 24882.
Courtesy of the American School of Classical Studies at Athens: Agora Excavations

eastern Aegean producers including Lesbos and the area around Klazomenai are rarely represented. These early fifth-century deposits include a surprisingly sparse representation of either local Attic jars or those from nearby sites to the west. A scatter of western Mediterranean Italian and Punic amphoras complete the assemblage attested in the early fifth century. Over roughly the second and third quarters of the fifth century, that wide range of sources seen in the Late Archaic period was constrained somewhat by the economic depression seen in much of Asia Minor and hence a reduction in the exports of most eastern Aegean producers with the exception of Chios. Imports from the northern Aegean continued unabated. Imports from the west also shrank, though an interesting continuity is seen in the admittedly scarce record of Punic imports. By the end of the fifth century and continuing through the first half of the fourth, the resurrected economies of coastal Asia Minor meant renewed amphora exports arriving in Athens from that region.

The most vivid impression we have of commerce using amphoras in the Classical Agora comes from the southeast corner. Seven well deposits in this area, spanning the last thirty years of the fifth century and the first decade or so of the fourth, contained numerous well-preserved jars and large fragments of others from all the major suppliers of the day. The finds stand out for their many examples of commercial graffiti: indications of price, capacity, or volume, and possibly contents of the amphoras. Although very recent excavations are starting to bring more such graffiti to light near the Classical shops at the southwest side of the Agora area, the southeast corner's density of such commercial markings, limited in time and space, is quite striking. Unlike the impression one derives from the literary sources suggesting commodity-specific zones of commerce, marketing in this area was not limited to sales of wine (and other amphora-borne goods). The well deposits also offer evidence for bone working, terracotta figurine, and other ceramic production/sales nearby. The brisk nature of business in the region is implied by how the wells were filled: the bones show little sign of weathering or gnaw marks from scavengers.

Despite this clear evidence for very active commerce around the Agora, and even quite intense interest in measurement as attested by the volumetric graffiti, the tools of transactions are still relatively rare. Among the finds from the Agora, very few bronze weights are attributed to the Classical period. Volumetric measures, rarely encountered in Athens before the fifth century, do become common in the fifth and fourth centuries, but most are found in the immediate region of the Tholos (see Fig. 25.2). This spatial concentration, along with official stamps or painted labels such as *demosion* ("of the people"), supports the view that these measures were used for official supervision rather than daily use by merchants spread over the marketplace. (See also Steiner, Chapter 25 in this volume.)

Hellenistic Athens

Over the last quarter of the fourth century and well into the third, clear patterns for the importation of amphoras and concentrations of commercial graffiti largely disappear. The various shops, especially at the northern end of the Agora, continue in operation, but the general picture from the archaeology of Athenian marketing is quite different from that of the Classical period. By the last quarter of the third century and then through the second century, construction projects geared toward commerce and the artifacts of marketing are again more plentiful. The later Hellenistic transport amphoras found in the Agora area, however, vividly demonstrate the changes to the economic landscape of Athens and the Greek world as a whole that had occurred over the preceding century.

Classical Athens had drawn imports from across the Mediterranean but particularly from the northern and eastern Aegean regions. By the late fourth century, many of the northern producers experienced significant setbacks due to Philip II's military expansion and general reorganization of the region. Thasos, one of the most prolific exporters of the Late Classical and Early Hellenistic amphoras, is represented through this period, though the stamps on these amphoras' handles bias their archaeological collection and retention. Amphora production in the Chalkidiki saw a hiatus over the last half of the fourth century, but production and exports to Athens resumed sometime in the third century. The eastern Aegean producers continued to be quite active, and their products do appear in Early Hellenistic deposits. No specific types, however, appear in great numbers, and new sources start to appear: central Greek types from just north of Attika, and Pontic types from Chersonesos and Sinope. Interestingly, early Rhodian amphoras, which are quite common in the eastern Mediterranean throughout the third century, are nearly absent from Athens.

By the last quarter of the third century, Athens seems to join in much more with the major trends in Hellenistic amphora production and shipping. Rhodian, Koan, and Knidian amphoras are the most common types in Athens, especially as one moves into the second century, as is the case at most Aegean and eastern Mediterranean sites. Chios and other producers on the nearby mainland are also often represented in the import record. Through this period, too, there is again a steady, though never overwhelming, presence of imports from Italy and the Punic West, including both the southern tip of the Iberian Peninsula and Tunisia (Web Fig. 17.2).

The mid-second century saw a boom of construction around the Agora that likely facilitated marketing and trade. The beginning of this movement toward a more 'commercialized' Agora can be seen in the early second-century dismantling of the Square Peristyle, the last of a series of likely lawcourts in the northeast corner of the Agora. In its place, the Athenians built a modest row of five two-room shops. At roughly the same time, pieces of the former lawcourt building were being used for new commercial buildings across the south end of the Agora. (See Harris, Chapter 28 in this volume.) The South Stoa II and Middle Stoa along with the small East Building closing the space all created an immensely long rectangular zone across the southern part of the Agora (see Map 6.1). The Middle Stoa appears to have been simply a long colonnade, open on both sides and without divisions for offices. The South Stoa and East Building have rooms appropriate for shops or offices. The Stoa of Attalos constructed along the east side of the Agora forms a right angle to this southern complex. This last building's monumental inscription indicates that the Stoa included retail space that would be rented from the city. With these buildings, the permanent facilities for marketing made an immense leap forward in the middle decades of the second century BC. Even if some of these rooms served as civic offices, the number of permanent shops and roofed areas for stalls was unprecedented for Athens.

Despite the more commercial appearance of the Agora area, and despite Athens' access to the major trunk routes of the Late Hellenistic Aegean, the archaeological record of Late Hellenistic marketing is quite different from that encountered in the Classical period. Commercial graffiti or dipinti (painted markings) are extremely rare, as are large dumps of discarded jars of the sort seen in the Classical well deposits. One does find large fragments or even complete amphoras in the Late Hellenistic period reused as packing around well shafts or other constructions. As suggested above, Classical amphoras were often emptied at the point of sale, with the contents being decanted into smaller vessels, and the jars eventually discarded in a convenient well shaft. The rarity of similar dumps of Hellenistic amphora debris may indicate that sales of amphora-borne goods now less often involved decanting into the consumer's vessel. Instead, sales involved the complete vessel and its contents, which the consumer then removed from the Agora area itself. Such a shift in retail practice would be facilitated by the greater precision of amphora capacities in the Late Hellenistic as opposed to the Classical period, thereby allowing for greater trust in individual containers.

Changes in the kinds of measuring devices available in Hellenistic Agora fit well with these shifts in other artifactual evidence for commerce. Volumetric dry measures become rare in the Hellenistic period, and those that are found do not carry the indications of official reference devices seen in the Classical period. Furthermore, the increased availability of permanent shops would allow for greater familiarity between buyers and trustworthy sellers, likewise increasing the security in somewhat larger purchases.

Not all transactions enjoyed the same level of improved trust. Bronze and especially lead weights are very common in the Hellenistic period (Fig. 17.2). All but six published examples are found on the west side of the Agora. The vast majority appear clustered just south of the so-called Strategeion, in and around the so-called State Prison, and further southeast still around a house that, by the Hellenistic period, was as much an industrial complex as living quarters.

Fig. 17.2 Lead weight, one-third of a stater, Athenian Agora, Hellenistic, Agora IL 315. The weight is decorated by an amphora in relief (upon which is shown a bearded figure seated on a throne), all surrounded by raised letters, TPITH[MOPION].
Courtesy of the American School of Classical Studies at Athens: Agora Excavations

Athenian Markets and Trade in the Aegean

As in so many areas of research on the ancient Greek world, an Athenocentric perspective risks obscuring what is in fact unique and unusual about Athens. The market buildings of the Classical period are so far quite modest compared with, for example, an immensely long series of fifth-century shops now uncovered at Argilos on the Thracian coast. Jumping to the Hellenistic period, the dense integration of shops, storerooms, and other commercial structures throughout the cityscape of Delos finds, so far, no match in Athens. While Delos may offer an unfair comparison, the architecture of commerce there reminds us what we may not yet be able to see under the modern, urban landscape of Athens. Sites throughout the Greek world offer up transport amphoras by the thousands, much as we have in Athens; however, the changing mix of locally produced jars and imported sources varies greatly from region to region. Undeniably, Athens stands out for the amount of text, whether ink or on stone, related to commerce. Athenian commercial graffiti, either the extended name-inscriptions of the eighth and seventh centuries or the commercial notations of the late fifth century, likewise, so far set Athenian marketing and trade apart from the rest of the Greek world. And yet, particularly in the Hellenistic period, while numerous other marketplaces across the Greek world offer up complete or fragmentary measuring tables (*sekomata*), only one fragmentary possible example is known from the Athenian Agora.

Conclusion

As research in ancient economies has shifted in its goals from classification and labeling toward more precise descriptions of performance and behaviors, documentation of the textual and archaeological evidence related to local or regional economies has taken on greater importance in recent decades. Although the evidence from Athens, particularly the literary and epigraphic sources, has long contributed to ancient economic history, the detailed story of changing behavior in Athenian markets and trade remains to be written.

Further Reading

Comprehensive studies of ancient Greek economies, including important historiographic essays, are now available with Scheidel et al. 2007 and Bresson 2016. For the relatively sparse evidence related to Early Iron Age markets and trade at Athens, Papadopoulos 2003. The commercial topography of Athens is discussed by Rotroff 2009. Thompson and Wycherley 1972 remain very useful for the literary evidence regarding the Agora. Townsend 1995 covers the remains along the east side of the Agora, including Hellenistic shops preceding the construction of the Stoa of Attalos. The commercial importance of the Stoa of Attalos is made clear by Kaye 2016. For the wine-selling area to the southeast, see Lawall 2000. On transport amphoras as evidence for Athenian trade, see Lawall 2013 and Tzochev 2016. The tools of commerce such as balance weights and other measuring devices are published in Lang and Crosby 1964; graffiti and dipinti are covered in Lang 1976, with further examples and discussion in Lawall 2000.

Bibliography

Bresson, A. 2016. *The Making of the Ancient Greek Economy: Institutions, Markets, and Growth in the City-States.* Princeton.

Kaye, N. 2016. "The Dedicatory Inscription of the Stoa of Attalos in the Athenian Agora. Public Property, Commercial Space, and Hellenistic Kings." *Hesperia* 85: 537–558.

Lang, M. 1976. *Graffiti and Dipinti.* Agora 21. Princeton.

Lang, M., and M. Crosby. 1964. *Weights, Measures, and Tokens.* Agora 10. Princeton.

Lawall, M.L. 2000. "Graffiti, Wine Selling, and the Reuse of Amphoras in the Athenian Agora, ca. 430 to 400 BC." *Hesperia* 69: 3–90.

——— 2013. "Transport Amphoras, Tribute, and Trade." In *Handels- und Finanzgebaren in der Ägäis im 5 Jh. v. Chr.*, ed. A. Slawisch, Istanbul, 103–120.

Papadopoulos, J.K. 2003. *Ceramicus Redivivus: The Early Iron Age Potters' Field in the Area of the Classical Athenian Agora*. Princeton.

Rotroff, S.I. 2009. "Commerce and Crafts around the Athenian Agora." In *The Athenian Agora: New Perspectives on an Ancient Site*, eds. J.M. Camp and C.A. Mauzy, Mainz am Rhein, 39–46.

Scheidel, W., I. Morris, and R.P. Saller, eds. 2007. *The Cambridge Economic History of the Greco-Roman World*. Cambridge.

Thompson, H.A., and R.E. Wycherley. 1972. *The Agora of Athens: The History, Shape, and Uses of an Ancient City Center*. Agora 14. Princeton.

Townsend, R. 1995. *The East Side of the Agora: The Remains beneath the Stoa of Attalos*. Agora 27. Princeton.

Tzochev, C. 2016. *Amphora Stamps from Thasos*. Agora 37. Princeton.

Additional resources to accompany this chapter can be found at: www.cambridge .org/NeilsRogers

18 | Coinage and Its Economic Implications

JOHN H. KROLL

When it comes to natural resources, Athens was the most richly endowed of all Classical Greek cities. Not only was it one of the very few cities whose territory contained precious metal-bearing ore, but the deposits of argentiferous lead ore in the Laurion region of southeastern Attika were so prolific and extensive that during the fifth and fourth centuries BC Athens was arguably the leading provider of silver within the central and eastern Mediterranean basin. We know this chiefly from the vast scale and wide dispersal of Athenian silver coinage as documented in recovered hoards. But for all its importance as an export commodity, coined Attic silver served more fundamentally as the essential currency in every kind of transaction in Athens' public and domestic economy, and, above all, provided the very foundation for Athens' rise to power in the early fifth century BC.

Mining and Minting

Silver in the Laurion region of southern Attika had been extracted from mediocre surface ores already in the Bronze Age. It was not until around 525 BC, however, that deep exploration with vertical shafts and tunneling located the incomparably rich vein of silver-bearing ore, known as the "Third Contact," that produced Athens' silver bonanza. Following this discovery, the Athenians designed and began to mint their familiar tetradrachms that display on obverses the helmeted head of their eponymous deity, Athena, and on the reverses her owl, a berry, and leaves of an olive sprig, and the abbreviation of the city's name, AΘE. Explicitly proclaiming their Athenian origin, the coins appear from the beginning to have been conceived for the export of surplus silver. Large consignments of them have been recovered in hoards in Sicily and Egypt dating to the early years of the fifth century.

Produced initially with elegance and care, these early owl coins gradually took on a simplified, often slapdash character (Fig. 18.1), as hurried mass production was required to keep up with the ever-increasing amount of silver that was being mined and rushed through the mint. Estimates from

(a)   (b)

Fig. 18.1a–b Two Archaic owl tetradrachms: (a) from the beginning of the owl coinage, 510s BC (Munich, Staatlichen Münzsammlung 141194, 17.24 g); (b) a hurriedly-minted specimen of the 480s BC (New York, ANS 1980.109.55, 16.97 g).
Courtesy of the Staatlichen Münzsammlung, Munich, and the American Numismatic Society

the number of known obverse coin dies engraved and used during the first two decades of the fifth century BC give a rough total of more than 180 talents (approximately, five metric tons) of coined silver per year.

So far as is known from the management of Attic silver mining in the fourth century, most of the silver remained the property of the private individuals who mined it, while the Athenian state captured a percentage of the silver through fees and taxes and by charging a minting fee of probably 5 percent for converting the bullion into coinage. In 483 BC, the state treasury had amassed about a hundred talents from mining revenues. Rather than allowing these profits to be divided up and shared among the citizenry, the Athenian statesman Themistokles persuaded the Assembly to spend it on the construction of a hundred or more warships, making Athens, almost overnight, a formidable sea power (Herodotos 7.144; *Constitution of the Athenians* 22.7). This pivotal decision led to the Athenians' prominent role in saving Greece from the Persian invasion of 480 and 479; to their subsequent organization of the alliance known as the Delian League; and, fairly quickly, to the hardening of this alliance into the Athenian naval *arche* (rule) or empire.

During the fifth-century era of Athenian imperial supremacy, the extraction and minting of Laurion silver expanded exponentially. By mid-century, the engraving of the coins' dies had become mechanical and repetitive, producing a relatively rigid, standardized style of Athena heads (Fig. 18.2), within a scale of minting that was immense. Current estimates suggest that production involved up to a hundred obverse owl tetradrachm dies per year, implying an annual output of over a million coins in an annual amount of silver in the neighborhood of a thousand talents.[1]

---

[1] Kallet and Kroll 2020, 25–26.

(a)   (b)

Fig. 18.2a–b Two 'standardized' owl tetradrachms: (a) mid-fifth century (New York, ANS 1968.34.43, 17.21 g); (b) showing less quality control, from later in the century (New York, ANS 1944.100.24211, 17.80 g). The eyes of Athena, which are depicted as if seen from in front, give these coins a conservative, partially archaizing character. Courtesy of the American Numismatic Society

Most of the Athenian tetradrachms found in collections and book illustrations today are of this voluminous, standardized type and come from large hoards that have been (and are still being) discovered in Egypt, Turkey, and other countries of the Near East.

Even if some of this mass minting included silver from sources in Thrace and from reminting of non-Athenian coinage that had come into Athens' possession, the silver mining and processing industries at Laurion were operating at maximum intensity, employing the labor (and requiring the daily feeding) of 10–15,000 slaves, a workforce larger than whole populations of some Greek states. (See Lewis, Chapter 15 in this volume.) Most of the slaves were forced to toil in the cramped mine corridors, unable to stand while chiseling away, centimeter by centimeter, the silver-bearing stone. Other slaves manned the workshops where the stone was pulverized by hammering and grinding and the lead-silver ore was initially separated from other minerals by settlement in flows of water in 'washeries.' Separation continued by smelting the residue in furnaces at extremely high temperatures, and the final removal of silver from the lead was achieved in other furnaces by the technique known as cupelling. Overall, the ore processing was a lengthy and complex procedure, and one that in the furnace stages polluted the air through the release of toxic ash and fumes, giving the mining district a reputation for unhealthiness (Xenophon, *Memorabilia* 3.6). In her valuable accounts of these methods and their truly industrial scale, Rihll observes that it took 16 kilograms of stone ore and 18 kilograms of firewood to obtain a single drachma (4.3 g) of silver.[2]

[2] Rihll 2001, 129, 133.

Extensive remains of furnace sites and washeries with their deep, accompanying cisterns are found throughout the mining region.

The capital for these activities came principally from the Athenian elite, some of whom owed their fortunes to their investments in mining, like the exceptionally rich Kallias of Alopeke, who was nicknamed "pit-wealthy" (*lakkoploutos*), and whose son, Hipponikos, was the owner of 600 slaves that he contracted out to mine operators. Similarly, the Athenian general Nikias was said to have owned a thousand mining slaves, renting each for an obol a day (Xenophon, *Revenues* 4.14).

With the Spartans' construction of a fort in northern Attika at Dekeleia in 413, this fifth-century era of seemingly unlimited Attic silver extraction and minting was brought to an end (Xenophon, *Revenues* 4.25). The more than 20,000 slaves said to have escaped to the fort must have included a great proportion of the mining workforce. Soon after, the Athenians suffered other serious losses which led them to exhaust their silver reserves and to turn to their remaining reserves in gold. In 407/6 they began to mint an owl coinage from gold removed from the statues of Nike in the Parthenon, and in 406/5 they voted to strike a second emergency coinage, this one of bronze coins that were merely clad with a thin veneer of silver. In other words, the city was nearly broke. In the spring of 405, the Spartan navy, by then generously financed with Persian backing, surprised and destroyed the Athenian fleet in the Hellespont and, after blockading the Piraeus, forced Athens to surrender in 404.

Athens' recovery over the following years was remarkably swift. The substitute bronze coinage was probably withdrawn and silver restored within a year or so after the city's capitulation. Even though the city treasuries were empty, there was at that time plenty of precious metal coinage being held in private savings, such as the three talents of Athenian silver and four hundred Kyzikene and Persian gold coins in the strongbox that the wealthy speech-writer Lysias kept in his house (Lysias 12.11).

A new silver owl coinage, characterized by a greater naturalism in the heads of Athena (Fig. 18.3a), was introduced in the 390s with silver that probably came from the reminting of older coins withdrawn from circulation, from a large subvention from the King of Persia (whose land at that time was being attacked by the Spartans), and from established mines that could be opened as soon as labor was procured.[3] For the rest of the fourth century, minting continued apace and included an extraordinary episode of

[3] Kroll 2011b.

(a)   (b)

Fig. 18.3a–b The two varieties of fourth-century owl tetradrachms: (a) 390s–353 BC
(New York, ANS 1959.137.3, 17.18 g); (b) "Pi-style," 353–ca. 300 BC (New York, ANS
1944.100.24557, 17.06 g). The lowered position of the alpha on the reverse officially
distinguished the pi-style tetradrachms from those of the earlier fourth-century type.
Courtesy of the American Numismatic Society

recoining in 353 BC, when the city was again impoverished by war.
Desperate to raise revenue, the Athenians passed a law that voided all
silver coinage in Attika and required that everyone bring in his coins for
restriking so that the state could capture a deducted minting fee of probably 5 percent when each person got his money back in reminted form.[4]
This newly restruck coinage (known today as the "pi-style" coinage because
of the shape of the ornament on the helmet of Athena) was officially
distinguished from the previous, now "demonetized" coinage by the
lowered position of the letter alpha on the coins' reverses (Fig. 18.3b).
However successful this recoining may have been fiscally, the necessity of
having to restrike the thousands of tetradrachms and drachmas in Attika
within a space of a few months produced coins of chunky and crude
irregularity, whose careless appearance became a recognized hallmark of
good Athenian silver for the rest of the century. Although never as prolific
as the owl coinage of the preceding century, in addition to their profuse
circulation in Attika,[5] the fourth-century tetradrachms of Athens continued to be exported overseas in quantity.

Writing in 355 and concerned with some of the same revenue problems
that led to the reminting law two years later, the Athenian author
Xenophon (*Revenues* 4.5–6.28) argued that, although the mining industry
at Laurion was then operating below its full, fifth-century capacity, this was
largely due to a shortage of slave labor and because miners had only
recently undertaken to search for new deposits to exploit. Nothing came
of Xenophon's recommendations that the state itself should invest in these

[4] Kroll 2011a.
[5] For a hoard of nearly 400 pi-style tetradrachms excavated in 2005 beneath the floor of a building
in the Athenian Agora, see Camp 2007, 658–660.

two areas, but a state program of expanding the number of working mines nevertheless was put into effect, as we can see from the inscribed fourth-century lists of fixed-term mine leases annually sold by the *poletai*, the Athenian board of magistrates responsible for selling public property. The number of newly leased mining concessions rose from seventeen in 367/6 to a record sixty-two-plus in 342/1 as the result of state encouragement through financial incentives.[6] But the numbers fell in the following decades. Even if some miners were successful – the mine of Epikrates cited in a speech by Hyperides (4.35) was alleged to have made a profit of 300 talents in three years – the industry as a whole went into decline as the mines were becoming less productive and shortages in the supply of grain drove up the expense of feeding the gangs of workers. The last *poletai* account dates from ca. 300 BC and, being very fragmentary, documents only one mine concession. Around this time, the minting of the pi-style coinage had been or was soon to be discontinued.

Two Athenian coinages of the early third century attest to the loss of domestically supplied silver. The first was the coinage that the Athenian tyrant and general Lachares minted to pay his mercenaries during a siege of Athens in 295; it was a pi-style gold coinage, struck from the gold that Lachares scandalously removed from the chryselephantine statue of Athena Parthenos, having "stripped Athena naked," and from other dedications on the Akropolis.[7] The second was a revival in the 280s of the Athena/owl silver coinage, but it was minted from foreign silver that several Hellenistic monarchs had given Athens in support of the city's efforts to free itself from Macedonian garrisons.[8]

Athenian Coinage in Attika and Abroad

Along with the preeminent Athenian denomination, the tetradrachm (17.4 g in weight), the Athenian monetary system included smaller denominations (Fig. 18.4), ranging from the drachma (4.35 g) to the obol (of which, at 0.72 g, there were six to a drachma), the half-obol, and the tiny quarter-obol (0.18 g). In the fourth century, the Athenians added more fractions – such as a diobol, a three-quarters of an obol, and a three-eighths of an obol – some of which may have been minted for specific state

[6] See Rhodes and Osborne 2003, no. 36 (when the sales were first inscribed on stone), and Hopper 1953, 216.

[7] Kroll 2011a, 251–254.

[8] Kroll 1993, 10.

Fig. 18.4a–f Smaller denominations, mid to late fifth century BC: (a) drachma (New York, ANS 1955.54.195, 4.29 g); (b) hemidrachm or triobol (ANS 1944.100.24384, 2.12 g); (c) quarter-drachm or trihemiobol (ANS 1944.100.24259, 1.04 g); (d) obol (ANS 1944.100.24270, 0.69 g); (e) hemiobol (ANS 1944.100.24272, 0.35 g); (f) quarter-obol (ANS 1941.153.578, 0.17 g). Three of the fractions have denominationally specific reverse types: the owl on triobols (b) stands erect and facing, the owl on trihemiobols (c) stands facing with wings spread, and the quarter-obol (f) is fittingly denoted by a crescent or quarter moon (which was borrowed from the reverses of Athenian tetradrachms, where it appears behind the owls' necks as an attribute of these nocturnal birds). All coins printed at scale; (f) is shown also in an enlargement.

Courtesy of the American Numismatic Society

distributions. For a limited time, they minted even a minuscule eighth of an obol (0.09 g).[9] Such small change was essential for the market expenses of daily living, and since it made up the currency that the average inhabitant of Athens was most accustomed to using, these drachmas, obols, and fractions had to be stamped out in huge numbers. Unlike tetradrachms, which were widely employed in foreign as well as local transactions, these smaller pieces ordinarily remained in Attika, serving domestic needs. From banter in Aristophanes (*Wasps* 790–793; *Ekklesiazousai* 817–822), we learn that Athenians routinely carried their change in their cheeks, which is understandable in a world where clothing lacked pockets (and hygiene was not an issue). About a dozen red-figure vases show a well-off Athenian holding out a small sack-like purse of coins to purchase a big amphora from a vendor of vases, or, in most cases, sexual favors from a boy or a woman.[10] The amphora in the scene probably cost about 1–2 drachmas, to judge from price graffiti scratched on other vases of similar size and quality.[11] But most pots were cheaper: you could get a nicely painted cup for less than an obol. (See also Rotroff, Chapter 19 in this volume.)

In the building accounts of the Erechtheion, a stonemason (free or slave) earned a drachma a day, the same as a hoplite on duty or a rower in the Athenian fleet during the height of the Athenian empire. Unskilled laborers received half this amount, and subsistence living was in the range of 1 or 2 obols daily. In order to ensure that poorer citizens could freely participate in public service, around the middle of the fifth century, democratic Athens introduced a payment of 2 obols to each of the hundreds of citizens who served as jurors in the large lawcourts that were empaneled on a daily basis. Later in the century the stipend was raised to 3 obols, and pay for members of the Council of 500 had also begun. After the Peloponnesian War, pay to encourage attendance in the Athenian Assembly was introduced at 1 obol per attendee and kept being raised until, by the 320s, it had reached a drachma with extra obols for plenary sessions. At that time as well, members of the Council were receiving 5 obols a day, and the state was paying for the daily maintenance of the magistrates and administrative boards (*Constitution of the Athenians* 24). The combined obligations that the state had to meet in these payments to its own citizenry represented just one segment of its annual budget, which was supported by revenues (about 400 talents in the late 340s; Demosthenes 10.38) in rents, fees, and taxes,

[9] Svoronos 1923, pl. 32.23.
[10] Von Reden 1995, pls. 3a–8c.
[11] Johnston 1974, 149.

particularly the lucrative customs duties levied on all maritime imports and exports in the Piraeus.

However, the amount of silver coinage held and circulating in the private economy of Athens was many times larger than that in public use and served in a much broader range of expenditures, which extended from an eighth-obol's worth of grapes or flowers at the market to bags of tetradrachms routinely needed for purchasing grain, timber, slaves, and other goods imported by the shiploads in the Piraeus. No matter where one looked in ancient Athens, coinage was ubiquitous.

To judge from hoards, moreover, it was also Athens' most sought-after item of export. As Xenophon observed in his *Revenues* (3.2–3):

> In most port cities merchants have to take on a return cargo because the local coinage is of no use elsewhere. At Athens, however, not only are there more desirable things to export than anywhere else but even if merchants do not want to load up with a return cargo of goods, it is excellent business to export coinage; for wherever they sell it, they will get more than they invested.

In most places "selling it" would mean exchanging it at favorable terms for local products: in Sicilian ports, grain; in Egyptian, grain, papyrus, and sail cloth; along the southern coast of Asia Minor, timber; in Levantine ports, spices and incense. But to purchase grain from ports along the northern Black Sea, merchants would have to "sell" their silver tetradrachms in a literal sense, since they first had to exchange their Attic silver for electrum-gold coins of Kyzikos, the traditional trade currency for doing business in that region. Not all of the exported owl silver arrived directly from Athens. Much spent abroad in Athenian military and naval operations or in Aegean trade would presumably have been collected by silver traders and conveyed to where the demand and price were greatest. Those "sold" in ports of the eastern Mediterranean tended to get drawn ever further into Asia along the established overland trade routes, and the numbers are impressive. Some twenty known hoards found in Sicily, Turkey, the Levant, Iraq, and Iran have yielded a total of approximately 20,000 Athenian tetradrachms.[12] It is important to add that a great many discovered hoards have never been reported, and that large new hoards of Attic tetradrachms continue to turn up with some frequency.

---

[12] Listed in Kroll 2011a, 156–157, and Kallet and Kroll 2020, appendix. See also Anderson and Van Alfen 2008.

In some regions the coins were prized simply for their silver, as a commodity. But the popularity of Attic tetradrachms in Egypt led to them becoming a de facto currency, specified as "Greek staters" in Egyptian accounting lists beginning in 412 BC.[13] Fourth-century dies for the minting of imitation Athenian owls have also been found in Egypt.[14] But the minting of such imitations was widespread elsewhere and ranged from the atrociously crude copies produced in the Arabian Peninsula to sophisticated imitations that can be hard to distinguish from authentic Athenian strikings.[15] It is intriguing to reflect that in distant parts of the ancient world many people knew of Athens solely from its far-flung money, and sometimes imitated it on the conviction that its appearance was the way that acceptable money was supposed look.

Through trade, some imitation owls came to circulate in Attika, prompting the Athenians in 375/4 to pass a law on how the state currency "approvers" (the *dokimastai*) – two expert public slaves, one seated among the money changers' tables in the Agora, the other in the Piraeus – should deal with such "foreign silver coins with the same stamp as the Attic."[16] According to a recently proposed restoration in the inscribed law, the "approver" was required to cut a notch in the edge of such coins.[17] Any coin that was found to be of silver-plated bronze or lead or made of debased metal was confiscated. A notched imitation of good silver, however, was to be returned to its owner, who was free to dispose of it as best he could.

With its proud monetary tradition of native silver and bad experience with token bronze coins at the end of the Peloponnesian War, Athens was slower than most Greek states to adopt the innovation of minting its smallest denominations in bronze. Such base metal coins could be minted in sizes more convenient for handling and were profitable to mint, since their legally supported value was far greater than the intrinsic value of their metal. Notably, when the Athenians did initiate a bronze coinage in the 350s, it was not identified as a coinage of Athens at all, but as a coinage in the name of the Eleusinian goddesses, Demeter and Kore, that was produced for the benefit of the huge crowds of visitors who thronged Athens each year to participate in the Great Mysteries.[18] The coins' designs (Triptolemos and a piglet, Fig. 18.5) pertain to the festival, and their legend

---

[13] Agut-Labordère 2016, 5.
[14] Meadows 2011.
[15] Van Alfen 2005, figs. 13.5–10.
[16] Rhodes and Osborne 2003, no. 25.
[17] Attic Inscriptions Online, no. 819 (www.atticinscriptions.com/inscription/RO/25), note 5.
[18] Kroll 1993, 26 and 27–39.

Fig. 18.5 Bronze Eleusinian Festival coin, depicting Triptolemos and a piglet, mid-fourth century BC.
Courtesy of Classical Numismatic Group, Inc., Mail Bid Sale 76 (12 Sept. 2007), no. 484

reads ΕΛΕΥΣΙ, an abbreviation that is most plausibly expanded "of the Eleusi[nians]," that is, "of the Eleusinian goddesses."[19] Later in the fourth century the legend was changed to ΑΘΕ ("of the Athe[nians]"), and soon the city began to mint a regular bronze coinage with Athena/owl types that within a generation replaced all denominations in silver below the hemidrachm or triobol.

These bronze coins were struck in the large square building in the southeastern corner of the Agora, labeled on all Agora plans as the Mint (see Map 6.1). To judge from the unstruck bronze coin flans and other debris on the floors, from at least the third century though Hellenistic times the structure was used exclusively for the minting of bronze coins. (See also Lawall, Chapter 17 in this volume.) The building, however, was constructed in the late fifth or early fourth century, and it is unclear why.[20] Although it could date from the 390s, when, after a break following the Peloponnesian War, Athens resumed the minting of silver, no sure traces of silver working have been found in its early levels. Consequently, the location of the mint or mints for the striking of the silver coinages of Athens from Late Archaic through Hellenistic times remains a mystery.

Further Reading

For a broader and more detailed survey of Athenian coinage, consult Van Alfen 2012, which is excellent and fully up-to-date. For an exploration of what coinage can reveal about the history of fifth-century Athens, see Kallet and Kroll 2020. In addition to the discussions of Rihll 2001 and Hopper 1953, other informative accounts of Athens' silver mining and processing industries will be found in Mee 2011 and Kakavoyannis 2005 (with an English summary, pp. 331–339). For the many aspects of the Athenian economy, there are illuminating treatments by Kallet 2007, Pritchard 2015, and throughout Bresson 2016.

---

[19] Nollé 2014, 287–288.
[20] Camp and Kroll 2001, 142–145.

Bibliography

Agut-Labordère, D. 2016. "De l'amidonnier contre de l'orge: le sens de la conversion des quantités dans les ostraca démotiques de 'Ayn Manâwir (Oasis de Kharga, Égypte)." *Comptabilités* 8: 2–8.

Anderson, L., and P.G. Van Alfen. 2008. "A Fourth Century BCE Hoard from the Near East." *American Journal of Numismatics* 20: 155–198.

Bresson, A. 2016. *The Making of the Ancient Greek Economy: Institutions, Markets, and Growth in City-States.* Princeton.

Camp, J.M. 2007. "Excavations in the Athenian Agora: 2002–2007." *Hesperia* 76: 627–663.

Camp, J.M., and J.H. Kroll. 2001. "The Agora Mint and Athenian Bronze Coinage." *Hesperia* 70: 126–162.

Hopper, R.J. 1953. "The Attic Silver Mines in the Fourth Century BC." *Annual of the British School at Athens* 48: 200–254.

Johnston, A.W. 1974. "Trademarks on Greek Vases." *Greece and Rome* 2: 138–152.

Kakavoyannis, E. 2005. *Μέταλλα εργάσιμα και συγκεχωρημένα. Η οργάνωση της εκμετάλλευσης του ορυκτού πλούτου της Λαυρεωτικής από την Αθηναϊκή δημοκρατία.* Athens.

Kallet, L. 2007. "The Athenian Economy." In *The Cambridge Companion to the Age of Pericles*, ed. L.J. Sammons, Cambridge, 70–95.

Kallet, L., and J.H. Kroll. 2020. *The Athenian Empire: Using Coins as Sources.* Cambridge.

Kroll, J.H. 1993. *The Greek Coins. Agora* 26. Princeton.

2011a. "The Reminting of Athenian Silver Coinage, 353 BC." *Hesperia* 80: 229–259.

2011b. "Athenian Tetradrachm Coinage of the First Half of the Fourth Century BC." *Revue Belge de Numismatique* 157: 3–26.

Meadows, A. 2011. "Athenian Coin Dies from Egypt: The New Discovery at Heracleion." *Revue Belge de Numismatique* 157: 95–116.

Mee, C. 2011. *Greek Archaeology: A Thematic Approach.* Chichester.

Nollé, J. 2014. "'Panegyris Coinages' – Eine moderne Geisterprägung." *Chiron* 44: 285–323.

Pritchard, D.M. 2015. *Public Spending and Democracy in Classical Athens.* Austin.

Rhodes, P.J., and R. Osborne. 2003. *Greek Historical Inscriptions 404–323 BC.* Oxford.

Rihll, T.E. 2001. "Making Money in Classical Athens." In *Economies Beyond Agriculture in the Classical World*, eds. D.J. Mattingly and J. Salmon, London, 15–42.

Svoronos, J.N. 1923–1926. *Les Monnaies d'Athènes.* Completed by B. Pick, Munich. Reprinted in 1975 with translated text as *Corpus of the Ancient Coins of Athens*, Chicago.

Van Alfen, P.G. 2005. "Problems in Ancient Imitative and Counterfeit Coinage." In *Making, Moving, and Managing: The New World of Ancient Economies, 323–31 BC*, eds. Z. Archibald, J. Davies, and V. Gabrielsen, Oxford, 322–354.

2012. "The Coinage of Athens, Sixth to First Century BC." In *The Oxford Handbook of Greek and Roman Coinage*, ed. W.E. Metcalf, Oxford, 88–104.

Von Reden, S. 1995. *Exchange in Ancient Greece.* London.

19 | The Ceramic Industry

SUSAN I. ROTROFF

And she [Athens] that set up the beautiful trophy at Marathon
invented the offspring of wheel, earth, and oven, pottery of highest
fame, a useful housekeeper.

Kritias, fr. B 2 West[2]

Ancient Athenians were surrounded by clay. Table and toilet vessels, kitchen crockery, and cooking pots were of fired clay, the family food supply was protected by ceramic storage jars, and clay oil lamps provided indoor lighting. Athenians drank water carried in clay jugs from wells that were lined with clay tiles or drawn from fountain-houses supplied by clay pipes. Attic wine was fermented in clay *pithoi* (jars), goats were milked into clay pails, and Attic bees laid up their honey in clay hives. Even the houses were largely of clay, and at the end of their lives, many Athenians were buried under cover of a few ceramic tiles in the company of terracotta grave gifts. The claim of the fifth-century poet and politician Kritias that Athens invented pottery is spurious, but items manufactured from clay were ubiquitous.

Products

Pottery is the best-known product of the ceramic industry. Modern museums are well stocked with the figured vases that were produced in Athens from the seventh to the fourth century BC. The high prices they command on the art market today reflect modern admiration, but they were not luxury objects in antiquity and furnished the cupboard of many a house. In the early sixth century, Attic potters adopted the black-figure technique invented at Corinth, featuring figures in silhouette with interior details added in incision. In the last quarter of the same century, they invented their own technique, red-figure, in which clay-colored figures with painted interior details stand out against a black background (e.g. see Fig. 1.1). The aesthetic peak of these techniques ran from before the middle of the sixth to the end of the fifth century, though red-figure survived until the end of the fourth century.

It was abandoned in the third century in favor of floral and geometric motifs painted in orange and white clay directly on the black surface (West Slope Ware). In the last quarter of the third century, a new production technique was added, making use of molds to produce relief decoration. Both this and West Slope decoration continued in use until the sack of Athens by the Roman general Sulla in 86 BC, which dealt a crushing blow to the industry; Athens would never again be a significant producer of fine pottery.

These decorated vases, used for dining and drinking and as containers for perfumed oil, cosmetics, and jewelry, gifts for the gods, and ritual equipment, are only the tip of the ceramic iceberg. Much more pottery was simply covered with a black gloss,[1] sometimes embellished with simple stamped designs but usually without any decoration at all. Black-gloss could account for 65–85 percent of the tableware in urban contexts, even more in rural households. It performed most of the same tasks as figured wares, though there were differences in emphasis; for example, kraters (mixing bowls for wine and water) were commonly figured, while small bowls and oil lamps were of black gloss. In the Archaic and Classical periods, vessels were meticulously formed and the gloss was lustrous and thick. Thereafter, less attention was paid to shaping, and the quality of the black gloss declined; its use was largely abandoned after the Sullan sack in 86 BC.

Vessels of a different type were used for food preparation and other household tasks, storage and transport of foodstuffs, and agricultural activities. They were made of a less refined version of the clay used for tableware; gloss was applied only occasionally, in simple decorative patterns or on the inside to reduce porosity. Nonetheless, some of these vessels were among the most challenging of the potter's products; the *pithos*, a huge, thick-walled storage jar, was proverbially the epitome of the potter's art (Plato, *Laches* 187b; *Gorgias* 514e). Cooking pots were made of yet another material, adapted to withstand heat by the addition of gritty temper. Utilitarian vessels of household and cooking ware might have accounted for as much as a third of the pottery of an urban house, much more on a farm in the countryside. Other common ceramic items include loom weights and spindle whorls, used by the women of the household to meet the family's textile needs.

[1] Gloss refers to the fused lustrous black slip that covers much Greek pottery. It is sometimes called a glaze, but it lacks the glassy component of a true glaze.

Fig. 19.1 Mold of a Hermes statue from an Athenian coroplast's workshop, with modern cast at right, Athenian Agora, late fifth–fourth century BC, Agora T 1295. Courtesy of the American School of Classical Studies at Athens: Agora Excavations

In another segment of the industry, figurine makers (coroplasts) made clay sculptures ranging from a few centimeters to half a meter in height, representing gods, human beings, and animals, among other subjects (Fig. 19.1). Common votives and grave gifts, they are also found in domestic contexts, where their role is not well understood. These were often decorated with added color to increase their lifelikeness.

Architecture was served by yet another branch of the terracotta business. From the Archaic period onwards, most Athenian buildings were roofed with ceramic tiles (marble was used on only the most lavish temples). The roofs of houses were made of up pairs of wide, flat pan tiles and narrow curved cover tiles, sometimes with a thin gloss coating, laid on a clay bedding. In Late Hellenistic times, a marble paradigm displayed in the Agora ensured that tiles were made in prescribed sizes, documenting state interest in the industry. Public buildings had more substantial roofs, with elaborately painted eaves tiles and antefixes adorning their edges and peaks (Fig. 19.2). Some roofs included figured acroteria at the peak and corners, rare examples of large-scale Athenian terracotta sculpture.

Fig. 19.2 Reconstruction of painted terracotta eaves tiles with antefixes of the Middle Stoa, Athenian Agora, second century BC.
Courtesy of the American School of Classical Studies at Athens: Agora Excavations

Production

Details about ceramic production can be gleaned from a variety of sources. Ancient writers provide random anecdotes, while a few figured pots and plaques illustrate potters' shops and working procedures, and excavation has revealed the remains of kilns and workshops. The practices of traditional artisans and experimental replication of the processes involved help to fill out the picture of ancient production.

There was a certain degree of specialization within the industry. Tile makers, because of the size of their products, had special firing needs. Workshop debris rich in molds for figurines hint at specialists, as does the fact that Hellenistic mold-made bowls and lamps do not share decorative motifs. Indeed, ancient Greek has words for lamp maker (*lychnopoios*) and figurine maker (*koroplathos*) as distinct from potter (*kerameus*). But the lines were not firmly drawn; the contents of kilns and workshop debris sometimes include a mixture of products, and specialists may have worked side by side in the same workshop. In any event, all followed the same sequence of steps toward the creation of a finished product, even if they employed different techniques to fashion that product.

The first step was the acquisition of materials. The clay sources have not yet been identified. Ancient testimonia cite Cape Kolias, on the coast about 10 km south of Athens, as an excellent source of clay (Athenaios 11.482b; Suda, s.v. *Koliados keramies*), but chemical and petrographic analysis have identified only one or two ancient objects that match modern clay there. Traditional potters worldwide report a preference for sources within 2 km of the workshop, which would put the clay beds well within the limits of modern Athens, under which they may lie buried. Possibly the beds were exhausted in antiquity, or the processing of the clay has so altered its chemical composition that it does not match the original.

Raw clay requires lengthy treatment before it can be put to use. First, it is pounded and broken into small pieces, and then left to soak; the lighter impurities rise and the heavier ones sink in a process known as levigation. The purified clay is decanted into another basin, allowed to dry, cut into blocks of manageable size, and left under cover to rest for as long as six months. The artisan then wedges or kneads it in small amounts to remove air bubbles before forming it into the desired object. The clay may also be altered by the addition of temper, and two or more clays may be mixed to produce a material that is best suited to the maker's purpose. The gloss applied to the surface is simply a more highly refined version of the clay, chemically identical to it but with smaller particles that cause it to react differently to the firing process.

The next stage is the formation of the artifact. Tile makers used molds and wooden cradles, while coroplasts and some lamp makers depended heavily upon two-piece molds made of clay or, later, plaster. Potters formed most of their vessels on the wheel. Small and simple shapes could be made in one or two steps, but the complex forms that make up much of the Greek potter's repertoire required a more complicated procedure. Pots more than 30 cm high had to be thrown in pieces and then assembled. The partially dried, leather-hard vessel would be upended and trimmed on the wheel to refine the shape or form a foot. Handles and often feet were made separately. The surfaces of fine pottery were burnished or polished and painted with *miltos*, a thin solution of iron-rich ochre that enhanced their color. Even in plain wares, care was taken to remove traces of the production process. Finally, the pot was covered with gloss or decorated according to the desired technique and left to dry thoroughly before firing.

Other techniques played only a small role. Archaic cooking pots depended on hand-processing by the beater-and-anvil method for their thin and heat-resistant walls, and the round bottoms of later cooking pots were often formed in molds. Special fine-ware shapes like *rhyta* and head-vases combined bodies made in two-piece molds with added feet, rims, and handles (see Fig. 14.1). Widespread use of the mold occurs only in the Hellenistic period, for the hemispherical relief bowl. It was made by throwing the vessel within an open mold, a technique perhaps borrowed from glass-making and a significant innovation; it was first applied to pottery production at Athens in the last quarter of the third century BC and continued in use into the Roman period. Molds were used to achieve certain types of decoration – usually in imitation of metalware – rather than to increase the pace of manufacture; nothing approaching the mass production of later times existed in the Attic pottery industry.

Pottery was fired in small kilns, using whatever fuel the potter could amass: olive pits, olive and vine prunings, straw, nut shells, dung, and, of course, wood. The estimate that it takes one ton of wood to fire a kiln with a capacity of one cubic meter illustrates the voracious demands of the process.

The striking contrast between the orangish-red clay and the black gloss that makes Attic figured pottery so attractive required a complex, three-stage firing process, rediscovered in the twentieth century through analysis and experimentation. The contrasting red and black colors depend upon the manipulation of the iron in the clay. In the first stage of firing, with oxygen freely circulating as the kiln heated, the clay body and slip remained red, reflecting the iron in the clay, which was in the form of ferric oxide. When the temperature had reached about 800 °C, the kiln master created a reducing atmosphere by covering the kiln's vents and adding green wood to the firing chamber. This oxygen-poor atmosphere precipitated the conversion of the red ferric oxide in the clay to ferrous oxide, which is black, while moisture from the green wood encouraged the formation of magnetic oxide of iron, also black in color. The gloss consequently turned black and the clay turned gray. At a temperature of about 950 °C, the gloss, with its smaller clay particles, fused into a shiny surface that could no longer be altered. The temperature was then reduced slightly and the vents opened; when oxygen entered the kiln, the portions of the pot that were not protected by the gloss turned red again, as oxygen bonded with iron within the clay body, but the fused surface of the gloss remained black. Ancient kiln masters were able to follow the progress of the firing through test pieces, fragments of pottery pierced with holes so that they could be withdrawn for inspection.

Attempts to understand the nature of Athenian ceramic workshops have focused largely on the figured vases, a tiny percentage of which bear the signatures of the artisans who produced them: so-and-so *epoiesen* (made) or so-and-so *egrapsen* (painted) [this pot]. The practice is largely limited to the period 570–450 BC. *Egrapsen* inscriptions identify the painter. *Epoiesen* inscriptions probably refer to the potter but may also identify the owner of the workshop – the two would often be the same. Further works of the signing painters can be identified through a study of the details of their work, and additional, anonymous painters have been recognized by the same means. Close to 40,000 vessels have been attributed to specific 'hands,' and patterns of collaboration between potters and painters provide clues to the structure of the industry.

Potters signed about twice as frequently as painters, suggesting that potting was the more highly regarded skill. Sometimes the same man both painted and potted the vase,[2] but more frequently a potter and painter collaborated. Changes in the numbers and relationships of collaborators show that, in the early part of the sixth century, as the figured vessel industry was growing from a local concern into a business with considerable exports, most potters performed both functions. Starting in the later years of the sixth century, more specialist painters are documented; in the fifth century, the industry was made up largely of potter owners, who probably also negotiated sales and oversaw the all-important step of firing, working with a number of different painters at any one time.

Various models have been proposed for the overall size and organization of the Athenian pottery industry. At one end, there may have been some small one-man or family enterprises. Positive evidence for the involvement of families comes from signatures in which a potter identifies himself as the son of a known potter and from ancient texts that confirm the expectation that potters teach their craft to their sons (Plato *Republic* 411d–e, 467a; *Protagoras* 328). In many shops, however, the workforce probably extended beyond the family and economically beyond the status of a household industry to a dedicated professional concern. Such a shop might

---

[2] All the names are male, but one woman is depicted painting a vase on a ca. 475 BC Attic red-figure *hydria* (water jar) in Vicenza (Banca Intesa 2) attributed to the Leningrad Painter (BAPD no. 206564; Noble 1988, figs. 2 and 206; Boardman 2001, 147, fig. 178), hinting that women participated in the work.

employ a crew of between five and ten, with a master potter in charge of workers with varying levels and kinds of skills. Workshops tended to cluster in specific neighborhoods, an arrangement that would have allowed them to share resources and equipment while remaining independent (D.P.S. Peacock's nucleated industry).[3] Ancient sources document larger enterprises dependent on slave labor for other crafts (between 20 and 120 slaves manufacturing couches, swords, and shields [Lysias 12.19; Demosthenes 27.9]), but ethnographic parallels and practical considerations (e.g. space, firing capacity of the kiln) suggest that potters' workshops were much smaller. (See also Lewis, Chapter 15 in this volume.)

The signatures described above provide hints to the social status of the craftsmen, at least in the sixth and fifth centuries. Many names are non-Athenian, such as Thrax (Thracian), Skythes (Skythian), Amasis (a Hellenized Egyptian name), while others are nicknames that are uncommon among the citizenry. Some may be slaves, and one identifies himself explicitly so,[4] but many were probably metics (resident non-Athenians). Prohibited by law from owning land, metics had to make their living in other ways and consequently made up a large percentage of the artisans and traders of the city. There were undoubtedly citizens among the potters as well. In the fourth century, one of them left behind this swaggering epitaph: "Bakchios son of Amphis ... of the deme Kerameis. All Greece judged Bakchios to be the first among those who know how to unite earth, water, and fire in the same object, and he won the crown in every competition that this city organized" (IG II² 6320). Bakchios also made at least one dedication to Athena Ergane, the patron of craftsmen (IG II² 2939, 4339), and he may be the same man who potted two Panathenaic prize amphoras in 375/4. His sons carried on the family business, emigrating to Ephesos, where they won a contract to produce pottery for that city in the third quarter of the fourth century.[5]

Bakchios clearly prospered, and some earlier potters, too, were sufficiently successful to make fine dedications on the Akropolis. But success was not assured. The firing process in particular was unpredictable, and as much as 30 percent of a kiln load might be lost to breakage. An anonymous ancient poem asks for the protection of Athena against five demons that can destroy the kiln and its contents.[6] The small number of known prices

---

[3] Peacock 1982, 38–43.
[4] For the admitted slave, see Canciani 1978.
[5] Wankel 1979–1984, no. 1420.
[6] Milne in Noble 1988, 186–196.

confirms that pottery was not expensive. The highest price recorded for a figured vase is 18 obols, but few vessels cost more than six, most much less. (See Kroll, Chapter 18 in this volume.) In the last third of the fifth century, fifty black-gloss *oxybapha* (small bowls) sold for 3 obols, a *bolsal* (drinking cup) for half an obol. It would take a lot of pottery to cover expenses and produce the standard day-wage of 6 obols (1 drachma) for each of the five to ten members of the workforce. Add to this the fact that pottery is a seasonal industry (the damp weather of winter makes it difficult to dry the pottery sufficiently), and it seems that many potteries must have barely broken even.

Estimates of the total workforce involved in the production of figured pottery in the fifth century range from 200 to 1,000; the lower number is probably closer to the truth. Although figured vases were labor-intensive, other shapes, like *pithoi*, may have taken just as long to produce, and black-gloss, household, and cooking wares were manufactured in much greater numbers. Add the coroplasts and the tile and lamp makers, and it is clear that many hundreds of workers were engaged in the ceramic industry as a whole – a considerable population, but far less than the number of agricultural workers or the workforce of the arms industry, with its hundred-slave factories.

The locations of workshops are documented by the remains of kilns and deposits of industrial debris. The kilns are round or rectangular structures measuring 1–2 m across, with a lower chamber for the fire, stoked through a short tunnel, and an upper chamber into which the pottery was loaded; the domed roof may have been built anew with each firing. Telltale workshop debris includes damaged and misfired pottery, test pieces, aggregations of molds, and kiln furniture (props to support pottery in the kiln).

Pottery was made all over Attika, but the city itself was the main production center. The traditional location of the industry is preserved in the place name Kerameikos, applied to an area including the Classical Agora and stretching northwest to and beyond the city walls. Pottery production is well documented in the area of the Agora in the Early Iron Age (tenth to seventh century).[7] Later on, potteries were located in clusters outside the walls. Their remains have been found to the northwest, in the classical deme of Kerameis, and along the roads leading to the Academy and the Kolonos Hippios (see Map 4.2). In the fourth century, production was concentrated instead to the southwest, beyond the Philopappos Hill,

---

[7] See Papadopoulos 2003.

and recently a Hellenistic kiln has been discovered in the little-explored area to the east of the city.[8] These suburban concentrations protected densely populated areas from the dangers of fire and pollution but left the potters vulnerable in times of war.

The Market

How did the craftsman get his products to his customers? In some cases, he could depend on advance orders. Tiles for public buildings would have been ordered ahead of time to the specifications of the architect; some are even stamped with the name of the structure and the tile maker. The Athenian state commissioned amphoras for the oil given as prizes at the Panathenaia every fourth year: an exacting and lucrative contract, awarded by competition, involving the production of about 1,400 large amphoras of a standard capacity, decorated in the black-figure technique (see Web Fig. 24.3). Official dry and liquid measures for market control (see Fig. 25.2), water clocks to time lawcourt speeches (see Web Fig. 28.2), and tableware for public dining rooms (see Fig. 25.1) must also have been state orders. Private customers, traders, and middlemen may have visited the workshop, but pots were also sent into the city, where they were displayed for purchase in heavily trafficked areas in or near the Agora.

Every resident of Attika required table and household ware, and there were few competing products; cups and plates might be made of wood, but metal was too expensive, as was glass before the invention of glass-blowing brought down the price in the first century BC. With an estimated population on the order of 250,000, there were plenty of buyers. At critical times – after the Persian sack, for instance – the demands on the ceramic industry must have been prodigious, as Athenians struggled to replace not only their crockery but also their tile-roofed homes (see Web Fig. 25.1). This catastrophe must have entailed the destruction of kilns and workshop installations as well as houses. The fact that the record of the closely dated figured pottery preserves no hint of the disaster is a testimony to the strength of the industry and the energy of its practitioners.

Fine pottery of the Archaic and Classical periods also commanded a significant export market. Beginning in the second quarter of the sixth

---

[8] Parlama and Stampolidis 2000, 210–213.

century, Attic fine wares are increasingly common on sites around the Mediterranean, from Spain to the Levant, around the Black Sea, in North Africa, and as far east as Persia; by the second half of the century, Athenian pottery was virtually without competition in this market. (See Lawall, Chapter 17 in this volume.) The mechanisms of the trade are poorly understood. Pottery rarely constituted the main cargo of a trading ship but traveled with commodities such as grain, wine, and oil along established trade routes. Although some have dismissed pottery as a mere space-filler, the trade was sufficiently profitable to make the trouble of packing and transporting pottery worthwhile, and it clearly developed its own overseas markets. Distribution of Attic pottery is not random: potters were directing their wares to specific destinations.

The question of who wanted this pottery, and why, is an intriguing one, with different answers depending on local conditions. Etruria, in central Italy, constituted the largest market for Athens' figured ware and the most intensely studied.[9] In rare instances, workshops tailored their products to foreign buyers; the potter who signed his vases as Nikosthenes produced amphoras and *kyathoi* (dipper-like cups) imitating the shapes of Etruscan bucchero pottery. In most cases, however, it is difficult to explain why the Athenian wares appealed to the Etruscan buyer, other than their beautiful craftsmanship. We do not even know whether the vases were purchased specifically to be placed in graves, where most have been found, or were used in the home before reaching that final destination. Most are of standard Attic shapes, and many are painted with scenes and details intended for Athenian buyers. A case in point is the painted names describing a person as *kalos* – beautiful (see Shapiro, Chapter 1 in this volume). They are commonly taken to name the most admired Athenian young aristocrats of the day, people the Etruscan buyers could neither have heard of nor cared about. Recent studies have made some headway in explaining the appeal of Attic pottery in terms of indigenous needs, customs, and beliefs.

Attic pottery lost most of its overseas market in the Early Hellenistic period, as styles changed, quality declined, and political developments impacted trading patterns. Athenian pots did not disappear completely from the international scene until the first century BC, but their numbers dwindled dramatically.

---

[9] See most recently Bundrick 2019.

Conclusions

Because of the nature of clay – ironically both fragile and indestructible – ceramics constitute some of the best evidence we have for any ancient Athenian industry. The objects reveal production procedures, and the pattern of broken fragments points to everything from the locations of workshops to the structure of trade. They tell of deeply traditional practices based on technologies inherited from the past and engaged primarily in the manufacture of the useful products to which Kritias alludes. What is extraordinary is that, for the relatively brief period of two centuries, some of its Attic practitioners rose above the level of the mundane to produce pottery of astounding quality and international appeal. This floruit coincides with the period of Athens' greatest power, giving credence to the notion that even commonplace products may reflect the trajectory of the city.

Further Reading

Boardman 2001 presents an authoritative if opinionated account of the history, styles, iconography, functions, economics, and techniques of fine Greek pottery (mostly figured). For a diametrically opposed view of the enterprise, see Vickers and Gill 1994. Publications of the Agora excavations offer a cross-section of humbler products: lamps and black-gloss, household, and cooking pottery (*Agora* vols. 4, 8, 12, 22, 29, and 33) of the seventh to the first century. On a specific Late Archaic assemblage of pottery from the Agora, see Lynch 2011. For figurines, see Thompson 1987 and Uhlenbrock 1990. Winter 1993 provides an introduction to Greek roofing systems down to the end of the Archaic period. Clay preparation, the construction of fine pottery, and the three-stage firing process are explained in Noble 1988 and Schreiber 1999, the latter written from the perspective of an experienced potter. For recent discussions of the size and structure of the Athenian figured pottery industry, see Stissi 2012 and Sapirstein 2013. Peacock 1982, though focused on Roman pottery, provides a model for stages of industrial development that is also applicable to the Athenian industry; Hasaki 2020 examines ancient pottery production, especially at Corinth. For ceramic kilns in ancient Greece see https://atlasgreekkilns.arizona.edu/. Most of the evidence for prices comes from graffiti (Johnston 1979) and the lists of confiscated items in the Attic Stelai (Amyx 1958). For a sample of the heated debate over the value of pottery and the nature and significance of the trade in figured ware, see: Boardman 1988, Vickers and Gill 1994, and Osborne 1996.

Bibliography

Amyx, D.A. 1958. "The Attic Stelai III: Vases and Other Containers." *Hesperia* 27: 163–307.

Boardman, J. 1988. "Trade in Greek Decorated Pottery." *Oxford Journal of Archaeology* 7: 27–33.

2001. *The History of Greek Vases*. London.

Bundrick, S.D. 2019. *Athens, Etruria, and the Many Lives of Greek Figures Pottery*. Madison.

Canciani, F. 1978. "Lydos, der Sklave?" *Antike Kunst* 21: 17–20.

Hasaki, E. 2020. *Potters at Work in Ancient Corinth: Industry, Religion, and the Penteskouphia Pinakes*. Princeton.

Johnston, A.W. 1979. *Trademarks on Greek Vases*. Warminster.

Lynch, K.M. 2011. *The Symposium in Context: Pottery from a Late Archaic House near the Athenian Agora*. Princeton.

Noble, J.V. 1988. *The Techniques of Painted Attic Pottery*. Rev. edn. London.

Osborne, R. 1996. "Pots, Trade, and the Archaic Greek Economy." *Antiquity* 70: 31–44.

Papadopoulos, J.K. 2003. *Ceramicus Redivivus: The Early Iron Age Potters' Field in the Area of the Classical Athenian Agora*. Princeton.

Parlama, L., and N.C. Stampolidis, eds. 2000. *Athens: The City Beneath the City: Antiquities from the Metropolitan Railway Excavations*. Athens.

Peacock, D.P.S. 1982. *Pottery in the Roman Word: An Ethnoarchaeological Approach*. London.

Sapirstein, P. 2013. "Painters, Potters, and the Scale of the Attic Vase-Painting Industry." *AJA* 117: 493–510.

Schreiber, T. 1999. *Athenian Vase Construction: A Potter's Analysis*. Malibu.

Stissi, V. 2012. "Giving the *Kerameikos* a Context: Ancient Greek Potters' Quarters as Part of the *Polis* Space, Economy, and Society." In *"Quartiers" artisanaux en Grèce ancienne: une perspective méditerranéenne*, eds. A. Esposito and G.M. Sanidas, Lille, 201–230.

Thompson, D.B. 1987. "Three Centuries of Hellenistic Terracottas." In *Hellenistic Pottery and Terracottas*, H.A. Thompson and D.B. Thompson, Princeton, 181–267.

Uhlenbrock, J.P. 1990. "The Coroplast and His Craft." In *The Coroplast's Art: Greek Terracottas of the Hellenistic World*, ed. J.P. Uhlenbrock, New Rochelle, 14–21.

Vickers, M., and D. Gill. 1994. *Artful Crafts: Ancient Greek Silverware and Pottery*. Oxford.

Wankel, H., ed. 1979–1984. *Die Inschriften von Ephesos*. 8 vols. Bonn.

Winter, N.A. 1993. *Greek Architectural Terracottas from the Prehistoric to the End of the Archaic Period*. Oxford.

20 | Sculpture and Its Role in the City

OLGA PALAGIA

> [Athens] has plenty of marble, out of which they make very fine
> temples and altars, as well as beautiful statues; it is also much in
> demand in the rest of Greece and abroad.
>
> Xenophon, *Ways and Means* 1.4

Ancient Athens was richly embellished with sculptures, erected in sacred
and public spaces both in the city and the countryside. The civic landscape
was dominated by images that glorified the human form. Cult statues of
divinities were placed in temples, which were also decorated with architectural sculptures illustrating the lives of gods and heroes.[1] Sanctuaries
received votive statuary as well as reliefs. Thus far, unique aspects of the
Akropolis votives in the Archaic period are equestrian statues and seated
scribes. Athens is also the only city to produce herms in this period
(Pausanias 1.24.3). Commemorative statues and *stelai*, all in marble, were
placed on the tombs of the elite from the early sixth century BC onward.[2]
The aim of funerary sculpture was not to reproduce the true likeness of the
deceased but the timeless qualities of the ideal human condition. With the
inception of the democracy around 508 BC, the Athenians invented honorary portraiture by producing idealized posthumous likenesses. Lifelike
portraits began to appear toward the end of the fifth century, but idealized,
posthumous portraits also continued to be produced until the Hellenistic
period. This survey focuses on sculptures set up in Athens and Attika in the
Archaic and Classical periods and produced either in bronze or in local
marble from Mt. Penteli and Mt. Hymettos.

Bronze

Bronze sculpture dominated public dedications from its inception in the
late sixth century BC until the end of antiquity. The most famous bronze

---

[1] The earliest architectural sculptures in Athens were carved of Piraeus limestone.

[2] The practice was banned twice by anti-luxury laws, first in the period 479–430 BC and again from
317 BC to the time of Augustus.

group in Athens, which also functioned as a symbol of the city, was the group of the Tyrannicides, Harmodios and Aristogeiton, who killed the tyrant Hipparchos in the course of the Great Panathenaia in 514 BC (Web Fig. 20.1). The group was commissioned from the sculptor Antenor after the expulsion of Hipparchos' brother Hippias in 509 BC and set up in the Agora. It was removed in 480/79 by the invading Persians, who understood the political significance of the statues. A replacement was created by Kritios and Nesiotes in 477/6 and, as the recipient of cult, became one of the most significant landmarks of ancient Athens. Like funerary sculpture, the group and its replacement were created posthumously and did not aim to reproduce the individual features of the honorands, who had become elevated to heroic status. Other bronze portraits of the Classical period standing in the Agora and on the Akropolis are documented by Pausanias (Book 1: 16.1; 23.3; 27.3; 28.4–5.), and by footprints left on inscribed statue bases.

By far the most famous bronze statue on the Akropolis was the colossal bronze Athena or *Athena Promachos* created by Pheidias, the greatest fifth-century Athenian sculptor, and dedicated by the Athenians after the Persian Wars, although its exact date is disputed (see Map 5.1, no. 6).[3] Cult statues could also be made of bronze, for example, the Athena and Hephaistos made by Alkamenes for the Hephaisteion, documented by expenditure accounts. The bronze statues of antiquity have all but vanished, because they tended to be melted down in order to recycle the material, not only in later periods but also in antiquity, as we learn from a fourth-century Akropolis inventory of damaged votive statues that were to be liquidated.[4] The exception to the rule is formed by bronze statues found in shipwrecks and, as far as Athens is concerned, by a cache of four monumental statues of the fourth century found in a rescue excavation in Piraeus (Web Fig. 20.2). They were presumably stored in anticipation of Sulla's siege of Piraeus in 86 BC, and were buried in the debris of the city's destruction.

Imported Marbles

Marble sculpture was introduced into Athenian sanctuaries as well as cemeteries from the Cycladic islands of Naxos and Paros around 600 BC.

---

[3] Palagia 2013.
[4] Harris 1992.

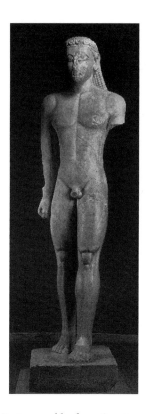

Fig. 20.1 *Kouros*, probably Parian marble, from Sounion, ca. 600 BC, Athens,
National Archaeological Museum 2720.
© Hans R. Goette

Some of the early imports are on a colossal scale, such as a group of *kouroi* dedicated to Poseidon at Sounion. The best-preserved *kouros* is about 3 m high (Fig. 20.1). Naxian and Parian sculptors brought to Athens their marbles, their tools, and their skills, providing the impetus for local talent to gradually develop a new formal language. The Naxian connection ran out of steam by the mid-sixth century, but the Athenians continued to import sculptors as well as marble from Paros well into the final decade of the fifth century. Parian masters in Athens contributed to the creation of an Attic style, even though they employed Parian marble, like Phaidimos, sculptor of the *kore* Phrasikleia in the sixth century, and Agorakritos, master of the Nemesis of Rhamnous in the fifth. After the late fifth century, imported marble was scarce until Thasian marble began to be employed primarily for imperial portraiture from the first century BC onward.

Pentelic Marble

In discussing the natural resources of Athens, Xenophon (*Ways and Means* 1.4) actually refers to Pentelic marble, which, by the fourth century, had come to dominate the markets not only in mainland Greece and South Italy but also in some of the satrapal courts of Asia Minor.[5] In the late fifth and fourth centuries, the architectural sculptures of the chief temples in the Peloponnese (Argive Heraion, Temple of Asklepios at Epidauros, Temple of Athena Alea at Tegea) and Delphi (Temple of Apollo), as well as the statues of the Mausoleion (except for some heads), were all in Pentelic marble.

The marble quarries on Mt. Penteli began to operate rather tentatively in the sixth century for the production of statuary. Pentelic marble has fine grains and is more compact than the coarse-grained and luminous Parian marble which held sway in the sixth and fifth centuries. The earliest sculptures in Pentelic marble were on a modest scale, judging by a miniature unfinished male statue (*kouros*) from the Dionysos quarry now in the British Museum. Among the first freestanding statues in Pentelic marble is the under-life-size "Pomegranate Kore," dedicated on the Akropolis in the second quarter of the sixth century.[6] The roughly contemporary sphinx that crowned a tall funerary monument at Spata, also in Pentelic marble, exhibits a robust style and a new confidence in local skills (Fig. 20.2).[7] A seated cult statue of Dionysos from Ikaria from the 520s is also of Pentelic marble.[8]

But it is only after the Persian Wars that the Pentelic marble quarries were exploited on a grand scale. After the defeat of the Persians at Marathon in 490, the Athenians began to construct a Doric temple of Athena on the Akropolis, entirely in Pentelic marble. Now known as the Older Parthenon, it remained unfinished on account of the Persian sack in 480/79. The same fate befell the monumental propylon to the Akropolis, which is known as the predecessor to Mnesikles' Classical Propylaia. In the mid-fifth century, the quarry industry was revived on Mt. Penteli for the building of the Temple of Hephaistos in the Agora. However, the architectural sculptures of the Hephaisteion (metopes, friezes, pediments, and

---

[5] But Sicily and, oddly enough, the Sanctuary of Zeus at Olympia persisted in their preference for Parian marble. On Sicily, see Marconi in Palagia 2019. On Olympia, see Palagia 2015b.

[6] Athens, Akropolis Museum 593. Palagia 2010, figs. 10–11.

[7] Athens, National Archaeological Museum 28. Despinis and Kaltsas 2014, no. 285.

[8] Athens, National Archaeological Museum 3072–3074 and 3897. Despinis and Kaltsas 2014, nos. 197–198.

Fig. 20.2 Sphinx once crowning a grave *stele*, Pentelic marble, from Spata, second quarter of the sixth century BC, Athens, National Archaeological Museum 28. © Hans R. Goette

acroteria) were all carved out of Parian marble, following regular practice, which continued throughout the fifth century with a few exceptions to be discussed below.

Massive exploitation of the Pentelic quarries is documented in the period 447–432 BC for the construction of the Parthenon from its foundations to its rooftiles, and its architectural sculpture (metopes, frieze, acroteria, and pediments) was entirely of Pentelic marble for the first time in Athenian history. (See Valavanis, Chapter 5 in this volume.) The annual building accounts of the Parthenon document payments to quarrymen and road builders as new roads were built every year to transport the marble blocks to the Akropolis. New roads imply new quarries, which were presumably constantly opened to supply the masons' needs. The building accounts of the pedimental sculptures record the employment of specialist stonemasons who blocked out the statues to reduce their weight for transport to the Akropolis. The artists who carved the pedimental statues are distinctly named as *agalmatopoioi*, and they commanded very generous fees.[9] The pedimental statues were carved in workshops on the Akropolis itself. This seems to have been standard practice, as very few unfinished

---

[9] The payment of 16,392 drachmas for the year 434/3 BC is recorded, but we do not know if it represents the annual fee.

statues were in fact found in the quarries of Attika. Apart from the small *kouros* in the British Museum mentioned above, there is also an Archaic seated statue and an unfinished dog, probably of the fourth century BC (Web Fig. 20.3).[10] All come from the quarry in Dionysos (on the far side of Mt. Penteli). Sculptors' workshops in Athens are documented by establishments on the outskirts of the Agora containing marble chips, unfinished sculptures and tools. The workshop of Mikion and Menon, for example, named after two of its owners, operated continuously from the fifth to the third centuries BC. One of the cisterns in the courtyard contained unfinished sculptures. Finally, a document relief of the late fifth century BC excavated in the Athenian Agora illustrates building activity with female figures, probably nymphs, shown measuring, drawing, and shifting a block with a lever in the presence of Athena.[11] (See also Lewis, Chapter 15 in this volume.)

The Parthenon was lavishly decorated with sculpture on an unprecedented scale. All ninety-two of its metopes were sculpted, an Ionic relief frieze was carved at the top of the exterior wall of the cella, possibly another frieze ran along the interior walls of the east porch, and the pediments carried over-life-size statues which were exceptionally finished and painted all round, even though their backs were not visible from the ground. The reception of these pediments in antiquity is remarkable: they caught the attention of Pausanias (1.24.5), who did not normally linger on architectural sculptures, and were also reflected in sculptures of the Roman period.

The cult statue of Athena Parthenos inside the Parthenon was made by Pheidias in 446–438 BC. It was about 11 m high, made of ivory and gold appliqués attached to a plaster core, and stood on a marble base decorated with a relief frieze, also of ivory and gold. Athena's shield and sandals carried mythological narratives.[12] Pheidias constructed his statue in a workshop built with spolia south of the Parthenon.

The Parthenon and its cult statue served as showcases of Athenian myths. Whereas the other sacred buildings erected in the second half of the fifth century on the Akropolis (the Propylaia, the Temple of Athena Nike, the Erechtheion) were also built of Pentelic marble, their architectural sculptures (except for the Propylaia, which had no sculptures) are in Parian marble (or gilded bronze in the case of the Nike temple's

[10] Dog, Kephisia Museum, ex Piraeus Museum 5760. Palagia 2011.
[11] Athens, Agora S 2495. Lawton 1995b.
[12] On the Athena Parthenos, see Palagia in Palagia 2019.

acroteria),[13] with the exception of the Caryatids in the south porch of the Erechtheion and the friezes of the Nike temple, which are in Pentelic marble. The architectural sculptures of the Temple of Ares in the Agora are also of Pentelic marble. This temple was originally in the Attic countryside (Pallene) and was moved to the heart of Athens in the time of Augustus. (See Rogers, Chapter 30 in this volume.) Two late fifth-century acroteria found in the Agora, of rather different styles but perhaps both from the Temple of Ares, are also of Pentelic marble.[14]

Among the dedications placed on the Akropolis in the fifth century, only a few survive, and these are of Pentelic marble. Notable among them is the statue of Prokne about to kill her son Itys, inspired by Attic drama. Pausanias (1.24.3) saw the statue and informs us that it was dedicated by Alkamenes, one of the chief sculptors of Athens in the High Classical period and a pupil of Pheidias. The implication is that Alkamenes was not only the dedicant but also the sculptor. Prokne's similarity to the Caryatids of the Erechtheion suggests that Alkamenes' workshop was probably involved in their creation. Another monumental statue in Pentelic marble dedicated on the Akropolis toward the end of the fifth century is a seated goddess, probably Athena.[15] It has been erroneously attributed to the west pediment of the Parthenon on account of size and marble, although its style, cubic structure, and the fact that it has a plinth (seated statues from the Parthenon pediments have no plinths) militate against this.

After the completion of the Parthenon, which released a considerable workforce of marble workers, and the lifting of the ban on grave reliefs at the inception of the Peloponnesian War around 431 BC, there is a new impetus in the use of documentary, votive, and funerary reliefs almost exclusively carved in Pentelic marble. In the last decades of the fifth century, two notable reliefs illustrate the coronation motif, the colossal Great Eleusinian Relief, where Kore crowns Ploutos or Triptolemos, and the coronation of Herakles by Nike.[16] Votive reliefs, as well as grave reliefs, became standardized in the fourth century, when they were produced by the thousands. Grave reliefs became increasingly larger and more elaborate, and their architectural frames expanded, adopting the form of shallow

---

[13] See Palagia 2000.

[14] Athens, Agora S 312; Gawlinski 2014, 56–58. Athens, National Archaeological Museum 1732; Kaltsas 2002, no. 163. On the friezes of this temple, see Stewart et al. 2019.

[15] Athens, Akropolis Museum 1363. Palagia 1993, 50–51, fig. 114.

[16] Eleusis relief, Athens, National Archaeological Museum 126; Clinton and Palagia 2003. Herakles relief, Athens, Akropolis Museum 1329; Palagia 2009, fig. 10.

temples. (See Shea, Chapter 10 in this volume.) A good case in point is the funerary monument of Prokles and Prokleides from the Kerameikos, which depicts father, mother, and son in solemn display, the father adopting the iconography of seated divine figures (Web Fig. 20.4).[17] Figures and frame rest on a pedestal made of dark grey Hymettian marble, a material that began to be exploited early but was soon overshadowed by Pentelic.

In the fourth century BC, the focus shifts from the Akropolis to the Agora. High-quality statues in Pentelic marble were set up in the Agora, e.g., an early fourth-century Aphrodite, a late fourth-century colossal Agathe Tyche, and the cult statue of Apollo Patroos by Euphranor (Web Fig. 20.5), state artist of Athens in the fourth century, dated to the 330s.[18] Pausanias (1.3.4) saw the Apollo and named its sculptor. Apollo Patroos is shown as the ancestral god of the Athenians through Ion; he is heavily clad as a performer, holding his kithara. The retrospective tendencies of his style are tempered by his high waist and elongated proportions. This is a Late Classical reinterpretation of the Pheidian ideal and appears to be invested with political as well as religious significance. It is reflected in contemporary Attic votive reliefs and remained popular in later periods, generating a number of Roman copies. But the greatest Athenian master of the fourth century was Praxiteles, whose works were shipped far and wide in the Greek world.[19]

Hymettian Marble

The quarries of Mt. Hymettos, producing fine-grained marble in various shades of grey, were in operation by the second quarter of the sixth century, as attested by some sculptured metopes and acroteria from the so-called Hekatompedon (H-architecture) on the Akropolis. High-quality Hymettian marble was also used in Attic funerary *stelai* of the same period; for example, a cavetto capital from Lamptrai (Web Fig. 20.6)[20] and a famous votive statue from the Akropolis, [Rh]ombos or the Calf-bearer.[21]

---

[17] Athens, National Archaeological Museum 737. Kaltsas 2002, no. 394.

[18] Aphrodite, Agora S 37; Stewart 2017, figs. 3a–b, 5, and 6 (here identified as Agathe Tyche). Agathe Tyche, Agora S 2370; Palagia 1994, fig. 1. Apollo Patroos, Agora S 2154; Palagia 2017, figs. 8.1 and 8.2.

[19] On Praxiteles, see Leventi in Palagia 2019.

[20] Athens, National Archaeological Museum 41. Despinis and Kaltsas 2014, no. 363.

[21] Athens, Akropolis Museum 624. Sturgeon (fig. 24) in Palagia 2006.

His inserted eyes are of Egyptian inspiration. The funerary statue of a horseman from Vari is also made of Hymettian marble (Web Fig. 20.7).[22] Hymettian marble for sculpture goes out of use toward the end of the Archaic period but will reappear, briefly, in the second half of the fourth century, for example in the dog from the precinct of Lysimachides of Kollytos at the Kerameikos cemetery.[23]

Conclusion

Bronze became the dominant medium for sculpture in Athens from the late sixth century BC on. It was popular for both portraiture and divine figures, but very few bronzes are extant because they were melted down, mainly in the Middle Ages, in order to recycle their material.

Marble sculpture in Athens was introduced from the islands of the Cyclades in the beginning of the sixth century BC. Athenian sculptors profited from the expertise of visiting masters and gradually developed their own style. The quarries of Mt. Penteli began to be exploited on a grand scale to serve the needs of the Periklean building program ca. 450. Even though the building accounts of the Parthenon record the trimming of pedimental statues at quarry level to reduce their weight for transport to the Akropolis workshops, the Pentelic quarries have yielded virtually no unfinished sculptures. Sculptors' activities in Athens are documented by debris in the industrial and domestic quarters on the outskirts of the Agora. Pentelic marble began to dominate the domestic market in the fourth century and continued, with few rivals, until Late Antiquity.

Further Reading

For the functions of sculpture in Athens, see Palagia 2015a, along with Hochscheid 2015 on the production of sculpture and its impact on the Athenian landscape. On bronzes, see Mattusch 1988. For the early marble sculpture in Athens, see Sturgeon in Palagia 2006; Palagia 2010; Sturgeon in Palagia 2019. For Classical sculpture in Athens, see Palagia in Palagia 2006. For Athenian sculpture in Parian marble, see Palagia 2000. For the quarries on Mt. Penteli, see Korres 2000 and 2001.

---

[22] Athens, National Archaeological Museum 79. Despinis and Kaltsas 2014, no. 266.

[23] Dog in the Kerameikos: Palagia 2011, 11, fig. 6. Grey marble was also produced in limited quantities and mainly for local use, in the Agrileza quarry near Sounion and the Kokkinaras quarry on Mt. Penteli. See: Goette 1991; Goette et al. 1999.

For workshops of marble sculptors in the Agora, see Lawton 2006 and Tsakirgis 2015. For reliefs, see Clairmont 1993, Lawton 1995a, and Comella 2002.

Bibliography

Clairmont, C.W. *Classical Attic Tombstones*. Vols. 1–7. Kilchberg.

Clinton K., and O. Palagia. 2003. "The Boy in the Great Eleusinian Relief." *Mitteilungen des Deutschen Archäologischen Instituts, Athenische Abteilung* 106: 201–222.

Comella, A. 2002. *I rilievi votivi greci di periodo arcaico e classico*. Bari.

Despinis, G., and N. Kaltsas, eds. 2014. *Εθνικό Αρχαιολογικό Μουσείο. Κατάλογος γλυπτών* 1.1. Athens.

Gawlinski, L. *The Athenian Agora: Museum Guide*. 5th edn. Princeton.

Goette, H.R. 1991. "Die Steinbrücke von Sounion in Agrileza-Tal." *Mitteilungen des Deutschen Archäologischen Instituts, Athenische Abteilung* 106: 201–222.

Goette, H.R., K. Polikreti, T. Vacoulis, and Y. Maniatis 1999. "Investigation of the Greyish-blue Marble of Pentelikon and Hymetus." In *Archéomatériaux. Marbres et autres roches*, ed. M. Schvoerer, Bordeaux, 83–90.

Harris, D. 1992. "Bronze Statues on the Athenian Acropolis: The Evidence of a Lycurgan Inventory." *AJA* 96: 637–652.

Hochscheid, H. 2015. *Networks of Stone: Sculpture and Society in Archaic and Classical Athens*. Oxford.

Kaltsas, N. 2002. *Sculpture in the National Archaeological Museum, Athens*. Athens.

Korres, M. 2000. *The Stones of the Parthenon*. Athens.

  2001. *From Pentelicon to the Parthenon: The Ancient Quarries and the Story of a Half-Worked Column Capital of the First Marble Parthenon*. Athens.

Lawton, C.L. 1995a. *Attic Document Reliefs*. Oxford.

  1995b. "Four Document Reliefs from the Athenian Agora." *Hesperia* 64: 122–130.

  2006. *Marbleworkers in the Athenian Agora*. Agora Picture Book 27. Princeton.

Mattusch, C. 1988. *Greek Bronze Statuary: From the Beginnings through the Fifth Century* BC. Ithaca, NY.

Palagia, O. 1993. *The Pediments of the Parthenon*. Leiden.

  1994. "No Demokratia." In *The Archaeology of Athens and Attica under the Democracy*, eds. W.D.E. Coulson, O. Palagia, T.L. Shear, Jr., H.A. Shapiro, F.J. Frost, Oxford, 113–122.

  2000. "Parian Marble and the Athenians." In *Paria Lithos*, ed. D.U. Schilardi and D. Katsonopoulou, Athens, 347–354.

  ed. 2006. *Greek Sculpture: Function, Materials, and Techniques in the Archaic and Classical Periods*. Cambridge.

  2009. "Archaism and the Quest for Immortality in Attic Sculpture during the Peloponnesian War." In *Art in Athens during the Peloponnesian War*, ed. O. Palagia, Cambridge, 24–51.

2010. "Early Archaic Sculpture in Athens." In *Scolpire il marmo*, ed. G. Adornato, Milan, 41–55.

2011. "An Unfinished Molossian Hound from the Dionysos Quarry on Mount Pentelicon." *Marmora* 7: 11–17.

2013. "Not from the Spoils of Marathon: Pheidias' Bronze Athena on the Acropolis." In *Marathon: The Day After*, eds. K. Buraselis and E. Koulakiotis, Athens, 117–137.

2015a. "The Functions of Greek Art." In *The Oxford Handbook of Greek and Roman Art and Architecture*, ed. C. Marconi, Oxford, 294–309.

2015b. "Dating the Corner Figures of the West Pediment and Questions Arising from the Use of Parian and Pentelic Marbles in the Sanctuary." In *New Approaches to the Temple of Zeus at Olympia*, ed. A. Patay-Horváth, Newcastle upon Tyne, 74–89.

2017. "Euphranor." In *Artists and Artistic Production in Ancient Greece*, eds. K. Seaman and P. Schultz, Cambridge, 124–140.

Palagia, O. ed. 2019. *Handbook of Greek Sculpture*. Berlin.

Stewart, A. 2017. "Hellenistic Free-Standing Sculpture from the Athenian Agora." *Hesperia* 86: 83–127.

et al. 2019. "Classical Sculpture from the Athenian Agora, Part 2: The Friezes of the Temple of Ares (Temple of Athena Pallenis)." *Hesperia* 88: 625–705.

Tsakirgis, B. 2015. "Tools from the House of Mikion and Menon." In *Autopsy in Athens*, ed. M.M. Miles, Oxford, 9–17.

Additional resources to accompany this chapter can be found at: www.cambridge.org/NeilsRogers

PART IV

Culture and Sport

21 | The Philosophical Schools

GEOFFREY BAKEWELL

The emergence of institutions dedicated to specific intellectual and prag-
matic ways of being in the world was a distinguishing feature of ancient
Athens. From their foundation in the fourth century BC, the philosophical
schools educated local adherents, drew immigrants and visitors from
around the Mediterranean, and played prominent cultural roles.[1]
Throughout the many centuries of their existence, the Academy, the
Peripatos, the Garden, and the Stoa competed with and complemented
one another on multiple levels. Considered as a whole, they offer an
invaluable approach to understanding ancient Athens, especially in the
Late Classical, Hellenistic, and Early Roman periods. Although the schools'
influence extended throughout the Imperial period and beyond, their
greatest *floruit* came before 86 BC, when Sulla's troops felled the groves
of the Academy and Lyceum and plundered the city (Plutarch, *Sulla* 12.3).
This chapter focuses on the formative fourth through second centuries BC,
and on how the intersection of Athenian topography with philosophical
practice turned the Academics, Peripatetics, Epicureans, and Stoics into
enduring models of how people should think, act, live, and die.

Strictly speaking, the Greek term *philosophia* denotes 'love of wisdom,'
and *schole* 'leisure.' These two concepts were first conjoined in a specific
historical context, namely that of Classical Athens. Following its turn to
democracy (ca. 508 BC), its sack by an invading Persian army (480 BC), and
its subsequent recovery and rise to empire, the city offered unprecedented
opportunities. Pythagoreans and rhetoricians from Magna Graecia to the
west, along with early scientific thinkers from Asia Minor to the east, all
converged in Athens seeking prestige, pupils, and pay. These visitors
caught the interest of leading citizens whose political and military responsibilities, together with their relatively abundant free time, made them eager
to explore in extended conversations the sayings of traditional authorities
like poets, lawgivers, and sages. The heady result helped transform the city
into "the education of Greece" (Thucydides 2.41.1).

---

[1] Haake (2010, 58–59) defines such schools, while Jones (1999, 228) discusses the ancient
terminology used to refer to them.

These innumerable exchanges occurred in a wide range of public and private settings. Plato's *Protagoras* provides an unforgettable picture of one such occasion. In this dialogue, set ca. 433/2 BC, visiting sophists hold court in the house of the wealthy aristocrat Kallias. Trailed by a rapt chorus of students, Protagoras paces the atrium, while Prodikos lectures others from the comfort of a fleecy bed. Sokrates then enters in comic fashion with his young friend Hipponikos, and proceeds to discuss with the visitors the lofty goals of education; as often, the men reach no clear conclusions. Aristophanes' comedy, *Clouds* (revised ca. 418–416 BC), places Sokrates on the receiving end of the ridicule; his "school" (*phrontistirion*, line 94) offers a distortedly hilarious glimpse of 'philosophy' as practiced in a fixed location *avant la lettre*. Taken together, Plato's dialogues and Xenophon's *Memorabilia* depict Athenians and foreigners regularly engaged in intellectual debate. As Haake notes, this "philosophizing was from the very beginning an integral part of a male elitist habitus."[2] Put differently, the activity was heavily gendered, and rested in large part on wealth deriving from the ownership of land and slaves, the exploitation of natural resources, and commerce.

Plato's Academy

Such was the general backdrop for Plato's foundation of the Academy. In the last decade or so of the fifth century BC, Athens suffered crushing military defeats and political coups. Following the restoration of democracy, its citizens were suspicious of both revolutionary religious sentiment and reactionary politics: one result was the trial and execution of Sokrates. His follower Plato, along with others, fled to nearby Megara, and thereafter made his first visit to Sicily. He returned to Athens in 387 BC and took up residence in an attractive extramural suburb north of the Dipylon Gate (Diogenes Laertius 3.7; see Map 4.2). This location, removed from the Agora and Pnyx, reflected his ambivalence, evident throughout the *Republic*, toward the involvement of philosophers in politics. But it was also close enough to the action to assure him a steady supply of visitors and interlocutors.[3] And the broad Kerameikos avenue leading to the Academy was lined with public funerary monuments of citizen warriors fallen on behalf of the city. These tombs were a visible reminder of the extent to

[2] Haake 2010, 76.
[3] Jones 1999, 232.

which traditional notions of excellence (*arete*), celebrated in epic poetry and questioned in tragedy, undergirded Plato's own thought. (See Shea, Chapter 10 in this volume.)

The Academy took its name from Hekademos, a local hero whose shrine is located by a boundary stone found in situ. Some of the site's physical particulars were described by the second-century AD traveler Pausanias (1.30); others have been revealed by modern excavations which began in earnest in 1929 and continued for another thirty-five years, but have been incompletely published.[4] The area boasted one of the three great public *gymnasia* of ancient Athens. Its precinct was walled off under the Peisistratids, and originally contained (at a minimum) a running track and wrestling ground. After the Persian retreat in 480, the general Kimon replanted the grounds, supplying them with water drawn from the nearby Kephissos River (Plutarch, *Kimon* 13.8). Sometime in the second half of the fourth century BC, a square peristyle was added; toward the end of the Hellenistic period, another building containing niches (*exedrai*) was constructed. Plato's choice of this spot for his school testifies not only to the elitist nature of the enterprise but also to the ways it was informed by gymnastics and athletics. His frequent wrestling and racing metaphors reveal the Academic life as marked by (psychic) exertion and competition for renown. And his followers were conspicuous in their stylish cloaks, tunics, and hats (Athenaios 544f–545a).

At the entrance to the Academy stood an altar to Eros (Pausanias 1.30.1). The god's presence highlighted the charms of youthful male bodies, and the ways homoerotic couplings could help or harm the soul (Plato, *Symposion* 210a–211c; *Phaedrus* 250e–253c). Inside were other altars to Prometheus, Hermes, Athena and Herakles, and the Muses (Pausanias 1.30.2). The last monument in particular was one reason earlier scholars like Wilamowitz considered the philosophical schools as legally recognized religious bands (*thiasoi*) organized around communal worship of the Muses.[5] More recently, however, others have shown that the schools are better understood as secular associations protected by Solonian law and dedicated to particular ways of life. In the Academy, men (and occasionally women; Diogenes Laertius 3.46) joined forces to undertake the sort of learning that lent meaning to life. But the nearby altars and statues also pointed to the tension between traditional understandings of the gods and

---

[4] See Panayiotopoulos and Chatziefthimiou in Kalligas et al. 2020, especially 28–31.
[5] Natali 2013, 78–80.

Plato's ongoing efforts to clarify the nature of the divine, and to reconcile it with the Forms that were central to his thought.

Plato ultimately acquired his own private property near the Academy *gymnasion*; together the two locales, public and private, formed the backdrop for the school's philosophical activity.[6] As founder, Plato framed problems and general themes for investigation, especially in politics, ethics, epistemology, mathematics, and ontology.[7] He also took the opportunity to write, and to read aloud from his works. His stated preference for discussion (*Phaedrus* 275d–276a; *Epistles* 7.344c) and the often aporetic and literary character of his dialogues made them particularly good to think with; students felt free to disagree with even primary tenets of his teaching (e.g. Aristotle, *Nicomachean Ethics* 1096a11–13).

Upon his death in 348/7 BC, Plato left behind a will bequeathing the Academy to his nephew Speusippos.[8] In turning to a relative, Plato highlighted the importance of family ties to the enterprise. As Wycherley noted, the first philosophical school was in many ways "a specialized extension of the Hellenic household."[9] For their part, students truly put their teachers on pedestals: a memorial to Plato complete with bust decorated the grounds of the Academy. And Speusippos and his own successors later dangled Plato's charismatic example as a lure for prospective pupils.[10]

Aristotle's Lyceum

The second great philosophical school of Athens was likewise connected with an Athenian *gymnasion*, the Lyceum. It, too, was extramural and riverine, located along the Ilissos River near the Diochares Gate, by a plain where the Athenian cavalry practiced maneuvers (see Map 4.2). For a long time, discrepancies among the ancient literary testimonia made identifying its precise location difficult.[11] But in the 1990s, building preparations for a modern art museum in downtown Athens revealed the remains of a

---

[6] Dillon 2003, 58–59; O'Sullivan 2002, 257.

[7] The fourth-century comic poet Epikrates (fr. 10) shows Plato and several followers hard at work, applying the method of collection and division to the pressing question of how best to classify a squash.

[8] The wills of the schools' founders, and of their successors, sometimes called scholarchs, are often preserved in the work of the third-century AD biographer Diogenes Laertius, and comprise an important resource for the study of ancient philosophy.

[9] Wycherley 1961, 55.

[10] Watts 2007.

[11] Ritchie 1989.

palaistra dating to the last quarter of the fourth century BC. This site, located along Rigillis Street between the Byzantine and Christian Museum and the National Garden, is now widely accepted as the Lyceum.[12] In antiquity and afterward, the term itself could refer to several things: the *gymnasion*; the informal instruction offered by Aristotle nearby; and the more formal philosophical establishment later established there by his student and successor Theophrastos. The Peripatos, as Theophrastos' school was known, took its name from a Greek word for a colonnaded building: here pupils could walk to and fro while pursuing their studies protected from the sun, wind, and rain.[13]

Originally from Stageira, Aristotle had as a young man been introduced to Plato and spent twenty years in the Academy; following his teacher's death, he quit Athens. Perhaps unhappy at being passed over for Speusippos, he then spent a dozen years abroad studying in Atarneus and Macedonia, working first with the tyrant Hermias, and later with the young Alexander the Great. Upon returning to Athens in 335, Aristotle kept a lower profile than either Sokrates or Plato had, in part because he and his associates were more inclined toward research than teaching. His followers were expected to know the works of Plato, and Aristotle himself regularly refers to the *Republic* and *Timaeus*. Like the Academy, the Peripatos promoted a spirit of intellectual tolerance. Yet the practice of oral dialectic, so essential for Plato, declined under Aristotle. He and his companions often preferred to study alone, or else lecture from their writings. What united the Peripatetics was the belief that the contemplative life (*theoretikos bios*) was ideal for human beings. Like the Academics, they paid no tuition, instead contributing voluntarily from their own wealth to make the good life possible for themselves and others.

The travels of Aristotle and his followers helped expand the boundaries of philosophical inquiry beyond fields traditionally explored by the Academy: literature and history received further attention, as did botany and zoology. Some Peripatetic work was moreover rooted in direct observation, or concerned with the collection and systematic organization of data (e.g. lists of winners at the Pythian Games, constitutional histories of numerous Greek city-states). Another methodological advance lay in the Peripatetics' use of the opinions of reputable authorities. Contrary to Plato's Sokrates, Aristotle thought that such *endoxa* contained elements

---

[12] Lygouri-Tolia 2002.

[13] On the ancient connection between walking and philosophy, see Montiglio 2000.

of truth, and frequently made them starting points for his own research on particular topics. The Peripatetics' respect for such sources, and their turn away from dialectic, made them more reliant on written materials capable of crossing temporal and geographical divides. Although Plato had accumulated a number of papyri, Aristotle's writings and library formed a pillar of the school that Theophrastos formally organized. After numerous vicissitudes, this collection eventually made its way to Alexandria, where it became a significant part of the Museum's holdings. The Peripatetics' methods also involved other aids to learning such as diagrams, maps, and globes.

Aristotle left Athens for the last time in 323, dying shortly afterwards. His will made extensive arrangements for his dependents and property, but his intellectual heir Theophrastos was also a metic (Diogenes Laertius 5.11–16). In addition to their non-citizen status, the two men shared a prominent connection with Macedonia that left the Peripatos politically vulnerable. After Athens' defeat at Chaironeia and occupation, Kassander eventually installed Theophrastos' student Demetrios of Phaleron as ruler of the city. The latter wasted little time in passing a law permitting Theophrastos to own immovable property. Following Demetrios' overthrow in 307 BC, popular anger flared up and resulted in the passage of Sophokles' law. This measure forbade philosophers to operate a school in the city without the express permission of the Assembly; they responded by emigrating in large numbers. The law was subsequently challenged and nullified, however, and the philosophers returned to Athens to usher in the heyday of their schools. The Peripatos resumed operations, and upon Theophrastos' death in 288, intellectual control passed to Strato (Diogenes Laertius 5.58).

Epicurus' Garden

The repeal of Sophokles' law created additional room for philosophizing. Epicurus was an Athenian who had been raised abroad but had done his ephebic training in Attika. After years of teaching in Mytilene and Lampsakos, in 307/6 BC, he returned to Athens (Diogenes Laertius 10.15). He acquired property a little north of the Dipylon Gate, and founded his own intellectual community known as the Garden. It differed from the nearby Academy and the Peripatos in that it occupied an exclusively private space; its sylvan setting was in keeping with Epicurus' dicta to avoid political involvement and preserve tranquility of mind. In the 1960s,

the remains of five life-sized statues from the Roman period were discovered near the intersection of Marathon and Achilles Streets. The fact
that two of them depict Epicurus, while a third shows another Epicurean
scholarch, likely Kolotes, strongly suggests that the Garden was located
nearby.[14]

These statues point to an aspect of philosophical life that differentiated
the Epicurean community from its competition. Reverence for their founders had certainly played an important role in defining the Academic and
Peripatetic communities (e.g. Diogenes Laertius 5.51, 53), but the sheer
number and size of Epicurus' statues, the devotion of his followers, and the
terms of his will all suggest that he was celebrated in the manner of an epic
hero. He claimed that he was self-taught (Diogenes Laertius 10.13), and he
and his followers showed little patience for other thinkers; two of his
successor Hermarchos' polemical works are entitled *Against Plato* and
Against Aristotle (Diogenes Laertius 10.25). Epicureanism was notable in
its lack of eclecticism and its hostility toward the philosophically omnivor-
ous: Timokrates, the brother of Epicurus' devoted explicator Metrodoros,
came in for particular abuse after defecting to the Stoa.[15]

Paradoxically, Epicureans' attacks on their rivals necessitated the collection of the latter's writings. Epicurus developed a library that, unlike
Aristotle's, remained firmly attached to his school (Diogenes Laertius
10.21). His own monumental work *On Nature* ran to thirty-seven unwieldy
volumes, portions of which are preserved on the papyri found in a Roman
villa at Herculaneum. The demand for a more condensed and easily
remembered version of his teachings eventually led Epicurus to the epis-
tolary approach. His letters to Herodotos, Pythokles, and Menoeceus are
preserved in Diogenes Laertius, and epitomize his work in different areas.
Epicurus also took advantage of his citizen status to have copies of his
writings and correspondence preserved in the Athenian archive at the
Metroon in the Agora, where they were available for public consultation.
(See Camp, Chapter 6 in this volume.)

Under Epicurus and his successors, philosophy was not just an intellectual matter but an all-encompassing way of life; the Garden was a residential community whose inhabitants ate and lived together (Diogenes
Laertius 10.11). As with the Academics and Peripatetics, Epicureanism
was in part a family affair, as the founder's parents and brothers all

---

[14] *ArchDelt* 26 (1971) A', 21–22; Clay 2009, 10, n. 3.
[15] Clay 2009, 17.

belonged to the school. In addition to accepting gifts, the Epicureans required contributions from wealthier members to facilitate the participation of others. The Garden was less exclusive than other schools with regard to gender and civic status; women (including courtesans) and slaves were conspicuously accepted as members. And the intimately shared lives of its adherents, together with their insistence on pleasure (rightly understood) as the highest good in life, contributed in no small part to later slanders against the school.

Epicurus died in 270, and left behind a will, a copy of which was also filed at the Metroon (Diogenes Laertius 10.16–22). This document was significantly more complex than the will of Plato or Aristotle.[16] On the one hand, it entrusted the Garden and his house in Melite to a pair of Athenian citizens, Amynomachos and Timokrates. But it also instructed them to place everything at the disposal of Epicurus' intellectual successor Hermarchos, and urged everyone to do their utmost "to preserve forever their common way of life" (Diogenes Laertius 10.17). The will also committed financial resources to support a number of cultic prescriptions. For one thing, Epicurus, his parents, and his brothers were all to be remembered yearly. This was in and of itself not unprecedented, but the community was also enjoined to hold monthly feasts honoring Epicurus and Metrodoros. Honors like this had traditionally been reserved for the gods, a potentially embarrassing fact for a philosophy that held (1) that the soul was mortal, and (2) that divine beings either did not exist or were indifferent to human affairs. The real point, however, was to offer Epicurus' life as a model to his followers, and they responded eagerly, placing images of the Master on cups, rings, and gems (Fig. 21.1).

Zeno's Stoa

The repeal of Sophokles' law likewise provided an opening for the last great philosophical school of Athens. Around 300 BC, Zeno of Kition (Cyprus) was delayed in Athens by shipwreck, and spent his enforced leisure reading the *Memorabilia* of Xenophon and following Krates the Cynic about the city (Diogenes Laertius 7.2–3). He subsequently began holding forth in the Painted Stoa (or Stoa Poikile), from which his followers eventually derived their name. The school's location in a public building within the Agora

---

[16] See Leiwo and Remes 1999.

Fig. 21.1 Portrait of a Greek philosopher, perhaps Epicurus, engraved gem, first to third centuries AD, London, British Museum 1923,0401.798.

signaled the Stoics' full-throated engagement with civic life (see Map 6.1). And the city repaid the compliment handsomely, passing a decree awarding him a golden crown and a tomb in the Kerameikos at public expense. Perhaps most provocatively, the Assembly allocated funds for copies of the decree to be inscribed and erected in two particular places: the Academy and the Lyceum (Diogenes Laertius 7.11–12)!

Our knowledge of the Stoa qua structure comes mainly from the ancient description by Pausanias (1.15) and ongoing excavations by the American School of Classical Studies at Athens.[17] The building was one of the first rebuilt in the Agora after the Persian sack, and its interior was decorated with famous painted panels celebrating military exploits: Theseus' defeat of the Amazons, the Greek conquest of Troy, the defining triumph at Marathon, and a recent Athenian victory over the Spartans at Oinoe (Fig. 21.2). The adornments also included shields taken from foes, above all the Spartans who had surrendered at Sphakteria in 425 BC. Like the paintings surrounding them, the Stoics emphasized bravery and civic duty, punctuating their philosophical points with exempla drawn from myth and history. And, again, like the paintings, their teaching was heavily gendered, with men proving superior to women by nature. The Agora location also offered an important link with the historical Sokrates, who had frequented the area and was a dominant influence on early Stoic thought. Finally, the proximity and prominence of many of the city's most important shrines, which were visible from the Stoa's south-facing main colonnade, fitted well

---

[17] Camp 2007 and 2015.

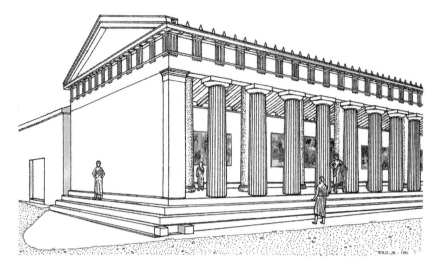

Fig. 21.2 Reconstruction of the Painted Stoa, Agora, ca. 400 BC.
Courtesy of the American School of Classical Studies at Athens: Agora Excavations

with the Stoics' general acceptance of prevailing views of the gods. The Stoa's central location brought in a steady supply of suitable pupils. Lacking private space of their own, Zeno and his successors held lively interactions not only with philosophical hopefuls but also hecklers and passersby. They thereby turned philosophy into a type of public performance, and paradoxically drew adherents by playing hard to get, even humiliating the occasional student.[18]

Conclusion

Perhaps the best way to underscore the importance of the philosophical schools in ancient Athens is to conclude with the mention of an embassy the city sent to Rome in the second century BC. Although the Roman Flamininus had proclaimed the freedom of the Greeks at Olympia in 196, Aemilius Paulus' defeat of the Macedonian ruler Perseus in 168 eventually led the Romans to divide Greece into a number of provinces that were incorporated into their empire. In 155, Athens was engaged in a territorial dispute with the neighboring town of Oropos, and ordered by an arbitrator to pay a penalty of 500 talents. The city chose to appeal the judgment to Rome, and sent as its spokesmen Karneades, Kritolaos, and Diogenes of

[18] Rihll 2003, 171–172.

Babylon, i.e. the heads of the Academy, Peripatos, and Stoa, respectively.[19] The ambassadors succeeded in having the fine reduced to 100 talents, and were rewarded with the gift of Athenian citizenship.

But the triumph of the schools was relatively short-lived. In 88 BC, Athens proved all too prone to the suasions of the Pontic ruler Mithridates and took his side in a rebellion against Rome; the ultimate result was the sack of Athens mentioned above. In addition to slaughtering many of the citizens, Sulla seized and brought to Rome the Library of Apellikon, which contained works by Aristotle and Theophrastos (Plutarch, *Sulla* 26). And by 79 BC, both the Academy and Garden had been largely reduced to objects of sentimental pilgrimage for Romans like Cicero and his friends (*De finibus* 5).[20] In the following decades, the city repeatedly wound up on the wrong side in Rome's civil wars, hosting first Brutus and Cassius and then Mark Antony. (See also Rogers, Chapter 30 in this volume.) While the philosophical schools continued to exist and indeed experienced a number of revivals under the Empire, they never regained their former luster, and were nominally closed by Justinian in AD 529.[21] But to this day their teachings and practices continue to educate and inspire, and the exploration and conservation of their physical traces remain abiding goals of archaeologists.

Further Reading

Rihll 2003 discusses the general dynamics of teaching and learning in ancient Athens, while Natali 2003 and Haake 2010 offer short overviews of the philosophical schools' topography and practices. On their various doctrines, see Long and Sedley 1987; on sculpted representations of philosophers, see Zanker 1995; on images of education on Athenian vases, see Oakley 2020, 103–112. For particulars regarding Plato's Academy, consult Caruso 2013 and Kalligas et al. 2020; for Aristotle and the Lyceum, Natali 2013. Clay 2009 examines Epicurus' Garden, and Kechagia 2010 the Stoa.

Bibliography

Camp, J.M. 2007. "Excavations in the Athenian Agora: 2002–2007." *Hesperia* 76: 627–663.

2015. "Excavations in the Athenian Agora: 2008–2012." *Hesperia* 84: 467–513.

---

[19] The absence of a representative from the Garden was doubtless due to the Epicureans' views on politics.

[20] On the end of the Academy, see Bonazzi in Kalligas et al. 2020.

[21] On their subsequent history see Natali 2003, 58–64.

Caruso, A. 2013. *Akademia: Archeologia di una scuola filosofica ad Atene da Platone a Proclo (387 a.C.–485 d.C.).* Athens.

Clay, D. 2009. "The Athenian Garden." In *The Cambridge Companion to Epicureanism*, ed. J. Warren, Cambridge, 9–28.

Dillon, J. 2003. *The Heirs of Plato: A Study of the Old Academy.* Oxford.

Haake, M. 2010. "Philosophical Schools in Athenian Society from the Fourth to the First Century BC: An Overview." In *Private Associations and the Public Sphere*, eds. V. Gabrielsen and C. Thomsen, Copenhagen, 57–91.

Jones, N.F. 1999. *The Associations of Classical Athens: The Response of Democracy.* Oxford.

Kalligas, P., C. Balla, E. Baziotopoulou-Valavani, and V. Karasmanis, eds. 2020. *Plato's Academy: Its Workings and Its History.* Cambridge.

Kechagia, E. 2010. "Rethinking a Professional Rivalry: Early Epicureans against the Stoa." *CQ* 60: 132–155.

Leiwo, M., and P. Remes. 1999. "Partnership of Citizens and Metics: The Will of Epicurus." *CQ* 49: 161–166.

Long, A.A., and D. Sedley. 1987. *The Hellenistic Philosophers.* Cambridge.

Lygouri-Tolia, E. 2002. "Excavating an Ancient Palaestra in Athens." In *Excavating Classical Culture: Recent Archaeological Discoveries in Greece*, eds. M. Stamatopoulou and M. Yeroulanou, Oxford, 203–212.

Montiglio, S. 2000. "Wandering Philosophers in Classical Greece." *JHS* 120: 86–105.

Natali, C. 2003. "Schools and Sites of Learning." In *The Greek Pursuit of Knowledge*, eds. J. Brunschwig and G.E.R. Lloyd, Cambridge, MA, 40–66.

    2013. *Aristotle: His Life and School*, ed. D.S. Hutchinson, Princeton.

Oakley, J.H. 2020. *A Guide to Scenes of Daily Life on Athenian Vases.* Madison.

O'Sullivan, L. 2002. "The Law of Sophocles and the Beginnings of Permanent Philosophical Schools in Athens." *Rheinisches Museum für Philologie* 145: 251–262.

Rihll, T.E. 2003. "Teaching and Learning in Classical Athens." *Greece & Rome* 50: 168–190.

Ritchie, C.E. 1989. "The Lyceum, the Garden of Theophrastus, and the Garden of the Muses: A Topographical Re-Evaluation." In *Φίλια ἔπη εἰς Γεώργιον Ε. Μυκωνάν δια τα 60 ἔτη του ανασκαφικού του ἔργου*, Τομος Γ', Athens, 250–260.

Watts, E. 2007. "Creating the Academy: Historical Discourse and the Shape of Community in the Old Academy." *JHS* 127: 106–122.

Wycherley, R.E. 1961. "Peripatos: The Athenian Philosophical Scene – I." *Greece & Rome* 8: 152–163.

Zanker, P. 1995. *The Mask of Socrates: The Image of the Intellectual in Antiquity.* Berkeley.

22 | Athletics, Democracy, and War

DAVID M. PRITCHARD

This chapter considers the paradox of elite athletics in Classical Athens. Although Athenian democracy may have opened up politics to every citizen, it had no impact on athletic participation. The athletes of this famous ancient democratic *polis* continued to be drawn from the upper class. Therefore, it comes as a surprise that non-elite Athenians judged athletics to be a very good thing and created an unrivaled program of local sporting festivals on which they spent a staggering sum of money. They also protected athletes and athletics from the public criticism that was otherwise normally directed toward wealthy citizens and their conspicuous activities. The work of anthropologists suggests that the explanation of this paradox lies in the close relationship that non-elite Athenians perceived between athletic contests and their own waging of war. The chapter concludes that it was the Athenian democracy's opening up of war to non-elite citizens that legitimized elite sport.

The Democratic Support of Athletics

The Athenian *demos* (people) lavished time and money on athletic contests. With justification the Athenians believed that they had more festivals than any other Greek state (e.g. Isokrates 4.45). They established most of their festivals with *agones* (contests) in the first fifty years of their democracy.[1] In doing so they introduced *agones* for musicians and choristers as well as for horse owners and athletes. Nevertheless, the *demos* clearly favored athletics, because they introduced it much more often than the other types of *agones*. Indeed, two-thirds of their fifteen competitive festivals had contests for athletes. It thus appears that the popularity of athletics closely paralleled the consolidation of the Athenian democracy.[2]

The most extensive program of contests was staged as part of the Great Panathenaia. (See also Miles and Neils, Chapter 24 in this volume.) In the

---

[1] Osborne 1993, 27–28, 38.
[2] Miller 2004, 233.

380s this four-yearly festival for Athena had thirty-nine contests for individual competitors in almost all types of competition (*IG* II^2 2311). Almost half of this festival's *agones* were for athletes in three different age classes. These events included all the standard ones of Greek athletics. For most of the Classical period, the Athenians staged the 'track and field' events of the Great Panathenaia on or near the *dromos* (racetrack) in the Agora. The *stadion* was a sprint from one end of this *dromos* to the other. The *diaulos* was two lengths of the racetrack, while the *dolichos* was a long-distance footrace of many lengths. The pentathlon consisted of five sub-contests: discus, javelin, the long jump with hand weights, the *stadion*, and wrestling. The Great Panathenaia had contests in wrestling, boxing, and the *pankration*. Of these three so-called heavy events, the *pankration* was the most brutal: this free-for-all sport had few rules, allowing kicks, chokeholds, and even blows to the genitals.

The Great Panathenaia also had *agones* for pyrrhic and dithyrambic choruses and for tribal teams of torch racers, sailors, and manly young men. In the torch race, each team had to run a relay race from the Academy (see below), outside the Dipylon Gate, to the Akropolis, while keeping their torch alight. The contests of this quadrennial festival were more numerous than those of the ancient Olympics. Eight other Athenian festivals had sporting contests. The annual games for the war dead, the Eleusinia, which was staged in three out of four years, and the four-yearly festival of Herakles at Marathon each had a large set of athletic, equestrian, and musical events.[3] Five other annual festivals also featured a single athletic or equestrian contest.[4]

The Athenian *demos* forced elite citizens to pay for a great deal of these competitive festivals. The torch racers of the Great Panathenaia, the Hephaisteia, and Prometheia competed and trained as part of teams that had been drawn from the Kleisthenic tribes. The cost of training each of these ten teams fell to an elite citizen serving as a *gymnasiarchos* or athletic-training sponsor (e.g. Xenophon, *Ways and Means* 4.35–37). A *choregos* or chorus-sponsor did the same for each of the choruses that competed in the state's dramatic and dithyrambic contests (e.g. *Constitution of the Athenians* 56.2–3). During the 350s, these festival liturgies added up to 97 annually, rising to 118 in the years of the Great Panathenaia.

In antiquity, the complaint was occasionally made that the Classical Athenians actually spent more on festivals than on wars (e.g. Demosthenes

[3] Kyle 1987, 44–47.
[4] Pritchard 2013, 95–96.

4.35–37; Plutarch *Moralia* 349a). Since the early nineteenth century, some ancient historians have viewed this accusation as fully justified.[5] It is undeniable that the Athenian democracy spent a large amount of money on *polis*-level festivals, but careful comparison of this spending with what was spent on the armed forces shows that this complaint is entirely incorrect. Indeed, what the Athenians spent on war manifestly dwarfed all other public expenditure combined. For example, in the 420s, public spending alone on the armed forces was 1500 talents (t.) on average per year.[6] During the 370s, the average total of all spending on war was more than 500 t.

In spite of this, the Athenian *demos* still placed a high priority on generously funding their festivals. They spent 25 t. on each celebration of the Great Panathenaia (Table 22.1).[7] The entire program of *polis*-administered festivals probably cost no less than 100 t. per year. This was a lot of money: it was comparable to the cost of running the democratic government itself.[8] The *demos* may have treated war-making as their top public priority, but they still clearly spent a large sum on their sporting festivals.

Athenian democracy also put great store in the public infrastructure for athletics. Leading politicians got ahead in their struggles for preeminence by taking care of the state's three *gymnasia* or athletics fields. They were located a short distance outside the city walls: to the northeast there was the Academy, to the southwest Kynosarges, and to the east the Lyceum (see Map 4.2). (See also Bakewell, Chapter 21 in this volume.) In the fifth century, Kimon spent his own money to provide proper running tracks and landscaping for the Academy (e.g. Plutarch, *Kimon* 13.7). Perikles used public funds to renovate the Lyceum (Harpokration, s.v. Lyceum). Alkibiades proposed a law concerning Kynosarges (e.g. *IG* I^3 134). In the fourth century, Lycurgus oversaw not only the completion of the first stone Theater of Dionysos but also the building of a new stadium for the Great Panathenaia and the renovation of the Lyceum (e.g. Pausanias 1.26.16). The Classical Athenians also witnessed a massive expansion in the number of privately owned *palaistrai* or wrestling schools (Plato, *Lysis* 203a–204e).

This public support of athletics was also reflected in Old Comedy. Surviving comedies can give the impression that simply everyone in the public eye was a victim of comic abuse. But an important study of the

---

[5] For example, see Csapo and Slater 1994, 141.
[6] Pritchard 2015, 92–111.
[7] Pritchard 2015, 28–51.
[8] Pritchard 2015, 51–90.

Table 22.1 *Cost of the Great Panathenaia in the 380s*

Public expenditure	12 t. 3,000 dr.
Market value of the olive oil for the prizes	5 t. 2,725 dr.
Festival liturgies	7 t. 2,000 dr.
10 athletic-training sponsorships for the torch race at 1,200 dr. each = 2 t.	
10 liturgies for the ship race at 1,500 dr. each = 2 t. 3,000 dr.	
9 chorus-sponsorships for the war dance at 800 dr. each = 1 t. 1,200 dr.	
6 chorus-sponsorships for the cyclic choruses at 300 dr. each = 1,800 dr.	
10 liturgies for the manliness contest at 800 dr. each = 1 t. 2,000 dr.	
Total	25 T. 1,725 dr.

Source: D.M. Pritchard

targets of the old comedians by Sommerstein shows that one group of conspicuous Athenians escaped such personal attacks: Athenian athletes.[9] In addition, in contrast to their treatment of other elite activities, the comic poets did not subject athletics to sustained parody or direct criticism. They manifestly assumed that athletics was an unambiguously good thing. For example, in the *Clouds*, Aristophanes linked the "old education" – of which athletics was the main component – with norms of citizenship and manliness (e.g. lines 961, 972–984, 1002–1032). Better Argument suggests that this traditional education flourished at the same time as two of the cardinal virtues of the Greek state, namely justice and moderation (960–962). It also nurtured "the men who fought at Marathon" (985–986).

During the Athenian democracy, playwrights, and public speakers generally depicted athletes and athletics in the same positive terms. Playwrights, of course, were members of the upper class, but their plays were staged in the Theater of Dionysos as part of the *agones* of two *polis*-sponsored festivals. The judging of these contests was formally in the hands of judges selected at random.[10] Nevertheless, victory ultimately depended on the vocal responses of the predominantly lower-class theatergoers (e.g. Demosthenes 18.265). The result was that the comic and the tragic poets had to tailor their plays to the outlook of lower-class citizens (e.g. Plato, *Laws* 659a–c, 700a–1b). Under the Athenian democracy, litigants and politicians faced a comparable performance dynamic: their *agones* (debates) were decided by the actual votes of lower-class

[9] Sommerstein 1996, especially 331.
[10] Csapo and Slater 1994, 301–305.

jurors, Assembly-goers, or councilors.[11] Consequently, they too had to negotiate the perceptions of poor Athenians (e.g. Aristotle, *Rhetoric* 1.9.30–31; 2.21.15–16; 2.22.3).

Therefore, the overwhelmingly positive treatment of athletes and athletics in Athenian popular literature is clear evidence of the high estimation that the Athenian lower class had of sport. This means that the preference that non-elite citizens showed for athletic *agones* in their state-sponsored program of festivals and their careful management of the public infrastructure for athletics can be attributed to their very positive evaluation of athletes and athletics.

The Paradox of Elite Athletics under the Athenian Democracy

For Athenian boys and young men, training in athletics took place only in the regular school classes of a *paidotribes* (athletics teacher). Isokrates explains how athletics teachers instruct their pupils in "the moves devised for competition" (15.183). They train them in athletics, accustom them to toil, and compel them to combine each of the lessons that they have learned (184–185). For Isokrates, this training turns pupils into competent athletic competitors as long as they have enough natural talent. Athletic trainers were most frequently represented in Classical texts or on Attic red-figure vases giving lessons in wrestling or in the other two 'heavy' events of boxing and the *pankration* (e.g. Aristophanes, *Knights* 490–492, 1238–1239; Plato, *Gorgias* 456d–e). This is not unexpected, because many of these teachers owned a *palaistra* (e.g. Aischines 1.10).

What is unexpected is that we also find them leading their students out to a *gymnasion*, where they would train them in the standard 'track and field' events of Greek athletics (Web Fig. 22.1). For example, in his *Statesman*, Plato outlines how there are in Athens, as in other cities, "very many" supervised "training sessions for groups" where instructions are given and *ponoi* (toils) expended not only for wrestling but also "for the sake of competition in the foot-race or some other event" (294d–e). It appears that athletics in Classical Athens consisted of two closely related activities: festival-based *agones* and the regular sports classes of athletics teachers. In Classical Athens, a boy studied athletics concurrently with the two other traditional disciplines of letters and music. Groups of students

---

[11] Pritchard 2019, 114–115.

going to sports classes would thus have been a common daily sight across the urban center.

Athenian democracy, importantly, did not finance or administer education. Consequently, each family made its own decisions about how long their boys would be at school and whether they would take each of the three traditional disciplines of education: athletics, music, and letters. The Athenians understood very well that the number of disciplines that a boy could pursue and the length of his schooling depended on his family's financial resources (e.g. Plato, *Protagoras* 326c). Money determined not only whether a family could pay school fees but also whether they could give their sons the *schole* (leisure) that they needed to pursue all three disciplines. Contemporary writers make clear that most poor citizens were unable to afford more than a few household slaves (e.g. Herodotos 6.137). Consequently, they relied on their children to help them to run farms or businesses. These writers were aware too how this child labor restricted the educational opportunities of boys (e.g. Isokrates 7.43–45; 14.48).

The result was that poor families decided to skip music and athletics, sending their sons only to the classes of a letter teacher.[12] It was only wealthy boys who received training in each of the three disciplines of education. Because the *demos* firmly believed that training in athletics was indispensable for creditable performance (e.g. Aischines 3.179–180), lower-class boys and youths would have been disinclined from entering athletic competitions in the first place. Therefore, in the Athenian democracy, athletes continued to be drawn predominantly – or possibly even exclusively – from the state's upper class.

There were, of course, other activities in Classical Athens, such as the drinking party, pederastic homosexuality, political leadership, and horsemanship, which were also exclusive preserves of the wealthy.[13] Yet, these upper-class pursuits differed from athletics in one critical respect: they were regularly criticized in Old Comedy and in the other genres of Athenian popular literature. Poor Athenians hoped, one day, to enjoy the lifestyle of the rich (e.g. Aristophanes, *Wasps* 708–711; *Wealth* 133–134), but they still had problems with the exclusive pursuits of this social class. Wealthy citizens, for example, were criticized for their excessive enjoyment of two elements of the *symposion* (drinking party): alcohol and prostitutes (e.g. Aischines 1.42). Non-elite Athenians were convinced that such a party

---

[12] Pritchard 2013, 34–83.
[13] Pritchard 2019, 62–63.

always came at the expense of a wealthy citizen's ability to pay for liturgies and the war tax (e.g. Lysias 14.23–25; 19.9–11).

The Cultural Overlap between Athletics and War

Classical Athenians thought of athletics and battle with a common set of concepts. No ancient writer comments on this cultural overlap, but anthropology suggests that it could explain the paradox of elite athletics in democratic Athens.[14] Anthropologists clearly show how common concepts can inform disparate activities and how large patterns of a culture can support each other. Lüschen infers from anthropological studies that "sport is indeed an expression of that socio-cultural system in which it occurs."[15] For him, sport not only evokes a society's values but also "socializes" toward them. On the basis of anthropological studies, Sipes has proven a new model about the sport–war relationship.[16] His cultural-pattern model views the "intensity and configuration" of aggression as "predominantly cultural characteristics." It establishes "a strain toward consistency in each culture, with similar values and behavior patterns, such as aggressiveness, tending to manifest in more than one area of culture." Sipes has established that cultural patterns "relative to war and warlike sports tend to overlap and support each other's presence."

The most fundamental cultural overlap lies in the fact that that battle and an athletic competition were each considered an *agon*, that is, a contest that was decided by mutually agreed-upon rules. The regular hoplite battle of Classical Greece was, to quote Vernant, "a test as rule-bound as a tournament."[17] Consequently, a Greek state informed another of its intention to attack by sending a herald (e.g. Thucydides 1.29.1). By agreement, their armies met in the topography that was best suited for Greek land warfare: an agricultural plain. After hours of hand-to-hand fighting, the decisive moment was the *trope* (turning), when the hoplites of one side turned around and ran for their lives (e.g. Euripides, *Children of Herakles* 841–842). The victors pursued them only for a short distance before returning to their next obligations on the battlefield. There they collected the bodies of their dead comrades, stripped the bodies of the enemy, and

---

[14] See Pritchard 2013, 20–30, with bibliography.
[15] Lüschen 1970, 87.
[16] Sipes 1973, 64–65.
[17] Vernant 1988, 38.

used some of the weapons and the armor that they had captured to set up a *tropaion* (trophy) on the exact spot where the *trope* had occurred (e.g. Aischylos, *Seven against Thebes* 277, 954). When the defeated had time to regroup, they sent a herald to those controlling the battlefield in order to ask for a truce for taking back their war dead (e.g. Thucydides 4.44, 97). Custom dictated that the victors could not honorably refuse this request, but asking for a truce was recognized as a decisive concession of defeat (e.g. Herodotos 1.82).

For Classical Athenians the *agones* (contests) of athletics and war also tested the moral fiber and the physical capacities of individual athletes and combatants.[18] Both activities were thought to involve *ponoi* (toils) and *kindunoi* (dangers). This popular view of athletics as dangerous was well justified. For example, the hand- and arm-bindings of a Greek boxer worked like knuckledusters: they were designed to protect his hands and to injure his opponent. The winner of a boxing bout emerged only when one boxer gave up or was bashed unconscious. In fact, boxers were occasionally killed (e.g. Pausanias 6.4.2; 8.40.3–5). The frequent depictions of them in Athenian vase-paintings show blood streaming from their faces (Fig. 22.1). The Athenians believed that victory was due to the *arete* (courage) of athletes and soldiers alike and the *kudos* (divine aid) of gods and demi-gods. By contrast, the defeat of a sportsman or a combatant was put down to his cowardice and was considered a source of shame.

This cultural overlap between the *agones* of athletics and war raised the evaluation that lower-class Athenians had of athletics in two distinct ways. The first was closely tied to the standing of *polemos* (war) in democratic Athens.[19] The Classical Athenians intensified and transformed the waging of war. They frequently attacked other democracies and killed tens of thousands of fellow Greeks. By the time the Athenian democracy was fully consolidated, *polemos* had come to dominate both their politics and their personal lives. War consumed more money than all other public activities combined and was waged more frequently than ever before. Lower-class citizens valued war more highly than any other secular activity. They saw themselves as more courageous on the battlefield than the rest of the Greeks, their motives for waging wars as always just, and the history of their state, from the age of the heroes, as a series of almost unbroken military victories.[20]

---

[18] Pritchard 2013, 176–188.
[19] Pritchard 2019, 153–157.
[20] E.g. Demosthenes 60.11; Lysias 2.55; Euripides, *Suppliant Women* 306–342, 378–380.

Fig. 22.1 Two pairs of boxers with referees, Attic red-figure *kylix*, ca. 490 BC, Toledo, Toledo Museum of Art 1961.26.
Courtesy of the Toledo Museum of Art, Gift of Edward Drummond Libbey

In democratic Athens, war was manifestly more prominent as a public activity than athletics. The Athenians, it is true, devoted a lot of time and money to athletic *agones*, but they devoted considerably more to their armed forces and actual military campaigns. Such campaigns typically involved many thousands of non-elite hoplites and sailors. (See Pritchard, Chapter 29 in this volume.) Nevertheless, the conception of these two activities as comparable meant that athletics was closely associated with a part of Athenian democracy's core business that was held in the highest possible esteem. The other conspicuous activities of the wealthy lacked such a close connection with *polemos*. This meant that the cultural overlap between sport and war gave athletics a real advantage over them in the evaluations that the *demos* regularly made of the elite's lifestyle.

Conclusion: Popular Empathy for Athletes

Athens of the fifth century extended military service and traditional representations of it to every stratum of the lower class, whereas before war had largely been an elite pursuit. Before the democracy, wars were waged infrequently and were initiated privately by upper-class faction leaders (e.g. Plutarch, *Solon* 9.2–3). The hoplites of each campaign numbered in the hundreds rather than the thousands and came predominantly from Athens' upper class. Scenes of warfare on Archaic Athenian black- and red-figure pottery demonstrate how upper-class Athenians drew on the values and the concepts of epic poetry to glorify their own soldiering.[21] Homer's heroes discuss how they will gain deathless renown and deathless memory of their youthfulness by bravely dying in battle (e.g. *Iliad* 12.318–328; 22.71–73). By his 'beautiful death,' a hero gains everlasting confirmation of his *arete*.[22] Painters sometimes represent this *arete* of the fallen hoplite by painting in a lion.[23] The lion was one of the animals that Homer used as a symbol of a hero's martial excellence (e.g. *Iliad* 5.782; *Odyssey* 8.161). Attic painters evoked a hero's attainment of the beautiful death by giving him alone long hair, which is, again, a characteristic of heroes in epic poetry (e.g. *Iliad* 2.443, 472).

The creation of a publicly controlled army of hoplites as part of the democratic reforms that Kleisthenes introduced at the end of the sixth century, the massive expansion of the public navy, and the introduction of pay for military service opened up war, like politics, to all non-elite citizens. Because of the real power that this social class wielded in Athenian democracy's legal and political forums, as well as at its dramatic contests, public speakers and playwrights found it necessary to represent the experiences of these new hoplites and sailors with the traditional moral explanation of victory on the battle- or sports-field.

This ideological democratization of war can be clearly observed in the public funeral for the war dead in Classical Athens. The bones of the fallen were placed in cypress caskets and displayed in Athens' Agora (Thucydides 2.34). On the day of the funeral they were carried to the public cemetery, where they were placed in "a beautiful and grandiose tomb" (Plato, *Menexenus* 234c). This cemetery was located between the Dipylon Gate and the Academy. Tombs for the war dead were occasionally adorned with images of soldiers killing opponents that evoked the *arete* of those being buried.[24] They also had epigrams explaining that the dead had put their *arete* beyond doubt, leaving behind an eternal memory of courage (e.g. *IG* I^3 1179.3, 8–9). Finally, each tomb displayed a complete list of the year's casualties (*IG* I^3 1142–1193). The funeral oration traditionally delivered

---

[21] Lissarrague 1990, especially 233–240.
[22] Loraux 2018.
[23] Lissarrague 1990, 71–96.
[24] Pritchard 2019, 156, fig. 4.3.

after the burial always outlined how the war dead had secured "the most beautiful death": by falling in battle for the state they had gained deathless renown and deathless remembrance not only of their *arete* but also of their youth. (See also Shea, Chapter 10 in this volume.)

This practical and ideological democratization of war created a second way for the cultural overlap between sport and war to impact positively on athletics. It meant that the Athenian *demos* not only closely associated athletics with the highly valued and the prominent public activity of war, but also had a strong personal empathy for what athletes actually did. They could see how such sportsmen displayed *arete* and endured *kindunoi* and *ponoi*, just as they themselves did when fighting for Athens. Together, these two ways fully account for why non-elite Athenians valued athletics and athletes as highly as they did, shielded both from public criticism, and showed a strong preference for athletic *agones* over other types of competition in their expanding program of festivals. In conclusion, the changes that non-elite Athenians made to the waging of war supported and legitimized elite athletics.

Further Reading

This chapter summarizes Pritchard 2013. The other monograph on Athenian athletics is the still indispensable Kyle 1987. On Greek athletics in general, see Phillips and Pritchard 2003, Miller 2004, and Christesen and Kyle 2014. For images of sport on Athenian vases, see Oakley 2020, 131–166. On Athenian competitive festivals, see Osborne 1993. For the most thorough treatment of the Great Panathenaia, see Shear 2021.

Bibliography

Christesen, P., and D.G. Kyle, eds. 2014. *A Companion to Sport and Spectacle in Greek and Roman Antiquity*. Malden, MA.

Csapo, E., and W.J. Slater. 1994. *The Context of Ancient Drama*. Ann Arbor.

Kyle, D.G. 1987. *Athletics in Ancient Athens*. Leiden.

Lissarrague, F. 1990. *L'autre guerrier: archers, peltastes, cavaliers dans l'imagerie attique*. Paris.

Loraux, N. 2018. "The 'Beautiful Death' from Homer to Democratic Athens." *Arethusa* 51: 73–89.

Lüschen, G. 1970. "The Interdependence of Sport and Culture." In *The Cross-Cultural Analysis of Sport and Games*, ed. G. Lüschen, Champaign, 85–99.

Miller, S.G. 2004. *Ancient Greek Athletics*. London.

Oakley, J.H. 2020. *A Guide to Scenes of Daily Life on Athenian Vases*. Madison.

Osborne, R. 1993. "Competitive Festivals and the *Polis*: A Context for the Dramatic Festivals at Athens." In *Tragedy, Comedy and the Polis: Papers from the Greek Drama Conference, Nottingham, 18–20 July 1990*, eds. A.H. Sommerstein, S. Halliwell, J. Henderson, and B. Zimmermann, Bari, 21–38.

Phillips, D.J., and D.M. Pritchard, eds. 2003. *Sport and Festival in the Ancient Greek World*. Swansea.

Pritchard, D.M. 2013. *Sport, Democracy, and War in Classical Athens*. Cambridge.
    2015. *Public Spending and Democracy in Classical Athens*. Austin.
    2019. *Athenian Democracy at War*. Cambridge.

Shear, J.L. 2021. *Serving Athena: The Festival of the Panathenaia and the Construction of Athenian Identities*. Cambridge.

Sipes, R.G. 1973. "War, Sport, and Aggression." *American Anthropologist* 75: 64–86.

Sommerstein, A.H. 1996. "How to Avoid Being a *Komodoumenos*." CQ 46: 327–356.

Vernant, J.-P. 1988. *Myth and Society in Ancient Greece*. Trans. J. Lloyd. New York.

Additional resources to accompany this chapter can be found at: www.cambridge
.org/NeilsRogers

23 | Theatrical Spaces

VALENTINA DI NAPOLI

> The Greeks cannot be said to have invented theatrical performance;
> they do, however, seem to have invented the western playwright, the
> dramatic poet whose written output stands in its own right as creative
> work.[1]

Theater is one of the most compelling aspects of Greek society and public
life. Strongly bound up with fundamental activities of the *polis*, it is an
Athenian invention which flourished particularly during the fifth century
BC, when the most famous tragedies and comedies were composed and
performed. The plays of Aischylos, Sophokles, and Euripides, as well as the
comedies by Aristophanes and Menander, have left a strong mark on
Western culture because of the themes they confront and the moral values
they express. It is not by chance that they are still read, performed, and
appreciated well beyond the narrow limits of a handful of specialists.

Dramatic performances of the Classical period were large-scale events in
which the public played a fundamental role, in the framework of rituals that
were always repeated, and yet were always new. The audience itself was
engaged in a shared experience where the actors and the chorus presented on
the stage gods and myths, war and politics, human feelings and weaknesses,
while having their heads wholly covered by masks and their bodies wrapped
in impressive garments, and all being framed by evocative stage settings.

The present chapter deals with the buildings that were constructed in
Athens in order to host these dramatic performances. Together with speech
and gestures, they created a theatrical space that allowed the audience to
experience the dramas physically. Before the earliest permanent structures
were built, theaters originally consisted of perishable elements and had a
provisional character. Greek architects subsequently found different solutions to the problem of building spaces suited to dramatic performances. In
the end, they invented the architectural category of the theater, which can
undoubtedly be numbered among the most lasting contributions of the
Greek world.

---

[1] Wiles 2000, 165.

Performing for Dionysos

The theaters of the Classical period were conceived from the beginning as the venue for the musical and dramatic contests in the wider context of the cult of Dionysos. Their originally religious character is indicated by the fact that the earliest theaters are mostly found within or close to sanctuaries dedicated to Dionysos. Different theories have been suggested about the origins of theatrical performances in Athens, all having a common feature: that the core of drama must be pursued in the ritual dances of masked people who sang the dithyramb in the company of the double flute, around an altar of Dionysos. Such rituals in honor of the god of not only wine and drunkenness, ecstasy, fertility, and death but also rebirth, a god who could temporarily subvert hierarchies and the social order, were regularly held in a place dedicated to dance (*orchesis*) and were characterized by strong mimetic features and by the intense participation of the entire community. Consequently, the birth of the architectural category of the theater stems from the need to accommodate such ritual dances and the public who followed them.

In the Archaic and Classical periods, Athens had more than one theatrical space. The earliest ones are the so-called orchestra in the Agora, whose identification is still debated, and the theater in the Sanctuary of Dionysos in the Lenaion, where the festival of the Lenaia was celebrated until it was moved to the theater in the Sanctuary of Dionysos Eleuthereus. Some ancient texts place the sanctuary of the Lenaion outside the city walls, while others seem to connect it, even if not directly, to the Agora, where no traces of this sanctuary have so far been identified. It is even possible, as some scholars suggest, that the Sanctuary of Dionysos in the Lenaion may be identical with the Sanctuary of Dionysos *en limnais*, where the festival of the Anthesteria (new wine) was held. Finally, the third Athenian theater is the one in the Sanctuary of Dionysos Eleuthereus on the southern slopes of the Akropolis, which is attested from at least the early fifth century BC onwards.

The Orchestra in the Agora

General agreement has been reached about the main elements of fifth-century theaters. They were open, unroofed structures, whose core was the dancing and performance area called the *orchestra* (dancing place). The orchestra could be reached from both sides by two wide, open passages called *parodoi*. The auditorium, called in Greek *theatron* (seeing place), was originally constituted by wooden bleachers (*ikria*), which could be either built against a slope or freestanding. The location of earlier theaters was frequently next to the slope of a hill, which supported the seating. Finally, on one side of the orchestra, opposite the audience, there might have been a scene building, called *skene* (tent), in the form of a temporary, wooden construction that constituted a sort of backdrop for the play and allowed the actors to enter and exit the scenic space.

Scholarly debate continues about the earliest dramatic space of Athens, often referred to as the orchestra in the Agora. Literary sources suggest that before the dramatic performances were held in the Theater of Dionysos on the southern slopes of the Akropolis, the public gathered and watched performances in the Agora. This Archaic structure, which existed in the sixth century BC, was possibly located next to a black poplar (*aigeiros*) and, according to later sources, consisted of wooden *ikria*. This theater, which precedes the one in the area of the Sanctuary of Dionysos Eleuthereus, is related by some scholars to another structure attested in the ancient sources, namely, the orchestra in the Agora, located not far from the statues of the Tyrant-Slayers (Timaeus, s.v. *orchestra*) and the place where books were sold (*PCG* 5, fr. 327.1). This orchestra should be placed in about the same area where six centuries later the Roman Odeion of Agrippa was built (see Map 5.1, no. 16). It was the venue for the musical contests of the Panathenaia, founded in 566 BC and including dances and dithyramb, and the City Dionysia, whose dramatic contests were inaugurated in 534 BC. The term "orchestra," in fact, derives from the verb *orcheomai* and indicates the place for the dances of the chorus. Thus, the orchestra in the Agora and the *ikria* next to the black poplar have become in literature a unitary element and the very same structure, which is strongly connected with the earliest dramatic contests and performances and to the cult of Dionysos in the Archaic period.

Attempts at locating more precisely this Archaic theatrical space have now been complicated by new topographical studies and by the American excavations in the Athenian Agora, which suggest that the Archaic agora (or 'old agora') was not in the same place as the Classical one and must instead be located in the area to the southeast of the Akropolis, not far from the area where the mid-fifth-century BC Odeion of Perikles was built. In this case, the old, Archaic agora, and not the Agora of the Kerameikos, which came into use after the end of the sixth or at the beginning of the fifth century BC, would be the location for the wooden *ikria* of the earlier Athenian theater. (See also Papadopoulos, Chapter 3 in this volume.)

This matter must remain, however, open until new, decisive evidence is found. This is also true for the question of the precise location of the other Archaic and Classical theater of Athens, the theater in the Sanctuary of Dionysos in the Lenaion.

The Theater of Dionysos

The Theater of Dionysos is located on the southern slopes of the Akropolis, in the area of the sanctuary dedicated to Dionysos Eleuthereus, of which it constitutes a vital element (see Map 5.1, nos. 12 and 13). It is the place where the plays of Aischylos, Sophokles, Euripides, Aristophanes, and many other playwrights were first performed. It might not be an exaggeration to say that it is the symbol itself of Classical Greek drama. Many efforts have been made at reconstructing its earlier phases, which are no longer visible because of both the many transformations it underwent during its long life and several catastrophic invasions that occurred in Late Roman times. As a consequence, contrasting hypotheses have been suggested about the form of the theater in the Classical period, which recent excavations in crucial parts of the monument and fresh studies with new perspectives have rejected or confirmed.

It is uncertain at which moment the earliest theatrical space was established on the southern slopes of the Akropolis. The fact, however, that literary sources mention the collapse of the *ikria* during a dramatic contest among Aischylos, Pratinas, and Choerilos in 500–497 BC (Suda, s.v. Pratinas)[2] makes it extremely likely that the first theater in the Sanctuary of Dionysos was a wooden structure of the early fifth century BC and had very probably been already built in the late sixth century BC.[3] The choice of this precise place instead of the flat, open space of the agora (be it either the Agora of the Kerameikos or the 'old agora') can be explained by both the proximity of the Sanctuary of Dionysos, where the cult of the god had been transferred from Eleutherai in about the mid-sixth century BC, and the need to prop the wooden structures of the auditorium against a sloping ground. This new location would have allowed a bigger and more solid wooden auditorium, as well as better audiovisual conditions. According to recent studies, and contrary to the traditional opinion, both the early

---

[2] A collapse of the *ikria* is attested also later, in the mid-fifth century BC, before Aischylos' departure for Sicily (Suda, s.v. Aischylos).

[3] The fact that the first official record of a dithyrambic contest is dated to the late sixth century BC also provides important evidence.

Fig. 23.1 Reconstruction of the Theater of Dionysos in the fifth century BC.
Courtesy of J.-C. Moretti. Drawing by N. Bresch

orchestra and the *parodoi* were roughly on the same place as the later ones and, most importantly, the orchestra of the first Theater of Dionysos was a rectangular or trapezoidal space enclosed on three sides by rectilinear wooden benches (Fig. 23.1). This hypothesis is reinforced by the recent discovery of post holes in the area of the auditorium, which confirm the presence of a structure made of wooden benches. Furthermore, some rectilinear inscribed stone blocks which are dated to the second half of the fifth century BC must be connected to later, very likely Periklean, renovations in the *prohedria* (honorary seats for distinguished audience members) of the wooden, still rectilinear, theater of the Early Classical period. During this earlier phase, the scenic space was created on the occasion of performances with removable wooden structures, as ancient drama did not depend on any sort of realistic stage set. At that time, the connection to the nearby Sanctuary of Dionysos, which was placed at a slightly lower level, was still very strong.

Although archaeological evidence for work in the period of Perikles (second half of the fifth century BC) is not abundant, it does show that the political leader must have envisaged a wider renovation program of the whole area with the aim of creating a cultural hub on the southern slopes of the Akropolis, including the construction of the nearby imposing Odeion (see below). Traces of the Periklean works in the Theater of Dionysos are evident in the *analemma* walls made of conglomerate stone, which replaced the older walls, probably made of polygonal masonry. Perikles' building program must have remained unfinished because of the poor economic conditions of Athens after the massive construction on the Akropolis and mostly due to the outbreak of the Peloponnesian War. Thus, the *analemma* walls made of stone must have coexisted for several decades with wooden benches for the spectators, until imposing renovation work occurred in the Late Classical period. At any rate, it is very likely that the Periklean auditorium already had huge dimensions, stretching nearly to the horizontal passage that divides the Late Classical theater into two sections.

From about the mid-fifth century BC, the scene building, the one which is linked to the *floruit* of Classical drama, became a more permanent structure which delimited the scenic space and the orchestra on its southern side and at the same time marked a symbolic separation from the cultic space of the sanctuary. Interesting clues to the Classical stage have been detected in the Late Classical scene building, which preserved the back wall of conglomerate stone, dated to the previous phase. Cuttings for the insertion of wooden beams show that the Periklean scene building was a mixed structure of wood and mudbrick above stone foundations. This is also confirmed by the reference in Xenophon, still in 360–355 BC, to timbers "as thick as those of the tragic stage" (*Cyropaedia* 6.1.54). An interesting feature is the stage machine, whose stone foundations (3×7 m) have recently been identified in the central area of the stage, on the same axis as the theater auditorium and bonded into the back wall of the scene building. According to a recent reconstruction, this *mechane* would have been a wooden two-masted structure resting on massive stone foundations. It is tempting to imagine that this machine was featured in Euripides' *Medea* (431 BC) to help the murderous mother escape, or in Sophokles' *Philoctetes* (409 BC) to hoist up the actor embodying Herakles, the divine agent who resolved the plot.

The ambitious building program which took place in the third quarter of the fourth century BC is mainly, but not exclusively, ascribed to the initiative of Lycurgus, who was responsible for the public finances of Athens in 336–324 BC.[4] This phase is marked by the building of a stone

---

[4] Lycurgus is also responsible for the construction of another building for entertainment, namely, the Panathenaic Stadium in the area of the Ilissos River. Meant to host athletic contests, it was first used for the Panathenaic Games of 330/29 BC.

theater and the creation of a circular space for the orchestra, which, from being the conceptual core of the dramatic action (as the place for the chorus), also became the geometric center for the whole construction. The new theater served several needs in a more functional way. Namely, it accommodated more easily the increased number of spectators, offered better acoustic and visual conditions during the performances, and at the same time constituted an exceptional means for displaying the city's wealth by giving a monumental appearance to one of the most important public places of Athens. The work needed was extremely demanding from a technical point of view, as it involved the excavation of the bedrock, the transportation to the site of a remarkable amount of artificial fill, the quarrying of more than 6,800 tons of Piraeus limestone for the seats, and the impressive carving of the rock of the Akropolis in order to obtain a sheer vertical face (*katatome*) at the back of the auditorium.

The circular orchestra, made of beaten earth until the Early Roman period, was 19.61 m in diameter and had a removable altar in the center for the libations to Dionysos before the theatrical contests. Around the orchestra, a deep underground canal was dug which collected the rainwater from the huge auditorium and was covered with stone slabs in the places corresponding to the stairs that delimited the *kerkides* (wedge-shaped tiers of seats).[5] The seats of the auditorium, made of Piraeus limestone, were divided horizontally into two unequal sections by the *peripatos*, that is, the walkway which ran beneath the Akropolis. The lower section consisted of sixty-seven rows of seats (excluding the *prohedria*) divided by fourteen staircases into thirteen *kerkides*, while the upper section was probably divided into ten *kerkides*. The presence of very thin lines on the fronts of the seats allows a reconstruction of a total number of as many as 19,000 spectators. The sixty-seven thrones of the *prohedria*, made of Pentelic marble, bore inscriptions assigning them to priests and priestesses. The most important throne, the one dedicated to the priest of Dionysos, was located at the bottom of the central *kerkis* of the auditorium and was decorated with depictions related to the cult of the god.

Statues of poets and winners of the musical contests were displayed in several locations around the theater. Lycurgus was a passionate admirer of Classical drama and the achievements of the Classical period; he was responsible for the first official copy of the works of the three tragedians. It is fitting, therefore, that he placed in the eastern *parodos* the standing

---

[5] During the performances, the remaining space of this underground canal was covered with wooden planks.

statues of Aischylos, Sophokles, and Euripides, displayed on the same base and next to the seated statue depicting the comic poet Menander (Web Fig. 23.1).[6] Furthermore, the *parodoi* acquired more importance thanks to the construction of monumental wooden Doric gateways. Another statue base, dedicated by the poet Astydamas after his victory in 340 BC, was incorporated into the end of the eastern retaining wall of the auditorium in such a way that it has been persuasively deduced that the construction of the stone auditorium had already begun before the time of Lycurgus, that is, under Euboulos (ca. 350 BC).

The Lycurgan scene building likely had two lateral projecting wings with columns in the Doric order,[7] and was provided on its front with painted wooden panels (*pinakes*), which created the illusion of the scenic space, together with three openings in the front wall of the *skene* and the flat roof. It is very probable that the Lycurgan scene building did not yet include a colonnade on its front. Most interestingly, the scene building of the second half of the fourth century BC preserved the back wall of conglomerate stone from the Periklean phase, as well as the earlier foundations for the stage machine. This suggests that the Periklean stage must have been very similar, from a functional and formal point of view, to the stone phase monumentalized some decades later, in the second half of the fourth century BC. It is therefore very likely that the Lycurgan stage crystallized into stone older architectural features, thus giving tangible form to a very conservative stage and scene building. This happened at a time when the performances of old tragedies had been included in the program of the musical contests (from 386 BC onwards) and the plays of Euripides, involving a wide use of the *deus ex machina*, were highly appreciated by the public, but also at a moment when newly built monuments, like the theater at Epidauros, were already suggesting innovations in theater design.

In a later phase, which can probably be dated to the Late Hellenistic period, the scene building was provided with a row of columns in the Doric order on its front (*proskenion*), and the lateral projecting wings became narrower, in order to allow the spectators to circulate more freely in the *parodoi*. Owing to the scanty architectural remains, it is unclear if the scene building had an upper floor during this phase.

The appearance of the Theater of Dionysos changed radically in the Roman Imperial period. The construction of marble monumental gateways

[6] See Ma 2015 on the statue of Menander.
[7] They are usually labelled *paraskenia* in modern literature, although the epigraphic sources do not attest the term in relation to these elements.

in the Ionic order has been attributed to the Augustan period. Works undertaken during the reign of Nero, on the initiative of Tiberius Claudius Novius, one of the most significant political personalities of Athens of that time, involved the construction of a two-story scene façade and of a low *pulpitum* (stage for the actors) in the Roman fashion, the paving of the orchestra with slabs of polychrome marbles, as well as the erection of a parapet around the orchestra aimed at protecting the public during the gladiatorial combats (AD 61/2). In the age of Hadrian, the scene façade was refurbished and embellished with statues depicting satyrs, silens, caryatids, and the emperor himself. Furthermore, the auditorium received thirteen statues of Hadrian, and special marble seats for the emperor and his entourage were placed in its central section. Later works in the Theater of Dionysos are dated to the late fourth and the fifth century AD, when a low stage (*bema*) made of reused material was built in the area of the former scene building and the orchestra was transformed into a waterproof pool for water spectacles. The construction of an early Christian basilica in the area of the eastern *parodos* (sixth century) marked the definitive abandonment of the theater, which was gradually buried under tons of debris.

The Odeion of Perikles

The Odeion of Perikles, on the southern slopes of the Akropolis, was the largest roofed building of the ancient Greek world (temples apart)[8] and nonetheless remains one of the lesser known. Although it is not a proper theatrical building, it is included here because of its close topographical and conceptual proximity with the Theater of Dionysos and the world of performances (Map 23.1). It was placed immediately to the east of the theater, with whose plan it has a close relationship, and was the venue for the *proagon*, or the official theatrical presentation which took place some days before the Great Dionysia in the presence of the *archon basileus*. Furthermore, the Odeion of Perikles hosted the musical contests of the Panathenaic Games. The name itself, *odeion*, is derived from the Greek term for ode. This building, which was completed in time for the Panathenaia of 446/5 BC, was intended to hold the musical contests of two major Athenian festivals. (See Miles and Neils, Chapter 24 in this

---

[8] It had a surface area of 4,280 m², whereas the Parthenon, for instance, has a surface area of 2,146 m² and the Olympieion a surface area of about 4,435 m².

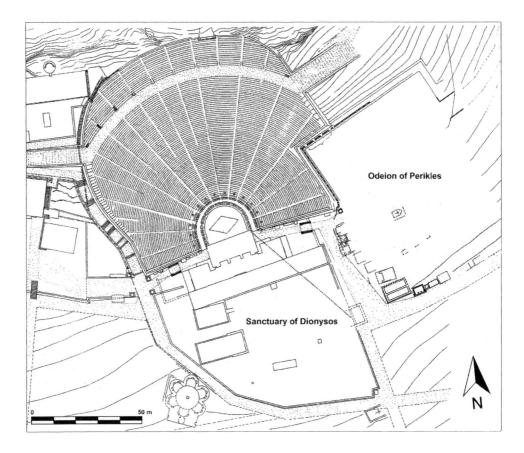

Map 23.1 Plan of the Theater of Dionysos and Odeion of Perikles, Athens.
Source: Greco 2010, fig. 88, adapted by D. Weiss

volume.) It was, however, a truly multifunctional building: literary sources attest that it was also used for different activities such as a tribunal, for political meetings, distributing wheat, philosophical debates, and probably also as a music school.

Covered by debris and modern houses, the Odeion of Perikles was excavated in the 1930s (northwestern and northeastern corners) and in the 1960s (southern columns), while its southeastern corner was found during rescue excavations in 2001–2002. Today, it is totally buried. Literary sources, confirmed by the remains, attest that this building was provided with many columns (*polystylon*) and was many-sided (*polyedron*). The texts also mention that the roof had been built with the wooden masts and yards from the Persian ships destroyed by the Greeks during the Battle of Salamis, and most of them connect the monument with

Perikles.[9] Actually, the Odeion of Perikles and the Theater of Dionysos must have been conceived of as a unit that was so intertwined that the construction of the former affected the shape of the eastern side of the auditorium of the theater.

The plan of the Odeion of Perikles is partially hypothetical. It was probably an almost square building, measuring about 62.40 m from east to west and a little more from north to south, and provided with 9 × 10 rows of columns which supported the hip roof. Some scholars place the entrance on the southern side, while others suggest the presence of a *propylon* on the eastern side. It is also debated whether the building had exterior walls or was instead an open, colonnaded hall. Wooden benches in the interior might have hosted about 3,000–4,000 people, although it is not certain whether spectators other than the actors and the officials of the City Dionysia were admitted to the Odeion during the *proagon*. The interior was at least partially decorated with wall paintings: the ones on the northwestern side, constituted by red bands on white ground and small panels bearing agonistic depictions (laurel crown, Panathenaic amphora, palm branch), have been discovered.

The building was partially refurbished in the mid-second century BC at the personal expense of a certain Miltiades of Marathon, *agonothetes* in the Panathenaic Games, who took care of the sections which needed repair (*IG* II^2 968, lines 47–48). During the attack by the Roman general Lucius Cornelius Sulla in 86 BC, the Odeion was burnt by the Athenians themselves in order to prevent the aggressors from using its wooden elements for their siege machines. It was then reconstructed according to the same plan, in 56 BC, by the king of Cappadocia, Ariobarzanes, who commissioned the work from two Roman architects, Marcus and Gaius Stallius, and to the Greek architect Menalippos (*IG* II^2 3426). The Odeion was probably destroyed in AD 267, when the Herulians invaded Athens. In any case, it no longer existed in the sixth century, when a Christian basilica was built in the area of the western section of the Odeion and above the eastern *parodos* of the Theater of Dionysos.

Conclusions

From the time when the earliest wooden *theatron* was built in Athens, a construction which must have caused significant problems with sight lines, capacity, and stability, the city felt the need of more permanent and reliable

---

[9] With the sole exception of Vitruvius (5.9.1), who ascribes the Odeion to Themistokles.

structures which could host the dramatic performances in the context of the annual musical contests in honor of Dionysos. Athens was then provided with an imposing structure that gradually grew and evolved, from wood to stone, and from rectilinear to semicircular. The Classical, mainly wooden, theater built during the time of Perikles (second half of the fifth century BC) was later replaced by the new, imposing stone theater built in the Late Classical period (second half of the fourth century BC) at the initiative of Euboulos first and Lycurgus later. The plans of both the Theater of Dionysos and the Odeion were adapted to the preexisting local road network on the southern side of the Akropolis, so that age-old roads in the area were respected and influenced, to a certain extent, the two monuments. The new, Late Classical theater, whose layout was centered on the geometric form of the circle, ensured improved optoacoustic results, which could better suit both the dramatic performances and the needs of the Assembly of the Athenian *demos* that took place there. Its technically demanding construction and the economic effort required made this new stone theater a tangible symbol of the city's wealth and power. The result was a building whose plan and function constitute not only a clear mark of deference toward the Classical tradition, but also one of the most important and enduring legacies of ancient Greece to the Western world.

Further Reading

The literature on this topic is rich and mainly in German and modern Greek. The problem of the 'old agora' and the topography of earlier Athens is analyzed in Miller 1995 (especially 218–219). Of the vast bibliography about the origins of drama, see Csapo and Slater 1994, 79–138, 286–301; Green 1994, especially 16–48; Connor 1996; Sourvinou-Inwood 2003, 141–172; Csapo and Miller 2007, 1–38; Kowalzig and Wilson 2013. Wiles 2000 is a good introduction to the art of Greek theater performance. On the Theater of Dionysos, in addition to the classic Pickard-Cambridge 1946, a recent presentation of the wooden theater can be found in Moretti 1999–2000 and in Papastamati-von Moock 2015, while for the Lycurgan phase, Papastamati-von Moock 2014 is very useful. On the Odeion of Perikles, see Robkin 1976; Miller 1997, 218–242; Shear 2016, 197–228 (for a discussion within the wider framework of Perikles' building activity). For a discussion of the theatrical spaces of Athens and Attika in the Roman period, see Di Napoli 2013, 7–25.

Bibliography

Connor, W.R. 1996. "Civil Society, Dionysiac Festival, and the Athenian Democracy." In *Démokratia: A Conversation on Democracies, Ancient and Modern*, eds. J. Ober and C. Hedrick, Princeton, 217–226.

Csapo, E., and M.C. Miller, eds. 2007. *The Origins of the Theater in Ancient Greece and Beyond.* Cambridge.

Csapo, E., and W.J. Slater. 1994. *The Context of Ancient Drama.* Ann Arbor.

Di Napoli, V. 2013. *Teatri della Grecia romana: forma, decorazione, funzioni. La provincia d'Acaia.* Athens.

Greco, E., ed. 2010. *Topografia di Atene. Sviluppo urbano e monumenti dalle origini al III secolo d.C. Tomo I: Acropoli – Areopago – Tra Acropoli e Pnice.* Athens.

Green, J.R. 1994. *Theater in Ancient Greek Society.* London.

Kowalzig, B., and P. Wilson, eds. 2013. *Dithyramb in Context.* Oxford.

Ma, J. 2015. "The Portrait of Menander in the Theatre of Dionysus and Its Neighbours." *Studi Ellenistici* 29: 235–239.

Miller, M.C. 1997. *Athens and Persia in the Fifth Century* BC: *A Study in Cultural Receptivity.* Cambridge.

Miller, S.G. 1995. "Architecture as Evidence for the Identity of the Early *Polis*." In *Sources for the Ancient Greek City-State, Symposium 1994,* ed. M.H. Hansen, Copenhagen, 210–244.

Moretti, J.-C. 1999–2000. "The Theater of the Sanctuary of Dionysos Eleuthereus in Late Fifth-Century Athens." *Illinois Classical Studies* 24–25: 377–398.

Papastamati-von Moock, C. 2014. "The Theatre of Dionysos Eleuthereus in Athens: New Data and Observations on Its 'Lycurgan' Phase." In *Greek Theatre in the Fourth Century* BC, ed. E. Csapo, H.R. Goette, R. Green, and P. Wilson, Berlin, 15–76.

2015. "The Wooden Theatre of Dionysos Eleuthereus in Athens: Old Issues, New Research." In *The Architecture of the Ancient Greek Theatre, Acts of an International Conference, Athens 2012,* eds. R. Frederiksen, E. Gebhard, and A. Sokolicek, Aarhus, 39–79.

Pickard-Cambridge, A.W. 1946. *The Theatre of Dionysus in Athens.* Oxford.

Robkin, A.L.H. 1976. "The Odeion of Perikles: Some Observations on Its History, Form, and Functions." PhD dissertation, University of Washington.

Shear, T.L. 2016. *Trophies of Victory: Public Buildings in Periklean Athens.* Princeton.

Sourvinou-Inwood, C. 2003. *Tragedy and Athenian Religion.* Lanham.

Wiles, D. 2000. *Greek Theatre Performance. An Introduction.* Cambridge.

Additional resources to accompany this chapter can be found at: www.cambridge .org/NeilsRogers

24 | Athenian Festivals

MARGARET M. MILES AND JENIFER NEILS

> Let us visit the gleaming land of Pallas, to see the ravishing country
> Of Kekrops with its fine men, gleaming . . .
> Where ineffable rites are celebrated, where
> The temple that receives initiates is thrown open during the pure mystic festival;
> And where there are offerings to the heavenly host,
> Temples with lofty roofs and statues,
> Most holy possessions for the Blessed Ones
> Well-garlanded victims for the gods, and feasts in all seasons.
> Aristophanes, *Clouds* 299–310 (trans. J. Henderson)

Of all the many religious festivals celebrated by the Athenians, two stand out as the largest, most costly, and most renowned: the Panathenaia held in honor of their city goddess Athena, and the Great Mysteries that honored the agricultural divinities Demeter and her daughter Persephone. These grand festivals attracted participants and spectators from all over the Mediterranean. They were celebrated for over a millennium, from at least the sixth century BC (the traditional founding date of the Panathenaia is 566 BC) until Late Antiquity. On such occasions, Athenians and their foreign guests marched in procession to the shrines of their most revered goddesses: the Akropolis in the heart of the *polis*, and Eleusis some fourteen miles (21 km) to the west, well outside the city walls.

These two major festivals were intimately embedded in the topography of Athens and its surrounding territory of Attika. Both processional routes began from neighboring gates at the city walls in the district Kerameikos, to the northwest of the city center (see Maps 2.1 and 4.2), and went in opposite directions. The Sacred Gate marks the start of the Sacred Way, which leads outside the city across the fertile Thriasian plain to the sanctuary at Eleusis. The Dipylon (double) Gate forms the beginning of the Panathenaic Way that transects the central market and civic area (Agora) and proceeds uphill and on to the Akropolis. The sensory experiences of these two processional routes must have been very different: one led though the autumnal countryside with its groves of olives trees and

332

cultivated fields, while the other traversed the bustling city center with its shops, lawcourts, and shrines in high summer. Also, the actual religious experience and end result of these festivals for the participants could not have been more different, as we shall see.

Eleusis and the Mysteries

Men and women, free or slave, Athenians and foreigners, young and old, all were welcome to become initiates into the Mysteries, as long as they could speak Greek and had not committed a blood-crime (such as murder). The initiation ceremony took place at night, in a large square hall called the Telesterion, with many interior columns and rock-cut steps along three inner sides so that devotees could stand or sit around the interior perimeter. The architectural concept is much like a very large Greek temple turned outside in, and elements of the Doric and Ionic orders were included in the design. The sanctuary and buildings were designed for privacy, and all initiates were sworn to keep secret what happened there. We get tantalizing hints about the events from ancient authors, and hostile comments from early Christian writers, who saw the Mysteries as competition. We know that 'things were enacted,' 'things were said,' and 'things were shown,' but no one ever revealed what these were. If initiates violated the oath of silence, they could be put to death; this actually happened to two Argive teenagers who tried to spy on the events. The mid-second-century AD traveler Pausanias (1.14.3, 1.38.7) says he was warned in a dream not to write about the city branch of the sanctuary or the main sanctuary at Eleusis, or even their buildings. Yet ancient authors agree that the experience shifted one's perspective on this life and the afterlife, and initiates could look forward to a better and happier existence. This eschatological understanding seems to be what the poet Pindar (fr. 137a) refers to: "blessed is he who has seen this and thus goes beneath the earth; he knows the end of life, he knows the beginning given by Zeus." Sophokles restates a passage in the *Homeric Hymn to Demeter* (480–482; ca. 600 BC): "Thrice blessed are those mortals who have seen these rites and enter into Hades: for them alone there is life, for all others is misery" (fr. 837 Radt). There were at least two stages of initiation, and individuals could attend multiple times if they wished.

The ritual reflects a soteriological myth involving abduction and resurrection. Hades, the Greek god of the underworld, absconded with a beautiful young girl, Persephone (called simply Kore in Athens). Her disappearance underground resulted in a severe famine caused by her bereft mother, the goddess Demeter. According to the *Homeric Hymn to Demeter*, the goddess, after much wandering in search of her lost daughter, took refuge at Eleusis, where she was welcomed by the ruling family. In return, she taught the Eleusinians the art of agriculture, ordered the king to build her a temple and an altar, and taught them her Mysteries, so that they could reenact them. When Zeus finally ordained that his daughter Persephone could rejoin her mother for all but one-third of the year, fertility returned to the land. A local hero of Eleusis named Triptolemos was commissioned to spread the cultivation of grain to the far reaches of the known world, and became a cultural hero who spread civilization from Athens outward (see Fig. 18.5). At a later date, the legendary Athenian king Erechtheus went to war and conquered the formerly independent Eleusis; once Eleusis became a part of Athens, the festival was adapted to promote Athenian interests, and Athens took credit for bringing renewed fertility to all of Greece and beyond. Each year, heralds were sent throughout Greece to announce the start of the festival, and to declare a truce, if necessary, so that non-Athenians could come and participate in the Mysteries.

In historic times, the Eleusinian Mysteries were ritually linked to central Athens by a Sanctuary of Demeter located just below the north slope of the Akropolis (see Map 6.1). Known as the City Eleusinion, it featured a Temple of Demeter (still unexcavated and under the modern neighborhood of Plaka), and a Temple of Triptolemos in a forecourt located on the Panathenaic Way. Here, priestesses deposited the Sacred Objects they brought to Athens from Eleusis, shortly before the nine-day festival began. Those seeking initiation participated in a round of sacrifices over several days, including a trip to the sea at Piraeus for a purifying bath followed by the sacrifice of a piglet. "Lend me three drachmas for a piglet, since I must be initiated before I die," says a character in one of Aristophanes' comedies (*Peace* 374–375). At 3 drachmas it was not a cheap offering, but the piglet was sacrificed and barbequed at Piraeus before the actual celebration of the Mysteries.

The Eleusinian Mysteries required a large number of supervisory cult personnel. Guides called mystagogues tutored the initiates during the spring, in a separate festival called the Lesser Mysteries, and accompanied them to Eleusis in their first initiation there. On the fifth day of the festival, the purified initiates (*mystai*) began their procession to Eleusis from the City Eleusinion, under the guidance of the so-called *Iacchagogos*. Iacchos was the personification of the shouts and hymns uttered by those in the procession – and by the fifth century BC, they numbered in the thousands. Following him were priestesses carrying the Sacred Objects in cylindrical boxes or *kistai*, back to Eleusis. The initiates came next, wearing myrtle crowns and carrying bundles of myrtle branches; myrtle is sometimes depicted on coins minted for the festival. The written sources tell us of various peculiar (to us at any rate) rites along the way such as tying yellow strings on the initiates' right wrists and left ankles (known as the *krokosis*), or the custom of masked dancers shouting obscenities at the initiates as they passed by (known as the *gephyrismos*), in a challenge to the normal social order typical of initiations. The key personnel for the actual celebration were chosen from two aristocratic families of Eleusis: the Eumolpidai provided the hierophant who conducted the nocturnal ceremony in the *anaktoron*, and the Kerykes supplied the *dadouchos*, or torch bearer.

Many festivals in Attika involved the use of special ceramic cult vessels, such as *krateriskoi* (small footed cups) at Brauron or Panathenaic prize amphoras, as we shall see below. At the sanctuaries of Demeter, archaeologists have uncovered distinctively shaped vases called *plemochoai*. A footed, carinated bowl with an out-turned rim, the *plemochoe* comes in a range of sizes, and typically had a lid. Athenaios (11.496a) tells how they were used: "They use it at Eleusis on the last day of the Mysteries, a day which they call *Plemochoai*; on that day they fill two *plemochoai*, and standing up they [over]turn one toward the east, the other toward the west, reciting a mystical formula over them." A dedicatory plaque found at Eleusis shows initiates dancing with *plemochoai* tied on their heads, and approaching the Two Goddesses (Fig. 24.1).[1] These vessels became a symbol of the Mysteries, and are featured on coins minted for the festival. A *plemochoe* is represented on a carved relief from an entrance in the City Eleusinion, now built into the Little Metropolis church in Athens (Web Fig. 24.1).

A recent reevaluation of pottery and finds from the Bronze Age at Eleusis has shown that, beneath the Archaic and Classical levels of the Telesterion, there were fragmentary remains of a building that stood apart from the rest of the area, and its surroundings were used for ritual deposits. Thus, the place itself was venerated for many centuries, even though the ritual as a Mystery cult within the city-state Athens (with a procession and initiation) must have taken shape in the early Archaic period. Were those early remains both a residence and a family shrine and, if so, to what degree may we consider it as continuity of cult across the so-called Dark Ages? This remains an open question. The Mysteries were celebrated for over a thousand years, until an imperial decree of

---

[1] Athens, National Archaeological Museum 11036.

Fig. 24.1 Ninnion Tablet, fourth century BC, Athens, National Archaeological
Museum 11036
© Deutsches Archäologisches Institut, Athen, Emile 634. Photograph: E. Seraf

AD 390/1 prohibited them, and the sanctuary at Eleusis was sacked and
destroyed by Goths around AD 395.

Exactly what was said and done during the final rites, and how people
interpreted what they learned certainly changed over time. The terminology and vocabulary of the Mysteries had a broad impact: on philosophers
such as Plato, and on many subsequent authors who built on his use of the
imagery, including early Christian authors who used the vocabulary of
"mysteries" for describing their new religious understanding. Cicero (who
was an initiate) says, "Athens has given nothing to the world more excellent or divine than the Eleusinian Mysteries" and that through initiation
"not only do we learn a way of living in happiness but also a way of dying
with greater hope" (*De legibus* 2.36).

Athens and the Panathenaia

Since Athena was the tutelary goddess of Athens, it is not surprising that
the city's major festival was held in her honor. She won this title in a

contest with her uncle and fellow Olympian, Poseidon, by producing the first olive tree, a scene which is depicted in the west pediment of the Parthenon. Poseidon was also worshiped on the Akropolis, in a joint cult with the Attic hero, Erechtheus. Just as at Eleusis, where the cult of a younger male, Triptolemos, enhanced the mission of Demeter, so the hero shrine of this early king, known as the Erechtheion, served as a second temple of the goddess Athena (see Map 5.1, no. 7). This temple, not the Parthenon, was the destination of the birthday gift to Athena, a newly woven garment known as the *peplos*, although it is depicted prominently on the east frieze of the Parthenon. (See Valavanis, Chapter 5 in this volume.)

The Panathenaic Festival, held every four years in honor of Athena, was modeled on the four Panhellenic Games held at Olympia, Nemea, Isthmia, and Delphi that honored male deities (Zeus, Poseidon, and Apollo). In addition to the usual elements of a religious ritual, such as a procession and sacrifice of animals followed by feasting, the Panathenaia included athletic and equestrian competitions, and contests for musicians, heralds, and rhapsodes (reciters of poetry). What made the Athenian games particularly distinctive were its intramural contests in which the ten Athenian tribes competed against each other in pyrrhic dancing, a torch relay, a regatta, a unique chariot race (the *apobates*), and even a 'Mr. Athens' or male beauty (*euandreia*) contest. (See also Pritchard, Chapter 22 in this volume.)

These events took place throughout the city in the days preceding the twenty-eighth of Hekatombaion, said to be Athena's birthday: horse and chariot racing in the hippodrome, the athletic contents in a stadium, the boat race in the Piraeus harbor, and the musical contests in an *odeion* (concert hall) built by Perikles on the south slope of the Akropolis. Some of the physical evidence for these locales has disappeared, but still prominent today is the Panathenaic Stadium, which was laid out by Lycurgus in the fourth century BC and seated 50,000 spectators.[2] We are told by ancient sources that the Periklean *odeion* was a replica in stone and timber of Xerxes' tent, captured from the Persians after the Battle of Plataia in 479 BC. (See Di Napoli, Chapter 23 in this volume.) Measuring approximately 60 meters per side and with up to ninety internal columns, it resembled a huge hypostyle hall not unlike the audience chamber at Persepolis. The closest parallel for this unusual building is the Telesterion at Eleusis which,

---

[2] This same stadium was rebuilt first by Herodes Atticus in AD 143/4 and later again as the venue for the first modern Olympics of 1896, and it is the terminus of the annual Athens Marathon. See Rogers, Chapter 30 in this volume.

as we have seen above, was a large square roofed building with internal supports. Both were built to accommodate large audiences and are unique to Athens.[3] In the fifth century BC, many spectators gathered in the Theater of Dionysos on the south slope of the Akropolis to observe a procession of expensive offerings to Athena brought by Athens' allies in the Delian League, a demonstration of Athens' hegemony in politics and cult.

   If the Parthenon's Ionic frieze reflects actual details of the Panathenaic Festival (as many believe it does), then equestrian events loomed large at the Panathenaia. That the festival included a parade of the Athenian cavalry is indicated by the 177 horsemen depicted on the Parthenon frieze (see Fig. 29.1). Xenophon (*On the Cavalry Commander* 3.2) recommends one in his treatise on horses: "As for processions, I think they would be most pleasing to the gods and spectators if they included a gala ride in the Agora. The starting point would be the Herms [northwest Agora] ... When the circuit is completed ... the next thing to do, I think, is to gallop at top speed by tribes to the Eleusinion." The chariot race known as the *apobates* (and unique to Athens) required armed warriors to leap on and off fast vehicles driven by charioteers who urged on the horses. This spectacular race took place in the Agora and was a crowd favorite, according to ancient sources. The race is depicted on both the north and south inner friezes of the Parthenon, and the north frieze shows the victor, possibly from the tribe named for the hero Erechtheus, being crowned. Having leapt off his chariot, he places his foot on a large rock, which is likely to be the prominent feature in the City Eleusinion known as the Rocky Outcrop (Web Fig. 24.2). We know that the race ended there, because the sloped terrain thereafter is too steep for chariots. This particular event might have been added to the program in the early fifth century BC, when suddenly it is represented for the first time on a number of cheap *lekythoi* (oil flasks), produced as souvenirs.[4]

   The Panathenaic competitions were also distinctive in offering lucrative prizes (as opposed to the more typical vegetal wreath), not only to the victor but also to second place winners. Most of these prizes consisted of

---

[3] The only other building in ancient Greece that resembles these two is the Thersilion at Megalopolis, built in the mid-fourth century BC as a meeting place for representatives of the Arkadian League.

[4] See Neils and Schultz 2012. There were also miniature Panathenaic-shaped amphoras produced in the fourth century BC; see Neils 1992, 44–45.

specially commissioned amphoras (two-handled jars) filled with olive oil pressed from Athena's sacred groves, and decorated with an image of a striding armed Athena on one side and an athletic or equestrian contest on the other (Web Fig. 24.3). Ever since their invention in the 560s BC, these special prize vases were painted in the black-figure technique, even though after about 500 BC most vase-painters used the newer red-figure technique. This distinctive vase thereafter became a symbol of the games at Athens, and as such appears in a variety of media including the coinage minted by the city. (See Kroll, Chapter 18 in this volume.) Panathenaic amphoras have been found in archaeological contexts across the Mediterranean, indicating that they were valued as souvenirs and antiques long after the sacred oil was consumed.

After the competitions, the grand procession, or *pompe*, took place. Participants began the day by congregating at the Dipylon Gate, the largest gate ever constructed in ancient Greece, and ended their day there feasting on the meat of the 100 cows (*hekatomb*) sacrificed to Athena. Some critics charged that these festivals were put on less for religious reasons than to satisfy the people's craving for meat, and Sokrates himself is said to have associated the Panathenaia with indigestion. In the fourth century BC, just within the Dipylon Gate, a long rectangular building was constructed for preparations for the festival. Appropriately called the Pompeion, it contained dining rooms and an open courtyard, possibly for housing a large ship cart on wheels which in later times carried the *peplos* like a sail to the foot of the Akropolis. (Excavations of the courtyard have uncovered postholes for the support of tents set up to shelter those boiling and consuming this vast quality of meat. See Costaki and Theocharaki, Chapter 4 in this volume.)

Since it is a later addition, the ship cart does not appear on the Ionic frieze of the Parthenon which constitutes the most detailed illustration of the Panathenaic procession in the mid-fifth century BC.[5] In addition to the many horsemen on parade and the chariots carrying the *apobatai* at full speed, the frieze depicts the main participants in a sacrificial procession: musicians, water-carriers, herdsmen with cows and sheep, women carrying incense burners, libation equipment, and a basket, and, over the main temple doorway, a priest and priestess with attendants. What at first glance is surprising is the presence of not just Athena, but all twelve Olympians seated in a semicircle watching the ceremony. The fact that the land gods

[5] On the iconographic evidence for the Panathenaic ship, see Wachsmann 2012.

Fig. 24.2 Panathenaic *peplos* being folded by priest and young boy, East Frieze of the Parthenon frieze (Block 5, Fig. Nos. 31–35), ca. 440 BC, London, British Museum 1816,0610.19.
© Hans R. Goette

(Ares, Demeter, Dionysos, Hermes) are on one side and the sea gods (Poseidon, Apollo, Artemis, Aphrodite) are on the other is almost certainly a subtle reference to the Parthenon as a thank-offering for the stunning Athenian victories over the Persians on land (Marathon) and on sea (Salamis).

The most obvious iconographic feature of the frieze that allows us to identify it as the procession of the Panathenaia is the robe being folded by a priest with the aid of a young boy (Fig. 24.2).[6] This special woolen *peplos* took nine months to weave and represented the battle of the gods against the giants in which Athena played a prominent role. Like sacrifice scenes in Greek art that never show the high point (i.e. the killing of the animal), we should probably read this scene as the time *after* the presentation of the garment, when the gift has been accepted and the ceremony is ending. Thus, the Parthenon frieze is a unique document, not unlike a documentary film strip, illustrating the entire procession in time and space from its beginning at the Dipylon Gate in the morning to its denouement on the Akropolis at the end of the day.

---

[6] The sex of the child is often debated, but it would have been crystal clear to any ancient viewer that he is male because of the shorter length of his garment. Females always cover their ankles, even young girls, as shown in the Girl with the Doves stele in New York (Metropolitan Museum of Art 27.45).

Processions

Spectacular processions of Olympian gods, on foot, cart, and chariot, are illustrated on early Athenian black-figured pottery, in celebration of the wedding of Peleus and Thetis (with the birth of Achilles as the eventual outcome). Processions conferred prestige, bound their starting and end points together, marked the annual cycle of religious events, and honored the gods, but were also simply fun for both participants and observers. The Sacred Way (Web Fig. 24.4), with the City Eleusinion as one terminus and signaled at the Kerameikos with its own gateway (separate from the Dipylon Gate), was used for three distinctive processions: for much of the Panatheniac procession, for the procession to Eleusis, and also for a third sacred procession, to Delphi, undertaken occasionally by Athenian envoys. The Sacred Way continued west across Attika and beyond into neighboring territories until it reached Apollo's sanctuary at Delphi, and so was 'international' in its extension. The route of the Sacred Way was designated by inscribed boundary markers, of which several are preserved (*IG* I^3 1095, 1096; *IG* II^2 2624).

Those Athenians who were not actually participating in the Panathenaic procession could watch it from wooden bleachers set up along the route. The Panathenaic Way goes gently uphill from the Dipylon Gate near the cemetery at the Kerameikos, moves past residential neighborhoods and into the Agora, where it leads diagonally up across the public space, passing stoas, small temples, the lawcourts, administrative buildings, namely the seat of the working Athenian democracy and the heart of the city. (See Camp, Chapter 6 in this volume.) Then it continues by the City Eleusinion's forecourt, and leads up toward the caves sacred to Pan, Zeus, and Apollo in the north face of the Akropolis. Bypassing the Areopagos and swinging around the Klepsydra, the road then turns steeply up the wide ramp to the Propylaia. There, all five doors were open to the grand procession that culminated on the top of the Akropolis, at Athena's altar between the Parthenon and the Erechtheion. Together with the other venues for competition noted above, we see that virtually all areas in the city, even Piraeus, were included as locales for this festival. The Athenian sculptor Pheidias chose to represent this festival on the inner frieze of the Parthenon, and for the first time on a temple the Athenians themselves are shown processing in honor of Athena. This frieze inspired later civic and ritual representations, such as the procession of the imperial family and Roman senate on the Ara Pacis in Rome.

Notably, the Eleusinian procession along the Sacred Way was supposed to be accomplished by prospective initiates on foot, despite the long distance. Although carts could be used on parts of the route for safe transport of the Sacred Objects, an inscription of 422 BC (*IG* I^3 79) calls for the construction of a bridge over the Rheitos stream, wide enough for the Sacred Objects to be taken securely on foot, but specifically not wide enough for a cart. Later in the fourth century BC, a law passed by Lycurgus mandated that no carts be used by women, with a fine as a penalty – and he was the first to have to pay the fine when his wife nonetheless went by cart ([Plutarch], *Lives of the Ten Orators* 842A). The initiands kept up their spirits with jokes and songs, and they frequently noted landmarks that recalled Demeter's own walk to Eleusis, and her suffering over the loss of her daughter. In effect, they were reenacting a part of Demeter's search for Persephone.

The Eleusinian processions are symbolized in architectural sculpture by the key figures, Hierophantids, a special class of priestesses who carried the *kistai* with the Sacred Objects. They are shown as caryatids, with arms upraised to hold their *kistai*, in two Roman-period marble entrance gates at Eleusis and at the City Eleusinion (Web Fig. 24.5). Pausanias (who must have been initiated himself) traveled along the route and described the landmarks, tombs and monuments he saw around AD 165, and his account is not only a first-hand glimpse of what could be seen then, but also a sort of exposition of the impact and widespread power of the Eleusinian deities, from the legendary past to more recent Athenian history. Several of the landmarks, such as the Sanctuary of Aphrodite on the saddle of Mt. Aigaleos, have been located and excavated, and it is still possible to walk the route along the Sacred Way (alongside heavy traffic).

Conclusion

Thus, the Panathenaia, or 'All-Athenian,' festival is an *exemplum* of '*polis* religion,' incorporating as it does all the citizens of Athens, women and metics (resident foreigners), and tribute-bearing members of the Delian League. With its lucrative prizes, it lured the best athletes, equestrians, and musicians to Athens every four years for a spectacle which was public, gustatory, and highly urban. The festival continued to be celebrated for centuries, well into the Roman Imperial period and far outlasting the civic structures of the *polis*: the cultural prestige of Athens provided forward momentum. As an open-air civic festival, it contrasts in many ways with the Eleusinian Mysteries, which offered personal well-being, while still enacting Athenian heritage and an age-old system of decorum, during intensely dramatic nocturnal events. The Eleusinian sanctuaries at Eleusis and below the Akropolis flourished in the Roman period, especially under Hadrian, when imperial patronage reconfigured the entrance courts with extensive additions and embellishment with *propyla*, fountains, and arches.[7] These two prominent festivals represent only a small part of the overall ancient Greek religious experience, yet they illustrate the range and variety of religious practice available to the residents of ancient Athens. It is no surprise that the Athenians were said to be more devout than any other Greeks.

Further Reading

The literature on these subjects is vast; a good place to start is Parker 2005. Attic processions are the subject of chapters in Friese 2019. Mylonas 1961 is still the *locus classicus* for the site of Eleusis, now supplemented by the extensive work of Clinton, in particular Clinton 1992 and 2005/2008. On the nature and modern study of Mystery religions, see Cosmopoulos 2003 and Bremmer 2014. For the argument that the ritual dates back to the Bronze Age, see Cosmopoulos 2015. The City Eleusinion is thoroughly published by Miles 1998. For a general overview of the Panathenaia, see Neils 1992 and 1996, and Neils and Tracy 2003; more comprehensive is Shear 2021. For discussion of the Telesterion and the Odeion of Perikles, see Shear 2016.

Bibliography

Bremmer, J. 2014. *Initiation into the Mysteries of the Ancient World.* Berlin.

Clinton, K. 1992. *Myth and Cult: The Iconography of the Eleusinian Mysteries.* Stockholm.

   2005/2008. *Eleusis. The Inscriptions on Stone: Documents of the Sanctuary of the Two Goddesses and Public Documents of the Deme.* 2 vols. Athens.

Cosmopoulos, M. 2015. *Bronze Age Eleusis and the Origins of the Eleusinian Mysteries.* Cambridge.

   ed. 2003. *Greek Mysteries. The Archaeology and Ritual of Ancient Secret Cults.* London.

Friese, W., et al., eds. 2019. *Ascending and Descending the Akropolis: Movement in Athenian Religion.* Aarhus.

Miles, M.M. 1998. *The City Eleusinion. Agora* 31. Princeton.

   2012. "Entering Demeter's Gateway: The Roman Propylon in the City Eleusinion." In *Architecture of the Sacred: Space, Ritual, and Experience*

---

[7] See Miles 2012, along with Rogers 2021 for an exploration of the sensory experience related to the processions and this space in the Roman period.

from Classical Greece to Byzantium, eds. B.D. Wescoat and R.G. Ousterhout, Cambridge, 114–151.

Mylonas, G. 1961. *Eleusis and the Eleusinian Mysteries*. Princeton.

Neils, J. 2001. *The Parthenon Frieze*. Cambridge.

— ed. 1992. *Goddess and Polis: The Panathenaic Festival in Athens*. Princeton.

— ed. 1996. *Worshipping Athena: Panathenaia and Parthenon*. Madison.

Neils, J., and P. Schultz. 2012. "Erechtheus and the Apobates Race on the Parthenon Frieze (North XI–XII)." *AJA* 116: 195–207.

Neils J., and S. Tracy. 2003. *The Games at Athens*. Agora Picture Book 25. Princeton.

Parker, R. 2005. *Athenian Religion: A History*. Oxford.

Rogers, D.K. 2021. "Sensing Water in Roman Greece: The Villa of Herodes Atticus at Eva-Loukou and the Sanctuary of Demeter and Kore at Eleusis." *AJA* 125.

Shear, J.L. 2021. *Serving Athena: The Festival of the Panathenaia and the Construction of Athenian Identities*. Cambridge.

Shear, T.L. 2016. *Trophies of Victory: Public Buildings in Periklean Athens*. Princeton.

Wachsmann, S. 2012. "Panathenaic Ships: The Iconographic Evidence." *Hesperia* 81: 237–266.

Additional resources to accompany this chapter can be found at: www.cambridge.org/NeilsRogers

25 | Eating and Drinking

ANN STEINER

The protocols and customs surrounding the consumption of food and drink are defining elements of any culture. Fortunately, both the material record and ancient texts yield significant information about what and how Athenians of the fifth century ate and drank. Commensality took place in connection with a broad spectrum of public and private events; social hierarchies, political positions, and cultural values were expressed and codified through these modes of public and private eating and drinking.

Written texts provide both direct and indirect information on these topics, but the majority of them focus on drinking and dining events that included only men, and, for the most part, men who were Athenian citizens. Women, children, foreign residents called metics, and slaves are less evident from this record, and information about them must be teased out with care. Poetry, from the comedies performed at public festivals to drinking songs, and prose sources, such as histories, medical and scientific writing, philosophy, speeches written for lawsuits, and public inscriptions, all contain relevant information. Evidence from material culture includes the ceramic shapes used for cooking, serving, and eating food and for the elaborate rituals surrounding drinking wine; the floorplans of physical spaces where Athenians ate, both public and private; physical remains of meals, both plant and animal; and the bones of Athenians themselves, revealing their overall nutritional palette and how it translates into a picture of the health of the population (see Liston, Chapter 13 in this volume).

In addition to this primary evidence, the work of social anthropologists on food and eating has contributed immensely to our understanding of how different types of commensality worked both to segregate and to knit together society. From the private house to the public sphere, we see many examples verifying that fifth-century Athenians understood and exploited the bonding effect of eating together and its importance in defining the relationships and values of social groups. The city mandated and hosted some shared meals alongside those that took place within private houses.

We know quite a bit about what food was available as well as the attitudes of the Athenians toward food and how it was consumed.

Eating and Health: Medical Texts

According to the Hippocratic corpus, a body of writing attributed to the fifth-century physician Hippokrates, Greeks were well aware of the links among food, eating, and health. Greek medical writing includes ample discussion of *diaita*, practices relating exclusively to food and drink and to the latter plus exercise.[1] Recovery from illness could require specific dietary practices, and drugs or medicines were usually added only after dietary measures proved unsuccessful. Various medical treatises list foods and their properties, methods of preparation, and preservation.

A few passages in ancient texts suggest that Athenians were aware that people of different cultures ate differently from the Greeks. In a well-known passage, Herodotos describes the eating customs of the Persians (1.133), stating that they ate fewer courses per meal overall, but more of them were desserts. Some Hippocratic sources make it clear that ancient Greeks considered themselves superior to others because they had the self-discipline to minimize sweet foods and to modify their diet if ill health required it.

Hippocratic writers considered the number of meals per day so defining for a people that they advised physicians when traveling to a new city to ask before anything else whether the population were *monositein* (single meal eaters) or not. For most Greeks, however, a daytime meal and a second meal in the evening were the common practice. Although *deipnon* is ordinarily assumed to be the evening meal, it could sometimes be eaten during the day, especially if diners were eager to consume wine (Aristophanes, *Cocalus* fr. 360). One scholar has proposed a widely accepted scheme which seems to fit the available evidence: for Athenians, *ariston* precedes *deipnon* and can be in the morning or afternoon; its timing then has an effect on when *deipnon* takes place. The latter takes place at different times depending on the season – earlier in winter than in summer, for example.[2] It seems that, in general, women and men did not eat together when outsiders were present, and both solitary eating and freeloading were seen as social sins.

---

[1] The discussion here relies on Jouanna 2012, 137–153.
[2] Wilkins 2000, 57–62.

Available Food

By the fifth century there was an extensive trade network, bringing to Athens a great assortment of food and drink from all over the Mediterranean: "as denizens of the world's greatest *emporion*, Athenian shoppers had access to nearly everything the ancient world had to offer, in terms of food, clothes, durable goods, and art."[3] Weather conditions caused the sea-lanes to be shut down for a good portion of the year, so many of the imports were available only in the summer months. Political conditions, especially those imposed by war, also had an impact on what could reach Athens. Nevertheless, in comedies written and performed in public festivals of the second half of the fifth century in Athens, the variety of food and drink described is staggering, suggesting that most Athenians were aware of this abundance and in some detail. It is also clear that many foodstuffs and methods of preparation mentioned in the comedies were considered rare and exotic, consumed mainly by the self-indulgent.

Because of Athens' location on the sea, it is natural to ask in particular what kinds of seafood its inhabitants ate, and scholars have analyzed the comic sources for information on the purchase, cooking, and consumption of fish. One key passage suggests that eating fish was a marker of extravagant behavior among elites and not readily available to those less well-off.[4] Eel, in particular, is consistently at the top of the hierarchy of fish delicacies, and its purchase and consumption are often markers of self-indulgence and profligacy. In fact, in contrast to the large number of species and dishes named in comedy, there is a very small percentage of fish remains found in contexts in the Agora in Athens.[5] Thus the prominence of discourse surrounding fish is contradicted by how little evidence of its consumption is extant. At the same time, mention of wild game is common, and physical evidence verifies its actual consumption.

Probing the comic sources more deeply, we see that the number of food categories and diversity within them are indeed impressive.[6] Grains (wheat, barley, bran, corn), legumes (beans, lentil, peas, chickpeas), seeds and nuts (sesame, almond, hazelnut, acorn), and dairy products (milk, cheese, eggs) are mentioned most often. Meats mentioned include both domestic

---

[3] Van Alfen 2016, 277. Wycherley 1957, 185–206, is a collection of ancient references to the numerous shops and stalls where one could purchase commodities in the ancient Agora of Athens.

[4] Davidson 1998, 226–227.

[5] MacKinnon 2014, 230–231.

[6] Lewis 2016, 381–388.

animals (cattle, pigs, boar, sheep, goat), game (rabbit or hare, fox, mole, rat, cat), and fowl (duck, goose, quail, partridge, dove, and eleven different types of songbirds). At least twenty-eight different species of fish are mentioned, with a total of forty-six when we consider the sub-varieties. To these we can add thirteen different types of shellfish as well as eel, octopus, squid, and cuttlefish. From the garden come snails, cicadas, and grasshoppers. Fruits, many fresh as well as dried, include a roster still familiar in Athens: olives, figs, apples, pomegranates, pears, dates, myrtle berries, strawberries, plums, and, of course, grapes. To the list of vegetables (garlic, onion, leek, cabbage, asparagus, cucumber, gourds, radish, beet, turnip, and lettuce), we can add edible plants and weeds (cress, chervil, mallow, horse parsley, honey clover, chicory, and vetch). Some wildflower blooms and blossoms are also cited as food.

The number of spices is testimony to the broad range of tastes available to the Athenian palette. Salt was king, but there is also reference to saffron, oregano, mint, anise, mustard, coriander, silphium, thyme, lavender, helle-bore, mastic, laurel, dropwort, surge, asphodel, fennel, mullein, saltbush, marjoram, and basil. Condiments include salt, brine, vinegar, garlic, honey, and fish sauce. Breads in at least five different formats, including sour-dough, are made from wheat, barley, and corn. At least sixteen different types of cakes, most apparently savory, are also named in comedies.

Physical evidence verifies in broad strokes what the comedies suggest. Faunal analysis of animal bones in the Agora confirms the prominence of pigs, sheep, goats, and cattle in that order, with an emphasis on juvenile animals – lambs, kids, and calves. Jokes in comedy suggest that the high fat content of grilled meat at religious festivals caused intestinal distress for individuals not used to its consumption. This tells us more about the rareness of eating broiled or roasted meat in comparison to the more everyday boiled stews. Based on the percentages of types of cooking pots preserved, stews and soups, no doubt lentil and pea, broth, and gruel as well as meat-based recipes, were commonly served.

Reconstructing the Athenian Diet

Study of faunal remains from three fifth-century Athenian cemeteries verifies that the Athenian diet was robust, including a significant level of protein consumption. Through stable isotope analysis of skeletons of slaves who worked the silver mines from the Attic cemeteries at Laurion, as well as two at the urban center, the Kerameikos, where elites were buried, and the Kotzia Square for Athenians of more modest means, a picture emerges of a diet of "terrestrial protein mostly from staples such as barley and wheat form[ing] the bulk of the Athenian diet, while $\delta^{15}N$ values show that meat and/or dairy products were an important part of the diet."[7] Marine sources are also identified. The percentage of marine food is low, consisting only of smaller fish such as sardines, anchovies, and gilt-headed sea bream, and thus confirms the evidence from excavated remains of seafood. Interestingly, there is little difference among the three social groups whose remains were tested. Even at the lowest position in the social order, slaves seem to have been well nourished, as were men, women, and children.

To accompany meals, wine and olive oil from diverse sources were abundantly available in Athens. As testimony, we have both the references to wine in comedies, where as many as nine production cities are mentioned, as well as the very substantial evidence of transport amphoras, containers for wine and oil exported and traded throughout the Mediterranean. (See Lawall, Chapter 17 in this volume.) Distinctive shapes, fabrics, and stamped impressions help to identify the sources of these wines. Diagnostic fragments from many contexts in the Agora in Athens dating to the sixth and fifth centuries confirm that wines from Attika, Corinth, the Aegean islands, and farther east include over half of those mentioned in comic texts.[8] Based on a comparison of contexts from private houses, magistrates' dining facilities, and debris thought to be from a tavern, the tavern diners had a more restricted range of wines from which to choose than other groups. In the fifth century, imports from the island of Chios, slightly northeast of Athens and very near the coast of modern Turkey, and from the site of Mende in Northern Greece, not far from Thessaloniki, are most numerous.

Thus, when we compare references in comic texts to physical and material remains, we draw the intriguing conclusion that elite cuisine and its sources from all over the Mediterranean were known throughout Athenian society, but were apparently inaccessible to most of its members. The broad food supply, visible in the raucous markets in the Agora, in comparison to which sectors of society were able to take advantage of it, thus becomes a lens through which to view Athens' role in Mediterranean trade as well as class distinctions and the dynamics of political power within the city itself.

---

[7] Lagia 2015, 126.
[8] Rotroff and Oakley 1992; Lawall 2000; Lynch 2013.

Eating in Houses

Private houses were the site of both the least- and best-known customs for Athenian eating and drinking. Several houses have been excavated, both near the city center and in the countryside.[9] (See Harrington, Chapter 9 in this volume.) In most cases, there is no clear indication that any particular room had an exclusive use as a kitchen, with a water supply and facilities for cooking, grilling, and baking. Instead, cooking pots are found in many different locations in the house, perhaps close to where they were stored when not in use. Portable hearths were the norm rather than fixed hearths, and they are found throughout domestic spaces, thus no doubt used both for grilling and warmth. Some scholars have hypothesized that a number of different spaces, including the central courtyard, could have accommodated cooking. The cooking pots from domestic contexts have small capacities, suggesting that meals for just a few people were prepared at one time.

Neither texts nor ceramic remains provide evidence that members of the household regularly ate at the same time in the way we conceive of a 'family meal' today. A few references in Athenian comedy indicate that wives at times served their husbands food at home; we do not know if the wives ate as well (e.g. Aristophanes, *Wasps* 610–612; *Knights* 42–60, 1164–1226; *Thesmophoriazousai* 468–470, 595). The little evidence we have suggests that meals were segregated by sex.[10] In sum, although women and children spent most of their time within the home, there is little information about when and how they ate. The family was an important unit for determining citizenship and inheritance of property, but to our knowledge the bonds among family members were not reinforced daily or even regularly with the experience of shared meals.[11]

In contrast, the private evening drinking party, the *symposion*, is one of the best known of all social events in Athenian culture. Some ancient Greek houses are equipped with a special room for these drinking parties hosted by male members of the household for their male friends, and such rooms have been linked with the word *andron* found in literary sources. These rooms feature an off-center door and sometimes a raised curb to

[9] Foxhall 2007, 235–242.
[10] Dalby 1993. This article is an excellent overview of literary sources for interaction between men and women on all occasions involving consumption of food and drink.
[11] Rawson 2011, a comprehensive anthology on the ancient Greek family, does not treat regular eating practices within the Classical household.

accommodate the correct arrangement of dining couches. *Andrones* held seven or eleven couches, allowing drinkers to recline either solo or in couples. Although rooms that look identical to private *andrones* have been identified in public spaces in Athens, there is almost no archaeological evidence for them in private houses in Attika. Any rectangular room, however, could be furnished as an *andron*, and the open courtyard may have been converted to a sympotic purpose as well.

Prior to the late sixth century, the *symposion* was an activity of elite men, but as the Athenian system of government became more democratic, men from lower strata of society adopted it as well. A 'drinking-together,' the *symposion* focused primarily on wine, not food; light snacks or simple meals, brought by the guests in baskets, were sometimes consumed before the drinking began. Poetry composed for *symposia*, and memorized and recited at them, focused on the pleasures of wine and sex in the sympotic context. Although the female members of citizen families did not join *symposia*, female entertainers, prostitutes, and courtesans could be present.

Athenian craftsmen created a substantial range of pottery shapes for use in *symposia*: large bowls in which to mix water and wine, a variety of cups for drinking, pouring vessels, and bowls and plates for food (Web Fig. 25.1). Although many of these are decorated with scenes of *symposia*, thus apparently uniting function and decoration, the images are overall highly idealized.[12] They can tell us what likely outfitted the sympotic space, but their language of imagery can be used as evidence for sympotic practice only with caution.

The *symposion* served both social and political functions. Its exclusion of women of citizen families reveals the male sphere as the locus of power and intellect. Events followed a script or template of events that encouraged a tension between equality and fierce competition among participants. Everyone reclined, but a 'symposiarch' or master of ceremonies was chosen to put to the vote the ratio of water to wine, a decision that dictated whether the point of the evening was to have a serious discussion or to get drunk. The symposiarch also decided who reclined on which couch. Both verbal participation and drinking proceeded 'to the right,' beginning with the first couch and progressing to the last. As activity moved around the room, the pressure built to come up with something novel and substantive or at least clever to say. Participants thus took turns in such diverse activities as intellectual discussions on a stated topic, poetry recitations and

---

[12] Indeed, some of the largest and most elaborate were exported to Italian buyers. See Rotroff, Chapter 19 in this volume.

improvisation, mock 'beauty pageants,' and performances by musicians and dancers. Sex of all sorts and in all combinations was part of sympotic experience for some Athenian men. (See Ormand, Chapter 26 in this volume.)

The group also decided on whether there would be a *komos,* a rowdy parade through the streets, after the party ended. Such public performances brought the private group into the eye of the community, for which there are accounts of vandalism that shocked the populace and resulted in legal action. Thus, bonds formed in sympotic groups could express themselves in politics (Web Fig. 25.2). Thucydides (8.54.4) tells us that sympotic groups' affinity played out "in law cases and contests for office."[13] Elite education and enculturation prepared young men for successful participation in the *symposion,* just as it did for public life. Even as the *symposion* became 'democratized,' men of middle and lower classes could find themselves outclassed and intimidated in a sympotic setting where men with elite backgrounds had an advantage.[14] Thus, the *symposion* is an excellent example of Dietler's "diacritical feast," a commensal event that relies on "differentiated cuisine and styles of consumption [that] naturalize and reify concepts of ranked differences in the status of social orders or classes."[15] General acceptance of the custom is clear; despite the fact that the *symposion* was linked to the wealthier class, fifth-century texts tell us that it was not perceived "as inimical to the democracy."[16]

Feasting in Public

Here, we consider commensality that took place in public, hosted by the *demos,* in some cases supplemented by funding from elites who were expected to use personal wealth to contribute to the welfare of the city. This type of commensality loosely fits the category that Dietler calls patron-role feasts, where there is no reciprocity required: the patron, the *polis,* maintains its superiority in its partnership with its citizens by providing literal nourishment on specified occasions that are controlled and carefully choreographed.[17] Thus, even those honored by the *polis* for

---

[13] Bowie 1997, 3.
[14] Bowie 1997, 3.
[15] Dietler and Hayden 2001, 85–88.
[16] Bowie 1997, 3.
[17] Dietler and Hayden 2001, 82–85.

exceptional service fall beneath the collective whole of the *demos* in the civic hierarchy, because they are the beneficiaries and not the hosts of these feasts.

Many public religious celebrations sponsored by the city included animal sacrifice and the consumption of food and wine. Cult officials might eat in public buildings in special dining rooms that were similar to the *andron* in private houses; for example, a lavish room for such dining was part of the monumental gateway to the Akropolis, and the officials for the Great Panathenaia may have eaten there (see Map 5.1, no. 3). The majority of festival participants, however, probably ate in the open or in temporary structures created for the occasion.[18] Some ritual celebrations required deviations from normal commensal practices; for example, on the middle day of the Anthesteria, a festival in honor of the god Dionysos, Athenians chugged undiluted wine from pitchers (*choes*) in silence in place of the polite, conversation-filled ingestion of diluted wine from special cups at the *symposion* (Web Fig. 25.3). This reversal of the norm, characteristic of the worship of Dionysos, helped to thrust into relief the social value of more typical, moderate wine drinking. Another reversal involves drinking by women. We have hints from architecture and written and visual sources that women on rare occasions may have reclined and consumed wine during the feasting that accompanied religious rites.[19]

Public Dining and Politics

By the fifth century, Athens fed its citizens in at least two additional ways: at the 'city hall,' or Prytaneion, where the ancestral hearth of the city was located in the Archaic agora, and at various dining facilities in the Classical Agora for magistrates serving the democracy, some of whom received a daily stipend to cover their meal expenses. This payment was a key part of the philosophy of the democracy, as it was intended to allow all Athenians, rich or poor, to participate in running the city. The meals at the Prytaneion were conceived as a benefit bestowed in gratitude for extraordinary service to the *polis*, a type of regular provision of meals known as *sitesis*.

---

[18] Cooper and Morris 1990.

[19] Peirce 1998 demonstrates how the imagery on a group of Athenian vases provides evidence for women engaging in a Dionysiac ritual that included a sacrifice of meat, its consumption, and a *symposion* followed by a revel.

Physical evidence for the oldest public dining room, the Prytaneion, has proved to be elusive (see Map 6.1).[20] Legend attributes its founding to the hero Theseus when he united the villages in Attika with the city center to create one *polis*, and it was functioning during the time of Solon in the sixth century. A credible current hypothesis for its location assigns some actual remains located in the 'old agora' at the east end of the Akropolis to it; this building is rectangular and very large, ca. 45 × 65 m. By the fifth century, both citizens and foreigners could be invited to dine there, either once or permanently. The qualifications for the honor of dining at the Prytaneion were established by law and voted on by the Assembly in the Classical period, but we have no information about how the list of those thus entitled was developed in the early history of the *polis*. The so-called Prytany decree (*IG* I[3] 131) specifies who was privileged to enjoy *sitesis* at the Prytaneion:

(1) The heroes Kastor and Polydeukes, elsewhere known as the Dioskouroi but as the Anakes by the Athenians (they were not present, of course, but a meal was laid out for them);
(2) The oldest male descendant of the tyrant-slayers, Harmodios and Aristogeiton, whose assassination of the tyrant Hipparchos opened the door to democracy;
(3) Seers or prophets whose work saved the city from peril;
(4) Victors in the Panhellenic Games whose achievements brought glory to Athens; and,
(5) By vote of the Assembly, exceptional leaders in the *polis*, including certain generals.[21]

By the end of the fifth century, one of the largest categories of diners offered one-time meals was foreign visitors and ambassadors. As non-citizens, their privilege was named *xenia*, an ancient term conveying the notion of hospitality more than honor or gratitude.

What were the meals like in this august setting? One source tells us that they were simple and sober, apparently not actually requiring much cooking or other preparation: "cheese, barley cake, tree-ripe olives, and leeks."[22] It is likely that menus were more ample by the Classical period, perhaps including meat. Likewise, there is no direct evidence for wine

---

[20] Kavvadias and Matthaiou 2014. All of the testimonia from ancient writers on this building and eating customs therein up to ca. 400 are collected in Miller 1978.

[21] Blok and Van 't Wout 2018 is the source for all of the information on the Prytaneion and the decree *IG* I[3] 131.

[22] Wilkins 2000, 177.

service, but it is reasonable to assume that it accompanied meals in the Prytaneion. One scholar interprets a passage in Herodotos (6.139) as indicating that couches furnished the *prytaneion*, just as they did *andrones* for private *symposia*, but even that passage is not decisive.[23]

The provision of meals to public officials at other dining halls was, in contrast, a necessity; long work days, for some as long as twenty-four hours, required meals. A late source gives us a general view of a perceived political benefit to including shared meals for public officials.[24] According to Athenaios (*Deipnosophistai* 4.185f–186a), "because wine seems to draw people into friendship by warming and relaxing the soul," the lawgivers were anticipating the Classical period dinner parties (i.e. *symposia*) when they mandated meals organized by tribes and communities, as well as cult-dinners, phratry-dinners, and those referred to as *orgeonika*. A shared meal was also a good way to enable cohesion among citizens quickly in a system where roles were determined by lot and terms lasted for a year. A closer look at the evidence for two different magistrates' dining halls provides us with a window into these shared meals and reveals the tensions between those who favored government by a small group of elites and those who sought to ensure a political system where every citizen had a voice and a vote.

The construction of a dining room for one group of magistrates, the *prytaneis* or 'presidents' of the Council of 500, took place at the very moment the group was created. The *Constitution of the Athenians* (43.3) tells us that the *prytaneis* ate in a round building (known as the Tholos) and prepared, with the Council, the agenda for meetings of the Assembly. Each tribe served 'in prytany' for one month of the year. Roughly a third of the fifty men stayed in the building from dusk one day until dusk the next to deal with emergencies or other business that came up outside of the normal workday. The building (Fig. 6.2) thus had to accommodate both eating and sleeping. The *prytaneis* most likely ate seated on a bench around the circumference of the building rather than reclining, as it is impossible to fit fifty dining couches around its circumference. The drinking and eating ware is simple; there are many identical examples of relatively few shapes in plain black-glaze pottery (Fig. 25.1). A number of these vessels are marked with an abbreviation for the word *demosion* which is translated

---

[23] Topper 2012, 21.

[24] Athenaios, a second-century AD writer, relied on much earlier sources for his encyclopedic work on the *symposion*. His work is used – with appropriate caution – to enlarge understanding of dining customs in Classical Athens.

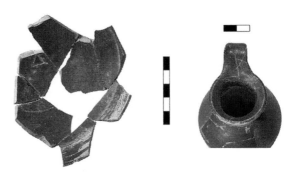

Fig. 25.1 Fragmentary drinking cup (left) and *olpe* (right), Tholos (Deposit G 12:22), Athenian Agora, ca. 450 BC, Agora P 10813, P 10819. These vessels show the *delta/epsilon* abbreviation, signifying that they belong to the *demos*.
Courtesy of the American School of Classical Studies at Athens: Agora Excavations. Image adapted by R. Bidgood

"belonging to the people," indicating that they were public property. Several of these shapes are identical in capacity to the Athenian standard measures that governed commercial activity in the Agora and were housed in the Tholos. Conforming to these standard measures must have ensured both tight control over the inventory of food and drink needed to provision the dining room as well as equal portions for the diners. The cooking ware tells us that meat formed a big part of the meals here, and it could be accompanied by stews. A large number of small bowls for spices are present, and drinking cups are simple bowls with handles.[25] The conventions of eating and drinking at the Tholos appear to express the values of equality and moderation that are key democratic ideals.

For a second dining establishment, about 50 m north of the Tholos, we have only a hint of its physical form but an enormous body of ceramic evidence for what and how magistrates ate there. This 'anonymous' magistrates' dining hall was likely to have served archons and/or cavalry officers. Among the thousands of ceramic fragments for storing, cooking, serving and consuming food and wine, many have the mark, "property of the demos," indicating they were public property. It likely began to serve its clientele by at least a decade before the Tholos was built, indicating it was already in use at the time the last tweaks to the democratic system were implemented. Because it overlaps for at least thirty-five years with the Tholos, it provides the opportunity to compare dining customs at the two public mess halls. Although the scanty architectural remains

---

[25] Steiner 2018 presents the earliest ceramic evidence from the Tholos.

tentatively associated with the debris are too fragmentary to reconstruct the setting for meals, the pottery decorated with figural scenes gives us a very good idea of their general tenor.[26] A significant percentage of the cups, mixing bowls, and pitchers are just like those used in private *symposia* (Web Fig. 25.4). Irreverent graffiti that appear to mock important political processes, such as ostracism and the regular publication of accounts and legal actions in public inscriptions, are scratched onto some ceramic fragments. The form and content of these inscriptions suggest that at times the behaviors of elites may have dominated and thus intimidated men from lower social classes, less experienced with this type of sympotic behavior.[27] This evidence highlights for us how the tensions between those who fully supported the democracy and those who resented its encroachment on elite power played out in at least one public dining room.

Taverns

It was also possible for all Athenians to buy a meal from a private owner in taverns, called *kapeleia*. The dining debris from a well in the southwest corner of the Agora has been identified as likely from a tavern.[28] The faunal debris indicates the consumption of expensive domestic mammals, such as sheep and lambs.[29] In ancient comedy, Athenian taverns have a negative reputation for cheating patrons and being the locus of scurrilous behavior. Perhaps this shady reputation explains why the material found in the debris includes bronze standard measures, engraved with "Property of the Athenian *demos*," identical to those that were 'official' measures stored in the Tholos. Prominent display and use of such containers may have been useful in negotiating claims from disgruntled customers (Fig. 25.2). Pitchers are the most common shape found in the Agora tavern, and, although there are a few examples of mugs and flat-bottomed cups in the debris, patrons may have brought their own drinking cups. Red-figured pottery in shapes associated with the boudoir is plentiful, suggesting the presence of women. As a result, scholars argue that the taverns may have been brothels as well. Thus, while women were obviously present in some taverns, both as prostitutes and their managers, we have no idea if and how they ate there.

[26] Rotroff and Oakley 1992 illustrate the material from this dining hall.
[27] Steiner 2002 includes extensive discussion of Talcott's earlier work on the material.
[28] Agora Deposit Q 15:2. See Lawall 2000 and MacKinnon 2014.
[29] MacKinnon 2014, 229.

Fig. 25.2 Official bronze measure (half-kyathos), from Agora deposit Q 15:2, ca. 400 BC (left); official clay measure (3 choinikes/12 kyathoi), from the Akropolis North Slope, ca. 450–425 BC. Agora B 1082 bis, AP 1103. Both bear inscriptions indicating they are the property of the *demos*.
Courtesy of the American School of Classical Studies at Athens: Agora Excavations. Image adapted by R. Bidgood

Conclusion

Athenians in the fifth century were healthy, ate well, and regarded overall moderation in the consumption of food as a virtue and essential to good health. An extensive array of food and spices was sold in the markets of Athens, much of it too expensive and/or rare to be available to the average citizen. The habits of private eating in households are not well understood, except for the men's *symposion*, which featured drinking wine more than eating food. The city hosted meals in at least three types of setting to achieve a variety of goals:

(1) In the Prytaneion, to honor those who had given extraordinary service to the *polis* or were its foreign guests;
(2) In a variety of dining establishments in the Agora, to feed magistrates whose positions required long work days; and
(3) At a substantial number of public festivals.

Taverns, privately run establishments where food and drink could be accompanied by prostitution, existed as well.

The importance of eating to our understanding of a culture is summed up in the frequently cited statement by Brillat-Savarin in his nineteenth-century classic work, *The Physiology of Taste*. "Tell me what you eat and I will tell you what you are." Tweaking this observation, we can add that *how* you eat is equally revelatory. Based on what their skeletons tell us, the fifth-century Athenians were uniformly well nourished, regardless of gender or social class. Their food was prepared and cooked in identical pots and pans, despite the fact that elites may have had a wider range of exotic imports and seafood than less affluent Athenians. It is in the details of *how* various groups ate that we learn about social hierarchies, political positions, and cultural values. For the ancient Athenians, the identity of the host, the menu, the basis on which you were present for the meal, the company with whom you ate, what vessels for serving and consuming it you used, and the position you adopted while you ate and drank all contribute to a portrait of the city and its inhabitants. For citizen men we know a great deal; women and children were crucial but not powerful, and about their commensal experience we know almost nothing. Elite individuals vied with the collective *demos* to host the eating and drinking that counted, just as a struggle between the few and the many persisted throughout the fifth century, when Athenian democracy was at its height.

Further Reading

To set ancient Athenian eating and drinking in a wider Mediterranean context, see Wilkins and Nadeau 2015. Dietler and Hayden 2001 provide theoretical background on communal feasting from a broad anthropological perspective. The seminal work on the ancient Greek *symposion* remains Murray 1990. Van den Eijnde et al. 2018 presents many facets of the history and impact of communal dining on the development of the *polis* in general. Glazebrook and Tsakirgis 2016 offers several case studies covering eating and drinking at Athenian taverns and brothels. The perceived relationship between ancient Greek diet and health is covered in Jouanna 2012, while Papathanasiou et al. 2015 provides an analysis of the physical evidence for nutrition in ancient Greece. Wilkins 2000 analyzes thoroughly the central role of food and eating as revealed in publicly performed comedies. Finally, Davidson 1998 explores how eating and drinking in combination with sexual behaviors are defining aspects of Athenian culture.

Bibliography

Blok, J., and E. Van 't Wout. 2018. "Table Arrangements: *Sitêsis* as a Polis Institution." In *Feasting and Polis Institutions*, ed. F. Van den Eijnde et al., Leiden, 181–204.

Bowie, A. 1997. "Thinking with Drinking: Wine and the Symposium in Aristophanes." *JHS* 117: 1–21.

Cooper, F., and S. Morris. 1990. "Dining in Round Buildings." In *Sympotica*, ed. O. Murray, Oxford, 66–85.

Davidson, J.N. 1998. *Courtesans and Fishcakes: The Consuming Passions of Classical Athens.* New York.

Dietler, M., and B. Hayden. 2001. *Feasts: Archaeological and Ethnographic Perceptions on Food, Politics, and Power.* Washington, DC.

Dalby, A. 1993. "Food and Sexuality in Classical Athens." In *Food, Culture, & History. Vol. I*, eds. G. Mars and V. Mars, London, 165–190.

Foxhall, L. 2007. "House Clearance: Unpacking the 'Kitchen' in Classical Greece." In *Building Communities: House, Settlement, and Society in the Aegean and Beyond*, eds. R. Westgate, N. Fisher, and J. Whitley, London, 233–242.

Glazebrook, A., and B. Tsakirgis, eds. 2016. *Houses of Ill Repute: The Archaeology of Brothels, Houses, and Taverns in the Greek World.* Philadelphia.

Jouanna, J. 2012. *Greek Medicine from Hippocrates to Galen: Selected Papers by Jacques Jouanna*, ed. P. Van der Eijk, Leiden.

Kavvadias, G., and A.P. Matthaiou. 2014. "A New Attic Inscription of the Fifth Century BC from the East Slope of the Acropolis." In *Αθηναίων επίσκοπος: Studies in Honour of Harold B. Mattingly*, eds. A.P. Matthaiou and R.K. Pitt, Athens, 51–72.

Lagia, A. 2015. "Diet and the Polis: An Isotopic Study of Diet in Athens and Laurion during the Classical, Hellenistic, and Imperial Roman Periods." In *Archaeodiet in the Greek World: Dietary Reconstruction from Stable Isotope Analysis*, eds. A. Papathanasiou et al., Princeton, 119–145.

Lawall, M.L. 2000. "Graffiti, Wine Selling, and the Reuse of Amphoras in the Athenian Agora, ca. 430–400 BC." *Hesperia* 69: 3–90.

Lewis, D.M. 2016. "Commodities in Classical Athens: The Evidence of Old Comedy." In *The Ancient Greek Economy: Markets, Households, and City-States*, ed. E. Harris et al., Cambridge, 381–398.

Lynch, K.M. 2013. *The Symposium in Context: Pottery from a Late Archaic House near the Athenian Agora.* Princeton.

MacKinnon, M. 2014. "Animals, Economics, and Culture in the Athenian Agora: Comparative Zooarchaeological Investigations." *Hesperia* 83: 189–255.

Miller, S.G. 1978. *The Prytaneion: Its Function and Architectural Form.* Berkeley.

Murray, O. 1990. *Sympotica: A Symposium on the Symposium.* Oxford.

Papathanasiou, A., M.P. Richards, and S.C. Fox, eds. 2015. *Archaeodiet in the Greek World: Dietary Reconstruction from Stable Isotope Analysis.* Princeton.

Peirce, S. 1998. "Visual Language and Concepts of Cult on the 'Lenaia Vases.'" *Classical Antiquity* 17: 59–95.

Rawson, B., ed. 2011. *A Companion to Families in the Greek and Roman World.* Malden, MA.

Rotroff, S., and J. Oakley. 1992. *Debris from a Public Dining Place in the Athenian Agora.* Princeton.

Steiner, A. 2002. "Private and Public: Links Between *Symposion* and *Syssition* in Fifth Century Athens." *Classical Antiquity* 21: 347–390.

2018. "Measure for Measure: Fifth Century Public Dining at the Tholos in Athens." In *Feasting and Polis Institutions*, ed. F. Van den Eijnde et al., Leiden, 205–232.

Topper, K. 2012. *The Imagery of the Athenian Symposium.* Cambridge.

Van Alfen, P. 2016. "Aegean and Levantine Trade, 600–300 BCE: Commodities, Consumers, and the Problem of Autarkia." In *The Ancient Greek Economy: Markets, Households, and City-States*, ed. E. Harris et al., Cambridge, 277–298.

Van den Eijnde, F., J. Blok, and R. Strootman, eds. 2018. *Feasting and Polis Institutions.* Leiden.

Wilkins, J. 2000. *The Boastful Chef: The Discourse of Food in Ancient Greek Comedy.* Oxford.

Wilkins, J., and R. Nadeau. 2015. *A Companion to Food in the Ancient World.* Chichester.

Wycherley, R.E. 1957. *Literary and Epigraphical Testimonia. Agora* 3. Princeton.

Additional resources to accompany this chapter can be found at: www.cambridge .org/NeilsRogers

26 | Sex and the City

KIRK ORMAND

> But you are taking refuge in the names of buildings, demanding that
> we provide a list, house-by-house, of where you sat [as a
> prostitute] . . . Houses and lodgings do not provide a name to those
> who live in them, but the inhabitants furnish places with the names of
> their own business practices. Where several men have rented a single
> dwelling, and share it, we call it an apartment house . . . and if ever
> somehow a doctor moves into one of the industrial buildings on the
> street, it is called a surgery . . . but if a pimp and *pornai* [move in],
> from the work itself it is called a brothel. Thus you have created many
> brothels by the recklessness of your behavior.
>
> Aischines 1.124

Where in ancient Athens did sexual activity take place, and how did those
spaces define, and become defined by, that activity? As the quotation from
Aischines' first oration indicates, the Athenians of the Classical period did
not designate certain spaces, or certain areas of the city, as appropriate to
extramarital sex. Rather, the social spaces of Athens were defined by the
activities that took place in them, whether those activities were domestic,
industrial, mercantile, or some combination of all three. In order to discuss
the role of sex in the city – the sexual topography of Athens, as it were – we
must begin with a taxonomy of different kinds of sex and the overlapping
spaces in which they might have occurred.

We have different types of evidence for sexual activity and its spaces:
literary, archaeological, and visual material all provide some indications of
what went on where. Each of these sources has its own limitations. Literary
sources, though invaluable for reconstructing imagined venues, tend to
represent ideals that are not always confirmed by the archaeological evidence.[1] The archaeological evidence is often frustratingly incomplete, to
the extent that it can be difficult to identify with any certainty a brothel as
distinct from a private house.[2] And while pottery depicts a range of sexual

---

[1] See for example, Tsakirgis in Glazebrook and Tsakirgis 2016, 21–24.
[2] See the useful collection of articles in Glazebrook and Tsakirgis 2016, especially the contributions
from Lynch, Ault, Lawall, and Glazebrook.

acts between different kinds of partners, sometimes idealized, other times deliberately parodic, it rarely gives much indication of the *space* in which those acts take place.[3] The discussion that follows examines what we know about different sexual situations, comparing and collating various kinds of source material wherever possible.

Domestic Sex

Husbands and wives engaged in sexual activity, ideally in the privacy of their own homes. A passage from Aristophanes' *Lysistrata* (916–965) gives us some details about imagined sexual activity between a husband and wife. Myrrhine, in pretending to get ready to have sex with her husband Kinesias, insists on various accoutrements: a bed, blankets, pillows, and proper perfume. Her husband, meanwhile, comically confesses to overwhelming desire for her. A line much earlier in the play (162–166) suggests that Athenian men could force their wives to have sex, but found forced sex unappealing, and the evidence suggests that mutually pleasurable sex was considered the ideal.

Several lawcourt speeches provide strong evidence that, under normal circumstances, a wife's quarters would have been secluded. In Lysias' first oration (1.9), for example, the defendant explains that his wife, whom he later caught in an act of adultery, had changed quarters with him, moving downstairs in order to be closer to their recently born child and wet nurse. The speaker clearly expects his audience to understand the normal arrangement of space, and hopes that they will not blame him for having moved his wife to a place where she would be more easily available to a predatory adulterer.[4] By way of contrast, in narrating the story of Neaira, a non-citizen sex worker, Apollodoros tells us that, at one point in her life, a man named Phrynion had purchased her services. A clear indication that Neaira was neither a citizen nor a wife was that Phrynion "had intercourse with her in public whenever he wished, anywhere at all, showing off his privilege to the onlookers" ([Demosthenes] 49.33). Wives, unlike Neaira, were supposed to keep their sexual activities rigorously private.

This emphasis on women's privacy, however idealized, stems from the role of citizen women in the Athenian state. From some time in the sixth century BC onwards, only the legitimate children of married couples had

---

[3] See especially Neils 2000; Smith in Glazebrook and Tsakirgis 2016.

[4] Tsakirgis in Glazebrook and Tsakirgis 2016, 24, points out that this picture of Euphiletos' house has been idealized for rhetorical purposes.

full rights in an *oikos* (or household), among them, the right to inherit the familial property. In 451/50, this definition of familial membership was extended to the Athenian *polis*; legislation introduced by Perikles stated that only the children of two married *astoi*, that is, Athenian citizens, had full citizenship rights.[5] Numerous legal speeches exist in which the descendants of a man (who may have had more than one sexual partner) dispute which of them is legitimate and has the right to the familial property. In Isaios 8, for example, the sons of the daughter of Kiron (who is not named, a protection of her private status as a citizen woman) argue that their father married her in public, gave a public banquet, and that after the birth of her male children he introduced them to his phratry (brotherhood). He also points out that the woman's fellow demeswomen chose her to preside at the religious festival of the Thesmophoria. All of this is adduced as evidence that the woman (a) was a legitimate daughter of Athenian citizens, (b) had been properly married to her husband, and (c) had therefore produced legitimate citizen sons – who now want to inherit. Given this careful structure of familial and political membership, the state and the family had a vested interest in limiting sexual access to citizen wives; an illegitimate child who was improperly recognized as legitimate constituted a threat to the *polis* and its households. (See also Patterson, Chapter 12 in this volume.)

And indeed, archaeological studies of fifth-century houses suggest that they were arranged so as to prevent passersby from having direct sight lines into the inner spaces that were normally the province of women.[6] A door opening to the street typically leads down a hallway to an open courtyard, off which are located several rooms, including *androns* (men's quarters and dining rooms), women's quarters, store rooms, and rooms that served as kitchens (see Map 9.1 and Harrington, Chapter 9 in this volume). As Tsakirgis points out, "since the courtyard was usually placed at the center of the house, anyone passing through it could be observed in her or his passage to another part of the house."[7] The layout of the house seems designed to provide protection from the outside world, and to allow observation of movements within.

Greek vase-painting provides further support in the form of vases that depict wedding processions or celebrations before the wedding. As Neils and Smith have shown, these paintings accentuate the door of the nuptial

---

[5] See the discussion in Patterson 1990, 61; Cox 1998, 134.
[6] Nevett 1999, 124; Tsakirgis in Glazebrook and Tsakirgis 2016, 14–19.
[7] Tsakirgis in Glazebrook and Tsakirgis 2016, 19.

bedroom, an otherwise unusual architectural feature on vases. The point of such depictions, however, is not realistic representation, but rather indication of the transition from public space to the private room behind the door.[8] Several Athenian vases show the importance of the door as a barrier: an *epinetron* (thigh cover for woolworking) from Eretria shows the bride leaning back on a couch, presumably within the *thalamos* with what appear to be double doors behind her, while looking outward to the group of friends who bring her wedding gifts, in a space that seems to be a courtyard; and a *chous* in New York depicts a young woman coming to the front door of a house while an unruly reveler threatens to break in from outside (Web Fig. 26.1).[9] The identity of the woman has been disputed: Neils has argued that a respectable citizen woman would not come to the door herself, especially at night (she carries a lamp).[10] As Smith points out, regardless of *her* status, "the door symbolizes the security of the interior/ home space that is under attack."[11]

Not all men were married, and while unmarried men could interact with sex workers in *porneia* (brothels), they could also have *pallakai* (unmarried women who engaged in long-term affairs with men) or *eromenoi* (young male lovers) live with them in their own homes. In his attempt to prove that Timarchos was a sex worker, Aischines (1.40–42) suggests that, at one point in his life, Timarchos went to live with men who supported his extravagant tastes in exchange for sex: Euthydikos, a physician who lived in the Piraeus, and a man named Misgolas who was known for his taste for singers and lyre-players. While the speaker stops short of saying exactly what Timarchos did, he does not hesitate to list the habits that would require financial support: expensive dinners, flute-girls, high-priced *hetairai*, and gambling. Timarchos had to exchange *something* for these services, the speaker says, and the implication is that he provides sexual services. And while married men would not have had *pallakai* in their own homes, Menander's comedy the *Samia* presents a father, Demeas, who has a live-in *pallake* named Chrysis; when he thinks that she has had an affair with his son, he threatens to turn her out of the house and send her to work in a *porneion*, a brothel. This is a work of fiction, but if the details of the plot are somewhat convoluted, the preliminary social setup presumably

[8] Neils 2000, 213; Smith in Glazebrook and Tsakirgis 2016, 160–164.
[9] Athens, National Archeological Museum 1629; BAPD no. 216971. New York, Metropolitan Museum of Art 37.11.19; BAPD no. 539.
[10] Neils 2000, 2011. *Contra* see Corner 2011, 65.
[11] Smith in Glazebrook and Tsakirgis 2016, 160.

presents a situation that would seem plausible in real life. In fact, the speaker in Antiphon's first oration (1.14) suggests that a man named Phileoneos intended to do the same (i.e. to send his *pallake* to a *porneion*).

The *oikos* could also be a scene for extramarital sex if a wife had an affair, an event that seems to have fueled deep paranoia on the part of Athenian men. Euphiletos, the speaker in Lysias' first oration, tells a lively narrative of gathering a group of friends on a night when he is supposed to be out of town. They sneak into Euphiletos' house to catch his wife in the act of sex with her adulterous lover: "Those going in first saw him still lying next to my wife, those behind saw him standing naked on the bed" (Lysias 1.24). In Aristophanes' *Thesmophoriazousai* (476–489), the Kinsman, disguised as a woman, tells the other women at the Thesmophoria about "her" first adulterous encounter, which takes place at night just outside the door of the house. This is a doubly fictional account: a lie told by a man pretending to be a woman, in a work of comedy – but the Kinsman's story is one that he presumes will have a ring of verisimilitude for his audience of women.

The case of Neaira ([Demosthenes] 59), perhaps the best known of ancient Greek sex workers to modern audiences, is the exception that proves the rule. If we can believe the speaker, Apollodoros, Neaira was living with Stephanos, an Athenian citizen, as if she were his legal wife. In this situation, Stephanos is said to have tried to pass off one of Neaira's daughters (Phano) as his legitimate child with another citizen woman, and to have married her as such to an Athenian citizen man (Phrastor). Phrastor, in turn, tried to introduce his son with Phano to his phratry, which would have constituted strong evidence that they (and in turn Phano, and thus Neaira) were citizens. We see, therefore, the kind of threat that a non-citizen woman could have constituted to the category of citizenship through sexual activity. In a later passage in the speech, Apollodoros alleges that Stephanos brought a suit for adultery against a man named Epainetos, whom he caught having sex with Phano. Epainetos, however, filed a countersuit on the grounds that Phano was a professional sex worker: "He cited the law, which does not allow one to arrest a man as a *moichos* who is with any women who sit in a brothel (*ergasterion*) or who sell themselves openly, and saying that the house of Stephanos was this, a brothel, and that this was their work, and that this was their primary trade" (59.67). Sex with a woman who was a prostitute, even if she turned out to be a citizen, could not be categorized as adultery, and the activity of commercial sex could implicitly define her husband's *oikia* as a "workshop" of sex, a brothel.

The *Symposion*

The *symposion*, an event in which men ate, drank, and listened to and recited music and poetry, was a particularly charged sexual event within the house. (What the houseowner's wife thought of these events is, like so much of women's lives in Athens, entirely lost to us.) It is clear from literary depictions of *symposia* as well as the evidence of vase-painting that female sex workers were often present, and that *auletrides* (flute-girls) were also sometimes available as paid sex workers. At the same time, the *symposion* is a marked site of pederastic eroticism. Hundreds of vases show men and youths reclining on couches, drinking together, and gazing with erotic intensity at each other. All of this sexual activity was marked, as Corner has argued, as extramarital.[12]

The sexual activity of *symposia* is particularly important as it relates to the idea of the *polis*. Scholarship for the last forty years has argued that *symposia* were set up as exclusive spaces in which men of homogeneous status (usually elitist) engaged in aristocratic play that was fundamentally opposed to the egalitarian leveling of the *polis*. (See Steiner, Chapter 25 in this volume.) As part of this play, the figure of the *hetaira*, a higher-class sex worker, was present, but her sexual favors were figured as gift exchange rather than commercial sales.[13] While much of this picture is undoubtedly correct, Corner has argued that there are aspects of the *symposion* that echo the sexual and social practices of the democratic *polis*. That is, while the *symposion* might have been set up to *exclude* the rabble outside, the men inside were treated to a paradoxical equality of status, marked in part by their equal access to the evening's *hetairai*. As Corner shows, Isaios (3.13, 3.15) refers to a woman who is claiming to be a legitimate wife as "a *hetaira* available to anyone who wished." The phrase "whoever wishes" is also used to invite speakers to speak at the Assembly. As Corner concludes, the *symposion* represented a unique politically hybrid space: "The liberty of extramarital sex that the *polis* afforded to men was normally to be exercised outside the household out of respect for the wife and the proper integrity of the *oikos*. The *symposion* represented a unique case of legitimately bringing that civic sexuality into the house."[14]

---

[12] Corner 2011, 65, 71.
[13] For example, see Kurke 1999, 178–199.
[14] Corner 2011, 70–71.

Sex outside the Home

As the situations discussed above demonstrate, men were not legally prevented from having sex outside of marriage. A man could not legally have sex with another man's wife or an unmarried citizen woman, but he could, without penalty, engage in sexual activities with sex workers of various kinds. We should note that the *polis* of Athens recognized sex work as a legitimate trade, and collected an annual tax on them (Aischines 1.119).[15] Still further, it has been argued that the Athenian state established state-run brothels with regulated prices, in a democratizing move: regardless of the wealth of a free Athenian citizen man, he could afford to enjoy the sexual favors of a local sex worker. A fragment of a comedy by Philemon ascribes the establishment of such brothels to the traditional lawgiver Solon; and though that in itself is not likely, Halperin argues that "what is important is not the literal truth or falsity of the story but the fact that it could be publicly told in classical Athens; even more important is the understanding of the relation between prostitution and democracy which it expresses." And as Halperin continues, "whether this was due to Solon or not, prostitution at Athens – unlike at Corinth – was proverbially cheap."[16] Indeed, we do know that legislation regulated the prices that could be paid to *auletrides*, who could be in high demand at *symposia*, and might have also sold sexual favors; when disputes arose over the hiring of a popular *auletris*, it was settled by the quintessentially democratic method of selecting lots (*Constitution of the Athenians* 50.2).[17]

Brothels could house male or female prostitutes, as the legal cases make clear. If an Athenian citizen man prostituted himself, he lost significant citizenship rights (the basis for the accusation in Aischines' *Against Timarchos*); a citizen woman similarly lost important civic and social privileges if recognized as having committed adultery or prostituted herself ([Demosthenes] 59.73, 85–87). Sex workers seem to have been distinguished on the basis of status, which no doubt corresponded to their working conditions: *pornai* were probably slaves, and worked in brothels or on the streets; *hetairai* (often translated "courtesans") were of higher status, could be daughters of citizens, and had some control over whom they sold their services to; *pallakai* engaged in longer-term relationships with men in exchange for material support. As scholars have shown,

---

[15] See the useful discussion in Glazebrook 2011, 48–49.
[16] Halperin 1990, 101; see the supporting arguments in Burnett 2012, 177.
[17] See the discussion in Glazebrook 2011, 47.

however, there is significant slippage between these terms, and any female sex worker could be called a *porne* as an insult.[18]

While visiting a sex worker in a brothel might not have had significant social consequences, it is clear that longer-term relationships with *hetairai* or *pallakai* were seen as a potential threat to individual Athenian households. Perhaps the most celebrated case is represented in Isaios 6, in which the son-in-law of a man named Euctemon sued for his wife's inheritance. Euctemon lived to the remarkable age of 96, and, at some point, it seems that he began an affair with a sex worker (*paidiska*) in the Piraeus named Alke. According to the prosecution, Euctemon then hired Alke to run his tenement house (*sunoikia*) in the Kerameikos (on which see below). We are not told explicitly that this tenement house functioned as a brothel, only that it was "near the gate, where wine is sold" (6.20), but that seems to be the implication. Over time, the speaker says, Euctemon began spending more and more time with Alke, even having meals there instead of with his family. Finally, "he was so reduced, either by drugs, or disease, or some other cause, that he was convinced by her to introduce the older of her two sons into his phratry under his own name" (6.21). The phrase about "disease, drugs, or some other cause," is a clear reference to an Athenian law that did not allow a man to dispose of his property if under the influence of disease, drugs, or the persuasion of a woman (cf. Demosthenes 46.14). We seem to have a case of a man living, in essence, in a state of bigamy: abandoning his wife and children to spend time with a woman identified as a former prostitute and set up as the manager of an apartment house that *may* have served as a brothel.

The apparent ubiquity of brothels as depicted in Athenian legal speeches has led to some recent excellent work on the locations of these businesses. It must be admitted outright that the identification of brothels (*porneia*) by the archaeological evidence is particularly tenuous.[19] To a large extent, this is due to the fact that brothels, as the passage from Aischines at the start of this chapter indicates, might have been housed in individual houses or apartment buildings, archaeologically indistinguishable from the residential houses around them. Nonetheless, several buildings have been identified as *porneia*, with varying degrees of certainty. Most scholars agree that Bau Z in the Kerameikos was a brothel (cf. Web Map 9.1), at least in its

---

[18] See Goldhill 2015, 185–186, with bibliography, for a useful discussion.

[19] See the excellent discussions of Glazebrook, Lynch, Lawall, and Ault in Glazebrook and Tsakirgis 2016.

third phase, in the late fourth century.[20] The particularly striking feature of the third phase is the addition of several small rooms south of the central courtyard, and an added entrance from the street at the southeast corner. These two features, in addition to the building's large size, relatively high assemblage of drinking and eating pottery, and finds of 163 low-denomination coins, suggest its use as a *porneion*. Ault argues that we should see the building serving the same purposes in its earlier two phases, partly on the grounds of likely continuity of function, and partly on the evidence for "robust feminine presence" in the form of finds associated with textile production.[21]

Two other buildings seem possibly to have been *porneia*: Bau Y, immediately southeast of Bau Z in the Kerameikos is a relatively wealthy building with two *andrones* opening onto a central peristyle courtyard. It has multiple cisterns and drains, which suggest capacity higher than needed for residential use, and, in one of the *andrones*, the graffito *Boubalion kale* ("Boubalion is beautiful") was found.[22] Another large building with a central courtyard and bathing facilities, near the Olympic equestrian center in the ancient deme of Myrrhinous, is "just off the main road leading to the port."[23] The building has been linked to prostitution (and possibly to celebration of Aphrodite) primarily because of a stone slab inscribed with the name NANNION, which was built into the second phase of the building; Nannion is the name of a famous fourth-century *hetaira*.

As has often been pointed out, none of these buildings seems to have served a single purpose, and in some cases "brothels" might be better identified as "taverns" where sex could also be purchased. But the buildings are not always associated with entertainment. In our most securely identified sex worker shop in the Kerameikos (Bau Z3), excavators found a large number of loom weights and other materials necessary for wool working. The strong suggestion is that this building served at least two commercial purposes, with sex work going hand in hand with textile production.[24] There is a distinct tendency in modern scholarship to assume that sex work was the identifying function of such buildings, and that the sex workers were engaged in textile production in their off hours; but there is no

---

[20] See Davidson 1998, 86–90; Glazebrook 2011, 39–43; Ault in Glazebrook and Tsakirgis 2016, with references to the excavation publication of Knigge 2005.

[21] Ault in Glazebrook and Tsakirgis 2016, 91. See also Harrington, Chapter 9 in this volume.

[22] Glazebrook 2011, 39–41; Ault in Glazebrook and Tsakirgis 2016, 93.

[23] Glazebrook 2011, 45.

[24] Ault in Glazebrook and Tsakirgis 2016, 85, 91; Glazebrook in Glazebrook and Tsakirgis 2016, 170.

compelling reason to assume that sex work was considered the primary industry.

Perhaps even more important is the suggestion that there were no areas of Athens particularly zoned (even informally) as red-light districts.[25] The fact that *porneia* might look more or less like private homes means that it is almost impossible to know exactly where they were located. Isaios 6 tells us that Alke worked as a sex worker in the Piraeus, and that Euctemon set her up in his apartment building in the Kerameikos. But we know from both archaeological and literary evidence that workshops of various sorts existed in residential neighborhoods; the workshop of Simon the cobbler, quite near a boundary stone marking the limits of the Agora, is a case in point. In his accusation against Timarchos (1.74), Aischines suggests that the listeners to his speech can see a group of men "sitting in the *oikemata*, engaging in this practice by their own admission." The passage suggests that they are physically visible from the Agora where, presumably, he was speaking.[26] In brief, we must assume that buildings that housed groups of sex workers could have been present anywhere in Athens. It is not surprising to hear that they are in Piraeus or by the Kerameikos. Sex work depends on traffic, and ports and city gates typically see both; the Kerameikos neighborhood sits just inside the city walls, by the Dipylon and Sacred Gates (see Maps 4.1 and 4.2).

Pottery also provides evidence of prostitution, but rarely gives us much detail about place or even practice. Kilmer points out that it is often difficult to distinguish prostitutes from respectable wives on pottery; in general, the presence of a man carrying a gift or a sack (presumed to contain money) is taken as an indication that the woman he is approaching is a sex worker.[27] One particularly interesting vase shows a scene that has been interpreted as two men approaching a sex worker: a woman sits in an interior space, clothed and holding a mirror (Fig. 26.1).[28] A young cloaked boy stands in front of her, and outside the portico are two men – one a bearded adult holding a money sack and a walking stick, the other unbearded and fully wrapped in a cloak. The relationship between the two potential "clients" cannot be determined, but the reading of the vase as a visit to a relatively upscale *porneion* or *oikema* seems secure.[29] Even here,

---

[25] Glazebrook in Glazebrook and Tsakirgis 2016, 170–175, 180–181.

[26] Glazebrook 2011, 41.

[27] See Kilmer 1993, 159–169.

[28] Tampa, Museum of Art 1986.070; BAPD no. 202666. See discussion by Neils 2000, 211–212.

[29] See Glazebrook 2011, 55 n. 9, for a list of vases showing likely brothel scenes.

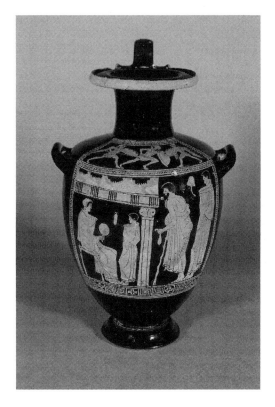

Fig. 26.1 Brothel scene, Attic red-figure *hydria*, attributed to the Harlow Painter,
ca. 470 BC, Tampa Museum of Art 1986.070.
Courtesy of the Tampa Museum of Art, Joseph Veach Noble Collection, Museum Purchase
in part with funds donated by Mr. and Mrs. James L. Ferman, Jr.

however, there are few architectural or social details; the primary distinction of space seems to be between the interior, where the presumed *hetaira*
sits, and the exterior street, signaled in part by the older man's walking
stick.

Adult men, married or single, might also have pursued romantic and
sexual relationships with younger men; the age of desirability was terminated by the appearance of secondary sex characteristics, particularly rough
facial hair or hair on the thighs. Though it has sometimes been argued that
such pederastic relationships were an affectation of the elite, the presence of
male prostitutes as well as references to such relations as common to all in
legal speeches makes this view untenable (e.g. Lysias 3.4). Since young men,
in contrast to unmarried women, were not expected to live lives of idealized
privacy, access to them would have been less severely restricted.

Aristophanes' *Clouds* (973–974) suggests that *gymnasia* were favorite cruising grounds for older men, and this is confirmed by the fact that Athenian laws required that *gymnasia* not open before sunrise or remain open after dark (Aischines 1.10). Of the more than 600 vases that show pederastic courtship scenes (very few show sex acts), many have strigils or other athletic instruments hanging from the imaginary "wall" behind the figures.[30]

Pederastic assignations could take place almost anywhere, however, and many of the vases showing pederastic affairs seem to be located either at *symposia* or in the street. Were certain areas of Athens particularly known as pederastic cruising grounds? Aischines' speech *Against Timarchos* provides unusually helpful evidence. At several points in the speech, Aischines (1.80) reminds the audience that when Timarchos had been on the *boule* (347/6 BC), whenever he mentioned the need to repair walls or a tower, "immediately you shouted and laughed, and you yourselves said the name of the deeds which you knew belonged to him." A little later in the speech, Aischines quotes a man named Autolykos who had spoken against a proposal by Timarchos to repair some buildings near the Pnyx. Autolykos, Aischines tells the jury, suggested that Timarchos was more familiar with the "deserted spots on the Pnyx" than the council of the Areopagos was. All of these references are evidence for well-known spots for sexual encounters. Walls and towers suggest areas at the outskirts (not unlike the Kerameikos); and the "deserted spots" on the hill of the Pnyx probably provided areas of privacy and cover.[31] Timarchos' notoriety extended to the idea that he frequented such places.

Conclusion

The sexual topography of Athens was varied, and differed according to the type of sex that was undertaken, and the relationship of that sex to the political entity that was Athens. Of paramount importance for the state was legitimate sex between married partners, normally conceived of as taking place in the protected space of the *oikos*. Only those sex acts could result in the generation of future citizens in mid-fifth-century Athens. But Athenian

---

[30] For images see Lear and Cantarella 2008, e.g. figs. 1.7A and 1.7B.
[31] Kamen 2018, 50–52.

men were not limited to marital sex, and relations with citizen young men, professional sex workers, or slaves of either sex were possible. The spaces in which such activities took place depended on several factors: availability to traffic, ready access to sex workers or pederastic partners, and the ability to provide a modicum of privacy.

Further Reading

The bibliography on ancient Greek sexual behavior is vast. Halperin et al. 1990 provides the standard constructionist view. Robson 2013 gives a readable and insightful overview, along with Ormand 2018, which also considers Roman sexual practices. The collections of Masterson, Rabinowitz, and Robson 2015 and Hubbard 2013 include excellent essays on a wide range of topics. The best recent work on the archaeological remains for Athenian sex work is the collection of Glazebrook and Tsakirgis 2016 (with references to earlier work). For perceptive essays on vases and sculpture, see the collection of Cohen 2000. Kilmer 1993 is the standard work on Attic red-figure erotica.

Bibliography

Burnett, A. 2012. "Brothels, Boys, and the Athenian Adonia." *Arethusa* 45: 177–194.

Cohen, B., ed. 2000. *Not the Classical Ideal: Athens and the Construction of the Other in Greek Art*. Leiden.

Cox, C.A. 1998. *Household Interests: Property, Marriage Strategies, and Family Dynamics in Ancient Athens*. Princeton.

Corner, S. 2011. "Bringing the Outside In: The Andron as Brothel and the Symposium's Civic Sexuality." In *Greek Prostitutes in the Ancient Mediterranean, 800 BCE–200 CE*, eds. A. Glazebrook and M. Henry, Madison, 60–85.

Davidson, J.N. 1998. *Courtesans and Fishcakes: The Consuming Passions of Classical Athens*. New York.

Glazebrook, A. 2011. "*Porneion*: Prostitution in Athenian Civic Space." In *Greek Prostitutes in the Ancient Mediterranean, 800 BCE–200 CE*, eds. A. Glazebrook and M. Henry, Madison, 34–59.

Glazebrook, A., and B. Tsakirgis, eds. 2016. *Houses of Ill Repute: The Archaeology of Brothels, Houses, and Taverns in the Greek World*. Philadelphia.

Goldhill, S. 2015. "Is There a History of Prostitution?" In *Sex in Antiquity*, eds. M. Masterson et al., London, 179–197.

Halperin, D.M., et al., eds. 1990. *Before Sexuality: The Construction of Erotic Experience in the Ancient Greek World*. Princeton.

Hubbard, T., ed. 2013. *A Companion to Greek and Roman Sexualities*. Malden, MA.

Kamen, D. 2018. "The Consequences of Laughter in in Aeschines' *Against Timarchos*." *Archimede* 5: 49–56.

Kilmer, M. 1993. *Greek Erotica on Attic Red-Figure Vases*. London.

Knigge, U. 2005. *Der Bau Z. Kerameikos* 17. Munich.

Kurke, L. 1999. *Coins, Bodies, Games, and Gold: The Politics of Meaning in Archaic Greece*. Princeton.

Lear, A., and E. Cantarella. 2008. *Images of Ancient Greek Pederasty*. New York.

Masterson, M., N.S. Rabinowitz, and J. Robson, eds. 2015. *Sex in Antiquity*. London.

Neils, J. 2000. "Others within the Other: An Intimate Look at Hetairai and Maenads." In *Not the Classical Ideal: Athens and the Construction of the Other in Greek Art*, ed. B. Cohen. Leiden, 203–226.

Nevett, L.C. 1999. *House and Society in the Ancient Greek World*. Cambridge.

Ormand, K. 2018. *Controlling Desires: Sexuality in Ancient Greece and Rome*. Revised edn. Austin.

Patterson, C. 1990. "Those Athenian Bastards." *Classical Antiquity* 9: 40–73.

Robson, J. 2013. *Sex and Sexuality in Classical Athens*. Edinburgh.

Additional resources to accompany this chapter can be found at: www.cambridge .org/NeilsRogers

PART V

Politics

27 | Associations

JAMES KIERSTEAD

The first problem confronting anyone approaching the topic of ancient associations is one of definition. What are we talking about when we speak of associations? The short answer is "groups of people who came together for some purpose, but which were neither families nor central state institutions" – religious societies, kinship groups, and that sort of thing. This is vague, but anything more specific than that quickly gets us into trouble. Take, for example, the definition offered by Tod in his entry on "Clubs, Greek" for the *Oxford Classical Dictionary* ('clubs' being a term previous generations of scholars sometimes used for what we now call 'associations'):

> The clubs here discussed may be defined as voluntary associations of persons more or less permanently organized for the pursuit of a common end, and so distinguishable both from the State and its component elements on the one hand, and on the other from temporary unions for transitory purposes.

Even in this short definition, there are a couple of things that would immediately rule out some of the groups that turn up in our evidence, and that have been discussed by modern scholars under the heading 'associations.' Was the group that put up an inscription (*IG* II^3 4.635) identifying itself only as 'the washers' or 'fullers' more or less permanently organized? We have no way of knowing – that inscription is the only evidence that remains of them.

Were all of Athens' associations 'distinguishable from the State'? That depends what one means by 'the State'; but it does seem that many of them were linked to the state in a way which makes discussion of them in terms of 'civil society' anachronistic (and this is an issue that also affects the distinction that some scholars have made between 'public' and 'private' associations). Even 'voluntary' might be problematic, since it may be that membership of some of these groups was expected of all citizens.

The Greek word that most closely corresponds to the way modern scholars use the term 'associations' is *koinonia*, which can refer to association in an abstract sense as well as to groups of people, and thus has some of the same semantic range of the English word. It is also used by Aristotle to discuss a set of groups that has considerable overlap with what we now speak of as 'Athenian associations' (*Eudemian Ethics* 7.9.3; *Nicomachean Ethics* 8.9.4–6): he mentions phratries, *orgeones*, tribes, demes, *thiasoi*, and *eranoi* (all staples of the modern literature on associations), as well as business partnerships and groups of sailors and soldiers (less well-defined groups, which also show up less in our evidence). Aristotle also tells us that these groups all "aim at some advantage" (*Nicomachean Ethics* 8.9.4), and, as we have seen, that they existed for some purpose is one of the only things that seems to unite all of the groups that are now discussed as 'associations.' So what kinds or purposes did they have, and what kinds of associations were there?

Athenian Associations: A Quick Guide

The aim of this section is to provide a brief overview of the different types of associations that were active in ancient Athens, from Archaic through to Hellenistic times. (A narrative of how things changed over that time is provided in the following section.) Though we have seen that no firm line can be drawn between 'private' and 'public' associations, it is nonetheless clear that some groups were more closely bound up with the state than others. Some groups even formed an integral part of the constitutional machinery, and have been analyzed as 'civic subdivisions' that were part of 'public organization.'[1] At the same time, though, these were also groups of people, and so they can and have also been viewed as 'associations.' We will start with groups of this sort; as we go on, the associations surveyed will get less public and more focused on kinship, religion, and other things. It is worth bearing in mind, however, that even the most official civic subdivisions also engaged in religious activities.

Demes

The 139 demes formed the basic administrative divisions of the Classical Athenian state (see Map 2.1). They were small settlements (with an average citizen population of around 300) that we would call 'villages' (in the countryside) or 'boroughs' (in the urban core). The constitutional role of

---

[1] Jones 1987.

the demes is described elsewhere in this volume (see Fachard, Chapter 2); but the demes also had personalities as communities. They had their own assemblies, and elected leaders called demarchs. Some had their own theaters, and put on plays as part of the dramatic festival known as the Rural Dionysia.[2] Demes played an active role in local religious life, sometimes in concert with other demes in cultic associations that had roots in Archaic times (see on Regional Associations below). Some of Athens' most important temples and sanctuaries were situated in demes – the Temple of Poseidon at Sounion and the Sanctuary of Demeter and Kore at Eleusis are only two examples.

Tribes

From Archaic times, Athens had the four tribes that were traditional for Ionian city-states, but it was the ten new *phylai* introduced by Kleisthenes around 508/7 that played a major role in the Classical *polis*. Like the demes, the tribes had an institutional role; and, like the demes, they can also be viewed as associations. There were shrines to the eponymous heroes of the various tribes, and this is where the tribal meetings that we hear of may have taken place.[3] Tribesmen could also meet at the monument to the ten eponymous heroes in the Agora (Web Fig. 27.1), where notices with tribe-specific information were posted. This might include military summons, since the tribes also formed divisions of the Athenian army, cavalry and navy.

Phratries

The phratries were mainly concerned with kinship, though this aspect of them was tightly bound up with their religious activities. Phratry members (*phrateres*) came together at a festival called the Apatouria, which involved sacrifices to Zeus Phratrios and Athena Phatria (Zeus and Athena of the phratries), among other activities. Citizens introduced their sons to their fellow *phrateres* at two ceremonies, the Meion and the Koureion (which probably took place in childhood and in adolescence, respectively); newly married members introduced their wives at the Gamelia.[4] The knowledge that phratries built up of lines of descent may have equipped them to play a

[2] Paga 2010.
[3] Jones 1999, 156–169.
[4] Lambert 1993, 141–190.

role in certifying young men for citizenship, and it may be that all Athenian citizens were expected to be members of phratries. We only know the names of nine or ten certain phratries, though there were probably more; this uncertainty has made any estimation of an average number of members impossible.

Gene

The *gene* were religious groups, although members also tended to claim common descent from a distant ancestor. Scholars used to see *gene* as closed, aristocratic clans, but in recent decades the tide has turned against this view.[5] Though some *gene* had a certain social prestige, others lacked it entirely, and alongside high-born members of *gene* (the fourth-century statesman Lycurgus, say), we also come across perfectly ordinary Athenians who were members of a *genos* (Phrastor of the Brytidai, who turns up at Demosthenes 59.49–63, is probably the best example). The main role that *gene* played in Classical Athens was to select priests for public cults, which they normally did by allotment.[6] At least a few *gene* must have existed in Archaic times, with the Kerykes even showing up in a fragment of Solon (fr. 88 Ruschenbusch). In Late Hellenistic times, the *gene* found a new life, and this time they *were* narrowly aristocratic clubs,[7] something that may have misled earlier generations of scholars about the true nature of their Classical antecedents. As with phratries, precise numbers for *gene* are difficult to come by, though one authoritative catalogue lists forty-seven "certain and probable" *gene* and thirty-three "uncertain and spurious" ones.[8]

Thiasoi

Thiasos was a word used of a variety of groups, mostly religious in nature. These range from formal organizations with officers to apparently more spontaneous bands of worshippers. The word could be used of groups that also went by the name of *orgeones*, and, on one or two occasions, may have been used of sub-groups of phratries.[9]

---

[5] Especially in the wake of Roussel 1976 and Bourriot 1976.
[6] Blok and Lambert 2009.
[7] Ismard 2010, 365–404.
[8] Parker 1996, 284–327.
[9] Lambert 1993, 81–93.

Orgeones

This is another more or less general word for groups that tended to be religious; an Alexandrian commentator (Harpokration, s.v. *orgeonas*) defines *orgeones* simply as "people who came together in honor of gods or heroes." Ferguson's distinction between citizen *orgeones*, which tended to be based in the urban center of Athens and to cultivate local heroes, and non-citizen *orgeones*, which worshiped foreign deities and clustered in the Piraeus, has remained influential, even if scholars have taken issue with it in various ways.[10]

Eranoi

Eranistai are mentioned by Aristotle in the discussion of *koinonia* that was quoted at the beginning of this chapter. He says there that they come together "for the sake of pleasure," but he also pairs them with *thiasoi*, which suggests a religious function, and the first appearance of the word in an inscription comes on a dedication to Zeus Philios (*IG* II² 2935). We may suspect then, that *eranoi*, like *orgeones* and *thiasoi*, provided an opportunity for fellowship and feasting in a religious context. The word *eranos*, though, could also mean a loan, and there is some evidence for groups of moneylenders banding together in so-called credit associations.[11] After the start of the Hellenistic period, the evidence for this sort of financial association dries up, and the presence of cultic associations with members calling themselves *eranistai* increases.

Regional Associations

These were associations of several demes for religious purposes – usually three or four demes, as names such as the Tetrapolis of Marathon, or the Tetrakomia of Phaleron, would indicate. These names might suggest that these organizations pre-dated the consolidation of an Athenian *polis* with villages known as demes – if they did not, it would be surprising to find local associations with names ending with *-polis* or *-komia* (from *kome*, a more traditional word for a village). Moreover, many of the regional associations consist of demes that were in different parts of the Kleisthenic system, suggesting that any links between them must have

---

[10] Ferguson 1944; Jones 1999, 249–267.
[11] Jones 1999, 308.

preceded it. In Classical times, these associations selected officers, ran festivals, and were associated with sanctuaries (for example, the League of Athena Pallenis and the sanctuary of the same name).[12]

Hetaireiai

Hetaireiai or *hetairiai*, often referred to as 'political clubs' by modern scholars, were small groups of male aristocrats of around the same age who met at each other's houses, usually for well-lubricated dinner parties. The names of some of the clubs, such as the Ithyphalloi (the Stiff Pricks) or Kakodaimonistai (the Evil Spirits, compare with today's Hell's Angels) suggest a certain rebelliousness vis-à-vis contemporary social norms (with the form of these names echoing – and sending up – the names of more conventional religious organizations).[13] The combination of an aristocratic and usually youthful membership with a contrarian spirit makes it unsurprising, in the context of democratic Athens, that these groups seem to have been generally hostile to the democratic state.[14] They are usually identified with the *synomosiai* that Thucydides (8.54.4) associated with the oligarchic takeover of 411, and that apparently swore oaths to be "ill-disposed towards the people" (Aristotle, *Politics* 5.7.19); by the second half of the fourth century, there was a law against anyone who sought to undermine the democracy or formed a *hetairikon* (Hyperides 4.8).

Philosophical Schools

The roots of the formal entities that we now know as 'philosophical schools' can be seen in the less formal sophistic movement of the fifth century. The schools per se were all founded in the fourth century or later, whether we are talking about schools like those of Antisthenes or Isocrates, which did not survive their founders' passing, or schools like Plato's Academy or Aristotle's Lyceum, which very much did. (See Bakewell, Chapter 21 in this volume.) Despite their reputation as standing somewhat apart from Athenian society (true of their physical location near the city walls), both of these last two schools were open to anyone who could pay for their own upkeep while attending them: we know of commoners, foreigners, and freedmen who studied there and we even hear of female

---

[12] Jones 1999, 234–242; Ismard 2010, 211–223.
[13] Jones 1999, 223–227.
[14] Calhoun 1913.

students at the Academy. The schools were headed by scholarchs, who were likely elected by school members.[15]

Other Groups

A few other associations have left some trace; for example, the *synodos*, first attested on an inscription from sometime after 229 BC (*IG II*^{2} 1322), and a kind of religious grouping that gradually supplants *thiasoi* and *orgeones* in the record. A number of groupings have left little in the way of epigraphic evidence; Aristotle, for example, references business partnerships as well as groups of sailors and soldiers. Mention is also made of messes (*syssitoi*), burial societies (in which members took care of other members' funerals), and groups of men who associated with the aim of 'plunder or trade.' This appears in a document known as *Solon's Law on Associations*, which brings us to the end of the list of groups that we can usefully say something about, as well as to the beginning of most chronologies of Athenian associations.

Athenian Associations through Time

Solon's *Law on Associations* is preserved in the sixth-century AD *Digest* (47.22.4), but most scholars accept it as a genuine piece of legislation from the early sixth century BC.[16] It states that internal decisions made by associations shall have force, so long as they do not conflict with the laws of the *polis*. This is a fairly peaceful beginning to the relationship between associations and the Athenian state, a relationship that would go through a number of different permutations in subsequent centuries. Solon's *Law* (if authentic) is good evidence for the existence of a range of associations even in Archaic times, since it mentions phratries, *orgeones*, and *thiasoi*, as well as (as we have seen) messes, burial societies, and groups of traders and plunderers. It is likely that many of the regional associations, and at least some *gene*, also existed before the time of Kleisthenes' reforms.

Kleisthenes' reforms, by adding a series of brand-new civic subdivisions such as the newly established demes and tribes, obviously played a major role in reshaping Athens' network of associations. But it is worth noting that Kleisthenes does not seem to have wiped the slate clean of previously existing groups. Rather, existing communities were repurposed (with

---

[15] Lynch 1972; Jones 1999, 227–234; Ismard 2010, 186–208.
[16] For example, see: Jones 1999, 34; Ismard 2010, 44–57.

preexisting villages fitted into the new system of demes), hooked up to the new machinery (with phratries probably now serving as antechambers to demes), or simply allowed to carry on in a kind of comfortable retirement, in the shadow of the new groups which replaced them (as with the old Ionian tribes, which seem to have continued to perform some religious functions).[17]

Perikles' Citizenship Law of 451 represents the first possible instance of the state moving into territory that had previously been monopolized by associations. By clearly defining the criteria for citizenship (two native-born Athenian parents), the *polis* restricted the previously unchallenged right of associations to incorporate new citizens as they saw fit (*Constitution of the Athenians* 26.4).[18] This was followed a few decades later by a transfer of financial power away from peripheral associations and towards a central institution. The central institution in this case was the Treasury of the Other Gods on the Akropolis, probably established around 434/3 BC, which consolidated a range of smaller treasuries overseen by peripheral religious groups into a single treasury in the heart of the city.[19]

An ancient legal institution was also centralized, sometime around the overthrow of the regime of the Thirty (404/3 BC). This was the 'jurors in the demes,' a body of thirty (then forty) men (three or four from each tribe) who, in the fifth century (and possibly even in the sixth: *Constitution of the Athenians* 16.5, 26.3) would travel around the demes making legal judgments. By the fourth century, they were based permanently in the urban center, with demesmen forced to come to them; and they were limited to cases involving less than 10 drachmas (53.2).[20]

Procedures for introducing new citizens were further centralized in 384, with grants of honorary citizenship having to be confirmed in a second Assembly meeting after the new citizens had been enrolled in a deme, tribe, and phratry; this made the associations' choice of who to include in their ranks formally subordinate to the will of the Assembly.[21]

There is also some evidence for centralization in the selection of magistrates and in taxation.[22] Magistrates were selected by lot, not in the demes but in the centrally based tribes, from around 388 BC on (*Constitution of the Athenians* 62.1), and the *eisphora*, a levy for the

[17] Ismard 2010, 84–121.
[18] Ismard 2010, 124.
[19] Samons 2000, 50–54.
[20] See also Sealey 1987, 58.
[21] Osborne 1981, 4.162–163, with Ismard 2010, 132.
[22] Whitehead 1986, 132.

military, was collected by central corporations called symmories rather than by demarchs from 378 on. Around 334, the set of phratries into which honorary citizens could be introduced was restricted, further tying these associations' hands. And in 330, demes and phratries were banned from awarding their own crowns (a mark of honor) at the City Dionysia, Athens' main dramatic festival (Aischines, *Against Ctesiphon* 3.41–45).

That, at least, is one possible narrative of the changing relationship between associations and the democratic state through the Classical period (though not one that everyone would accept).[23] By the Hellenistic period, the associations which had been such a feature of democratic Athens were beginning to dry up – or, at least, the evidence for them was. Inscriptions produced by demes peak in the late fourth century but collapse in the third, so much so that by the beginning of the second century they have disappeared completely. *Thiasoi* turn up in inscriptions from the mid-fifth century on, but have vanished by the end of the third. And *orgeones* are attested from the fourth century on, but by the mid-second century are nowhere to be seen.[24]

It is at this point in the second century that we see the reemergence of the *gene* – now no longer in the form they took during the democracy, but as aristocratic clubs dominated by a few families, who were often able to keep the priesthoods on offer within their own lines of descent.[25] An association that had once had a democratic character during the democracy now had an aristocratic one during the ascendancy of the aristocratic republic of Rome. This is only one of the considerations that has prompted scholars to ask what impact Athens' associations and its democracy might have had on one another.

Associations and Democracy

We can start with the simple observation that many of the groups above were democratic structures of a small-scale and localized sort – the *gene* chose priests by allotment, as we have seen; and the demes had their own assemblies and elected leaders. It is also worth recalling that demes and tribes formed an integral part of the democracy's constitutional machinery.

---

[23] See also Jones 1999, esp. 40–45; Ismard 2010, 122–145. Lambert, *per litteras*, is unconvinced.
[24] Kierstead 2013, 237–251.
[25] Ismard 2010, 365–404.

But where does this leave the other associations? Was there some relationship between the set of associations as a whole and the democracy?

Nicholas Jones believes that Athens' associations represented a 'response to democracy,' by acting as sites of social inclusion for people who were excluded from Athens' formal political institutions (i.e. women, slaves, and foreigners). Jones argues, for example, that, alongside the "constitutional deme" that was restricted to male citizens, we can speak of a "territorial deme" that also included non-citizens resident in the area.[26] In the years since Jones' work, there have been frequent attempts to find evidence for interaction between citizens and non-citizens in Athenian associations. That there was some sort of interaction is beyond doubt; and yet solid evidence of citizens and non-citizens both having regular membership in the same associations in the Classical period has proven more elusive.[27] Although there are one or two possible examples of interaction before 323 BC, most of the evidence for non-citizens in Athenian citizen associations comes from afterwards. Why this is the case is unclear, but there are essentially two possibilities: either mixed associations of citizens and non-citizens existed before the Hellenistic period, but the evidence (for whatever reason) fails to reflect that; or citizen associations only started to include non-citizens in the Hellenistic period.

If we go with the first option, we then need to have some sort of account of how it came about that evidence for mixed associations is largely absent from the Classical evidence. Several suggestions have been made: that this simply reflects the fact that most of our inscriptions come from the end of the Classical period; that associations made efforts around that time to publicize their inclusive credentials to stay on the right side of the democratic state; or that they felt able to be open about their activities only after the reversal of a legislative program to bring them under stricter control by the state. If we instead embrace the second option, a natural question is why these groups only started to include non-citizens from the Hellenistic period on. Here, again, a number of theories have been advanced: that centuries of democracy eventually made Athenian society more inclusive; that, as traditional descent-based associations withered away, new, more cosmopolitan groups associated with foreign gods emerged to take their place; or that, with the decline of Athens' democracy, citizens had less and less motivation to keep non-citizens out of associations that were traditionally linked to Athenian citizenship.

[26] Jones 1999, esp. 51–150.
[27] For this and the next few paragraphs, see Kierstead forthcoming, with the literature cited there.

That certain associations were linked to Athenian citizenship in the Classical period can itself be seen as part of the relationship between these groups and the democracy. After all, only citizens were allowed to take part in the city's formal political institutions, and it is clear that the key vote on a young man's citizen status was taken by the demes (*Constitution of the Athenians* 42.1–2). Moreover, it would appear that confirmation by a phratry could pave the way to registration in a deme; and even that involvement in a *genos*, *orgeon*, or *thiasos* might smooth one's adoption into a phratry. If this model is correct, an obvious question is why there were three gateways to citizenship where one would have sufficed. One possible answer is so that citizens could be certified as belonging to the Athenian community in three different ways: in terms of cult (shown by activity within a *genos*, *orgeon*, or *thiasos*), of descent (certified by affiliation with a phratry), and in terms of the political community of adult male citizens (confirmed by the deme).[28] (See also Kellogg, Chapter 11 in this volume.)

In this account, the associations' certification of new citizens as sound in these different respects would have sent a powerful signal to other citizens that they could be trusted. That associations built up trust between citizens in other ways – for example, simply by bringing Athenians together in various sorts of regular cooperation – has been a feature of more than one account of the relationship between associations and democracy in Athens. Johnstone has offered a slightly different version of this theory, in suggesting that associations and other institutions allowed Athenians to act *as if* they trusted one another (i.e. they facilitated interaction even in the absence of trust).[29]

A different, but complementary, approach has been to stress associations' power to build up personal networks, networks which helped information to spread within the *polis*, to construct a kind of public space, and even to disperse power in a way that helped the city do without a strongly coercive state apparatus. An Athenian citizen, by virtue of his belonging in a range of groups, was not simply a subject of the Athenian state, but a member of religious traditions, of a family lineage, of a local community, and more besides; and, perhaps partly by virtue of these associations, he was also a participant in a democratic *polis*.[30]

[28] Kierstead 2018.
[29] Johnstone 2011, especially 3.
[30] Ismard 2010, especially 411.

The fly in the ointment for anyone who sees the associations as having helped sustain the democracy are the *heteireiai* and *synomosiai* that are associated with the oligarchic coup of 411 BC. These, however, seem to have been relatively small in number, at least compared with the many more democratic associations we have evidence for from throughout the Classical period. That many of these associations – the *gene* above all – changed their nature from Archaic to Hellenistic times, apparently in some sort of relationship with the form of government in the city as a whole, may well then be a mark of how tightly, and enduringly, these groups were bound up with the history of the Athenian *polis*.

Further Reading

A few overviews of Athens' associations and their role in the *polis* have appeared relatively recently. Jones 1999 (a seminal work) marshals the evidence in support of a number of interesting and original hypotheses, though not all of these have found ready acceptance. Ismard 2010 is a magisterial overview of the evidence within a stimulating, if sometimes somewhat complex, theoretical framework. Johnstone 2011 is an idiosyncratic, independent-minded, and highly original discussion of a range of Athenian groups and institutions. Kierstead 2013 investigates the role that associations might have played in building up trust, dispersing authority, and hence in sustaining the democracy.

For individual associations, there is still much to be learned from the standard works, even if some appear dated. These are Whitehead 1986 on demes, Lambert 1993 on phratries, Bourriot 1976 on *gene*, Ferguson 1944 on *orgeones* (still influential), and Calhoun 1913 on *hetaireiai* (still valuable, especially for these groups' political activities). Roussel 1976 (along with Bourriot 1976) played a key role in overturning an older view of associations as holdovers from an atavistic past, presenting them instead as part and parcel of the developing *polis*. The debate over Athens' associations, their nature, and their relationship with the democracy continues unabated. Scholars currently active in this field include Stephen Lambert, Josine Blok, Claire Taylor, Alex Gottesman, Sara Wijma, Ilias Arnaoutoglou, Nikolaos Papazarkadas, Vincent Gabrielsen, and several others.

Bibliography

Blok, J., and Lambert, S. 2009. "The Appointment of Priests in Attic *Gene*." *ZPE* 169: 95–121.

Bourriot, F. 1976. *Recherches sur la nature du génos. Étude d'histoire sociale athénienne. Périodes archaïque et classique*. Lille.

Calhoun, G.M. 1913. *Athenian Clubs in Politics and Litigation*. Austin.

Ferguson, W.S. 1944. "The Attic Orgeones." *Harvard Theological Review* 37: 61–140.

Ismard, P. 2010. *La cité des réseaux: Athènes et ses associations, VIe–I^e siècle av. J.-C.* Paris.

Johnstone, S. 2011. *A History of Trust in Ancient Greece.* Chicago.

Jones, N.F. 1987. *Public Organization in Ancient Greece: A Documentary Study.* Philadelphia.

   1999. *The Associations of Classical Athens: The Response of Democracy.* Oxford.

Kierstead, J.C. 2013. "A Community of Communities: Associations and Democracy in Classical Athens." PhD dissertation, Stanford University.

   2018. "Incentives and Information in Athenian Citizenship Procedures." *Historia* 68: 26–49.

   Forthcoming. "Non-Citizens in Athenian Associations." In *New Approaches to Greek Institutional History*, ed. M. Canevaro, Edinburgh.

Lambert, S.D. 1993. *The Phratries of Attica.* Ann Arbor.

Lynch, J.P. 1972. *Aristotle's School: A Study of a Greek Educational Institution.* Berkeley.

Osborne, M.J. 1981. *Naturalization in Athens.* Brussels.

Paga, J. 2010. "Mapping Politics: An Investigation of Deme Theatres in the Fifth and Fourth Centuries BCE." *Hesperia* 79: 351–384.

Parker, R. 1996. *Athenian Religion: A History.* Oxford.

Roussel, D. 1976. *Tribu et cité. Étude sur les groupes sociaux dans les cités grecques aux époques archaïque et classique.* Paris.

Samons, L.J. 2000. *Empire of the Owl: Athenian Imperial Finance.* Stuttgart.

Sealey, R. 1987. *The Athenian Republic: Democracy or the Rule of Law?* Berkeley.

Whitehead, D. 1986. *The Demes of Attika, 508/7–ca. 250 BC: A Political and Social Study.* Princeton.

Additional resources to accompany this chapter can be found at: www.cambridge.org/NeilsRogers

28 | Rule of Law and Lawcourts

EDWARD M. HARRIS

> For men to be happy they must be ruled by the voice of law, not the
> threats of a man; free men must not be frightened by accusation, only
> by proof of guilt; and the safety of our citizens must not depend on
> men who flatter their master and slander our citizens but on our
> confidence in the law.
>
> Hyperides, Epitaphios 25

The Athenians of the Classical period strongly believed in the rule of law.
According to Thucydides (2.37), Perikles in his Funeral Oration praised his
fellow citizens for obeying those in office and the laws, especially those
established to help victims of injustice. When the young men of Athens
became ephebes at age 18, they swore to follow the established laws, the
magistrates who give prudent orders, and any laws that might be established prudently in the future. The Athenians did not find the rule of law in
conflict with democracy: Aischines (3.6) says that as long as the Athenians
obey the laws, democracy remains safe. On the other hand, when the courts
allow themselves to be distracted by irrelevant charges, the laws are
ignored, and democracy is destroyed.

Equality, Accountability, and Accessibility

The Athenians' conception of the rule of law shared many features in
common with the modern concept. First, they believed in the principle of
equality before the law. In fact, there was a provision enacted in 403/2 BC
that stated, "It is not permitted to enact a law directed at an individual
unless that same law applies to all Athenians" (Andokides 1.87). In
Euripides' play *The Suppliant Women* (433–434, 437), Theseus, the king
of Athens, announces that "when the laws are written, both the powerless
and the wealthy have equal justice, and the lesser man with justice on his
side prevails over the powerful man." Second, the Athenians thought that
all officials should be accountable before the law. Every official in Athens
had to present records of his financial transactions to a board of *logistai*
(accountants), and anyone who wished could bring a charge against an

official before the *euthynoi* (auditors) (*Constitution of the Athenians* 48.4–5). Even Perikles, the leading politician in Athens at the beginning of the Peloponnesian War, was deposed from his office as general and fined (Thucydides 2.65). Third, the rule of law required that all statutes and legal procedures be accessible to all. The Athenians made their laws and decrees readily available by inscribing the most important ones on *stelai* and placing them in central locations.[1] As Sickinger has observed, no litigant speaking in an Athenian court complained that it was difficult to find the laws he needed.[2] The Athenians also attempted to make their laws clear and easy to read. Fourth, the Athenians tried to make their legal procedures fair and transparent. Defendants had to be presented with the charges against them and had the right to present documents and witnesses to prove their innocence. As we will see, the Athenians went to great lengths to ensure that judges would be impartial and not influenced by bribes. Fifth, the Athenians believed that there should be no punishment without law. In fact, there was a rule that officials could not apply a law which had not been written down, that is, enacted by the Assembly and included in the lawcode (Andokides 1.87). Laws went into force on the day they were enacted and could not be applied retroactively. In fact, many laws explicitly state that they are to go into effect "henceforth" (*to loipon*) and not be used about actions in the past. One must not make the mistake of believing that the Athenians had popular sovereignty in the fifth century BC, and the sovereignty of law only started in the fourth century BC.[3] The ideal of the rule of law went back to Solon and continued after Kleisthenes' reforms of 508 BC right down into the Hellenistic period.

Enacting Laws

The first laws of Athens were enacted by Drako in the late seventh century and by Solon when he was appointed as lawgiver in 594 BC (*Constitution of the Athenians* 5–12). These laws were preserved on *axones* (tablets turned on an axle) and *kurbeis* (boards) and put on display in the Agora. (See also Meyer, Chapter 7 in this volume.) During the fifth century, the Athenians enacted temporary measures, granted privileges to individuals, and passed

[1] Many of these *stelai* have been preserved and are on display in the Athens Epigraphical Museum or in the Agora Museum.
[2] Sickinger 2004.
[3] Harris 2016.

permanent measures in the Assembly. Anyone could propose legislation, and all proposals approved by a majority went into effect. To prevent a measure from being repealed at a subsequent meeting of the Assembly, the proposer might add an entrenchment clause, which imposed heavy penalties on anyone who proposed to annul or alter the measure. In general, however, no legal distinction was made between temporary measures and legislation designed for the long term. Starting in the year 410/9 there was a review of the laws of Drako and Solon, which lasted until 400/399 BC. A group of officials called the *anagrapheis* found the texts of the laws and submitted them to the Assembly, which either rejected them or voted to retain them and then have the texts inscribed on *stelai* (*IG* I³ 104.3-9 [409/8 BC]).

After the restoration of the democracy in 403/2 BC, the Athenians enacted several important measures about laws and legislation. A distinction was now made between decrees (*psephismata*) and laws (*nomoi*). Decrees (*psephismata*) were either temporary measures, such as a decision to send a military expedition or an embassy, or measures to grant privileges or honors to individuals, such as a crown for meritorious public service.

Laws (*nomoi*) were general rules applying to everyone on a permanent basis. Decrees were still passed in the Assembly by a majority vote, but a new, more complex procedure, as recorded in Demosthenes (20 and 24), was created to enact laws. It involved several steps:

(1) A preliminary vote in the Assembly could take place at any time during the year to permit proposals for new laws.

(2) All new proposals for laws had to be placed in front of the Monument of the Eponymous Heroes in the Agora (see below) so that everyone could read them.

(3) The secretary was to read out all proposals submitted at every meeting of the Assembly until *nomothetai* were appointed.

(4) During the third meeting of the Assembly after the preliminary vote, the people were to discuss and pass a decree about the appointment of *nomothetai*.

(5) Public advocates (*synegoroi)* were to be elected to defend any laws to be repealed before the new laws could be enacted.

(6) Any laws contrary to the new proposals for laws had to be repealed by a public action against inexpedient laws.

(7) If the person who proposed a new law did not follow these rules, anyone who wished could bring a public action against him on a charge of enacting an inexpedient law.

All laws were passed at a meeting of the *nomothetai*, which was a meeting of the Assembly convened for the special purpose of enacting laws. The aims of these procedures were to ensure that permanent measures were not passed hastily or without proper deliberation and that statutes not contradict one another. As Demosthenes (20.93) observes, "opposing laws are repealed so that there is one law for each subject. This avoids confusion for private individuals, who would be at a disadvantage in comparison to people who are familiar with all the laws." There was also an annual procedure to remove contradictory laws held by the *thesmothetai* (Aischines 3.38). This concern for consistency and transparency is one of the hallmarks of the Athenian rule of law.

Judges and Their Oath

A pool of six thousand judges (*dikastai*) was selected to decide cases every year. Some scholars have translated the Greek word *dikastes* with the English term "juror," but this translation is both inaccurate and misleading. In Common Law countries, such as the United Kingdom and the United States, there is a distinction between judges, who are public officials with long-term appointments who enforce procedural rules during the trial, and jurors, who are average citizens and serve only to hear a single case and decide only questions of fact relating to the guilt or innocence of the defendant. In a modern court, only the judge can speak during the trial to give instructions to the litigants, and the jurors must remain silent. The *dikastes* in an Athenian court served for at least an entire year and gained considerable experience deciding cases. Like a modern judge at a bench trial, the Athenian judge decided both issues of law and legal interpretation and issues of fact. Finally, the Athenian *dikastes* did not have to remain silent but could shout at litigants who were not observing the informal rules governing behavior in court (Aischines 2.4). It would be a mistake to call Athenian judges 'amateurs.'

Starting around 450 BC, judges were paid 2 obols a day, a payment which was raised to 3 obols by the 420s BC. Since an Athenian could earn more by working on a public project or in his own workshop, the payment was meant to provide only for subsistence. In his play *Wasps*, Aristophanes gives the impression that most judges were older men like Philokleon and his friends, and this may have reflected reality. Each judge was given a bronze token, which was about 11 by 2 cm and 2 mm thick and was stamped with the individual's name and an owl, but after around 350 BC the tokens for judges were made of boxwood (*Constitution of the Athenians* 63.4).[4] Once a judge ended his year of service and did not continue, the token might be given to another judge whose name was stamped over the former name.

The judges swore an oath, which contained four main promises.[5] First, they swore to vote in accordance with the laws and decrees of the Athenian people. This meant that they did not make ad hoc judgments about the conduct of defendants, but applied consistent principles to every case. Just as today, this was a key aspect of the rule of law. Second, the judges swore to vote only about the charges in the indictment (*engklema*). This meant that the judges would vote only about the question: Did the defendant violate the substantive rule in the law under which the case was brought? In other words, if the defendant was charged with theft, the judges would vote whether the defendant had stolen the item(s) indicated by the accuser and not about his general reputation or behavior (Antiphon 5.11). Third, the judges pledged to vote with their most honest judgment. This had two aspects: the judge would decide honestly and without being influenced by dishonest considerations, and when there were no relevant laws to guide his decision, he would decide according to his most just opinion. This pledge did not give the judges the right to ignore the law when voting, but only covered cases in which the law gave no clear instructions. But in almost all cases the law did provide clear guidance, and this clause was only invoked twice in the roughly one hundred speeches of the Attic orators preserved in the medieval manuscripts (Demosthenes 20.118–119; 39.39–40). Fourth, the judges swore to vote without favor or hostility, in other words, without taking their personal attitudes towards the litigants into consideration. This bound them to act impartially, another key feature of the rule of law both today and in antiquity.

Lawsuits

When an accuser wished to bring a case against an opponent, he might first propose private arbitration, that is, an informal, out-of-court means of dispute resolution. If the litigants could agree on several arbitrators and the issues to be decided, the arbitrators would try first to reconcile the parties or, if mediation did not succeed, give a decision, which was considered

[4] For more on these tokens, see Kroll 1972.
[5] Harris 2013, 101–137, 353–357.

binding. If the litigants could not agree to private arbitration, the accuser would summon the defendant to appear before the relevant magistrate on a certain day and bring along two witnesses to prove that he had actually delivered the summons. If the charge were homicide or impiety, for instance, the accuser would present his charge to the *archon* called the *basileus* at the Stoa Basileios.[6] The Stoa was located in the northern part of the Athenian Agora between the Painted Stoa and the Stoa of Zeus (see Map 6.1). The empty bases for many *stelai* containing laws were found in front of the Stoa and can still be seen there today (Web Fig. 28.1).

When the two parties met before the magistrate, the accuser submitted the *engklema* to the magistrate, which recorded his own name, the name of the defendant, the type of action he was initiating, and the charges against the defendant. If the defendant denied the charges, he submitted a written statement to that effect called an *antigraphe*. The magistrate then examined the plaint to determine whether the charges were brought in a case that lay within his jurisdiction and whether the charges against the defendant followed the language of the relevant statute. If the magistrate accepted the case, he posted a copy of the plaint before the Monument of the Eponymous Heroes in the Agora (Demosthenes 21.103). This monument was on the eastern side of Agora and after around 350 BC was in front of the Metroon and the New Bouleuterion (see Map 6.1, Web Fig. 27.1). Its central location ensured maximum publicity for legal business. The magistrate next conducted a hearing called the *anakrisis*, at which the litigants could question each other about aspects of the charge. The magistrate might also require that changes be made to the plaint. At the end of the *anakrisis*, the magistrate assigned the case to a specific court on a specific day.

The two main categories of charges in Athenian law were private charges (*dikai*) and public charges (*graphai*). In a private charge, one individual claimed that another person had violated his rights and asked for a payment of damages. This charge, however, could be brought only by the person whose rights were violated. If the amount claimed by the plaintiff was less than 1,000 drachmas, the case was heard by 201 judges; if more than 1,000 drachmas, by 401 judges. In a public charge, anyone who wished could bring a charge against someone who committed an offense threatening the entire community. These public offenses included treason, theft of public funds, accepting bribes as an official, passing an illegal

---

[6] This was the official who received the charge of impiety made by Meletos against Sokrates in 400/ 399 BC.

decree (*graphe paranomon*), falsely claiming to be a citizen, and failing to perform military service. This kind of charge also included serious offenses against individuals, such as *hybris*. In some cases, the Athenians elected prosecutors to bring a public case. In general, however, there was no office in the Athenian democracy equivalent to the District Attorney in modern states. For public charges, the democracy relied mainly on volunteers. On the other hand, these prosecutors were often politicians like Demosthenes or Hyperides who had much experience in public affairs. In most cases, however, the accuser in a public case gained nothing from a conviction. One exception was in cases of denouncing property of public debtors who had not paid fines (*apographe*), in which the successful prosecutor received a percentage from the sale of the debtor's property. Foreigners and metics could also bring both private charges and public charges. If the accuser in a private suit was a metic or foreigner, however, he would bring his charge before the archon called the polemarch and not one of the regular officials in charge of the courts. In his Funeral Oration (Thucydides 2.39.1), Perikles boasts that Athens was open to the world; the Athenians did not construct walls to keep foreigners out. One of the ways the Athenians implemented this ideal was by providing metics and foreigners with access to their courts. This was especially important for attracting skilled laborers and merchants who wished to import and export goods. Normally women were represented in court by their husbands or male relatives, but, in some cases, they may have initiated private cases.

Around 400 BC, the Athenians instituted a set of public arbitrators. If someone brought certain types of private suits, the accuser and the defendant would first go before a public arbitrator, an Athenian citizen who was 59 years old. The public arbitrator would try to mediate the dispute, but if he did not succeed, he would give a decision. The litigants could accept the decision, which was binding. If one of the litigants did not accept the decision, the arbitrator put the testimonies of the witnesses, the challenges, and other documents in two *echinoi* (ceramic jars), one for the accuser and one for the defendant, and attached the judgment of the arbitrator. The case was then sent to one of the regular courts, but neither litigant could introduce new evidence at the trial.

Judge Selection

Every day when the courts met, which could be as often as 300 days a year (Aristophanes, *Wasps* 660–665), there was a selection of judges. In the fifth century, the 6,000 judges were probably divided into ten sections, with sixty from each tribe, and assigned to specific magistrates for the entire year. If not all 6,000 were needed on a given day, the magistrates would select only those who arrived first and exclude latecomers (Aristophanes, *Wasps* 233–234, 240, 303–305, 689–690). Probably after 403 BC, there was a selection made every day, but the judges were assigned to courts by lot. The judges would enter by a gate assigned to their tribe and give their bronze tokens to an archon. The archon took ten tokens, one from each tribe, to select a committee who would become judges and select the other members. This committee placed the bronze tokens in two *kleroteria*, which were made of marble and contained slots with five columns each or ten in total, one for each tribe (Fig. 28.1).[7] Along one side of each *kleroterion* was a metal tube. The committee determined how many judges would be needed that day and selected a number of white balls and black balls to be placed in the metal tube. If a white ball fell next to a row of five plaques in the *kleroterion*, the men who owned those tokens would be assigned to a case that day. If a black ball fell next to a row in the *kleroterion*, the men with tokens in that row would have their tokens returned and go home. After this selection was made, the judges were assigned to different courts by lot. The magistrates assigned to preside over different courts were also selected by lot to prevent bribery. This complex system reflects the Athenians' desire to achieve fairness and impartiality in legal proceedings.

Trials

At the start of the trial, the clerk would read out the plaint. This would keep the judges and the litigants focused on the legal charges in the case and discourage them from being distracted by irrelevant issues. In a private case, the accuser would speak first, followed by the defendant. Then the accuser would speak again, followed once more by the defendant. The litigants could present witnesses and written documents, which were read by the clerk, to support their cases. A litigant might present a challenge to his opponent asking him to submit his slave for torture to obtain evidence. In the extant orations, there is not one example of an opponent accepting this challenge, but there is no reason to doubt that torture was often used to

---

[7] For more on the *kleroteria*, see Dow 1939.

(a)

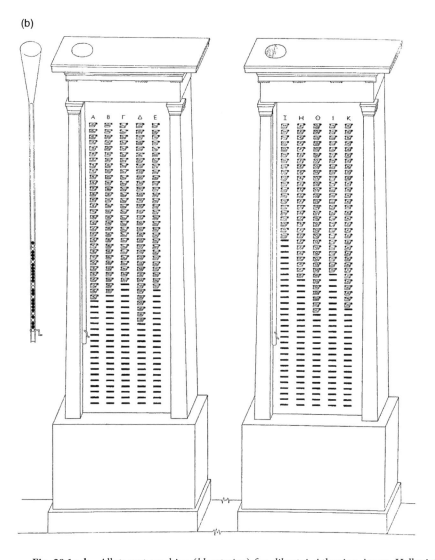

(b)

Fig. 28.1a–b Allotment machine (*kleroterion*) for *dikastai*, Athenian Agora, Hellenistic:
(a) wooden *pinakia* inserted in a *kleroterion*, (b) restored drawing of *kleroteria*.
Agora I 3967.
Courtesy of the American School of Classical Studies at Athens: Agora Excavations

gain information (Demosthenes 48.14–17). In one case, the Areopagos Council arrested Antiphon, a metic, tortured him and put him to death after he confessed (Demosthenes 18.132–133).

In a public case, the accuser and the defendant each spoke once, but the speeches were much longer. Speeches were timed by the water clock (*klepsydra*), and fragments of one have been found in the Agora excavations (Web Fig. 28.2).[8] Litigants in private cases were given a relatively short time according to the amount claimed, about forty minutes being the maximum allowed. In public cases, the day was divided into three parts, the first given to the accuser, the second to the defendant, and the third to determining the penalty (see below). It has been calculated that the accuser and the defendant could each speak up to three hours. Litigants were expected to present their own cases, but they might ask a supporting speaker (*synegoros*) to speak on their behalf for either several minutes or for their entire time allotted.

After the speeches were finished, the secretary of the court would read out the charges again, and then the judges would vote.[9] In the fifth century, each judge would receive a pebble, which he dropped into either of two urns, one for the accuser and one for the defendant. To ensure a secret ballot, there may have been a cover hiding the openings of the urns so that no one could see into which urn the judge dropped his pebble. Sometime in the early fourth century BC, a new way of voting was created. Each judge received two bronze ballots, each of which resembled a small wheel with an axle in the middle (Fig. 28.2). The center of the axle in the ballot for the accuser was hollow, that for the defendant solid. The judge, placing each ballot between his thumb and forefinger to make sure no one knew how he was voting, would then place one ballot in the urn for votes to be counted and discard the other in an urn for spare ballots.

The decision was made by a simple majority; there were no separate rules for private and public cases. This meant that it was much easier for an accuser in democratic Athens to gain a conviction in a public case than it is for a public prosecutor to win a criminal case in a modern court, in which all twelve jurors must vote unanimously for conviction. For instance, Sokrates was tried on a public charge of impiety and was convicted by only thirty votes out of several hundred; almost half the judges voted to acquit (Plato, *Apology* 36a). If the court voted to convict a defendant on a public charge, a second vote took place to determine the penalty. The

---

[8] See Young 1939 on the *klepsydra*.
[9] Boegehold 1995, 27–28, 209–211.

Fig. 28.2 Inscribed ballots of *dikastai*, Agora, fourth century BC. Agora B 1056, B 146, B 728, B 1058, B 1055.
Courtesy of the American School of Classical Studies at Athens: Agora Excavations

accuser would propose one penalty, and the defendant would propose another. The possible penalties ranged from death or permanent exile and confiscation of property to the loss of certain civic rights or a fine. The court then voted a second time to choose one of the penalties proposed by the litigants. For instance, after Meletos convicted Sokrates of impiety, he proposed the death penalty, and Sokrates proposed a fine of 30 *mnai*, which was equivalent to 3,000 drachmas (Plato, *Apology* 38b). The court then voted for the death penalty, and Sokrates was escorted to prison and ordered to drink hemlock several days later. Harsh penalties were not unusual; the Athenians convicted many generals and politicians and sentenced them to death, large fines, or permanent exile. The historian Thucydides may have been tried and sent into exile. Imprisonment was not normally imposed as a penalty.

Types of Charges

The Athenians were very concerned about litigants abusing the legal system to pursue personal vendettas and imposed serious penalties for accusers bringing frivolous cases. If the accuser in a private case lost, he had to pay a penalty of one-sixth of the amount claimed (*epobolia*) in his plaint. If the accuser in a public case did not gain at least one-fifth of the votes, he had to pay a fine of 1,000 drachmas and lost the right to bring any public cases in the future. These penalties and other measures helped to discourage litigants from using the courts to carry on feuds.

There were special procedures for homicide, because this was the most serious crime against an individual and was thought to cause religious pollution.[10] If a murderer was not punished and remained in the city's territory, the pollution might cause plagues or other disasters (Antiphon

---

[10] See Harris 2015 on the role of pollution in Athenian law.

5.82–83). For instance, in Sophokles' play *Oedipus Tyrannos*, the intentional killing of Laius caused the plague in Thebes, which could only be removed by the execution or permanent exile of the murderer. Homicide was a private charge and could be brought only by the relatives of the victim. When an accuser initiated the charge, he had to swear a solemn oath that the charges were true, calling down destruction on himself, his relatives, and his household if it were not (Antiphon 5.11–12). The charge was presented to the *archon basileus*, who made a proclamation banning the defendant "from lustral water, libations, bowls of wine, holy places, and the marketplace" (Demosthenes 20.158). To avoid pollution, trials for homicide were not held inside buildings but were tried in the open air (Antiphon 5.11).

There were four basic categories of homicide tried by different courts. First, there was intentional homicide tried at the Areopagos, the most respected court in Athens. The penalty was either death or permanent exile and confiscation of goods. Second, there was the charge of involuntary homicide, in which the defendant caused the death of the victim against his will. The penalty was exile until the defendant could convince the relatives of the victim to grant him pardon and perform a purificatory sacrifice to remove his pollution. This charge was tried at the Palladion, which also tried charges of plotting a murder, which was brought in cases in which someone attempted to commit murder. (See also Costaki, Chapter 33 in this volume.) If the defendant admitted that he had committed murder, but claimed that he did it justly or according to the laws, he was tried at the Delphinion. This included cases in which someone caught a man seducing or committing sexual violence against his wife or female relative. Trials at the Palladion and Delphinion were tried by *ephetai*, special judges appointed by lot. If someone was in exile for involuntary homicide and was accused of another murder, he was tried at a curious court located in Phreatto, a seaside area of the Piraeus. The accuser and judges stood on the shore while the defendant presented his case in a boat moored offshore, which could not have contact with the land. This was done to prevent the defendant from spreading his pollution to Attika.

Conclusion

The laws and legal procedures of the Athenians attempted to implement the rule of law by ensuring fairness in trials, equality before the law, and the accountability of all officials. There were certainly shortcomings to the Athenian system of justice (one-day trials, low burden of proof in public cases, lack of jury selection, no appeals procedure), but the Athenian courts did to a large extent protect the rights of citizens, metics, and free foreigners. In this way, the legal system helped to maintain order and enforce communal values.

Further Reading

The major sources for Athenian law are the *Constitution of the Athenians* and the Attic orators; see especially Canevaro 2013. On democracy and the rule of law, see Harris 2006 and 2013. For a detailed treatment of Athenian legal procedure, see Harrison 1971, although some of the details are out of date. MacDowell 1978 is a basic introduction to Athenian law and legal procedure. For a review of recent scholarship on ancient Greek law, see Harris 2018.

Bibliography

Boegehold, A. 1995. *The Lawcourts at Athens: Sites, Buildings, Equipment, Procedure, and Testimonia. Agora* 28. Princeton.

Canevaro, M. 2013. *The Documents in the Attic Orators: Laws and Decrees in the Public Speeches of the Demosthenic Corpus.* Oxford.

Dow, S. 1939. "Aristotle, the Kleroteria, and the Courts." *Harvard Studies in Classical Philology* 50: 1–34.

Harris, E.M. 2006. *Democracy and the Rule of Law in Classical Athens. Essays on Law, Society, and Politics.* Cambridge.

2013. *The Rule of Law in Action in Democratic Athens.* Oxford.

2015. "The Family, the Community, and Murder: The Role of Pollution in Athenian Homicide Law." In *Public and Private in Ancient Mediterranean Law and Religion*, eds. C. Ando and J. Rüpke, Berlin, 11–35.

2016. "From Democracy to the Rule of Law? Constitutional Change in Fourth Century BCE Athens." In *Die Athenische Demokratie im 4. Jahrhundert: zwischen Modernisierung und Tradition*, ed. C. Tiersche, Stuttgart, 73–87.

2018. "Some Recent Developments in the Study of Ancient Greek Law." *Journal of Ancient Civilizations* 33: 187–266.

Harrison, A.R.W. 1971. *The Law of Athens: Procedure.* Oxford.

Kroll, J.H. 1972. *Athenian Bronze Allotment Plates.* Cambridge, MA.

MacDowell, D.M. 1978. *The Law in Classical Athens.* London.

Sickinger, J.P. 2004. "The Laws of Athens: Publication, Preservation and Consultation." In *The Law and the Courts in Ancient Greece*, eds. E.M. Harris and L. Rubinstein, London, 93–109.

Young, S.H. 1939. "An Athenian Klepsydra." *Hesperia* 8: 274–284.

Additional resources to accompany this chapter can be found at: www.cambridge .org/NeilsRogers

29 | Armed Forces

DAVID M. PRITCHARD

On the eve of the Peloponnesian War, Perikles famously advised the Athenians how they could win (Thucydides 2.13.1–8). He reassured Assembly-goers that they already had the required funds and armed forces for victory. First, Perikles mentioned the 13,000 hoplites, and then the 1,200-strong cavalry and the 1,600 archers. The last corps of which he spoke was the navy of 300 triremes. What lies behind Pericles's famous numbers? What constitutes the legal status of these corps members and their social background? How were they recruited into their corps and subsequently mobilized for campaigns? What are each corps' history and organization? By comparing all military branches, this chapter reveals the common practices that the *demos* (people) used to manage their armed forces. It explains the common expectations that they brought to this management.

Hoplites

The hoplites (armed foot soldiers) of Classical Athens were divided into ten *taxeis*, or units. With one *taxis* for each of the ten tribes, a unit was often simply called a *phyle*, or tribe. The division of Athenians into tribes was a one of the democratic reforms of Kleisthenes.[1] Soon after 506 BC, he divided Attika into three regions. In each region, neighboring demes were grouped together into ten *trittyes* (thirds). A tribe had one *trittys* from each of the three regions. The Athenians believed that Kleisthenes had made them stronger militarily (e.g. Herodotos 5.78–79). It is likely that a public army of hoplites was another of his reforms. Greek hoplites typically fought as part of a coalition army; when they did, those from a *polis* (city-state) formed a distinct contingent. A detachment from Classical Athens was divided into *phylai* (tribes). In land battles, Athenian hoplites thus always fought beside fellow *phyletai* (tribesmen). In the 480s, the Athenians

---

[1] Hansen 1991, 34–35. See also the chapters of Fachard and Kierstead, Chapters 2 and 27 in this volume.

created a board of ten taxiarchs to command their hoplite *taxeis*. It was the *taxiarchos* who subdivided his tribe's hoplites into *lochoi* or subunits. The number of a tribe's *lochoi* varied in relation to how many hoplites Athens had put into the field.[2]

The hoplites were the first branch of the armed forces that Perikles mentioned in his last prewar speech (Thucydides 2.13.6–7). The 13,000 of them who were liable for active service were the largest corps after the navy. Perikles distinguished them "from both the oldest (*hoi presbytatoi*) and the youngest (*hoi neotatoi*) and all the metics who were hoplites." This second group of hoplites normally only manned the city walls and Attika's forts. Hansen's work on ancient Greek demography establishes that there were 60,000 citizens in 432/1.[3] (See also Kellogg, Chapter 11 in this volume.) Certainly, the *neotatoi* were the precursors of the fourth-century ephebes, who were 18- and 19-year-olds (*Constitution of the Athenians* 42.1–5). The *presbytatoi* were most probably 50 to 59 years of age.[4] In the table of age distribution that Hansen uses, those aged between 20 and 49 years represent 72.7 percent of adult males.[5] In 432/1, the number of Athenians in this age-band would have been 43,620. The 13,000 active-service hoplites therefore represented 29.8 percent of them.

This 30 percent came from relatively prosperous families. Athens probably began to pay hoplites at the same time as it did sailors in the 470s. By 433/2, the regular *misthos* (pay) for both was 1 drachma (dr.) per day. Nevertheless, each hoplite had to purchase his own equipment. This was not cheap, because a shield and a spear cost up to 30 dr. and bronze armor up to 100 dr. His ownership of a slave is further evidence of his prosperity. Thucydides believed that every Athenian hoplite brought along a slave (e.g. 7.75.4). The Athenians judged it unsafe to arm slaves for land battles and so used them only as baggage-carriers. In Classical Athens, it cost about 200 dr. to buy a slave.[6] Even for a skilled laborer, who earned 1 dr. per day, this was expensive. Unsurprisingly many poor citizens did not own a slave (e.g. Lysias 24.6; see also Lewis, Chapter 15 in this volume.)

The old argument was that the *telos* of an Athenian determined the corps in which he served.[7] In the 570s, Solon had divided the Athenians into four such *tele* or income classes (e.g. *Constitution of the Athenians* 7.3).

---

[2] Crowley 2012, 36–39.
[3] Hansen 1991, 55.
[4] Christ 2001, 404.
[5] Hansen 1986, 12–13.
[6] Pritchard 2015, 84–85.
[7] Spence 1993, 180–182.

Service as a hoplite, it was argued, was the duty of every member of his third lowest *telos*. This class, called *zeugitai* (yoke-men), produced at least 200 *medimnoi* of agricultural produce.[8] The top two *tele* were called 'the 500-*medimnoi* men' and the *hippeis* (horsemen). It was long argued that they had to serve as, respectively, trierarchs and horsemen. Members of the lowest class, who were called *thetes* (hired laborers), were free to volunteer to be sailors or archers. In the last twenty years, the study of ancient Greek agriculture has refuted this old argument. Van Wees puts beyond doubt that a *zeugites* needed 8.7 hectares in order to qualify for his *telos*.[9] Because Attika only had 96,000 hectares of arable land, there was simply not enough for all 13,000 active-service hoplites to be *zeugitai*. When van Wees factors in the land that the other income classes owned, it emerges that the top three *tele* provided only half of the hoplites. On the eve of the Peloponnesian War, the other half were *thetes*. *Telos* membership, it appears, played no role in the recruitment of hoplites.

Instead, a non-elite Athenian probably simply chose whether he would be a hoplite, an archer, or a sailor, when, as an 18-year-old, he was registered as a citizen in his deme. If he decided to be a *hoplites*, this choice was written beside his name in the *lexiarchikon grammateion* (e.g. *IG* I³ 138.1–7), which was the register that a demarch maintained of adult Athenians in his deme. Before a campaign, each taxiarch drew up the *katalogos* (conscription list) for his tribe. He got the names of conscripts by asking the demes in his *phyle* to nominate them. Commanders were not supposed to conscript hoplites who had recently served. Each tribe's *katalogos* was displayed under the statue of its eponymous hero in the Agora (see Web Fig. 27.1). The statues of the tribal heroes formed a monument that served as the state's noticeboard. On display, too, was the date when the conscripts had to muster and where they had to do so. Most often they mustered in the athletic field of the Lyceum, which was just outside the city walls (see Map 4.2 and Bakewell, Chapter 21 in this volume), but musters could also be held in, for example, the Agora or the meeting place of the Assembly on the Hill of the Pnyx. In the last two locations, *horoi* (boundary markers) have been found, whose inscriptions state that a *trittys* of a tribe ends and another *trittys* of the same tribe or the next tribe begins. These *horoi* presumably helped the *taxiarchos* to call the roll of his tribe.[10]

---

[8] The *medimnos* was a dry measure of around 52 liters.

[9] Van Wees 2001, 47–54.

[10] Pollux 8.115; Christ 2001, 407.

Horsemen

The second corps that Perikles mentioned in his last prewar speech was the cavalry (Thucydides 2.13.8). In 432/1 it consisted of 1,000 *hippeis* (horsemen) and 200 *hippotoxotai* or mounted archers. The *hippeis*, who were always citizens, were likewise divided into ten tribal units. Each *phyle* of 100 horsemen was commanded by a *phylarchos* or phylarch, and two *hipparchoi* (hipparchs) commanded the corps as a whole. *Hippeis* were conscripted for a campaign in the same way as hoplites: their names were placed on a tribal *katalogos*. When he compiled a conscription list, however, a phylarch had access to what a taxiarch never did: a central record of *hippeis*. Athens simply did not have enough secretaries to maintain a central record for 13,000 hoplites, but could do so for the cavalry because of its much smaller size.

The cavalry corps was most probably created in the 450s.[11] Initially it had only three units of 100 *hippeis* each. The Parthenon, which was completed by 438/7 BC, provides a firm date by which the cavalry had been expanded to ten units. This branch participated in the *pompe* (procession) of the Great Panathenaia (e.g. Xenophon, *On the Cavalry Commander* 3.1–2; see Miles and Neils, Chapter 24 in this volume), which was the focus of this temple's north (Fig. 29.1) and south friezes. The Parthenon's south frieze most clearly depicts ten distinct units of *hippeis*, which have different uniforms. (See also Valavanis, Chapter 5 in this volume.) This is surely a depiction of the ten tribes of the expanded corps.

Serving as a horseman was much more demanding than being a hoplite. Each *hippeus* had to buy his own warhorse and a horse for his slave *hippokomos* or groom, and together the two horses probably cost him 500 dr. His service was also a full-time commitment, because *hippeis* had constantly to train and always to be ready for deployment; this training took place in or around the *asty* or urban center. Corps members regularly paraded in the Agora or, for example, in one or another of the athletic fields outside the city walls. In order to find enough recruits for their expanded corps, the *demos* decided to give them two subsidies. The first was a *katastasis* (setting-up loan) so that a recruit could buy his warhorse; the second was a *misthos* of 2 dr. per day year-round. Because a *hippeis* needed only 1 dr. for the fodder of his two horses,[12] he could take home the same amount as a hoplite.

[11] Bugh 1988, 41–44.
[12] Spence 1993, 290–295.

Fig. 29.1 Horsemen in Panathenaic procession, North Frieze of the Parthenon (Block 37, Fig. Nos. 96–99), ca. 440 BC, Athens, Akropolis Museum 862. © Hans R. Goette

Solon's income classes played no role in the recruitment of horsemen.[13] This explains why *hippeis* in our sources are members of either his second highest *telos* or the cavalry (Thucydides 3.16.1; Aristophanes, *Knights* 225, 550). The term was never simultaneously used to describe both groups. Instead, service as horsemen was a legal requirement of "those who were most able in terms of money and physical capacity" (Xenophon, *On the Cavalry Commander* 1.9–12). Indeed, hipparchs could compel 20-year-olds who met these criteria to join up. There was a very good reason for the first criterion: the 500 dr. that a *hippeus* had to spend on his horses was at least five times what a hoplite paid for his equipment, the equivalent of two years of wages for a skilled laborer. While the state lent him the money for his own horse, he had to pay this loan back after 10 to 15 years, when he retired from the corps. (See also Smith, Chapter 14 in this volume.) This would have been daunting to everyone except those who knew that they would inherit enough to cover a *katastasis*.

---

[13] Bugh 1988, 20–34.

Therefore, it is unsurprising that Aristophanes believed that all 1,000 *hippeis* belonged to the elite.[14] Demography seems to confirm his belief. Horsemen were aged between 20 and 32.5 years, and in the age distribution table that Hansen uses, they account for 37.2 percent. In 432/1 there were, in this age-band, 22,320, of which the 1,000 horsemen were 4.5 percent. This is slightly less than the 5 percent of Athenians who were wealthy.[15] Simply belonging to the elite made a physically fit young Athenian liable for cavalry service.

The horses that the 200 mounted archers rode were owned by the state. After 412/11, when the *demos* began to reduce pay for the corps, the *hippotoxotai* always earned twice as much as the 1,000 horsemen. This heavier subsidization suggests that the *hippotoxotai* were much less able to bear the cost of corps membership, and it strengthens the case that they did not belong to the elite. Athenians certainly served as mounted archers (e.g. *Constitution of the Athenians* 24.3). Nevertheless, they did not serve beside the *hippeis* in the ten tribes; rather they formed their own unit under the direct command of a hipparch (Xenophon, *Memorabilia* 3.3.1). We last hear of mounted archers in the 380s.

Archers

In 432/1 BC, the third corps that Perikles mentioned were the 1,600 archers (Thucydides 2.13.8). The Athenians had no *toxotai* (archers) at the Battle of Marathon in 490/89. Because, ten years later, they could put such soldiers on their triremes at Salamis (e.g. Aischylos, *Persians* 454–461), this corps must have been created in the 480s. In 483/2, Themistocles convinced the Athenians to expand massively their public navy (Thucydides 1.14.1–2). The 200 triremes that they had after this shipbuilding was Greece's largest public navy. Archers had a great deal to contribute on their decks: they could kill enemy rowers from a distance and help to stop any hostile boarding of their triremes. The *demos* probably saw archers as a good way to increase the military advantages that they sought. It is thus likely that they decided to create the archer corps as part of their naval expansion in the late 480s.

---

[14] E.g. *Knights* 225, 266, 579–580, 842, 1369–1372. Pritchard 2018b, 447–448.
[15] Pritchard 2010, 13.

The Athenians in this corps were undoubtedly *thetes*, because, as we will see, they had joined up as a way of escaping dire poverty.[16] Nevertheless, there is no evidence that their membership of this *telos* had made them liable for archer service. *Toxotai* presumably joined the corps on a voluntary basis as hoplites did theirs. The *demos* also created a board of *toxarchoi* or archer corps commanders (e.g. *IG* I³ 1186.20). The small size of their corps allowed these commanders to maintain a central record of members.[17] *Toxarchoi* were required to draw up a *katalogos* of conscripts for each land or naval campaign.[18] Therefore, conscription was common across the terrestrial branches of the armed forces. In other respects, however, the archer corps was differently organized. Many corps members were actually metics.[19] Because membership of a *phyle*, in Classical Athens, was a prerogative of citizenship, the inclusion of metics ruled out the corps' organization by tribes. Indeed, it is not clear that *toxotai* even had regular units.

The *demos* may have understood the military advantages that their archer corps gave them, but they still held archers in low regard. The Athenians believed that a brave man bore *kindunoi* (dangers) in spite of the personal risk.[20] In bearing them, he accepted the possibility of death in battle. In land battles, archers, by contrast, ran away when the enemy got too close (e.g. Thucydides 2.79.6). Because they could shoot their arrows from a safe distance, they bore much lower risks. This meant that archers appeared not to meet the popular definition of *arete* (courage), and playwrights and public speakers did not fail to point this out (e.g. Euripides, *Herakles* 158–164, 187–204). Therefore, the first reason why the *demos* esteemed archers to be lowly was that they judged them to be cowards. The second reason is that they saw archery as a predominantly barbarian mode of combat; in the eyes of the *demos*, the main combat mode of the Persians was archery. In fact, many or possibly even most of the metics in the archer corps were non-Greeks.[21]

Trundle rightly asked why some Athenians chose to be archers in spite of this low regard.[22] The *demos* considered *toxotai* to be the poorest branch of the army (e.g. *IG* I³ 138.3–4). It is possible that what attracted citizens to

---

[16] For citizens as *toxotai*, see e.g. Lysias 34.4; *IG* I³1032.168–171.
[17] Pritchard 2018a, 92.
[18] Meiggs and Lewis 1988, 23.23–26.
[19] *IG* I³ 138.3, 6–7; Pritchard 2019, 69.
[20] Lysias 2.12, 15, 20, 23, 25; Thucydides 2.39.1, 4; Pritchard 2018c, 239.
[21] Thucydides 8.98.1–2; *IG* I³ 1172.35–37.
[22] Trundle 2010, 143–144.

it was pay and the fact that it cost less than hoplite service. But the same was the case with the navy. In addition, the *demos* held sailors in much higher regard, seeing them as no less courageous than hoplites.[23] Yet, the archer corps offered much better employment conditions.[24] Athens required *toxotai* to be ready for immediate deployment and always to be practicing their perishable skill. To meet comparable requirements, horsemen were employed full-time. There is good evidence that archers enjoyed the same conditions (e.g. *Constitution of the Athenians* 24.1–2). Sailors, by contrast, earned pay only for their days on the high seas.

The answer to Trundle's good question is that some poor Athenians chose to be archers, because they needed full-time employment. Yet offering such steady jobs did not come cheaply. In 432/1, archers also earned 1 dr. per day; consequently, their *misthos* used up 10 percent of the state's annual budget.[25] After the Peloponnesian War, Athens found it immensely difficult to pay for such recurring costs. By the time of the Corinthian War (395-387 BC), budget problems had forced the Athenians to disband the archer corps.

The policing of Classical Athens was in the hands of 300 Scythian archers.[26] The Athenians probably first purchased these *demosioi* (public slaves) in the mid-fifth century. These archers were commanded by the executive committee of the democratic *boule* (Council). Their main duty was to act as bouncers in the Assembly. They moved citizens loitering in the Agora towards the Pnyx, when an Assembly meeting was about to start and, when the executive committee ordered them, they threw out unruly Assembly-goers. At other times, they made arrests or stood guard in the Agora or, for example, on the Akropolis. The last mention of this force occurs in a comedy of the 390s (Aristophanes, *Ekklesiazousai* 143, 258–259).

Sailors

The last force that Perikles mentioned in his prewar speech was the navy with its 300 triremes (Thucydides 2.13.8). It was the duty of all citizens to

---

[23] Aischylos, *Persians* 337–347, 357–360, 386–401; Aristophanes, *Knights* 563–573; Lysias 2.24, 33, 40, 42–43, 47–48; Pritchard 2019, 109–137.

[24] Pritchard 2019, 74–76.

[25] In 432/1, this budget was 1,000 t. (Xenophon, *Anabasis* 7.1.27).

[26] Pritchard 2019, 76–78.

Fig. 29.2 Trireme, Attic marble relief, ca. 410–400 BC, Athens, Akropolis Museum 1339.
© Hans R. Goette

fight for the state.[27] In 432/1, two-thirds of them met this duty by serving in the navy. In the first several years of the Peloponnesian War, Athens regularly had 20,000 sailors at sea simultaneously. The 200-strong crew of a standard Athenian trireme was divided into four groups, two of which were the four *toxotai* and the ten *epibatai* (e.g. Thucydides 2.23.1–2). The third group consisted of the six petty officers (e.g. *IG* I³ 1032.35–46, 156–167). These officers were called collectively *he hyperesia* (the assistance) because they assisted the trireme commander. The fourth group were the 170 *nautai*. The trireme got its name from the three levels of the benches on which these rowers sat. The *demos* judged that the *thranitai*, who sat on the top bench, contributed the most. A trireme had sixty-two top bench, fifty-four middle bench, and fifty-four lower bench rowers (Fig. 29.2).

A trireme crew was led by a *trierarchos* (trireme commander). What differentiated this command from other forms of military service was the huge cost. The state left the recruitment of *nautai* to individual trierarchs. While it paid the *misthos* of sailors, *trierarchoi* who wanted the best of them paid more than this wage, and at sea trierarchs also paid for ship repairs and replacement rowers. The average attested cost of a trierarchy

[27] Aristophanes, *Wasps* 117–120; Lysias 16.17; Pritchard 2019, 45, 101–102.

was 4,436 dr.[28] Therefore, it is easy to understand why the *demos* made the trierarchy one of the two liturgies that the wealthy were obliged to perform. Each year, the generals drew up a list of those who might be conscripted for the trierarchy.[29] He who was conscripted was exempted from being so again for two years. The wealthy thus met their military duty by alternately serving in the army and the navy. In order to keep track of his expenses, a trierarch always maintained a detailed crew list. In 405/4, the *demos* honored the sailors of their eight triremes that escaped from the sea battle at Aegospotami.[30] They did so by setting up a monument with their crew lists; what survives of this *stele* provides the crew lists of four of these warships (*IG* I³ 1032).

Epibatai were regular members of the hoplite corps who were serving in a fleet.[31] While marines were volunteers, there still needed to be a roll call in order to ensure that all had kept their promise to serve. For the sake of this call, the Athenians installed the same *horoi* in their naval harbor at Zea (see Map 16.1, see also Steinhauer, Chapter 16 in this volume.) as they had in the other muster grounds for hoplites: *trittys* markers (*IG* I³ 1127–1130). If *epibatai* also embarked *trittys* by *trittys*, on a single trireme, they should have come only from one *phyle* or two in the official order of the tribes. *IG* I³ 1032 recorded the deme names of citizen sailors. Because a citizen's deme determined his tribe, it lets us test this hypothesis. On each of this *stele*'s triremes the marines were scattered right across the tribes. They, clearly, had not embarked by tribes. The employment of metics in the archer corps simply ruled out the use of tribes for embarking the conscripted *toxotai*.

The most important petty officer on a trireme was the *kybernetes*, or helmsman. He controlled the steering oars and so, with the help of the *proirates* (bow officer), navigated the trireme. These two petty officers had five deckhands each. The orders of the *kybernetes* were relayed to the rowers by the *keleustes* (rowing master), who, along with the *auletes* (*aulos* or flute player), set the rowing speed. The final two petty officers were the *naupegos* (shipwright) and the *pentekontarchos* (pursuer). Because a trireme could not function without *he hyperesia* (assistants; Thucydides 8.1.2), the Classical Athenians preferred to reserve these indispensable roles for fellow citizens. Their mobilization had two stages: in the first, the state conscripted the required number of *hyperesiai,* and in the second the

[28] Pritchard 2015, 97, 128 n. 40.
[29] Gabrielsen 1994, 68–74.
[30] Pritchard 2019, 84–88.
[31] Pritchard 2019, 42–43.

trierarchs competed with each other to hire the best of these conscripts by offering bonuses. Because this second stage ruled out any role for the *phylai*, it is not surprising that each *hyperesia* on *IG* I³ 1032 came from non-contiguous tribes.

Rowers were never formally recruited into the armed forces. Rather, they simply turned up in the Piraeus when a fleet was just about to depart. Trierarchs competed with each other to hire the best of these volunteers. Most of the *nautai* whom they hired were fellow Athenians; indeed from 433 to 426 there were normally 50 percent more Athenians in this branch of the armed forces than were required for the fleets of any particular year. In spite of this, a trierarch always had to hire non-citizens in order to find his 170 *nautai*. Most of these foreigners were metics, but others were simply from other *poleis* (city-states) in the Athenian empire. While the Athenians never used slaves in land battles, they found that giving them an oar was safe, and so trierarchs also employed slave rowers.[32]

Since these commanders relied on non-citizen rowers, many Athenian *nautai* clearly did not row every year. This suggests that their service pattern was similar to that of hoplites and trierarchs: after serving in a fleet, they had a rest for a year or two. The use of the market to mobilize rowers and the non-citizen status of many of them ruled out tribal organization.

Common Practices across the Armed Forces

In all branches of the armed forces, Solon's income classes played no roles. It was simply the obligation of every citizen to serve in one branch or another. Non-elite Athenians were free to choose the corps that best suited them. Elite citizens did not have the same choice. The *demos* made it compulsory for them to serve as trierarchs, and as young men they were legally obliged to join the cavalry corps. *Telos* membership thus had no impact on an Athenian's military obligation nor the branch in which he served. Conscription was also not limited to the top three income classes. As many hoplites, for example, came from Solon's fourth *telos*, their conscription lists always included *thetes*. Since the *demos* did not expect to fight all the time, in their eyes, a citizen who did so periodically fulfilled his duty to fight for the state. Therefore, they granted hoplites who had

---

[32] Pritchard 2019, 99–101; *IG* I³ 1032.105–133, 227–275, 357–399, 449–484.

recently served a legal right to a rest. They judged it enough for Athenian rowers to serve periodically. For every corps, the Athenians created written records of those corps members who served on a campaign. For the land forces, corps or unit commanders maintained these records; for the navy, this responsibility generally fell to individual trierarchs. In conclusion, tribal organization was less common than previously believed in the armed forces; because membership of a tribe was a right that only citizens enjoyed, those corps that had non-citizens as members could not be so organized. The only Athenians who fought alongside fellow tribesmen were hoplites and cavalrymen.

Further Reading

This chapter summarizes Pritchard 2019, 28–137, where many of the specific sources from the playwrights and the orators can be found. For more on the hoplites, see Christ 2001 and Crowley 2012. On the horsemen, see Bugh 1988, Spence 1993, and Pritchard 2018b. For the archers, see Trundle 2010, 145–152, and Pritchard 2018a. On naval personnel, see Gabrielsen 1994 and Pritchard 2018c. For depictions of warfare on Athenian vases, see Oakley 2020, 167–188.

Bibliography

Bugh, G.R. 1988. *The Horsemen of Athens*. Princeton.
Christ, M.R. 2001. "Conscription of Hoplites in Classical Athens." CQ 51: 398–422.
Crowley, J. 2012. *The Psychology of the Athenian Hoplite: The Culture of Combat in Classical Athens*. Cambridge.
Gabrielsen, V. 1994. *Financing the Athenian Fleet: Public Taxation and Social Relations*. Baltimore.
Hansen, M.H. 1986. *Demography and Democracy: The Number of Athenian Citizens in the Fourth Century* BC. Herning.
     1991. *The Athenian Democracy in the Age of Demosthenes: Structure, Principles, and Ideology*. Cambridge, MA.
Meiggs, R., and D.M. Lewis. 1988. *A Selection of Greek Historical Inscriptions to the End of the Fifth Century* BC. Rev. edn. Oxford.
Oakley, J.H. 2020. *A Guide to Scenes of Daily Life on Athenian Vases*. Madison.
Pritchard, D.M. 2010. "The Symbiosis between Democracy and War: The Case of Ancient Athens." In *War, Democracy, and Culture in Classical Athens*, ed. D.M. Pritchard, Cambridge, 1–62.
     2015. *Public Spending and Democracy in Classical Athens*. Austin.
     2018a. "The Archers of Classical Athens." *Greece & Rome* 65: 86–102.
     2018b. "The Horsemen of Classical Athens: Some Considerations on Their Recruitment and Social Background." *Athenaeum* 106: 405–419.

2018c. "The Standing of Sailors in Democratic Athens." *Dialogues d'histoire ancienne* 44: 231–253.

2019. *Athenian Democracy at War*. Cambridge.

Spence, I.G. 1993. *The Cavalry of Classical Greece: A Social and Military History with Particular Reference to Athens*. Oxford.

Trundle, M. 2010. "Light Troops in Classical Athens." In *War, Democracy, and Culture in Classical Athens*, ed. D.M. Pritchard, Cambridge, 139–160.

Van Wees, H. 2001. "The Myth of the Middle-Class Army: Military and Social Status in Ancient Greece." In *War as a Cultural and Social Force: Essays on Warfare in Antiquity*, eds. T. Bekker-Nielsen and L. Hannestad, Copenhagen, 45–71.

Reception

30 | Roman Athens

DYLAN K. ROGERS

> Athens has been a delight to me, when it comes to the city and its
> decoration and the love that its people show you, a certain kind of
> goodwill they have for us.
>
> Cicero, *Letters to Atticus* 5.10.5

Visiting Greece in 79 BC, Marcus Tullius Cicero, the famous Roman orator, statesman, and writer, was captivated by the splendor of the ancient city of Athens. Walking in the footsteps of the philosophers and improving his Greek, Cicero, like countless other young Roman men, experienced a city that was tantamount to a political backwater. After the Roman conquest of Greece in the second century BC by Titus Quinctius Flamininus and Lucius Mummius, Greek culture, both visual and literary, began to permeate life on the Italian peninsula, prompting the Latin poet, Horace, in the Augustan period, to proclaim "Conquered Greece (*Graecia capta*) took captive her savage conqueror and brought her arts into rustic Latium [the region around Rome]" (*Letters* 2.1.156–157).[1] Having lost its power gained in the Classical period, especially during the subsequent, turbulent Hellenistic era, Athens still remained, however, a cultural capital in the Mediterranean – and had consequently become a de facto university town. Indeed, Cicero, reflecting on the monuments and history of the city, proclaimed "I really do love Athens itself!" (*Letters to Atticus* 6.1.26).

Athens was a complex urban center in the Roman period. The city was naturally in a unique situation upon the arrival of the Romans: namely, there was already a preexisting urban footprint (Map 30.1). In the early first century BC, the Athenians sided with Mithridates VI Eupator in a series of wars against the Romans, which would eventually cause the Roman general, Lucius Cornelius Sulla, to besiege the city and Piraeus in 86, thus bringing Athens fully under Roman control, including Roman building activity.[2] The city also constantly lived in the shadow of its Classical past, imbuing it with a cultural cachet that saved it from countless political

---

[1] See Waterfield 2014 for an engaging account of the Roman conquest of Greece.
[2] On the extent of the Sullan siege of Athens, see Rogers forthcoming.

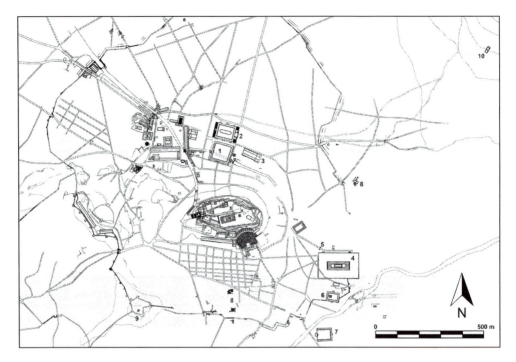

Map 30.1 Plan of Roman Athens, ca. AD 160. 1. Roman Agora. 2. Library of Hadrian. 3. Pantheon?
4. Temple of Olympian Zeus. 5. Arch of Hadrian. 6. Panhellenion? 7. Kynosarges Gymnasion.
8. Houses. 9. Philopappos Monument. 10. Hadrianic Fountain on Lykabettos. Note that the Odeion of
Herodes Atticus was dedicated between AD 160–174.
Courtesy of E. Papi, adapted by D. Weiss

missteps that destroyed other Greek cities at the hands of the Romans.
Further, the city chose the wrong side in a number of instances of political
infighting in the first century, including picking Pompey over Julius Caesar,
Brutus and Cassius over Octavian (later the emperor Augustus), and Mark
Antony over Octavian. Athens lacked the political status it once had, especially given that the Romans established Corinth as the capital of the
province of Achaia, which encompassed much of the Greek mainland, by
46 BC.[3] Athens' glorious past is often credited with saving it from destruction, which would then allow the city under the Roman Empire to flourish,
in a sense living in its own glorious present. During the Roman period, the
city saw bursts of construction projects that altered the physical landscape of
the urban center, creating a space that could be recognizably Roman while
still retaining the imprint of the Classical period – which is still visible today.

[3] Shear 1981; Raja 2012, 93–95.

Life in the city of Athens under the Romans was cosmopolitan and constantly in flux. When examining the material and visual culture of Roman Athens, whether at the hands of imperial or local private benefactions (or euergetism), a number of themes emerge, including political and ideological, religious, and cultural and educational motivations of individuals, which are explored in this chapter. In terms of building activities, the Romans first began construction and renovation projects in the urban center (especially around the Agora and the Akropolis); then by the second century, new public and domestic spaces were being created outside the historic city center – thus demonstrating how Athens was to be dramatically transformed under the Romans. Further, Athens and its inhabitants in this time period would also be caught between two epochs, in which local identity struggled between the fifth century BC and the Roman present. Athenian identity under the Romans was not only unique but also collective, in that the Athenians themselves still managed to fit into the growing imperial apparatus of the Romans. For example, a cuirass statue of the emperor Hadrian, found in the Athenian Agora, shows the goddess Athena being crowned by two Nikai (Victories), while she stands on the She-wolf, suckling Romulus and Remus – the symbol par excellence of the city of Rome (Fig. 30.1).[4] Two worlds collide here, thus illustrating the blending of visual cultures in the city of Athens.

Early Imperial Activity in Athens

As the first century BC progressed, especially after Sulla, Athens appeared to be a city with a depressed economy and minimal cultural production.[5] But over the course of the century, Athens received a series of monetary benefactions from individual Romans. For example, Pompey the Great is reported to have given fifty talents to the city in 62 BC (Cicero, *Letters to Atticus* 6.1.25). After prompting from Herodes of Marathon (the grandfather of Herodes Atticus), the Eponymous Archon of 60/59, Julius Caesar gave another fifty talents to build a commercial marketplace in Athens in the year 51. At the time, it seems that Athens lacked a public space directly tied to commercial activities, and in 69, when pirates sacked the island of Delos, Athens received an influx of merchants – thus prompting the need for a commercial marketplace. But after the Battle of Pharsalus in 48,

---

[4] Athens, Agora S 166. See Camp in Vlizos 2008, 87–88.
[5] For example, see various chapters in Hoff and Rotroff 1997.

Fig. 30.1 Statue of Hadrian, marble, Athenian Agora, between AD 117 and 138, Agora S 166.
Courtesy of the American School of Classical Studies at Athens: Agora Excavations

Caesar demanded the money back (along with other monetary gifts he had given to other Greek cities).

It appears, however, that before the Athenians gave the money back, they began construction of what would later be called the Roman Agora (Map 30.1, no. 1). Connected by a street to the Athenian Agora that lies directly to the west, the Roman Agora is a square-shaped Ionic colonnaded portico, which allowed for shops to line the periphery. The site of the new Roman Agora was a space that already had buildings constructed during the Hellenistic period, including the famous Tower of the Winds and perhaps a stoa to the east. On the west side of the Roman Agora, at the main entrance opening to the street leading to the Athenian Agora, a monumental gateway was installed, dedicated to Athena Archegetis (Athena the Founder; Web Fig. 30.1). The inscription mentions that the funds for the marketplace and the gate came from Julius Caesar and Augustus under the archonship of Nikias, which dates the completion of the Roman Agora to 11–9 BC (*IG* II² 3175). Atop the gateway, cuttings suggest the existence of an equestrian statue of Lucius Caesar, one of the heirs of Augustus, which might have been dedicated by his brother, Gaius Caesar, after Lucius' death in 2 BC.[6] Given its proximity to the nearby Athenian Agora, the relationship between the two spaces is much debated. Relying on the testimony of the second-century AD travel writer, Pausanias, many suggest that the older Agora had become a de facto museum in the Roman period, a testament to the glories of the Classical past. Others now argue that it is impossible to discern what exactly occurred in the Agora during the Roman period from the available evidence.[7] At the very least, political and administrative activities still happened there, given that the Agora had already had these spaces for centuries.

The emperor Augustus visited Athens on three occasions, in 31, 19, and 12 BC, initiating building or restoration projects. On the Akropolis, there are a few indications of Augustan building activity.[8] It appears that the Erechtheion underwent renovations under Augustus, perhaps illustrating the religious piety that he stressed in rebuilding religious structures (e.g. *Res gestae divi Augusti* 25). East of the Parthenon, an Ionic circular monopteros (7.35 m in diameter), dedicated to the cult of Roma and Augustus, was installed in either 20/19 or 19/18 BC (see Map 5.1, no. 10). Using the same architectural style as the Erechtheion and echoing the age-old Greek tholos form, this monument served as a bridge between Athenian and Roman identities.[9] However, its placement on the east side of the Parthenon, the main entrance to the temple and the main space for cultic activity, was a disruption to the topography of the Akropolis. Further, the Classical style of the structure was then connected to the cult of the emperor and the city of Rome – making strong connections between Athens and the imperial capital for all to experience. After Augustus, other members of the Julio-Claudian dynasty would restore other parts of the Akropolis, including Nero's restoration of the east façade of the Parthenon and Claudius' completion of the monumental staircase leading to the Propylaia.[10]

---

[6] Hoff 2001.

[7] Shear 1981; *contra* Dickenson 2017, 396–397. See also Baltes 2020.

[8] For overviews of Augustan building activities in Athens, including the Akropolis, see Stephanidou-Tiveriou in Vlizos 2008, and Raja 2012, 105–120. See also Spawforth's 2012 analysis of local Greek culture under Augustus.

[9] Morales 2016.

[10] There is evidence for a now-lost Neronian inscription on the east façade of the Parthenon, which was reconstructed in the twentieth century (*IG* II² 3277). For more, see Williams 2013, 80–88.

p. 88

In the Athenian Agora, two major monuments were installed in the Augustan period, in addition to other smaller monuments and renovations that occurred in this space (see Map 6.1). First, a Classical temple of Athena was transplanted from Pallene in the Attic countryside, and installed on the northern side of the Agora, just south of the Altar of the Twelve Gods. A so-called itinerant temple, in that it literally moved, this structure was rededicated to Ares, presumably making a connection to the Temple of Mars Ultor in the Forum of Augustus in Rome. There is speculation that the temple also received a dedication to one of the heirs of Augustus, Gaius Caesar, after his death, which would fit in well with the eastern Mediterranean tradition of ruler cults.[11] Second, immediately south of the Temple of Ares, a two-story Odeion was donated by Marcus Vipsanius Agrippa, running on a north–south axis, parallel to the Panathenaic Way. Agrippa, the right-hand man of Augustus and victorious admiral of the Battle of Actium, was known for his construction and infrastructure projects in Rome, and it is believed that this Odeion was commissioned by Agrippa on his visit to the city between 16 and 14 BC. The impressive structure, designed as a covered theater, provided space for musical performances and recitals among other events, thus stressing the ways in which Roman buildings altered the educational and cultural landscape of Athens. Further, the Odeion's size, with its daring roofing structure that spanned nearly 25 m, hints at the alterations that Roman monumentality made in Athens, by physically and visually dominating the Agora. As on the Akropolis, in the city center of Athens, Roman building projects not only disrupt the preexisting spaces, but also speak to the implications of the Roman presence here (e.g. religious and cultural motivations of the Romans).

Hadrian: New *Oikist* of Athens

A self-professed *philhellene*, the emperor Hadrian (reigned AD 117–138) is known for his extensive travels throughout the Roman Empire, and particularly for his three extended stays in Greece in 124/5, 128/9, and 131/2. During these excursions, Hadrian initiated a number of construction projects all over Greece, but paid special attention to Athens itself, notably with the completion of the Temple of Olympian Zeus (the Olympieion),

---

[11] Raja 2012, 109. See also Stewart 2016.

and construction of a Pantheon, library, *gymnasion*, and an aqueduct (see Map 30.1). There is ample epigraphic evidence of the appreciation owed on the part of the Athenians toward Hadrian; many name him "Founder (*Oikist*) and Savior" of the city.[12] Indeed, near the entrance of the Olympieion at one of the gates of the ancient Themistoklean walls, a large Roman arch was installed. This thin one-bayed arch of the Corinthian order mentions on the west side, facing the city center, "This is Athens, the city of Theseus," while on the east side it states, "This is the city of Hadrian, not of Theseus" (*IG* II² 5185). The Athenians equated Hadrian with Theseus, a founding hero of the mythical past of Athens – thus elevating him to heroic status. Indeed, it is known that the Athenians added an eleventh tribe in honor of Hadrian to their traditional ten, going so far as to erect a statue of him onto the Monument of the Eponymous Heroes in the Athenian Agora.

The Arch of Hadrian alludes to a new quarter of the city of Athens (Map 30.1, no. 5). It is in this period that the city moves outside the ancient walls, particularly to the north and east, where the National Gardens and Syntagma Square are today. There are a number of domestic structures, baths, and sanctuaries from the Hadrianic period and later that are suggestive of a new district, an opulent neighborhood in the city (Map 30.1, no. 8).[13] Further evidence to support the fact that this area began to transition into a more upscale neighborhood is found on the major road to the west of the modern National Gardens (Amalias Avenue today). Once lined with funerary monuments, the area ceased to function as a cemetery, with the influx of new building activity.[14] In addition, Roman domestic construction, on top of earlier Greek houses, can be seen in the neighborhood that lies underneath the Akropolis Museum today.[15] The houses also stretch into the fourth and fifth centuries along with other houses on the slopes of the Areopagos Hill, attesting to the continued occupation of Athens through the Late Antique period.

Arguably, one of the most important benefactions of Hadrian was the installation of a new aqueduct and fountains in Athens. (See also Stroszeck, Chapter 8 in this volume.) Hadrian initiated the construction on his first visit to Athens in 125, and it was completed by his successor, Antoninus

---

[12] See Lagogianni-Georgakarakos and Papi 2018, 140–141.

[13] Zachariadou in Vlizos 2008. See also the various excavations tied to the construction of the Athens Metro (Parlama and Stampolidis 2000).

[14] Giatroudaki, Servetopoulou, and Panayotopoulos in Vlizos 2008.

[15] Saraga in Di Napoli et al. 2018; Eleftheratou 2019.

Pius, in 140. Tapping the water sources of the Parnes Mountains to the north of the city, the Hadrianic aqueduct ran nearly 20 km into the city. The system is known for being a long, continuous tunnel, and, in addition, the tunnel collected water from other springs along its route to the city, ensuring a constant and plentiful water supply (with a daily discharge of over 30,000 m^3).[16] The tunnel, with shafts located at intervals to allow for maintenance and cleaning, and its water were in use until at least the 1930s, when a new water source was tapped in the area of Marathon. The aqueduct entered the city in the modern neighborhood of Kolonaki, on the slopes of the Lykabettos Hill, at an elevation of 136 m above sea level. At Dexameni Square (literally Reservoir Square), a basilica-style fountain-house was constructed with Roman concrete (*opus caementicium*) and barrel vaulting (Map 30.1, no. 10). Its tetrastyle Ionic façade supported a Syrian arch.[17] The structure functioned as a settling tank (with a 2,400–3,600 m^3 capacity), allowing the water to filter out any impurities, before being channeled into three sections of the city below. The water was able to supply a plethora of activities in the city, including a Hadrianic-period fountain installed along the Panathenaic Way in the Agora and numerous bath buildings, whose construction and popularity soared in the period after the completion of the aqueduct.[18]

Further, under Hadrian, several important cultural and educational facilities were conceived and built. Directly north of the Roman Agora lies the Library of Hadrian (Pausanias 1.18.9; Map 30.1, no. 2). Originally built on the remains of Hellenistic domestic structures (which are still visible today), the Library was probably inaugurated in 132. The structure consists of a large rectangular *quadriporticus* (a four-sided covered colonnade) that measures 82 by 60 m, with a large decorative pool in the center of the courtyard (Fig. 30.2). The west façade, facing modern Monastiraki Square, is marked by its freestanding Phrygian marble Corinthian columns, an order that instantly evokes 'Romanitas.' On the east side of the *quadriporticus* is a large room that some argue would have held papyri or book scrolls; on the northern and southern edges of the east side are two rooms that could have functioned as audience halls, complete with seating. Thus, in the heart of the city, Hadrian commissioned a multipurpose public building that could be used for learning and cultural events. In addition,

---

[16] Chiotis in Aristodemou and Tassios 2018.

[17] Leigh 1997. The current Dexameni was built in the nineteenth century using the ancient reservoir plan and was in use well into the twentieth century.

[18] On the Hadrianic fountain in the Agora, see Leigh in Aristodemou and Tassios 2018.

Fig. 30.2 Digital reconstruction of the Library of Hadrian, with the Roman Agora and the Pantheon in the background.
Source: Photorealistic image by D. Tsalkanis and C. Kanellopoulos

during this period, the *gymnasia* of Athens received special attention. Hadrian himself was probably responsible for a new *gymnasion* in the area of Kynosarges, south of the Olympieion (Map 30.1, no. 7). The management of *gymnasia* of the city also received renewed interest from local elites. The training of young men (ephebes) in Classical Athens included physical, military, and educational activities; however, by the time of Hadrian, the training had shifted primarily to physical and educational (especially in philosophy, grammar, and rhetoric). And it was the local men placed in charge of the *gymnasia* (*kosmetai*) who would have financed the *gymnasia* themselves, along with appointing and paying the instructors.[19] These *kosmetai* set up portrait busts of themselves in the *gymnasia*, thus promoting their own euergetism, while stressing their inalienable connection to the past models of education in Athens (Web Fig. 30.2). Under Hadrian, it seems that Athens flourished once again as a place of learning that Cicero two-and-a-half centuries earlier had celebrated.

Finally, Hadrian made an indelible mark on the religious landscape of the city. In 124/5, in an act of piety, he initiated the completion of the Temple of Olympian Zeus that was started under the Peisistratids in the

[19] Lagogianni-Georgakarakos and Papi 2018, 158–161.

sixth century BC (Map 30.1, no. 4). Upon its inauguration in 132 (*IG* IV^2 384), the temple was one of the largest dedicated to Zeus in the Greco-Roman world (43 × 110 m), with 104 Corinthian columns of colossal height (nearly 17 m). Surrounding the temple, a large *temenos* (128 × 205 m), or precinct, was constructed on heavily terraced walls, which buttressed the complex against the slopes of the Ilissos River valley to the south. Dedicated by cities throughout the Greek world, numerous statues of Hadrian were installed around the edges of the precinct.[20] Some believe that the statues were connected to the Panhellenic League (a federation of thirty-three Greek cities) that was instituted around the time of the inauguration of the Olympieion. While there does not seem to be an overt political function to the League, except for forging ties between Rome and the Greek East, Athens served as the League's capital, thus elevating the city's status and prestige in the Empire. The headquarters of the League have not yet been located: some argue that it was in the *temenos* of the Olympieion or in a so-called Panhellenion, another *quadriporticus* in the Ilissos River valley (Map 30.1, no. 6). There is also evidence that the League incorporated the Eleusinian Mysteries into their celebrations, reviving the cult, which had gone nearly dormant since the first century BC.[21]

Local Elites in Athens

Following the example of Hadrian, Athenian elites in the second century also made their mark around the city of Athens, through public benefactions and other modes of self-commemoration. While euergetism by members of the local elite class routinely occurred in Athens before and after the arrival of the Romans, there was a marked increase of monumentality during the Roman period. In the Agora, a library was installed directly south of the Stoa of Attalos by a certain Titus Flavius Pantainos and his family around the year 100 (see Map 6.1). The complex consisted of a large square room that opened onto a peristyle, providing a pleasant place for reading and discussing literature. An inscription found in the

---

[20] Pausanias 1.18.6; Camia, Corcella, and Monaco in Di Napoli et al. 2018.

[21] After Hadrian and into the reign of the Severans, the entrance forecourt of the Sanctuary of Demeter and Kore at Eleusis was repaved and new gateways and arches and a Hadrianic fountain were constructed. The architectural style of these new structures mimicked the Classical fifth-century architecture of Athens, which, as has been argued, stems in part from the growth of the Second Sophistic, a literary movement that hailed the values of Classical Athens. See Miles 2012 and Rogers 2021.

excavations of the building reveals part of the library's regulations (which still prevail today!): "No book shall be removed since we have sworn an oath. [The library] is open from the first to the sixth hour" (Web Fig. 30.3).[22] Situated at the heart of the old Agora of the city, along the Panathenaic Way, this library would have added to the cultural ambience of Athens, especially its popularity as a cultural capital for young Roman men.

Local elites often promoted their bi-cultural identities, illustrating the international and cosmopolitan nature of Athens. The city had a mix of inhabitants that drew on not only notions of local Greek and Roman identities, but also those from farther east in the Roman Empire. For example, Gaius Julius Antiochos Epiphanes Philopappos (AD 65–116), a prominent citizen of Athens, was actually a descendant of the last king of Commagene (modern Armenia), which was made a Roman province in AD 70. Philopappos went on to become consul of Rome in AD 109 and afterwards settled in Athens. Following his death, a mausoleum was constructed for him high on the Hill of the Muses, southwest of the Akropolis (Map 30.1, no. 9; Web Fig. 30.4). The two-story façade depicts Philopappos in a chariot, during the procession for his inauguration as consul on the lower story. Above, niches contain a heroic-clad seated figure of Philopappos and his grandfather, Antiochos IV. Unique in the Roman world, this grand monument atop a hill is reminiscent of tomb placement in Commagene, while the sculptural program (of a procession and a seemingly divine figure of Philopappos) takes inspiration from the Arch of Titus in Rome, with its own procession and deified Titus.[23] Further, Philopappos made a lasting impression on the city of Athens, as his family was granted the right to construct a funerary monument not only within the city walls, but also in a conspicuous position for all to see, then and today. Indeed, the prominence of the monument interacts visually with earlier choregic monuments above the nearby Theater of Dionysos, illustrating the phenomenon of local elites throughout the Roman Empire competing for attention and recognition in urban settings. Thus, Philopappos successfully altered the landscape of the city, while also creating a monument not seen elsewhere in the Roman world that extolled his multifaceted identity.

Herodes Atticus (AD 101–178) was also a prominent member of the Athenian elite during the second century. He was a Greek who was able to

---

[22] Agora I 2729.
[23] Kleiner 1983.

craft a bi-cultural identity, stemming from his lineage, which he traced back to Erechtheus, one of the ancient kings of Athens, and the time he spent in Rome as a Roman citizen (even serving as a tutor to the young Marcus Aurelius and later as consul in AD 143), as well as his marriage to a Roman woman, Aspasia Annia Regilla. Herodes, the wealthy descendant of the Herodes of Marathon who received money from Caesar for the Roman Agora, had a number of estates throughout Greece, including at Eva-Loukou in Arkadia, at Marathon, and in the area of Kifissia on the outskirts of Athens.

In the city itself, Herodes constructed a number of structures that are still in use today. After the Odeion of Agrippa was partially destroyed in the middle of the second century, Herodes took the opportunity to build his own larger and grander concert hall on the south slopes of the Akropolis (see Map 5.1, no. 16). It was dedicated between AD 160 and 174 in memory of his wife after her death. The structure could hold 5,000 spectators, with an expansive roofing system that spanned nearly 50 m – a true feat of Roman ingenuity in construction, with wooden timbers that do not have intermediate supports.[24] The Odeion made an unforgettable mark on the topography of the south slope of the Akropolis, with its sanctuaries and Theater of Dionysos – indeed, placing the magnificent benefaction of Herodes at the forefront of the cultural, political, and religious nexus of the historic city center. While dedicated in memory of his wife, the Odeion is a testament to the self-promotion practices of members of the imperial elite in the Greek East, who used their own money to promote their own interests, while also improving the surrounding urban areas. In a similar vein, Herodes also rebuilt the Panathenaic Stadium, on the banks of the Ilissos River, in AD 143/4. Using the remains of the fourth-century BC Stadium of Lycurgus, which held the athletic competitions associated with the Panathenaic Festival, Herodes reconstructed the stadium in marble and enlarged it to be able to hold nearly 50,000 spectators – a number that could rival the capacity of the Colosseum in Rome. It was again refurbished for the first modern Olympic Games in 1896, and it is affectionately referred to by modern Athenians as the *Kallimarmaro*, or the Beautiful Marble, given its continued importance in the topography and cultural landscape of the city. (See also Bridges, Chapter 32 in this volume.)

---

[24] Korres 2015.

Postscript: After the Romans and Their Legacy

After the patronage of Hadrian and Herodes in the second century, the city of Athens saw a marked decrease in monumental building programs. For the most part, though, Athens continued on as a cultural center in the eastern half of the Mediterranean. Under the emperor Valerian (reigned AD 253–260), parts of the fortification walls were shored up in the eastern half of the city (Map 4.1). In the year AD 267, however, the Heruli, a group of barbarians from the area north of the Black Sea, sacked the city. Athens responded by building a new wall system, using materials from destroyed structures, in the city center, stretching out from the north slope of the Akropolis. Because the Post-Herulian Wall narrowly constricted the size of the city, Athenians could probably use the walls in the event of a future attack, while still inhabiting the city that had grown under the Romans over two centuries before.

In subsequent centuries, Athens continued to live in the shadow of its former self, especially in the Late Antique period, into the Byzantine period, and during Frankish domination, before the fall of Athens to the Ottomans in 1458. There would be at least two other invasions that would make their mark on the city, the Visigoths in 396 and the Slavs in 583/4. But Athens remained a center for rhetorical and philosophical studies, drawing the likes of the writer Libanios and the future emperor Julian. Sometime after AD 400, a large palace was built on the site of the ruined Odeion of Agrippa in the Agora, although not much is known about its function. Some philosophical schools have been identified in the city, which often took shelter in domestic spaces, such as the Omega House in the Agora, on the slopes of the Areopagos Hill. The schools were closed, however, in AD 529 by an imperial decree of Justinian. Then, Christian building activity took root in the city, including the conversion of the Parthenon into a Church of the Theotokos (the Mother of God) Atheniotissa, and the installation of a church in the courtyard of the Library of Hadrian. Over time, some of the Roman monuments of Athens would also be quarried for their building materials, such as the Temple of Ares in the Agora and the famed Phrygian columns of the Library of Hadrian. During the Middle Byzantine period (ninth to thirteenth centuries), Athens continued to flourish, as recent excavations of domestic and commercial structures in the city center (especially around the Agora) suggest. Numerous churches built on traditional cross-in-square plans popular in this period can be found throughout the city. For example, the Church of Panagia Gorgoepikoos (known as the Little

Metropolis), which sits today in the shadows of the nineteenth-century Orthodox Cathedral, contains numerous spolia, or reused architectural or sculptural materials, dating from antiquity onwards, making the church a unique example of the incorporation of ancient building materials still visible today in Athens (see Web Fig. 24.1). Finally, in 1204, following the sack of Constantinople by the Crusaders, Athens came under Frankish domination, which is marked by an increase in fortifications, especially around the Akropolis – until the arrival of the Ottomans.

The Roman imprint on the city of Athens and its inhabitants (of past and present) is omnipresent. In terms of the built environment of Roman Athens, emperors and the local elite permanently altered the city, providing monuments that not only drew inspiration from the Classical period but were also markedly Roman, usually in terms of form and function. The multiethnic identities of those living in Athens allowed for the construction of a unique urban environment in the Roman Empire, namely a *polis* that promoted its glorious past and its present. The political and ideological, religious, cultural and educational projects of the Romans impacted the life of Athenians in the Roman period, elevating the status of the city to one of the cultural capitals of the Mediterranean. Further, many of the large-scale building projects of the Roman period are still used and enjoyed on a daily basis by the inhabitants and visitors to Athens – illustrating the ongoing social and cultural impact of the Roman presence in Greece.

Further Reading

Over the course of the last three decades, scholars have begun to pay greater attention to the city of Athens in the Roman period, a time often overlooked in light of the glories of the Classical period. Important edited volumes on a range of topics include Hoff and Rotroff 1997, Ostenfeld 2002, Vlizos 2008, Caliò et al. 2012, Dijkstra et al. 2017, and Di Napoli et al. 2018. See the work of the Roman Seminar in Athens, which hosts an annual international lecture series on topics related to Roman Greece (http://sites.google.com/view/romanseminar), along with the Ancient Athens 3D project for digital reconstructions of monuments of Roman Athens and other time periods of Athenian history (www.ancientathens3d.com). For a succinct discussion of the monuments installed in the city under the Romans, see Raja 2012, 92–135, including issues related to regional identity, along with Rous 2019, especially 198–209, and Yegül and Favro 2019, 579–595. Late Hellenistic Athens is explored in Habicht 1997. On issues related to Athens under the rule of Augustus, see for example Spawforth 2012. The role of Hadrian and Athens can be found in a number of new publications, including Lagogianni-Georgakarakos and Papi 2018. See Tobin 1997 for a discussion of the construction projects of Herodes

Atticus. Those interested in learning more about Christian Athens can turn to the work of Baldini (e.g. in Caliò et al. 2012); on Byzantine Athens, see most recently Bouras 2017; and on Ottoman Athens, see Georgopoulou and Thanasakis 2019.

Bibliography

Aristodemou, G.A., and T.P. Tassios, eds. 2018. *Great Waterworks in Roman Greece: Aqueducts and Monumental Fountains, Function in Context.* Oxford.

Baltes, E.P. 2020. "A Monumental Stepped Statue Base in the Athenian Agora." *Hesperia* 89.2: 339–377.

Bouras, C. 2017. *Byzantine Athens: 10th–12th Centuries.* London.

Caliò, L.M., E. Lippolis, and V. Parisi, eds. 2012. *Gli Ateniensi e il loro modello di città.* Rome.

Dickenson, C.P. 2017. *The Evolution of Public Space in Hellenistic and Roman Greece (c. 323 BC–267 AD).* Leiden.

Dijkstra, T.M., I.N.I. Kuin, M. Moser, and D. Weidgenannt, eds. 2017. *Strategies of Remembering in Greece Under Rome (100 BC–100 AD).* Leiden.

Di Napoli, V., F. Camia, V. Evangelidis, D. Grigoropoulos, D.K. Rogers, and S. Vlizos, eds. 2018. *What's New in Roman Greece? Recent Work on the Greek Mainland and the Islands in the Roman Period.* Athens.

Eleftheratou, S. 2019. *Μουσείο Ακρόπολης: η ανασκαφή.* Athens.

Georgopoulou, M., and K. Thanasakis, eds. 2019. *Ottoman Athens: Archaeology, Topography, History.* Athens.

Habicht, C. 1997. *Athens from Alexander to Antony.* Cambridge, MA.

Hoff, M.C. 2001. "An Equestrian Statue of Lucius Caesar in Athens Reconsidered." *Archäologischer Anzieger* 4: 583–599.

Hoff, M.C., and S.I. Rotroff, eds. 1997. *The Romanization of Athens.* Oxford.

Kleiner, D.E.E. 1983. *The Monument of Philopappos in Athens.* Rome.

Korres, M. 2015. *The Odeion Roof of Herodes Atticus and Other Giant Spans.* Athens.

Lagogianni-Georgakarakos, M., and E. Papi, eds. 2018. HADRIANUS-AΔPIANOΣ: *Hadrian, Athens, and the Gymnasia.* Athens.

Leigh, S. 1997. "The 'Reservoir' of Hadrian in Athens." *Journal of Roman Archaeology* 10: 279–290.

Miles, M.M. 2012. "Entering Demeter's Gateway: The Roman Propylon in the City Eleusinion." In *Architecture of the Sacred: Space, Ritual, and Experience from Classical Greece to Byzantium*, eds. B.D. Wescoat and R.G. Ousterhout, Cambridge, 114–151.

Morales, F.A. 2016. "The Monument of Roma and Augustus on the Athenian Acropolis: Imperial Identities and Local Traditions." In *Imperial Identities in the Roman World*, eds. W. Vanacker and A. Zuiderhoek, London, 141–161.

Ostenfeld, E.N., ed. 2002. *Greek Romans and Roman Greeks: Studies in Cultural Interaction.* Aarhus.

Parlama, L., and N.C. Stampolidis, eds. 2000. *Athens: The City beneath the City: Antiquities from the Metropolitan Railway Excavations.* Athens.

Raja, R. 2012. *Urban Development and Regional Identity in the Eastern Roman Provinces, 50 BC–AD 250: Aphrodisias, Ephesos, Athens, Gerasa.* Copenhagen.

Rogers, D.K. 2021. "Sensing Water in Roman Greece: The Villa of Herodes Atticus at Eva-Loukou and the Sanctuary of Demeter and Kore at Eleusis." *AJA* 125.

Forthcoming. "Sulla and the Siege of Athens: Reconsidering Crisis, Survival, and Recovery in the First Century BCE." In *The Destruction of Cities in the Ancient Greek World: Integrating the Archaeological and Literary Evidence,* eds. S. Fachard and E.M. Harris. Cambridge.

Rous, S.A. 2019. *Reset in Stone: Memory and Reuse in Ancient Athens.* Madison.

Shear, T.L., Jr. 1981. "Athens: From City-State to Provincial Town." *Hesperia* 50.4: 356–377.

Spawforth, A.J.S. 2012. *Greece and the Augustan Cultural Revolution.* Cambridge.

Stewart, A. 2016. "The Borghese Ares Revisited: New Evidence from the Agora and a Reconstruction of the Augustan Cult Group in the Temple of Ares." *Hesperia* 85.3: 577–625.

Tobin, J. 1997. *Herodes Attikos and the City of Athens: Patronage and Conflict Under the Antonines.* Amsterdam.

Vlizos, S., ed. 2008. *Athens during the Roman Period: Recent Discoveries, New Evidence.* Athens.

Waterfield, R. 2014. *Taken at the Flood: The Roman Conquest of Greece.* Oxford.

Williams, D. 2013. *The East Pediment of the Parthenon: From Perikles to Nero.* London.

Yegül, F., and D. Favro. 2019. *Roman Architecture and Urbanism: From the Origins to Late Antiquity.* Cambridge.

Additional resources to accompany this chapter can be found at: www.cambridge.org/NeilsRogers

31 | Early Travelers and the Rediscovery of Athens

ROBERT K. PITT

Looking out over the modern city from the top of Mt. Lykabettos or Philopappos Hill, the topographer of today is faced with a blanket of concrete and asphalt stretching up to the mountainous sides of the bowl in which Athens lies. The picture even a hundred years ago was unimaginably different, but the twentieth century brought waves of migrants, fleeing wars and driven from their homelands. As the population exploded and the capital expanded, the landscape of the ancient city was covered, save for the areas of major excavation and heritage sites around the center and the chance discoveries of rescue projects in more recent times.

One result of this modern development for the field of topography is a reliance on the writings of the so-called early travelers who visited Athens from the last days of the Byzantine Empire up to the War of Independence and the foundation of the Greek State in the early nineteenth century, but are particularly well represented from the late seventeenth century on. They form a fascinating group of merchants, grand tourists, diplomats, scholars, artists, and relic hunters, each in search of traces of the physical remains of Athens' glorious past; they were almost exclusively Western Europeans, and most came armed with a classical education. Many left disappointed with the meager village they found clustered around the Akropolis, their progress impeded by what they saw as ignorant priests and corrupt Turks, but they were captivated by the great marble monuments remaining from antiquity. The records of their journeys, published as well as kept in scattered archives, preserve a vital source for a lost world. In this chapter, we will explore some of the more important travelers for the topography of the ancient city in the order in which they arrived and will attempt to understand the motives and goals behind their labors and publications.

Before the Ottoman Conquest

During the Byzantine period, Christian pilgrims flocked to Athens, as its cathedral of the Theotokos Atheniotissa (the converted Parthenon) was one of the most important pilgrimage sites in the empire. A lively set of writings and correspondence survives for the final decades of this era in the works of the Metropolitan bishop of Athens, Michael Choniates. In office from 1182 to 1205, he wrote scathing appraisals of the city in his day from his residence atop the Akropolis. It alone was singled out for praise, seeming as it did "to bestride the very peak of heaven."[1] But in 1204, the Fourth Crusade and the capture of Constantinople resulted in the dividing up of many Greek lands among the conquering knights, and within a year the unhappy lot fell to Choniates to deliver the city over to the Burgundian Otto de la Roche as the first 'Duke of Athens.' It was during the following two-and-a-half centuries of Frankish rule – as the various European rulers were called, in turn French, Catalan, and Italian – that our first Western travelers came to Athens. Perhaps the earliest to leave a systematic account was the Italian notary Niccolò da Martoni, who took a tour of the city's antiquities in 1395, writing a Latin account of his findings that includes the first eyewitness description of the Parthenon and the treasures housed within it since Pausanias.

But the most influential traveler of the period was the indefatigable Cyriacus (or Cyriac) of Ancona (ca. 1391–ca. 1453), a merchant and scholar who took great pleasure in the monuments of antiquity during his many years of extensive travels around the eastern Mediterranean. Cyriacus was in Athens in 1436 and 1444, and although only a fraction of his manuscript letters and diaries has survived, his contribution has led him to be called 'the father of classical archaeology'; he sketched and described the Olympieion (calling it Hadrian's Palace, as many later travelers would also), the Hephaisteion (a Temple of Mars), the Parthenon and Propylaia, and the Tower of the Winds: "we revisited the octagonal temple of Aeolus, which has at the top of the walls eight winged figures of the winds" (trans. Stoneman 2010, 30). His particular interest was in epigraphy, and he is frequently the earliest source to record important inscriptions, such as the dedication from the Monopteros of Rome and Augustus on the Akropolis, and the Greek and Latin texts on the Philopappos Monument, two of which he alone preserved before they were destroyed. A prime example of an Italian humanist and antiquarian, sponsored by cardinals and popes, Cyriacus at the very end of his life may even have been in the camp of Mehmet the Conqueror at the fall of Constantinople in 1453, witnessing that watershed moment in history. His writings preserve a unique snapshot of Athens just before the Frankish Dukes surrendered the city in 1456, after which the Ottoman conquest would throw a veil over

---

[1] For Choniates at Athens, see Kaldellis 2009, 145–165.

Athens that very few outsiders would penetrate for the next 200 years; so much so that the German classicist Martin Crusius (Kraus) was moved in 1573 to enquire of Greek correspondents in Istanbul whether the city of Athens actually still existed. Academic curiosity for the history, monuments, and topography of Athens was not dulled by the lack of autopsy, and scholars in Western Europe continued to gather together information from ancient literature, none more so than the Dutch philologist Johannes Meursius (van Meurs) (1579–1639), whose collections of sources on Athens would prove essential reading material for travelers of later generations attempting to link the snippets of text with the remains on the ground.[2]

Monks, Diplomats, and Scholars in the Seventeenth Century

The isolation of Athens from the eastern pilgrimage trails and trade routes gradually relented during the course of the 1600s, in part because of improved French diplomatic and economic relations with the Ottoman empire under Louis XIV. The Turkish victory at the Siege of Candia (Crete) in 1669 ended a long war with Venice, and diplomatic missions were soon thriving, such as that of the French ambassador to the Porte, the Marquis de Nointel. Possessed of a thirst for classical antiquity and a collecting zeal, he traveled widely around Turkey and Greece, visiting Athens in November 1674. His extensive entourage boasted researchers, antiquaries, stonemasons (with equipment for removing marbles), and artists, including one once identified (perhaps incorrectly) as Jacques Carrey, whose drawings of the Parthenon sculptures are an invaluable record of the monument before the great explosion of 1687, when Venetian cannon struck the powder stores held inside.

A French order of Capuchin monks had established a mission at Athens in 1658 that provided hospitality to a great many travelers over the centuries, including Lord Byron, who took advantage of the reading room created inside the Lysikrates Monument that had been incorporated within the walls of the monastery (Web Fig. 31.1). The Capuchins were evidently keen antiquarians, sending information on the ancient remains to scholars in Paris and elsewhere, and preparing the first plan of the ruins of Athens, which they freely distributed; it would provide the basis for a number of published plans of the city.

---

[2] J. Meurs, *Atticarum Lectionum, Libri vi, in quibus antiquitates plurimae, nunc primum in lucem erutae, profereuntur*, Leiden 1617; *Athenae Atticae. Sive, de praecipuis Athenarum Antiquitatibus, Libri iii*, Leiden 1624.

Diplomats stationed at Athens appear as important figures in travel literature well into the nineteenth century, acting as guides, hosts, interlocutors, and
antiquities agents, such as the French (and later English) consul Jean Giraud
in the late seventeenth century. He would be influential during the sojourn of
two travelers whose works became the standard texts on the city's remains for
the next century, Spon and Wheler. The Lyonnais doctor and antiquary Jacob
Spon (1647–1685) abandoned his medical practice and traveled to Rome in
order to further his studies of the ancient world in 1674, the same year he had
edited and seen through to publication *Relation de l'état present de la ville
d'Athènes*, a work by Jacques-Paul Babin, a Jesuit missionary living in Turkey,
that had been sent to him in Lyon. Babin had visited Athens five times, and
his reflections on the state of the city's tangible past would be one of the first
such eyewitness accounts of its kind to be printed. It spurred Spon to travel
and see for himself what remained of Athens.

While in Rome, Spon was fortunate enough to meet a kindred spirit in
George Wheler (1651–1724). They decided to travel together to Greece,
initially with two further Englishmen, Giles Eastcourt and Francis Vernon,
but they separated at Zakynthos and the latter pair did not fare well.
Eastcourt died of a fever on the way to Delphi, and Vernon was murdered
in Isfahan over an argument about a penknife, a reminder of the ever-
present dangers of travel in the East. Whilst in Venice, Spon received a
copy of a curious volume purportedly by a Frenchman well acquainted
with the situation at Athens called La Guilletière, whose letters home were
published by his brother Georges Guillet de Saint-George (1624–1705) as
Athènes ancienne et nouvelle (Paris 1675), but this was in fact a fabrication
of Guillet cobbled together from classical texts (from Meursius), correspondence with the Capuchin monks in Athens, and sheer flights of fancy.
The book, however, proved immensely popular, running in two years to
three editions and an English translation, and encouraging Guillet to
compose an equally spurious account of a journey to the Peloponnese,
Lacedemone ancienne et nouvelle (Paris 1676). Spon and Wheler had the
book with them during their explorations of Athens in 1676, and Spon
would expend much energy and ink over the remainder of his short life in a
heated and much-publicized polemic with Guillet, who adamantly stuck to
his fantasy, even accusing Spon of never having stepped foot in Athens.[3]

---

[3] See G. de Saint-Georges, *Lettres écrites sur une dissertation d'un voyage de Grèce publié par
M. Spon*, Paris 1679; J. Spon, *Réponse à la critique publiée par M. Guillet sur le Voyage de Grèce
de Jacob Spon*, Lyon 1679.

Spon brought out his own account of his Greek travels in 1678, *Voyage d'Italie, de Dalmatie, de Grèce et du Levant*, a work of great integrity and learning that would place Athenian topographic research on firm scientific ground (Map 31.1). Spon was well acquainted with ancient literature, combining primary sources and observations of monuments and landscape with critiques of previous scholarship and including a great many inscriptions recorded by himself and others. His basic topographic methodology would be imitated by many who followed. Wheler's own account of their travels, *A Journey into Greece*, was published in 1682. With the exception of observations on religion (he became an Anglican cleric) and botany (an interest of several early travelers), it is almost entirely taken from Spon, and yet rather unfairly remained a more popular work. However, it did include an important map of Attika that Wheler had created using a mariner's compass to take triangulations of the topography. Like Cyriacus, their timing was fortuitous, as the resumption of Venetian hostilities, with the invasion of the Morea by Morosini in 1685, would again make travel problematic in Greek lands. Military conquest did, however, bring with it further cartographic advances, as the defenses of Greek towns were mapped by Venetian engineers, whose plans would often accompany

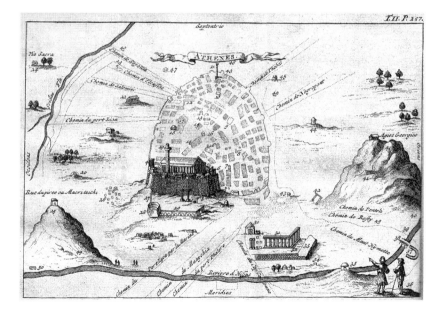

Map 31.1 Plan of Athens in J. Spon, *Voyage d'Italie, de Dalmatie, de Grèce et du Levant* (1678).
Source: R.K. Pitt

volumes on the capture of Athens in 1687. The famous cartographer Vincenzo Coronelli was particularly successful in producing copious editions of plans and maps of Greece, including two of Athens based on those of Spon and Guillet, although a more influential and accurate plan based on the work of Venetian engineers was included in Fanelli's *Atene Attica* (Venice 1707).

Towards Scientific Investigation: The Eighteenth Century

Arguably the greatest single contribution of any mission for the topography and monuments of Athens was the work of James Stuart (1713–1788) and Nicholas Revett (1721–1804). This pair of architects and artists had met in Italy where, in mingling with the grand tourists and diplomats of the day, they were able to raise funds to extend their journey to Greece. Between 1751 and 1753, with professed aims of empirical truth and accuracy, they set about to record the standing architecture of Athens with a level of detail that had not previously been attempted, producing superb architectural plans of the principal remains as well as beautiful views of the city and aspects of contemporary life (by Stuart). Back in England, the Society of Dilettanti agreed to publish the results of their work, although the production would take a very long time, volume one of *The Antiquities of Athens* being published in 1762, the first of five magnificent folio volumes (Stuart would die before the second volume was produced in 1789, although with a title page dated to 1787, and the series was not completed until 1830). The influence of these volumes was profound and helped to fuel the Greek revival movement in Britain, with versions of Greek temples and copies of the Caryatid porch or Lysikrates Monument popping up in the architectural landscape of Britain, some built by Stuart and Revett themselves. The level of accuracy in their plans and detailed drawings exposed the beauty and quality of ancient Greek art and architecture to an eager public who previously had had access only to Roman types and copies. Their travels would also inspire the Society of Dilettanti, an aristocratic drinking club "for which the nominal qualification is having been in Italy, and the real one, being drunk," as Horace Walpole would quip, to aim higher in its pursuit and dissemination of the knowledge of ancient Greece. Stuart and Revett were elected themselves in absentia in 1751.

Stuart and Revett were beaten to publication by Julian-David Le Roy in 1758 with his volume *Les Ruines des plus beaux Monumens de la Grèce*, which depicts many of the same monuments as *The Antiquities of Athens*

Fig. 31.1 The Temple of Artemis Agrotera above the Ilissos, from J. Stuart & N. Revett, *The Antiquities of Athens*, Vol. 1, London 1762.
Source: R.K. Pitt

but in a wholly different manner. Where Stuart and Revett aimed for accuracy, Le Roy cared more for the romance of the scene, adding numerous inaccuracies that would stir controversy and lead Stuart and other Dilettanti members to lengthy attacks against the work. Such disputes led travelers' writings to become obsessed with correcting their predecessors, in a spirit of both national competition and a striving for true depictions of the monuments and sites of Greece.

Stuart and Revett's mission has preserved for us several monuments that would later be damaged or lost entirely, such as the Ionic Temple of Artemis Agrotera above the Ilissos (Fig. 31.1). The building was in large part still standing in the 1750s, having been converted into a church, but it was subsequently demolished for its building material, which was incorporated into the last circuit wall of Athens constructed under the Ottoman Voivode Hadji Ali Haseki in 1778. This act of vandalism also claimed a bridge over the Ilissos River opposite the Panathenaic Stadium, and the façade of the Nymphaeum of Hadrian on Mt. Lykabettos. They would also document for the first time traces of polychromy on the ancient architecture they studied. Stuart followed Spon in meticulously researching the ancient literary sources for the buildings he measured, and improved several identifications such as the Temple of Olympian Zeus (which others had taken for the Pantheon or Palace of Hadrian), although the Library was still a mystery (a Stoa of Hadrian), and the Odeion of Herodes Atticus was erroneously published as the Theater of Dionysos.

The success of Stuart and Revett's work led the Dilettanti to raise funds for a sponsored expedition on behalf of the Society principally to record the antiquities on the west coast of Asia Minor and in Greece. The Society drew up a brief for the travelers, who were "to make exact plans and measurements, to make accurate drawings of the bas-reliefs and ornaments ... copying all the inscriptions you shall meet with, and keeping minute diaries," although they were instructed not to interfere with the continuing publication of *The Antiquities of Athens*. This Ionian Mission became the first such sponsored enterprise with the specific aim of recording the state of the ancient remains, and the Dilettanti placed at its head Richard Chandler (1738–1810), a talented classicist and epigraphist who had been chosen on the basis of his excellent publication of the antiquities of the University of Oxford (*Marmora Oxoniensia*, Oxford 1763). Chandler was joined by Revett and the painter William Pars (1742–1782); the group set out for the east on their two-year mission in 1764, spending longer in Athens than planned when a plague broke out in Smyrna. It was at Athens that Chandler increased his remit from observing to collecting, purchasing specimens of architecture, sculpture, and inscriptions that included two pieces of the Parthenon frieze and an important building account of the Erechtheion (the 'Chandler *stele*'). On his return to London, Chandler deposited these marbles (eventually donated to the British Museum) along with the notebooks and drawings of the expedition with the Society of Dilettanti, who then allowed him to publish first the inscriptions he recorded (*Inscriptiones Antiquae*, Oxford 1774) and his travel diaries (*Travels in Asia Minor*, Oxford 1775; *Travels in Greece*, Oxford 1776), before editing the results of the expedition along with Revett and Pars as the first two parts of *Ionian Antiquities* (London 1769–1797). As with *The Antiquities of Athens*, the series continued for some time, encompassing in Volumes III to V a further Ionian mission undertaken by the Dilettanti, whose members were William Gell, Francis Bedford, and John Gandy, and for Attika one particularly important book of their architectural plans of Eleusis, Rhamnous, Sounion, and Thorikos (*The Unedited Antiquities of Attica*, London 1817).

The most influential of Chandler's works was undoubtedly the *Travels*, which would run to several editions and translations, demonstrating a wide public interest in classical lands; they would act as guidebooks for Asia Minor and Greece for almost a century. The approach was logical and scientific, if not exactly page-turning. Chandler moves from the literary texts to the notices of early travelers, before expounding on the present state of the ruins, often accompanied by lengthy passages of Pausanias or an inscription in translation to help flesh out a reconstruction of the locale. His use of inscriptions is particularly noteworthy: he identifies monument types and groups them into categories, such as the choregic dedications, and attempts to date them by the presence of archon names or by their alphabets and letter shapes.

The Early Nineteenth Century

The two decades leading up to the War of Independence witnessed an explosion of travel to Greece. Fueled by romantic ideas about the West's classical heritage, poets, painters, and tourists poured into Athens, a great many publishing their travel diaries. Most would differ fundamentally in outlook from their eighteenth-century predecessors, such as Chandler, who seems dry and scholarly in comparison to the new wave of travelers in search of the beauty and inspiration that Hellenic lands and ideals had to offer. Some stand out, however, for their contributions to Athenian topography, such as Edward Dodwell, whose superb detailed views of Athens preserve a uniquely accurate account of the contemporary city. Perhaps the most remarkable of the early foreign topographers was Colonel William Martin Leake (1777–1860), whose travels around the eastern Mediterranean as soldier, diplomat, prisoner, and antiquarian provided the basis for several volumes on ancient Greek lands, which with military precision corrected the errors of previous travelogues. His work on Athens remained a foundational text for the topography of the ancient city up to the studies of Walther Judeich (1859–1942).[4]

Travelers had for centuries taken information about Athens from long-term residents, whether from the Capuchin monks or the English and French diplomats stationed in the city, and none would be more influential for the study and collecting of Athenian antiquities than Louis-François-Sébastien Fauvel (1753–1838). Fauvel had traveled extensively in the eastern Mediterranean, partly as a member of the scientific and artist entourage of the Comte de Choiseul-Gouffier, French ambassador at Istanbul. He would eventually secure a diplomatic mission himself, and his residence in

[4] W.M. Leake, *The Topography of Athens: With Some Remarks on Its Antiquities*, London 1821 (2nd edn. 1841); W. Judeich, *Topographie von Athen*, Munich 1931.

Athens was an essential call for the travelers of the day, hosting visitors among paintings of Athens and the antiquities he had excavated and collected (Web Fig. 32.2). Fauvel acted as a guide to the monuments of the city, and funded much of his activities as a wily dealer in antiquities for his foreign clients. Many of his detailed notes on the monuments and inscriptions of Athens were lost, and the remainder (in the Bibliothèque nationale in Paris) he did not manage to publish, but his influence is principally to be seen in the plan of Athens he produced around 1787 or later, copies of which were circulated and eventually published (Map 31.2). His detailed records of the city's surviving remains provide crucial documentation before much of the city was destroyed in the ensuing War of Independence. During the hostilities between Greeks and Ottomans, the urban fabric was bombarded, resulting in many deaths and the almost total devastation of the lower town, Fauvel's house, and its ancient contents.

Fauvel, in fact, forms a link between the world of the travelers and the succeeding generations of professional archaeologists of the new Greek

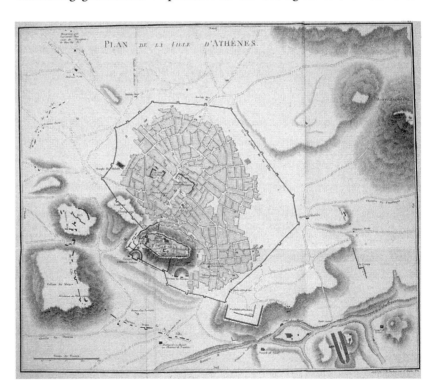

Map 31.2 Plan of Athens by Fauvel published in G.-A. Olivier, *Atlas pour servir au voyage dans l'Empire othoman, l'Égypte et la Perse*, Paris 1807, pl. 49.
Source: R.K. Pitt

State in his tutoring of the young Kyriakos Pittakis (1798–1863), who had fought in the war against the Ottomans. Pittakis went on to become one of Greece's first archaeological overseers, organizing restoration efforts on the Akropolis, setting up the earliest public collections of marbles, and playing an instrumental role in the founding of the Archaeological Society at Athens in 1837. (See also Costaki, Chapter 33 in this volume.) With the creation of archaeological bodies to rescue and protect the monuments of Athens, and dedicated men such as Pittakis to record the discoveries being made, studies of the topography and history of the ancient city were placed on a solid footing, and the publications and pillaging of travelers gave way to systematic and salvage excavations and an accompanying academic dialogue that continues unabated up to the present.

Further Reading

For Athenian monuments and sources in the Byzantine period, see Kaldellis 2009 and Bouras 2017. For detailed bibliographic information of the publications of the early travelers to Greece, see Paton 1951, Weber 1952 and 1953, Navari 1989, and for a collection of images from these works, Tsigakou 2007. The story of travels to Athens is told by Laborde 1854, and travelers within their intellectual and cultural context are discussed in Tsigakou 1981, Stoneman 2010, and Constantine 2011. Accounts of individual travels and missions include: for Cyriacus of Ancona, Bodnar 1960 and Chatzidakis 2017; for the Dilettanti Society, Kelly 2009; for Stuart and Revett, Weber Soros 2006; for Dodwell, Camp 2013; and for Fauvel, Zambon 2014.

Bibliography

Bodnar, E.W. 1960. *Cyriacus of Ancona and Athens*. Brussels.
Bouras, C. 2017. *Byzantine Athens: 10th–12th Centuries*. London.
Camp, J.M. 2013. *In Search of Greece: Catalogue of an Exhibit of Drawings at the British Museum by Edward Dodwell and Simone Pomardi*. Los Altos, CA.
Chatzidakis, M. 2017. *Ciriaco d'Ancona und die Wiederentdeckung Griechenlands im 15. Jahrhundert*. Wiesbaden.
Constantine, D. 2011. *In the Footsteps of the Gods: Travellers to Greece and the Quest for the Hellenic Ideal*. London.
Kaldellis, A. 2009. *The Christian Parthenon: Classicism and Pilgrimage in Byzantine Athens*. Cambridge.
Kelly, J.M. 2009. *The Society of Dilettanti: Archaeology and Identity in the British Enlightenment*. New Haven.
Laborde, le comte Léon de. 1854. *Athènes aux XVᵉ, XVIᵉ et XVIIᵉ siècles*. Paris.

Navari, L. 1989. *Greece and the Levant: The Catalogue of the Henry Myron Blackmer Collection of Books and Manuscripts.* London.

Paton, J. M. 1951. *Chapters on Mediaeval and Renaissance Visitors to Greek Lands.* Princeton.

Stoneman, R. 2010. *Land of Lost Gods: The Search for Classical Greece.* London.

Tsigakou, F.-M. 1981. *The Rediscovery of Greece.* London.

     2007. *Athens through the Eyes of Artists-Travelers 16th–19th Centuries.* Athens.

Weber, S.H. 1952. *Voyages and Travels in the Near East Made During the XIX Century.* Princeton.

     1953. *Voyages and Travels in Greece, the Near East and Adjacent Regions Made Previous to the Year 1801.* Princeton.

Weber Soros, S., ed. 2006. *James "Athenian" Stuart: The Rediscovery of Antiquity.* New Haven.

Zambon, A. 2014. *Aux origines de l'archéologie en Grèce: Fauvel et sa méthode.* Paris.

Additional resources to accompany this chapter can be found at: www.cambridge.org/NeilsRogers

ROBERT A. BRIDGES JR.

The story of post-antique Athens is a very different one from the stories of such cities as Rome and Constantinople/İstanbul, both of which retained their roles as centers of secular and religious power and as places of pilgrimage from antiquity until modern times. Athens continued to play a major role in the intellectual history of both East and West as well, but as a name, an idea/ideal, rather than as a physical entity until the time of its reentry onto the European stage in the early nineteenth century.

The Background

Athens declined as a center of political influence during the later Roman Empire but still maintained a certain degree of intellectual clout due to the continuing presence there of the schools of rhetoric and philosophy. When these were shut down by Justinian in AD 529, the city was reduced to the rank of a small provincial center and suffered to a greater or lesser extent from the ongoing 'barbarian invasions' in the middle years of the Byzantine Empire. There seems to have been a certain late flourishing in the period around AD 1000, but the city was never again to reach a point of significant cultural or political influence.

After the Fourth Crusade of 1204, a series of Frankish dynasties under the overall sovereignty of the kings of Sicily and later the kings of Aragon established the Duchy of Athens, first ruled by the Burgundian de la Roche and de Brienne families from 1205 until 1311. This was followed by a takeover by the Catalan Company from 1311 until 1388, and finally by the Florentine Acciaioli dynasty from 1388 until the Ottoman conquest of 1456, with a short Venetian interval from 1395 to 1402. During all these periods, the city was restricted to a small settlement around the north slope of the Akropolis enclosed by the rebuilt third-century post-Herulian fortification wall, corresponding more or less to the area occupied by the modern district of Plaka. The Akropolis itself served as the seat and residence of the ruling dynasty.

The period of the Ottoman domination of the city (*Tourkokratia*) saw considerable expansion of the city to the north.[1] The Ottoman governors and garrison still resided on the Akropolis itself and the Muslim inhabitants of the city clustered in the area immediately below. The Greek population occupied the area further north of this and remains of a surprising number of churches can be dated to this period. The Ottoman city was initially unfortified, except for the Akropolis itself, until after the Venetian siege by Morosini of 1687/88 that nearly destroyed the Parthenon. In the period immediately preceding the Greek War of Independence, the city included 1,930 families, with over 75 percent of its population being Greek Orthodox.

The Greek War of Independence

The Greek War of Independence broke out in March 1821. The combatants in the war were many and varied. The local inhabitants (the autochthons) were made up of a mix of landlords, town notables, seamen, merchants, members of the Orthodox clergy, peasants, and brigands, all of whom hoped to profit politically and economically from the expulsion of their Ottoman overlords. The foreigners (the heterochthons) included members of the Greek diaspora and philhellenes of various nationalities, all of whom were steeped both in classical culture and in the ideas and ideals of the Enlightenment and the French Revolution.

Almost from the outset of the revolution, a series of National Assemblies were called with the avowed purpose of administering the new nation state and establishing a constitution for it.[2] Count Ioannis Kapodistrias was named head of state in 1827, and the provisional capital of the new democracy was established in the Peloponnesian port of Nauplion. Previously, Kapodistrias, a native of Corfu, had served as Foreign Minister to Alexander I, Tsar of Russia and, as such, had traveled extensively in Western Europe. He was a master of diplomacy and intimately familiar with the current European political situation. In addition to a series of administrative measures designed to bring Greece in line with current European practices, he was also concerned

---

[1] On Ottoman Athens, see most recently Georgopoulou and Thanasakis 2019.
[2] Assemblies were held in Epidauros in late 1821, in Astros in 1823, in Epidauros, Aigina, and Troezen in 1827, in Argos in 1829, and in Nauplion in 1831.

with the physical rebuilding of the war-ravished country and called upon a number of European-trained architects and planners to carry out a far-ranging series of projects – land redistribution, refugee housing, construction of schools, and planning new towns to cater to the needs of the population displaced by the ongoing hostilities. In the current context, it was his administration that commissioned two young German-trained architects in 1831 to produce a detailed topographical plan of Athens and its surviving monuments of the ancient, medieval, and Ottoman periods, as well as a plan for its redevelopment (see below).

After Kapodistrias' assassination in 1831 and the ensuing political upheaval, the 'Protecting Powers' (Great Britain, France, and Russia) held a conference in London in 1832 to determine the future of the new state. No Greek representatives were included in the proceedings. It was decided that a monarchy should be installed and the throne was offered to the 17-year-old prince Otto of Wittelsbach, younger son of King Ludwig I of Bavaria, one of the leading philhellenes of the day. The Treaty of Constantinople in 1832 between the Protecting Powers and the Ottoman Empire formally recognized the independence of the new kingdom and fixed its borders. Otto arrived in Nauplion in February of 1833.

The problem of a capital city for the new kingdom was a matter of some concern. Nauplion, Argos, Tripolis, the Isthmus of Corinth, Megara, and Piraeus all had their advocates, and many believed that any decision about a capital could only be deemed a temporary one, since the obvious capital for a kingdom of all the Greeks could only be 'the City' – Constantinople. However, Ludwig I's decision, seconded by the members of Otto's Bavarian regency, prevailed, and, on September 18, 1834, Athens was officially declared the capital of the Kingdom of Greece.

Athens had suffered enormously during the years of the war. In 1821, an uprising of the local residents had expelled the Ottoman garrison from the Akropolis, but the Ottoman troops returned in 1826 (Fig. 32.1) and, after a siege of almost a year, recaptured the Akropolis, where they were to remain in control until late March 1833.[3] The local Athenian population

---

[3] A famous general in the Greek War of Independence, Ioannis Makriyannis (1797–1864), wrote his memoirs of the war, which he later had illustrated with 24 watercolor paintings by Dimitrios Zographos. For more on Makriyannis and illustrations of these paintings, see Georgopoulou 2018.

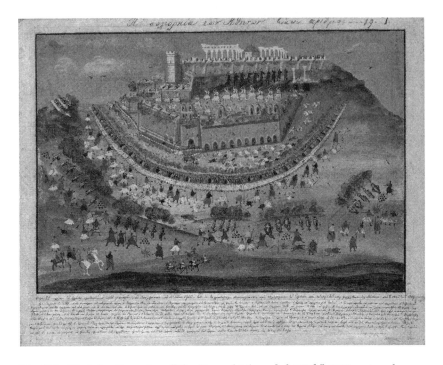

Fig. 32.1 Dimitrios Zographos, "The Siege of Athens [of 1826]," 1836, watercolor on cardboard, 50 × 63 cm. Commissioned to accompany the *Memoirs* of Ioannis Makriyannis.
Courtesy of the American School of Classical Studies at Athens: Gennadius Library

abandoned the city, which had been reduced to a field of ruins, only to make a hesitant return and begin reconstruction in 1831 after the establishment of the newly independent state. An often-cited reference by Christopher Wordsworth in his "Athens and Attica: Journal of a Residence There" describes the state of affairs in 1832/33:

> The town of Athens is now lying in ruins. The streets are almost deserted: nearly all the houses are without roofs. The churches are reduced to bare walls and heaps of stones and mortar. There is but one church in which the service is performed. A few new wooden houses, one or two of more solid structure, and the two lines of planked sheds which form the bazar [*sic*] are all the inhabited dwellings that Athens can now boast. So slowly does it recover from the effects of the late war.

From a medium-sized town of some 12,000 inhabitants at the beginning of the war, the city had been reduced to no more than 4,000 souls when Otto arrived in his new capital in 1834.

The Kleanthes and Schaubert Plan

Stamatios Kleanthes and Eduard Schaubert arrived in Athens in 1831 and began work on their survey of the city and its surviving monuments.[4] The result of their topographical research was a proposed plan for the reconstruction of Athens. It took into account all the surviving monuments and used them as the framework on which to build a modern royal capital, one which would be worthy of the city's glorious past, with all necessary administrative and civic structures for a projected population of 40,000 people. It followed the contemporary Late Baroque formulae of other such new capitals as Versailles and Washington, DC, featuring broad tree-lined boulevards and grand open spaces lined with monumental public structures forming impressive vistas connecting to the surrounding landscape.

The basis of the plan (Map 32.1) was a right triangle composed of two major avenues, one (modern Stadiou Street) determined by the axis of the ancient Panathenaic Stadium, the other (modern Peiraios Street) a continuation of the direct route to the port of Piraeus. (See also Map 4.2.) This right angle was bisected by a major north–south avenue (modern Athinas Street) leading visually to the Propylaia of the Akropolis. The intersection of these three major arteries (modern Omonia Square) was to be occupied by the projected royal palace, allowing a visual dialogue between the seat of the new monarchy and the glories of the ancient past. The central north–south avenue was to be flanked by parallel avenues leading to the Tower of the Winds (modern Aiolou Street) and the Areopagos (never constructed). Along this central tree-lined axis were major open squares accommodating the theater, a casino, stock exchange, commercial establishments and, farther along, the central markets. Two other major streets were to cross this central axis at right angles, both anchored by surviving monuments from the city's past – current Evripidou Street, with the eleventh-century Church of Agioi Theodoroi at one end and the sixth-century Church of Agios Ioannis stin Kolonna at the other, and the current Ermou Street with the eleventh-century Church of Panagia Kapnikarea at about its

---

[4] Kleanthes was born in Kozani and later moved to Bucharest. He fought with Alexandros Ypsilantis in his unsuccessful campaign against the Ottoman forces in 1821 before moving to Vienna and Leipzig to study architecture and then on to Berlin, where he studied with Karl Friedrich Schinkel. Schaubert was born in Breslau, where he studied before joining Schinkel's classes in Berlin.

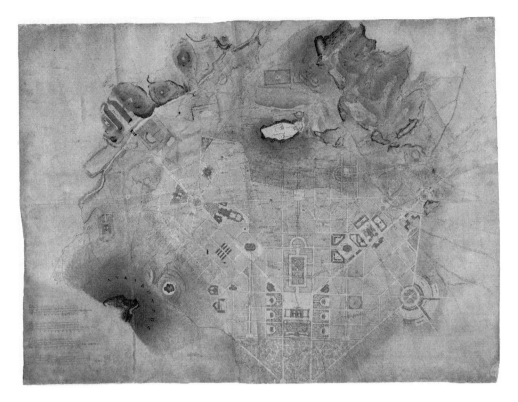

Map 32.1 S. Kleanthes and E. Schaubert, "Second Plan for the New City of Athens," 1833.
© Deutsches Archäologisches Institut, Athen, Neg. 72.3354

mid-point. Both these transverse streets terminated in large planted squares where they intersected the two diagonal avenues framing the plan. Ministries, the Parliament buildings, and various other governmental offices were located on either side of the palace along the two major diagonal venues.

A further feature of the Kleanthes and Schaubert plan was the provision of an open, unbuilt archaeological zone on the north slope of the Akropolis which was to include almost the entire area of the modern Plaka district. This area had been primarily occupied in pre-revolutionary times by the Muslim population of the town, and thus few returning Athenians could lay claim to building lots in the area. The idea was to set this zone apart for future excavations, after which time it could be landscaped and become a promenade area for both the local population and for visitors interested in the antiquities of the city. The plan was submitted to Otto's government and accepted by the same royal decree that named Athens as the capital of the realm in the summer of 1833.

Modifications to Kleanthes and Schaubert's Plan

The realization of Kleanthes and Schaubert's plan got off to a rocky start. As they had already warned in the memorandum attached to their proposal, land values increased dramatically with the declaration of Athens' new status. The local population had begun to return to the city after the independence of the new state and had already started to rebuild their shattered homes, thus making expropriations for the creation of the new streets and squares in the area of the preexisting city considerably more complicated and expensive. Otto's government was seriously short of cash. The plan was also criticized by the local residents as overambitious, and so, in 1834, Otto's father, King Ludwig, dispatched one of his court architects, Leo von Klenze, to Athens to examine the situation on the ground. The upshot of this visit was a revision, although not a total abandonment, of the original scheme. The major avenues were reduced in width and the squares reduced in size. The principal alteration was the relocation of the proposed royal palace and associated governmental buildings from the northern apex of the triangle to its western corner, in the area of the ancient Kerameikos. Thus, the palace gardens could be directly in contact with the archaeological zone. While a certain number of economies were occasioned by the reduction in size of the interventions in the area of the existing city, the overall financial condition of the country rendered von Klenze's proposal unrealistic as well.

King Ludwig himself paid a visit to Athens in 1835, accompanied by yet another of his court architects, Friedrich von Gärtner. During this visit, Ludwig and von Gärtner took matters in hand and finalized the plan for the new capital. The site of the palace was moved yet again, this time to the eastern apex of the triangle, and its design was assigned to von Gärtner. The overall triangular layout of the original scheme was retained, although with some drastic reductions. The new streets which had already been driven through the old town and partially paved (Athinas, Aiolou, and Ermou) were retained, but the third parallel north–south street and the other projected *percements* were abandoned, as was the entire area of the archaeological zone, which had already begun to be built up by the returning residents. The foundations for the new palace were begun in January of 1836.

King Ludwig's direct interventions were crucial for the final developments of the plan for the new capital. It was he who declared that the surviving monuments of the city's past should all be preserved and that no modern structures should be constructed to conflict with them, thus, in effect, vetoing another proposal for the construction of the royal palace – Schinkel's plan to situate the palace on the Akropolis itself. (See also Costaki, Chapter 33 in this volume.) It was also Ludwig who provided the funds for the construction of the palace, a stripped-down version of von Gärtner's project without the added decorative elements envisioned by the architect.

Building the New Nation

One of the fundamental aims of the new government was to create a sense of unified nationhood among the disparate groups of the population. The governing classes were, for the most part, foreign-educated and had been raised with a reverence for all things ancient Greek. The local population, on the other hand, had only the vaguest notion of their Classical heritage and, after three-and-a-half centuries of Ottoman rule, considered that what made one 'Greek' was a commitment to the Orthodox Church and a certain independent attitude vis-à-vis the government. The key to resolving this difficulty was thought to be education and a concurrent desire to connect all the disparate factions of the nation with the Classical Greek past.

This scheme manifested itself in a variety of ways. From 1833 on, various sources had proposed a revival of the Olympic Games as a symbol of the connection of the new kingdom with its heroic past and, as early as 1837, Otto proclaimed that there should be a "national gathering with contests in agriculture, industry and athletic games." Although he did not use the words 'Olympic Games,' the choice of events (discus, javelin, long jump, foot races, wrestling, chariot racing) makes clear that they were the inspiration. These games did not take place until sometime later, although a wealthy member of the Greek diaspora in Romania, Evangelis Zappas, offered to cover their expenses, including the excavation of the ancient stadium and its rebuilding and refurbishing in marble. The financial contribution was gratefully accepted, but the monies were deployed else-where. The first games of 1859 were a haphazard affair, held in one of the city's squares, and a woeful flop. However, those of 1870 were held in the ancient stadium, were a great success, and paved the way for the first official International Olympic Committee games of 1896 – also held in the ancient stadium, now fully refurbished with marble seating. (See also Rogers, Chapter 30 in this volume.)

Public education, however, was the major thrust, and so, after construction work began on the palace, the next major architectural project to be undertaken in 1839 was the University, designed by the Danish architect Hans Christian Hansen, who had been appointed court architect in 1834. This was followed by a spate of school buildings, many of them monumental structures paid for by wealthy members of the Greek diaspora and, for the most part, designed by foreign-trained Greek architects.

One of the government's most far-reaching measures was the establishment of an official language for the country, one which could be used in the public education sector as a means of ensuring that the local speakers of a variety of often mutually incomprehensible dialects that had developed during the Byzantine and Ottoman epochs would have a common tongue. The chosen idiom was known as *Katharevousa*, the purified language. This was a linguistic invention proposed by various members of the Greek diaspora during the pre-revolutionary period and brought to its definite form by Adamantios Korais in the late eighteenth century. He sought to free the common vernacular (*Dimotiki*) from the accumulation of foreign vocabulary which it had acquired over the course of the centuries. It was based on a hypothetical language directly descended from the Classical Attic Greek of the fifth century BC without any external influences. Although *Katharevousa* was never declared the official language of the new kingdom, it was used exclusively in government proceedings, official documents, and as the basis for the educational system.[5] This situation continued until 1976 when, in the immediate post-junta era, linguistic reform measures declared that *Dimotiki* should be the sole language of education at all levels.

Greece did not institute a formal school of architecture until 1917, although the Royal School of Arts, founded in 1837, served as a training ground for engineers. Therefore, the architects of the major buildings of the new capital were either foreigners or foreign-trained Greeks, educated in the prevailing modes of architectural expression of the late eighteenth and early nineteenth-century academies of France, Germany, or Italy. Less ostentatious projects were often handled by military or civil engineers or simple builders.

---

[5] Well into the twentieth century, *Katharevousa* was the language of university instruction and, more bothersome for the students, university written exams. The proponents of *Katharevousa* versus *Dimotiki* were often divided along political lines: conservatives, royalists, and the clergy siding with the purified form of the language, while leftists, some major literary figures, and the public masses favored *Dimotiki*.

Public Buildings

The earliest public buildings of the new capital were, for the most part, minor administrative buildings necessary for the functioning of the government (the royal printing office in 1834 and the mint in 1836) or utilitarian structures (the military and municipal hospitals in 1836). Almost all the major projects envisioned by Otto's government were cultural institutions – the University in 1838, the Observatory in 1842, the Academy in 1859 (Web Fig. 32.1). Notably missing from the list are the monumental governmental buildings which formed a prominent feature of the Kleanthes and Schaubert plan – the only exception being the Parliament building on Stadiou Street, begun in 1858. Other later civic buildings also normally adhered to the so-called Neoclassical style: the town hall in 1872, the Polytechneion in 1873, the Zappeion exhibition hall in 1874, the National Archaeological Museum in 1886, and the National Library in 1888, as well as orphanages, schools, and hospitals.

The early official buildings of the capital are remarkable for their adherence to Classical models – often including direct quotations of elements from surviving ancient monuments. Thus, the University reproduces the Ionic columns of the Propylaia, the Academy quotes liberally from the Erechtheion, and the National Library's central section is a direct copy of the Temple of Hephaistos, albeit on a reduced scale. This is not altogether surprising, since many of the architects commissioned to construct these buildings had initially come to Athens as part of their post-educational grand tour and had studied, or directly participated in, the excavations on the Akropolis and the restorations of its monuments. The single exception to this Neoclassical monopoly of civic architecture is the neo-Byzantine eye clinic of 1848 by Hans Christian Hansen next to the University.

Religious Buildings

While most governmental, civic, educational, and cultural buildings of the nineteenth century stayed close to ancient prototypes in their exterior design, religious structures were another matter. As noted above, the number of churches surviving from the pre-revolutionary period was vastly reduced. Of the 129 churches recorded in the mid-1820s, only twenty-four survived after the final expulsion of the Ottoman troops, with another seventeen in ruins. In addition to shoring up existing Orthodox churches and building new ones for the expanding Greek population, the Protecting

Powers also desired places of worship for their co-religionists. King Otto was Roman Catholic, Queen Amalia was Protestant, and the nation as a whole was overwhelmingly Greek Orthodox. A new Roman Catholic cathedral was built in neo-Renaissance style on plans by Leo von Klenze (1853–1865); an Anglican church in neo-Gothic style was constructed following plans by Charles Cockerell and Christian Hansen (1839–1843); a surviving eleventh-century Byzantine church was restored and redecorated for use by the Russian Orthodox community (1847–1855). The construction of the Greek Orthodox cathedral on plans by Theophil Hansen (the brother of Christian Hansen) in neo-Byzantine style was begun in 1842.[6] Other major new ecclesiastical constructions in various neo-Byzantine idioms were also constructed along the major avenues of the new city: Agia Eirini (1847) and Panagia Chrysospiliotissa (1863) on Aiolou Street; Zoodochos Pigi (1846) on Akadimias Street; and, in newly created squares in the area of the old city, Agios Georgios Karytsi (1845).

Domestic Architecture

The earliest houses of Athens were simple rebuildings of the houses of the Ottoman period. They usually consisted of one- or two-story structures clustered around open courtyards, often overlooked by a deeply recessed loggia. Street façades were plain and undecorated. With the influx of members of the Bavarian court and other newcomers to the city, a new type of dwelling made its appearance. Individual two-story houses without courtyards but with architecturally articulated façades became the rule. This fashion was increasingly adopted by the local populace to create what one now has a tendency to consider the 'traditional' Athenian house with a façade embellished with classical elements (often mass-produced elements of terracotta) with a central, slightly projecting balcony held up on marble consoles and enclosed by wrought iron railings, and a lively roofscape enriched by terracotta antefixes and even life-sized sculptures. Local terracotta, marble, and wrought iron industries were kept busy mass-producing architectural elements, which could be applied with greater or lesser appropriateness to what were basically vernacular buildings.

   With the growing population of the city and the arrival of wealthy members of the Greek diaspora, competition among architects and proprietors became more and more intense and architectural articulation became

---

[6] Lack of funds and changes of designs/architects (Dimitris Zezos, Panagis Kalkos, François-Louis-Florimond Boulanger) delayed completion until 1862.

increasingly elaborate, with a preference for town mansions influenced by the flamboyant style associated with the Parisian École des Beaux-Arts.

The architecture of Athens was dominated by the work of Ernst Ziller, another German architect who came to Athens in 1861 and stayed there until his death in 1923. Initially, he was involved in the completion of works begun by others, but during the latter part of the nineteenth century, his exuberant mix of classical and Renaissance elements made him much in demand, and his numerous churches, palaces, theaters, and especially private residences transformed Athens into a modern European metropolis. The relatively sober Neoclassical and neo-Byzantine buildings of the early years of the new capital were now being upstaged by a much more eclectic mix of elements drawn from a wider range of sources and periods.

Decline of Neoclassicism

Neoclassicism was not entirely dead, however. It continued to be used for official buildings, mostly hospitals and educational institutions, down to the end of the century. It has been periodically revived in later periods, in relatively pure form for new constructions (e.g. the Gennadius Library of 1926) or for revamping eclectic nineteenth-century buildings for government use (the transformation of Ziller's romantic Andreas Syngrou Mansion into the Neoclassical Ministry of Foreign Affairs during the 1930s) or as an inspiration for a more modern idiom (as in the United States Embassy of 1959–1961 by Walter Gropius interpreting the architecture of the Parthenon through a Bauhaus lens, Web Fig. 32.2). By and large, however, the fourth Congrès International d'Architecture Moderne (CIAM) of 1933 (which later produced the famous "Charter of Athens" under the direction of Le Corbusier) and the writings of modern architectural critic Sigfried Giedion provided local Athenian architects with direct access to the avant-garde of Western Europe and marked the end of the revivalist movements of the nineteenth century.

Further Reading

For more on the development of architecture in modern Athens and Greece, see Tzonis and Rodi 2013. On the history and development of Athens as a city and capital of Greece, see Travlos 1981, Bastéa 2000, Papageorgiou-Venetas 2001 (in Greek, but well illustrated), and Beaton 2019 (with previous bibliography); further, see Hamilakis 2007 on the relationship between modern Greece and its ancient past. See Scully 1963 for an entertaining exploration of the relationship between Kleanthes and the Duchess of Plakentias. The Akropolis in the nineteenth century has been presented by Carter 1979 and Tomlinson 1987. The work of Danish architects in Athens in the nineteenth century has been explored by Bendtsen 1993 and Cassimatis and Panetsos 2014 (in Greek), along with Kardamitsi-Adami 2006 on the architecture of Ziller. Biris and Kardamitsi-Adami 2005 offers a lavishly illustrated introduction to Neoclassical architecture in Greece. Dumont 2020 explores the neighborhood of Vrysaki in Plaka that was razed with the start of the excavations of the Athenian Agora in 1931.

Bibliography

Beaton, R. 2019. *Greece: Biography of a Modern Nation.* Chicago.

Bendtsen, M. 1993. *Sketches and Measurings: Danish Architects in Greece, 1818–1862.* Copenhagen.

Bastéa, E. 2000. *The Creation of Modern Athens: Planning the Myth.* Cambridge.

Biris, M., and M. Kardamitsi-Adami. 2005. *Neoclassical Architecture in Greece.* Athens.

Carter, R. 1979. "Karl Friedrich Schinkel's Project for a Royal Palace on the Acropolis." *JSAH* 38.1: 34–46.

Cassimatis, M.Z., and G.A. Panetsos. 2014. *'Hellenische Renaissance': The Architecture of Theophil Hansen (1813–1891).* Athens.

Dumont, S. 2020. *Vrysaki: A Neighborhood Lost in Search of the Athenian Agora.* Princeton.

Georgopoulou, M., ed. 2018. *Ioannis Makriyannis: Vital Expression.* Athens.

Georgopoulou, M., and K. Thanasakis, eds. 2019. *Ottoman Athens: Archaeology, Topography, History.* Princeton.

Hamilakis, Y. 2007. *The Nation and Its Ruins: Antiquity, Archaeology, and National Imagination in Greece.* Oxford.

Kardamitsi-Adami, M. 2006. *Classical Revival: The Architecture of Ernst Ziller, 1837–1923.* Athens.

Papageorgiou-Venetas, A. 2001. *Αθήνα: Ένα όραμα του Κλασικισμού.* Athens.

Scully, V. 1963. "Kleanthes and the Duchess of Piacenza." *JSAH* 22.3: 139–154.

Tomlinson, R.A. 1987. "The Acropolis of Athens in the 1870s: The Evidence of the Alma-Tadema Photographs." *Annual of the British School at Athens* 82: 297–304.

Travlos, J. 1981. "Athens after the Liberation: Planning the New City and Exploring the Old." *Hesperia* 50.4: 391–407.

Tzonis, A., and P. Rodi. 2013. *Greece, Modern Architectures in History.* London.

Additional resources to accompany this chapter can be found at: www.cambridge.org/NeilsRogers

33 | Urban Archaeology: Uncovering the Ancient City

LEDA COSTAKI

The existence of modern Athens lies in a paradox. The very reason for its choice as the capital city of Greece in 1833 – its glorious Classical past – became a thorn in the side of development and modernization. The constant conflict between new construction and old antiquities overshadows the history of Athenian urbanization. Any modern city built over an ancient site is bound to wrestle with this challenge. However, because Athens is considered the cradle of Western civilization and the Classical past lies at the heart of the Greek national narrative, Athenian antiquities are surrounded by an aura of sanctity, unlike that of any other city.[1]

Urban Archaeology after 1834

The impression given by the town after the War of Independence was one of ruins, chaos, and misery. At the time of liberation, the archaeology of Athens was largely unknown, despite the hordes of European travelers who had passed by over the centuries, producing accounts and drawings of varying quality and reliability. (See Pitt, Chapter 31 in this volume.) Besides the Akropolis with the Parthenon, most of the other standing monuments in the city were variously identified, while attempts to locate the sites mentioned in Pausanias' *Periegesis* and to reconstruct the ancient topography presented many discrepancies. To mention but a few examples, the Odeion of Herodes Atticus was identified as the Theater of Dionysos, the Temple of Olympian Zeus as the Palace of Hadrian, and the Library of Hadrian was known as the Temple of Zeus.

With the formation of the Greek state came large-scale excavations on the Akropolis, along its slopes, and in the lower city to reveal the standing Classical monuments so much venerated by foreigners and locals alike. As had happened so often in the past after widespread destructions, the city had to be cleared of masses of debris and accumulated ruins. In the lower city, it was more a matter of rescuing works of art and inscriptions from

---

[1] Hamilakis 2007; Bastéa 2000.

their reuse as building materials or from being sold and relocated. From the same period and in the context of early designs for a new city plan dates the initial discussion for the creation of an archaeological zone. Stamatis Kleanthes and Eduard Schaubert, as well as Leo von Klenze (1834),[2] envisioned an area around the Akropolis free of buildings for the creation of an archaeological park; however, the pressing housing needs of a fast-growing population and the state of chaos that prevailed in the city soon cancelled all such plans. (See Bridges, Chapter 32 in this volume.) When the government in 1834 asked the German archaeologist and Ephor of Antiquities of Greece, Ludwig Ross, to define specific sites with antiquities around the Akropolis which were absolutely in need of protection and had to be expropriated, Ross, along with his Greek colleague, Kyriakos Pittakis, selected thirteen sites. This list had to be drastically condensed to five, never to be officially ratified and implemented.[3] It was only in the late 1990s that the vision for the unification of archaeological sites of Athens began to be implemented. It constitutes the second most radical change in the archaeological landscape of the city following the creation of the Agora archaeological site and park in the 1930s.

The history of Athenian urban archaeology is associated with certain figures who dedicated their lives and work to the field. In the early years, the founding fathers of Greek archaeology, K. Pittakis, P. Eustratiades, and Stephanos Koumanoudes saved, recorded, and protected what they considered their ancestors' heritage. They fought vehemently against the destruction of antiquities, whether by halting illegal quarrying of the hills with remains of ancient habitation, by saving marble antiquities from being thrown in the lime kilns, or by collecting any important finds from private plots during the opening of foundations for new houses. The twentieth century saw the reorganization of the Greek Archaeological Service, which entered a new era of more systematic work and better structured record keeping in 1960 under the General Director of Antiquities, J. Papademetriou. The reappearance of the *Archaiologikon Deltion*, the official journal of the Service, after a lapse of almost thirty years, was a major achievement of those years and remains an invaluable source of information. In the first volume of this new period (*ArchDelt* 16, 1960), six excavations were reported from Athens, including the Academy of Plato, with three plans and a few photographs.

---

[2] For the early plans of the new city, see Korres 2010.
[3] Biris 1995, 61–62.

The twentieth century also saw milestone works by Walther Judeich and John Travlos. Although Judeich's *Topographie von Athen* (1905/1931) set the solid foundations for all future research in the city, it was, undoubtedly, John Travlos (1908–1985) who became the leading figure of Athenian topography over the last century.[4] With his two seminal books, Πολεοδομική εξέλιξις των Αθηνών (1960) and the *Pictorial Dictionary of Ancient Athens* (1971), he shaped our knowledge of Athenian topography. Although not a member of the Archaeological Service himself, he seems to have been present at every rescue excavation in the city, having access to all new discoveries, drawing plans, and keeping notes. His personal papers housed in the Archives of the Archaeological Society at Athens provide not only valuable insights on his work but also on his commitment to plotting new information. One particular sketch of the excavation at Menandrou and Sapphous Streets was made on Christmas day 1968!

Creation of Archaeological Sites

The creation of the archaeological sites in the city as we know them today started in the nineteenth century with the clearing of all later additions on the Akropolis and the gradual excavations of the standing monuments of the lower city. The first five officially declared archaeological sites were the areas around the Theseion (later correctly identified as the Temple of Hephaistos), the Lysikrates Monument, the Roman Agora, the 'Prytaneion' (Diogeneion), the Stoa of Attalos, and the 'Giants' of the Agora. Other major areas were yet to be included in the archaeological plan of the city. The well-preserved Library of Hadrian was excluded, since the bazaar and infantry barracks existed there. To the southeast of the Akropolis, the Olympieion with the Arch of Hadrian had always been in the outskirts of the city and was never enveloped by the urban fabric. Free of later additions, the area was mostly defined by the laying out of adjoining roads. The Panathenaic Stadium also lay outside the built environment, its concave shape ever visible on the slopes of the Ardettos Hill. It was eventually excavated by the architect Ernst Ziller in 1868–1869 and rebuilt in Pentelic marble for the first modern Olympic Games of 1896. Despite extensive quarrying that scarred the Hill of the Muses (Philopappos Hill), the Pnyx, and the Hill of the Nymphs, these hills to the west of the Akropolis were equally isolated and untouched by the new capital city.

[4] See Kokkou 2020 for a biography of Travlos.

Monuments of the Byzantine, Frankish, and Ottoman periods fell victim to the cleansing operations that took place across the city, despite the fact that already in 1837 a decree had been passed for the protection of medieval remains in Athens. After the demolition of the Frankish tower of the Propylaia in 1874 and the grand excavations of 1885–1890 by P. Kavvadias, the Akropolis assumed the appearance that it more or less has today. It had already become, in 1835, the first archaeological site with an entrance fee.

Piecemeal exploration of the ancient city is a recurring phenomenon revealing an important parameter of its urban archaeology: multiple excavations by different people have been carried out on the same site, often after long intervals, or have been left incomplete. As a result, there is no consistency in the archaeological documentation, which hinders any attempt to reconstruct the contexts of a disturbed and complex stratigraphy in a city with continuous habitation over thousands of years. Along the south slope of the Akropolis, the Theater of Dionysos was cleared by Eustratiades from 1861 to 1867 and the Odeion of Herodes Atticus earlier on by Pittakis (1848–1857). However, it was Koumanoudes who undertook large-scale excavations from 1876 to 1879 to reveal the remaining monuments (Stoa of Eumenes, Asklepieion, and other sanctuaries) and to shape the area as we know it today. The Odeion of Perikles was cleared and identified some decades later in 1918 by P. Kastriotis, while the propylon of the Sanctuary of Dionysos was excavated only in 2001. This last discovery had repercussions on other topographical problems, since it secured the eastern terminus of the Street of the Tripods.

The Theater of Dionysos is a typical example of the long process undertaken to recover the emblematic monuments of Athens. The first attempt to excavate it dates to 1837–1838 (Archaeological Society), but the first substantial remains were revealed in 1840–1841. The *koilon* was cleared from 1859 to 1861 (J.H. Strack and E. Ziller) and was continued by Eustratiades (1861–1867), while more trenches were opened by Wilhelm Dörpfeld in 1925. Travlos excavated the east *parodos* in 1951, and the Greek Archaeological Service returned for a number of years in the late 1980s. (See also Di Napoli, Chapter 23 in this volume.)

The history of excavations of the Roman Agora and the Library of Hadrian is as long and disjointed, while even today parts of these monumental complexes remain unexcavated beneath modern buildings. For much of its later history, the Library of Hadrian housed public buildings of commercial or military use and was thus integrated in the life of the new city. After the fire of 1884 destroyed the bazaar, it was possible for

Koumanoudes to excavate the eastern part of the complex and to securely
identify the building (1885–1886). The most recent excavation has been in
the basement of the Aiolos Hotel at the corner of Aiolou and Adrianou
Streets in 2011; it has revealed large sections of the south and east walls and
the floor of the Library.[5]

The excavations of the Roman Agora started with a number of expropriations of private houses west of the Tower of the Winds.[6] Work started in
1890–1891, and soon it became obvious that for the excavation of this very
large building, major interventions would be necessary, making the whole
operation rather complicated and difficult, namely: abolishing
Epameinondas Street, demolishing a Turkish bath, removing the military
bakery in the Fetiye Mosque, and demolishing a small Catholic church and
a number of houses. The West Propylon (Gate of Athena Archegetis; see
Web Fig. 30.1), which had always stood in the heart of the city, had not
previously been identified as part of the complex and was known as the
Gate to the Bazaar. When it was clear that the ancient building under
excavation should be associated with the four columns of Athena
Archegetis, it was determined that the whole area in between should be
excavated. However, it was never possible to expropriate all the houses, and
part of the Roman Agora still lies under a number of nineteenth-century
buildings. Excavations were renewed in 1910 under the supervision of
P. Kastriotis and A. Philadelpheus, with successive operations in 1931, in
1940–1942 by the Italians during the Occupation, in 1963–1964 by
A. Orlandos and P. Lazaridis, and by the Archaeological Service off and
on from 1955 to 1991.[7] The most recent addition to the site has been the
excavation of the plot on the north side known as Kalamia (2000–2003).

A number of scholars, both Greeks and foreigners, have been occupied
with the study of the architecture of the colossal Temple of Zeus, opening
trenches throughout the area. However, the major topographical question,
whether the precinct was included within the circuit of the Themistoklean
city wall, was only clarified with Travlos' excavations in 1956–1959. Travlos
located a city gate of Themistoklean date to the north of the precinct built
of poros limestone column drums from the earlier Peisistratid Olympieion.
The important area to the south of the Olympieion bounded by the Ilissos
River was excavated from 1893 until 1962 by various Greek excavators.

[5] *ArchDelt* 66 (2011) B', 46–63.
[6] *PAE* 1890, 11–17; *PAE* 1891, 7–10.
[7] Mallouchou-Tufano 2000.

The quest for the famous public monuments of the ancient city dictated the selection of specific plots to be expropriated and explored. Typical is the example of the excavations for the Bouleuterion. In 1851, the house and plot of one L. Psoma near the (now demolished) Hypapante Church in Plaka were expropriated and excavated at the suggestion of Pittakis, who believed it to be a promising candidate for the location of the Bouleuterion.[8] When K. Kourouniotes returned to excavate in this plot in 1910, the antiquities were identified as part of the Late Roman Wall, and later the American excavations would bring to light the City Eleusinion in this area.

The ancient cemeteries, especially the most famous ones, were another pole of attraction for early archaeologists. Already in the nineteenth century, individuals were digging their fields in the area of Agia Triada in northwest Athens in search of the beautiful funerary monuments of the Kerameikos cemetery and the famous Dipylon Gate. Official excavations started randomly in 1860 and more systematically in 1863 by the Archaeological Society under Pittakis and Eustratiades, who made efforts to rescue chance finds and to expropriate private plots. Due to the deep fill in the area, this is one of the few places where Classical monuments, especially funerary monuments, were found standing in situ as they were set up in antiquity. It was some years later, in 1872, that the Dipylon Gate, the Sacred Gate, and the city wall were revealed and thereby provided a fixed point for the rest of the topography of Athens. When the excavations were passed over to the German Archaeological Institute in 1913, most of the public monuments (fortifications, Pompeion, fountain-house) and the Street of the Tombs had already come to light. It was up to the Germans to meticulously excavate the extensive necropolis, the shrines, the road to the Academy, and the Kerameikos *horoi*. The houses in the area of the Sacred Gate were only excavated in the 1970s. The ongoing excavations continue to reveal unexpected finds, while research interest has shifted to themes such as water management and cults in the Kerameikos.[9]

The shaping of the archaeological landscape peaked in the first half of the twentieth century when a large area in the heart of the old city was expropriated to give place to the excavations of the ancient Agora by the American School of Classical Studies. The expropriation and demolition of the Vrysaki neighborhood (1931–1939) in search of the Athenian Agora,

---

[8] The Bouleuterion was eventually excavated on the west side of the Agora by the American School of Classical Studies in 1934; see Shear in *Hesperia* 4 (1935) 340–370.

[9] Stroszeck 2017 and Chapter 8 in this volume.

the civic center of Athenian democracy, constitutes a massive operation and an unparalleled milestone in the transformation of the urban landscape, with a major impact on the local population, giving the historic center of Athens its current appearance.[10]

The creation of archaeological parks and the consolidation of archaeological sites in Athens has been a slow progress on a rough and rutted road.[11] The clash between the Archaeological Service and the inhabitants has not always been on matters of property, but also on views about public benefit and accessibility to areas of recreation, the prime example being the Philopappos Hill.[12] Some sites were only defined in the twenty-first century, while the most recent addition to the list of sites is the archaeological park of the Lyceum on Rigillis Street. The importance of the Lyceum as the School of Aristotle was such that all plans for the construction of a Museum of Modern Art were cancelled; when the rescue excavation was completed, the area was landscaped and opened to the public.

As a result, in the early twenty-first century the extent of archaeological sites and parks in Athens covers a surface area of ca 1 km^2. Despite the sites' visibility in the modern urban landscape and the contribution that their systematic exploration has made to our knowledge of ancient Athens, it is daily rescue excavations that have been silently uncovering the palimpsest of the city for over a century in more than 1,500 excavation sites.

Rescue Excavations

Rescue excavations, the most common type of archaeological fieldwork in the city today, are usually short-term operations conducted by the Greek Archaeological Service under heavy pressure prior to construction, usually on private plots. More ambitious, longer-term projects are the result of large-scale public works such as the construction of the Athens Metro or the new Akropolis Museum.[13] The results are published as preliminary reports in journals, such as the *Archaiologikon Deltion*. Rescue excavations

[10] A thorough study with photographic documentation of this neighborhood is now available in Dumont 2020.
[11] Papageorgiou-Venetas 1994.
[12] The heated debate on whether the Western Hills of Athens constitute an archaeological site that should be fenced and protected or a recreational green area open to the community is a recurrent issue.
[13] Excavations for the Athens Metro lasted from 1992 to 1998, for the new Akropolis Museum at the Makriyannis plot from 1997 to 2003.

with their limitations and problems lie at the core of urban archaeology: they are incidental, fragmented, dispersed, and not initiated by a research question.[14] In the words of a Greek archaeologist, "these excavations lack primary meaning."[15]

It is unfortunate that the process of excavating ancient Athens follows the pace of modern construction work. Sites are excavated in a piecemeal fashion and are randomly distributed throughout the city with some areas, including the north-northwest and south-southeast, having been more extensively explored than others, thus giving the false impression that they were more densely built in antiquity. Ever since the early plans of Kleanthes, Schaubert, and von Klenze failed to keep the area to the north of the Akropolis free of buildings for future excavations, the history of archaeological research in Athens is far from being a planned and sched-uled activity. For most of the nineteenth century, the major archaeological achievements in the lower city came from the opening of foundations for houses and other buildings and were mostly chance finds, not the products of stratigraphical operations. An example of the type of breakthroughs that provided reference points for the topography of the city includes the inscribed base of the Euboulides monument that is mentioned in Pausanias' description (1.2.5) and was found in situ when the house of Doctor Treiber was being built on Ermou and Agion Asomaton Streets in 1837.[16] Thanks to this discovery, the route from the Kerameikos to the Agora was established at a time when neither of these two sites had been excavated. Also, along the north side of the city, the line of the ancient city wall, which was not previously known, was established due to two excav-ations for the foundations of private houses in 1872.[17]

Building activity in the twentieth century was very intense after the late 1950s, a fact that is reflected in the increasing numbers of salvage excav-ations that hit a peak in the twenty years between 1960 and 1980,[18] with a record of 107 excavations reported in *ArchDelt* 29 (1973–1974) B' (Map 33.1). Roughly, in the 1960–1970s, the construction of apartment buildings on private plots dominates, while from the 1980s on, an escalation of large-scale infrastructure works can be observed, such as road building (e.g. the construction of the Lenormant-Konstantinoupoleos Avenue overpass) and

---

[14] Karagiorga-Stathakopoulou 1988, 87–90; Parlama 1996, 45–47.
[15] C. Karouzos in a 1936 article in *Nea Estia*.
[16] Travlos 1981, 395.
[17] Sites Th27 and Th35 respectively in Theocharaki 2020.
[18] 1960–1970: 425 excavations reported; 1970–1980: 443 excavations reported.

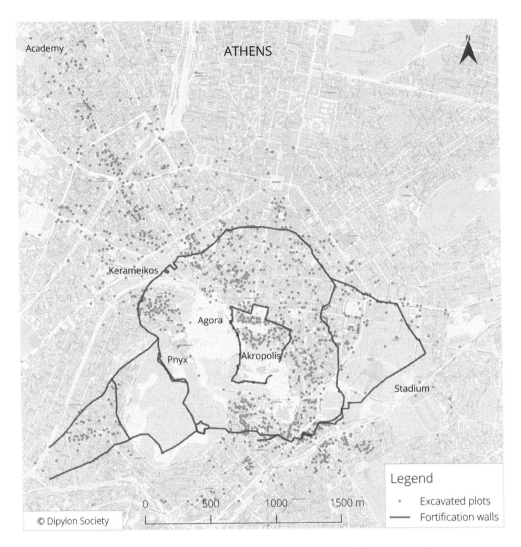

Map 33.1 Map of distribution of rescue excavations in Athens since the late nineteenth century.
© Dipylon Society/Stamatina Lampraki

the construction of underground parking facilities (e.g. at Kotzia Square).
Consequently, there is an increase in the complexity and the challenges of
these rescue excavations. In the 1990s the construction of the Athens
Metro, combined with the building of the new Akropolis Museum at the
Makriyannis plot south of the Akropolis, the Unification of Archaeological
Sites project, and the massive public works in preparation for the
2004 Athens Olympic Games, generated extensive excavations and a score
of new data at an unprecedented scale. It is no surprise that to date this
material has not been fully processed.

A major flaw of rescue excavations is spatial limitation that does not allow full recovery. This results in partially excavated features and inadequate exploration of architectural remains. It is not uncommon to reveal the continuation of a feature or structure in subsequent operations, when the originally excavated part no longer exists and the connection between the two might be easily missed, especially since a considerable lapse of time separates the relevant operations. Excavation finds are isolated from each other and from their spatial context, so that it is often difficult to associate them with neighboring finds, monuments, and topographical features.[19] The interpretation of such diffuse and fragmented data is extremely difficult and can only be facilitated by the digital mapping of the excavations.[20]

The sheer bulk of the material, its fragmented nature, and incomplete investigation impedes moving from excavation to data collection, analysis, and interpretation. Very often the results of such rescue excavations have not been studied in a comprehensive way in their historical and topographical context. This lack of archaeological interpretation perpetuated by the lack of proper stratigraphic excavation and recording system may explain why, for so many rescue excavations, all we have are short excavation reports.[21]

The importance of stratigraphy became apparent at the turn of the nineteenth century with the pioneering work of Dörpfeld, who introduced new methods. He excavated the valley between the Akropolis west slope and the Pnyx, bringing to light a neighborhood of ancient Athens with streets, houses, shrines, fountains, and a complex water management system (1891–1898). In a city with continuous habitation for over thirty-five centuries, the stratigraphy is inevitably complicated. Deposits can be quite deep in Athens, reaching 10 m in places. The Eridanos River was found 7.5 m beneath modern ground level at Monastiraki Square, and the deposits at the Kerameikos are ca. 8 m deep below the level of modern Ermou Street. Perhaps the most significant single period rise in the elevation of the ground level in the city (ca. 2 m in places) occurred after the War of Independence in the nineteenth century and is due to the cleaning operations after years of war.

---

[19] See for example the associated excavations at 3 Makri Street (1972) and 4 Tzeraion Street (1953) in the Makriyannis area. Almost twenty years separate the two excavations, so that the relation of the exposed features could not have been recognized at the time.

[20] Such a project is now being undertaken by the Dipylon Society for the study of ancient topography (https://dipylon.org/en/2018/06/12/mapping-the-antiquities-athens/).

[21] For example, elevations are always given in relation to the modern street or sidewalk level (and not in mASL).

Overall, we are still lacking well-established stratigraphic sequences to interpret depositional processes and to document the diachronic development of habitation across the city. For example, how do the Persian destruction deposits at the Agora compare to finds from elsewhere in Athens? In the seventy volumes of the *ArchDelt*, very few references are made to such contexts. With the exception of Archaic spolia used in the construction of the Themistoklean city wall that provide indirect evidence for the destruction of the city by the Persians, it seems that only two instances have been securely identified with this historic event, and both concern the destruction of small roadside shrines.[22] Has the debris attributed to the cleanup that followed the Persian destruction of the city not been identified, or are we to assume that the destruction was not as widespread as the written sources indicate? The best attested destruction layers are those attributed to Sulla's sack of the city in 86 BC and the subsequent cleanup, and to the Herulian invasion in AD 267, with occurrences evenly distributed throughout the city.

Despite their shortcomings, there can be no doubt that rescue excavations have contributed decisively to our knowledge of Athenian topography. The finds cover all aspects of life in the city: public and religious buildings, residential quarters, industrial installations, and burial grounds. Occasionally, rescue excavations have provided information even on the geomorphology of the area.[23]

Contribution of Rescue Excavations to Our Knowledge of Athenian Topography

One of the oldest and most recalcitrant problems in Athenian topography is the location of the Prytaneion and the old agora, since most of the monuments of Archaic Athens lie beneath the modern city in the neighborhood of Plaka. The breakthrough discovery for untangling the Archaic topography was a Hellenistic decree honoring the priestess of Aglauros that came to light in 1980.[24] Despite certain dissenting voices, the inscription is believed to have been found in situ. As a result, the large cave on the east

---

[22] At 29 Poulopoulou Street and 18–20 Vasilis Street in northwest Athens, see *ArchDelt* 33 (1978) B', 10–12 and *ArchDelt* 34 (1979) B', 26–27, respectively.

[23] For example, the discovery of the Eridanos River bed at Syntagma Square and its second-century AD vaulted channel at Monastiraki (Metro excavations).

[24] *SEG* 23.115; Dontas 1983, 48–63.

slope of the Akropolis is now associated with the Aglaurion, and that in turn is used as a fixed point for moving the location of a number of early civic buildings further to the east.[25] Although claims have been made for identifying the Prytaneion with the remains excavated in the square of Agia Aikaterini,[26] there is no consensus and, actually, newer epigraphic evidence that turned up in a 2001 rescue excavation at 32 Tripodon Street points to a location closer to Agios Demetrios Katephoris.[27]

A prime example of a fragmented monument that has been reconstructed from data provided by rescue excavations is the city wall of Athens. (See Costaki and Theocharaki, Chapter 4 in this volume.) A major public monument of paramount importance for the history and topography of the city, the city wall remained in service with continuous repairs and modifications for many centuries, a true landmark of the city. It has been revealed over the years at about 180 excavated sites throughout modern Athens. However, the city wall has left very few discernible traces in the modern urban fabric and can hardly be conceived today as a single monument in its spatial context.[28] Among the many instances of its excavation, the gate that was found at Erechtheiou Street was an important discovery in 1955; before then, we did not know of the existence of a gate in the south stretch of the wall between the Hill of the Muses and the elusive Phaleric Gate. Issues of its construction, dating, and course have been clarified thanks to numerous excavations.

In a similar manner, the street network has been excavated gradually in a haphazard way in about 300 excavation sites, with data accumulating over the years. Stretches of the same street excavated in different plots on different occasions are being pieced together to reconstruct routes, histories of use and destruction, and everyday life in the city. The case of the Street of the Tripods is characteristic, with stretches found in plots along modern Tripodon, Vyronos, and Prytaneiou Streets and Lysikratous Square.

In the southern part of the city, rescue excavations have uncovered a large Late Classical public building first found in the 1960s and tentatively identified by Travlos as the Palladion, one of the lawcourts of Athens.[29] New excavations in 2012 at 10 Makri Street revealed the southern part of the peristyle court, while clay ballot boxes and a bronze ballot reinforced

---

[25] Among others, see Shear 1994.

[26] Schmalz 2006.

[27] Kavvadias-Matthaiou 2014. In the area of Erechtheos and Kyrrestou Streets, see Kroustalis 2013, 13–15.

[28] Theocharaki 2011 and 2020.

[29] Travlos 1971, 412–416.

the identification of the building as a lawcourt. (See Harris, Chapter 28 in this volume.)

Nearby, at the Makriyannis plot, extensive excavations over a number of years and on different occasions have brought to light an entire residential quarter of ancient Athens,[30] with its streets, water management system, houses, and various installations providing a layered history of this area from prehistoric times to the twelfth century AD.[31] Part of this excavation is now visible at the basement of the Akropolis Museum. Throughout the city, walls, floors (packed earth, mosaic, or paved), hearths and ovens, wells, and household shrines attest to continuous habitation and verify the extent and density of the residential districts. Similarly, kilns, casting pits, furnaces, garbage pits, and cisterns provide evidence for a robust industrial world. Pottery and coroplast workshops, dyeing installations, and metallurgical workshops, have been found almost everywhere in the city, often in association with cemeteries or roads through gates in the city wall, but also within the walled urban area.[32] Although there seems to be a concentration in the northwest beyond the Agora and in southern parts of the city, this might be misleading, owing to the random distribution of excavation sites.

Two out of the three *gymnasia* of Athens have come to light in rescue excavations. Parts of a large Hadrianic peristyle building have been excavated in various plots south of the Ilissos River and are identified with the *gymnasion* at Kynosarges.[33] What is thought to have been the *palaistra* of the Lyceum Gymnasion was excavated on Rigillis Street in eastern Athens in 1996.[34] The *gymnasion* at the Academy in northwest Athens was mostly excavated in a systematic project funded by Panagiotis Aristophron during the 1930s in 'search of Plato's Academy' and again from 1955 to 1963. However, a most important piece of evidence for the location of this site, the boundary stone of the Academy, was found in situ

---

[30] Third Ephorate of Prehistoric and Classical Antiquities (1985–1986); restoration of Weiler building (1985–1986); First Ephorate of Prehistoric and Classical Antiquities (1987–1989); University of Athens (1986–1997 with intervals); Metro Excavations (1993–1996); construction of Akropolis Museum (1997–2003).

[31] Eleftheratou 2019.

[32] See, for example, many pottery workshops in the Petralona district, bronze casting workshops at Syntagma Square (Parlama and Stampolidis 2000, 155–156) and pottery workshops found at 78 Peiraios Street (*ArchDelt* 56–59 [2001–2004] B', 234–235).

[33] Despite the finds made by members of the British School at Athens at the end of the nineteenth century, the site of the Archaic/Classical *gymnasion* remains elusive.

[34] Lygouri-Tolia 2002.

in a rescue excavation in 1967.[35] (See also Bakewell, Chapter 21 in this volume.)

When we come to the burial grounds of the city, the evidence is overwhelming, with graves being discovered in the hundreds around the external perimeter of the city wall, bearing witness to extensive and long-lived cemeteries.[36] Two mass burials of about 150 individuals excavated during the Metro excavations for the Kerameikos station at Iera Odos and Peiraios Streets (1993–1998) have been associated with the victims of the plague (430–426 BC) and, thus, linked to a historic event during the Peloponnesian War (Thucydides 2.47.3).[37] In conjunction with the finds of the large cemetery at Amerikis Street and Syntagma Square in eastern Athens, our views on the development of the Classical cemeteries of the city need to be reconsidered. (See also Shea, Chapter 10 in this volume.)

The find at 35 Salaminos Street (1996–1998) in the Metaxourgeio district in northwest Athens is notable, because it sparked again the long-standing and heated discussion about the location of the Demosion Sema, the famous public cemetery of ancient Athens where the war dead were buried. Apparently, four narrow oblong structures were identified as a monumental complex of *polyandria* bordering the road from the Dipylon Gate to the Academy.[38] All four were dated to 430–420 BC on the basis of fine red-figure vases and white-ground *lekythoi* (perfumed oil flasks) found in the area. On either side of the Dromos to the Academy, over fifty sites have been excavated mostly along modern Plataion Street, but no conclusive evidence on the location of the Demosion Sema has been put forth.

In the religious domain, data provided by rescue excavations are equally precious. In fact, we can legitimately ask what our knowledge of the religious landscape of Athens would be without the evidence from the rescue excavations. Aside from the testimonia from numerous inscriptions that have been found attesting to cults otherwise unknown, there is now concrete evidence for smaller temples and shrines dispersed throughout the urban fabric, some of which are not mentioned in the written sources. These highlight aspects of popular religion and supplement our knowledge

---

[35] At the corner of Aimonos and Tripoleos Streets, *ArchDelt* 22 (1967) B', 46.

[36] At Kotzia Square alone, 653 graves were excavated (*ArchDelt* 53 [1998] B', 67–68); 159 graves at 10 Diamantopoulou Street (*ArchDelt* 56–59 [2001–2004] B', 208–214), and 267 graves at 3 Amerikis Street (*ArchDelt* 53 [1998] B', 61–65). It is not uncommon to find forty to fifty graves in a single plot.

[37] Baziotopoulou-Valavani 2002.

[38] *ArchDelt* 52 (1997) B', 52–56; *ArchDelt* 61 (2006) B', 102–104.

of the official state religion as performed in the large temples of
the Akropolis.

Among the numerous examples, the discovery of the Sanctuary of
Herakles Pankrates near the Ilissos River in eastern Athens in a rescue
excavation by J. Meliades in 1952–1954 stands out, not only because of its
rich finds but also for adding to our knowledge of the topography of this
unexplored area.[39] Meliades also excavated the important Sanctuary of the
Nymphe to the south of the Akropolis during the landscaping of the area in
front of the Odeion of Herodes Atticus in 1955–1959. In 1958,
J. Threpsiades excavated the Sanctuary of Artemis Aristoboule in a rescue
excavation in the neighborhood of Theseion.[40] It comprised a small temple,
an altar, and a *temenos* wall, and was identified on the basis of a votive
inscription (Agora I 6969) with the Sanctuary of Artemis Aristoboule that
was founded, according to Plutarch, by Themistokles after the naval battle
at Salamis (Plutarch, *Themistokles* 22; *On the Malice of Herodotos* 37). In
the same neighborhood, two small shrines have come to light close to the
line of the city wall, both constructed in the late sixth century BC.[41]

At the site of the Temple of Artemis Agrotera on the south bank of the
Ilissos River, continuing excavations in 2012 and 2014 have brought to
light a votive inscription, fragments of relief decoration, and the foundations of a second temple that most likely belong to the Sanctuary of Zeus
Meilichios.[42]

However, by far the longest and most fascinating history of discovery is
that of the Pythion, the Sanctuary of Apollo Pythios in southeast Athens.
The inscribed crowning of the Archaic altar was found in 1877, and
132 years later, in 2009, a joining fragment was found in a rescue excavation which helped securely identify the location of the sanctuary southwest of the Olympieion and within the Themistoklean city wall.[43] The
inscription (*IG* I^3 948) on the altar confirms Thucydides' claim (6.54.6–7)
that Peisistratos the Younger, son of the tyrant Hippias and grandson of
the tyrant Peisistratos, had dedicated the altar of Apollo Pythios during his
archonship in 522/1 BC. However, as with so many finds of the nineteenth
century, it was difficult to ascertain the exact location of the original

---

[39] At the intersection of Vasileos Georgiou and Vasileos Konstantinou Streets.

[40] At Herakleidon and Neleos Streets (J. Threpsiades and E. Vanderpool in *ArchDelt* 19 (1963) A'
Meletai, 26–36).

[41] One at 29 Poulopoulou Street and the other at 18–20 Vasilis Street. For a detailed discussion of
small roadside shrines in Athens, see Costaki 2008.

[42] Litsa 2015.

[43] For the new fragment see http://greekepigraphicsociety.org.gr/may-2011/#more-463.

fragments of the crowning and to associate them with subsequent discoveries.[44]

The remains of religious buildings and sacred sites combined with evidence from the street network can help in the reconstruction of the routes that specific processions followed during religious festivals. There is also a route followed not by a religious procession, but by a famous traveler of the second century AD that has been the subject of debate in modern scholarship. It is the route taken by Pausanias and used frequently in order to identify excavated monuments in the city. Away from the civic center and the large temples lies a distinctive example of his description coming alive. As Pausanias is walking from the city to the Academy, after he has described the state burials (Demosion Sema), he mentions the tomb of the orator Lycurgus, son of Lykophron (1.29.15). A rescue excavation at 56 Vasilikon and Kratylou Street revealed the family grave plot of Lycurgus of the deme Voutadai, as attested by a group of inscribed funerary markers.[45] This find bears more significance than just attesting the family names and genealogy of Lycurgus; it is one of those fascinating moments in Athenian scholarship when evidence from ancient literary sources, epigraphy, and archaeology coincides.

With the constant flow of new archaeological data and research, we have gained new monuments, new finds, and new identifications, but we have also revised identifications and reexamined interpretations of the past in a city that never ceases to surprise us. One of the more recent is the stunning Archaic sculpture that came to light in 2002 at the Kerameikos, a site that has been excavated for over 100 years. All the pieces were in secondary use, set as fill in the course of the Sacred Way a few meters outside the Sacred Gate. Also, the Hekataion in the Kerameikos is now identified as the Sanctuary-Oracle of Apollo Paian, with an omphalos in its courtyard and the first instance of hydromancy in Athens.[46] In the Agora, a site continuously excavated since 1931, the building in the southwest corner that was long believed to have been the Heliaia, one of the lawcourts of Athens, has been in the last twenty years reinterpreted as the Aiakeion.[47] The identifications of the State Prison and the Strategeion have also been challenged in the light of new finds. A large hoard of fourth-century BC Athenian silver

---

[44] Matthaiou (2011) presents all evidence and reconstructs the history of research that documents the location of this important sanctuary.

[45] *ArchDelt* 34 (1979) B', 18–20; Matthaiou 1987, 31–43.

[46] Stroszeck 2017, 120–123.

[47] Stroud 1998.

tetradrachms that was buried in a shallow pit beneath the floor of one of the rooms of the so-called Strategeion was found in 2004, suggesting the identification of the building as the Poleterion or as a commercial establishment. The results of a rescue excavation in the bed of the Athens–Piraeus railway in 2011 came to complement and change our understanding of a previously partially excavated feature. This was a row of square stone sockets in line with the Panathenaic Way that had been interpreted as a starting-line of an early racetrack, but is now proven to be part of a temporary roped-off enclosure (*perischoinisma*). (See also Camp, Chapter 6 in this volume.) Although the famous civic buildings, such as the Tholos, the Bouleuterion, and the Metroon, have been securely anchored in the main square of the Agora, it remains to be seen whether the stoa that is currently being excavated on the north side of Adrianou Street is indeed the famous Stoa Poikile.

The cases above exemplify what can be considered as a great divide in the history of excavations in the city. On one hand, many of the large-scale systematically excavated archaeological sites yielded widely read corner-stone publications. On the other hand, evidence provided by so many important rescue excavations is still to be fully processed and pieced together. Such processing would allow us to address a number of questions: Which parts of the city have been more fully explored and which less? Which plots have been excavated more than once and how do these multiple interventions affect the archaeological record? What remains are preserved in basements of modern buildings? Who are the principal archaeologists involved? And how has our knowledge of Athenian topography evolved since the last major comprehensive work (Travlos 1971)?

If we return to the image of the city, a question arises. How do antiquities interact with the modern city fabric? Antiquities in a megalopolis like Athens are fragmented and, in turn, fragment the modern city fabric. They are threatened by the expanding metropolis, and at the same time they impose restrictions on the city's plan and growth. A broader study of the functional role of archaeological sites, standing monuments, and excavated antiquities on private plots is necessary.[48] The display of antiquities (copies and originals) in many of the Metro stations constitutes an important innovation in the history of Athenian archaeology. The same is true with

---

[48] Papageorgiou-Venetas 1994, 247–250, discusses the controversy of archaeological sites in 'living' historic urban centers.

the integration of ancient architectural remains in the design of modern buildings in such a way as to be visible by passersby. The modern pedestrian can gaze through these windows into the past of the city. Antiquities have always marked the cityscape of Athens, infinitely linked to the city's urban form.

Further Reading

Petrakos has published extensively on the history of Greek archaeology, the contributions of individual prominent archaeologists, and the role of institutions, such as the Archaeological Society of Athens (e.g. Petrakos 2011, 2013). Hamilakis 2007, Bastéa 2000, and others discuss the role of antiquities in the construction of the Greek national narrative in a growing corpus of scholarship. On the early history of the foreign archaeological schools in Athens, see Whitling 2019. Archaeological reports of rescue excavations and new finds can be found in the annual volumes of the *Archaiologikon Deltion* and online (http://chronique.efa.gr). Judith Binder (1923–2013) had a deep knowledge of Athenian archaeology, especially the literary sources concerning the city. An avid opponent of Travlos, she challenged many of his identifications of ancient monuments. She has left two unpublished major resources on the study of Athens: *The Monuments and Sites of Athens: A Sourcebook* and *The Monuments and Sites of Athens as They Were Seen, Described, and Investigated from 1102 to 1997*, focusing on the history of excavations in the city. The most recent survey of the topography of ancient Athens can be found in the volumes of the *Topografia di Atene* by Greco (2010–2015).

Bibliography

Bastéa, E. 2000. *The Creation of Modern Athens. Planning the Myth.* Cambridge.

Baziotopoulou-Valavani, E. 2002. "A Mass Burial from the Cemetery of Kerameikos." In *Excavating Classical Culture: Recent Archaeological Discoveries in Greece*, eds. M. Stamatopoulou and M. Yeroulanou, Oxford, 187–201.

Biris, K.H. 1995. *Αι Αθήναι από του 19ου εις τον 20ο αιώνα.* Athens.

Costaki, L. 2008. "'Πάντα πλήρη θεών είναι': παρόδια ιερά στην αρχαία Αθήνα." In *Μικρός Ιερομνήμων: Μελέτες εις Μνήμην Michael H. Jameson*, eds. A.P. Matthaiou and I. Polinskaya, Athens, 145–166.

Dontas, G. 1983. "The True Aglaurion." *Hesperia* 52: 48–63.

Dumont, S. 2020. *Vrysaki: A Neighborhood Lost in Search of the Athenian Agora.* Princeton.

Eleftheratou, S. 2019. *Μουσείο Ακρόπολης: η ανασκαφή.* Athens.

Greco, E., eds. 2010–2015. *Topografia di Atene. Sviluppo urbano e monumenti dalle origini al III secolo d.C.* 5 vols. Athens.

Hamilakis, Y. 2007. *The Nation and Its Ruins: Antiquity, Archaeology, and National Imagination in Greece*. Oxford.

Karagiorga-Stathakopoulou, T. 1988. "Δημόσια έργα και ανασκαφές στην Αθήνα τα τελευταία πέντε χρόνια." *Ηόρος* 6: 87–108.

Kavvadias, G., and A.P. Matthaiou. 2014. "A New Attic Inscription of the Fifth Century BC from the East Slope of the Acropolis." In *Αθηναίων επίσκοπος: Studies in Honour of Harold B. Mattingly*, eds. A.P. Matthaiou and R.K. Pitt, Athens, 51–72.

Kokkou, A. 2020. *Ιωάννης Τραυλός. Η ζωή και το έργο του*. Athens.

Korres, M., ed. 2010. *Οι πρώτοι χάρτες της πόλεως των Αθηνών*. Athens.

Kroustalis, E.S. 2013. "Η αναθηματική επιγραφή *IG* II² 2877 και η οικία του προξένου Giraud." *Γραμματείον* 2: 11–16.

Litsa, M. 2015. "Ζευς Μειλίχιος εν Άγρας." *Γραμματείον* 4: 49–52.

Lygouri-Tolia, E. 2002. "Excavating an Ancient Palaestra in Athens." In *Excavating Classical Culture: Recent Archaeological Discoveries in Greece*, eds. M. Stamatopoulou and M. Yeroulanou, Oxford, 203–212.

Mallouchou-Tufano, F. 2000. "Από τον 19° στον 21° αιώνα: μεταμορφώσεις του αρχαιολογικού τοπίου στην Αθήνα." In *Αθήναι: από την κλασική εποχή έως σήμερα (5ος αι. π.Χ.-2000 μ.Χ.)*, eds. C. Bouras et al., Athens, 308–343.

Matthaiou, A.P. 1987. "Ηρίον Λυκούργου Λυκόφρονος Βουτάδου." *Ηόρος* 5: 31–43.

——— 2011. "Το Πύθιον παρά τον Ιλισσόν." In *Έπαινος Luigi Beschi*, eds. A. Delivorrias, G. Despinis, and A. Zarkadas, Athens, 259–271.

Papageorgiou-Venetas, A. 1994. *Athens: The Ancient Heritage and the Historic Cityscape in a Modern Metropolis*. Athens.

Parlama, L. 1996. "Οι σωστικές ανασκαφές των Αθηνών και προβλήματα πολεοδομίας της αρχαίας πόλεως." In *Αρχαιολογία της πόλης των Αθηνών: επιστημονικές – επιμορφωτικές διαλέξεις*, ed. E. Grammatikopoulou, Athens, 45–55.

Parlama, L., and N.C. Stampolidis. 2000. *Athens: The City Beneath the City: Antiquities from the Metropolitan Railway Excavations*. Athens.

Petrakos, V.C. 2011. "Περίγραμμα της ιστορίας της Ελληνικής Αρχαιολογίας." *Ο Μέντωρ* 100: 7–44.

——— 2013. *Πρόχειρον Αρχαιολογικόν, 1828–2012*. Athens

Schmalz, G.C.R. 2006. "The Athenian Prytaneion Discovered?" *Hesperia* 75: 33–81.

Shear, T.L. 1994. "Ισονόμους τ' Αθήνας εποιησάτην: The Agora and the Democracy." In *The Archaeology of Athens and Attica under the Democracy*, eds. W.D.E. Coulson et al., Oxford, 225–248.

Stroszeck, J. 2017. *Ο Κεραμεικός των Αθηνών. Ιστορία και Μνημεία εντός του αρχαιολογικού χώρου*. Bad Langensalza.

Stroud, R.S. 1998. *The Athenian Grain-Tax Law of 374/3 BC*. Princeton.

Theocharaki, A.M. 2011. "The Ancient Circuit Wall of Athens: Its Changing Course and the Phases of Construction." *Hesperia* 80: 71–156.

2020. *The Ancient Circuit Walls of Athens*. Berlin.

Travlos, J. 1971. *Pictorial Dictionary of Ancient Athens*. New York.

        1981. "Athens after the Liberation: Planning the New City and Exploring the Old." *Hesperia* 50: 391–407.

Whitling, F. 2019. *Western Ways: Foreign Schools in Rome and Athens*. Berlin.

Index

Made in the USA
Las Vegas, NV
20 August 2021